Study Guide

for use with

Economics

Seventeenth Edition

Paul Samuelson
Professor Emeritus,
Massachusetts Institute of Technology

William Nordhaus
Yale University

Prepared by

Laurence Miners
Fairfield University

Kathryn Nantz
Fairfield University

Boston   Burr Ridge, IL   Dubuque, IA   Madison, WI   New York   San Francisco   St. Louis
Bangkok   Bogotá   Caracas   Kuala Lumpur   Lisbon   London   Madrid   Mexico City
Milan   Montreal   New Delhi   Santiago   Seoul   Singapore   Sydney   Taipei   Toronto

McGraw-Hill Higher Education

A Division of The McGraw-Hill Companies

Study Guide for use with
ECONOMICS
Paul Samuelson, William Nordhaus

Published by McGraw-Hill/Irwin, an imprint of the McGraw-Hill Companies, Inc., 1221 Avenue of the Americas, New York, NY 10020. Copyright © 2001, 1998, 1995, 1992, 1989, 1985, 1980, 1976, 1973, 1970, 1967, 1964, 1961, 1958, 1955, 1951, 1948 by the McGraw-Hill Companies, Inc. All rights reserved.

1 2 3 4 5 6 7 8 9 0 CUS/CUS 0 9 8 7 6 5 4 3 2 1 0

ISBN 0-07-237225-7

www.mhhe.com

"To our kids: Zach, Hilary, and Hannah; Sarah and Scott."

TABLE OF

CONTENTS

CHAPTER

The Fundamentals of Economics

I. CHAPTER OVERVIEW

In this beginning chapter basic economic concepts are discussed. The first part of this chapter has been designed to provide a rough outline of what the discipline of economics is all about. The primary objective here is to give you the "lay of the land," as well as a feel for why people would ever want to concern themselves with the study of economics in the first place. We need to consider how, in broad and general terms, such a study should be conducted.

In the second part of the chapter the three main problems of economic organization are presented and discussed. In the last section there is a discussion of the production-possibility frontier that every society faces. Together, these sections help to describe the constraints placed on all economies as they deal with the problem of scarcity.

Finally, there is an appendix to this chapter, focusing on the use of graphs in economic analysis. Basic equations related to the use and interpretation of graphs are presented. Following the format of your text, there is an appendix to this chapter in the *Study Guide* that you can use to review this material.

II. LEARNING OBJECTIVES

After you have read Chapter 1 in your text and completed the exercises in this *Study Guide* chapter, you should be able to:

1. Recognize that while there are numerous specific examples of economic problems and decisions, they are all illustrations of the b*asic definition of economics: Economics is the study of how societies use scarce resources to produce valuable commodities and distribute those commodities among various people.*
2. Understand the *what,* the *how,* and the *for whom* of economic decision making.
3. Define the three primary inputs in the production of outputs: land, labor, and capital.
4. Distinguish between microeconomics and macro-economics.
5. Understand and avoid the common fallacies in economic reasoning.

6. Distinguish between positive and normative economics.
7. Understand the concept of *productive efficiency* and how it relates to both the use of **inputs** and the basic definition of economics.
8. Use the **production-possibility frontier** to illustrate the choices that societies face.
9. Understand the concept of **opportunity cost** and explain its relationship to the production possibilities frontier.

III. REVIEW OF KEY CONCEPTS

Match the following terms from column A with their definitions in column B.

A	B
__ Scarcity	1. The branch of economics concerned with the overall performance of the economy.
__ Efficiency	2. Commodities or services, such as land, labor or capital, that are used by firms in their production processes.
__ Free goods	3. Measurement of cost based on the value of the next-best forgone alternative.
__ Economic goods	4. Using the economy's resources as effectively as possible to satisfy people's needs and desires.
__ Macroeconomics	5. Describes the facts and behavior of an economy.
__ Microeconomics	6. Assuming that what is true for part of a system is also true for the whole system.
__ Normative economics	7. Commodities and resources that we value are limited in supply.
__ Positive economics	8. Goods and services that result from the production process.

1

___ Laissez-faire

___ Inputs

___ Outputs

___ *Post hoc* fallacy

___ Fallacy of composition

___ Opportunity cost

9. A market economy in which the government has almost no role.

10. Assuming that one event causes another simply because it happens first.

11. Goods that we value that are limited in supply.

12. Involves value judgments and ethical precepts about an economy.

13. Commodities and resources that are available without limit.

14. Branch of economics concerned with the behavior of individual entities such as markets, firms, and households.

IV. SUMMARY AND CHAPTER OUTLINE

This section summarizes the key concepts from the chapter.

A. Introduction

1. Economics exists as a discipline of study because the "things" that we value in our world are not available in a limitless supply. These "things" include, but certainly are not limited to, raw materials and resources, clean air and water, and all types of manufactured goods and services. If everyone in the world had all they could possibly hope for, there would be no need for economics.

2. Economics is the study of how societies use scarce resources to produce valuable commodities and distribute them among different people.

3. In an attempt to meet the (unfulfilled) needs of people, economies strive to produce goods and services efficiently. When an economy is producing efficiently, it cannot produce more of one good without producing less of another.

4. Within the study of economics, a significant distinction is made between the behavior of individual components of an economy (individuals, households, firms, industries, etc.), on the one hand, and the functioning of the economy taken as a whole, on the other. The former, called **microeconomics**, looks at the small building blocks of a larger system. How are vegetable prices set? How do people negotiate their employment contracts? These are the types of questions that are asked in the study of microeconomics.

5. By way of contrast, **macroeconomics** focuses on broader sorts of questions. What is the relationship (if any) between the rate of unemployment and the rate of inflation? What should we expect to see as a consequence of enormous federal government budget deficits? These are typical macroeconomic issues.

6. The textbook distinction between microeconomics and macroeconomics is somewhat less clear in reality. Unemployment, for example, is not just a national problem, but a household problem as well. When is an industry so large that an analysis of its response to a certain tax treatment is a question of macroeconomics rather than microeconomics? Recognizing this blurring is not, however, nearly as important as recognizing that macroeconomic and microeconomic views of how the world behaves must be consistent with each other.

7. Even though economics is a social science, economists often use a scientific approach when tackling economic problems. They identify economic problems, formulate theories, collect and analyze data, and use **econometrics**, a specialized branch of statistics, in an attempt to accept or refute economic theories. As in any scientific investigation, efforts are made to control for other factors related to the problem under consideration. For example, if we are interested in explaining the relationship between the price of CDs and the quantity purchased by a consumer, we would want to hold the consumer's income constant. Normally, we would expect that when the price of a product goes up, the quantity demanded will fall. However, it is possible that a consumer may coincidentally get a better paying job or a raise in pay just as the firm is increasing the price of CDs. So unless we hold income constant we may conclude that when price increases the consumer will demand more CDs.

8. "*Post hoc*" is Latin for "after this." Just because one event precedes another, it does not mean that it caused the events that follow. This is the *post hoc* fallacy. Finally, the **fallacy of composition** says that what is true for the part is not necessarily true for the whole. For example, one firm may cut prices to steal customers away from competitors and make more profit. On the other hand, if all firms cut prices, they may wind up stealing customers from no one and wind up losing money due to lower revenues.

B. The Three Problems of Economic Organization

1. Since we are faced with both scarcity and the wants of the people, each society must decide "what" goods and services to produce. No country has enough resources to meet *all* the wants of *all* its citizens. Scarcity means that choices have to be made.

2. "How" deals primarily with the production process. Typically, there may be several different ways of producing a particular product. For example, a painter could use a compressor and spray gun to paint a building. Alternatively, the painter could hire several workers with paintbrushes to help with the work. Depending upon the availability (and cost) of these alternative **inputs**, either method could prove to be the best way to do the job. **Technology**, or the knowledge used to combine inputs, is also an important factor in determining *how* to produce outputs.

3. Finally, society must determine who will get the outputs that are produced. This is the "for whom" part of the

economic problem. This is a very difficult decision, and often issues of fairness and equity come into play when deciding how to distribute a nation's output.

4. There are two fundamentally different ways that societies use to address these three problems. In a **market economy** individuals and private firms make the major decisions about *what, how,* and *for whom.* In a **command economy** these decisions are made by the government. No contemporary society falls completely into either of these polar categories. Rather, all societies are **mixed economies,** with elements of both market and command decision making.

C. Society's Technological Possibilities

1. Firms use **inputs** to produce goods and services, which are called **outputs.** The three main categories of inputs are **land, labor,** and **capital.**

2. The *land* includes the earth itself and all the precious (and scarce) **natural resources** that we get out of it. In our congested world we need to broaden our definition of "land" beyond natural resources and include **environmental resources** such as air, water, and climate. These, too, are becoming scarce and are often adversely affected by our production decisions.

3. *Labor* consists of all human time spent in production. There are skilled workers and unskilled workers. There are managers and assembly line workers. There are doctors, lawyers, engineers, and even economists. Labor is both the most familiar and the most crucial input for an advanced industrial economy. Resources and capital may be imported—every country has its own labor force.

4. *Capital* resources are durable goods, the output of some previous production process, which are then used to produce other goods and services. Examples of capital goods include factories, trucks, computers, washing machines, compressors, and spray guns for paint.

5. Economists often use diagrams to explain economic concepts. The *production possibility frontier (PPF)* is used to illustrate the concept of scarcity and the production choices that society faces.

6. **Opportunity costs** measure the cost of doing something in terms of the next-best alternative that is given up. The opportunity cost of going to college is four (or more) years of work, plus the next-best way of using the money spent on tuition and fees. In a two-good *PPF* world, the opportunity cost of producing more of one commodity is the amount of the other good that must be given up. Because economic resources are scarce, society is forced to make choices. The cost of these choices can be measured in terms of opportunity cost.

V. HELPFUL HINTS

1. All economic issues and problems ultimately relate back to the idea of scarcity. Since we are faced with scarcity, we must make choices. Look back at the eight definitions/examples of economics at the beginning of the textbook chapter. Make sure you see how they relate to the concept of scarcity.

2. All decisions therefore relate in some sense to economics. On a personal level, your time (like your income) is a scarce resource and you continually decide how best to use it. The decision to stay in bed an extra hour, or go to class, or study, or eat breakfast is ultimately tied back to the concepts of scarcity and choice. The sooner you buy into and grasp this most basic notion of economics, the happier you (and your instructor) will be!

3. Inputs are often referred to as **factors of production.** The two expressions can be used interchangeably.

4. Capital is one of those terms (there will be others) that have special meaning for economists. To the noneconomist, "capital" is often used synonymously with money. It is not uncommon for business associates to talk of the capital they have invested in a project. For students of economics, however, capital is a factor of production. It is itself an output from some previous production process. Remember, capital is something physical, like a piece of equipment, that firms use as an input to produce goods and services. Money is not capital.

5. The terms *outputs* and *goods and services* can be used interchangeably.

6. Economists frequently use diagrams, like the production-possibility frontier (*PPF*), to simplify and explain concepts. The *PPF* illustrates the tradeoff that society faces when it produces one good instead of another. Of course, in reality, an economy produces thousands of goods. In a three-dimensional *PPF* diagram, a third axis could be added to show the tradeoff among three goods. While no one can draw a four-dimensional diagram, conceptually the interpretation is the same as for our two-dimensional diagram.

7. Economics is an inexact science, and unlike the natural sciences, experiments are usually not performed in a controlled environment. Always take care to know what is and what is not being held constant. Make sure that you understand the *post hoc* fallacy and the fallacy of composition too.

8. **Opportunity cost** is a very important term in economic analysis. Economists are always measuring costs and benefits, and weighing the pros and cons of economic decisions. Opportunity costs provide a useful way to measure the cost of a particular economic decision. Remember, opportunity costs are measured in terms of the next-best foregone alternative, not in terms of money. This concept is used over and over again in economics.

VI. MULTIPLE CHOICE QUESTIONS

These questions are organized by topic from the chapter outline. Choose the best answer from the options available.

A. Introduction

1. Economics is concerned primarily with:
   a. money.
   b. determining corporate profits and losses.
   c. the allocation of scarce resources.
   d. balancing your checkbook.
   e. all of the above.

2. When Samuelson and Nordhaus write that "goods are limited while wants seem limitless," they mean that:
   a. people are basically greedy and not willing to share.
   b. the government needs to redistribute output.
   c. current methods of production are inefficient.
   d. there is no simple solution to the basic economic problems of scarcity and unlimited human wants.
   e. none of the above.

B. The Three Problems of Economic Organization

3. Which of the following are economic goods?
   a. Atlantic Ocean sea water.
   b. Iowa farm land.
   c. California coast line.
   d. All of the above.
   e. All of the above, except **a**.

4. The *post hoc* fallacy occurs when:
   a. one problem follows another.
   b. you think something that is true for one unit is true for all.
   c. many variables may change at the same time and you fail to adjust for the changes.
   d. you assume one event was caused by another simple because the other event occurred first.
   e. economists from different schools of thought approach the same economic problem.

5. The fallacy of composition occurs when:
   a. one problem follows another.
   b. you think something that is true for one unit is true for all.
   c. many variables may change at the same time and you fail to adjust for the changes.
   d. you assume one event was caused by another simply because the other event occurred first.
   e. economists from different schools of thought approach the same economic problem.

6. The problem of failing to hold other things constant occurs when:
   a. one problem follows another.
   b. you think something that is true for one unit is true for all.
   c. many variables may change at the same time and you fail to adjust for the changes.
   d. you assume one event was caused by another simple because the other event occurred first.

   e. economists from different schools of thought approach the same economic problem.

7. The three fundamental questions of economic organization are:
   a. closely related to the concept of scarcity.
   b. not nearly as important today as they were at the dawn of civilization.
   c. *what, how,* and *why.*
   d. *land, labor,* and *capital.*
   e. all of the above.

8. The economic problem of *what* goods to produce:
   a. may be a problem for any individual firm seeking to make a profit but is not in any sense a problem for society as a whole.
   b. can be illustrated as the problem of choosing a point on the production-possibility curve.
   c. arises only when the stock of productive resources is very small.
   d. arises only when all productive inputs are so specialized that each can be used only in the production of one good and no other.
   e. none of the above.

9. The economic problem of *how to* produce goods would not exist:
   a. if the required proportions of inputs were fixed for all commodities, so substitution of one input for another input in production would be impossible.
   b. if production had not been carried to the point where there was full employment of all the economy's resources.
   c. if the economy's stock of capital were small relative to its labor force.
   d. in a technically advanced society, since proper technology would have established the best possible method of producing each good.
   e. in any circumstance, because the problem of how to produce goods is an engineering problem throughout and not an economic problem.

10. Which of the following statements applies to a mixed economy?
    a. There is confusion and a lack of organization.
    b. The allocation of resources changes from production period to production period.
    c. There are no real examples of truly mixed economies.
    d. Mixed economies include aspects of both market and command economies.
    e. None of the above statements apply.

C. Society's Technological Possibilities

11. Capital is:
    a. the same as money.
    b. the headquarters of economic planning.
    c. both an input and an output.

d. all of the above.

e. none of the above.

12. Land, labor, and capital are:.

a. available only in finite amounts.

b. used to produce outputs.

c. the primary factors of production.

d. combined with technology in the production process.

e. all of the above.

13. Which of the statements below does *not* apply to the production-possibility frontier, or *PPF*?

a. The *PPF* is closely related to the concept of scarcity.

b. Quantities of inputs are measured along the axes of the *PPF*.

c. The *PPF* may shift over time.

d. Movements along the *PPF* may occur as the allocation of resources changes.

e. Technology may change the shape of the *PPF*.

14. Which of the statements below is a reason why an economy might produce a level of output that is beneath its production-possibility frontier?

a. The available resources are not equally suited to the production of both outputs.

b. The available body of technological knowledge is not being fully utilized.

c. Society prefers one product over the other.

d. In reality, economies produce thousands of goods not just two.

e. There are no frontiers left anymore.

15. Which of the following statements is false? When an economy is on its *PPF*:

a   more of one product cannot be produced without sacrificing some of the other.

b. resources are fully employed.

c. the economy is producing with *productive efficiency*.

d. consumers will have all that they need.

e. a strike by workers will move the economy beneath the *PPF*.

16. Which of the following statements could be used to explain an outward shift in the production-possibility frontier?

a. There is an increase in technology.

b. The population of the country increases.

c. The country decides to postpone current consumption in favor of capital investment.

d. New natural resources are discovered under the ocean.

e. All of the above apply.

17. Which of the following are measured along the axes of a *PPF* graph?

a. quantities of productive inputs or resources.

b. quantities of finished commodities.

c. values of finished commodities.

d. all of the above.

e. none of the above.

18. Each and every point in a production-possibility diagram (whether on the curve or off it) stands for some combination of the two goods produced. With a given input stock, some of these points are attainable, while others are not. Specifically, with respect to production, the economy *could* operate:

a. anywhere on the curve and only on the curve.

b. anywhere on the curve or anywhere inside it (below and to the left).

c. anywhere on the curve, inside it, or outside it.

d. all of the above.

e. none of the above.

19. In order to shift the *PPF* out (above and to the right), an economy would have to:

a. somehow increase its stock of inputs.

b. remove some incompetent bureaucrats from their jobs.

c. eliminate the sources of significant abuse of monopoly power.

d. all of the above.

e. none of the above.

20. If an economy did somehow add to its input stock, or if it did discover new production techniques, then the production-possibility curve would:

a. remain unchanged.

b. move appropriately inward and to the left.

c. move appropriately outward and to the right.

d. all of the above.

e. none of the above.

Please use Figure 1-1 to answer questions 21 through 24.

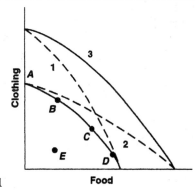

Figure 1-1

21. On the dark production frontier labeled *ABCD,* which point corresponds to the economy's valuing food most heavily?

a. A.

b. B

c. C.

d. D.

e. E.

22. A shift in the dark *PPF* curve to the position indicated by the line marked "1" would be appropriate to illustrate:
    a. a change in the tastes of the population whereby its members want more food produced and less clothing.
    b. the appearance of some new resources useful only in the clothing industry.
    c. an improvement in technology applicable to both industries.
    d. a change in the production mix involving an increase in clothing output and a decrease in food output.
    e. the development of a better technology in the food industry alone.

23. Which alternative in question 22 would have applied if the dark *PPF* had shifted to position 2?
    a.
    b.
    c.
    d.
    e.

24. Which alternative in question 22 would have applied if the dark *PPF* had shifted to position 3?
    a.
    b.
    c.
    d.
    e.

Please use Figure 1-2 to answer questions 25 through 27.

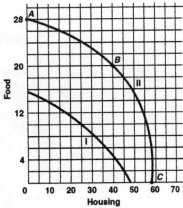

Figure 1-2

25. As the economy moves from point *A* to point *B*:
    a. it gives up 8 units of housing and gains 40 units of food.
    b. it gives up 8 units of food and gains 40 units of housing.
    c. idle resources become fully employed.
    d. the economy becomes more efficient.
    e. there is a breakthrough in technology.

26. As the economy moves from point *B* to point *C*:
    a. it gives up 20 units of food and gains about 17 units of housing.
    b. it gives up 20 units of housing and gains about 17 units of food.
    c. idle resources become fully employed.
    d. the economy becomes more efficient.
    e. there is a breakthrough in technology.

27. Assume that an advance in technology is responsible for the shift from *PPF I* to *PPF II*. It appears that technology
    a. affected both industries equally.
    b. had a relatively greater influence on the food industry.
    c. had a relatively greater influence on the housing industry.
    d. was actually destroyed.
    e. none of the above.

28. The concept of opportunity cost is:
    a. useful only when discussing the production possibility frontier.
    b. used to measure costs in terms of the next-best alternative.
    c. measured in dollars and cents.
    d. used only by professional economists.
    e. none of the above.

29. The opportunity cost of repairing the roads in town could be:
    a. putting an addition on the school.
    b. purchasing new snow removal equipment.
    c. changing from a volunteer to a full-time fire department.
    d. any of the above, depending upon which is the next-best alternative.
    e. none of the above.

VII. PROBLEM SOLVING

The following problems are designed to help you apply the concepts that you learned in the chapter.

A. Introduction

1. To exercise your understanding of the distinction between *micro*economics and *macro*economics, consider the following list of publications. Each appears in a footnote somewhere later in the textbook. On the basis of the content suggested by the titles, indicate whether you expect the research to be primarily related to *micro* or *macro* economics. Use the letters **MI** for *micro*, and **MA** for *macro*.
    a. Arthur Okun, *The Political Economy of Prosperity*
    ___
    b. Orley Ashenfelter, "Union Relative Wage Effects," in Stone and Petersen (eds.), *Econometric Contributions to Public Policy* ___

c.   Edward Denison, "Is U.S. Growth Understated because of the Underground Economy? Employment Ratios Suggest Not," *Review of Income and Wealth* ___
d.   R. J. Gordon, "Inflation, Flexible Exchange Rates and the Natural Rate of Unemployment," in M. N. Baily (ed.), *Workers, Jobs and Inflation* ___
e.   A. A. Berle, Jr., and Gardner Means, T*he Modern Corporation and Private Property* ___

B. The Three Problems of Economic Organization

2.   This question focuses on the difference between *normative* and *positive* economic statements. Indicate which of the following are statements of *normative* (**N**) or *positive* (**P**) character.
a.   Taxes should be progressive. ___
b.   Taxes discourage work effort. ___
c.   Inflation tends to be high when unemployment is low. ___
d.   Inflation is less harmful than unemployment. ___
e.   Pollution restraints cost jobs. ___
f.   Pollution restraints are worth the cost. ___

C. Society's Technological Possibilities

Capital is essential to any modern economy, and a heavy reliance on capital is a characteristic of successful advanced economies in the world today.
3.   Circle *all* the following *that qualify* as capital:
a.   An oil refinery.
b.   An issue of General Motors stock.
c.   Cash in a business owner's safe.
d.   A screwdriver used by a carpenter.
e.   Money borrowed by a business firm from a bank to expand its operations.
f.   A steel-ingot inventory held by a steel company.
g.   Unsold automobiles held by an auto manufacturer.
· h.   An inventory of groceries held by a supermarket.
4.   Any developed nation possesses a large stock of capital, and much of each day's productive effort goes into maintenance and expansion of that stock. Consequently, today's productive effort to maintain and expand capital is signifi-

cantly devoted to satisfying (**yesterday's / today's / tomorrow's**) needs, while the consumer goods actually enjoyed today result from (**yesterday's / today's / tomorrow's**) effort.
5.   Circle as many of the following as are correct:
a.   The larger the available stock of capital, the larger the output of consumer goods that is possible.
b.   In terms of a production-possibility frontier, additions to the stock of capital can push the frontier upward and outward.
c.   A decision to produce or to not produce more capital goods is not part of the decision of *what* goods to produce.
d.   In a fully employed economy, a decision to produce more capital goods today must go hand-in-hand with a decision to produce fewer consumer goods in the current period..

Consider the production-possibility curves drawn in Figure 1-3. Use the different *PPFs* to answer questions 6 through 10. In each panel the *lighter* schedule represents an *original* curve, while the *darker* schedule represents what happens to the frontier after something has *changed* the economy.
6.   Suppose that scientific invention increased the productivity of resources used only in the production of X Which panel most accurately reflects this development? ___
7.   Many scientists believe that we are exhausting our natural resources. Assume that natural resources used to produce X are being depleted, but that the production of Y, at least for the time being, is not affected. ___
8.   Assume that the labor force grows and the new workers receive specialized training to produce commodity Y. ___
9.   Technological knowledge increases and both industries benefit, more or less equally, from the new technology. ___
10.   A war depletes some of the resources used to produce X. ___

VIII. DISCUSSION QUESTIONS

Answer the following questions, making sure that you can explain the work you did to arrive at the answers.

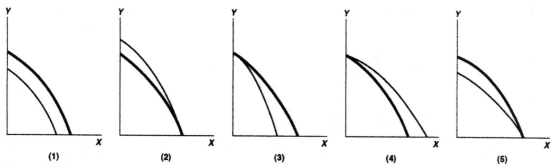

(1)   (2)   (3)   (4)   (5)

Figure 1-3

Table 1-1 shows the production possibilities for the country of Economainia for two commodities: apartments and bread. At each production point listed in Table 1-1, all of Economainia's resources are fully employed and all the available technological knowledge is being utilized.

TABLE 1-1 Economainia's Production Possibilities

Apartments (thousands of units)		Bread (millions of loaves)
0	A	30
6	B	29
2	C	26
18	D	22
24	E	16
30	F	0

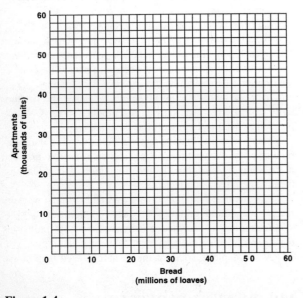

Figure 1-4

1. Use Figure 1-4 to plot the points and draw Economainia's *PPF*. Use the letters from the table (A through F) to label the points on your *PPF*. Before you start, note how the axes on the diagram are labeled.

2. Is point *C* a point of productive efficiency? Please explain. What about points *A*, *B*, *D*, *E*, and *F*?

3. Find the point where Economainia is producing 16,000 apartments and 10,000,000 loaves of bread. Label this point *G*. Assuming that your *PPF* remains where it is (at least for now), list two reasons why Economaninia could be producing at point *G*.

4. Is point *G* a point of productive efficiency? Please explain.

5. Suppose Economaninia's *PPF* shifts so that it now goes through point *G*, and not points *A* through *F*. Draw this new *PPF* on your diagram. What could have caused this shift in the *PPF*?

6. Find the point where Economaninia is producing 50,000 apartments and 50,000,000 loaves of bread. Label this point *H*. Given your current *PPF* can Economaninia actually produce this combination of goods? Please explain why, or why not.

Suppose some changes occur in the Economaninia economy such that a new set of production possibilities becomes possible. Table 1-2 lists the new production options.

TABLE 1-2 Economaninia's New Production Possibilities

Apartments (thousands of units)	Bread (millions of loaves)
0	50
6	48
12	46
18	40
24	40
30	34
36	16
42	0

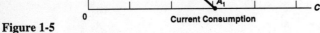
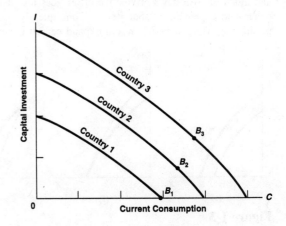

Figure 1-5

7. Add these points to your diagram and draw Economaninia's new *PPF.* Give two reasons for the shift in the *PPF.*

8. Given your new *PPF,* can Economaninia now product at point *H*? Please explain.

The next two questions refer to Figure 1-5, which is also Figure 1-5 in your textbook.

9. Explain the difference between points A_1, A_2, and A_3 in panel (*a*).

10. What is the relationship between the three points in Figure 1-5 (*a*) and the three *PPFs* in Figure 1-5 (*b*)?

11. When an economy decides to produce more capital goods, must it usually (at least for the time being) produce fewer consumer goods? Why, or why not?

12. List the opportunity costs associated with going to college for four years. Explain why the amount spent for room and board should or should not be included in your list.

IX. ANSWERS TO STUDY GUIDE QUESTIONS

III. Review of Key Concepts

7	Scarcity
4	Efficiency
13	Free goods
11	Economic goods
1	Macroeconomics
14	Microeconomics
12	Normative economics
5	Positive economics
9	Laissez-faire economy
2	Inputs
8	Outputs
10	*Post hoc* fallacy
6	Fallacy of composition
3	Opportunity cost

VI. Multiple Choice Questions

1. C 2. D 3. E 4. D 5. B 6. C
7. A 8. B 9. A 10. D 11. C 12. E
13. B 14. B 15. D 16. E 17. B 18. B
19. A 20. C 21. D 22. B 23. E 24. C
25. B 26. A 27. B 28. B 29. D

VII. Problem Solving

1. a. MA
   b. MI
   c. MA
   d. MA
   e. MI
2. a. N
   b. P
   c. P
   d. N
   e. P
   f. N
3. a, d, f.
4. tomorrow's, yesterday's
5. a, b, d.
6. (3)
7. (4)
8. (5)
9. (1)
10. (4)

VIII. Discussion Questions

1.

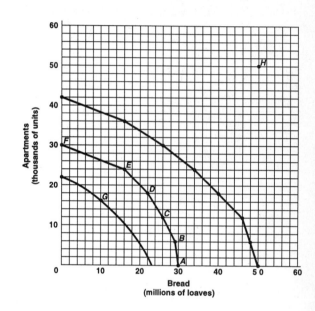

Figure 1-4

2. Point *C*, as well as points *A, B, D, E,* and *F,* all represent points of productive efficiency. Society is on its frontier. There is full employment of all resources and the only way to produce more of one good is by producing less of the other.

3. Economainia could be at *G* due to unemployment (of any resource) or some other inefficiency, such as strikes or political turmoil.

4. Since point *G* is beneath society's frontier, it represents a point of *in*efficiency—society could do better.

5. A leftward shift in the *PPF* can occur when society depletes or loses resources.

6. Point *H* is currently unattainable. Economainia has neither the resources nor the technological know-how to produce at point *H*.

7. The *PPF* may shift to the right due to advances in technology or the discovery or acquisition of more resources.

8. Point H is still unattainable. Society can produce either 42,000 apartments and no bread, or 50,000,000 loaves of bread and no apartments.

9. As the economy moves from A_1 to A_3, it is giving up or trading current consumption goods for capital goods. The increase in capital goods will enable this economy to produce more goods and services in the future. All the points in Figure 1-5 (a) represent points of full employment and efficient use of the available technology.

10. As the economy allocates more resources to capital investment in Figure 1-5 (a), it is providing for more economic growth in the future. The points A_1, A_2, and A_3 represent three different choices, made by three different countries with equal resource endowments. Country 1 decides to allocate all its resources to current consumption. It does not grow, and the PPF in Figure 1-5 (b) is similar to the one in Figure 1-5 (a). Countries 2 and 3 allocate more resources to capital investment. The more resources that are allocated to capital the more the economy grows, and the further out to the right the PPF shifts in the future.

11. Yes. Resources are scarce, and tradeoffs occur. While allocating more resources to capital goods will help an economy grow and produce more of both consumer and capital goods in the future, it must sacrifice some current consumption. This is not a huge problem. Since the production of capital goods is typically financed (at least in part) by saving, households send a signal to producers that they do not need consumer goods in the present. They are postponing consumption until some point in the future, when the capital investment will enable the economy to produce more.

12. The opportunity costs of going to college include the next-best use of your time, probably the money lost from not working at a market job, and the next-best use of the money spent on tuition, books, and fees, perhaps some financial investment. The amount spent for room and board is not part of opportunity cost. Regardless, of how the four years are spent, living expenses must be paid. Of course, if there is a substantial difference between college and non-college living costs, the alternative use of any extra costs should be included.

APPENDIX TO CHAPTER

How to
Read Graphics

I. CHAPTER OVERVIEW

Economics makes extensive use of graphs and charts. They appear in nearly every chapter of the text, and the appendix to Chapter 1 in the text is included to provide the reader with a basic review of their foundation. This associated appendix extends that review.

Graphs and charts are tools with which the fundamental notions of economic reasoning can be illustrated, exercised, and stretched. Graphs provide an easy context within which to explore many economic phenomena that would otherwise require pages of prose. To proceed without a minimal understanding of graphs would be to proceed at a great disadvantage; it would be like playing defense in basketball with both hands tied behind your back.

This appendix is designed to present both a brief review of the basics of graphical analysis and some small insight into its usefulness. If you are already comfortable with graphs, you may still want to scan this appendix for a glimpse of things to come. Graphs are used in economics, most fundamentally, to illustrate how sets of numbers are related to each other.

II. LEARNING OBJECTIVES

After you have read the appendix to Chapter 1 in your text and completed the exercises in this *Study Guide* chapter, you should be able to:

1. Interpret economic relationships that are presented in diagrams and graphs.
2. Plot your own diagrams using (economic) data.
3. Evaluate the slopes of curves.
4. Understand the relationship that exists between variables that are plotted in a graph.
5. Use an equation to describe a linear relationship between two variables.

III. REVIEW OF KEY CONCEPTS

Match the following terms from column A with their definitions in column B.

A	B
__ Slope	1. A straight line that just touches, but does not cross, a curved line at a particular point. Used to measure the slope of the curve at that point.
__ Intercept	2. Indicates a direct relationship between two variables such that they both move (increase or decrease) in the same direction.
__ Origin	3. A diagram illustrating how a variable has changed with the passage of time. Time is measured on the horizontal axis in this diagram.
__ Positive slope	4. The point of intersection between a line on a diagram and the vertical axis.
__ Negative slope	5. Horizontal and vertical lines on a diagram that aid in plotting points.
__ X axis	6. Vertical axis on a diagram. Measurement along this axis is from bottom to top.
__ Y axis	7. The change in the variable on the vertical axis per unit of change in the variable on the horizontal axis.
__ Grid lines	8. A plot of pairs of points, used to visualize the relationship between two variables.
__ Tangent	9. Indicates an inverse or indirect relationship between two variables such that they move in opposite directions. (When one increases, the other decreases and vice versa.)
__ Scatter diagram	10. Horizontal axis on a diagram. Measurement along this axis is from left to right.

11

__ Time-series   11. The bottom, left-hand corner,
   diagram   or beginning point of reference in
                           a graph.

Note to Students *Since the emphasis in this appendix is to give you practice working with graphs, we are changing our usual format at this point to give you more practice working through examples of graphs.*

IV. EXAMPLES

Example One: Study Hours and Leisure Hours

Suppose that you decide to plan your working day. A considerable part of each 24 hours must be given over to sleep, meals, and class attendance. Suppose that these matters take up 14 hours per day. This leaves the remaining 10 hours to divide between study, on the one hand, and leisure and recreation, on the other.

That 10 hours could be divided in an infinite number of ways. At one extreme would be 10 hours for leisure and 0 hours for study. This particular time allocation must be considered unsatisfactory in the sense that its pursuit tends to lead to unpleasant interviews with the dean of students. It is, nonetheless, a possible allocation of time. At the other extreme would be 10 hours for study and 0 for leisure and recreation, i.e., the typical week before examinations allocation. Between the two extremes is a wide selection of alternatives. Among these choices are the allocations indicated in Table 1A-1.

TABLE 1A-1

	A	B	C	D	E	F	G
Leisure hours	10	8	7	6	4-1/2	2-1/2	0
Study hours	0	2	3	4	5-1/2	7-1/2	10

Table 1A-1 shows two sets of numbers. One set gives the number of possible study hours; the other gives the corresponding number of leisure hours (given a total of 10 hours to allocate between leisure and study). The numbers are, in other words, inexorably tied to one another; each study-hour number is paired with a leisure-hour figure. It is always this type of pairing process that a graph illustrates. The leisure-study tradeoff provides a perfect example. All the pairs in Table 1A-1 are characterized by one relationship: the sum of the hours spent studying and the hours spent relaxing must always equal 10.

All these points are captured somewhere along the line *AG* in Figure 1A-1 (assuming that negative numbers of hours are not allowed) . To see how, notice that the vertical line at the left of Figure 1A-1 and the horizontal line at the bottom are the axes against which the pairwise linkage is to be charted. Each is divided off with a number scale, and the meaning of the numbers is indicated by the labels: Hours of Study Time" (horizontally) and "Hours of Leisure Time" (vertically).

The slanting line carrying points labeled *A* through *G* has already been identified as the actual graph of the leisure-study relationship. Each point identified along that line corresponds to a pair in Table 1A-1. Take point *B*. for example. Point *B* in Table 1A-1 pairs 2 hours of study with 8 hours of leisure time. The dashed lines in Figure 1A-1 do the same thing. Passing down from point *B* to the study-time horizontal axis, note that 2 hours is associated with point *B*; moving left to the leisure-time vertical axis, similarly note that 8 hours is associated with point *B*. Table 1A-1 and Figure 1A-1 illustrate the same thing, for point *B* and every other point along the line.

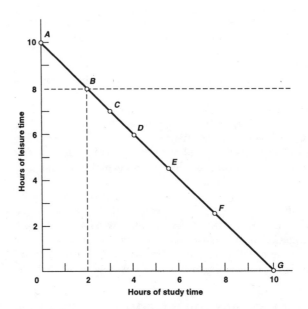

Figure 1A-1

1. In Figure 1A-1, point *B* stands for the combination of 2 hours of (**study / leisure**) and 8 hours of (**study / leisure**).
2. In Figure 1A-1, leisure hours are measured (**vertically / horizontally**) and study hours are measured (**vertically / horizontally**).
3. Point *D* stands for __ hours of leisure and __ hours of study; 9 study hours and 1 leisure hour would be a pair indicated by a point between points (**A and B / D and E / F and G**).
4. The rate at which study hours can be turned into leisure time is __ hour(s) for every 1 hour of study time sacrificed.
5. The slope of the line in the diagram is __.
6. Take any point inside the triangle formed by the three lines (*AG* and the two axis lines). The pair of measurements for any such point:
    a. must together total more than 10.
    b. must together total less than 10.
    c. must together total 10.

d. may total more than 10 or less than 10.

7. Which alternative in question 6 correctly describes the pair of measurements belonging to any point outside line *AG* (above and to the right)? (**a / b / c / d**)

8. If we redid this example by assuming that there were a total of 11 hours to allocate, rather than 10, what would happen to line *AG* (as the line indicating all possible combinations) ?

    a. It would move outward (i.e., upward and to the right), remaining parallel to the present line.

    b. It would move inward (i.e., downward and to the left), remaining parallel to the present line.

    c. Its position would not change.

    d. It would pivot or rotate outward on point *A*.

Example Two: Money, Apples, and Oranges

Suppose that someone particularly interested in either apples or oranges decides that he will allocate $40 to the purchase of one or the other, or both. Let apples cost $2 per bushel, and let oranges cost $1 per dozen. Table 1A-2 records a few possible combinations of apples and oranges that this person might consider. Notice, for example, that devoting the entire $40 to apples would allow him to bring 20 bushels of apples home (point *A* in Table 1A-2). Devoting the entire $40 to oranges would allow him to bring 40 dozen oranges home (point *G* in Table 1A-2). Other intermediate combinations, designated elsewhere in Table 1A-2, would also be possible and should not be ignored. It is likely, in fact, that these intermediate points would be preferred to "specializing" exclusively in the consumption of one fruit or the other.

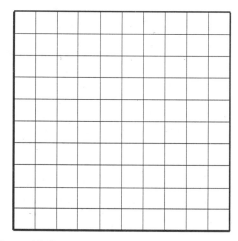

Figure 1A-2

TABLE 1A-2

	A	*B*	*C*	*D*	*E*	*F*	*G*
Apples (bushels)	20	18	15	10	5	2	0
Oranges (dozens)	0	4	10	20	30	36	40

Figure 1A-2 is blank save for a series of vertical and horizontal "grid lines," used to help locate the point that matches up with any given pair of numbers. On Figure 1A-2, draw a graph that illustrates the points in Table 1A-2. First label your axis lines. Then pick a scale for each of the axes, i.e., choose how much distance you are going to use to represent 1 bushel of apples and 1 dozen oranges. With these scales in mind, plot the seven points of Table 1A-2 and label each with its letter identification. They should all lie along a straight line much like the one drawn in Figure 1A-1. After you have satisfied yourself that they do, draw the entire line by connecting the points. This "smoothing" allows the graph to reflect all the points that you could have marked off if you had the time and patience—all combinations of oranges and apples (including fractions) that could be purchased with $40. The concept introduced in the last line above bears repeating. Looking back at Figure 1A-1, note that you cannot possibly find any combination of two positive numbers which add up to 10 that does not appear somewhere on line *AG*. Line *AG* includes every possible pair that satisfies this linking rule. Moreover, line *AG* can be trusted in another respect: it contains no point that does not meet the linking rule. In other words, line *AG* is an exact graphical representation of the "sum-to-10 rule" in the sense that (1) it includes *all* points that satisfy this rule, and (2) it includes *only* points that satisfy this rule. Similarly, the line that *you* drew in Figure 1A-2 includes *all* the combinations of apples and oranges which cost $40 and *only* those combinations which, indeed, cost $40.

9. In this example, our fruit lover would have loved to have purchased 20 dozen oranges and 20 bushels of apples. He (**could / could not**) do that, however, because he had (**more than enough money / insufficient funds**).

10. That combination, i.e., 20 of each fruit, would cost ___.

11. In the study-leisure example, the rate of exchange between study time and relaxation time was ___ hour devoted to studying for every 1 hour of forgone relaxation. In the apples-oranges example, the tradeoff is ___ dozen oranges for every bushel of forgone apples.

Example Three: The Guns-or-Butter Diagram

The first graphical diagram that you encountered in the text was the guns-or-butter chart of Chapter 1. As shown in Table 1A-3 (reproduced from Table 1-1 in the text), it involves pairs of figures once again.

TABLE 1A-3

	A	*B*	*C*	*D*	*E*	*F*
Butter (millions of pounds)	0	1	2	3	4	5
Guns (thousands)	15	14	12	9	5	0

The background of the guns-or-butter case is fundamentally one of scarcity. The economy has only a limited and fixed stock of machinery, labor, and all the other things needed to produce such items as guns or butter. Some of these resources can be used in the production of either commodity. Labor, for instance, can be transferred from the production of guns to the production of butter, or vice versa (with due allowance for the training time that might be required to make labor proficient in its new location). If labor were switched from, say, work on guns to work on butter, the result would be an increase in the output of butter and a corresponding reduction in the output of guns. If resources were fully employed, the inevitable cost of getting more of one commodity must, by extension of this example, always be a reduction in the supply of another.

The "guns-or-butter" metaphor first arose in Nazi Germany. By the end of the 1930s, Hitler's government had turned so much of German industry toward rearmament that there were shortages of some civilian goods, butter among them. The late and generally unlamented Hermann Goering made a famous speech in which he sought to appease the public's complaints by declaring, "We must choose between guns and butter!" Some choice.

As a further exercise in graph drawing, draw the guns-or-butter diagram for yourself in Figure 1A-3 using the figures in Table 1A-3. As before, first label your two axes. Measure quantity of guns in the vertical dimension (as the text does) and quantity of butter horizontally. Ordinarily, you want to make use of all the space available on a graph. In Figure 1A-3, the maximum butter quantity to be recorded is 5 (million pounds); so put 5 at the bottom right-hand corner. There are 15 little squares sitting on the horizontal axis line; if 5 goes below the end of the fifteenth square, then 1 must go below the end of the third one, 2 below the end of the sixth, and so on. As to guns, your maximum is 15 (thousand); so put 15 at the top left, with the smaller numbers below. Notice that (in the matter of graph distances) your

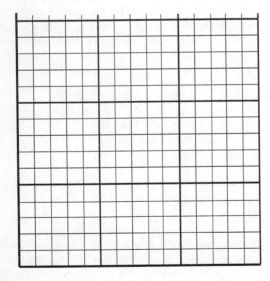

Figure 1A-3

two number scales can be different. Here, the same distance in inches which measures 5 million pounds of butter (horizontally) records 15,000 guns (vertically).

Having put labels and numbers on your axes, indicate on the graph the six points in the table. (This is known as plotting the points.) Identify them by letter and join them with a smooth curve. You have now completed a graph of the guns-butter production-possibility frontier (*PPF*). What can you learn from this graph? Why was it worth the trouble? Four different observations spring to mind:

1. The area of the graph above and to the right of the frontier (the curved line *ABCDEF*) represents more desirable but unattainable territory. Points in that region represent larger guns-butter combinations than those represented by the frontier line, but they are unattainable unless or until the economy acquires more productive agents or develops better techniques for using what it has. The process of economic growth can be represented as a gradual outward shifting of the frontier.

2. The graph area below and to the left of the frontier is fully attainable. If the economy's actual guns-butter production were to be represented by a point in this area, it would signify (a) that the economy was not fully using all its available resources, or (b) that although it was employing them fully, it was somehow failing to use them to the best advantage. We assume that the economy can reach any point on the frontier without disrupting its social order and without undue strain on its productive agents and that its people will want production to reach this line. Both of the two commodities are scarce relative to the desire for them.

3. If both the unattainable area above the curve and the undesirable area below the curve were removed from consideration, then only the frontier would remain. The decision which people in this economy (or their leaders) must somehow make about what to produce can thus be represented as the problem of deciding which point along the frontier *ABCDEF* to choose. To describe this as a "guns-or-butter" decision can be a bit misleading; it suggests (all) guns or (all) butter. If both guns and butter were desirable, though, it is most likely that points *A* and *F* would both be rejected in lieu of some intermediate point such as *C* or *D*.

4. In actual life, decisions about what to produce have been being made for a long time, and they are still being made. A decision of this nature is not something that can be made only once and then forgotten, for tastes change and so do productive conditions. It is a little more realistic, then, to think of an economy which is currently operating at some point such as *D*, and which might, for example, be disposed to spend its "peace dividend" and move toward having a little more butter. This would mean a movement away from point *D* and toward point *E*.

12. The figures in the guns-or-butter table represent (**maximum / minimum**) combinations of these two commodities that some imaginary community could produce per unit of time. The figures stand for (**money values / physical quantities**) of guns and butter.

13. If all available resources or inputs were devoted to butter production, butter output would be ___ million pounds and gun output would be ___ thousand guns. If the economy wished to have 9000 guns per period, butter output could not exceed ___ million pounds.

14. Suppose that the community is producing a total of 1 million pounds of butter. If it wants to increase this by another 1 million pounds, then the required decrease in gun production would be ___ thousand. If the community were producing 4 million pounds of butter and wanted to increase this by 1 million (to a total of 5 million), then the required decrease in gun production would be ___ thousand.

15. Suppose that the community is producing 15,000 guns and is considering a reduction to 14,000. The change would make possible a butter increase of ___ million pounds. Alternatively, if the community currently produces 9000 guns and decides on a reduction to 5000, then a butter increase of ___ million pounds would be possible. If gun production were to be increased from 9000 to 10,000, this increase of 1000 would call for a reduction in butter output of approximately ___ million pounds.

Notice that your two answers in question 14 were different, indicating that the cost of butter in terms of guns changed as more butter was produced. This notion will be important later.

One essential distinction that pervades economic thought is the difference between movement along a curve and shifts of a curve. It has already been noted in the context of the guns-or-butter example of Table 1A-3 that a society disposed toward having a little more butter could move from a point like D toward a point like E. Notice, however, that such a move clearly indicates that more butter means fewer guns. Point D represents 3 million pounds of butter and 9000 guns; point E represents 4 million pounds of butter but only 5000 guns. Without any increase in resources or advances in technology, this sort of movement along the PPF is society's only option.

When the things which are normally held constant in the construction of a curve are allowed to change, however, the entire curve can actually shift. Suppose, for example, that the economy whose guns-or-butter tradeoff was represented in Table 1A-3 was to discover a better way to make butter—a way that would use fewer resources that are applicable to the production of guns. Table 1A-4 reflects such a change.

Compare Tables 1A-3 and 1A4. The technological improvement reflected in Table 1A-4 shows that butter production doubles for any given level of gun production except the maximum.

Table 1A-4

	A'	B'	C'	D'	E'	F'
Butter (millions of pounds)	0	2	4	6	8	10
Guns (thousands)	15	14	12	9	5	0

Hint In general, if a variable that is important to the analysis of some issue changes *and* it is *not measured on one of the axes* of your diagram, then this will cause the curve to shift. In the example at hand, there was a change in technology. (Note, technology is not measured on the axes of the PPF; just guns and butter are.) Since technology is very relevant to this analysis, the PPF will shift when technology changes. Alternatively, a change in guns or in butter will not cause the PPF to shift; rather, as we trade guns for butter, we move along the PPF.

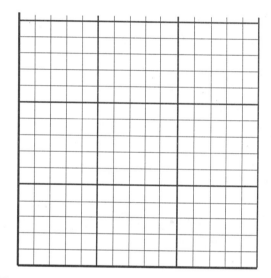

Figure 1A-4

Graph the production-possibility frontier defined in Table 1A-4 on Figure 1A-4. (We suggest using one box for each thousand guns and 1.5 boxes for each million pounds of butter, but feel free to use your own judgement in setting up the diagram. Be sure to label your axes.) Label the points and smooth the curve. Now replicate your graph of the production-possibility frontier from Table 1A-3 on Figure 1A-4. The frontier should have shifted out in moving from Table 1A-3 to Table 1A-4 for every level of gun production but one—the one in which no butter at all is produced so that 15,000 guns can be   manufactured. That makes sense, though, because the technological advances in the production of butter increase the opportunities of the economy except in the case where it ignores the new butter technology and specializes entirely in the production of guns. Movement from D to E is no longer necessary. Shifting from D to D' increases butter production to 4 million pounds even though gun production holds at 9000.

Example Four: Slope—Straight Lines

One way to describe a straight-line relationship between some variable X and another variable Y is to assert that X and Y are linked so that any given change in X always generates exactly the same change in Y. Starting with X and Y occupying some initial positions, we often ask, 'What would happen to Y if X were to change its position (i.e., its value)?" In a more useful way, perhaps, we might ask, "What change in Y would be forthcoming if X were to increase or decrease by 1 unit?"

To get a picture of what is going on, think of starting somewhere on a straight-line graph and making little movements to the right in two stages. Think, in particular, first about making a strictly horizontal movement of sufficient length to indicate a 1-unit increase in the X value. Since the move was horizontal, the Y value will not have changed. Then think about a vertical movement up or down to signify a change in Y of a very special dimension: a vertical distance precisely equal to the amount of movement required to return to the straight line. For example, in either of the two little diagrams composing Figure 1A-5, the true path traced out is $ABDE$, but the movement from B to D can be considered in two parts. First, there is a probing movement from B to C (the 1-unit change in X which takes the point momentarily off its true path along the line). Then there is a second, correcting movement from C to D (the matching change in Y required to get back on the line). If $BC's$ length indicates a 1-unit increase in X, then $CD's$ length must indicate the rate at which Y must change in response to X to stay on the straight line. On the graph, this vertical measure of the change is called the slope of the line $ABDE$.

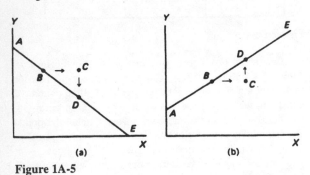

(a)   (b)

Figure 1A-5

Several points about the slope of a line should now be clear:

1. *Slope* is always a number that measures a *rate of change*. It is the amount by which some variable Y must change in response to a 1-unit change in X if we are to stay on the same straight line.

2. If the graph line is straight, one single number measures its slope at any and all points. This is just another way of saying that a straight line is one whose direction does not change.

3. The slope always assumes a negative value if the X-Y relation is an inverse one—one in which a positive increase in X requires a reduction in Y. Both the study-leisure (Figure 1A-1) and the apples-oranges (Figure 1A-2) examples qualify, and both straight lines drawn in those two diagrams have negative slopes. In terms of what we draw, therefore, the slope is negative if the graph falls down to the right. Conversely, the slope is positive and the line climbs up toward the right if the X-Y relation is a direct one.

Now consider a little more fully the technique for measuring or illustrating graphically the slope of a straight line. We have said that the slope of either graph line $ABDE$ in Figure 1A-5 is measured by the length of CD. This assumes that BC is of a length equal to 1 unit of X. We could equally well have said that slope is measured by the fraction CD/BC, with the lengths of CD and BC representing the numbers for which they stand. Since BC corresponds to the number 1, CD/BC reduces to CD anyway. The only objection to defining slope to be CD/BC is that at first it seems needlessly clumsy; but measuring slope as the more general fraction CD/BC is a reminder that the Y movement (CD) can be considered only relative to the amount of movement envisioned in the variable X (BC).

Some people find it helpful to think of slope as "the rise over the run." The "rise" is the vertical distance involved; in Figure 1A-5's terms, the rise is CD. The "run" is the horizontal distance; it is BC in Figure 1A-5's terms. So the "rise over run" rule would, in this instance, cause us to place CD over BC.

It is tempting to associate the measure of slope with the steepness with which the graph line rises or falls, so a steeply tilted line is often assumed to be one with a high slope value, positive or negative. Sometimes this conclusion is valid, but don't overlook the fact that the steepness with which a graph line rises or falls depends in part on the scale chosen for the graph. Diagrams (*a*) and (*b*) in Figure 1A-6 both portray exactly the same relationship, and either is a perfectly respectable illustration. Notice, however, that the horizontal scale has been stretched in (*b*) in comparison with that used in (*a*). This stretching makes the line look flatter in (*b*) than in (*a*) even though the slope in both cases is +1/2.

The trick is that relative steepness accurately reflects relative slope only when the scales are the same. When you have two lines on the same graph, therefore, you can certainly say that the steeper line has the larger slope, in absolute value—more negative if the two lines are negatively sloped and downward-sloping or more positive if the two lines are positively sloped and upward-sloping. In Figure 1A-6(*c*), for example, line I has a slope of 4, line II has a slope of 2, and I

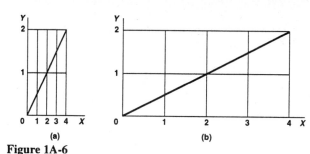
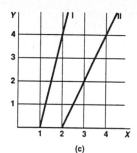
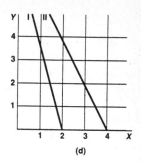

Figure 1A-6

is clearly steeper than II. In Figure 1A-6(d), line I has a slope of -4, line II has a slope of -2; the number 4 is still greater than 2 -and -4 is more negative than -2, so line I is again steeper than line II.

Figure 1A-7 contains six different graphs. In each, the variable X signifies the magnitude being measured horizontally, and Y signifies the magnitude being measured vertically. Use the letters beneath the diagrams to answer questions 16 through 25. Some questions may have more than one correct answer.

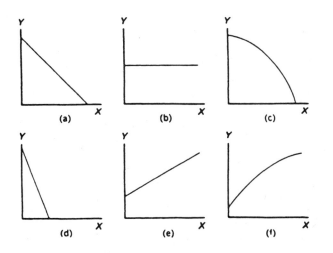

Figure 1A-7

16. Diagrams (**a** / **b** / **c** / **d** / **e** / **f**) illustrate an inverse relation between X and Y.

17. In diagram (**a** / **b** / **c** / **d** / **e** / **f**), Y's response to a change in X is zero.

18. The X-Y relation is positive rather than inverse in diagram(s) (**a** / **b** / **c** / **d** / **e** / **f**).

19. Among the diagrams illustrating an inverse relation, the slope is constant in diagram(s) (**a** / **b** / **c** / **d** / **e** / **f**).

20. The diagram best suited to illustrate the relation between an adult's daily food intake in calories, measured along the X axis, and his or her weight, measured along the Y axis, would be (pick two which could be correct) (**a** / **b** / **c** / **d** / **e** / **f**).

21. The relationship between a child's age (X) and height (Y) would probably be illustrated best by (**a** / **b** / **c** / **d** / **e** / **f**).

22. The most probable relation between the number of study hours you put in before a given examination (X) and the examination grade you can expect to earn (Y) is illustrated best by (or is supposed to be illustrated best by) diagram(s) (**a** / **b** / **c** / **d** / **e** / **f**).

23. Assume, in diagram (d), that the graph line meets the Y axis at 10 units and that it meets the X axis at 5 units. (You may want to write these figures on the diagram.) A 1-unit increase in X must therefore be accompanied by a (**0** / **.5** / **1** / **2** / **4** / **10**) unit (**increase** / **decrease**) in Y.

24. In diagram (b), let the graph line meet the Y axis at 4 units. When the value of X is 0, then the value of Y must be (**0** / **1** / **2** / **4** / **can't tell**). Similarly, when the value of X is 10, then the value of Y must be (**0** / **1** / **2** / **4** / **can't tell**).

25. In diagram (e), let one point on the graph line represent the point where $X = 0$ and $Y = 4$. This point on the diagram is called the (**intercept** / **origin** / **slope**). Let another point on the graph line represent the point where $X = 3$ and $Y = 5$. These two points indicate an underlying relation which holds that every single unit increase in the value of X must be accompanied by (**an increase** / **a decrease**) in the value of Y equal to (**.25** / **.33** / **1** / **3** / **4**).

Note **If you find yourself stuck on any of these questions, or if you have answered incorrectly, do not be too concerned: the unfamiliar is seldom easy. Go back and review earlier material if necessary, until you are reasonably sure you understand why each answer is correct.**

26. Slope is a measure of the rate at which the value of Y changes for each change of (**0 units** / **1 unit** / **the same number of units**) in the value of X.

27. When a graphed line has the same slope value throughout, we can be certain that the line is (**curved** / **rising** / **straight** / **falling**).

28. We can graphically illustrate or measure slope of a line by using a right-angled triangle immediately above or below the graph line. Slope is the fraction or ratio obtained by

putting the length of the (**vertical / horizontal**) side of the triangle over the length of the (**vertical / horizontal**) side.

29. When an X-Y relation is inverse, then its graphical illustration will look like the path of a point which (**falls / rises**) as it moves to the right. The slope value of such a relation is (**positive / zero / negative**).

30. In diagram (*b*) of Figure 1A-7, the slope of the line illustrated is (**positive / negative / zero / impossible to tell**).

31. Two positions of X on a straight graph line are 5 and 7. What is the value of slope if the corresponding values for Y are:

a.   5 and 7? (**-3 / -2 / -1/ 0 / 1 / 2 / 3 /infinity**)
b.   4 and 2? (**-3/ -2/ -1/ 0 / 1 / 2 / 3 / infinity**)
c.   2 and -2? (**-3 / -2 / -1 / O / 1 / 2 / 3 / infinity**)
d.   4 and 4? (**-3 / -2/ -1 / 0 / 1 / 2 / 3 / infinite**)
e.   -2 and -8? (**-3 / -2 / -1 / 0 / 1 / 2 / 3 / infinity**)
f.   -8 and -2? (**-3 / -2 / -1 / 0 / 1 / 2 / 3 / infinity**)

Example Five: Equations for Straight Lines

While a picture is often worth a thousand words, a single equation can completely describe a linear relationship between two variables. Assume there are two variables, X and Y, and they are linearly related. The following equation can be used to describe their relationship:

$$Y = a + bX$$

where a is the intercept of the line and b is its slope. (You may recall that the intercept is the point where a line crosses the Y, or vertical axis.) Look, for example, back at Figure 1A-1 in this appendix which illustrates the relationship between leisure time and study time. The Y axis intercept of that line is 10 and the slope is -1. Therefore, the equation for that line is:

$$Y = 10 - 1X$$

32. Look at Figure 1A-2 which illustrates the relationship between apples and oranges. Write an equation which completely describes this relationship. (Unlike in the leisure and study-time example, the slope in this diagram is not -1. So there are two possible answers, depending upon which fruit you plotted on the vertical axis.)

---

33. Look at Figure 1A-7, panel (*e*). Suppose that the Y intercept is 3 and the slope of the line is 2. Write the equation for this line.

---

34. Look at Figure 1A-7, panel (*b*). Suppose that the Y intercept is 4. Write the equation for this line. (*Hint*: What is the slope of a horizontal line?)

In addition to writing equations from lines drawn on graphs, you can also formulate equations from tables of data. Once you derive the equation, it is very easy to precisely plot

the line! Suppose you are presented with the following data for Y and X:

TABLE 1A-5

Y	X
22	20
25	25
28	30

At this point, we know neither the slope nor the intercept of this linear relationship. The relationship is a positive one, however (Y and X increase together).

The first thing we need to do is find the slope. As we move down the table, Y always increases by 3 units and X always increases by 5 units. So the slope, measured by the *change* in Y over the *change* in X is +3/5, or +0. 6. At this point we can write the equation for the line as:

$$Y = a + 0.6X$$

To solve for the intercept, a, we can pick *any pair of Y* and X numbers from Table 1A-5 above. For example, pick the 28 and the 30. Substitute these numbers into our equation and solve for a.

$$28 = a + 0.6(30)$$
$$28 = a + 18$$
$$28 - 18 = a$$
$$10 = a$$

The data in Table 1A-5 can now be represented with the following equation:

$$Y = 10 + 0.6X$$

This is a very powerful statement! Even though the table includes only three pairs of numbers, you can now solve for any value of Y as long as you are told what the corresponding value of X is.

35. When X is 85, Y will be equal to ___. Unless you have either a very large table or a very large piece of graph paper, it is difficult to determine the answer without the equation.

Example Six: Slope—Curved Lines

A curved line is one whose slope continually changes; i.e., the amount of change in Y required to accommodate a 1-unit change in X varies according to the position from which this change begins. Consider the curved line ABCDEF in Figure 1A-8. Suppose we are at point B. If we know the exact X and Y values associated with every point on this line, then we should have no difficulty in learning what the changes in both X and Y would be as a result of moving from point B to point E. Moreover, we could put the usual right-angled triangle underneath the line segment between B and E, with corners at points B and E, and from it develop a value for the slope—a value called the *arc slope* from B to E.

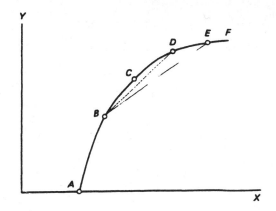

Figure 1A-8

The arc slope would not, however, be the slope of the curved line itself; it would really measure the slope of the straight line running between points *B* and *E*. We would get a different and somewhat higher slope figure if we dealt similarly with a change from point *B* to point *D*, and a still different value for a change between points B and C.

For some purposes, it is quite sufficient to know the arc slope from point *B* to *E*, or to *D*, or to *C*. For other problems, however, it can be essential to know the value of the slope of the curved line exactly at some point like point *B*.

Does it make sense to speak of the slope of a line precisely at a single point? Certainly point *B*, considered in isolation, has no slope and no direction. When point *B* is considered as part of the line *ABCDEF*, however, its slope is another matter. The slope of the line is a measure of the direction in which it runs, computed in terms of the scales on the two axes. Think for the moment of *ABCDEF* as the path traced by a moving automobile traveling around a curve. The direction of the automobile changes continually, since it follows the curve, but we can say that the automobile is headed in a specific direction at any specific moment, like the exact moment when it passes over point *B*. We can certainly do so in the sense that a compass mounted on the car's dashboard at that exact moment would give an exact reading.

But how is this direction at *B* to be indicated on a piece of graph paper? The accepted answer is quite simple: by a *tangent* drawn to the curved line at point *B*. The tangent to a curved line is itself, by definition, a straight line; it does not cross the curved line, and it touches it at only one point. By inspection of Figure 1A-9(a), for example, it is easy to see how the slope of the tangent line *FJ* is to be considered as a measure of the slope of the curved line at point *B*; and line *GH* does the same for point *D*. We can then, of course, apply the usual right-angle technique for computing the slope of each straight line.

What does this slope mean? Figure 1A-9(b) redraws the guns-or-butter production-possibility frontier from Table 1A-

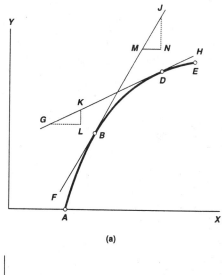

(a)

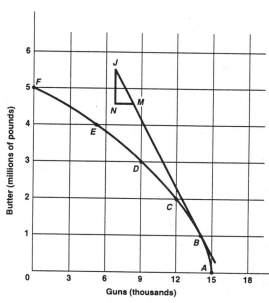

(b)

Figure 1A-9

4. At point *B*, a tangent line is drawn, and its slope, — (*JN/MN*), represents the slope of the guns-or-butter schedule at point *B*. It is, intuitively, a reflection of how many guns need to be sacrificed to increase the production of butter not by 1 million pounds but by 1 pound—a much smaller number. In reality, the slope of the line at point *B* is the sacrifice in guns required to finance a minuscule increase in butter production; and after all, 1 pound is a small quantity when it is compared with 1 million pounds.

36. Figure 1A-10 consists of eight separate diagrams, each illustrating a small segment of a graph line. In each, the

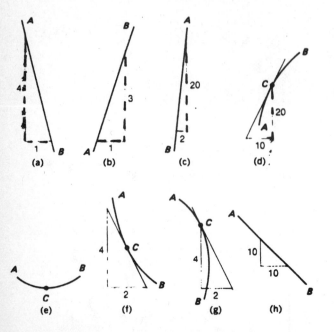

Figure 1A-10

numbers indicate the length of the adjacent straightline segment. Use the numbers in parentheses below to indicate the slope of line *AB* in each of the panels, (*a*) through (*h*). Where line *AB* is curved, it is the slope at point *C* that is desired. Circle the correct answer for each panel.

a. (-4 / -3 / -2 / -1 / 0 / 1 / 2 / 3 / 4 / 10 / infinity)
b. (-4 / -3 / -2 / -1 /0 / 1 / 2 / 3 / 4 / 10 / infinity)
c. (-4 / -3 / -2 / -1 / 0 / 1 / 2 / 3 / 4 /10 / infinity)
d. (-4 / -3 / -2 / -1 / 0 / 1/ 2 / 3 / 4 / 10 / infinity)
e. (-4 / -3 / -2 / -1 / 0 / 1 / 2 / 3/ 4 / 10 / infinity)
f. (-4 / -3/ -2 / -1 / 0 / 1 / 2 / 3 / 4 / 10 / infinity)
g. (-4 / -3 / -2 / -1 / 0 / 1 / 2 / 3 / 4 / 10 / infinity)
h. (-4 -3 / -2 / -1 / 0 / 1 / 2 / 3 / 4 / 10 / infinity)

Example Seven: Two or More Lines on a Graph
So far our discussion has run in terms of the interpretation of a single line on a graph. But most text diagrams will include two or more lines, usually intersecting at one or more points on the graph. The supply-and-demand diagrams of Chapter 3 in your textbook are good examples. The demand line, or demand curve, is drawn as usual—from two sets of figures paired together. Table 1A-6 provides one example of a demand curve.

Table 1A-6 shows a relationship between the quantities of wheat that buyers in some market would demand (i.e., be prepared to buy) if the price were to stand at any one of five possible levels.

TABLE 1A-6

	Price of Wheat (per bu)	Quantity Demanded (million bu per month)
A	$5	9
B	4	10
C	3	12
D	2	15
E	1	20

It does not matter whether this is a real market or an imaginary one. The precise figures in the table are not especially important, either. This schedule is intended simply to illustrate the reasonable (and important) notion that as the price of wheat falls, buyers probably will want to buy a larger total amount than they did before. In other words, quantity of wheat bought should be expected to be inversely related to the price of wheat.

It is also possible to prepare another schedule, indicating what sellers of wheat (the producers of wheat, the suppliers of wheat) are prepared to do. In this case, it seems reasonable to assume that if the price were to go up, then suppliers would try to supply a larger quantity because the higher price would generate a higher return on their efforts. Alternatively, if the price were to fall, then they would choose to supply less. Table 1A-7 represents this different relation, showing quite clearly that the quantity of wheat supplied is directly related to the price of wheat.

TABLE 1A-7

	Price of Wheat (per bu)	Quantity Supplied (million bu per month)
A	$5	18
B	4	16
C	3	12
D	2	7
E	1	0

At this stage, it is not particularly essential that you fully understand the ideas conveyed by the demand and supply schedules. What matters for the moment is that you recognize something familiar in the construction: the demand curve consists of two sets of inversely related figures, neatly paired one with the other; the supply curve consists of two sets of positively related figures, equally neatly paired with each other. This means that each can be depicted as a line on a graph—and both can even be depicted together on the same graph.

Why? Despite their differences, there is a fundamental similarity between the two schedules. Although they represent the attitudes or the intentions of two entirely different groups of people, *the two schedules match one another in that one column refers to price and the other to quantity.*

It is only because they match in this respect that both can be depicted on the same graph. If we are to make any sense out of two or more lines on the same graph, these lines must refer to the same kinds of things, measured in the same kinds of units.

In Figure 1A-11, draw the lines corresponding to these two schedules. (Plot the five points for each schedule and join them with a smooth curve.) Label your demand curve *DD* and your supply curve *SS*.

Your two lines should cross at one point and one point only: the point signifying a price of $3 per bushel and a quantity of 12 million bushels. Its significance is that at this level of price, and no other, the intentions of buyers and the intentions of sellers match. In these circumstances, the price of $3 will be called an "equilibrium price," and the quantity of 12 million bushels an "equilibrium quantity." At a price of $3, buyers want to purchase exactly the 12 million bushels that suppliers are willing to deliver.

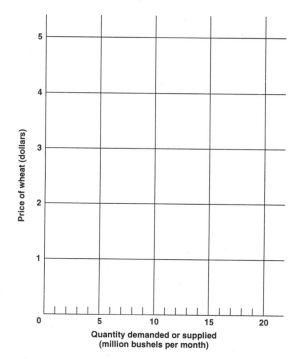

Figure 1A-11

V. REVIEW

37. One point on a graph indicates a value for *X* of 4 and a value for *Y* of 10. Another point indicates that *X* = 5 and *Y* = 8. If these two points are joined by a straight line, then the slope of that line is ___.

38. The slope of a straight line is -3. Movement from one point to another along that line results in an increase in *Y* from 10 to 16. What was the associated change in *X*? It must have (**risen / fallen**) by (**6 / 3 / 2 / 1 / 0.5**).

39. A line on a graph appears as the upper half of a circle: it starts out at the origin of the graph, rises, and then falls, until finally it drops to the horizontal axis from which it started.

Which of the following correctly describes the slope of this line as it moves from the origin to the right?

a.   It will have a changing but positive slope value throughout.

b.   It will first have a negative slope (toward the left-hand side), and its value will grow larger as the line proceeds to the right. Eventually, though, the slope will turn positive.

c.   It will first have a positive slope, and its value will grow larger as the line proceeds to the right. Eventually, though, the slope will turn negative.

d.   It will first have a positive slope, but its value will diminish as the line proceeds to the right. The slope will eventually reach a value of zero at the top of the semi-circle, and then it will turn negative.

40. In Figure 1A-11, the *DD* curve has a (**negative / positive**) slope. Its value is (**constant / changing**) throughout the line. The *SS* curve in this figure has a (**negative / positive**) slope. Its value is (**constant / changing**) throughout the line.

VI. CONCLUSION

Graphs were made to help people grasp ideas with as little expenditure of time and effort as possible; but if you want to take advantage of this device, you must learn the rules and you must ask the right questions:

1.   What does the graph measure on each axis? What are the labels on the axes? Each line on a graph indicates some kind of relation or linking rule between the two sets of numbers.

2.   Which way does the line run? Does it fall to the right or rise to the right? If it falls, then the relation between the two sets of numbers is an inverse one—as one rises, the other falls. If it rises to the right, then the two sets of numbers move in the same direction and represent a direct relationship.

3.   Is the line straight or curved? If it is straight, the ratio of the change in the value of *Y* to the change in the value of *X* is constant. If the line curves, this ratio varies.

4.   If there are two or more lines on a graph, then there are two or more schedules in the background. What kind of relationship is involved in each schedule, and why is it important to bring the schedules together on the same graph? Usually the two lines cross one another at some point, and usually this intersection is important because at this point the two schedules match one another.

5.   If the variables under consideration change, should you move along the curve or will the curve shift? Generally, if the variable that is changing is measured along one of the axes in the diagram, then you move along the curve. If some other relevant variable changes, say technology in the *PPF*

analysis, then the curve will shift to illustrate the change. The importance of understanding this concept—the difference between movements along and shifts in curves—cannot be stated too strongly.

VII. ANSWERS TO STUDY GUIDE QUESTIONS

III. Review of Key Concepts

7   Slope
4   Intercept
11 Origin
2   Positive slope
9   Negative slope
10 X axis
6   Y axis
5   Grid lines
1   Tangent
8   Scatter diagram
3   Time-series diagram

IV. Examples

1. study, leisure
2. vertically, horizontally
3. 6, 4, F and G
4. 1
5. -1

6. b
7. a
8. a
9. could not, insufficient funds
10. $60
11. 1, 2

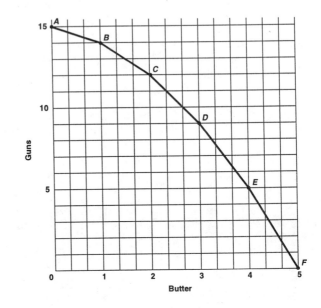

Figure 1A-3

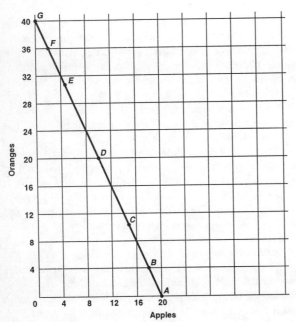

Figure 1A-2

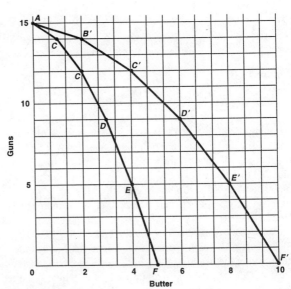

Figure 1A-4

12. maximum, physical quantities
13. 5, 0, 3
14. 2, 5
15. 1, 1, .33
16. a, c, d
17. b
18. e, f
19. a, d
20. e, f
21. f
22. e
23. 2, decrease
24. 4, 4
25. intercept, an increase, .33
26. 1 unit
27. straight
28. vertical, horizontal
29. falls, negative
30. zero
31. a. 1
    b. -1
    c. -2
    d. 0
    e. -3
    f. 3
32. If apples (AP) are on the vertical axis: AP = 20 -0.5 ×
OR.
    If oranges (OR) are on the vertical axis: OR = 40 -2.0 ×
AP.
33. $Y = 3 + 2X$
34. $Y = 4$
35. 61
36 a. -4
   b. 3
   c. 10
   d. 2

e. 0
f. -2
g. -2
h. -1

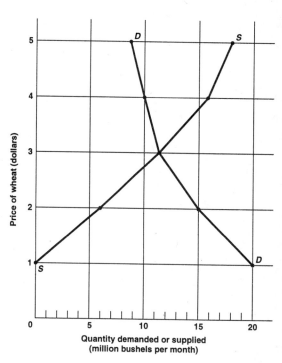

Figure 1A-11

37. 2
38. fallen, 2
39. d
40. negative, changing, positive, changing

CHAPTER

Markets and Government in a Modern Economy

I. CHAPTER OVERVIEW

This chapter introduces a series of fundamental ideas and concepts which define the essence of the economic problem and the source of economic opportunity for an advanced economy. They are important because they form the foundation for the analysis of a market economy. The tools and methods that you learn here will be carried throughout the text and developed in greater detail as you make your way through the course. It is essential, therefore, that you grasp each of them before you proceed.

II. LEARNING OBJECTIVES

After you have read Chapter 2 in your text and completed the exercises in this *Study Guide* chapter, you should be able to:

1 Describe what is meant by the term **market** and describe the process of achieving **equilibrium** in a market economy.

2. Use your definition of market equilibrium to address three basic economic problems that confront all societies.

3. Explain how the price system works as an **invisible hand**, allocating goods and services in a market economy.

4. Understand the importance of (a) specialization, (b) the division of labor, (c) money, (d) factors of production, and (e) capital and property rights in the functioning of a modern economy.

5. Use a **circular-flow diagram** to illustrate the relationships between agents and markets in a modern economy.

6. Make a case for government intervention in a mixed market economy in order to promote **efficiency, equity,** and **macroeconomic growth** and **stability**.

III. REVIEW OF KEY CONCEPTS

Match the following terms from column A with their definitions in column B.

A

__ The market mechanism

__ Market equilibrium

__ Perfect competition

__ The invisible hand

__ Specialization and division of labor

__ Capital

__ Efficiency

__ Equity

__ Monopoly

__ Externalities

__ Fiscal policy

B

1 A market structure in which a commodity is supplied by a single firm.

2. Involves issues of "fairness" in the distribution of income.

3. Productive inputs that include all durable produced goods that are in turn used in production.

4. Arrangements whereby buyers and sellers interact to determine the prices and quantities exchanged of a commodity.

5. The use of economic resources that produces the maximum level of satisfaction possible with the given inputs and technology.

6. The balancing of supply and demand in a market.

7. A government's program with respect to its own spending and taxation.

8. Situations in which production or consumption yields positive or negative effects on outside parties.

9. A method of organizing production whereby each group of people concentrates its efforts on a particular set of tasks.

10. With each participant pursuing his or her own private interest, a market system works to the benefit of all.

11. Markets in which no firm or consumer is large enough to affect market price.

IV. SUMMARY AND CHAPTER OUTLINE

This section summarizes the key concepts from the chapter.

A. What Is a Market?

1. A market economy has at its heart the actions of buyers and sellers who exchange goods and services with one another. There is no higher authority that directs the behavior of these economic agents; rather, it is the *invisible hand* of the marketplace that allocates final goods and services, as well as factors of production.

2. Buyers and sellers receive signals from one another in the form of prices. If buyers want to buy more of a good, prices rise and sellers respond by supplying more to the marketplace. If buyers want to buy less of a good, prices fall and sellers respond by supplying less to the marketplace. This is what is meant by the term *invisible hand*. Prices rise and fall naturally as people change their behavior; there is no need for a higher authority. Price signals tell sellers what to do with their production levels.

3. Market equilibrium occurs when the price is such that the quantity that buyers are interested in purchasing is equal to the quantity that sellers are interested in supplying to the market.

4. The market mechanism allows an economy to simultaneously solve the three economic problems of *what, how,* and *for whom.* Consumers indicate their preferences over *what* is produced through their willingness to pay for a good or service. Firms respond to this by considering the mix of final products that will maximize their own profits, that is, the difference between their revenues from sales and their production costs. This must involve the question *how,* since firm production costs are determined by the prices of inputs and technology used in the production process. Once these questions have been addressed, *for whom* is found to be those consumers who have the money to pay for the goods and services produced.

B. Trade, Money, and Capital

1. Advanced economies use complex systems of trade in order to accumulate the bundle of goods and services that the people in that economy want to consume. People produce the goods and services that they can produce most efficiently, and then they trade their excess for other items that they need.

2. Money is *not* an input or factor of production. Consumers and firms use money in order to more efficiently carry out market transactions; it is a kind of lubricating oil that allows the machinery of an economy to operate with a minimum of friction.

3. In this course, the term *capital* does *not* refer to money. Instead, the term refers to productive inputs that have, themselves, been manufactured. The notion of capital includes durable items like blast furnaces, factory buildings, machine tools, electric drills, jack hammers, and so on. It also includes stocks of semifinished goods. These are goods which are on the way to becoming consumer goods but which are still manufactured inputs to be used in later stages of the production process.

4. Capital accumulation is an important determinant of economic growth. An economic system that builds a strong capital base is investing in a factor of production that will make all other factors more productive, or useful. Capital is typically privately owned in a market economy, so that private individuals can make decisions about its use. Because these individuals will directly benefit from the use of their capital, they have some incentive to make sure that it is employed efficiently.

C. The Economic Role of Government

1. In the real world, markets do not always operate as smoothly as we might like. Market imperfections lead to a wide range of problems, and governments step in to address them.

2. Governments intervene in a market economy in order to promote *efficiency.*

   a. Market allocations are only efficient when conditions of *perfect competition* hold; this means that no firm or consumer is large enough to affect input or output market prices. When there are many small firms in a market, competition forces all firms to operate with lowest possible costs and prices.

   b. Market allocations become inefficient when *externalities* occur. Externalities are the positive or negative effects on outside parties that production or consumption in an industry yields. For example, when people receive education, schools and students benefit, but so do others in the community who now have neighbors who are better educated.

   c. Market allocations often do not work well, if at all, in the case of public goods. A *public good* is something that is nonrival (my consumption of the good does not exclude your consumption of it) and that can be collectively consumed (we can both enjoy it at the same time). Because it is difficult, or at least expensive, to exclude consumers once the good is available, these types of goods are often provided by the government. One example is snow removal. Once the street has been plowed, everyone on the block can use it; however, it is very impractical to charge residents every time they use the plowed street.

3. Governments intervene in a market economy in order to promote *equity,* or fairness, in the distribution of resources and income. This is a difficult concept because there is no universal definition of fairness. Markets distribute goods and services to those who have the money to purchase them, not necessarily to those who need or deserve them the most.

4.   Governments intervene in a market economy in order to promote *macroeconomic growth and stability*. Fiscal policies of government (the power to tax and spend) and monetary policies (the power to adjust the money supply and interest rates) help to move an economy along a stable path, avoiding periods of excessive inflation and unemployment.

V. HELPFUL HINTS

1.   Over the past few years, monumental changes have taken place around the world that have led to the development of market economies. The Soviet Union collapsed of exhaustion and Russia and the newly-independent states are in the process of initiating market reforms. China now allows many small farmers to exchange their products in markets. These large economies, formerly dominated by central economic planning, found that the old (command) system did a poor job of alleviating the problems of scarcity.

2.   Markets do not provide the only solutions to economic problems. In fact, some economies use goodwill and/or command to motivate resources that are commonly owned by the group. For example, the *kibbutz* system in Israel encourages collective consumption as well as joint ownership of the means of production. These small, intentional communities have provided very efficiently and equitably (according to group standards) for the needs of their citizens.

3.   It is easy to assume that when a market economy is operating efficiently it is also providing an equitable distribution of income and opportunity. However, this is not always the case. In the United States, some people inherit wealth and property from their relatives, while others inherit nothing. Likewise, while some people have the opportunity to attend Harvard University, others are not even able to complete high school before they must enter the work force. These factors are not always determined by the market and at times may lead to distributions that seem very unfair to some people.

VI. MULTIPLE CHOICE QUESTIONS

These questions are organized by topic from the chapter outline. Choose the best answer from the options available.

A. What Is a Market?

1.   Markets can occur:
   a.   whenever buyers and sellers of the same product can communicate with one another.
   b.   only if buyers and sellers have some form of currency to use for exchange.
   c.   only if the government steps in and regulates the behavior of buyers and sellers.
   d.   all of the above.
   e.   none of the above.

2.   If a commodity such as peanuts becomes overstocked, sellers will:
   a.   raise their prices in order to make up for the fact that sales are lower.
   b.   raise their prices in order to increase the demand for peanuts.
   c.   lower their prices hoping to lure additional buyers into the marketplace.
   d.   lower their prices in order to encourage competition from rival firms.
   e.   grow more peanuts next year to make up for losses this year.

3.   A market equilibrium is defined as occurring when:
   a.   government has balanced the forces of demand and supply
   b.   the price is such that the quantity that buyers want to buy is equal to the quantity that sellers want to sell.
   c.   price and quantity are equal.
   d.   prices are rising.
   e.   prices are falling.

4.   The three economic problems of *what, how,* and *for whom* goods shall be produced apply:
   a.   mainly to totalitarian or centrally planned societies, in which the problem of planning arises directly.
   b.   only (or principally) to free enterprise or capitalist societies, in which the problem of choice is most acute.
   c.   only (or principally) to less developed societies, since development alone is largely a question of dealing with these three problems.
   d.   to all societies, regardless of stage of development or form of political organization.
   e.   to none of the above necessarily, since they are problems for the individual business firm or family not for society.

5.   There cannot be a problem of *what* goods to produce if:
   a.   the supply of a productive resource is very small, so it must be devoted to the production of goods selected from a set of essential necessities.
   b.   production has not yet reached the stage at which the law of diminishing returns begins to operate.
   c.   the supply of productive resources is sufficiently large to make possible the production of some luxury goods.
   d.   each productive input is so specialized that it can be used only in the production of one good and no other.
   e.   production can be carried on under conditions of decreasing or constant cost, rather than increasing cost.

6.   The "invisible hand" refers to:
   a.   the role of government in the marketplace.
   b.   a system of taxation that redistributes wealth from the rich to the poor.
   c.   the fact that individuals, pursuing their own self-interest, achieve the best good for all when operating in a market economy.

d.　a production system whereby each individual performs the task to which he or she is best suited.

e.　a production system whereby each country produces the products that best suit each particular resource base.

B. Trade, Money, and Capital

7.　An example of specialization in production can be seen when:

a.　wheat is produced in the United States and exchanged for autos produced in Japan.

b.　most of the potatoes produced in the United States are grown in Idaho and Maine, where the soil and climate are optimal for their production.

c.　faculty in a university teach courses in their areas of expertise.

d.　all of the above.

e.　none of the above.

8.　Specialization (or division of labor) is rampant in a modern economy because it increases the output obtainable from a given resource supply. The consequences of specialization include (circle as many as are correct):

a.　the exchange of goods.

b.　the use of money.

c.　social interdependence.

d.　an intensified law of scarcity.

e.　possibly a sense of alienation on the part of members of the society involved.

9.　Capital, in an economic sense, includes all the following *except*:

a.　inventory on a grocer's shelf.

b.　a $100 bill.

c.　ten new computers that are being used by your university's accounting department.

d.　a new hammer that is purchased by a carpenter.

e　a new boiler that is used to heat your student center cafeteria.

10.　Money is *not* counted as part of capital because it:

a.　is essential to production.

b.　has no part to play in production.

c.　is not actually useful in production, although it is essential to have money in order to buy the real inputs that are needed for production.

d.　is counted as part of labor.

e.　none of the above.

11.　When reference is made to "a capitalist economy," the speaker is probably contemplating an economy:

a.　in which most capital goods are privately owned.

b.　in which the stock of capital is large relative to the population of that economy.

c.　that is under communist or socialist direction, so property rights to the capital flow to the government.

d.　suffering from high and increasing rates of inflation.

e.　that has limited economic resources with which to work.

12.　Due in part to the heavy use of automobiles in the United States this century, Congress passed the Clean Air Act in 1991. Basically, this act is an attempt to:

a.　encourage specialization in production.

b.　better define property rights over use of the air.

c.　prohibit division of labor in the production of power in the United States.

d.　eliminate property rights over the use of the air.

e.　none of the above.

13.　Examples of globalization could include (circle all that apply):

a.　the use of American-made airplane engines in Airbus planes.

b.　import taxes levied against goods produced in other countries.

c.　quotas imposed on imports into the United States.

d.　Italian citizens working in the German economy.

e.　Japanese financial institutions lending to American firms.

C. The Economic Role of Government

14.　The philosophy of laissez-faire means that:

a.　government controls the economy through a central planning board.

b　firms are allowed to monopolize industries in the economy to make greater profits.

c.　barter is used instead of money to make all transactions.

d.　the government uses taxing and spending policies to redistribute income and wealth.

e.　government interferes as little as possible in economic affairs.

15.　Government's role in a modern economy is to:

a.　ensure efficiency.

b.　correct an unfair distribution of income.

c.　promote economic growth and stability.

d.　all of the above.

e.　none of the above.

16.　Perfect competition means that:

a.　all goods and services have prices and are traded in markets.

b.　no firm or consumer is large enough to affect the market price.

c.　each industry is controlled by a single, monopolistic firm.

d.　**a** and **b**.

e.　all of the above.

17. Many governments subsidize primary research because it often benefits all citizens, even those who are not actively involved in research. This makes primary research a(n):
   a. negative externality.
   b. private good.
   c. public good.
   d. efficient good.
   e. equity good.

18. A government policy that aims to provide a more equitable distribution of resources might involve:
   a. decreasing transfer payments.
   b. abolishing progressive taxation.
   c. providing national health insurance.
   d. subsidizing housing for low-income families.
   e. any of the above, depending on the definition of equity used by the economy.

19. Milton Friedman is an economist who believes strongly in:
   a. the ability of markets to provide efficient solutions to economic problems.
   b. the need for government intervention in order to make markets work efficiently.
   c. the need for protectionist legislation in order to save domestic jobs.
   d. fiscal and monetary policies that will "fine tune" the economy across the business cycle.
   e. government provision of public goods.

VII. PROBLEM SOLVING

The following problems are designed to help you to apply the concepts that you learned in this chapter.

A. What Is a Market?

1. Determine whether the following events would lead to store shelves that are **understocked** or **overstocked,** and explain the effect of this on prices in a market economy.
   a. Flooding in the midwest destroys a large portion of the corn crop. Will store shelves tend to be **understocked** or **overstocked** with corn? Prices will go (**up / down**).
   b. Your college wins the NCAA basketball championship. Will bookstore shelves tend to be **understocked** or **overstocked** with sweatshirts? Prices will go (**up / down**).
   c. Scientists find that much of the popcorn sold at movie theaters is bad for our health. Will theaters tend to be **understocked** or **overstocked** with popcorn? Prices will go (**up / down**).

2. Draw a circular-flow diagram in the space below, showing the interaction between households and firms in goods markets and in input markets. Use your diagram to show how this market economy would answer the *what, how,* and *for whom* questions that face all societies.

B. Trade, Money, and Capital

3. Many people have speculated that the Soviet Union's demise was a result of its investing too many resources in military equipment and too few resources in capital products.
   a. Draw a hypothetical production-possibility frontier (from Chapter 1) in Figure 2-1. (Assume that as you try to specialize in the production of either good, it becomes increasingly harder to produce additional units of it.) Explain why you would expect the frontier to have the shape it does.

_____

_____
_____

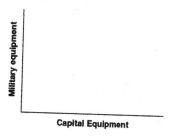

Figure 2-1

   b. As this economy produces increasingly more military goods, what happens to the *PPF*? Carefully explain. Given this information, why might you have predicted the eventual demise of the Soviet Union? Explain.

_____

_____
_____

C. The Economic Role of Government

4. Consider the following events. Do they indicate a movement **toward** or **away from** the notion of laissez-faire?

    a. President Ronald Reagan fires the nation's striking air traffic controllers. **(Toward / Away from)**

    b. President Bill Clinton supports the notion of nationalized health insurance. **(Toward / Away from)**

    c. British Prime Minister Margaret Thatcher "privatizes" national industries, like British Airways, by selling them to private investors. **(Toward / Away from)**

    d. The Federal Reserve takes actions to decrease the money supply, thereby increasing interest rates. **(Toward / Away from)**

    e. The government requires all auto manufacturers to install safety belts in newly produced automobiles. **(Toward / Away from)**

    f. The FTC breaks up Microsoft, on the grounds that the company has too much monopoly power. **(Toward / Away from)**

VIII. DISCUSSION QUESTIONS

Answer the following questions, making sure that you can explain the work you did to arrive at the answers.

1. For the past several decades, governments have been taking steps to preserve the environment. Recently, a new policy initiative has emerged that uses basic economic concepts to provide incentives for polluters. Markets have emerged in which pollution "rights" are traded between "owners" of these rights. Government authorities establish maximum amounts of pollutants that firms can emit into the air on a region-by-region basis. They then dole these rights out to firms in the area, who are allowed to emit pollutants only as long as they own the rights to emit them.

    a. Using this information, explain how markets for pollution rights emerge. How are property rights established, and why is it important to establish these property rights?

    b. Why might this policy fail to provide incentives for firms to limit pollution to the greatest extent possible? Explain.

2. If money is not categorized as capital by economists, why do we use money in an economic system at all? What purpose does it serve? Explain.

3. Discuss the pros and cons of promoting laissez-faire in an economic system. Would you be in favor of such a policy? Why or why not?

4. Define what is meant by the term *equity*. Why is it difficult for economists to come up with a definitive definition of an equitable distribution of resources? Explain.

5. Define what is meant by the term *progressive taxation*. How might this help to provide a more equitable distribution of income?

IX. ANSWERS TO STUDY GUIDE QUESTIONS

III. Review of Key Concepts

4	The market mechanism
6	Market equilibrium
11	Perfect competition
10	The invisible hand
9	Specialization and division of labor
3	Capital
5	Efficiency
2	Equity
1	Monopoly
8	Externalities
7	Fiscal policy

VI. Multiple Choice Questions

1. A   2. C   3. B   4. D   5. D   6. C
7. D   8. A, B, C, E   9. B   10. C   11. A
12. B   13. A, D, E   14. E   15. D   16. B
17. C   18. E   19. A

VII. Problem Solving

1.   a. understocked, up
     b. understocked, up
     c. overstocked, down

2.

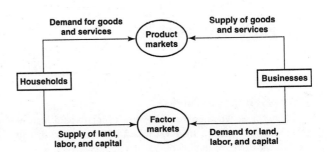

3.   a. Resources are not equally suited to the production of both commodities. Starting at point *A* in Figure 2-1, a relatively large amount of capital equipment is produced as society gives up military equipment. However, as more and more capital equipment is produced, the resources that are left are less and less suited to the production of them. Consequently, more and more military equipment must be given up.

    b. As the Soviet economy produced more and more military goods, less and less capital equipment was available for its firms. Furthermore, some of the resources that were being used to produce military goods were much better suited to the production of other commodities. It became increasingly more difficult to efficiently and equitably distribute the capital equipment, that was available. Finally, the economy collapsed.

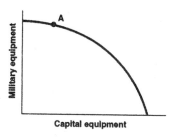

Figure 2-1

4. a. away from
   b. away from
   c. toward
   d. away from
   e. away from
   f. away from

VIII. Discussion Questions

1. a. Each firm in an industry is given the right to pollute a certain (limited) amount of air. If a firm pollutes more than its limit, it can be fined by the government. In essence, each firm "owns" a certain amount of air. If a firm pollutes more than what it "owns," it can expect to be penalized. However, if a firm does not pollute all the air it is allowed to, it can sell its remaining allotment to another firm. In this way the firm that reduces pollution is rewarded, and firms' that pollute excessively are penalized. By establishing property rights for air, firms are given an incentive to take care of what they "own."

   b. As long as firms are given property rights to a certain amount of air, they may have little incentive to reduce pollution beneath their allotment. Firms are essentially told that a certain amount of pollution is free.

2. Money is very useful as a medium of exchange. When sellers accept it as a means of payment, it eliminates the need to provide the seller with some desirable (from the seller's perspective) commodity that the buyer may not have. Sellers can use the money they receive to purchase the commodities they desire.

3. *Pros*: Freedom of choice in occupations and production; low taxes mean that the successful retain most of their rewards; society, not the government, decides how to allocate resources.

   Cons: No program of economic stabilization; no provision for the production of public goods; less consumer protection; no oversight of externalities.

4. *Equity* deals with fairness. Economists have difficulty with this concept because we all have different tastes and preferences as well as different needs and abilities. Should individuals be rewarded according to their efforts or according to their needs? The answer to this question entails subjective evaluation.

5. *Progressive taxation* occurs when the *percent* of income that is paid in taxes increases with increases in income. The very wealthy would pay the highest percentage of their income in taxes. These tax revenues could be redistributed by the government to the poorest families. This would make the distribution of income more equitable.

CHAPTER

Basic Elements of Supply and Demand

I. CHAPTER OVERVIEW

This chapter lays the foundation for the rest of your course by describing the interaction between buyers and sellers in a market economy. Properly framed, almost any economic question can be approached from a supply-and-demand perspective; because resources are limited but wants are unlimited, the magic of the market is to direct signals between people who are looking to consume and people who are looking to produce. Our implicit assumption is that *prices* carry this information between buyers and sellers, and hence prices are discussed as the most important factor determining behavior on both sides of the market.

II. LEARNING OBJECTIVES

After you have read Chapter 3 in your text and completed the exercises in this *Study Guide* chapter, you should be able to:

1. Define **demand** in a market using words, tables, and diagrams.
2. Illustrate the **shifts in demand** caused by changes in factors other than price that influence a consumer's willingness to purchase.
3. Explain the difference between changes in demand and changes in quantity demanded.
4. Define **supply** in a market using words, tables, and diagrams.
5. Illustrate the **shifts in supply** caused by changes in factors other than price that influence a firm's willingness to produce and sell.
6. Explain the difference between changes in supply and changes in quantity supplied.
7. Use the concepts of **shortages** and **surpluses** to illustrate the natural tendency of a market to move toward equilibrium.
8. Show the effects of shifts in supply or demand using diagrams.

III. REVIEW OF KEY CONCEPTS

Match the following terms from column A with their definitions in column B.

A	B
__ Effective demand	1. One explanation for an increase in labor supply.
__ Increase in supply	2. A factor other than price that changes supply.
__ Consumer income	3. A factor other than price that changes demand.
__ Technology	4. One reason why we have an upward-sloping supply curve.
__ Prices of substitutes	5. The quantities of a good demanded per unit of time at alternative prices, all else being fixed.
__ Immigration	6. An increase in this factor will shift demand to the right.
__ The laws of diminishing returns	7. The price and quantity at which there is no surplus or shortage.
__ Equilibrium level of output	8. Occurs when the price of a product falls.
__ Surplus	9. Occurs when the quantity supplied is greater than the quantity demanded.
__ Decrease in quantity supplied	10. The recent explosion of computer technology has caused this.

IV. SUMMARY AND CHAPTER OUTLINE

This section summarizes the key concepts from the chapter.

Many forces can operate to push the observed price of any given commodity higher or lower: changes in people's tastes, changes in their incomes, changes in the costs of production, changes in the prices of substitute products, changes in government policy, etc. For example, the price of tickets to see a Grateful Dead concert might fall if their music becomes less popular, if the incomes of music lovers fall, if the price of guitars doubles, if the price of Rolling Stones concerts falls, or if the government decides to place taxes on concert tickets.

In order to assess the impact of any of these single events, we need to divide these forces into two groups: those that have their initial impact on the demand side of the market and those that have their initial impact on the supply side of the market.

A. The Demand Schedule

1. When economists refer to the *law of downward-sloping demand,* they are speaking of a particular kind of behavior among buyers that is observed with so few exceptions that it can be designated as a "law" of behavior.

2. It is essential to keep in mind that a demand curve is a conditional schedule; it answers an "if this, then that" type of question. It shows, in particular, that if the price of some good were to stand at some specified level, then consumers would be willing to purchase the indicated quantity.

3. The quantity of a good or service that is read from a demand curve does not depend at all upon whether or not that quantity is feasible to supply at the given price. It reflects only the desires of consumers who worry only about their own preferences and what they can afford.

4. Remember that price is not the only factor that influences consumers' decisions to buy. Average income, number of buyers, price and availability of related goods, and tastes and preferences all define the behavior of buyers in markets. Any changes in these factors will cause the demand curve to shift.

B. The Supply Curve

1. The *supply schedule* (and *supply curve*) for a commodity shows the relationship between its market price and the amount of that commodity that producers are willing to produce and sell, other things being held equal.

2. The quantity of a good or service that is read from a supply curve does not depend upon whether or not people want to buy that much. It reflects only the ambitions of suppliers who worry only about their costs and their anticipated profits (given the quoted price).

3. Technology, input prices, prices of related goods, and government policy all define the behavior of sellers. Thus, changes in any of these factors will cause the supply curve to shift.

C. Equilibrium of Supply and Demand

1. The division between buyers and sellers is nearly absolute. In all but a very few exceptional cases, economic forces *directly* influence either the demand side of a market or the supply side of a market, *but not both.*

2. Market-clearing equilibrium prices are achieved when the quantity supplied matches the quantity demanded.

3. When the quantity demanded exceeds the quantity supplied, the resulting shortage pushes the price up toward equilibrium. On the other hand, when the quantity demanded is less than the quantity supplied, the resulting surplus pushes the price down.

4. When we draw demand and supply schedules, we are defining a relationship between quantities demanded or supplied and the relative price of the product. When relative prices change, consumers or producers change their behavior *along* the demand and supply curves. Demand and supply curves shift only when a factor *other than* the own-price of the product has changed.

V. HELPFUL HINTS

Understanding demand-and-supply diagrams is crucial to understanding how a market economy operates. Simply memorizing all the movements and shifts in curves that can be applied to different market situations does not work well. For your part as a student, it takes thoughtfulness and practice. Nevertheless, there are several guidelines that can help you in your study of markets.

1. Whenever you are confronted with a supply and demand problem (even in a multiple choice or true/false problem), *draw* the appropriate diagram and use it to illustrate the changes that you anticipate in the market. The discipline of envisioning the graph will help you keep track of what is changing and what is staying the same, first on the demand side and second on the supply side. You will find it easier to avoid errors caused by confusing changes in quantities demanded and supplied (movement along curves) with changes in demand and supply (shifts of curves).

2. In *any* diagram, if a variable that is measured on one of the axes changes, the curve will not shift. You simply move along the curve to measure the response to the change in the variable. For example, in demand-and-supply diagrams, price is measured along the vertical axis. According to this rule, if there is a change in price, the curves will not shift. After all, in order to draw the demand and supply curves in the first place, we had to know how much would be demanded or supplied at each price. If *any other* variable changes and it has bearing on the market, then a curve will shift.

3. When demand and supply curves shift, think of these shifts in terms of *left* and *right,* rather than up or down. Up usually implies there is more of something rather than less. However, when supply curves shift up, less is being supplied at every price. To avoid this pitfall, think of shifts in terms of *left* and *right.*

4. When equilibrium is reached in a market, this means that the market clears; that is, all consumers who are willing to pay the market price are able to find the product. Producers sell all they are willing to bring to market at that price. Market equilibrium does not necessarily mean, however, that all consumers or producers are completely satisfied with the equilibrium position. Some consumers may want to purchase the commodity but may not be able to afford the market-clearing price. I may *want* to purchase an Infinity automobile, but I am currently "priced out" of that market. Automobile manufacturers, on the other hand, may *want* to produce more luxury automobiles but refrain from doing so because they think the established market price is too low.

5. *Excess demand* means the same thing as *shortage*.
6. *Excess supply* means the same thing as *surplus*.

VI. MULTIPLE CHOICE QUESTIONS

These questions are organized by topic from the chapter outline. Choose the best answer from the options available.

A. The Demand Schedule

1. A demand curve for widgets shows:
   a. how people's spending patterns change as their income changes.
   b. that people spend more money on widgets as the price of widgets increases.
   c. the quantity of widgets that would be purchased per unit of time at each alternative price, holding other factors influencing demand fixed.
   d. that firms are willing to supply more output, per unit of time, as prices increase.

2. As the price of airline tickets increases, the:
   a. demand for airline tickets increases.
   b. supply of airline tickets decreases.
   c. quantity of tickets demanded decreases.
   d. quantity of tickets supplied decreases.

3. The law of downward-sloping demand holds that:
   a. a surplus of goods will cause price to fall.
   b. people normally buy more of a good as their incomes rise.
   c. the quantity of a good that consumers willingly purchase increases as the price of the good falls.
   d. the quantity of a good purchased will decrease as it goes out of style or is replaced by something of better quality.

Use Figure 3-1 to answer questions 4 through 7.

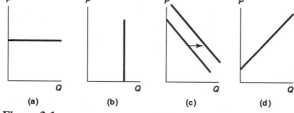

Figure 3-1

4. A patient must purchase some exact quantity of a particular drug (no less, no more) and will pay any price in order to obtain it. Which of the diagrams best illustrates this demand curve?
   a. (*a*)
   b. (*b*)
   c. (*c*)
   d. (*d*)

5. The government declares that it is prepared to purchase any and all gold supplied to it by domestic gold mines at a price of $410 an ounce. Which of the diagrams best illustrates this demand curve?
   a. (*a*)
   b. (*b*)
   c. (*c*)
   d. (*d*)

6. An increase in consumers' money incomes prompts them to demand a greater quantity of good X at any price. Which of the diagrams best illustrates this demand curve?
   a. (*a*)
   b. (*b*)
   c. (*c*)
   d. (*d*)

7. I can buy *any amount* of sugar in my local supermarket at a fixed price of 40 cents per pound. No matter how much I buy, I always pay the same price per pound. Which of the diagrams best illustrates this supply curve?
   a. (*a*)
   b. (*b*)
   c. (*c*)
   d. (*d*)

8. Any of the following could cause an increase in the demand for Wheaties *except*:
   a. a decrease in the price of wheat used to produce cereal.
   b. a new report from the Surgeon General suggesting that wheat helps to cure sunburns.
   c. a picture of a popular sports figure, such as Michael Jordan, on the Wheaties box.
   d. an increase in the price of a competing cereal, such as Cheerios.

9. Suppose that the demand curve for commodity X shifts to the left. One reasonable explanation for this shift would be:
   a. the supply of X has decreased for some reason.
   b. the price of X has increased, so people have decided to buy less of it than they did before.
   c. consumer tastes have shifted in favor of this commodity, and they want to buy more of it than they did before at any given price.
   d. the price of X has fallen, so people have decided to buy more of it than they did before.
   e. none of these events.

10. Four of the five events described below might reasonably explain why the demand for beef has shifted to a new position. Which one is not a suitable explanation?
    a. The price of some good which consumers regard as a substitute for beef has risen.
    b. The price of beef has fallen.
    c. Money incomes of beef consumers have increased.

    d.   A widespread advertising campaign is undertaken by the producers of beef.

    e.   There is a change in people's tastes with respect to beef.

11. When applied to the demand for commodity X the phrase "other things equal," or "other things constant," means that:

    a.   the price of X is held constant.

    b.   both buyer incomes and the price of X are held constant.

    c.   buyer incomes, tastes, and the price of X are held constant.

    d.   all factors that might influence the demand for X including the price of X are held constant.

    e.   none of the above.

12. If IBM and Compaq computers are substitutes, a decrease in the price of IBM PCs will cause:

    a.   a decrease in the demand for Compaq computers.

    b.   an increase in the demand for IBM computers.

    c.   an increase in the supply of IBM computers.

    d.   an increase in the supply of Compaq computers.

B. The Supply Curve

13. The supply curve describes:

    a.   an inverse relationship between price and quantity supplied.

    b.   a direct relationship between income and quantity supplied.

    c.   a cyclical relationship between consumption and savings.

    d.   a direct relationship between price and quantity supplied.

14. An increase in the cost of materials needed to produce snow skis causes the following change in the snow ski market:

    a.   the demand curve shifts to the right.

    b.   the supply curve shifts to the left.

    c.   both the demand and supply curves shift to the left.

    d.   neither curve shifts.

15. Consider the producer who makes leather shoes and leather purses. An increase in the price of leather shoes would cause:

    a.   a decrease in the supply of leather purses.

    b.   movement along the supply curve for purses.

    c.   a shift in the demand curve for leather shoes.

    d.   the supply curve for leather shoes and the supply curve for purses to shift to the left.

16. The demand for snowboards has increased recently as more people have taken up the sport. This will cause the supply curve for snowboards to:

    a.   shift to the left.

    b.   shift to the right.

    c.   remain the same.

    d.   decrease next year.

17. Supply curves are typically "positively sloped." The meaning conveyed by any such curve is that:

    a.   any increase in costs of production will result in a movement up along the supply curve.

    b.   the lower the price, the larger the supply that consumers are prepared to buy.

    c.   the higher the price, the larger the quantity suppliers will wish to sell.

    d.   the larger the quantity suppliers have to sell, the lower the price they will have to quote in order to dispose of it.

    e.   none of the above.

18. Which of the following will *not* help to determine the position of the supply curve?

    a.   Technology

    b.   Resource costs.

    c.   Consumer income.

    d.   Government taxes.

C. Equilibrium of Supply and Demand

19. Equilibrium in a market indicates:

    a.   the price at which quantity supplied equals quantity demanded.

    b.   that every buyer who wants to buy can buy at the equilibrium price, and every seller who wants to sell can sell at the equilibrium price.

    c.   there is no tendency for price to change.

    d.   all of the above.

    e.   none of the above.

20. In prosperous times, *both* the equilibrium price *and* the quantity of some commodity X may go up simultaneously. Such a situation:

    a.   is one of the few recognized exceptions to the law of downward-sloping demand.

    b.   is precisely what the law of downward-sloping demand says is to be expected.

    c.   is the consequence of a demand curve running from southwest to northeast.

    d.   cannot be explained by means of ordinary supply-curve and demand-curve analysis.

    e.   is caused by a rightward-shifting demand curve and a stable supply curve.

21. Beef supplies are sharply reduced because of drought in the beef-raising states, and consumers turn to pork as a substitute for beef because they believe there are health benefits. *In the beef market,* these two phenomena would be described in terms of supply and demand as:

    a.   a leftward shift in the demand curve.

    b.   a leftward shift in the supply curve.

    c.   a rightward shift in the demand curve.

    d.   a rightward shift in the supply curve.

    e.   both the supply curve and the demand curve will shift to the left.

22. Which alternative in question 21 would be correct with respect to the events described had that question asked about *the pork market*?

    a.

    b.

    c.

    d.

    e.

23. Let the initial price of a good be $5. If buyers wish to purchase 4000 units per week at that price while sellers wish to sell 5000 units per week, then:

    a. price will tend to increase in the future.

    b. firm output will tend to increase in the future.

    c. price and output will tend to remain the same in the future.

    d. price will tend to decrease in the future.

    e. something is wrong—this could not happen.

Figure 3-2 shows conditions in the market for home heating oil last year. The initial equilibrium position in the market is shown by price P_1 and quantity Q_1. Please use the diagram to answer questions 24 and 25.

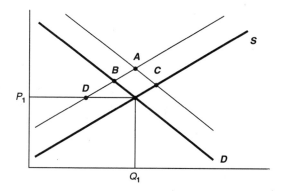

Figure 3-2

24. This winter has been unusually cold and snowy in the northeast, with a record number of snowstorms. The new equilibrium in the market for home heating oil is best represented by point:

    a. *A.*

    b. *B.*

    c. *C.*

    d. *D.*

25. At the old equilibrium price, there now exists a(n):

    a. shortage.

    b. surplus.

    c. equilibrium.

    d. excess supply.

Table 3-1 contains data pertaining to the market for mountain bikes. Please use the data to answer questions 26 and 27.

TABLE 3-1

Price	Quantity Supplied (weekly)	Quantity Demanded (weekly)
$100	1000	4000
200	2000	3500
300	3000	3000
400	4000	2500
500	5000	2000

26. The equilibrium price in this market is:

    a. $100.

    b. $200.

    c. $300.

    d. $400.

27. The equilibrium quantity exchanged in this market is:

    a. 2000 bikes.

    b. 3000 bikes.

    c. 4000 bikes.

    d. 5000 bikes.

28. A recent *Wall Street Journal* article (6/24/93) details the increased popularity of "Doc Martens" shoes and boots among college-aged students. This fad has had a big impact on the market for Reebok sneakers, a substitute for Doc Martens. We would expect the equilibrium:

    a. price of Reeboks to fall and the equilibrium quantity exchanged to increase.

    b. price and quantity of Reeboks exchanged to increase.

    c. price and quantity of Reeboks exchanged to decrease.

    d. price of Reeboks to increase and the equilibrium quantity exchanged to decrease.

VII. PROBLEM SOLVING

The following problems are designed to help you to apply the concepts that you learned in this chapter.

1. For each of the following statements, put a **T** if the statement is *true,* an **F** if the statement is *false,* and a **U** if you are *uncertain* about the validity of the statement.

A. The Demand Schedule

____ a. The substitution effect tells us that people will buy more as prices fall because their purchasing power is increasing.

____ b. The demand for cars has increased in the past 50 years because the price has fallen.

____ c. When demand decreases, the price falls, so supply shifts to the left.

B. The Supply Curve

____ d. Over the past few years, the price of compact disc players has fallen, and at the same time firms are supplying many more compact disc players. The law of supply is invalid in this case.

___ e.   An improvement in technology will cause the supply curve to shift to the right.

___ f.   If the price of Pepsi goes up, it is likely that the market supply curve for Coke will shift to the right.

___ g.   If the wages of autoworkers increase, the supply of automobiles will shift to the left.

C. Equilibrium of Supply and Demand

___ h.   Markets for goods are defined by the behavior of suppliers who determine prices and output levels.

___ i.   If the actual price in a market is above the equilibrium price, we would expect to see downward pressure on output and price.

___ j.   In a market economy, goods are allocated by the price system to those people who can afford them.

2.   Table 3-2 focuses on the factors that will shift either the demand curve or the supply curve. In each case, determine which curve will shift, and write in **demand** or **supply** as appropriate; then write in whether the shift will be to the **right** or the **left**. In addition, determine whether equilibrium price and output will be **higher** or **lower**. The first case has been completed as an example.

TABLE 3-2

Shift Factor	Demand or Supply	Shifts	Left or Right	Price Will Be	Output Will Be
a. Population increases.	demand	shifts	right	higher	higher
b. Input prices go up.	___	shifts	___	___	___
c. Tariffs are removed.	___	shifts	___	___	___
d. Average income falls.	___	shifts	___	___	___
e. Technology improves.	___	shifts	___	___	___
f. Product becomes more desirable/popular.	___	shifts	___	___	___

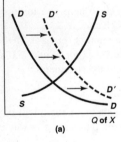
(a)

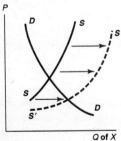
(c)

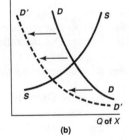
(b)

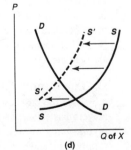
(d)

Figure 3-3

3.   This problem deals with shifts in demand and supply curves. Figure 3-3 illustrates four different shifts in demand or supply. Take a moment to consider each shift.

Table 3-3 considers changes that occur in seven different markets. Determine which diagram—(a), (b), (c), or (d)—is most appropriate for each market. Then identify the specific *shift factor* that caused the curve to shift. Finally, determine whether equilibrium price and output will be *higher* or *lower*. The first case has been completed as an example.

TABLE 3-3

Change in Market	Diagram	Shift Factor	Price Will Be	Output Will Be
a. Good X is clothing that has gone out of style	b	change in taste shifts DD left	lower	lower
b. Pollution tax on supplier	___	_____	___	___
c. Opening of market to foreign buyers	___	_____	___	___
d. Price of substitute good falls	___	_____	___	___
e. Market structure requires more advertising	___	_____	___	___
f. A 10% across-the-board income-tax cut	___	_____	___	___
g. Robot makes production more efficient	___	_____	___	___

4.   This problem deals with the market for fish and the effect of a papal decree issued by Pope Paul VI in 1966 which gave local Catholic bishops the authority to allow Roman Catholics to eat meat on Fridays. We will use hypothetical data to analyze the effect of the decree on the market for fish. (For a more accurate analysis see Frederick W. Bell, "The Pope and the Market for Fish," *American Economic Review* 58 [December 1968], pp. 1346-1350.)

Table 3-4 presents market data for the price per pound of codfish (measured in dollars) and the quantity demanded and supplied at those prices (measured in thousands of pounds) . (*For the time being, ignore the column on the right labeled "New Quantity."*)

a.   Every time the price of codfish decreases by 60 cents per pound, the quantity demanded increases by _____.

b.   Every time the price of codfish decreases by 60 cents per pound, the quantity supplied decreases by _____.

TABLE 3-4

Price	Quantity Demanded	Quantity Supplied	New Quantity
$3.00	0	15	0
2.40	2	12	0
1.80	4	9	2
1.20	6	6	4
.60	8	3	6
0	10	0	8

c. On Figure 3-4, plot the market demand and supply curves.

d. What are the equilibrium price and quantity in this market? _____

e. Now suppose the papal decree is issued. Which curve will be affected by this change?

_____

f. Which *shift factor* will cause the curve to shift?

_____

Suppose the column labeled "New Quantity" in Table 3-4 represents the change in the market.

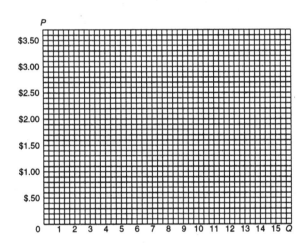

Figure 3-4

g. Plot the new curve on Figure 3-4. (Is there any doubt about which curve shifted?)

h. Approximately, what are the new equilibrium price and output? _____

i. What type of change would have resulted in a movement along the demand curve and *not* a shift in it?

_____

j. Will the supply curve shift as a result of the papal decree? Will the quantity of fish supplied change? Explain. _____

_____

5. What would happen to used-car prices in a recession as family incomes fall? The first three columns in Table 3-5

can be used to illustrate *price, quantity supplied,* and *quantity demanded* before the recession hits the economy.

TABLE 3-5

Price	Quantity Supplied	Quantity Demanded	New Quantity
$500	100	400	_____
600	150	300	_____
700	200	200	_____
800	250	100	_____
900	300	0	_____

a. Use the grid in Figure 3-5 to plot the supply and demand curves in this market.

b. Determine the equilibrium price and output.

_____

c. At what price would the quantity supplied fall to zero? _____

d. What is the price axis intercept of the supply curve?

_____

e. What are the slopes of the supply and demand curves? _____

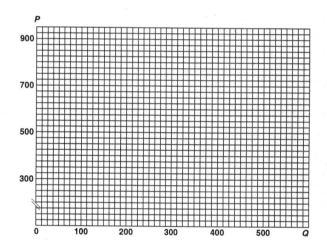

Figure 3-5

One special feature of this market is that households, or consumers, are both suppliers and demanders of used cars. When the recession comes a new relationship is established between *price* and *quantity.* Suppose a new relationship is established between price and quantity as shown in Table 3-6.

TABLE 3-6

P	Q
$500	55
700	155
900	255

f.   Use these numbers to fill in the last column in Table 3-5. Note that there are gaps in your data!

g.   Calculate and then fill in the missing numbers in the column.

h.   Add this new curve to your diagram in Figure 3-5.

i.   Approximately, what are the new equilibrium price and output? _____

j.   For what reason(s) did the curve shift?

_____

_____

k.   Can you think of any reasons why the curve might shift in the opposite direction instead?

_____

_____

l.   Finally, suppose, as a result of the recession, some households decide to purchase a used car rather than a new one. Suppose further that some households that were previously planning to buy a used car decide to postpone the purchase of a car altogether. Assume that this second change dominates, or is stronger than, the first one mentioned. Illustrate this change in your diagram in Figure 3-5 and explain the effect it will have on market price and output. _____

_____

_____

6.   The last market example that Samuelson and Nordhaus discuss in this chapter focuses on the supply of and demand for workers, or labor. *Labor, land,* and *capital* are considered the *primary factors of production* that firms use to produce goods and services. The exchange of the factors of production takes place in *factor* markets. Goods and services, on the other hand, are exchanged in *product* markets. To make sure that the functions of these markets are clear to you, we suggest that you review the circular-flow diagram of a market economy (Figure 2-1) in Chapter 2 of the text.

In the *factor* market for labor, the roles of individuals and firms are reversed from their positions in the *product* market. In the factor market, individuals are the suppliers of labor services, and firms are now the consumers or demanders of labor services. Workers will supply more of their labor services at higher prices or wage rates, and all other things held equal, firms will demand more labor services as wages fall.

Figure 3-6 illustrates demand and supply curves for labor in a competitive market. As indicated, the equilibrium market wage is $5 (per hour).

a.   If the wage rate were beneath the equilibrium wage, would you expect either the demand or supply curve to shift? Explain why or why not. _____

_____

_____

b.   If the wage rate were beneath the equilibrium wage, what forces would move the market toward equilibrium?

_____

_____

c.   Suppose the government passed a law which said that all workers in this industry must be paid at least $6 per hour. Would you expect either the demand curve or the supply curve to shift? Explain why or why not.

_____

_____

_____

d.   Assuming that there are no other changes, describe the effect that this legislation would have on wages, employment, and unemployment in this market.

_____

_____

_____

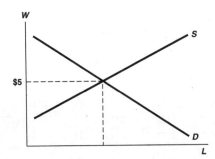

Figure 3-6

VIII. DISCUSSION QUESTIONS

Answer the following questions, making sure that you can explain the work you did to arrive at the answers.

1.   Explain why the market supply curve for any commodity has a positive slope.

2.   Explain why the market demand curve for any commodity has a negative slope.

3.   Explain the importance of the concept "all other things held equal" in supply-and-demand analysis.

4.   Suppose that we are studying the market for cornflakes. Suppose further that during the summer of 1999 the following events both occur: (1) The weather in the farm belt is extraordinarily hot, with very little rain; and (2) A new research study is published and widely disseminated which proves that eating cornflakes makes people healthier and adds years to their lives. Figure 3-7 illustrates the initial equilibrium position in the cornflake market.

a.   Show how the two events described above will change this market.

b.   Can you say what will happen to the equilibrium price in this market? Please explain your answer.

c.   Can you say what will happen to the equilibrium quantity in this market? Please explain your answer.

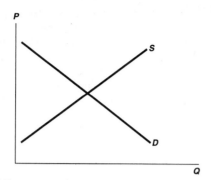

Figure 3-7

5. In the last section of the chapter, Samuelson and Nordhaus discuss "rationing by prices."
   a. What exactly does this mean?
   b. What other methods can societies use to ration goods and services?

IX. ANSWERS TO STUDY GUIDE QUESTIONS

III. Review of Key Concepts

5	Effective demand
10	Increase in supply
3	Consumer income
2	Technology
6	Prices of substitutes
1	Immigration
4	The law of diminishing returns
7	Equilibrium level of output
9	Surplus
8	Decrease in quantity demanded

VI. Multiple Choice Questions

1. C 2. C 3. C 4. B 5. A 6. C
7. A 8. A 9. E 10. B 11. E 12. A
13. D 14. B 15. A 16. C 17. C 18. C
19. D 20. E 21. E 22. C 23. D 24. C
25. A 26. C 27. B 28. C

VII. Problem Solving

1. a. F
   b. F
   c. F
   d. F
   e. T
   f. F
   g. T
   h. F
   i. T
   j. T
2. b. supply, left, higher, lower

c. supply, right, lower, higher
d. demand, left, lower, lower
e. supply, right, lower, higher
f. demand, right, higher, higher

3. b. (*d*) Increase in costs shifts *SS* left. higher, lower
   c. (*a*) Increase in the number of buyers shifts *DD* right, higher, higher
   d. (*b*) Decrease in substitute's price shifts *DD* left. lower, lower
   e. (*d*) Increase in costs shifts *SS* left. higher, lower
   f. (*a*) Increase in income shifts *DD* right. higher, higher
   g. (*c*) Increase in technology shifts *SS* right. lower, higher

4. a. 2 (thousand)
   b. 3 (thousand)
   c.

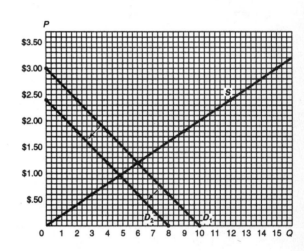

Figure 3-4

d. $P_1 = 1.20 per pound.
   $Q_1 = 6$ thousand pounds.
e. Demand will shift to the left.
f. Consumers' tastes and preferences will be affected by the decree.
g. See Figure 3-4.
h. P_2 is approximately $0.96 per pound.
   Q_2 is approximately 4.8 thousand pounds.
i. If there is a change in the price of codfish, consumers will move along the demand curve.
j. The papal decree will cause the demand curve to shift, not the supply curve. Producers will move down the existing supply curve to the new demand curve. If as a result of the lower prices, less profits are made, this may encourage firms to exit the industry. If and when this occurs, the supply curve will shift to the left. But

the papal decree has no direct effect on the position or shape of the supply curve

5. a.

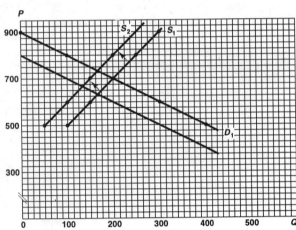

Figure 3-5

b. $P_1 = \$700$.
    $Q_1 = 200$.
c. $300.
d. $300.
e. Slope of supply = 2.
    Slope of demand = -1.

TABLE 3-5

f. g.	Price	Quantity Supplied	Quantity Demanded	New Quantity
	$500	100	400	55
	600	150	300	105
	700	200	200	155
	800	250	100	205
	900	300	0	255

h. See Figure 3-5.
i. P_2 is approximately $730.
    Q_2 is approximately 162.
j. Automobile owners are holding on to their cars longer during the recession. Perhaps their pay has been cut or they have lost their jobs.
k. If household income falls dramatically, people may be forced to sell their cars for money. (This would probably be a depression.)
l. See Figure 3-5. The demand curve will shift to the left. Market price and output will both fall.

6. a. Neither curve will shift. Since the wage rate is measured along the Y axis, you would move along the curves to the equilibrium wage.
    b. There would be an excess demand for labor. Firms would want to hire more workers than they could find.

As wages rose, more workers would seek employment, and firms would demand fewer workers.
c. Neither curve will shift. There will be an excess supply of labor if the wage is raised to $6 an hour.
d. Wages, for those who found work, would be higher. Unemployment would increase because firms would lay some previously employed workers off, and more people would be looking for work.

VIII. Discussion Questions

1. If firms are to produce more output, they will have to bid resources away from other industries. Their costs go up, so to produce more, they must be paid more.
2. As consumers purchase commodities, the additional satisfaction they receive from additional units begins to decrease. So their willingness to pay for the commodity declines as well.
3. It is very difficult to explain how the economy works if we cannot (at least in the classroom) hold other things equal. When more than one change occurs at a time, it becomes impossible to explain causal relationships.
4. a.

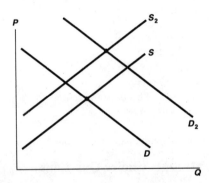

Figure 3-7

b. Since people recognize health benefits, and since supply has been reduced, the price will go up.
c. We cannot be certain about quantity. Consumers want more. Firms want to supply less. Whichever curve shifts more will dominate and determine the direction of the change in output.
5. a. In a market system, goods and services are rationed by the marketplace. Consumers "vote" with their dollars and determine what will be produced.
    b. An alternative rationing plan can be imposed by the government. This is a command economy. Remember, all societies are faced with scarcity and must devise some way to ration goods and services.

CHAPTER

Applications of
Supply and Demand

I. CHAPTER OVERVIEW

There is a common expression among people who think about economic issues: "It's all a matter of supply and demand." This expression is, for the most part exactly correct. Properly framed, the essence of most economic questions can be approached using the basic market analysis you learned in Chapter 3; properly interpreted, the answer to almost any question concerning resource allocation can be explained in terms of supply-demand intuition.

In Chapter 3 you learned the laws of supply and demand, and you became familiar with the effects of changes in supply and demand on market prices and quantities exchanged. For example, you found that when demand increases in a market, prices rise and quantities exchanged increase.

This leads naturally to the related question: "By how much?" How large are the responses to changes in the market, and upon what does this responsiveness depend? This chapter will provide you with the tools you need to answer this question and with the opportunity to apply your tools in the arena of policy-making.

II. LEARNING OBJECTIVES

After you have read Chapter 4 in your text and completed the exercises in this *Study Guide* chapter, you should be able to:

1. Define the term **price elasticity of demand.**
2. Discuss the factors that determine whether price elasticity of demand is **elastic, unitary-elastic,** or **inelastic,** and compare consumer behavior in the short run and the long run. Describe elastic and inelastic regions that exist along most demand curves.
3. Calculate price elasticity of demand using a **method of averages** and interpret your result.
4. Explain, using diagrams, the relationship between total revenue and price elasticity of demand.
5. Define the term **price elasticity of supply.**
6. Discuss the factors that determine whether price elasticity of supply is **elastic, unitary-elastic,** or **inelastic,** and compare producer behavior in the short run and the long run.

7. Calculate price elasticity of supply using a method of averages, and interpret your result.
8. Apply supply, demand, and elasticity concepts to the following situations and markets: (a) agriculture markets, (b) taxes, and (c) price ceilings and price floors.

III. REVIEW OF KEY CONCEPTS

Match the following terms from column A with their definitions in column B.

A	B
__ Price elasticity of demand	1. The ultimate economic impact or burden of a tax.
__ Price elasticity of supply	2. Legal maximum price that sellers can charge for a good or service as defined by government.
__ Elastic demand	3. Demand or supply is infinitely responsive to changes in price.
__ Inelastic demand	4. The multiplicative product of price and quantity sold.
__ Unit-elastic demand	5. Measures the percentage change in quantity demanded of a good when its price changes.
__ Perfectly elastic	6. Legal minimum price that sellers can receive for a good or service as defined by government.
__ Perfectly inelastic	7. Percentage change in quantity demanded is less than percentage change in price.
__ Total revenue	8. Demand or supply is not responsive at all to changes in price.
__ Tax incidence	9. Percentage change in quantity demanded is greater than percentage change in price.
__ Price ceiling	10. Measures the percentage change in quantity supplied of a good when its price changes.
__ Price floor	11. Means that total revenue will not change when the price of the good changes.

IV. SUMMARY AND CHAPTER OUTLINE

This section summarizes the key concepts from the chapter.

A. Elasticity of Demand and Supply

1.   Any elasticity that you encounter in economic analysis measures, in *percentage terms,* the responsiveness of some economic variable to a change. All elasticities are designed to answer the question "How much?" For example, we know from the law of demand that as price falls, quantity demanded increases. *Price elasticity of demand* describes the *percentage change* in quantity demanded of a product caused by some *percentage change* in its price. Thus, price elasticity of demand helps us to describe movement along a demand curve. Because it is expressed in percentage terms and is hence devoid of all scale measurements, it can be used to compare consumer responsiveness across goods and at different price levels.

2.   Price elasticity of demand between any two points on a demand curve can be calculated using the following formula:

$$E_D = \frac{\text{percentage change in quantity demanded}}{\text{percentage change in price}} =$$

$$\frac{[(Q_2 - Q_1) / ((Q_2 + Q_1) / 2)]}{[(P_2 - P_1) / ((P_2 + P_1) / 2)]}$$

Notice that the numerator and the denominator both contain *percentage* changes rather than *absolute* changes in quantities and prices. These percentage changes (and any percentage change, for that matter) are found by taking an absolute change and dividing it by a reference point. For example, to find percentage change in quantity demanded, find the difference between the initial and final quantities at two points on your demand curve. Divide this difference by your reference point, which in our case will be the *average* quantity. This gives you the percentage change in quantity demanded. Follow the same method for the percentage change in price; divide the absolute difference in prices by the average price. Plug these values into the equation above to find a coefficient for price elasticity of demand between two points on your demand curve.

Notice that the sign of this coefficient will always be *negative.* That is, as long as the demand curve is downward-sloping, there will be an inverse relationship between price and quantity demanded. Therefore when you interpret this coefficient, just look at its *absolute size,* or *absolute value.* Ignore the negative sign and simply ask yourself if the coefficient is greater than, less than, or equal to 1.

3.   a.   Demand is defined as *elastic* when the percentage change in quantity demanded is *greater than* the percentage change in price. ($E_D > 1$)

b.   Demand is defined as *inelastic* when the percentage change in quantity demanded is *less than* the percentage change in price. ($E_D < 1$)

c.   Demand is defined as *unit elastic* when the percentage change in quantity demanded is *equal to* the percentage change in price. ($E_D = 1$)

4.   The demand for any good is *more elastic* when there are more substitutes available, when the item is considered to be more a luxury than a necessity and when a longer time frame is considered. Demand for most goods will be *more elastic in the long run than in the short run,* since a longer time frame allows consumers to search more carefully for substitutes.

5.   Demand curves that are flat tend to be relatively more elastic than demand curves that are steep. However, all linear demand curves are elastic at the top, are unitary elastic at their midpoint, and are inelastic at the bottom. Notice that when prices are high, the same *percentage change* means a greater *absolute change* in price. For example, suppose the price of a good is $1.00. A 10 percent increase in price means the new price is $1.10. Suppose the price of a good is $100. The same 10 percent increase in price means the new price is $110! Consumers tend to be more responsive to a $10 change in price than to a $.10 change in price.

6.   *Price elasticity of supply* describes *how much* quantity supplied increases when the price of a product rises. Thus, it helps us to describe movement along a supply curve.

7.   Price elasticity of supply between any two points on a supply curve can be calculated using the following formula:

$$E_S = \frac{\text{percentage change in quantity supplied}}{\text{percentage change in price}}$$

$$\frac{[(Q_2 - Q_1) / ((Q_2 + Q_1) / 2)]}{[(P_2 - P_1) / ((P_2 + P_1) / 2)]}$$

Price elasticity of supply takes the same general form as price elasticity of demand. Again, you are using percentage changes in the numerator and denominator rather than absolute changes, and again, you are using average quantity supplied and price for your reference points.

8.   The supply of any good is *more elastic* when there is greater flexibility in the production process, allowing increases in output without significant increases in the price of inputs, and when a longer time frame is considered.

B. Applications to Major Economic Issues

1.   Elasticities help to determine the impact of government policies because they describe the responsiveness of agents in the economy to change.

2.   When the government decides to levy a tax, the *incidence* of the tax describes who bears its ultimate economic burden, buyers or sellers. The larger portion of the tax tends to be paid by the side of the market that responds more *inelastically* to changes in price. For example, if demand is relatively inelastic, consumers will not alter their buying patterns significantly when price increases, giving sellers the opportunity to pass the tax onto the consumers without fearing large decreases in sales. As demand becomes more elastic, sellers have to worry about larger and larger decreases in sales when they raise prices.

3.   Prices are sometimes fixed by law. *Price floors* are legal minimum prices; they hold prices artificially above equilibrium to protect sellers. For example, minimum wages set by governments hold wages above equilibrium in order to achieve policy objectives. *Price ceilings* are legal maximum prices; they hold prices artificially below equilibrium to protect buyers. For example, in markets for gasoline the government has considered holding prices low to protect consumers.

V. HELPFUL HINTS

l.   Elasticities make an important contribution to the study of economics. As we have seen, they help to define responsiveness to changes at the margin. You will find many interesting uses for the concept of elasticity as you make your way through this course.

2.   The elasticity of demand is *not* the slope of the demand curve. Remember that the slope of the demand curve as we draw it always measures the *absolute change* in the price divided by the *absolute change* in the quantity demanded between any two points on the curve. Elasticity, on the other hand, is the *percentage change* in quantity demanded divided by the *percentage change* in price. There is a relationship between these two concepts, but they are not the same thing.

3.   The elasticity of demand is *not* constant as you move down a linear demand curve. Remember that the same percentage changes result in smaller absolute changes as you move down the curve; consumers tend to be less responsive to smaller changes in price than they are to larger changes.

4.   Some of the most fun and challenging uses for economics are in the area of government policy. By applying basic economic concepts, you can get a feel for the impact of policy in the areas of taxation and price controls, among others. However, remember that policymakers often have normative economic goals that they are trying to achieve. For example, using the positive economics generated in this chapter, you can see that minimum wage policy raises wages and costs for firms and also restricts employment. This may seem inefficient. However, wages do increase for some workers; as an antipoverty measure, it may achieve desired results. The bottom line is that good policymakers have to consider both positive and normative economics.

5.   Remember, the person who actually sends the tax money into the government (producer or consumer) may not be the one actually *bearing the burden* of the tax. The burden is determined by the relative elasticities of the supply and demand curves. For example, taxes on gasoline are most often collected by suppliers. However, when a new tax is levied by government, prices on the gas pumps often rise, indicating that consumers are bearing at least some of the burden of the new tax.

VI. MULTIPLE CHOICE QUESTIONS

These questions are organized by topic from the chapter outline. Choose the best answer from the options available.

A. Elasticity of Demand and Supply

1.   The price elasticity of demand equals the:
   a.   absolute price change divided by the absolute quantity change between two points on a demand curve.
   b.   percentage change in revenue divided by the percentage decrease in price.
   c.   percentage change in revenue divided by the percentage increase in quantity demanded.
   d.   percentage change in quantity demanded divided by percentage change in price.
   e.   slope of the demand curve.

2.   Suppose Mr. Gray has budgeted a fixed amount of money to buy eggs. Within a certain range of prices, he will spend neither more nor less than this amount of money on eggs, regardless of the price. His demand in this price range would properly be designated as being:
   a.   in equilibrium.
   b.   perfectly elastic.
   c.   perfectly inelastic.
   d.   highly inelastic, but not perfectly so.
   e.   unit-elastic.

Use the following information to answer questions 3 and 4: The Dark Movie Theater raised the price of popcorn from $2.00 per barrel to $2.30 per barrel. This caused the quantity of barrels sold to fall from 100 per day to 80 per day.

3.   At this time, the price elasticity of demand for popcorn could be estimated to be:
   a.   -.52.
   b.   -1.
   c.   -1.59.
   d.   -1.9.
   e.   -66.67.

4.   The Dark Movie Theater will see its total revenues from popcorn sales:
   a.   rise.
   b.   fall.
   c.   double.
   d.   remain the same.
   e.   fall to zero.

5. When the words "total revenue" are used in any discussion of demand curves, they refer to:
    a.   the profit, after deduction of costs, that the suppliers of a good or service earn from selling to consumers.
    b.   the total amount of money consumers will spend on a good at any particular price.
    c.   the gross income suppliers will receive from government.
    d.   the quantity of a good that is associated with any particular price.
    e.   nothing; the words "total revenue" cannot have any meaning in relation to demand curves.
    Figure 4-1 indicates the demand for air travel between New York City and Chicago. Use it to answer questions 6 and 7.

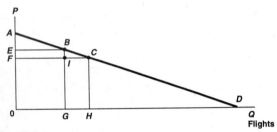

Figure 4-1

6. At point *B*, total revenue is represented by area:
    a.   *EBGO*.
    b.   *AOD*.
    c.   *FCHO*.
    d.   *AEB*.
    e.   *EBIF*.
7. Between points *B* and C demand is:
    a.   relatively elastic.
    b.   relatively inelastic.
    c.   perfectly elastic.
    d.   perfectly inelastic.
    e.   unit-elastic.
8. If a 10 percent reduction in a commodity's price brings a 5 percent increase in the amount of *money people spend* to buy that commodity, then in this region of the demand curves price elasticity of demand is:
    a.   elastic.
    b.   unit-elastic.
    c.   inelastic although not perfectly so.
    d.   perfectly inelastic.
    e.   perhaps any of these—the information given is insufficient to determine elasticity.
9. If a 10 percent reduction in price causes a 5 percent increase in the *quantity* of a commodity that people buy, then in this region of the demand curve, price elasticity of demand is:

a.   elastic.
b.   unit-elastic.
c.   inelastic, although not perfectly so.
d.   perfectly inelastic.
e.   perhaps any of these—the information given is insufficient to determine elasticity.
10. Which of the following observations would indicate that demand for a good is price-inelastic?
    a.   The good in question is more of a necessity than a luxury for most people.
    b.   There do not exist good substitutes for this good.
    c.   The time period allowed for responding to a change in price is very small.
    d.   All or any of the above.
    e.   None of the above.
11. Betty notices that no matter how many paper cups she buys, she always pays the same price per cup. This means that the supply curve which confronts her is:
    a.   perfectly inelastic.
    b.   perfectly elastic.
    c.   unit-elastic.
    d.   elastic, but not necessarily perfectly elastic.
    e.   none of these things, necessarily
12. A perfectly inelastic supply curve would be shown in the ordinary supply-and-demand graph as a:
    a.   vertical line.
    b.   horizontal line.
    c.   straight line, but neither horizontal nor vertical.
    d.   curved line.
    e.   any of the above.
13. Which alternative in question 12 would be correct for the graphical portrayal of a perfectly inelastic demand curve?
    a.
    b.
    c.
    d.
    e.
14. If a demand curve displays unitary price elasticity throughout its entire length, then the demand curve is:
    a.   a straight line, and total expenditure by buyers is the same at all prices.
    b.   not a straight line, and total expenditure by buyers falls as price falls.
    c.   a straight line, and total expenditure by buyers first increases and later decreases as price falls.
    d.   not a straight line, and total expenditure by buyers rises as price falls.
    e.   none of the above is correct.
    Use the diagrams in Figure 4-2 to answer questions 15 and 16.
15. A patient must purchase some exact quantity of a particular drug (no more, no less) and will pay any price, if necessary, in order to obtain it. Which of the five dia-

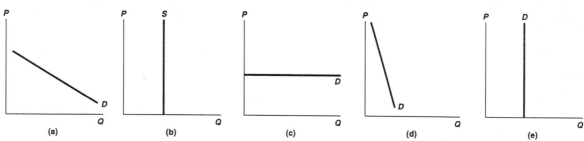

Figure 4-2

grams could be used to illustrate this situation?
a.
b.
c.
d.
e.

16. Over the past century, consumers of food in the United States have not purchased much more to eat, in spite of the fact that tremendous improvements in technology have led to lower real food prices. Which of the five diagrams could be used to illustrate this situation
a.
b.
c.
d.
e.

B. Applications to Major Economic Issues

17. For farmers, improvements in technology this century have been a mixed blessing. Farmers have seen:
a. large increases in supply and large increases in prices of agricultural products.
b. large increases in demand and large increases in prices of agricultural products.
c. large increases in supply and large decreases in prices of agricultural products.
d. small decreases in supply but large increases in demand; these two forces offset one another.
e. none of the above.

18. Which of the diagrams in Figure 4-3 reflects the effect of crop restrictions when they are placed on markets for agriculture products?
a.
b.
c.
d.

19. The government levies an excise tax of 5 cents per unit sold on the sellers in a competitive industry. Both supply and demand curves have some elasticity with respect to price. When this tax is represented on the supply-and-demand diagram, the entire:
a. supply curve shifts upward by exactly 5 cents, but (unless demand is perfectly elastic) the market price remains constant.
b. supply curve shifts upward by less than 5 cents, but (unless demand is highly elastic) the market price rises by the full 5 cents.
c. supply curve shifts downward by less than 5 cents and the market price falls.
d. supply curve shifts upward by exactly 5 cents, but (unless supply is perfectly elastic) the market price rises by less than 5 cents.
e. demand curve shifts upward by exactly 5 cents, but the market price rises by less than 5 cents.

20. Suppose that the demand curve for wheat is perfectly inelastic with respect to price. If a tax of 50 cents per bushel sold were imposed on the market and collected by producers, then price would:
a. rise, but by less than 50 cents, and there would he

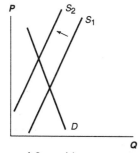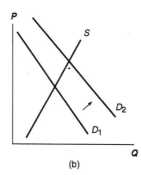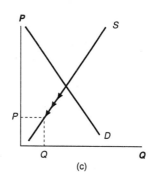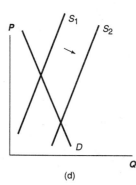

Figure 4-3   (a)   (b)   (c)   (d)

some reduction in the quantity bought and sold.

b. rise by the full 50 cents, but there would be no reduction in the quantity bought and sold.

c. rise, but by less than 50 cents, and there would be no reduction in the quantity bought and sold.

d. rise by the full 50 cents, and there could definitely be a reduction in the quantity bought and sold.

e. fall, but by less than 50 cents, and there would be some reduction in the quantity bought and sold.

21. The change brought about by the tax levy described in the question above could be described as a decrease in:

a. supply followed by an increase in quantity demanded.

b. quantity supplied followed by a decrease in quantity demanded.

c. supply followed by a decrease in demand.

d. quantity supplied followed by a decrease in demand.

e. none of the above.

22. Suppose the government imposes an additional tax of $1.00 per bottle of whiskey. In response to this tax, the market price rises from $12.00 to $12.63 per bottle. From this information, you can say that:

a. the supply curve is relatively more inelastic than the demand curve.

b. the demand curve is relatively more inelastic than the supply curve.

c. price elasticity of demand and supply are equal.

d. the sellers bear the entire burden of the tax.

e. none of the above.

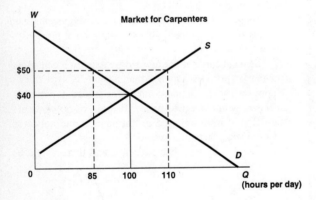

Figure 4-4

Use Figure 4-4, which describes a hypothetical market for carpenters, to answer questions 23 through 25.

23. Suppose the government passes a law stating that carpenters must be paid no less than $50 per hour. This sort of price control would be called a(n):

a. price ceiling.

b. price floor.

c. wage subsidy.

d. tax.

e. equilibrium price.

24. Between the old equilibrium and the new minimum wage, price elasticity of demand is:

a. -.66.

b. -.73.

c. -1.37.

d. -1.50.

e. none of these.

25. Between the old equilibrium and the new minimum wage, price elasticity of supply is:

a. .43.

b. .66.

c. 1.00.

d. 2.33.

e. none of these.

26. Energy price controls are a type of:

a. tax.

b. price floor.

c. subsidy.

d. price ceiling.

VII. PROBLEM SOLVING

The following problems are designed to help you apply the concepts that you learned in the chapter.

A. Elasticity of Demand and Supply

1. Please complete the following statements with the correct answers:

a. If we say that "demand is highly price-elastic," we mean that any price reduction would produce a relatively (**large / small**) (**increase / decrease**) in purchases and that a price rise would yield a relatively (**large / small**) (**decrease / increase**) in buying.

b. To describe supply as "decidedly price-inelastic" would mean that any price increase would cause a relatively (**large / small**) (**increase / decrease**) in quantity offered for sale and that any price reduction would produce a relatively (**large / small**) (**increase / decrease**) in the quantity supplied.

2. Table 4-1 shows demand for hamburgers at Sam's Drive-In at prices from $8 to $0.

TABLE 4-1

Price	Quantity Demanded	Total Revenue	Price Elasticity of Demand
$8	0		
7	2		
6	4		
5	6		
4	8		
3	10		
2	12		
1	14		
0	16		

a. Use the numbers in Table 4-1 to draw a demand curve in Figure 4-5.

b. Calculate the total revenue received by Sam's at each price in Table 4-1.

c. Plot the total revenue curve along with your demand curve.

d. Calculate the price elasticity of demand at the midpoint between the prices listed in Table 4-1. Use your diagram and explain the relationship between price, elasticity of demand, and total revenue.

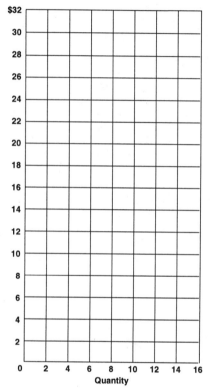

Figure 4-5

3. Use your answers to question 2 to complete the following:

a. Notice the interesting behavior of the total revenue curve as you move down the length of the straight-line demand curve. As price falls, total revenue (**remains the same at all quantities / falls throughout the entire price range / rises first, reaches a peak, and then falls / falls first, reaches a minimum, and then climbs**) .

b. If the price falls from $7 to $6, total revenue (**rises / stays the same / falls**). How is this possible when the lower price means that each unit that was purchased at $7 is now purchased at $6? For the 2 units demanded at $7, lowering the price by $1 results in $2 less revenue being collected. The lower price means a larger quanti-

ty is demanded. Is the revenue collected from the sale of these extra units enough to overcome the initial loss just noted? Four units are demanded if the price is $6— an increase in the quantity demanded—yielding an additional $___ in revenue. In this case, the increase in revenue generated by selling more units (**is / is not**) enough to offset the initial loss.

c. Now suppose that the price falls from $4 to $3. Selling the units demanded at $4 for a dollar less results in a revenue loss of $__. The associated increase in the quantity demanded of units brings a counterbalancing revenue gain of $__. The loss (**outweighs / exactly balances / falls short of**) the gain, and total revenue (**falls / stays the same / increases**).

4. Complete the following:

a. If an increase in demand is sudden and suppliers have no reserve inventories on hand, then no greater quantity can be offered immediately, despite the price rise. In this case, the supply curve would have to be shown as (**perfectly elastic / perfectly inelastic**).

b. Given a little time, suppliers can adjust to a demand surge by working their plant and equipment harder (e.g., by adding an extra shift of workers) . The result of this increase in supply would be the new (**long-run / short-run**) equilibrium.

c. If the shift in demand is sustained, then existing and potential new suppliers have even more time to build new plants and install new equipment. There is a further increase in the supply. Finally, an equilibrium price indicating (**long-run / short-run**) equilibrium may be reached.

d. Note carefully that all this is just a statement about price elasticity of supply. It says that the degree of responsiveness of supply to a price change will depend on the amount of adjustment time suppliers can have. The longer this time period, the (**higher / lower**) will be the price elasticity (the elasticity coefficient) of supply.

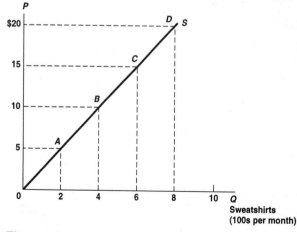

Figure 4-6

The same sort of relationship between elasticity and time (**can / cannot**) be defined for the demand side.

5. Suppose Figure 4-6 shows the supply curve in the market for sweatshirts at Anywhere State University.

   a. The slope of this supply curve is ___.

   b. The price elasticity of supply between points *A* and *B* is___; between *B* and *C* is___; and between *C* and *D* is ___.

   c. (advanced concept) The equation for this supply curve is: _____.

   d. (advanced concept) The relationship between the slope of a supply curve and its elasticity at a given point can be described as follows: _____

_____.

B. Applications to Major Economic Issues

6. One of the most heavily taxed consumer products in the United States, and in many other countries, is cigarettes. Figure 4-7 shows a hypothetical representation of this market:

   a. Initially, the equilibrium price is $___ and the equilibrium quantity exchanged is ___ packs per day.

   b. The federal government is discussing the idea of increasing the tax on cigarettes in order to finance a universal health care system. Suppose the government decides to levy a $1-per-pack tax. Show the impact of this on the market using Figure 4-7.

   c. After the tax is levied, the equilibrium price becomes approximately $__ and the equilibrium quantity exchanged is approximately ___ packs per day.

   d. In this case, the buyers must pay approximately $___ of the new tax and the sellers must pay approximately $___ of the new tax. The government will

collect $___ per day.

   e. Carefully compare the relative price elasticities of supply and demand in this price range. How can you explain the division of the tax that you calculated in part d?

7. Price controls have been used by many governments in order to achieve policy objectives. Sometimes, as in the case of price supports in the dairy industry, policymakers are trying to protect sellers' incomes. Other times, as in the case of rent control, policymakers are trying to protect buyers from high prices.

Consider Figure 4-8. The equilibrium price of *X* is $___ and the equilibrium quantity is ___ units. Suppose the government is considering a number of policy options designed to restrict consumption to 500 units. First, it could impose a price (**ceiling / floor**) of $___; the quantity demanded would then be ___ units, but the quantity supplied would be ___ units. A (**shortage / surplus**) of ___ units would result in the short run. Second, the government could set a production quota at 500 units; suppliers would receive a price of $___ for every unit that they sold. Finally, the government could issue ration tickets and announce that one ticket and no more than $5 would be required to purchase 1 unit of *X*. If the tickets could be bought and sold, they would command a price of $___. Carefully explain why this is true.

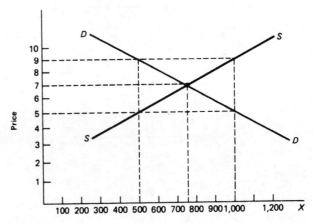

Figure 4-8

VIII. DISCUSSION QUESTIONS

Answer the following questions, making sure that you can explain the work you did to arrive at the answers.

1. Are the following statements true or false?

   a. If demand is price-elastic, then a 10 percent increase in price is associated with a reduction in the quantity demanded of more than 10 percent. This means that quantity is falling faster than price is rising,

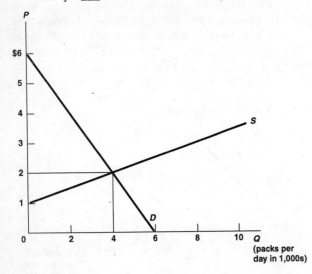

Figure 4-7

and total revenue will fall. **(T/F)**

b. If demand displays unitary price elasticity, then a 10 percent increase in price is matched by a 10 percent increase in quantity demanded. This means that total revenue will remain unchanged. **(T/F)**

c. If demand is price-inelastic, then a 10 percent increase in price is associated with a reduction in the quantity demanded of less than 10 percent. This means that total revenue will actually rise with the price. **(T/F)**

2. Put **(E)** for price-elastic, **(U)** for unitary-elastic, or **(I)** for price-inelastic in the blanks below according to which term most accurately describes each demand situation:

___ a. Price falls from $6 to $5 and revenue falls from $60 to $55.

___ b. Price falls from $6 to $5 and revenue stays the same.

___ c. Price climbs from $5 to $6 and quantity purchased falls from 80 to 60.

___ d. Price drops from $6 to $5 and there is no increase in quantity demanded.

___ e. Price climbs from $300 to $301 and there is no reduction in quantity demanded.

___ f. Price climbs and revenue climbs by $10.

___ g. Price climbs from $5.00 to $5.01 and people stop buying the stuff completely.

3. Although we have discussed the extreme case of a good that has a perfectly inelastic demand in all price ranges, there are very few goods that can be categorized in this way. Why is this? Explain.

4. Carefully explain why all linear demand curves have elastic, unit-elastic, and inelastic regions. Given this, and the relationship between elasticity and total revenues, which of the following two firms is more likely to increase the price of its product: (a) a producer of canned soup, whose price elasticity of demand is currently -.5; or (b) a producer of fur coats, whose price elasticity of demand is currently -3.8?

5. An example in your textbook discusses the relationship between price elasticity of demand and airline pricing policies. Low-elasticity business travelers are charged higher prices than are higher-elasticity vacation travelers. Explain the form that this sort of pricing policy might take. Can you think of another market in which price differentials exist for consumers with different price elasticities of demand?

6. (a) Use a diagram to show the impact of a price ceiling in the market for butter. Why might government policymakers adopt such a plan? Can you think of any time during this century when this policy might have been appropriate?

(b) Now use a diagram to show the impact of a price floor in the market for butter. Why might government policymakers adopt such a plan? Can you think of any time during this century when this policy might have been appropriate?

7. During the summer of 1993, severe flooding in the midwestern United States destroyed corn, wheat, and soybean crops. During the summer of 1994, severe flooding in the southeast destroyed a large portion of the peanut and cotton crops. Use supply-and-demand diagrams to show the effects of this flooding if demand is relatively inelastic in the markets for these agriculture products. Now, show the effects of this flooding if the demand for these agriculture products is relatively elastic. Explain the difference, and make predictions concerning farm incomes in light of these disasters.

IX. ANSWERS TO STUDY GUIDE QUESTIONS

111. Review of Key Concepts

5	Price elasticity of demand
10	Price elasticity of supply
9	Elastic demand
7	Inelastic demand
11	Unit-elastic demand
3	Perfectly elastic
8	Perfectly inelastic
4	Total revenue
1	Tax incidence
2	Price ceiling
6	Price floor

VI. Multiple Choice Questions

1. D 2. E 3. C 4. B 5. B 6. A
7. A 8. A 9. C 10. D 11. B 12. A
13. A 14. E 15. E 16. D 17. C 18. A
19. D 20. B 21. E 22. B 23. B 24. B
25. A 26. D

VII. Problem Solving

1. a. large / increase
      large / decrease
   b. small / decrease
      small / increase

2. a and b: see table.

TABLE 4-1

Price	Quantity Demanded	Total Revenue	Elasticity of Demand
$ 8	0	$ 0	xxx
7	2	14	15.00
6	4	24	4.33
5	6	30	2.20
4	8	32	1.29
3	10	30	.77
2	12	24	.45
1	14	14	.23
0	16	0	.07

c.   see Figure 4-9.

d.   As price falls in the elastic portion of the demand curve, total revenue increases. As price falls in the inelastic portion of the demand curve, total revenue decreases.

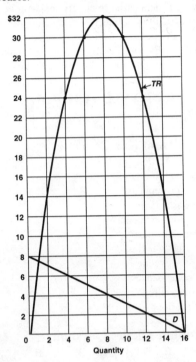

Figure 4-9

3.   a.   Rises first, reaches a peak, and then falls.
     b.   Rises, $12, is.
     c. $8, 2 units, $6, outweighs, falls.
4.   a.   perfectly inelastic
     b.   short-run
     c.   long-run
     d.   higher, can
5.   a.   2.5
     b.   1, 1, 1
     c.   Price = 2.5 × Quantity
     d.   Elasticity = (1/slope) × (P/Q)
6.   a. $2.00, 4000 packs per day
     b.   Shift the supply curve to the left by the amount of the tax.
     c. $2.75, 3000
     d. $.75, $.25, $3000
     e.   Demand is relatively more inelastic, so buyers pay more of the tax.
7. $7.00, 750, floor, $9.00, 500, 1000, surplus, 500, $9.00, $4.00. Buyers are willing to pay as much as $9.00 for 500 units of the item; if the price is $5.00 then people will be willing to pay as much as $4.00 for the tickets.

VIII.   DISCUSSION QUESTIONS

1.   a.   T
     b.   F
     c.   T
2.   a.   I
     b.   U
     c.   E
     d.   I
     e.   I
     f.   I
     g.   E
3.   For most goods and most consumers, price eventually reaches a level beyond which further consumption is impossible.
4.   At higher prices, the same percentage change in price is a larger absolute change; thus consumers are more responsive to it. The producer of canned soup is more likely to raise price. Because demand is inelastic, a price increase will lead to higher total revenues.
5.   Vacation travelers must stay over a Saturday night in order to guarantee lower fares. In movie theaters, adults pay more for tickets than children do.
6.   a.

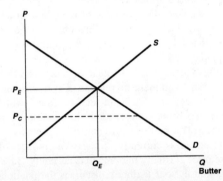

A price ceiling in the market for butter might be appropriate if the government is trying to protect buyers from high prices. This might have happened during World War II, when much of the economy's productive capacity was directed toward military equipment and away from consumer products.

     b.

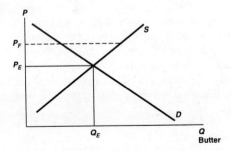

A price floor in the market for butter might be appropriate if the government is trying to protect sellers from low prices. This might be used currently, as new technology in the dairy industry threatens to bring prices and farm income down further.

7.

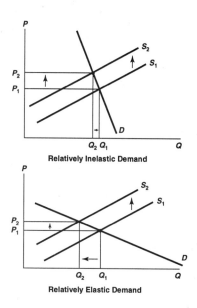

Relatively Inelastic Demand

Relatively Elastic Demand

In either case, a significant decrease in supply will raise prices and reduce the quantities of the goods exchanged. If demand is elastic, the price change will be relatively small while the quantity change is relatively large. If demand is inelastic, the price change will be relatively large while the quantity change is relatively small. For those farmers unaffected by the floods, incomes will rise as long as demand is inelastic.

CHAPTER

Demand and Consumer Behavior

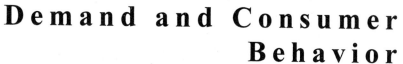

I. CHAPTER OVERVIEW

Now that you know the basics of market behavior, you are ready to do more in-depth analysis of the demand curve. This chapter asks, "What makes consumers tick?" and provides you with an opportunity to apply consumer theory to different situations. In a market economy consumer theory is very important; just think about the number of firms and agencies that exist to sell a whole host of products to consumers! Firms compete fiercely for the dollars that consumers bring to the marketplace. The theory that this chapter develops will give you some clues as to the nature of this competition.

Consumer theory formalizes behavior that should be very familiar to you. You, your classmates, your friends, and their families are all consumers who ordinarily have only a limited amount of money to spend in any given period of time on the goods and services that they need or want. Each good has a market price which usually cannot be altered by bargaining or haggling. You must decide which goods to buy and how much of each good to buy knowing from the quoted prices that each purchase will exhaust part of your limited income or budget, but also knowing what you like and what you do not like. Chapter 5 involves careful analysis of this decision-making process.

II. LEARNING OBJECTIVES

After you have read Chapter 5 in your text and completed the exercises in this *Study Guide* chapter, you should be able to:

1. Define **total utility** and **marginal utility** and explain the difference between these two measures of consumer satisfaction.
2. Explain the **law of diminishing marginal utility** and its importance in economic analysis.
3. Show that an individual's utility is maximized for a given income when the marginal utility derived from the last dollar spent on each good is the same for all goods purchased.
4. Express the utility-maximizing rule mathematically, and show how it combines with the law of diminishing

marginal utility to produce downward-sloping demand curves.
5. Define **substitution** and **income effects** and explain how they work to produce downward-sloping demand curves.
6. Explain how **market** demand curves are derived from the horizontal summation of **individual** demand curves.
7. Describe the **paradox of value** and resolve it through application of the utility-maximizing rule.
8. Discuss what is meant by the term **consumer surplus**, and illustrate the concept using examples and a demand curve.

III. REVIEW OF KEY CONCEPTS

Match the following terms from column A with their definitions in column B.

A	B
__ Utility	1. Denotes the percentage change in quantity demanded divided by the percentage change in income, all else held fixed.
__ Marginal utility	2. Represents the sum of the individual demands at each price.
__ Utilitarianism	3. Given two goods, an increase the price of one causes a decrease in the demand for the other.
__ Law of diminishing marginal utility	4. Explains why the price of a diamond is greater than the price of a gallon of water.
__ $MU_1/P_1 = MU_2/P_2 = ... = MU$ per \$ spent	5. States that when the price of a good rises, consumers will tend to substitute other goods for the one whose price is rising in order to satisfy their needs less expensively.
__ Market demand	6. Measures the want-satisfying power of a good or service.
__ Income elasticity	7. Given two goods, an increase in the price of one causes an increase in the demand for the other.

__ Substitutes

__ Complements

__ Substitution
effect

__ Income effect

__ Demerit goods

__ Paradox of
value

__ Consumer
surplus

8.   States that as the amount of a good consumed increases, the marginal utility of that good tends to diminish.

9.   Measures the increase in total utility when an additional unit of a good is consumed.

10. The gap between the total utility of a good and its total market value.

11. "The greatest happiness of the greatest number."

12. Denotes the impact of a price change on a good's quantity demanded that results from the effect of the price change on consumers' real income.

13. Describes the market basket of goods that will bring the consumer maximum satisfaction.

14. Goods whose consumption is deemed harmful.

IV. SUMMARY AND CHAPTER OUTLINE

This section summarizes the key concepts from the chapter.

A. Choice and Utility Theory

1.   Utility measures the want-satisfying power of a good or service. Marginal utility is the rate at which utility changes as *each additional unit* of a particular good is consumed. As with other marginal concepts, marginal utility measures the change in a total value when an additional unit of something else is used.

2.   The law of diminishing marginal utility holds that as the amount of a good consumed increases, the *marginal* utility of that good tends to diminish. That is, the more you have of any one thing, the less an additional unit of it is worth to you. This ties nicely into the *paradox of value* discussed later in the chapter. People are not willing to pay much for an additional gallon of water because they have so much of it that an additional gallon has a low marginal utility. However, notice that when water becomes more scarce, as it does during droughts or in deserts, the price climbs, reflecting the fact that consumers under these circumstances place a higher value on additional gallons of it.

3.   Utility is an important concept for economists, but there is no *cardinal* measure of it. That is, there is no scale or instrument upon which utility can be measured. Instead, we rely on *ordinal* measures, which simply rank items relative to one another. For example, instead of saying that I get 10 utils from consuming an apple and 5 utils from consuming a banana, I can only say that I get more utility from an apple

than from a banana. This type of ordinal measure is sufficient for economists to use utility theory to develop an understanding of consumer behavior.

B. Consumer Equilibrium Condition

1.   Utility is maximized subject to a budget constraint if the ratios of marginal utility to price for all goods are equal, i.e., if the marginal utility of the last dollar spent is the same regardless of where it is spent. Stated differently, utility maximization requires that for any goods X and Y:

$$MU_X / P_X = MU_Y / P_Y$$

2.   Utility theory helps to explain why demand curves are generally downward-sloping, as was argued in Chapters 3 and 4. As the price of good X *falls,* the quantity of X consumed *rises,* and so MU_X *falls* with price.

3.   Substitution and income effects also help to explain the negative correlation between price and quantity demanded. *Substitution effects* describe the fact that as prices change along a demand curve, consumers substitute relatively cheaper goods into their market baskets. *Income effects* describe the fact that as prices change along a demand curve, money income is held fixed, but real income or purchasing power changes. This means that consumers are not able to buy as much at higher prices.

For example, suppose a consumer increases her purchases of apples from 4 to 6 when the price of apples falls from 50 cents to 25 cents per apple. She purchases more apples and substitutes them into her market basket in place of oranges, bananas, and other fruit that is now relatively more expensive. (Substitution effect.) She is able to buy more apples because she has more purchasing power. When the price was 50 cents, she spent a total of $2.00 on 4 apples. The same 4 apples now cost only $1.00! She has an additional $1.00 of purchasing power to spend on apples, or any other good in her market basket, even with no increase in her budget. (Income effect.)

C. From Individual to Market Demand

1.   Market demand curves reflect, for any price, the total quantity demanded across many individuals. They are the "horizontal sum" of individual demand curves.

2.   As illustrated in Chapter 3, the demand for a good *shifts* when any factor other than the price of the good itself changes. When money income changes, demand curves shift; the magnitude of this shift depends upon *income elasticity,* which measures the percentage change in quantity demanded resulting from some percentage change in income. When prices of other goods change, demand curves shift; the magnitude of this shift depends upon *cross price elasticities,* which measure the percentage change in quantity demanded resulting from some percentage change in the price of another good.

3. Goods can be either *normal* or *inferior.* With a normal good, as income increases, demand increases (or shifts to the right). With an inferior good, as income increases, demand decreases (or shifts to the left). For example, for many people cars and stereos are normal goods. For many people, used clothes and Spam are inferior goods. Remember, though, that definitions of normal and inferior goods are subjective and based upon individual preferences.

4. Goods can be related in two different ways. *Complements* are goods that are consumed together. *Substitutes* are goods that are consumed in place of one another. Goods are independent when the consumption of one does not depend on or affect consumption of the other.

5. *Demerit goods* are goods whose consumption is deemed harmful. Governments sometimes intervene to discourage consumption of such goods; for example, in the United States the government prohibits the sale and use of certain addictive drugs, such as heroin and cocaine.

D. Paradox of Value

1. The *paradox of value* addresses the somewhat counterintuitive observation that water costs less than diamonds in spite of the fact that water sustains life and diamonds are often simply decorative. This can be explained by the fact that water is relatively abundant, and hence in great supply, but diamonds are relatively scarce. Note that the *total* utility from water is greater than the *total* utility from diamonds.

E. Consumer Surplus

1. Consumer surplus represents the difference between what people would have been willing to pay for a given quantity of some good, one unit at a time, and how much they actually had to pay in a market quoting one price for all units. Remember that a demand curve represents the maximum amount that consumers would be willing and able to pay for each unit of a good. Also remember that from our model, there is a single market price paid for all units of a good exchanged. (Price dispersion will be discussed in a later chapter.) This means that consumers typically receive a "surplus;" that is, some consumers receive value from a good or service in excess of the amount that they paid for it.

V. HELPFUL HINTS

1. Utility theory would be much more concrete if we could somehow *measure* utility, or consumer satisfaction. Just think, we could then ask consumers to strap their "utilmeters" onto their wrists before they walk into the grocery store or mall, and they could simply purchase those goods that bring the highest utilmeter reading per dollar spent. For example, a consumer in the cookie aisle of the grocery store could choose between the Oreos and the Chips Ahoy by holding each one in turn and checking to see which product got the highest number of utils.

This might be nice, but this sort of cardinal representation of utility is not possible. Utility is a subjective notion. It changes over time; some things that you like now you may not have liked or needed as a child. (Coffee or beer, for example?) If I say, "I got a marginal utility of 200 from the last cookie I ate," it would be impossible for you to place this on a meaningful scale. Thus, we have to be happy with ordinal measures of utility, that is, with our ability to say "I like A better than B" or "I like B better than A" or "I like A and B exactly the same amount." This sort of measurement is fine for our purposes as economists.

2. Grab a box of cookies, or a bag of potato chips, or something else that you like to eat and think carefully about the concepts of total utility, marginal utility, and the law of diminishing marginal utility. The marginal utility of, say, cookies is the additional satisfaction that you get from consuming each additional cookie. The total utility you get is the total of the marginal utilities from each cookie; that is, when you have finished your snack, total utility is the total amount of satisfaction that you got from eating those cookies. The law of diminishing marginal utility should hold; as you eat more and more cookies, eventually your marginal utility will fall. Does this principle hold for you?

3. Income elasticities and cross price elasticities are very similar to price elasticities of supply and demand that you learned about in Chapter 4. However, there are some important differences. Price elasticities of demand and supply measure moves *along* a demand or a supply curve, because price is measured on the Y axis. Income elasticity and cross price elasticities measure *shifts in* the demand curve as factors other than the price of the product are changing. This is an important distinction to make.

4. Notice that the *sign* of an income elasticity or of a cross price elasticity gives you important information. A positive income elasticity means that a good is normal, but a negative income elasticity means that a good is inferior. A positive cross price elasticity means that the two goods are substitutes, but a negative cross price elasticity means that the two goods are complements.

VI. MULTIPLE CHOICE QUESTIONS

These questions are organized by topic from the chapter outline. Choose the best answer from the options available.

A. Choice and Utility Theory

1. The marginal utility of a commodity is:
   a. an indication of the last use to which the commodity has been put or the use to which it would next be put if more were available.
   b. equal to the price of that commodity.
   c. the ratio of the total utility generated by consuming that commodity to the total utility of all other commodities that are consumed.

d.   the extra utility yielded by consuming each successive unit of that commodity.

e.   the same thing as the total utility derived from consuming that commodity.

2.   If the marginal utility of a commodity is zero, then:

a.   total utility for this commodity has reached a maximum.

b.   the commodity in question has no utility; i.e., it is not one that consumers want to use.

c.   the paradox of value must have been reached.

d.   the consumer has reached his or her equilibrium position with respect to purchase of this commodity

e.   total utility for this commodity must be zero also.

3.   The law of diminishing marginal utility states that:

a.   as the amount of a good consumed increases, the total utility of that good tends to diminish.

b.   as the amount of a good consumed decreases, the total utility of that good tends to diminish.

c.   as income increases, marginal utility tends to diminish.

d.   as the amount of a good consumed increases, the marginal utility of that good tends to diminish.

e.   when the price of a good increases, marginal utility tends to diminish.

Use the following information to answer questions 4 and 5. Albert consumes five Oreo cookies. The *marginal* utility of the first cookie is 10 utils; of the second, 12 utils; of the third, 8 utils; of the fourth, 3 utils; and of the fifth, -2 utils

4.   When he consumes these five cookies, his *total* utility from cookies is:

a.   -2 utils

b.   1 util.

c.   31 utils

d.   35 utils.

e.   not enough information to calculate total utility.

5.   The law of diminishing returns sets in after the:

a.   first cookie.

b.   second cookie.

c.   third cookie.

d.   fourth cookie.

e.   fifth cookie.

B. Consumer Equilibrium Condition

6.   When a consumer is maximizing his or her utility subject to the constraint of income and given prices, then the:

a.   total satisfaction derived from each commodity must equal the total satisfaction derived from ever other commodity.

b.   ratio of the total satisfaction derived from any commodity to the price of that commodity must be equal for all commodities.

c.   satisfaction derived from the last tiny unit of each commodity bought must be equal for all commodities.

d.   ratio of the total satisfaction derived from any commodity to the total expenditure on that commodity must be equal for all commodities.

e.   none of the preceding descriptions is necessarily correct.

7.   The equilibrium condition for a consumer who is spending all of his or her budget on two commodities, A and B, is given by:

a. $MU_A = MU_B$

b. $MU_A / P_B = MU_B / P_A$

c. $MU_A / P_A = MU_B / P_B$

d. $P_A = P_B$

e.   none of the above.

8.   You have $20 per week available to spend as you wish on commodities A and B. The prices of these commodities, the quantities you now buy, and your evaluation of the utility provided by these quantities are recorded in Table 5-1. You are currently spending your entire weekly budget.

TABLE 5-1

	Price	Bought	Total Utility	Marginal Utility
A	$.70	20	500	30
B	$.50	12	1 000	20

For maximum satisfaction, you should buy:

a.   less of A and more of B.

b.   the same quantity of A but more of B.

c.   more of A and less of B.

d.   more of A and the same quantity of B.

e.   the same amount of A and B.

9.   The price of good X is $1.50 and that of good Y is $1.00. If a consumer considers the marginal utility of Y to be 30 utils, and is maximizing utility with respect to purchases of X and Y, then he or she must consider the marginal utility of X to be:

a.   15 utils

b.   20 utils

c.   30 utils.

d.   45 utils.

e.   not enough information to tell.

10.   If, in question 9, the figure of 30 utils had been the *total* (rather than marginal) utility of Y, which alternative would be correct with respect to the total utility of X?

a.

b.

c.

d.

e.

11.   Homer does not have to work on Saturday, and he is trying to decide how to spend his afternoon. He decides

that he can either watch TV or play baseball with Bart. The *total utility* that he would derive from each pursuit is independent of the other and is given in Table 5-2.

TABLE 5-2

Hours Spent	Total Utility	
	TV	Baseball
1	16	10
2	24	18
3	31	24
4	37	30

If Homer has 4 hours to allocate between TV and baseball, what combination would he choose to maximize his utility?

a. 4 hours of baseball.
b. 3 hours of TV and 1 hour of baseball.
c. 2 hours of TV and 2 hours of baseball.
d. 3 hours of TV and 1 hour of baseball.
e. 4 hours of TV.

12. In question 11, at this utility-maximizing combination of TV and baseball, the marginal utility of:
a. TV is 8 and of baseball is 8.
b. TV is 24 and of baseball is 18.
c. TV is 40 and of baseball is 28.
d. TV is 31 and of baseball is 24.
e. both goods are indeterminate.

13. The income effect captures which of the following economic phenomena?
a. If money incomes fall, people will purchase less of any given commodity.
b. A decrease in the price of a major purchase has an effect similar to an increase in income, and this may prompt people to buy more of that good.
c. The quantity of a good purchased may actually decrease as people's incomes rise.
d. As people's incomes rise, they save proportionately more out of income, so they actually spend a smaller fraction of their incomes.

e. If the price of a good drops, it is as though the prices of all other goods have risen, in relative terms, so smaller quantities of those other goods will tend to be bought.

14. You regard goods X and Y as substitutes. If the price of X rises and neither good is inferior, the *income effect* should induce you to purchase:
a. more Y only if the price of X is less than the price of Y.
b. less of good Y.
c. the same amount of Y.
d. more Y only if the price of X is greater than the price of Y.
e. none of the above.

15. Which alternative in question 14 would have been correct if it had referred to the *substitution effect* rather than the income effect?
a.
b.
c.
d.
e.

16. A consumer moves to a new equilibrium position as a result of some change either in market price or in income. In this new equilibrium situation, marginal utilities are all lower than they were in the old equilibrium situation. Tastes or preferences are unchanged. This consumer is:
a. definitely worse off in the new situation.
b. definitely better off in the new situation.
c. worse off in the new situation if income has changed, but not otherwise.
d. better off in the new situation if price has changed, but not otherwise.
e. better off or worse off in the new situation; the information given does not necessarily indicate one or the other.

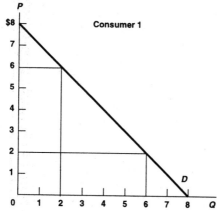

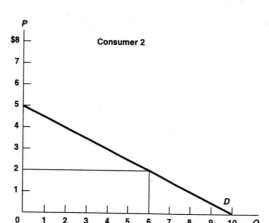

Figure 5-1

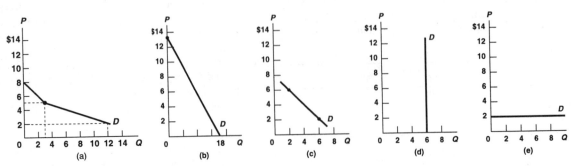

Figure 5-2

C. From Individual to Market Demand

17. The market demand curve is the:
    a. vertical summation of the individual demand curves.
    b. horizontal summation of the individual demand curves.
    c. equilibrium price and quantity exchanged in the market at a given point in time.
    d. relatively inelastic portion of the individual demand curve.
    e. individual demand curve with the highest elasticity of demand at every price.

18. Suppose a market is composed of two consumers with the demand curves shown in Figure 5-1.
    The market demand curve is given by which panel of Figure 5-2:
    a.
    b.
    c.
    d.
    e.

19. A consumer's demand curve for any given commodity is most likely to shift to the right with:
    a. an increase in the price of substitutes or a decrease in the price of complements.
    b. an increase in the price of either substitutes or complements.
    c. a decrease in the price of substitutes or an increase in the price of complements.
    d. a decrease in the price of either substitutes or complements.
    e. none of these cases.

20. Suppose that the income elasticity of demand for new houses is 2.3. If consumer incomes increase by 2 percent, you could expect the quantity of new houses to:
    a. increase by 2.3 percent.
    b. increase by 2 percent.
    c. increase by 4.6 percent.
    d. decrease by 1 percent.
    e. decrease by 4.6 percent.

21. Suppose that when the price of Coke increases by 2 percent, the quantity of Bacardi Rum purchased increases by 4 percent. (Assume everything else is held fixed.) This means that the:
    a. income elasticity of demand is 2 and the goods are complements.
    b. cross price elasticity is 2 and the goods are substitutes.
    c. cross price elasticity is -.5 and the goods are complements.
    d. price elasticity of demand for Coke is -2 and the goods are complements.
    e. price elasticity of demand for Bacardi is .5 and the goods are substitutes.

D. Paradox of Value

22. The paradox of value occurs because:
    a. prices of commodities are not always proportional to the total satisfaction that they give us.
    b. it is impossible to explain the price of a commodity in terms of either demand factors alone or supply factors alone.
    c. it is impossible to explain why people's tastes are what they are or why they vary from one person to the next.
    d. prices of commodities always perfectly reflect the amount of value that they bring to the consumer.
    e. none of the above.

23. The paradox of value is best illustrated by which of the following?
    a. The quantity of diamonds demanded increases as price decreases.
    b. Suppliers are willing and able to supply more water when the price increases, everything else held fixed.
    c. Consumers must pay more for diamonds than they pay for water, even though water is a necessity and diamonds are a luxury for most people.
    d. Consumers will substitute diamonds into their market basket when the price of diamonds falls.
    e. Diamonds and water do not mix.

24. The demand for addictive substances is highly dependent on past consumption. For heavy users of cocaine, demand is:
a. highly inelastic so that government prohibition has little impact on price.
b. highly elastic so that government prohibition has a great impact on price.
c. highly inelastic so that government prohibition has a great impact on price.
d. highly elastic so that government prohibition has little impact on price.
e. perfectly elastic since users can get all they want to consume at the market price.

E. Consumer Surplus
25. Consumer surplus is defined as the:
a. difference between the total utility of a good and the maximum amount that consumers are willing to pay for it.
b. difference between the total utility of a good and the market price.
c. sum of the total utility of a good and its market price.
d. total revenue that producers receive from selling a particular good.
e. sum of the marginal utilities for all consumers of a good.
26. The idea of "consumer surplus" reflects the notion that:
a. the gain consumers obtain with some purchases exceeds the gain suppliers obtain from selling.
b. purchasing many goods is a real bargain for consumers, because they would have been willing to pay more than they actually do in order to get them.
c. the marginal utility of the first units of a product consumed may exceed the total utility which the product supplies.
d. total utility increases either when consumer incomes rise or when the prices they must pay for goods fall.
e. when demand is price-inelastic, buyers can obtain a larger quantity for the expenditure of less money.
Use Figure 5-3 to answer questions 27 and 28.

27. If this good is provided for free, consumer surplus will be:
a. $5.
b. 10 units.
c. $16.
d. $25.
e. $50.
28. If the price of this good is $2, consumer surplus will be:
a. $2.
b. $9.
c. $12.
d. $25.
e. $50.

VII. PROBLEM SOLVING

The following problems are designed to help you apply the concepts that you learned in this chapter.

A. Choice and Utility Theory
1. a. If the total utilities associated with the consumption of 1, 2, and 3 units of B were to be, respectively, 100, 160, and 200, then the corresponding marginal utilities would be _____, _____, and _____.
b. Which of the following sets of total utility figures (designated for 1, 2, 3, and 4 units of B consumed) illustrates the idea of diminishing marginal utility?
(1) 200, 300, 400, 500.
(2) 200, 450, 750, 1100.
(3) 200, 400, 1600, 9600.
(4) 200, 250, 270, 280.
c. Which of the following sets of marginal utility figures (once again defined for 1, 2, 3, and 4 units of B consumed) would likewise illustrate the diminishing marginal utility principle?
(1) 200, 150, 100, 50.
(2) 200, 300, 400, 500.
(3) 200, 200, 200, 200.

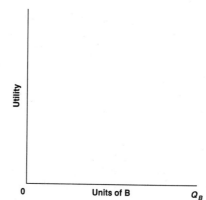

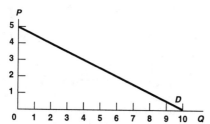

Figure 5-3

Figure 5-4

TABLE 5-3

Total Units	Apples (Total Utility)	Apples (Marginal Utility)	Bananas (Total Utility)	Bananas (Marginal Utility)	Cherries (Total Utility)	Cherries (Marginal Utility)
1	10	——	100	——	6	——
2	19	——	150	——	12	——
3	27	——	175	——	18	——
4	34	——	187	——	24	——
5	40	——	193	——	30	——
6	45	——	196	——	36	——
7	49	——	197	——	42	——
8	52	——	197	——	48	——

(4) 200, 250, 270, 280.

d. In Figure 5-4, plot the total and marginal utility curves for the set of marginal utility figures that you chose in part **c**.

B. Consumer Equilibrium Condition

2. In Table 5-3, three sets of total utility values are described for Betty White, who is using apples, bananas, and cherries to make a fruit salad. The three sets of utility values are assumed to be independent of one another. That is, the amount of utility you get for any given quantity of apples is not affected by the amount of bananas or cherries you happen to be consuming. This is not necessarily true in real life; apples and bananas might, for example, be close substitutes. The assumption of independence is made here only for the sake of simplicity and clarity.

a. Complete the information on marginal utilities for apples, bananas, and cherries in Table 5-3.

b. Suppose that Betty has $15 per week to spend on these three types of fruit. These are the only goods available, or at least the only goods in which Betty has any interest. Let the price of apples be $1 per unit, the price of bananas be $2 per unit, and the price of cherries be $1 per unit. How much of each fruit should Betty purchase for maximum satisfaction with her $15? Carefully explain your reasoning.

c. Suppose that all prices double and that Betty's budget doubles. That is, the price of apples is $2.00, the price of bananas is $4.00, the price of cherries is $2.00, and Betty has $30 to spend. How does her utility-maximizing decision change? Explain.

_____

_____

_____

_____

3. Two "effects" explain why more of a commodity is bought if its price falls and why less is bought if its price rises. In this question and the one following, we use the idea of marginal utility to examine in detail the nature of these two effects.

a. Specifically, these effects are (1) the (**substitution / institutional**) effect and (2) the (**envy / income**) effect.

Table 5-4 shows the levels of total utility (*TU*) associated with different quantities of commodities X and Y, measured in satisfaction units. (Commodities X and Y are the only ones you can buy, or the only ones in which you are interested.) Calculate the MU of X and Y.

TABLE 5-4

No. of Units Consumed	MU of X	TU of X	MU of Y	TU of Y
3	32	348	20	130
4	——	376	——	148
5	——	400	——	164
6	——	420	——	178
7	——	436	——	190
8	——	448	——	200
9	——	456	——	208
10	——	461	——	213
11	——	464	——	216

b. Suppose that the prices of X and of Y are $2.40 and $1.00, respectively, and that you have just $20 per period to spend. Given the data in Table 5-4, what will your equilibrium or maximum-satisfaction X-Y combination be? In this situation, you will buy ___ units of X and ___ units of Y. The total utility you obtain, from X and Y combined, will be ___.

c. Now let the price of X drop from $2.40 to $1.00. The price of Y is still $1.00, and you still have $20 to spend. What will your new equilibrium position be; you will now buy ___ units of X and ___ units of Y.

In the new situation, the quantity of X has (**increased / decreased**). This is not surprising, since X's price has fallen. The quantity of Y has (**increased / decreased**). Why this should happen is not immediately obvious. Y's price has not fallen; indeed, the price of Y has risen relative to the price of X.

d. What has happened is this: In part **b** you were spending considerably more than half your income on X. The reduction in X's price considered in part **c** had an effect similar to a substantial rise in your income; in fact, your total satisfaction level has climbed from the original total of 600 utils to (**620 / 664 / 670 / 674**) utils. How so? *You have used the practical equivalent of a*

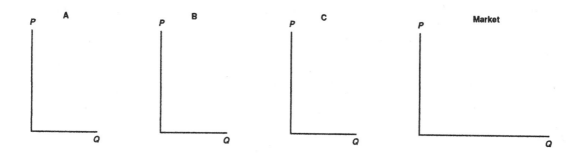

Figure 5-5

larger income to buy more X and more Y.

When X's price falls, there are two effects that operate on your desire to purchase X and Y. Insofar as X and Y are substitutes, you will be disposed to buy (**more / less**) Y and more X. But countering this is the income effect just discussed, which makes you inclined to buy (**more / less**) X and (**more / less**) Y. In this case, the income effect won out over the substitution effect. Had X and Y been "better" substitutes for one another, then the quantity of Y chosen might have fallen instead of rising.

C. From Individual to Market Demand

4. a. Table 5-5 records the quantities of some good X that each of three people demand for a variety of prices. Fill in the column indicated for the market demand schedule if these are the only three people interested in X at any price.

TABLE 5-5

Price	Individual A	Individual B	Individual C	Market Demand
$8	2	0	0	—
7	3	0	1	—
6	4	0	3	—
5	5	0	5	—
4	6	1	7	—
3	7	3	10	—
2	8	5	14	—

b. On the diagrams in Figure 5-5, plot the demand curves for each of the consumers, and plot the market demand curve.

E. Consumer Surplus

c. From your diagrams in Figure 5-5, you can see that if the market price is $4., consumer surplus is $___ for individual A, $___ for individual B. and $___ for individual C.

d. If the market price increases to $5, total consumer surplus in this market changes from $___ to $___.

VIII. DISCUSSION QUESTIONS

Answer the following questions, making sure that you can explain the work you did to arrive at the answers.

1. A consumer has $50 per week to spend on either commodity X, whose price is $5, or commodity Y, whose price is $4. For each of the four cases below, indicate whether or not this consumer is "at equilibrium," i.e., deriving the maximum-attainable satisfaction. If you lack sufficient information to answer, explain why. If you know the consumer is not at equilibrium, indicate the required direction of movement (e.g., "buy more of X and less of Y," "buy less of X and more of Y," "buy more of both," etc.).

   a. Purchases are now 2 of X and 10 of Y. Total utility of X at this level is 500 utils; total utility of Y is 400 utils

   b. Purchases are now 6 of X and 5 of Y. Total utility of X at this level is 400 utils, and the marginal utility of X is 60 utils. Total utility of Y is 800 utils, and the *MU* of Y is 30 utils.

   c. Purchases are now 6 of X and 5 of Y. The *MU* of X at this level is 25 utils; the *MU* of Y is 20 utils

   d. Purchases are now 6 of X and 4 of Y. The *MU* of X at this level is 25 utils; the *MU* of Y is 20 utils.

2. What does it mean when we refer to utility as an "ordinal" measure, rather than a "cardinal" measure? What contribution did Jeremy Bentham make to utilitarianism? Explain.

3. Mr. Economist says, "Consumers always find their optimal bundle of consumer goods when the marginal utility of the last unit of each good is equal." Do you agree?

4. Tables 5-2 and 5-3 in your textbook list estimates of price elasticities of demand and income elasticities for various goods.

   a. Income elasticity for automobiles is listed as 2.5. If incomes rise by 5 percent, what will happen to the quantity of automobiles demanded? Are automobiles an inferior good?

   b. The income elasticity for margarine is -.2. If income falls by 2 percent, what will happen to the quantity of margarine demanded? What type of good is margarine?

c. The price elasticity of demand for medical insurance is .31. If the quantity demanded has fallen by 10 percent, what must have happened to the price? What type of good is medical insurance?

5. As the environment becomes increasingly polluted, communities have to pay increasingly more money for clean air and clean water. Does this mean that the paradox of value is no longer valid?

6. In recent years, California has toyed with the idea of legalizing the purchase and sale of marijuana. Given what you know about consumer demand and addictive substances, would you recommend this policy change? Why or why not?

7. Consumer surplus is defined as the difference between what consumers are willing to pay and what they actually pay for a good or service. Why do firms not capture this surplus? That is, why do firms not charge people the maximum amount they are willing to pay, rather than a market-determined price?

IX. ANSWERS TO STUDY GUIDE QUESTIONS

III. Review of Key Concepts

6   Utility
9   Marginal utility
11 Utilitarianism
8   Law of diminishing marginal utility
13 $MU_1/P_1 = MU_2/P_2 = . . . = MU$ per \$ spent
2   Market demand
1   Income elasticity
7   Substitutes
3   Complements
5   Substitution effect
12 Income effect
14 Demerit goods
4   Paradox of value
10 Consumer surplus

VI. Multiple Choice

1. D 2. A 3. D 4. C 5. B 6. E
7. C 8. C 9. D 10. E 11. C 12 A
13. B 14. B 15. E 16. B 17. B 18. A
19. A 20. C 21. B 22. A 23. C 24. C
25. B 26. B 27. D 28. B

VII. Problem Solving

1. a. 100, 60, 40
    b. 4
    c. 1
    d. See Figure 5-4.
2. a. See Table 5-3.
    b. Betty will maximize her utility by setting the ratios of the marginal utility to the price equal for all goods. This results in her purchasing 5 units of apples, 4 units of bananas, and 2 units of cherries.
    c. If all prices and her budget double, Betty's utility-maximizing decision will not change. The ratios of the marginal utilities to the prices of the products still fall, but the increase in income will allow her to purchase more goods.

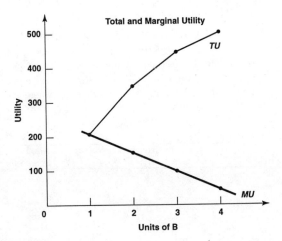

Figure 5-4

TABLE 5-3

Total Units	Apples— Total Utility	Apples— Marginal Utility	Bananas— Total Utility	Bananas— Marginal Utility	Cherries— Total Utility	Cherries— Marginal Utility
1	10	10	100	100	6	6
2	19	9	150	50	12	6
3	27	8	175	25	18	6
4	34	7	187	12	24	6
5	40	6	193	6	30	6
6	45	5	196	3	36	6
7	49	4	197	1	42	6
8	52	3	197	0	48	6

3. a. substitution, income
   b. 5, 8, 600 units
   c. 10, 10, increased, increased
   d. 674, less, more, more
4. a.

TABLE 5-5

Price	Individual A	Individual B	Individual C	Market Demand
$8	2	0	0	2
7	3	0	1	4
6	4	0	3	7
5	5	0	5	10
4	6	1	7	14
3	7	3	10	20
2	8	5	14	27

b. See diagram.

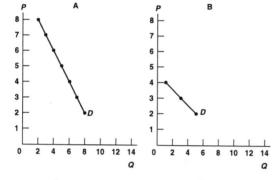

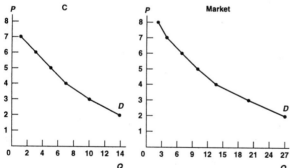

Figure 5-5

c. 14, 0, 9
d. 23, 13

VIII. DISCUSSION QUESTIONS

1. a. Not enough information to tell. Need marginal utility data.
   b. Not at equilibrium. Buy more X and less Y.
   c. At equilibrium. *MU/P* are equal for the two goods.
   d. Not at equilibrium. *MU/P* are equal for the two goods, but there is income left over.
2. Ordinal measures involve rankings; cardinal measures involve absolute numbers based upon some well-defined, universal scale. Jeremy Bentham proposed that society should be organized so as to generate the "greatest good for the greatest number." This led to the development of social policies designed to generate the greatest utility for society .
3. No. The optimal bundle of goods is found where the ratio of the marginal utility of one good to its price is equal to the ratios of the marginal utilities of all other goods to their prices.
4. a. The quantity of automobiles demanded will rise by 12.5 percent. Automobiles are not an inferior good; as income rises, consumption increases.
   b. The quantity of margarine demanded will rise by .4 percent. Margarine is an inferior good.
   c. The price must have increased by 32.26 percent. Medical insurance is a necessity
5. No. The prices of water and air are rising because people's marginal utility of clean air and water is rising.
6. Since many users of marijuana tend to be casual users with highly elastic demands, higher prices induced by government prohibition encourage them to substitute into legal drugs like alcohol and tobacco. Hence, legalizing the purchase and sale of marijuana may lead to a marginally lower price, but a dramatically increased quantity demanded.
7. It is difficult for firms to capture consumer surplus because it is difficult for them to determine how much money a consumer would be willing to pay for a good or service.

APPENDIX TO CHAPTER

Geometrical Analysis of Consumer Equilibrium

I. APPENDIX OVERVIEW

The purpose of this appendix is the same as that of Chapter 5: to explain how consumers can use their fixed incomes to their own best advantage, given their own personal tastes, when faced with market prices. It begins with the same description of the consumer's dilemma—namely, that consumers allocate a scarce budget to maximize utility—and it reaches the same results. In fact, only the method of description is different; the problem of maximizing satisfaction subject to a budget constraint is illustrated on a single graph.

So why bother? To be sure, the graph deals with a very simple case in which only two goods are involved, but the geometry will nonetheless reveal with increased clarity the general nature of making choices among many goods in the face of scarcity. The content of the analysis is not, in other words, confined to the two-good case that can be drawn on a piece of graph paper.

More important, though, the geometric approach frees us from the assumption of cardinal utility, an assumption which many economists dislike. The geometry assumes, instead, that people can display their preferences simply by ranking possible combinations of goods. Constructing the geometry of consumer decision making requires only that consumers are able to express a preference between two or more alternative combinations of any number of goods, i.e., that they are able to say which combination of goods they want. An approach that features consumers' ranking of preferences as the driving force behind demand theory is far easier to swallow than one that relies on consumers' abilities to quantitatively evaluate consumption bundles.

II. LEARNING OBJECTIVES

After you have read the appendix to Chapter 5 in your text and completed the exercises in this *Study Guide* appendix, you should be able to:

1. Define (a) an **indifference curve** and (b) an **indifference map**.
2. Explain why indifference curves will tend to vary from one individual to the next.

3. Show that it would be impossible for an indifference curve representing normal preferences to run in the southwest-to-northeast direction.
4. Describe what is meant by a **budget constraint**.
5. Explain how the **budget constraint** shifts when income changes or when one of the two prices changes.

III. REVIEW OF KEY CONCEPTS

Match the following terms from column A with their definitions in column B.

A	B
__ Indifference curve	1. Shows the combinations of two goods that cost the same amount of money, given a pair of market prices.
__ Law of substitution	2. Implies that the slope of the indifference curve declines as you move toward the southeast.
__ Substitution ratio	3. The scarcer a good, the greater its relative substitution value; its marginal utility rises relative to the marginal utility of the good that has become plentiful.
__ Budget constraint	4. Shows the combinations of two goods that bring equal utility to the consumer.
__ $MU_A/P_A = MU_B/P_B$	5. Defines the number of units of good Y that must be given up when you get another X in order to hold utility fixed in a given region of an indifference curve.
__ Convexity of indifference curves	6. Describes the optimal market basket for the utility-maximizing consumer, given market prices and income.

IV. SUMMARY AND APPENDIX OUTLINE

This section summarizes the key concepts from the appendix.

A. The Indifference Curve

1. An *indifference curve* plots combinations of two goods which generate the same level of satisfaction. The shape and slope of an indifference curve depend on individual preferences and reflect the subjective notion of utility.

2. Indifference curves most often run from northwest to southeast because more of one good must always be associated with less of another if total satisfaction is to remain constant. Put a different way, more of two goods (without any sacrifice) is usually thought to increase utility; linear movement away from the origin must therefore be associated with increased satisfaction.

3. *Indifference maps* are sets of indifference curves, each representing a different level of utility The indifference curves in a map are concentric to one another, due to the fact that each curve must represent just one level of utility.

B. Budget Constraints

1. A *budget constraint* plots combinations of goods that cost the same amount of money. Its slope reflects relative prices, so it rotates as the price of one good changes, and shifts parallel as income changes.

2. Any bundle *on or under* a budget constraint could be purchased by the consumer. Bundles on the curve represent exhaustion of the total budget; bundles below the curve represent expenditure of less than the total budget; bundles above the curve are too expensive for the consumer.

C. Consumer Equilibrium

1. Utility is maximized when the slope of an indifference curve equals the slope of a budget constraint at a point of tangency between the two. This means that the ratio of the marginal utilities of the two goods is equal to the ratio of the prices of the two goods.

2. When *income* changes, the budget constraint will shift parallel, reflecting a new set of consumption options. When the *price* of one of the goods changes, the budget constraint will pivot, reflecting a new set of consumption options. In either case, a new tangency solution will emerge, reflecting a new optimal bundle of goods for the consumer who is facing a different constraint.

V. HELPFUL HINTS

1. Indifference curves are sometimes difficult to understand because utility is such a slippery concept. Focus on the fact that indifference curves simply illustrate *preferences*. They describe how a consumer feels about two goods.

2. Common properties of indifference curves are as follows: Indifference curves for most goods are downward-sloping, reflecting a tradeoff between the two goods with utility held fixed. Indifference curves are convex to the

origin, reflecting the law of diminishing marginal utility. Indifference curves that are further from the origin generate higher levels of utility, since they may contain more of both goods. Indifference curves never cross; if they did, preferences would be ill-defined.

3. The general shape of indifference curves says a lot about consumer preferences. If curves in a map are relatively *steep* (Figure 5A-1), then the consumer is willing to give up relatively large amounts of y to get another x, holding utility fixed. This means that the consumer exhibits a preference for x. On the other hand, if curves in a map are relatively *flat*, then the consumer is willing to give up relatively small amounts of y to get another x, holding utility fixed (Figure 5A-2). This means that the consumer exhibits a preference for y.

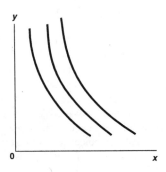

Figure 5A-1

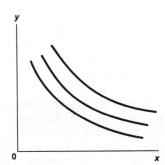

Figure 5A-2

4. Another way to interpret the tangency solution is that it represents the point at which the *subjective* tradeoff between two goods, given by the ratio of the marginal utilities, is equal to the *market-determined* tradeoff, given by the ratio of the prices.

VI. MULTIPLE CHOICE QUESTIONS

These questions are organized by topic from the appendix outline. Choose the best answer from the options available.

A. The Indifference Curve

1. An indifference curve describes:
    a. combinations of two goods that cost the same amount of money.
    b. quantities of a good that are demanded at each alternative price level.
    c. combinations of two goods that bring the same amount of utility to the consumer.
    d. combinations of two goods that an economy can produce, given full employment and efficiency, stable technology and a fixed resource base.
    e. combinations of two goods that are preferred to one another.
2. The position and shape of any indifference curve for a particular consumer are governed by:
    a. his or her tastes and by the amount of income defining the budget constraint.
    b. the prices of the goods purchased only.
    c. tastes, by the amount of income available, and by the prices of the goods purchased.
    d. the prices of the goods purchased and by the amount of income available, but not by tastes.
    e. his or her tastes only.
3. You are told that an indifference curve involving goods X and Y runs from southwest to northeast. Your response to this statement is that this:
    a. must indicate an increase in the consumer's income.
    b. is impossible because it would indicate that the consumer gets no satisfaction from either good X or good Y.
    c. would indicate that the consumer is indifferent to both of the goods.
    d. must indicate a change in the price of either X or Y.
    e. would indicate that the consumer must be given additional units of Y if utility is to remain constant when he or she gets an additional unit of X.

B. Budget Constraints

4. The position and shape of any budget constraint are governed by:
    a. the consumer's tastes and by the amount of income defining the budget constraint.
    b. the prices of the goods purchased only.
    c. tastes, by the amount of income available, and by the prices of the goods purchased.

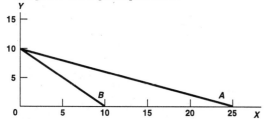

Figure 5A-3

d. the prices of the goods purchased and by the amount of income available, but not by tastes.
e. the consumer's tastes only.

Use Figure 5A-3 to answer questions 5 through 7.

5. If the price of Y is $5 and the price of X is $2, budget constraint A represents a total expenditure of:
    a. $5.
    b. $10.
    c. $15.
    d. $50.
    e. $100.
6. A shift in the budget constraint to curve B could occur because:
    a. the price of X has increased.
    b. the price of Y has decreased.
    c. income has increased.
    d. preferences have changed.
    e. the prices of both X and Y have decreased.
7. The new:
    a. price of X is $25.
    b. price of Y is $25.
    c. income is $35.
    d. price of X is $2.
    e. none of the above.

C. Consumer Equilibrium

8. On an indifference-curve map, a consumer's approach to the equilibrium position is properly described as follows. The consumer:
    a. moves to that point on the budget line representing the combination of goods having the highest money value.
    b. moves to that point on the budget line where the slope of the budget line equals the ratio of the two prices.
    c. moves along the budget line until the extra utility supplied by one good is just equal to the extra utility supplied by the other.
    d. picks the highest-valued indifference curve which is attainable along the given budget line.
    e. picks the highest-valued budget line which intersects the given indifference curve.
9. One of the following five statements describing indifference-curve analysis is incorrect. Which one?
    a. Each point on an indifference curve stands for a different combination of two goods.
    b. Each point on a budget line stands for a different combination of two goods.
    c. All the points on an indifference curve stand for the same level of satisfaction.
    d. All the points on a budget line cost the same amount of money.
    e. All the points on an indifference curve cost the same amount of money.

10. Suppose Al is currently consuming bundle Z in Figure 5A-4. To increase his utility without going beyond his budget constraint, he should:
   a. consume more A and less B.
   b. consume more B and less A.
   c. consume more of both A and B.
   d. decrease his consumption of both goods.
   e. purchase none of either A or B.

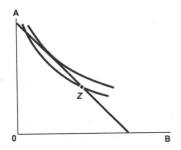

Figure 5A-4

11. If all prices and income double, the utility-maximizing consumer will:
   a. double his consumption of both goods.
   b. not change his consumption bundle.
   c. cut his consumption of both goods in half.
   d. change his preferences.
   e. none of the above.

VII. PROBLEM SOLVING

The following problems are designed to help you apply the concepts that you learned in this appendix.

A. The Indifference Curve

1. a. *Indifference curves* are intended to depict a consumer's tastes. Any single indifference-curve line, such as the ones in Figure 5A-5, is made up of a series of points. Each point on such a line stands for a different (**amount of money / level of satisfaction / combination of two commodities**). What these points—all the points on any one indifference curve—have in common is that they all represent the same (**amount of money / level of satisfaction / combination of two commodities**) in the eyes of the consumer.

   b. We can represent a consumer's *indifference map by* drawing any one or two of (**several / an infinite number of**) indifference lines or curves. Given any two such indifference curves, the one lying farther from the graph's origin must stand for the (**higher / same / lower**) level of satisfaction.

   c. On Figure 5A-5, draw a 45° line from the origin of the graph. The four points at which this line crosses the four indifference curves indicate four different clothing-food combinations. The farther the indifference curve lies from the origin, the larger is the indicated level of consumption of both food and clothing and thus the higher the level of utility (recall that marginal utility is always positive, so supplements in the consumption of any good without some sacrifice of another must improve utility).

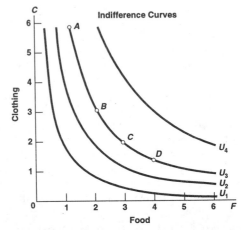

Figure 5A-5

   d. If two different clothing-food combinations lie on the same indifference curve, then the second must represent more food and less clothing (or vice versa) than the first. (You cannot be at the same level of satisfaction as before if you have more food *and* more clothing or if you have less food *and* less clothing.) This is indicated by the fact that any single indifference curve runs in a generally (**northeast-to-southwest / northwest-to-southeast**) directions

2. In Figure 5A-6, draw some sample indifference maps for the following preferences. *(Hint:* The common properties of indifference curves listed above may not hold for these consumers.)*

Figure 5A-6

   a. Larry goes out to buy drinks for the department picnic. He does not care whether he buys Coke or Pepsi; to him, these two goods are perfect substitutes.

   b. Sam always has to consume one green egg with one slice of ham. If he gets an additional egg, he will not eat it until he gets another slice of ham. If he gets an additional slice of ham, he will not eat it until he gets another egg.

c. (advanced concept) Sally sells financial portfolios to wealthy clients. These portfolios have two characteristics: they have some expected profit potential and they have some amount of risk attached to them. Sally's clients desire portfolios that earn high profits, but they like to avoid risk whenever possible. That is, they desire a portfolio that earns high expected profits, and they must be compensated in order to take additional risk.

B. Budget Constraints

3. Turn now to what you *could* buy (regardless of your tastes) if you were provided with a given income and faced with a particular set of prices. In the simple two-good case discussed here, all purchasable combinations can be represented by a straight line on a graph—the *budget line* or *consumption-possibility line* in Figure 5A-7.

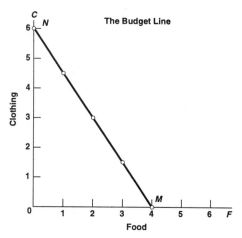

Figure 5A-7

Be sure you understand the information which this budget or consumption-possibility line is intended to convey. Each and every point on this line stands for a different (**amount of money income / level of satisfaction / combination of the two commodities**). The combinations are all different, but they all have one thing in common: given the prices specified, they (**can all be purchased for the same amount of money / all stand for the same level of satisfaction**). You can move up or down this budget line as you wish; all the points located there cost the same amount of money. Which point should you choose? That is a matter of taste. The various food-clothing combinations on the budget line are not equivalent in the sense of generating the same level of satisfaction. You should pick the combination which you like *most*—the combination which *maximizes your satisfaction.*

C. Consumer Equilibrium

4. Consider the indifference map shown in Figure 5A-8. This map represents Donna's preferences for salmon and swordfish.

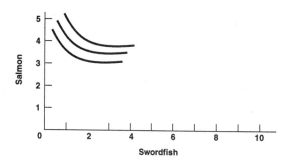

Figure 5A-8

a. Describe Donna's preferences. Which good would you say that she prefers, given the shape of the indifference curves above? _____.

b. Suppose that the price of swordfish is $5 per pound and the price of salmon is $10 per pound. Donna has $50 to spend on swordfish and salmon. Draw her budget constraint in the diagram above.

c. (advanced concept) Write the equation for Donna's budget constraint. _____.

d. What is the optimal combination of salmon and swordfish for Donna to buy with her $50? Mark it as point A in your diagram, and explain why it is better for Donna than any other combination, given her constraint.

5. In the upper part of Figure 5A-9, the line AB_0 is a consumer's initial budget line, and E_0 is his or her equilibrium point thereon. The curved line is an indifference curve for this consumer, and it is tangent to the budget line at this E_0 point. (The two other curved lines are also indifference curves.) The price of good X is $4 along constraint AB_0.

a. The consumer's income or budget must be ____.

b. The price of good Y must be ____.

c. The budget constraint shifts from position AB_0 to position AB_1. Such a shift could be caused only by a(n) _____

d. Quantitatively, what change is indicated by the shift from AB_0 to AB_1? Is it the price of X, the price of Y, or income that has changed? What is the new value? ____

e. If a further shift in the AB line occurs, from AB_1 to AB_2, what explains it? _____.

f. Use the lower part of Figure 5A-9 to show the demand curve of the consumer discussed in the preceding questions for commodity X. This demand curve is to be drawn given the particular level of income and price of good Y indicated by the preceding questions. Plot three points on this curve, correctly indicating the consumer's demand for X in these circumstances. *(Hint:* What price or prices of X must go with the three indifference curves illustrated? What quantity or quantities of X will be bought? Join these three points with a smooth curve.)

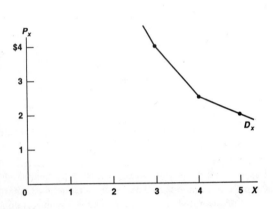

Figure 5A-9

VIII. DISCUSSION QUESTIONS

Answer the following questions, making sure that you can explain the work you did to arrive at the answers.

1. Indifference curves can never cross. Why not?
2. Indifference curves are typically convex to the origin. Why is this? Describe what happens as a consumer moves down and around the indifference curve to the southeast.
3. Consider Figure 5A-10. Suppose a consumer is currently at point *A*. What would you recommend to increase his or her utility? Suppose a consumer is currently at point *B*. What would you recommend to increase his or her utility? Finally, since market basket *C* has more of both goods and is

on a higher indifference curve, why doesn't the consumer choose it?
4. Rich states: "An individual demand curve can be derived from an indifference map and a set of budget constraints. All you have to do is change the level of income and check to see how the optimal market basket changes." Do you agree?

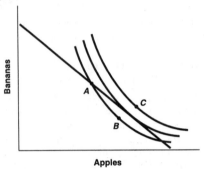

Figure 5A-10

IX. ANSWERS TO STUDY GUIDE QUESTIONS

III. Review of Key Concepts

4	Indifference curve
3	Law of substitution
5	Substitution ratio
1	Budget constraint
6	$MU_A / P_A = MU_B / P_B$
2	Convexity of indifference curves

VI. Multiple Choice Questions

1. C   2. E   3. E   4. D   5. D   6. A
7. E   8. D   9. E   10. A   11. B

VII. Problem Solving

1. a.   combination of two commodities, level of satisfaction
    b.   an infinite number of, higher
    c.   northwest-to-southeast
2. See Figure 5A-6.
3. combination of the two commodities, can all be purchased for the same amount of money

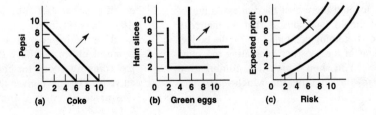

Figure 5A-6

4. a. Her indifference curves are relatively flat, so it looks like she prefers salmon. She is not willing to trade much salmon for swordfish as she moves around the indifference curves, holding utility fixed.
    b. See diagram.

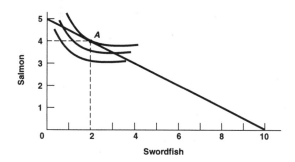

Figure 5A-8

c. Salmon = 5 -.5 (Swordfish)
d. Donna will buy four pounds of salmon and two pounds of swordfish. Even though swordfish is cheaper, Donna likes salmon better and buys more of it.
5. a. $20
    b. $4
    c. decrease in the price of X.
    d. $2.50 = P_x
    e. $2 = P_x
    f. See Figure 5A-9.

VIII. DISCUSSION QUESTIONS

1. Indifferent curves can never cross. If they did, a single point would represent two different levels of utility

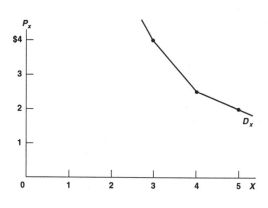

Figure 5A-9

2. Indifference curves are convex to the origin due to the law of substitution. As the consumer trades increasingly more of one good, say apples, for another good, say bananas, the marginal utility of the remaining apples rises. At the same time, since bananas are becoming more plentiful, their marginal utility is falling. Thus, the consumer needs greater and greater numbers of bananas to replace the utility lost when yet another apple is sacrificed.
3. If the consumer is currently at point A, I would recommend consuming more apples and fewer bananas. This will move the consumer to a higher indifference curve with no change in the level of expenditure. At point B, the consumer is not using the entire budget. The consumer cannot afford the bundle represented by point C.
4. Rich is not correct. In order to derive a demand curve, you need an indifference map and a set of budget constraints, each representing a different price for good whose demand curve you want to draw.

CHAPTER 6

Production and Business Organization

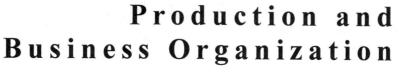

I. CHAPTER OVERVIEW

This chapter begins a discussion of the concepts economists use to investigate the purpose of forming any business: production and subsequent supply of goods and/or services to consumers. Remember the supply curve that you generated back in Chapter 3 of this *Study Guide*. It defined a relationship between the *price* of a product and the *quantity* of that same product that producers are willing and able to produce in a given time period. You will add to this relationship by exploring first the fundamental relationships that describe a production process, and second the most common organizational structures of firms in the U.S. economy. You will be answering two basic questions: What characteristics are common to most production processes? How are firms defined and organized?

II. LEARNING OBJECTIVES

After you have read Chapter 6 in your text and completed the exercises in this *Study Guide* chapter, you should be able to:

1. Define a production function and relate it to the notions of (a) **total product**, (b) **marginal product**, and (c) **average product**.
2. Explain the **law of diminishing marginal returns**. Define constant, increasing and decreasing returns to scale, and relate each to the law of diminishing marginal returns.
3. Compare and contrast the measures of total productivity and the productivity of a particular input. Relate both to technological change and the law of diminishing marginal returns.
4. Distinguish between the **short run** and the **long run** in the context of production.
5. State and explain the stylized facts that describe the growth of the aggregate U.S. economy since the turn of the century. Describe why it can be said that the experience of the United States over the past two decades has not been as profitable as its experience over the century taken as a whole.
6. Explain the differences between the three major

forms of business organization: **proprietorship, partnership**, and **corporation**.
7. Describe three reasons why firms exist in a modern economy.
8. Define the term **unlimited liability** as it applies to business organization, and explain the propensity of large businesses to be incorporated.
9. List the advantages and/or disadvantages of each of the three business forms.

III. REVIEW OF KEY CONCEPTS

Match the following terms from column A with their definitions in column B.

A	B
___ Production function	1. Holds that we will get less and less extra output when we add additional units of an input, all other inputs held fixed.
___ Total product	2. Occurs when a balanced increase in all inputs leads to a less-than-proportional increase in total product.
___ Average product	3. A period of time in which firms can adjust production by changing variable factors but not fixed factors such as capital.
___ Marginal product	4. Tells you how much output you will get from a given amount of inputs.
___ Law of diminishing marginal	5. Occurs when new engineering knowledge improves production techniques for existing products.
___ Constant returns to scale	6. The extra product or output added by 1 extra unit of input while other inputs are held constant.
___ Increasing returns to scale	7. Arise when an increase in all inputs leads to a more-than-proportional increase in the level of output.

___ Decreasing
    returns to scale

___ Short runl

___ Long run

___ Network

___ Adoption
    externality

___ Process
    innovation

___ Product
    innovation

___ Productivity

8. Different people are linked together through a particular medium.

9. Occurs when new or improvedproducts are introduced in the marketplace

10. Designates the total amount of output produced, in physical units.

11. Denotes a case where doubling the use of all inputs leads to a doubling of output.

12. A period sufficiently long so that all factors, including capital, can be adjusted.

13. Measures the ratio of total output to a weighted average of inputs.

14. Measures total output divided by total units of an input.

15. Consumers derive benefits from a number of other consumers who adopt the good.

IV. SUMMARY AND CHAPTER OUTLINE

Chapter 6 is divided into two related parts. Section A describes the theory of production; this will provide a basis for your understanding of production costs, as well as firm output decisions. Section B discusses business organization in the United States, helping to explain how and why firms do business.

A. Theory of Production and Marginal Products

1. A *production function* describes a relationship between total product or output of a firm and the employment of inputs.

2. The *average product* of an input is total output divided by the level of employment of that input. The *marginal product* of an input is the rate at which total output *changes* as employment *changes by* one unit—all other inputs held constant.

3. Marginal product declines in the short run due to the *law of diminishing returns*. This law states that as you continue to add variable inputs to a fixed capital base, eventually marginal product will fall.

4. *Returns to scale is* a long-run concept that reflects the response of total output to *proportionate* changes in *all* inputs. Diminishing marginal productivity (which is a short-run concept) can be consistent with increasing, decreasing, or constant returns to scale.

5. Time period is critical in defining the sort of adjustments available to firms. In the *short run*, the firm has time to manipulate the employment of some inputs (e.g., labor), but the capital stock is usually assumed to be fixed. Use of all inputs, including the capital stocks and embodied technology can be altered only in the *long run*.

6. When technological change occurs, the production function of the firm may shift. *Process innovation* leads to changes in production methods, while *product innovation* leads to the development of new products for the marketplace.

7. *Productivity* measures the amount of output produced per unit of input; productivity growth measures the rate of growth in the level of productivity.

B. Business Organization

1. Business establishments can be organized as individual proprietorships, as partnerships, or as corporations.

2. Businesses exist for three important reasons. First, firms exist to exploit economies of mass production, i.e., to take advantage of specialized equipment, assembly lines, and division of labor. Second, entrepreneurs can raise capital more effectively when businesses are carefully structured. Third, the production process is organized more efficiently when managers direct the activities of all inputs within a firm.

3. Corporations allow owners to limit their potential liability to the amount they have invested, but this structure usually requires owners to release the reigns of control to a management team.

V. HELPFUL HINTS

1. Make sure that you take time to carefully plot a production function, along with its related average and marginal cost curves. Practicing this exercise will help you to understand the relationships between inputs and output that characterize most production functions.

2. Remember that the law of diminishing returns is a *short-run* concept, because you are adding *variable* inputs to a fixed capital base. This differs from decreasing returns to scale, which involves the changes in output associated with increasing the use of *all* inputs, including capital. A change in a capital base always involves a long-run decision.

3. The law of diminishing returns is compatible with increasing, decreasing, and constant returns to scale; this can be difficult to understand. Returns to scale and marginal productivity refer to two distinct things: returns to scale reflect what happens when there is a proportional change in *all* inputs; marginal productivity reflects what happens when there is a one-unit change in only *one* input (all the others are held fixed).

4. When referring to the products that a firm produces, economists use the terms "total product" and "output" synonymously.

VI. MULTIPLE CHOICE QUESTIONS

These questions are organized by topic from the chapter outline. Choose the best answer from the options available.

A. Theory of Production and Marginal Products

1. A production function describes:
   a. how input prices change as the firm changes its output level.
   b. how much output you will get from a given amount of inputs.
   c. the level of output that firms should optimally produce at each price level.
   d. a relationship between prices and quantity demanded.
   e. all the above.
2. The average product of an input is given by the following ratio:
   a. change in total product/total product.
   b. change in the employment of one input/change in the employment of all inputs.
   c. total employment of all inputs/total employment of one input.
   d. total product/total employment of one input.
   e. change in total product/change in the employment of one input.

   The following data describe a short-run production function for ABC, Inc., which hires workers to produce widgets. Use Table 6-1 to complete questions 3 through 7.

TABLE 6-1

Quantity of Labor (Workers)	Total Product (Daily)
0	0
10	50
20	150
30	350
40	500
50	600
60	650
70	650
80	640
90	620

3. The marginal product of the first 10 workers is:
   a. 0.
   b. 5.
   c. 10.
   d. 50.
   e. 500.
4. When ABC, Inc. changes its utilization of labor from 40 to 50 workers, the marginal product is:
   a. 0.
   b. 5.

c. 10.
d. 50.
e. 500.
5. The average product of 50 workers is:
   a. 12.
   b. 50.
   c. 100.
   d. 600.
   e. cannot be determined without more information.
6. Diminishing returns set in sometime between:
   a. 10 and 20 workers.
   b. 20 and 30 workers.
   c. 30 and 40 workers.
   d. 40 and 50 workers.
   e. 70 and 80 workers.
7. From this production function, you can see that over this range of production ABC, Inc., experiences:
   a. increasing returns to scale.
   b. decreasing returns to scale.
   c. constant returns to scale.
   d. diminishing marginal utility.
   e. none of the above can be determined from this data.
8. The law of diminishing returns holds that:
   a. the total product of any input must eventually reach a maximum and fall as the employment of that input increases.
   b. the average product of any input must eventually reach a minimum and rise as the employment of all inputs increases proportionately.
   c. the marginal product of any input should eventually begin to decline as the employment of that input increases.
   d. the marginal product of any input should eventually begin to fall as the employment of all inputs increases proportionately
   e. the average product of any input should rise before it falls as the employment of that input increases.
9. If a production process displays diminishing returns for all inputs, then:
   a. it cannot display constant returns to scale.
   b. it must display decreasing returns to scale.
   c. it cannot display increasing returns to scale.
   d. all the above are true.
   e. none of the above is true.
10. If the marginal product of an input is positive, but decreasing as more and more of the input is employed, then:
   a. total product has reached a maximum and is declining.
   b. total product is increasing but at a slower and slower rate.
   c. average product must be declining.
   d. the firm should produce less output.
   e. the firm must be operating in the long run.

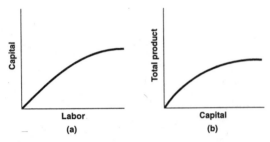
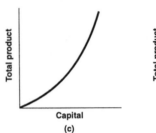

Figure 6-1

11. If the average product of some input is observed to be higher than its marginal product, then the:

a. marginal product must be increasing with the employment of that input.

b. marginal product must be moving toward the average product.

c. average product must be increasing with the employment of that input.

d. average product must be falling with the employment of that input.

e. total product must be falling with the employment of that input.

12. Which of the following adjustments to economic circumstance might a firm be able to accomplish in the long run?

a. Adoption of a new computer-based production technology that replaces 50 percent of the labor working the assembly lines.

b. Increased capacity utilization accomplished by hiring a third shift of workers.

c. Reduction of the work force by 30 percent in the face of stiff foreign competition.

d. Adoption of cost-cutting measures throughout middle management.

e. All the above are possible in the long run.

13. As a matter of historical record, it is widely agreed that:

a. total productivity in the United States has risen, on average, by nearly 0.5 percent per year since the turn of the twentieth century.

b. labor productivity has increased in the United States faster than total productivity over the past nine decades, even though the ratio of capital stock to labor force has remained remarkably constant.

c. the rate of growth of total productivity in the United States over the past 20 years has averaged almost 1 percentage point less than the average over the past 90 years.

d. the rate of return on capital has increased dramatically in the United States since the turn of the twentieth century due in part to technological innovation.

e. none of the above statements is true.

14. A total product curve has been drawn on a piece of graph paper. If a second curve is drawn to reflect technological progress which makes labor more productive, then this second curve will appear everywhere:

a. below the original curve and be flatter.

b. above the original curve and be flatter.

c. below the original curve and be steeper.

d. above the original curve and be steeper.

e. above the original curve *until* diminishing returns set in.

15. Consider the production functions shown in Figure 6-1. Which function displays diminishing marginal returns to capital?

a. (*a*)

b. (*b*)

c. (*c*)

d. (*d*)

e. all these functions display diminishing returns.

16. A newtork occurs when:

a. economies of scale occur in production.

b. different people are linked together through a particular medium.

c. the law of diminishing returns sets in for a production process.

d. firms find an advantage in investing in product innovations.

e. production costs fall as output increases.

17. When I decide to use e-mail to correspond with my business associates, I help to create:

a. economies of scale.

b. diseconomies of scale.

c. diminishing returns.

d. an adoption externality.

e. none of the above.

18. Important features of networks include:

a. they are "tippy".

b. history matters.

c. the winner often takes all.

d. all of the above.

e. none of the above.

B. Business Organization

19. There are important reasons why production in most economies is organized within the firm. These reasons include the ability to:

a. take advantage of mass production.

b. raise revenues.

c. hire management to organize production more efficiently.

d. all of the above.

e. none of the above.

20. The term "limited liability" is frequently used in enumerating the characteristics of a corporation. It means that:

a. any officer of the corporation is strictly limited in his or her ability to speak for the corporation and commit it to any liability.

b. once shareholders have paid for their stock, they have no further financial obligation, regardless of how much trouble the corporation gets into.

c. the corporation's liability to pay dividends to its stockholders is a limited one, since it need pay them only if it has earned a profit.

d. there are certain obligations which a corporation can legally refuse to pay.

e. the corporation has only a limited obligation to meet claims made by any single person or firm against it.

21. Five people own equal shares in a partnership. Unlimited liability holds that each of those five people is responsible for:

a. 20 percent of the partnership's debts, up to the amount he or she has invested in the business.

b. 20 percent of the partnership's debts, no matter how large the amount.

c. 100 percent of the partnership's debts, no matter how large the amount.

d. a percentage of the partnership's debts, determined by the initial ownership share.

e. none of the partnership's debts.

22. Today's most common ownership and control arrangement for large American corporations is best described by which of the following statements?

a. The professional managers are also the group owning a majority or near-majority of stock, so they can make all major decisions without real consideration of the wishes of minority stockholders.

b. The professional managers make all the major decisions, and the board of directors does not usually intervene unless it is losing confidence in those managers.

c. The professional managers control the company on all matters of importance, except they do not make basic decisions on such matters as production, new plants, and new products, these being left to the board of directors as stockholder representatives.

d. The board of directors makes the decisions on all matters of real importance; the role of the professional managers is confined to routine matters.

e. The stockholders rather than the board of directors make major decisions through voting-power control exercised at stockholder meetings.

TABLE 6-3:

	4 Units of Capital Employed				8 Units of Capital Employed		
Labor	TP	MP_L	AP_L	Labor	TP	MP_L	AP_L
0	0		undefined	0	0		undefined
		22				—	
1	22		—	1	22.5		—
		20				—	
2	42		—	2	44		—
3	60	—	—	3	64.5	—	—
4	76	—	—	4	84	—	—
5	90	—	—	5	102.5	—	—
6	102	—	—	6	120	—	—
7	112	—	—	7	136.5	—	—
8	120	—	—	8	152	—	—
9	126	—	—	9	166.5	—	—
10	130	—	—	10	180	—	—

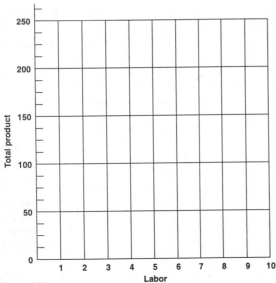

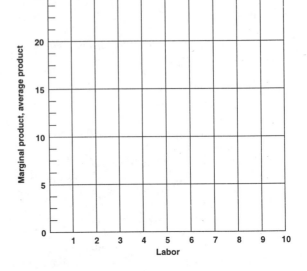

Figure 6-2

VII. PROBLEM SOLVING

The following problems are designed to help you apply the concepts that you learned in this chapter.

A. Theory of Production and Marginal Products

1. Consider a production function that relates the quantity of some good produced (X) with the quantities of capital (K), labor (L), and material (M) employed. Indicate in the blanks provided in Table 6-2 whether each stated formula applies to the total product, the marginal product, or the average product of capital, labor, or material. Use MP_K, for example, to indicate the marginal product of capital; AP_L the average product of labor; etc. If the stated definition applies to none of the possible combinations, write "N/A" (for "not applicable").

TABLE 6-2

Formula	Terms Describing Formulas
Change in K/change in X =	————
Change in X/quantity of L =	————
Quantity of X/quantity of K =	————
Change in X/change in L =	————
Quantity of X =	————
Quantity of K/quantity of M =	————
Change in X/change in K =	————
Quantity of K/quantity of X =	————

2. Table 6-3 provides the data for a production function that relates the employment of capital (K) and labor (L) to maximum output levels of some good Y.
　　a. Fill in the blanks for the marginal and amperage products of labor given capital employment of 4 units and 8 units.
　　b. Graph the total product curves for both levels of capital employment in the left panel of Figure 6-2. (Use different-colored pencils or pens to differentiate the two cases.) Graph the marginal and average product curves for both cases in the right panel of Figure 6-2. (Use the same colors.)

3. Refer again to the data from problem 2. Suppose that 3 units of labor are employed and that the capital stock increases from 4 units to 8 units. How does labor productivity, measured in terms of output per unit of labor, change as the capital stock increases? Carefully explain. Describe the difference between short-run and long-run decision making in the context of this table.

VIII. DISCUSSION QUESTIONS

Answer the following questions, making sure that you can explain the work you did to arrive at the answers.

1. Assume that the law of diminishing returns always holds. Are the following statements true or false (T or F)? Why?
　　____ a. If average product exceeds marginal product, then average product must be rising.
　　____ b. If marginal product is equal to average product,

average product must be maximized.

___ c. When marginal product is maximized, total product is also maximized.

___ d. Diminishing returns set in where total product begins to fall.

2. Indicate whether you would expect the following actions to be taken by a firm in the short run (SR) or in the long run (LR):

___ a. Adopting a new, computerized productiontechnique that involves reworking the assembly line.

___ b. Adopting a new, computerized production technique that improves inventory control.

___ c. Having 50 percent of the employees work overtime, amounting to an extra 10 hours per week per worker.

___ d. Reopening an existing assembly line located closer to a new and developing market.

___ e. Reworking the technology of the assembly technique to reduce material waste by 50 percent.

___ f. Increasing the work force by 10 percent to increase capacity utilization by 5 percent.

___ g. Doubling all inputs to take advantage of increasing returns to scale.

3. Which of the following empirical statements are true (T) and which are false (F) in regard to the experience of the aggregate U.S. economy?

___ a. Total productivity has risen in the United States by an average rate of 1.5 percent per year throughout the twentieth century.

___ b. On average, labor productivity grew faster than the 1.5 percent annual rate of growth of total productivity throughout the twentieth century.

___ c. The return to capital has held remarkably steady in the United States since the beginning of the twentieth century.

___ d. Since 1970, there has been a decline in the rate of growth of the real wages that support the American standard of living.

4. Since all the statements recorded in question 3 are true, there must be an economic justification for each that is consistent with the fundamentals of production. Match each of the following with the empirical statement that it helps explain:

a. The rate of technological progress nearly matched the rate at which diminishing returns affected capital. *a/ b / c / d*

b. Sustained technological progress accounted for sustained growth in overall productivity. *a / b / c/ d*

c. The capital stock of the United States grew faster than the number of hours of labor supplied throughout most of the twentieth century. *a / b / c / d*

d. The rate of growth of total productivity has declined against historical trends. *a / b / c / d*

5. The computer industry has undergone tremendous change over the past 10 years, with IBM tumbling from a near-monopoly position to its current place among a large number of competitors. Discuss the changes that have gone on in this industry as *process* innovations and *product* innovations. How is each of these significant in its own way?

6. In a recent *New York Times* article (2/16/97), economist Paul Krugman argued, "Technology, not global competition, is the principal cause of American income inequality... The onslaught of technology puts a premium on highly skilled people, driving up their wages but not those of the less skilled" Using the concepts from this chapter, explain the relationship between technology and labor productivity. Why might improvements in technology help to create more inequality in the distribution of income?

7. Professors Samuelson and Nordhaus pose the following question in the text: "How should government antitrust policy treat monopolists like Microsoft who have been the fortunate winners in the network race?" Given recent landmark antitrust decisions regarding Microsoft, how have policy makers answered this questions? Using what you know about the economic benefits and costs of networks, critique the government's course of action. Do you think they have done the right thing?

8. Explain three reasons why firms exist. What factors might reduce the importance of these? Explain.

9. Suppose you are organizing a new company, CompuTek. Your firm is going to produce personal computers, competing with the likes of IBM, Compaq, Dell, etc. List the three alternative firm organizational structures and discuss the pros and cons of these structures in this case. Which organizational structure is best for CompuTek? Explain.

IX. ANSWERS TO STUDY GUIDE QUESTIONS

III. Review of Key Concepts

4	Production function
10	Total product
14	Average product
6	Marginal product
1	Law of diminishing marginal returns
11	Constant returns to scale
7	Increasing returns to scale
2	Decreasing returns to scale
3	Short run
12	Long run
8	Network
15	Adoption externality
5	Process innovation
9	Product innovation
13	Productivity

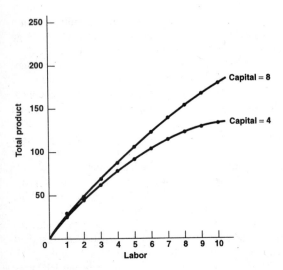

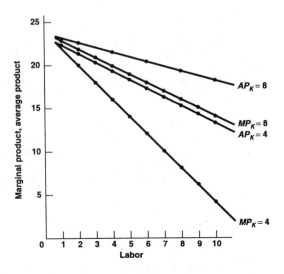

Figure 6-2

VI. Multiple Choice Questions

1. B   2. D   3. D   4. C   5. A   6. C
7. E   8. C   9. E   10. B   11. D   12. E
13. C   14. D   15. B   16. B   17. D   18. D
19. D   20. B   21. C   22. B

VII. Problem Solving

1. N/A, N/A, AP_K, MP_1, TP, N/A, MP_K, N/A
2. a.

TABLE 6-3

4 Units of Capital Employed				8 Units of Capital Employed			
Labor	TP	MPL	APL	Labor	TP	MPL	APL
0	0	-	-	0	0	-	-
1	22	22	22	1	22.5	22.5	22.5
2	42	20	21	2	44.0	21.5	22.0
3	60	18	20	3	64.5	20.5	21.5
4	76	16	19	4	84.0	19.5	21.0
5	90	14	18	5	102.5	18.5	20.5
6	102	12	17	6	120.0	17.5	20.0
7	112	10	16	7	136.5	16.5	19.5
8	120	8	15	8	152.0	15.5	19.0
9	126	6	14	9	166.5	14.5	18.5
10	130	4	13	10	180.0	13.5	18.0

b.   See Figure 6-2.
3.   If the capital stock increases from 4 to 8 units, output per unit of labor, or the average product of labor, increases firm 20 to 21.5. Total product increases from 60 to 64.5 units and the marginal product of the third worker increases from 18 to 20.5. This must be a long-run decision, since there is a change in the capital base.

VIII. Discussion Questions

1.   a.   F.   Average product must be falling when marginal product is less than average product. The average falls only when the marginal is pulling it down.
b.   T.   If the marginal is greater than the average, it pulls the average up. If the marginal is less than the average, it pushes the average down. The only place they can be equal is when the average is neither rising nor falling.
c.   F.   When total product is maximized, marginal product is zero.
d.   F.   Diminishing returns set in where marginal product begins to fall.

2.   a.   LR
b.   SR
c.   SR
d.   LR
e.   LR
f.   SR
g.   LR

3.   a.   T
b.   T
c.   T
d.   T

4.   a.   c
b.   a
c.   b
d.   d

5.   Process innovations include all of the changes made in the methods used to make computers. Significant engineering methods that have improved production techniques

would be included as process innovations. Product innovations include all of the changes made in the computers themselves. New shapes and styles, new components, and new capabilities—all of these have changed the computer market. Both process and product innovations have made the industry more competitive. Process innovations have allowed companies to manufacture computers more easily and cheaply. Product innovations have given consumers much more variety in the marketplace.

6.   In order to make technology useful, workers must have enough education and training to use it in the workplace. Technological innovations have made some workers much more productive because they understand its importance and how to use it. Their marginal product curves slide upward. However, less skilled workers are at an even greater disadvantage; even though their marginal product curves may be unchanged by technological advance, in relative terms they are worse off. They become even more firmly entrenched in the low end of the labor market, falling even further behind those who are better educated.

7.   Recent decisions indicate that policy makers have decided that the benefits derived from having a common operating system in the computer industry are outweighed by the fact that Microsoft is a near monopoly. The government has decided that competition in the marketplace is better for consumers in this case.

8.   Firms exist in order to take advantage of economies of mass production, to raise resources, and to provide management of production tasks. As people have quicker and broader access to information, tasks that have historically been performed in firms might be provided by individual entrepreneurs.

9.   Your computer company could be organized as an individual proprietorship, as a partnership, or as a corporation. Sole proprietorships are usually small, have limited access to resources, and require a tremendous amount of personal effort. A partnership combines the talents of several individuals but requires the partners to accept the risk inherent in unlimited liability . Corporations have access to lots of capital and spread risk across large numbers of people; however, they are subject to double taxation, which limits profitability.

CHAPTER 7

Analysis of Cost

I. CHAPTER OVERVIEW

This chapter continues the discussion of firm production and short-run supply decisions by exploring the nature of costs. A firm's production costs are determined by its level of output and are represented along a total cost schedule. Given the law of diminishing returns, these costs also depend critically upon the particular combination of inputs used in the production process. As you can imagine there are many ways to build any product, and it is the firm's job to choose the most efficient method from among the options available! The major objective here is for you to obtain a solid understanding of an economist's perspective of cost accounting so that subsequent descriptions of market structure will make sense.

The chapter is divided into three sections. First, the short-run cost function is described and then integrated into the short-run production theory developed in Chapter 6. Second, the nature of business accounting is outlined. Third, the notion of opportunity cost is explained to differentiate the accountant's definition of costs from that used by economists.

II. LEARNING OBJECTIVES

After you have read Chapter 7 in your text and completed the exercises in this *Study Guide* chapter, you should be able to:

1. Define and describe **total cost, fixed cost, variable cost, marginal cost**, and **average cost**, understanding what these measures of cost are designed to reflect and how they are related to one another.
2. Derive the associated average and marginal cost statistics from total, fixed, and variable cost.
3. Explain the link between productivity and cost.
4. Demonstrate precisely why marginal cost *always* intersects average cost at the minimum of any U-shaped average cost curve.
5. Demonstrate why production costs are minimized when inputs are hired in combinations such that the ratios of their marginal products to their prices are all equal.

6. Explain carefully the information that a **balance sheet** is intended to convey. List the major categories appearing on the two sides of a balance sheet and indicate the meaning (or definition) of each of those categories.
7. List the major items appearing on an **income statement**. Indicate the information that an income statement is intended to convey.
8. Explain the role of depreciation in the correct and accurate construction of an income statement.
9. Define the term **opportunity cost** and apply it to management decisions made by firms and individuals.

III. REVIEW OF KEY CONCEPTS

Match the following terms from column A with their definitions in column B.

A	B
__ Total cost function	1. The ratio of the marginal product of an input to its price is equal for all inputs.
__ Average cost	2. The extra cost required to produce 1 extra unit of output.
__ Marginal cost	3. A variable that represents change per unit of time.
__ Least-cost rule	4. Total cost divided by the number of units produced.
__ Income statement	5. Shows the minimum attainable costs of production, given a particular level of technology and set of input prices.
__ Balance sheet	6. Represents the level of a variable.
__ Assets	7. A statement showing revenues, costs, and profits incurred over a given time period.
__ Liabilities	8. A statement of a firm's financial position as of a given date, showing assets equal to the sum of liabilities and net worth.
__ Net worth	9. The value of the next best use for an economic good.

__ Opportunity cost	10. A physical property or intangible right that has economic value.
__ Stock	11. Debts or financial obligations owed to other firms or persons.
__ Flow	12. Total assets minus total liabilities.

IV. SUMMARY AND CHAPTER OUTLINE

This section summarizes the key concepts from the chapter.

A. Economic Analysis of Costs

1. *Total costs* include all costs incurred when a firm produces and sells a product; this chapter concentrates on short-run cost functions so there are two possible categories of costs. *Variable costs* are those costs whose total amount varies with the quantity of inputs used and output produced. *Fixed costs* are those costs that must be paid by the firm even if its output is zero. Note that in the long run, all costs are variable, since all inputs are variable.

2. *Marginal costs* measure the increase in total cost resulting from a l-unit increase in output. Like marginal product (from Chapter 6), marginal costs focus on the effect of incremental changes.

3. *Average costs* measure the per unit costs of production at any given level of output. You can find average variable cost, average fixed cost, or average total cost; all these concepts share the common characteristic of being per unit measures.

4. The law of diminishing returns, which you learned in Chapter 6, also speaks to the nature of a firm's costs. As the firm increases production, additional variable inputs are added to a fixed capital base; as marginal product begins to fall, marginal costs will begin to rise. Cost curves are U-shaped when short-run returns increase in the early range of production but eventually start to rise as output increases and more of the variable inputs are employed.

5. Profit-maximizing firms will attempt to choose the combination of inputs that allows them to produce with minimum costs. This combination will be such that the marginal productivity *of the last dollar spent* on each input is equal for all inputs used in the production process.

B. Economic Costs and Business Accounting

1. The *balance sheet* is a stock concept, or a snapshot of a firm's financial health—it reflects the economic condition of an economic enterprise at some prescribed point in time. The balance sheet begins by listing the firm's assets; that is, everything it owns, including cash, buildings, equipment, inventory, and so on.

2. The *income statement* is a flow concept, or a motion picture—it reflects growth or problems over a given period of time. Its primary function is to record how much profit (or loss) the company earned from its sales during some particular period.

3. *Depreciation* is a way of measuring the annual cost of a capital input that the company owns. Although the firm does not have to write a check to itself when its own capital equipment is used, it must recognize that equipment wears out as it is used in the production process. Capital equipment will eventually have to be replaced, and prudent managers do indeed make allowances for this in their budgets.

4. The firm's "worth" is not likely to be the same figure as the total monetary value of its assets. Any debts owed to others—the firm's liabilities—must be deducted to get an accurate portrait of financial health. The resulting figure is *net worth,* the difference between the total value of assets and the total value of liabilities.

C. Opportunity Costs

1. *Opportunity costs* measure the value of a resource at its next-best alternative use. As long as a resource is at least as useful as it would be in its next-best alternative use, economists can be sure that no reallocation would improve the overall efficiency of the firm (or even the economy).

2. If markets are functioning properly the price of the last unit of output sold is just equal to its opportunity cost. This means that the amount that a buyer is willing and able to pay is exactly equal to the value of the item at its next-best alternative use; there is no more productive use for the resources used to make that marginal unit of output.

V. HELPFUL HINTS

1. Marginal product and marginal costs both measure the effect of incremental changes. However, they differ in an important way. Marginal product measures the addition to total product, or output, when an additional *unit of an input is hired.* By contrast, marginal cost measures the addition to total cost when an additional *unit of output is produced.* Remember, "margin" means change.

2. Note that marginal cost, even though it is a per unit cost measure, is not the same thing at all as average cost. To illustrate the difference, consider some baseball or softball statistics. A batter has a batting average that indicates the number of hits he or she has gotten out of his or her total number of trips to the plate. Any average is calculated by dividing some *total* by the appropriate *number* of something else. (For example, a batting average is found by dividing *total* at-bats by the *number* of hits. A class average on a test is calculated by dividing the *total of* all the test scores by the *number* of students who took the test.) The marginal productivity of that batter would indicate how successful that batter was *at the very last trip he or she made to the plate.* Remember, "margin" means change.

3. The law of diminishing returns tells us that as we add additional units of a variable input to a fixed capital base, eventually marginal product will fall. This generates a downward-sloping marginal product curve and also generates an upward-sloping marginal cost curve. Think of it this way: As a firm attempts to increase production in the short run, it becomes increasingly *more difficult* to extend production; hence, it becomes increasingly *more expensive* to extend production.

4. Throughout this discussion, we are assuming that the firm is attempting to minimize production costs. This is consistent with profit maximization but does not necessarily imply that the firm is maximizing profits. There are things to be considered on the revenue side of the ledger before we can make any claims about profits; notice that a firm could be producing with minimum costs, but if it gives its product away for free, it will not earn any profits!

VI. MULTIPLE CHOICE QUESTIONS

These questions are organized by topic from the chapter outline. Choose the best answer from the options available.

A. Economic Analysis of Costs

1. If *AVC* rises with output, each increment in cost would have to be ___ the previous average to push the average higher.
   a. greater than
   b. equal to
   c. less than
   d. twice as large as
   e. one-half as large as

2. Fixed costs facing any firm in the short run include:
   a. any cost whose total is established at the time the input is purchased.
   b. the minimum cost of producing any given quantity of output under the most favorable operating conditions.
   c. any cost whose per unit charge has been settled for some future period, such as a long-term wage contract with a labor union.
   d. total expenses which must be covered even if nothing is produced.
   e. none of these things.

3. Marginal costs facing any firm considering a change in output represent:
   a. extraordinary overtime charges that must sometimes be paid to increase output.
   b. the cost incurred even if the firm produces zero output.
   c. the difference between the total cost actually incurred to produce any given output and the smallest possible total cost of producing that output.
   d. the increase in total cost that accrues from a 1-unit increase in quantity produced.

   e. the increase in total cost that accrues from any increase in quantity produced, whether 1 unit or more.

4. Suppose that the property taxes paid by a firm on its plant are increased; i.e., suppose that its fixed costs increase. As a result, the marginal cost curve for this firm would move:
   a. to the right.
   b. to the left.
   c. upward.
   d. downward.
   e. not at all.

5. Total cost in a certain plant, at an output level of 1000 units daily, is $4900. If production is reduced by 1 unit, total cost would be $4890. Within this output range:
   a. average cost is greater than marginal cost.
   b. average cost and marginal cost are approximately equal.
   c. marginal cost is greater than average cost.
   d. we cannot compare average and marginal cost, since we cannot derive marginal cost from the given information.
   e. we cannot compare average and marginal cost, since we cannot derive average cost from the given information.

Use Figure 7-1 to answer questions 6 through 8.

Figure 7-1

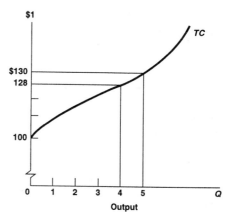

6. At five units of output, the *average fixed cost is*:
   a. $5.
   b. $20.
   c. $26.
   d. $100.
   e. $130.

7. The *marginal cost* of the fifth unit of output is:
   a. 0.
   b. $2.00.
   c. $2.60.
   d. $6.00.
   e. $30.00.

8. The *average variable cost* of five units of output is:
   a. 0.
   b. $2.00.
   c. $2.60.
   d. $6.00.
   e. $30.00.
9. Let average costs be minimized at output X_0. Which of the following statements is also true at X_0?
   a. Average variable cost will be equal to total fixed cost.
   b. Profit for the firm must be at its maximum level.
   c. Marginal cost will be equal to average variable cost.
   d. Marginal cost will be equal to average cost.
   e. None of the above is necessarily true at X_0.
10. If marginal cost exceeds average cost within a certain range of plant output, then any increase in output within that range should cause average cost to:
    a. rise.
    b. fall.
    c. rise or fall, depending upon the change in variable cost.
    d. remain constant.
    e. rise, fall, or remain constant, depending upon market conditions.
11. In a certain plant, marginal cost is $2.00 at 400 units of output weekly and it is $2.50 at 500 units of output. If output increases within this 400-to-500 range, then average cost:
    a. must rise.
    b. must fall.
    c. must remain constant.
    d. may fall, may rise, or both, but cannot remain constant throughout this output range.
    e. must fall and then rise.
12. If a firm has employed all its inputs so that the ratios of marginal product to price are the same for all inputs, then:
    a. the marginal product of each input is equal to its price.
    b. the firm is producing the maximum-profit output at minimum cost.
    c. the firm is producing the maximum-profit output, but it may or may not be producing that output at minimum cost.
    d. the firm may or may not be producing the maximum-profit output, but it is producing its present output at minimum cost.
    e. the firm may or malt not be producing the maximum-profit output, and it may not even be producing its present output at minimum cost.
13. The production function alone will tell a firm:
    a. what it will cost to produce any given quantity of output.

    b. the maximum-profit level of output.
    c. the various combinations of inputs that should be used in order to produce any given quantity of output most efficiently, i.e., at the least money cost.
    d. the various combinations of inputs that could be used in order to produce any given quantity of output.
    e. none of these.
14. A, B, and C are inputs employed to produce good X. If the quantity of A used were increased, then we would ordinarily expect A's marginal product to:
    a. increase, in all circumstances.
    b. increase if the quantities of B and C were left unchanged, but not necessarily to increase if the quantities of B and C were increased in the same proportion.
    c. decrease in all circumstances.
    d. decrease if the quantities of B and C were left unchanged, but not necessarily decrease if the quantities of B and C were increased in the same proportion.
    e. decrease if the quantities of B and C were increased in the same proportion, but increase if the quantities of B and C were left unchanged.
15. A firm employs inputs A and B so that the marginal product of A is 60 and the marginal product of B is 40. The prices of A and B are $4 and $9, respectively. Assuming that A and B are the only inputs involved, this firm is:
    a. producing its present output at minimum cost but definitely is not earning maximum possible profit.
    b. not producing its present output at minimum cost and is not earning maximum possible profit.
    c. producing its present output at minimum cost but may or may not be earning maximum possible profit.
    d. not producing its present output at minimum cost but nevertheless is earning maximum possible profit.
    e. possibly in any of the positions just described—the information furnished is insufficient to tell.
16. In question 15, change the price of input A from $4 to $3. If all the other information still applies, which alternative in question 15 is now correct?
    a.
    b.
    c.
    d.
    e.

B. Economic Costs and Business Accounting

17. A particular income statement records no depreciation expense for a piece of machinery, even though that machinery was used for production during the year. This accounting procedure could be justified:
    a. if the company did not find it necessary to spend money on the maintenance or repair of the machine during the year.

b. if depreciation entries totaling the original cost of the machine had already been made on earlier income statements.

c. if sales for the year were below normal, so the company decided not to charge any depreciation cost for the year.

d. if the company responded to an increase in market prices by estimating that the money worth of the machinery was unchanged even though it underwent some physical depreciation through use during the year.

e. by recognizing that depreciation entries are properly made on the balance sheet, not the income statement.

18. A balance sheet must always "balance" because:

a. total assets must equal total liabilities when both are properly specified.

b. net profit is defined as total revenue minus total expenses.

c. the definition of net worth is total assets minus total liabilities.

d. current assets plus fixed assets must equal current liabilities plus long-term liabilities.

e. the definition of net worth is capital stock plus retained earnings.

19. A company's total assets at the end of 1999 were $100,000, and its total liabilities were $70,000. At the end of 2000, its total assets were $115,000, and its liabilities totaled $75,000. It paid dividends totaling $15,000 in 2000. Assuming no change in its capital stock, its net profit after taxes for 2000 must have been:

a. $10,000.
b. $15,000.
c. $20,000.
d. $25,000.
e. $30,000.

20. A company's 2000 income statement shows a net profit earned (after taxes) of $200,000. This means that on its end-of-2000 balance sheet, as compared with its end-of-1999 balance sheet:

a. the total of assets should be up by $200,000, and so should the total of liabilities plus net worth.

b. retained earnings should be up by $200,000 minus the total of dividends paid.

c. current assets minus current liabilities should be up by $200,000.

d. cash on hand minus expenditures for new fixed assets should be up by $200,000.

e. net worth should be up by $200,000 minus the total of any bond interest paid.

21. A company's total assets were $600,000, and its total liabilities were $400,000 at the end of 2000. At the end of 2001, its total assets were $550,000, and its total liabilities were $200,000. During 2001, it (a) paid a dividend of $50,000 and (b) sold additional shares of its own stock for $100,000. With these figures, its net

profit after taxes for 2001 must have been:

a. zero.
b. $50,000.
c. $100,000.
d. $150,000.
e. $200,000.

C. Opportunity Costs

22. Opportunity costs are defined as:

a. the value of a resource at all its alternative uses.

b. fixed costs of production that must be paid even if output is zero.

c. the addition to total cost when the firm increases output by one unit.

d. the value of a resource at its next-best alternative use.

e. none of the above.

23. The opportunity cost of a new parking lot at your college is:

a. the cost of all the expenses that must be incurred to produce it.

b. determined by the value of the resources at their next-best alternative use.

c. the amount of depreciation on machinery and equipment that must be allowed for the production of the lot.

d. salary expenses for the laborers who produce it.

e. determined by the fees charged people who park in the new lot.

VII. PROBLEM SOLVING

The following problems are designed to help you apply the concepts that you learned in this chapter.

A. Economic Analysis of Costs

1. In the blanks below, put **V** if you think the item would contribute to *variable cost* and **F** if you think it would be part of *fixed cost* in the short run.

___ a. The cost of purchasing raw materials.

___ b. Depreciation on machinery when the rate of production is considered to be the primary source of depreciation.

___ c. The annual fire-insurance premium on plant buildings.

___ d. A tax levied on the firm for each hour of labor employed.

___ e. Depreciation on machinery when time rather than quantity of output produced is considered to be the factor principally responsible for the depreciation

___ f. Salaries paid to supervisors on an annual basis.

___ g. Local property taxes on buildings.

___ h.   The cost of purchasing electric power to run the machines.

___ i.   The cost of maintaining an active research-and-development department.

___ j.   A royalty paid for the use of certain machines according to number of units produced.

___ k.   Extra pay for overtime work by labor.

2.   The numbers in Table 7-1 indicate the estimated total cost incurred in producing quantities of output from 0 to 20 units weekly. This firm produces widgets using labor and a fixed capital base.

TABLE 7-1

Output	Total Cost	Total Variable Cost	AVC	ATC	AFC	MC
0	50	—	X	X	X	X
2	70	—	—	—	—	—
4	85	—	—	—	—	—
6	95	—	—	—	—	—
8	100	—	—	—	—	—
10	110	—	—	—	—	—
12	125	—	—	—	—	—
14	145	—	—	—	—	—
16	170	—	—	—	—	—
18	200	—	—	—	—	—
20	235	—	—	—	—	—

a.   Fill in the missing figures for total variable cost, *AVC* (average variable cost), *ATC* (average total cost), and *AFC* (average fixed cost).

b.   Fill in the missing figures for *MC* (marginal cost) . *Hint:* Remember that marginal cost is change in total cost divided by *change in quantity.*

c.   Plot the total cost, total variable cost, and fixed cost curves in Figure 7-2. Make sure to label your diagram carefully.

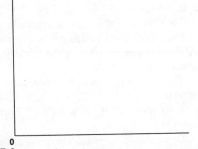

0

Figure 7-2

d.   Plot the *AVC, ATC, AFC,* and *MC* curves in Figure 7-3. Again, make sure to label your diagram carefully.

3.   Suppose the firm described in Chapter 7 of your text is a farm that produces fresh tomatoes in greenhouses. It can use varying quantities of energy and labor in the short run. Increasing the amount of energy used to run the greenhouse will improve the yield of the tomato plants; increasing the number of laborers employed to weed and care for the plants will also increase the yield. The firm finds that the daily marginal productivity of these inputs is as shown in Table 7-2.

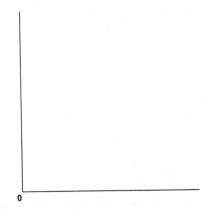

0

Figure 7-3

TABLE 7-2

Units of Labor Employed	Marginal Product	Units of Energy Employed	Marginal Product
1	10	1	20
2	12	2	25
3	14	3	22
4	13	4	17
5	11	5	10
6	8	6	1
7	3	7	-10

a.   At what level of employment does diminishing returns set in for labor? for energy? Explain.

_____

_____

_____

b.   If workers are paid $4 per unit, and energy costs $11 per unit, and the firm has $57 to spend on inputs, what is the optimal mix of labor and energy for this firm to employ? Explain.

_____

_____

_____

c.   Suppose an oil embargo causes the price of energy to rise. What will happen to the optimal mix of labor and energy? Explain in general terms.

_____

_____

_____

B. Economic Costs and Business Accounting

4. In December 1999, the Utter Confusion Manufacturing Company was formed, with the sale for cash of 5000 shares of common stock at $10 apiece.

a. In Table 7-3, show this firm's balance sheet as of December 31, 1999. Assume that the proceeds from the entire $50,000 stock sale were still held in cash and that no other transactions had yet taken place.

TABLE 7-3

Assets	Liabilities and Net Worth
Cash .... $___	Liabilities .... $___
	Net worth:
	Capital .... $___

Now suppose that the firm's operations during 2000 can be described as follows:

1. Money received (all in cash):
   a. Sales of merchandise manufactured, $115,000
   b. Bonds sold (100 bonds @ $1000), $100,000
2. Money paid out (all in cash):
   a. Machinery purchased, $170,000
   b. Raw materials purchased for use, $50,000
   c. Wages paid to labor, $24,000
   d. Interest paid on bond issue, $10,000

All raw materials purchased were fully used up in manufacturing before the end of the year (i.e., the closing inventory of raw materials was zero). All goods manufactured during 2000 were sold during 2000 (i.e., zero finished goods remained in the closing inventory). Depreciation on machinery was estimated at 10 percent, or $17,000. (The machinery was worth $170,000 when it was purchased on January 1. It was estimated as being worth only $153,000 on December 31. It was partly "used up" or worn out by use during the year, but that does not mean a cash outlay of $17,000.) The interest rate paid on the bonds is 10 percent. Note that item 2.D. above shows interest paid as $10,000, so it must be true that the bonds were floated (i.e., that the $100,000 was borrowed) on January 1, 2000.

b. How much cash did Utter Confusion have on December 31, 2000? (*Hint:* Start with the $50,000 raised from the sale of stock. Add the money received from sales of merchandise and bonds, listed above; then deduct the various cash outlays also listed.)

c. Draw up the firm's balance sheet for December 31, 2000, in Table 7-4. There are three steps involved:

(1) Run through the information above for assets held at the end of the year; they will have to be listed at their proper value on that date. (*Hint:* You have already dealt with cash; you should find only one other asset.)

(2) Do the same for liabilities. (*Hint:* You should find only one.)

(3) Repeat the process one more time for net worth. Remember that net worth must be whatever figure is needed to bring the balance sheet into balance. Follow the convention of dividing net worth between capital and retained earnings. Leave financial capital at $50,000 (because no more stock was sold during the year). Let retained earnings be the line within net worth that is manipulated to perform the balancing act.

TABLE 7-4

Assets (thousands)			Liabilities and Net Worth (thousands)		
Current: Cash ...... $___			Current liabilities: .... $___		
Fixed:			Long-term liabilities:		
Machinery	$___		Bonds .... $___		
Less: dep'n. allowance			Net worth:		
	$___	$___	Capital	$___	
		$___	Retained earnings	$___	$___
					$___

5. In this question you will use Table 7-5 to develop the firm's income statement for 2000 using the information already furnished in question 4.

Hint: Remember that this income statement should (a) record revenue earned from sales in 2000, (b) deduct the costs of making and selling the goods in question from this revenue, and (c) show the income (or profit) remaining after that deduction. It should also indicate the disposition of that profit (paid out as a dividend, or retained within the business). The sales figure is obviously $115,000. Raw materials purchases and wages are clearly expense items to be subtracted from sales revenue.

TABLE 7-5

Sales		$___
Less manufacturing cost of goods sold:		
Raw materials bought	$___	
Labor cost (wages)	$___	
Dep'n. on machinery	$___	$___
Gross profit		$___
Deduct bond interest		$___
Net profit and addition to retained earnings		$___

C. Opportunity Costs

6. Farmer Jones is trying to decide how to use 10 acres of land in her side yard, and she needs help from you. She could either rent it out to the local college to use for extra parking (the college is willing to pay $500 per year for this), or she could plant vegetables on the property. She estimates that direct costs for plants, water, labor, and fertilizer will total $375; revenues from the sale of the vegetables will total $825. What would you recommend? What are her

opportunity costs in this case? How much profit will she earn? Explain.

_____

_____

_____

VIII. DISCUSSION QUESTIONS

Answer the following questions, making sure that you can explain the work you did to arrive at the answers.

1. Suppose that in a given class of students, the average examination grade is always 70. Now we add a few new students (some extra, or "marginal," students) to this class. They are weaker students; they always score between 50 and 55 on examinations. What will happen to the class average? What can you say about the relationship between the marginal and the average grades in this class?

2. Are the following statements true (T) or false (F)?
   a. Average costs are minimized when marginal costs are at their lowest point. T / F
   b. Because fixed costs never change, average fixed cost is a constant for each level of output. T / F
   c. Average cost is rising whenever marginal cost is rising. T / F
   d. A firm minimizes costs when it spends the same amount of money on each input. T / F

3. Explain the difference between a balance sheet and an income statement. Why do accountants need both of these documents to fully understand a firm's financial position?

4. Return to the balance sheet for Hot Dog Ventures, Table 7-6 in your textbook. Suppose that the firm decides to borrow $45,000 to purchase a new computerized cash register. How would you adjust the balance sheet to account for this? Explain.

5. Is the following statement true or false: "The opportunity cost of spilling oil in the Atlantic Ocean is zero because no one pays to sail or swim there." Please explain.

6. The federal government owns thousands of acres of land in the western United States. It is trying to determine the appropriate price to charge for use of this land. (Cattle ranchers, mining companies, and others often rent this space from the government.) How would such a rent be determined? What sorts of costs would have to be considered by the government? Explain.

IX. ANSWERS TO STUDY GUIDE QUESTIONS

III. Review of Key Concepts

5	Total cost
4	Average cost
2	Marginal cost

1	Least-cost rule
7	Income statement
8	Balance sheet
10	Assets
11	Liabilities
12	Net worth
9	Opportunity cost
6	Stock
3	Flow

VI. Multiple Choice Questions

1. A 2. D 3. D 4. E 5. C 6. B
7. B 8. D 9. D 10. A .22. D 12. D
13. D 14. D 15. B 16. C 17. B 18. C
19. D 20. B 21. C 22. D 23. B

VII. Problem Solving

1. a. V
   b. V
   c. F
   d. V
   e. F
   f. F
   g. F
   h. V
   i. F
   j. V
   k. V

2. a. See table.

TABLE 7-1

Output	Total Cost	Total Variable Cost	AVC	ATC	AFC	MC
0	50	0	X	X	X	X
2	70	20	10.00	35.00	25.00	20.00
4	85	35	8.75	21.25	12.50	17.50
6	95	45	7.50	15.83	8.33	5.00
8	100	50	6.24	12.50	6.25	2.50
10	110	60	6.00	11.00	5.00	5.00
12	125	75	6.25	10.42	4.17	7.50
14	145	95	6.79	10.36	3.57	10.00
16	170	120	7.50	10.63	3.12	12.50
18	200	150	8.33	11.11	2.78	15.00
20	235	185	9 25	11.75	2.50	17.50

   b. See table.
   c. See Figure 7-2.
   d. See Figure 7-3.

3. a. For labor, diminishing returns set in after three units. For energy, diminishing returns set in after two units.
   b. The firm will use six units of labor and three units of energy. At this point, the ratios of the marginal product of each input to its price are equal.

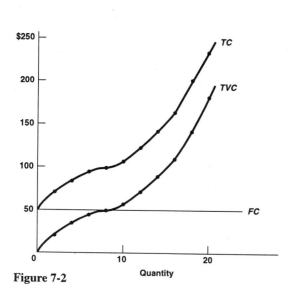

Figure 7-2

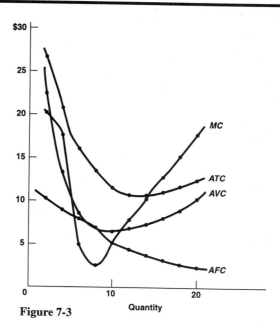

Figure 7-3

c.   If the price of energy rises, the firm will tend to find an optimal bundle of inputs containing more labor and less energy.

4.   a.   See Table 7-3.

TABLE 7-3

Assets		Liabilities and Net Worth	
Cash	$50,000	Liabilities	$0
		Net worth:	
		Capital	$50,000

b. $11,000
c.   See Table 7-4.

5.   See Table 7-5.

TABLE 7-5

Sales		$115,000
Less manufacturing cost of goods sold:		
Raw materials bought	$ 50,000	
Labor cost (wages)	$ 24,000	
Dep'n. on machinery	$17,000	$ 91,000
Gross profit		$ 24,000
Deduct bond interest		$ 10,000
Net profit and addition to retained earnings		$ 14,000

TABLE 7-4

Assets		Liabilities and Net Worth		
Current: Cash	$11,000	Current liabilities:		$ 0
		Long-term liabilities:		
		Bonds		$100,000
Fixed:		Net worth:		
Machinery	$170,000	Capital	$50,000	
Less: dep'n.		Retained		
allowance:	$17,000 .... $153,000	earnings	$14,000	$ 64,000
Total Assets	$164,000	Total Liabilities		$164,000

6.   Farmer Jones should rent the land. The opportunity cost of farming it herself is the $500 she could earn if the resource is used at its next-best alternative. Since she would only earn $450 from her own farming, she should rent the property

VIII. Discussion Questions

1.   The average will fall. Since the marginal scores are below the average, they will pull the average down.

2.   a.   False. Average costs are minimized when average costs equal marginal costs.

b.   False. Average fixed costs are total fixed costs divided by quantity of output. Therefore, average fixed costs fall as output increases.

c.   False. As long as marginal costs are below average costs, they are pulling the average cost down.

d.   False. A firm minimizes costs when it sets the ratios of marginal product to input price equal for all inputs.

3.   A balance sheet summarizes a company's financial position at a particular point in time. An income statement

summarizes a flow of financial activity over a period of time. Thus each statement provides a different type of information to an accountant or financial managers.

4. Fixed assets would increase by $45,000, with the cash register listed as an additional piece of equipment. Current liabilities would also increase by $45,000, with the loan appearing as an additional accounts payable.

5. This statement is false. The opportunity cost is defined by what the resources would have provided if they were used in their next-best alternative. The opportunity cost of using the water as a dumping ground might be enjoyment that people would have gotten from the recreational opportunities that would have been available in clean water.

6. An appropriate rent could be determined by considering the opportunity cost of using the land at its next-best alternative. The government would have to consider what it is giving up when it rents the land to private individuals. For example, the government might use the land as a national park.

APPENDIX TO CHAPTER

Production, Cost Theory, and Decisions of the Firm

I. APPENDIX OVERVIEW

This appendix extends one of the topics from Chapter 7: How does the firm choose the least-cost input combination to use in the production process? In the chapter, you learned that the least-cost combination of inputs will be characterized by the *least-cost rule,* which means that the ratio of an input's marginal product to its price will be equal for all inputs used in the production process. That is, the productivity of the last dollar spent on each input will be equal for all inputs.

If we limit the number of inputs to two (e.g., labor and land), the production function can be illustrated, with labor on the *X* axis and land on the *Y* axis, by a series of *equal-output lines,* or *isoquants.* Each of these lines represents all of the combinations of labor and land that can be used to produce a particular level of output. On the same diagram, we may also easily draw any number of *equal-cost lines,* or *isocosts.* Each of these lines represents all of the combinations of labor and land that cost the same amount of money. Taken in combination, these two sets of curves will succinctly describe the process of cost minimization.

II. LEARNING OBJECTIVES

After you have read the appendix to Chapter 7 in your text and completed the exercises in this *Study Guide* appendix, you should be able to:

1. Define and illustrate (a) an **equal-cost line** and (b) an **equal-product line**.
2. Draw sets of equal-cost lines and equal-product lines, and describe the process of moving from one curve to the next.
3. Explain why the minimum-cost combination of inputs is found at the point of tangency between an equal-cost line and the equal-product line for a particular output level.

III. REVIEW OF KEY CONCEPTS

Match the following terms from column A with their definitions in column B.

A	B
__ Equal-product curves	1. MP_x / MP_y, where x and y are two inputs used in a production process.
__ Equal-cost curves	2. Indicate all the different combinations of two inputs that yield the same quantity of output.
__ Substitution ratio	3. $MP_x / MP_y = P_x / P_y$, where *x* and *y* are two inputs used in a production process.
__ Least-cost tangency	4. Indicate all the different combinations of two inputs that cost the same amount of money.

IV. SUMMARY AND APPENDIX OUTLINE

This section summarizes the key concepts from the chapter appendix.

1. Production functions define relationships between inputs and outputs. They operate something like recipes by describing minimum input requirements, processes, and output expectations.
2. The law of diminishing marginal productivity, as you learned in Chapter 6, states that as you add variable inputs to a fixed input base, eventually the marginal product of the variable input will fall. This is illustrated in Table 7A-1 of the text. As you move across a given land row, you are adding workers to a fixed amount of land and you can see that the marginal product of labor falls.
3. Given input prices and a production function, it is possible to find the least-cost input combination for a particular output level by summing the total cost for each input.
4. In order to illustrate the process of finding the least-cost input combination for a particular output level, economists have developed two sets of curves. *Equal-product curves* indicate all the different combinations of two inputs that can be used to produce a particular level of output. *Equal-cost curves* indicate all the different combinations of two inputs that cost the same amount of money, given fixed input prices.
5. Once the firm has determined its optimal level of output and identified the associated equal-product curve, the least-cost combination of inputs will be found where this

equal-product curve is *tangent to* the lowest equal-cost curve. This means that the slope of the equal-product curve is equal to the slope of the equal-cost curve, given the definition of a tangency; i.e., $MP_x / MP_y = P_x / P_y$, where x and y are two inputs used in the production process. Note that this expression can be easily rewritten as $MP_x / P_x = MP_y / P_y$, and the illustration yields the same interpretation that was made verbally in Chapter 7, namely, that the productivity of the last dollar's worth of *each* input must be equal at the least-cost combination of inputs.

V. HELPFUL HINTS

1.   Production functions are not as mysterious as they may seem. Take a look at a boxed cake mix, or the directions for assembling a gas grill: They list raw materials, or pieces, that must be used in a production process, and they provide some directions that, when followed, will yield a finished product. In some sense, the functions that we refer to in this chapter have the same properties.

2.   You may have trouble understanding why the slope of an equal-product line must be $-MP_L/MP_K$, when labor is the X axis variable and capital is the Y axis variable. Here is a rough explanation: The slope of a line is often referred to as "rise over run," i.e., the change in the Y axis variable over the change in the X axis variable between two points. Suppose that when capital is reduced by 1 tiny unit, labor must be increased by 2 tiny units in order to hold output fixed and stay on the equal-product line. That would make the slope of the equal-product line -1/2 because at this point a unit of capital is *twice* as productive as a unit of labor; it takes 2 units of labor to make up for the output lost when 1 unit of capital is taken away. When capital was reduced, output fell—by an amount dictated by MP_K. The amount of labor needed to make up that output loss was dictated by MP_L.

3.   The tangency solution is a generally useful concept in economic analysis. The slope of the equal-product line represents the rate at which one input can be substituted for another *depending on how productive each input is at the margin*. The slope of the equal-cost line represents the rate at which one input can be substituted for another *given market prices*. Thus, the slope of the equal-product line—the ratio of the marginal productivities—is determined by the productivity of the inputs with this particular production function, while the slope of the equal-cost line—the ratio of input prices—is determined by market forces that are most often out of the firm's control.

VI. MULTIPLE CHOICE QUESTIONS

Choose the best answer from the options available.
1.   An equal-cost line describes the various:

a.   quantities of output that a firm will produce at alternative output prices.
b.   quantities of two inputs that would cost the same amount as the prices of the inputs change.
c.   combinations of two inputs that a firm could purchase for a given level of expenditure.
d.   combinations of two inputs that a firm could employ to produce some given quantity of output.
e.   combinations of inputs that bring equal utility to the firm.

2.   Which alternative in question 1 correctly describes an equal-product line?
a.
b.
c.
d.
e.

3.   Each and every point on an *equal-product curve* stands for a different:
a.   combination of two inputs, all of which can be purchased at the same total expense.
b.   quantity of output, all of which cost the same to produce.
c.   combination of inputs, all of which can be employed to produce the same level of output.
d.   production function, all of which use the same combinations of inputs.
e.   combination of outputs, all of which can be purchased at the same total expense.

4.   A diagram showing a set of equal-product curves illustrates the firm's:
a.   total cost function.
b.   minimum cost level of output.
c.   profit-maximizing level of output.
d.   production function.
e.   utility function.

5.   The slope of an equal-cost line is a measure of the:
a.   ratio of the price of the factor on the vertical axis to the price of the factor on the horizontal axis.
b.   ratio of the price of the factor on the horizontal axis to the price of the factor on the vertical axis.
c.   various outputs which may be produced at a given cost.
d.   total cost of producing a given output.
e.   marginal productivity of one of the factors.

6.   Consider Firm X's production function. It uses 2 workers and 1 unit of capital to produce 10 units of output. Additional workers, or additional units of capital, are not useful unless the inputs are obtained in the above ratio. Firm X will have equal-product curves that are:
a.   straight lines.
b.   L-shaped.
c.   curved, and convex to the origin.
d.   curved, and concave to the origin.

e.   any of the above.

Use Figure 7A-1 to answer questions 7 through 9.

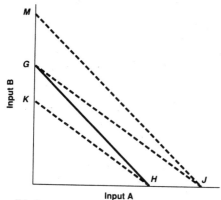

Figure 7A-1

7.   Line *GH* is an equal-cost line for inputs *A* and *B*. A shift of *GH* to a position such as *GJ* could be caused by a(n):
  a.   decrease in the price of input *A* with no change in the price of *B*.
  b.   increase in the price of both inputs.
  c.   decrease in the price of input *B* with no change in the price of *A*.
  d.   increase in the price of input *B* with no change in the price of *A*.
  e.   proportionate reduction in the price of both inputs.

8.   Suppose that the equal-cost line *GH* shifts to position *MJ* (with no change in the total cost). Which alternative in question 7 would correctly explain this shift?
  a.
  b.
  c.
  d.
  e.

9.   Suppose that the equal-cost line *GH* shifts instead to position *KH*. Which alternative in question 7 would correctly explain this shift?
  a.
  b.
  c.
  d.
  e.

10. What do we assume is held *constant* when an equal-cost line is drawn?
  a.   Total expenditure on input *A*.
  b.   Total expenditure on input *B*.
  c.   Quantity of the product produced.
  d.   Total expenditure on either *A* or *B* but not both.
  e.   Total expenditure on the two inputs combined.

11. Had question 10 referred to an equal-product rather than an equal-cost line, which alternative in that question would have been correct?

  a.
  b.
  c.
  d.
  e.

12. Equal-product lines and equal-cost lines have one property in common: Any point on either of these two lines is intended to mark some:
  a.   quantity of finished total output.
  b.   amount of total cost expressed in dollars.
  c.   combination of physical quantities of inputs.
  d.   pair of input prices.
  e.   amount of total sales revenue in dollars.

13. When the difference between the fixed-proportions (FP) and variable-proportions (VP) cases (with respect to the use of inputs in production) is illustrated by means of equal-product curves or lines, it shows up as follows: The equal-product curve is a:
  a.   straight line in the FP case, but it is a right angle in the VP case.
  b.   right angle in the FP case, but it is a curved line in the VP case.
  c.   curved line in the FP case, but it is a right angle in the VP case.
  d.   right angle in the FP case, but it is a straight line in the VP case.
  e.   curved line in the FP case, but it is a straight line in the VP case.

14. The points of tangency between equal-product and equal-cost curves are important because they indicate:
  a.   for any given level of output, the lowest possible equal-cost line that can be reached, i.e., it indicates minimum cost for that output.
  b.   for any given level of outlay on factors, the highest possible equal-product line that can be reached, i.e., it indicates the maximum output that can be obtained for that outlay of money.
  c.   the maximum-profit output level.
  d.   the minimum possible level of output that can be attained for any given outlay of money.
  e.   both **a** and **b**.

Figure 7A-2 illustrates a production function involving the employment of inputs *X* and *Y*. The two curved lines are equal-product lines for outputs of 300 and 420 units. *AB* and *CD* are equal-cost lines. *AB* marks a cost outlay of $36. Please use this information to answer   questions 15 through 21.

15. From examination of *AB*, the price of *X* must be:
  a. $2.50.
  b. $4.50.
  c. $5.50.
  d. $6.00.
  e. $8.00.

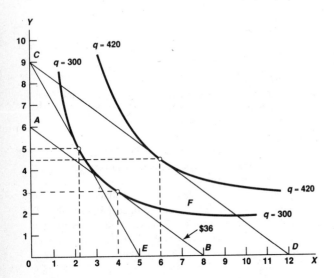

Figure 7A-2

16. From examination of *AB*, the price of *Y* must be:
    a. $2.50.
    b. $4.50.
    c. $5.50.
    d. $6.00.
    e. $8.00.
17. The minimum total cost of producing 300 units of output is:
    a. $36.
    b. $45.
    c. $54.
    d. $100.
    e. $160.
18. The average cost of producing 300 units (given the firm has chosen the minimum cost combination of inputs) is:
    a. 5 cents per unit.
    b. 10 cents per unit.
    c. 12 cents per unit.
    d. 15 cents per unit.
    e. 60 cents per unit.
19. The quantities of *X* and *Y* used to produce 300 units of output at minimum cost could be:
    a. 2.25 of *X* and 5 of *Y*.
    b. 4 of *X* and 3 of *Y*.
    c. 5 of *X* and 9 of *Y*.
    d. 8 of *X* and 6 of *Y*.
    e. none of the above.
20. Given the above prices of *X* and *Y*, equal-cost line *CD* must indicate a total outlay of:
    a. $36.
    b. $45.
    c. $54.
    d. $100.

e. $160.
21. Suppose that equal-cost line *CD* (still signifying the same total cost amount as before) shifts to position *CE*. This would indicate a(n):
    a. decrease in the price of *X*
    b. increase in the price of *X*
    c. decrease in the price of *Y*.
    d. increase in the price of *Y*.
    e. none of the above.
22. Farmer Jones is using labor and land in her production process; she grows corn on her 40 acres of land. The law of diminishing returns tells us:
    a. as she adds workers to her fixed amount of land, eventually the marginal product of land will fall.
    b. as she adds workers to her fixed amount of land, eventually the marginal product of labor will fall.
    c. that the average product of labor will remain constant in the short run.
    d. there are no variable inputs in the short run.
    e. as she spends more money on land and labor, marginal product will fall only in the long run.

VII. PROBLEM SOLVING

The following problems are designed to help you apply the concepts that you learned in this appendix.

1. Suppose Figure 7A-3 describes a production process in which output is produced using alternative quantities of labor and capital.

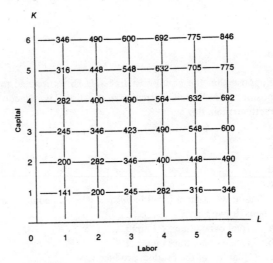

Figure 7A-3

a. Show in Figure 7A-4 the various capital-labor combinations that will produce an output of 346 units. Join these points with a smooth curve. Repeat the process for outputs of 490 and 282. For identification, label the three curves $q = 282$, $q = 346$, and $q = 490$.

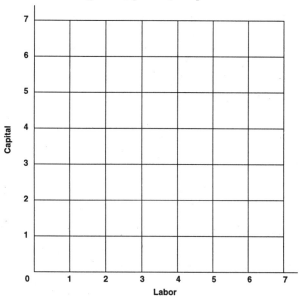

Figure 7A-4

b. You can add equal-cost lines to your figure above. Suppose that labor costs $2 per unit and that the rental cost of capital is $3, and further suppose that the firm has $12 to spend on these two inputs. Use this information to draw an equal-cost curve. (*Hint*: You know that your equal-cost curve will be a straight line, since the slope is constant. So, plot the two axis-intercepts and connect them to get your line; that is, plot the point representing $12 worth of labor and no capital and the point representing $12 worth of capital and no labor. Connect these two points with a straight line.)

c. One point on your equal-cost line is 1.5 units of labor and 3 units of capital. The output which this combination would produce, according to your production function above, is (**more than / less than / equal to**) 280 units? Explain. _____.

d. Draw another equal-cost line parallel to the previous one, but this time draw it so that it just touches your 282 equal product curve at one point. About what combination of inputs will this curve represent? How much money will the firm spend? _____.

2. Suppose a firm uses labor and capital to produce output.
a. If the price of labor is $50 per unit and the price of capital is $75 per unit, what will the firm 's equal-cost curve look like when it is spending $500? Draw the curve in Figure 7A-5 and label it curve 1.
b. If the price of labor falls to $45 per unit, what happens to the firm's equal-cost curve? Show the new curve in Figure 7A-5 and label it curve 2.

c. Return to the specifications for curve 1. If the firm decides to spend $750 instead of $500, what happens to the firm's equal-cost curve? Show the new curve in Figure 7A-5 and label it curve 3.

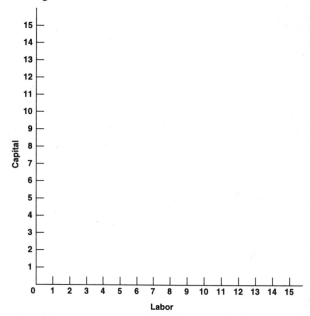

Figure 7A-5

d. Summarize the results of the above changes. What happens to the firm's options when these types of changes occur? _____
_____.

VIII. DISCUSSION QUESTIONS

Answer the following questions, making sure that you can explain the work you did to arrive at the answers.

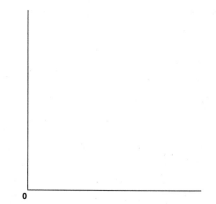

Figure 7A-6

1. The Sit Tite Chair Company uses labor and capital to produce wooden kitchen chairs. After carefully considering their production function, they find that they can produce a single chair using *any combination* of labor and capital, as long as they use 4 units of inputs. That is, they can produce a single chair using 4 units of labor, or 4 units of capital, or 3 units of capital and 1 unit of labor, etc. In Figure 7A-6, show the firm's equal-product curves for 1, 2, 3, and 4 chairs.

2. Is the following statement true or false: "A firm's production function is illustrated by a set of equal-product curves; these curves alone determine the optimal level of output for the firm, and the optimal input combination for the firm."

3. Is the following statement true or false: "A firm will always choose the optimal input combination where the marginal product of all inputs is zero." Please explain.

4. Suppose that a firm is producing widgets using capital and labor. The firm finds that it is currently spending all of its budget, and that the MP_L/MP_K is greater than P_L/P_K. What would you tell the firm to do? Illustrate its current position in Figure 7A-7 using equal-product and equal-cost curves.

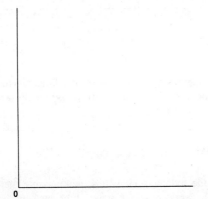

Figure 7A-7

IX. ANSWERS TO STUDY GUIDE QUESTIONS

III. Review of Key Concepts

2	Equal-product curves
4	Equal-cost curves
1	Substitution ratio
3	Least-cost tangency

VI. Multiple Choice Questions

1. C	2. D	3. C	4. D	5. B	6. B
7. A	8. E	9. D	10. E	11. C	12. C
13. B	14. E	15. B	16. D	17. A	18. C
19. B	20. C	21. B	22. B		

VII. Problem Solving

1. a. See Figure 7A-4

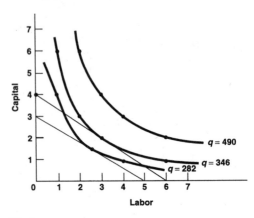

Figure 7A-4

    b. See Figure 7A-4.
    c. More than
    d. Approximately 1.8 units of capital and 2.4 units of labor. The firm will spend approximately $10.20.

2. a. See Figure 7A-5.

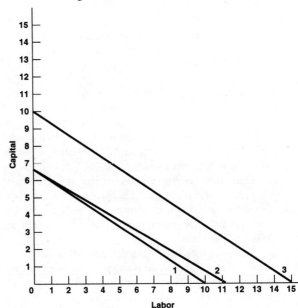

Figure 7A-5

    b. See Figure 7A-5.
    c. See Figure 7A-5.
    d. When prices change, the least-cost curve pivots. When the level of expenditure changes, the curve shifts parallel. The firm is able to produce more output with

the same level of expenditure when the price of input *X* falls. (Part *b*.) The firm is able to produce more output with a greater level of expenditure. (Part *c*.)

VIII. Discussion Questions

1. See Figure 7A-6.

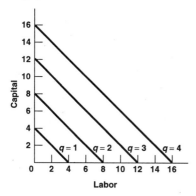

Figure 7A-6

2. False. In addition to equal-product curves, a decision maker would also need equal-cost curves to determine the optimal level of output for the firm.

3. False. The firm will set the ratios of marginal product to the price of each input equal to find the optimal combination of inputs.

4. Use more labor and less capital. This will allow the firm to increase output while spending the same amount of money. (See Figure 7A-7.)

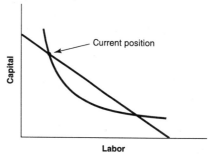

Figure 7A-7

CHAPTER

Analysis of Perfectly Competitive Markets

I. CHAPTER OVERVIEW

How do firms decide what prices to charge and what quantities to supply in the marketplace? Armed with the analytical tools acquired in Chapters 6 and 7, you are now ready to tackle this question. As you will see in the next few chapters, your answers will depend on the competitive environment that the firm faces, as well as the nature of the production process.

In this chapter, we will ask how the *competitive* firm chooses its optimal quantity to produce when confronted by a market which "calls out" some price over which the firm has no control. The link between production costs and the output decision will be based upon an assumption that firms are motivated primarily by a desire to maximize their profits. It will, in particular, be assumed that every firm chooses its optimal level of output for any price by maximizing the difference between the revenue that it can earn by selling the targeted output at the given price and the cost required to produce that output. Our study will provide insight into not only the firm's individual and market supply curves but also the structural and efficiency properties of competitive markets.

II. LEARNING OBJECTIVES

After you have read Chapter 8 in your text and completed the exercises in this *Study Guide* chapter, you should be able to:

1. Describe the characteristics of a **perfectly competitive industry**, and explain how these characteristics limit the sphere of economic variables over which a single competitive firm has influence.
2. Identify the **profit-maximizing goal** of the individual perfectly competitive firm, and indicate decision rules through which each firm can achieve this goal.
3. Review the notions of total cost, fixed cost, variable cost, average cost, and marginal cost.
4. Derive the **supply curve** of a competitive firm from the marginal cost curve.
5. Explain the **break-even** and **shutdown** conditions and their relevance to the competitive marketplace.

6. Explain the long-run and short-run equilibrium conditions for the competitive firm and the competitive market.
7. Explain why and under what conditions the supply curve might be (a) horizontal, (b) upward-sloping, (c) vertical, and (d) backward-bending.
8. Provide examples of markets in which these special cases of supply may be relevant.
9. Explain the efficiency of perfect competition in terms of (a) marginal cost and marginal utility and (b) consumer surplus and social welfare.
10. Contrast **efficiency** with **equity** as goals of an economic system, and discuss the role of each goal in developing policy.

III. REVIEW OF KEY CONCEPTS

Match the following terms from column A with their definitions in column B.

A	B
__ Price-takers	1. No possible reorganization of production can make anyone better off without making someone else worse off.
__ $P = MC = MR$	2. Implies that the quantity supplied will not change as prices change.
__ Zero-profit point	3. Occur when firms or individuals ignore the full social costs of their actions.
__ Shutdown point	4. Implies that there is a direct relationship between price and quantity supplied in an industry.
__ Economic profits	5. Firms that are so small relative to the size of the market that they perceive their demand curve to be perfectly elastic.
__ Competitive industry supply curve	6. Leads to no change in price as a firm or industry expands output in the long run.
__ Constant cost supply	7. Profit-maximizing output condition for a perfectly competitive firm.

___ Increasing
    cost supply

___ Pure economic
    rent

___ Backward-bending
    supply

___ Perfectly elastic
    supply

___ Allocative
    efficiency

___ Externalities

___ Equity

8. Involves issues of fairness in the allocation of resources.

9. Occurs when there exists a direct relationship between price and quantity supplied at low prices, but an indirect relationship between price and quantity supplied at high prices.

10. Price equals average total cost.

11. Price is equal to average variable costs.

12. The price of a factor of production that is fixed in total supply.

13. The horizontal summation of the individual firm's marginal cost curves. (Above minimum AVC)

14. Occur when price is greater than average total costs.

IV. SUMMARY AND CHAPTER OUTLINE

This section summarizes the key concepts from the chapter.

A. Supply Behavior of the Competitive Firm

1. A *perfectly competitive industry is* characterized by many small firms, each so small that no single firm can affect market price. Firms produce a homogeneous product so that consumers view all firms' outputs as perfect substitutes. These two characteristics together lead individual firms to perceive demand as perfectly elastic. Finally, competitors can easily enter or exit the industry.

2. Firms operating in perfectly competitive markets are *price-takers*; this means they take the market price as given and choose the output that maximizes profit. That output is q^*, defined in Figure 8-1.

3. The *supply curve* for an individual competitive firm is its marginal cost curve above minimum *AVC*; quantity supplied will be zero when price falls below minimum *AVC*.

4. The *zero-profit point* occurs where price is equal to minimum *ATC*. At this point, economic profits are zero and $P = MC = \min ATC$.

5. The *shutdown point* occurs where price is equal to minimum *AVC*. If price falls below this point, firms can minimize their losses in the short run by producing no output and paying only their fixed costs. If price is below *AVC* and a firm continues to produce, losses will include not only fixed costs but also a portion of variable costs.

B. Supply Behavior in Competitive Industries

1. The supply curve for a competitive market can be found by horizontally adding the quantity supplied by each firm in the market at each price.

2. In the short run, firms in a perfectly competitive industry can earn economic profits, break even, or earn losses. However, in the long run, the break-even point defines competitive equilibrium. Firms will enter the market when prices are higher (attracted by positive economic profit), shifting the short-run industry supply curve out and lowering the price along the market demand curve; firms will (eventually) exit the market in response to lower prices (repelled by negative profit), shifting the short-run industry supply curve in and raising the price along the market demand curve . Thus the *zero economic profit condition* must be expected by all firms in a perfectly competitive industry—$P = MR = MC = \min ATC$ in the long run.

3. The *long-run industry supply* may be upward-sloping if increased competition leads to increases in input prices; may be downward-sloping if increased competition leads to decreases in input prices; or may be horizontal if increased competition leads to no change in input prices.

C. Special Cases of Competitive Markets

1. Generally, an increase (decrease) in the demand for a commodity, holding the supply curve fixed, will raise (lower) the price of a commodity and increase (decrease) the quantity sold. An increase (decrease) in the supply of a commodity, holding demand fixed, will lower (raise) the price and increase (decrease) the quantity sold.

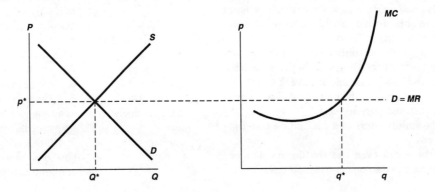

Figure 8-1

2.   In spite of these general rules, we sometimes have to reconsider our market model because the behavior of buyers or sellers is constrained in some way.   Consider the following four special cases:

   a.   When the firm operates under conditions of constant costs, as the firm or industry expands output in the long run, it expects no increases in the cost of inputs. This might happen because the inputs are abundant and widely available, or because production technology allows production to be expanded indefinitely without causing inefficiencies.

   b.   When the firm operates under conditions of increasing costs and diminishing returns, as the firm or industry expands output in the long run, increased competition for inputs puts upward-pressure on the prices of those inputs. This will lead to an upward drift in the price of the product.

   c.   In some cases, the firm sells a product or uses a resource that is fixed in total supply. From the perspective of our model, this means that the supply curve is perfectly inelastic. Consider the impact of an increase in demand for such a product. Since supply cannot fluctuate at all, price changes will reflect the full impact of the demand change. Consider the example of beachfront property in Connecticut; the supply of it is fixed, so increases in demand will result in higher prices but not in greater quantities of land available.

   d.   Finally, consider a backward-bending supply curve. This means that at relatively low prices, suppliers increase quantity supplied with increases in price, but at relatively high prices suppliers decrease quantity supplied with increases in price. This may seem counterintuitive, but consider labor markets. As a supplier of labor, you might be willing to supply (happily!) more hours of labor effort per week at higher wages. However, at some point, you may begin to feel "wealthy" enough to "buy" yourself some extra leisure time as wages continue to climb. This may help to explain why many doctors and dentists close their offices on Wednesday afternoons!

D. Efficiency and Equity of Competitive Markets

1.   *Allocative efficiency* occurs when no possible reorganization of production can make anyone better off without making someone else worse off. This means that there can be no reallocation of resources without lowering the utility of at least one person in the economy.

2.   If we assume that utility can be approximately measured by the dollar value that people are willing to pay, perfectly competitive markets lead to $P = MC = MU$, and thereby produce allocatively efficient solutions to the problem of resource allocation.

3.   Perfectly competitive markets serve to synthesize the needs and desires of buyers with the marginal costs of production represented by the supply curve, producing allocatively efficient solutions to resource allocation problems. *However,* providing an efficient market is not an easy task; externalities and monopolies are important sources of inefficiency, to name a few. Market failures can and do occur.

   Further, efficiency is *not* the only goal of an economic system. In fact, many societies encourage government intervention in markets in order to promote *equity*, or fairness, in the distribution of resources. There is no guarantee that equitable distributions are necessarily efficient or that efficient distributions are necessarily equitable.

V. HELPFUL HINTS

1.   The perfectly elastic demand curve of the competitive firm is often difficult to understand at first glance. The key here is that, in reality, the market demand curve *is* downward-sloping as one would expect; it is the *position of the firm relative to the market* that causes demand to *appear* to be perfectly elastic from the perspective of a small, individual producer.

2.   In this discussion, we assume that the firm's objective is to *maximize profits*. Note that there are other perfectly reasonable objectives that firms might have. For example, many not-for-profit organizations, such as hospitals, churches, and even many universities, exist in a market economy; the goals of these firms might be to serve the community or provide for social welfare. In other cases, firms aggressively market their products and try endlessly to increase sales and market share, seeming to maximize revenues or production rather than profits. In some cases, CEOs of companies seem to be interested in maximizing their own salaries rather than the profitability of the enterprises that employ them.

   In spite of these alternative objectives, profit maximization is a good starting point for analysis, because profits do an important job in a market economy. Profits signal to other resource owners that opportunities exist, and the absence of profits signals that opportunities do not exist, in certain industries. In many cases, other objectives are consistent with profit maximization; even if firms are not consciously striving to maximize profits, they often act *as if* they are.

3.   Economists measure profits differently than do accountants. Accounting profits exist when revenues *more than cover explicit costs* of production. Economic profits may or may not exist at this point. Economists further require that revenues cover *implicit costs,* or opportunity costs, when measuring profitability.

4.   Notice the parallel between the derivation of the market supply curve and the market demand curve. In both cases, individual curves are *added horizontally;* given a market

price, sum up the quantities supplied by all firms in the market. This yields a single point on the market supply curve.

5. Some students wonder about the final unit produced by the profit-maximizing firm, the unit for which $MC = MR$. It is true that the firm "breaks even," at the margin, on this unit. However, as long as marginal revenue is *greater than* marginal cost, the firm has an incentive to expand output. The equality tells the firm that, since marginal costs are rising, further increases in output are not wise. The equality serves as an important signal to the firm that they should not produce any additional units of output.

6. Remember that horizontal, vertical, and backward-bending supply curves are *special cases*. They do not occur frequently. In most markets, quantity supplied varies directly with output price.

7. Remember from Chapter 4 that the more *inelastic* side of the market will bear the greater burden of any new tax. In a market with a perfectly inelastic supply curve, the suppliers will bear the *complete* burden of the tax, since they cannot in any way alter supply in response to the price change. The buyers' price is not affected by the tax; the sellers' price falls by the amount of the tax.

8. One last word on efficiency versus equity: Economists spend lots of time talking about efficiency because we have found ways to define and measure it that are reasonably objective. Equity is a much more difficult concept because its definition is normative, or opinion-based. How would you define a *fair* distribution of income or resources? Would it be based upon equalities? Upon need? Upon hours worked? Or upon equal access to the resources available? All of these can be perfectly acceptable definitions, so it becomes incumbent upon each individual or society to determine the appropriate definition for themselves or their group. Often, this decision is based on cultural or societal norms. For example, in the United States, we often define fairness as equal access, whereas many of the socialist states define fairness as equality in distribution. In any case, in spite of the fact that we have a hard time defining it, equity is an important goal of an economic system, and we must not ignore it in our analyses.

VI. MULTIPLE CHOICE QUESTIONS

These questions are organized by topic from the chapter outline. Choose the best answer from the options available.

A. Supply Behavior of the Competitive Firm

1. All of the following characterize a perfectly competitive industry *except*:
   a. there are many firms in the industry.
   b. firms produce a homogeneous product; that is, any firm's product is a perfect substitute for any other's.
   c. there is extreme price competition among the competitors in the industry
   d. there is free entry and exit into and out of the industry
   e. all of the above describe perfect competition.

2. A firm that is maximizing profits under short-run conditions of perfect competition will:
   a. set average total cost equal to price.
   b. produce the output for which its average cost is at the lowest attainable level.
   e. produce the output for which average variable cost is just equal to market price.
   d. make its total revenue just equal to its fixed cost.
   e. take none of the above actions, necessarily.

3. The profit-maximizing rule for a firm in perfect competition is "price equal to marginal cost." This rule means that a firm should:
   a. increase output until price has risen to equal marginal cost.
   b. increase output until price has fallen to equal marginal cost.
   c. increase output until marginal cost has fallen to equal price.
   d. increase output until marginal cost has risen to equal price.
   e. decrease price until price equals marginal cost.

4. A firm operates under conditions of perfect competition. At its present level of output, *all* the following have a value of *$1*: the price it is charging, its marginal cost, and its average total cost. Marginal cost would rise with any increase in output. This firm:
   a. is definitely at its maximum-profit position
   b. is definitely not at its maximum-profit position.
   e. may or may not be at its maximum-profit position; we need to know average variable cost.
   d. may or may not be at its maximum-profit position; we need to know total cost and total revenue.
   e. may or may not be at its maximum-profit position; we would need to know total fixed cost.

5. A firm operating in a perfectly competitive industry is producing a daily output which supports total revenue equal to $5000. That output is its profit-maximizing output. The firm's average total cost is $8, its marginal cost is $10, and its average variable cost is $5. Its daily output is:
   a. 200 units.
   b. 500 units.
   c. 625 units.
   d. 1000 units.
   e. impossible to tell from the information furnished.

6. The fixed cost for the firm described in question 5 is:
   a. $10.
   b. $100.
   c. $500.
   d. $1500.

e. impossible to tell from the information furnished.

7. The daily profit earned or loss incurred by the firm in question 5 must be:
   a. a loss of $500.
   b. neither profit nor loss; the firm just breaks even.
   c. a profit of $500.
   d. a profit of $1000.
   e. impossible to tell from the information furnished.

8. A firm operating in a perfectly competitive market produces and sells 200 units of output daily at a price of $7.00. Its average cost is $4.99. If it were to increase output and sales to 201 units daily, average cost would rise to $5.00. To maximize its profit, and from the information supplied, this firm should:
   a. increase its output, since marginal cost (*MC*) is approximately $6.00.
   b. reduce its output, since *MC* is approximately $6.00.
   e. remain at its present output, since *MC* is approximately $7.00.
   d. certainly not reduce its output, and probably increase it, since average cost is less than the price.
   e. increase its output, since *MC* is approximately $5.01.

9. A firm must sell its product at a market price of $1.90. Its present operating figures are as follows: average cost, $2.00; marginal cost, $1.50; average variable cost, $1.50; total fixed costs, $500 per period. By the rules of maximum profit (or minimum loss) for a competitive firm, this firm would:
   a. definitely increase its present output level.
   b. definitely reduce its present output level.
   c. remain at its present output position.
   d. shut down.
   e. perhaps increase or perhaps decrease its output— the one critical figure needed to make this decision is lacking.

10. Because of a city tax reduction, the total fixed cost a firm must pay is reduced by $500 monthly. The firm operates in conditions of perfect competition. If the firm seeks to maximize its profit, this cost reduction should (at least in the short run) result in:
    a. a reduction in price.
    b. an increase in output.
    c. an increase in price.
    d. a reduction in output.
    e. no change in output or in price.

11. The supply curve of a firm in perfect competition is the same thing as:
    a. its entire marginal cost curve.
    b. a part of its marginal cost curve.
    c. its average cost curve.
    d. the region of its average cost curve over which *AC* rises or remains constant as output increases.
    e. none of these.

12. A firm operating in circumstances of perfect competition faces a market price of $10. It is producing 2000 units of output daily at a total cost of $19,000. This firm:
    a. should increase its output to improve its profit position.
    b. should reduce its output to improve its profit position.
    c. should shut down to minimize its loss.
    d. may or may not be at the output level yielding maximum profit—the information furnished is not sufficient to cover this point.
    e. is apparently now at its maximum-profit position.

13. Suppose that the firm described in question 12 sees its total cost climb to $19,010 as it increases its output to 2001 units. Would this additional information change your answer to that question? The correct alternative would now (or still) be:
    a.
    b.
    c.
    d.
    e.

14. A firm operating in a perfectly competitive industry finds that its total revenue does not cover its total cost at its best possible operating position (for any nonzero output). This revenue is, nonetheless, more than sufficient to cover fixed cost. This firm:
    a. is incurring a loss and would improve its position by shutting down.
    b. is incurring a loss but minimizes that loss by continuing to operate at its present position in the short run.
    c. is incurring a loss but could reduce or perhaps remove it by increasing its production and sales.
    d. is incurring a loss but the information given is not sufficient to indicate whether it would minimize that loss by continuing to operate or by shutting down.
    e. made be incurring a loss or earning a profit—the information furnished is insufficient to tell.

15. Which alternative in question 14 would have been correct had that question specified that the firm's total revenue (although still insufficient to cover total cost) was more than sufficient to cover its total variable cost?
    a.
    b.
    c.
    d.
    e.

16. A firm is operating in circumstances of perfect competition. It is producing that quantity of output at which average total cost is at its minimum level in the short run. This firm:
    a. must be at its maximum-profit output level but may or may not be charging the best price it could get for that output.

b.   must be at its maximum-profit output level and need not reconsider its price, since this is a market price over which it has no control.

c.   is not at its maximum-profit position and should increase its output.

d.   is not at its maximum-profit position and should decrease output.

e.   may or may not be at its maximum-profit position—the information furnished is insufficient to tell.

17. Economists refer to the "break-even point" for a competitive firm. This break-even point occurs at the output level where:

a.   marginal cost (MC) equals average cost (AC).

b.   average variable cost (AVC) equals average fixed cost (AFC).

c.   MC equals AVC.

d.   AC equals AVC.

e.   MC equals AFC.

18. Economists refer to the "shutdown point" for a competitive firm in the short run. This shutdown point occurs at the output level where:

a.   marginal cost (MC) equals average cost (AC).

b.   average variable cost (AVC) equals average fixed cost (AFC).

c.   MC equals AVC.

d.   AC equals AVC.

e.   MC equals AFC.

B. Supply Behavior in Competitive Industries

19. Suppose Figure 8-2 represents a perfectly competitive firm's cost structure. If the industry consists of 100 identical firms, then the quantity supplied across the entire industry at a price of $10 is:

a.   0.

b.   150.

c.   1500.

d.   15,000.

e.   none of the above.

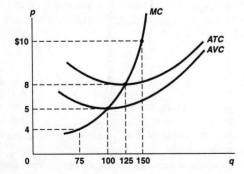

Figure 8-2

20. If the short-run marginal cost curve of a typical firm in a competitive industry should fall continuously over a substantial range of increasing outputs, then you should expect that:

a.   new firms would enter that industry.

b.   the profit earned by this typical firm could be expected to rise.

c.   the marginal cost of this firm should exceed its average cost through the output range in question.

d.   the total amount of fixed cost which this firm must pay should fall.

e.   perfect competition is likely to give way to imperfect competition.

21. The long-run equilibrium condition, "price equal to minimum average total cost," used in the theory of perfect competition, is a rule that:

a.   the firm need not consider in the short run but must obey in the long run if it wants to choose the output level that will maximize its profit.

b.   the firm must obey in the short run only if it wants to choose the output level that will maximize its profit.

c.   firms need not consider in either the short or the long run. The condition indicates a situation toward which all firms will be pushed in the long run.

d.   any profit-maximizing firm must adhere to in both the short run and the long run.

e.   is only relevant in markets for agricultural products.

22. Figure 8-3 represents the position of the perfectly competitive firm. In the long run, the firm can expect to be producing:

a. Q_1 and charging a price of P_1.

b. Q_2 and charging a price of P_1.

c. Q_2 and charging a price of P_2.

d. Q_3 and charging a price of P_2.

e. Q_3 and charging a price of P_1.

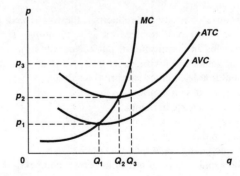

Figure 8-3

23. Given the usual downward-sloping shape of a market demand curve, what should be the effect of a tax on inputs that increases the marginal cost schedule (at every output) of each firm in a competitive industry on the market price and total output?

a. Price up and quantity up.

b. Price up and quantity down.

c. Price down and quantity up.

d. Price down and quantity down.

e. Cannot tell from the information given.

C. Special Cases of Competitive Markets

24. An increase in supply will lower price unless:

a. supply is perfectly inelastic.

b. demand is perfectly elastic.

c. it is followed by an increase in quantity demanded.

d. demand is highly inelastic.

e. both demand and supply are highly inelastic.

25. If a good is produced under constant-cost conditions, the effect of a $1 tax on each unit sold would probably be to:

a. raise price to consumers by $1.

b. raise price to consumers by less than $1 if demand is elastic.

c. require that the entire tax be paid by producers unless demand is perfectly elastic.

d. raise price to consumers by less than $1 if demand is inelastic.

e. none of these.

26. "Increasing costs" means:

a. the same thing as perfectly inelastic supply.

b. that as price increases, so does quantity supplied in the long run.

c. any shift to the right in a supply curve due to an increase in input prices.

d. any shift to the left in a supply curve following an increase in demand.

e. none of the above, necessarily.

27. If the revenue received by a factor of production is classed as a *pure economic rent*, and if the demand for this factor declines, then the price of this factor will:

a. fall, but the quantity bought and sold will be unchanged.

b. fall, and the quantity bought and sold will fall.

c. be unchanged, but the quantity bought and sold will fall.

d. be unchanged, and the quantity bought and sold will be unchanged.

e. none of these is true.

28. Perfectly elastic supply indicates:

a. constant cost.

b. increasing cost.

c. decreasing cost.

d. that revenue received by suppliers is designated as economic rent.

e. that a certain fixed supply will be offered no matter what the price may be.

29. If a commodity's return is in the nature of a pure economic rent and a tax is imposed on the commodity, then the:

a. incidence of the tax is borne wholly by the suppliers, and price to the buyers will not change.

b. incidence is borne wholly by the buyers.

c. incidence will be shared between the suppliers and the buyers.

d. output of the commodity will fall and its price will rise.

e. output of the commodity will not fall but its price will rise.

D. Efficiency and Equity of Competitive Markets

30. Allocative efficiency occurs when:

a. a consumer is on the boundary of the production-possibility frontier.

b. no possible reorganization of production can make anyone better off without making someone worse off.

c. any possible reorganization will improve welfare for all.

d. income is being redistributed through taxation.

e. marginal revenue is greater than marginal cost.

31. Suppose the U.S. government decides to place a $100 tax on all people in the economy who earn over $20,000 per year. This tax money would be redistributed to those who earn less than $20,000 per year. This policy would:

a. be allocatively efficient because it would take from the more wealthy and give to the less wealthy.

b. not be allocatively efficient because it is a redistribution that makes some people worse off.

c. not be allocatively efficient because $100 is not enough money to equalize incomes.

d. improve the distribution of income under any definition of equity or efficiency.

e. decrease the total utility of the society.

32. Market inefficiencies can come from:

a. externalities.

b. monopolies.

c. imperfect information.

d. all the above.

e. none of the above.

33. Producer surplus measures:

a. the excess of revenues over costs of production.

b. economic profits.

c. the difference between what consumers are willing to pay and what they actually pay for a good or service.

d. the output produced in a perfectly competitive market in excess of what is demanded.

e. none of the above.

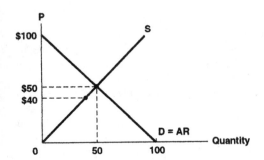

Figure 8-4

34. Using Figure 8-4, producer surplus in this perfectly competitive market is:
    a. $0
    b. $100
    c. $1,000
    d. $1,250
    e.   none of the above.
35. Using Figure 8-4, total surplus in this perfectly competitive market is:
    a. $0
    b. $100
    c. $1,000
    d. $1,250
    e. $2,500
36. If the government imposes a price ceiling of $40 on the market illustrated in Figure 8-4, producer surplus in this perfectly competitive market will fall to:
    a. $100
    b. $500
    c. $800
    d. $1,000
    e.   none of the above, producer surplus is always zero in a perfectly competitive market.

VII. PROBLEM SOLVING

The following problems are designed to help you apply the concepts that you learned in this chapter.

A. Supply Behavior of the Competitive Firm

1. State, and describe the importance of, three important characteristics of a perfectly competitive market:
    a. _____
    b. _____
    c. _____
2. Table 8-1 records a wide variety of cost and revenue information for various levels of output and two possible price specifications. It shows the total revenue obtained at

each price for various quantities of output from 10 to 20, as well as the profit to be earned from each of these outputs. Complete the blanks in this table.

  a.   From Table 8-1 it is clear that the profit-maximizing output for a price of $11.20 would be (**12 / 14 / 16 / 18 / 20**) units. At this output, average cost would be $___ and marginal cost would be approximately $___.

  b.   At a price of $8.80, profit-maximizing output would be (**12 / 14 / 16 / 18 / 20**), with average cost equal to $___ and marginal cost approximately equal to $___.

3. Now consider Figure 8-5. The three horizontal lines shown there indicate the demand curves facing a profit-maximizing competitive firm which correspond to three possible market prices.

  a.   For example, if price were $H0$, then the firm could move anywhere along D_1D_1. If $H0$ were the market price, then the firm would produce and sell quantity (**0F / 0E / 0G**). Note that in this position, the firm would be (**earning a positive economic profit / just breaking even / incurring a loss**).

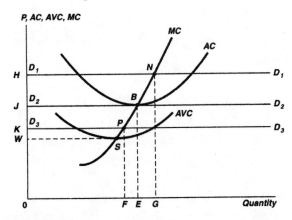

Figure 8-5

  b.   If price happened to be $J0$ then the firm's demand curve would be (**D_1D_1 / D_2D_2 / D_3D_3**), and its maximum-profit output would be (**0F / 0E / 0G**) . It would then be (**earning a positive economic profit / just breaking even / incurring a loss**).

  c.   If price were $K0$, the firm's best possible position would be to produce (**nothing / output 0F / output 0E**). In this position, its loss would be (**less than / equal to / greater than**) the amount of its fixed cost.

  d.   If price fell so low that it did not even cover average variable cost, then the firm would do better to cease operations entirely. On Figure 8-5, the boundary of this shutdown price zone is marked by price (**$H0$ / $J0$ / $K0$ / $W0$**). This price is (**greater than / equal to / less than**) the minimum level of (**average variable / average fixed**) cost.

4. Figure 8-6 shows marginal cost, average cost, and average revenue for a particular firm operating in a perfectly competitive market. The firm wishes to operate so as to maximize its profit.

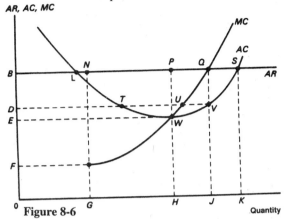

AR, AC, MC

Figure 8-6

a. At what level of output will the firm operate?
    (1) 0G   (2) 0H   (3) 0J   (4) 0K   (5) B0.
b. Which of the following correctly indicates the price at which it would sell its product?
    (1) 0G   (2) D0   (3) BF   (4) 0K   (5) B0.
c. Which correctly indicates the level of average cost at this maximum-profit output?
    (1) PH   (2) VJ   (3) SK   (4) DV   (5) EW.
d. Which correctly indicates the level of marginal cost at the maximum-profit output?
    (1) 0G   (2) D0   (3) BF   (4) 0K   (5) B0.
e. Which rectangle correctly indicates the total cost of producing the maximum-profit output?
    (1) DVJ0   (2) BQJ0   (3) BPH0   (4) BSK0   (5) EWH0.
f. Which rectangle correctly indicates the firm's total revenue at the maximum-profit output?
    (1) DVJ0   (2) BQJ0   (3) BPH0   (4) BSK0   (5) EWH0.

g. Which rectangle correctly indicates total profit earned at this output?
    (1) BQJ0   (2) DVJ0   (3) BQVD   (4) BPH0   (5) None.
5. This is a more difficult problem. You have been employed as a consultant on profit maximization. Each row of Table 8-2 provides you with some information about the operation of a different competitive firm. You are to sort through the information provided, and make a recommendation of what the firm should do given its own particular circumstance. Answer in each case by recording *one of* the numbers 1 through 7 in the last column according to the following code:
    1 = Firm is now at correct position.
    2 = Firm should increase price.
    3 = Firm should decrease price.
    4 = Firm should increase quantity of output and sales.
    5 = Firm should decrease quantity of output and sales.
    6 = Firm should shut down operations.
    7 = A nonsense case—figures supplied are inconsistent and could not all be correct.

The same number may, of course, be used more than once. Enough information is provided in each case despite the blanks. *Hint:* There is at least one "nonsense" case, in which the numbers provided are inconsistent and could not possibly be correct; in such cases, tell your clients they should audit their records!

B. Supply Behavior in Competitive Industries

6. Suppose the short-run marginal cost curves for two types of producers of corn are as shown in panels (a) and (b) of Figure 8-7. Suppose further that there are 50 of each type producer in this perfectly competitive market.
    In panel (c) of Figure 8-7, show the *market* supply of corn. The equilibrium price of corn in this market is $___ per bushel, and the equilibrium quantity exchanged is ___ bushels.

TABLE 8-1

	Cost Data			Revenue Data				
				Price = $11.20		Price = S8.80		
Quantity	Total Cost	Average Cost	Marginal Cost	Revenue	Profit	Revenue	Profit	
10	$100.50	$____		$____	$11.50	$____	$____	
			$____					
12	111.50	____		134.40	____	____		
			____					
14	124.50	____		156.80	32.30	____	____	
16	140.50	____	____	179.20	____	____	____	
18	162.50	____	____	____	____	____	____	
20	202.50	____	____	____	____	____	____	

TABLE 8-2

Case	Price	Q of Output	Total Revenue	Total Cost	Total Fixed Cost	Total Variable Cost	Average Cost	Average Variable Cost	Marginal Cost	With Increase in Output, MC Would	Answer
a.	$2.00	10,000		$16,000			At minimum level			Rise	
b.			$10,000			$2,000	$4.00	$3.00	$6.00	Rise	
c.	2.00	2,000			2,000	$5,000			2.00	Fall	
d.			6,000	6,000		4,500	At minimum level	0.75		Rise	
e.	5.00	2,000						5.25	5.00	Rise	
f.			20,000	18,000			3.60		4.00	Rise	
g.		4,000	16,000	16,000			At minimum level	5.00	3.00	Fall	
h.	4.50				9,000	12,000	5.25	At minimum level		Rise	
i.		3,000	9,000					3.25	3.00	Rise	
j.		2.000	16,000			3,000		7.00	8.00	Rise	

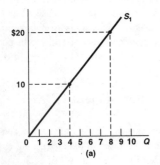

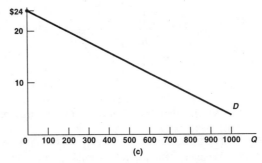

(a)   (b)   (c)

Figure 8-7

7. Consider the ABC Textile Firm, which operates as a perfectly competitive producer of cloth in the market. Diagrams in Figure 8-8 describe a hypothetical market for textiles, and the position of ABC relative to the market in long-run equilibrium.

a. Suppose there is a decrease in the worldwide demand for cloth, as people's tastes and preferences move in the direction of leather clothing. Show the impact of this change in the diagrams in Figure 8-8. The equilibrium price will (**increase / decrease**). ABC Textiles will (**increase / decrease**) its price-per-bolt and (**increase / decrease**) quantity supplied.

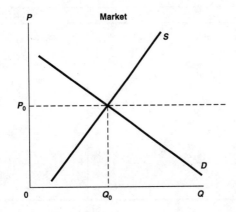

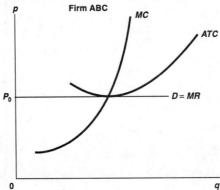

Figure 8-8

b. If the textile industry is a constant-cost industry, what will restore it to an equilibrium position, and what will be the nature of that new position? Show this new equilibrium in the diagrams in Figure 8-8. The new equilibrium price is (**higher than/ lower than / the same as**) the original price, and the new quantity exchanged in the market is (**higher than / lower than / the same as**) the initial equilibrium quantity.

C. Special Cases of Competitive Markets

8. The significance of a supply curve which is positively sloped is that, in the event of an increase in demand, we would expect quantity bought and sold to (**increase / remain unchanged / decrease**) and price to (**increase / remain unchanged / decrease**).

There are numerous exceptions to this general rule. Supply curves can be flat or vertical, for example. There can also be backward-bending supply curves, that is, supply curves with regions that are negatively sloped. Figure 8-9 shows three different supply curves. Each illustrates a different case discussed in the text. "E" is case 1, "U" is case 2, and "I" is case 3.

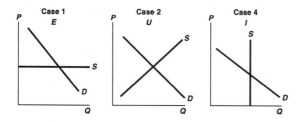

Figure 8-9

a. The case in which quantity supplied would respond neither to a price increase nor to a price decrease is (**E / U / I**).
b. The case in which suppliers are prepared to sell an infinite number of different quantities at the prevailing price is (**E / U / I**).
c. Suppose an increases in buyer incomes pushed each of the demand curves of Figure 8-9 to the right. The expected result would be a change in price and/or quantity bought and sold. For each alternative presented below, circle one or more answers, as appropriate. ("N" signifies that the outcome described fits none of the three panels of Figure 8-9.)
Given this increase in demand:
   (1) Price will rise in the case(s) illustrated in panel(s) (**E / U / I / N**).
   (2) Quantity bought and sold will increase in panel(s) (**E / U / I / N**).
   (3) Both price and quantity will increase in panel(s) (**E / U / I/ N**).

9. Consider the market for beachfront rental property in Malibu, California. Suppose the supply is *perfectly inelastic*, due to the limited supply of land and new zoning laws that prohibit further building on existing property. There are 20 apartments in existence today. Suppose the demand in this market is give by Table 8-3.

TABLE 8-3

Apartment Price (per month)	Quantity of Apartments Demanded
$2,000	0
1,500	100
1,000	200
500	300
0	400

a. Draw the demand and supply curves in Figure 8-10. What is the equilibrium price and quantity of apartments exchanged in this market? Label this equilibrium on your diagram.
b. How does the concept of *pure economic rent* relate to your diagram above?
c. Suppose the town of Malibu needs some extra income for a new park, and they decide to increase taxes on beachfront property owners by $100 per apartment. What impact will this have on the market? What will happen to buyers' prices? To sellers' prices? To the quantity of apartments exchanged? Show the effects of this event in Figure 8-10.

Suppose that instead of being perfectly inelastic, the supply curve is given by the information in Table 8-4.

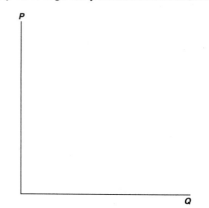

Figure 8-10

TABLE 8-4

Apartment Price (per month)	Quantity of Apartments Demanded
$2,000	400
1,500	300
1,000	200
500	100
0	0

d. Plot the old demand curve and the new supply curve in Figure 8-11. Show and describe how the same $100 tax would be divided between buyers and sellers.

e. Compare and contrast your answers to parts **c** and **d**.

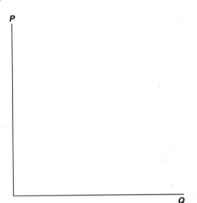

Figure 8-11

D. Efficiency and Equity of Competitive Markets

10. Figure 8-12 depicts demand/marginal utility curves for some good X for two different people (A and B) on the left side and supply/marginal cost curves for X for two different firms (I and II) on the right. Assume that these two people and two firms represent the entire market for X and that the market is competitive. Carefully draw the market supply and demand curves for X on the middle graph of Figure 8-12, and fill in the blanks in Table 8-5 for the resulting equilibrium.

a. Notice in Table 8-5 that the efficiency condition that $MU = MC, = P$ (**is / is not**) satisfied for both firms and both individuals. Total consumer surplus at equilibrium is $___.

b. Suppose that an economic planner wants to call out a single price for X that would generate an allocation of consumption and work effort that would maximize total consumer surplus in the X market. What price and quantity would be specified? $___ and ___.

TABLE 8-5

	Price	Quantity Demanded (units)	Quantity Supplied (units)	Marginal Utility/ Marginal Cost
Market	$___	___	___	MU = MC= $___
Individual A		___		MU = $___
Individual B		___		MU = $___
Firm I			___	MC = $___
Firm II			___	MC = $___

VIII. DISCUSSION QUESTIONS

Answer the following questions, making sure that you can explain the work you did to arrive at the answers.

1. Using diagrams show the relationship between the perfectly competitive market and a single firm operating in that market. Why is this relationship so important?

2. Given the usual downward-sloping shape of a market demand curve, what is the impact of a tax that affects only the *fixed cost* of every firm in a competitive market on the price charged and the quantity supplied by each competitive firm?

3. Ms. Smith says, "In the long run, since economic profits are zero, firms will have no incentive to produce output in a perfectly competitive market. Why would anyone produce and sell a product if they are going to earn no profits?" Do you agree?

4. During the summer of 1994, severe floods in the southeastern portion of the United States did great damage to the peanut crop. Use diagrams to show the effects of this disaster on the market for peanuts (assuming that the market was in long-run equilibrium before the flood) and on the farms that were not damaged by floodwaters. What happened to the equilibrium price and quantity exchanged in the market? What happened to profits for those farms not affected by the flood? What sorts of dynamics would you expect in the future?

5. List a new example of a market or industry that might have a perfectly elastic supply curve.

6. List a new example of a market or industry that might have a perfectly inelastic supply curve.

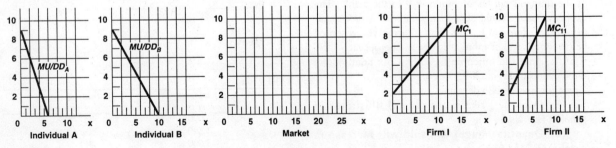

Figure 8-12

TABLE 8-1

| | Cost Data | | | Revenue Data | | | |
| | | | | Price = $11.20 | | Price = $8.80 | |
Quantity	Total Cost	Average Cost	Marginal Cost	Revenue	Profit	Revenue	Profit
10	$100.50	$10.05		$112.00	$11.50	$88.00	-12.50
12	111.50	9.29	$ 5.50	134.40	22.90	105.60	- 5.90
14	124.50	8.89	6.50	156.80	32.30	123.20	- 1.30
16	140.50	8.78	8.00	179.20	38.70	140.80	.30
18	162.50	9.02	11.00	201.60	39.10	158.40	- 4.10
20	202.50	10.13	20.00	224.00	21.50	176.00	- 26.50

7. What would happen if *both* supply and demand were downward-sloping? Would you necessarily have a market equilibrium? Use a diagram to illustrate your answer.

8. What sorts of factors would help to determine whether or not an individual's labor supply curve bends backward?

9. Would the curve depicting your personal supply of labor ever bend backward? If so, at what wage level would the "bend" occur?

10. Mr. X says: "I know a dentist who increased her prices and then decided to play golf, rather than work, on Wednesday afternoons. This must contradict the law of supply?" Comment.

11. Compare and contrast the terms *efficiency* and *equity*. Are these two goals of most economic systems consistent with one another? Can you think of times when pursuit of efficiency might hamper equity, or when pursuit of equity might hamper efficiency?

IX. ANSWERS TO STUDY GUIDE QUESTIONS

III. Review of Key Concepts

5	Price-takers
7	$P = MR = MC$
10	Zero-profit point
11	Shutdown point
14	Economic profits
13	Competitive industry supply curve
6	Constant-cost supply
4	Increasing-cost supply
12	Pure economic rent
9	Backward-bending supply
2	Perfectly inelastic supply
1	Allocative efficiency
3	Externalities
8	Equity

VI. Multiple Choice Questions

1. C 2. E 3. D 4. A 5. B 6. D
7. D 8. C 9. A 10. E 11. B 12. D
13. E 14. D 15. B 16. E 17. A 18. C
19. D 20. E 21. C 22. C 23. B 24. B
25. A 26. B 27. A 28. A 29. A 30. B
31. B 32. D 33. A 34. D 35. E 36. C

VII. Problem Solving

1. a. There are many small firms, so many that no single firm can affect the market price with its decisions.

   b. There is a standardized product, so that every firm's product is a perfect substitute for every other firm's product.

   c. Firms can enter or exit the industry easily and at relatively low cost.

2. See Table 8-1
   a. 18, $9.02, $11.00
   b. 16, $8.78, $8.00

3. a. 0G, earning a positive economic profit
   b. D_2D_2, 0E, just breaking even
   c. output 0F, less than
   d. W0, equal to, average variable

4. a. (3)
   b. (5)
   c. (2)
   d. (5)
   e. (1)
   f. (2)
   g. (3)

5. Listed here are the lines of reasoning that produce answers to this question.

   a. Get AC from Q and TC; AC = $1.60. Get MC from the fact that AC is at minimum; MC = $1.60. P>MC, therefore increase output. Answer: 4.

   b. Get AFC from AC and AVC; AFC = $1.00. Get Q from AFC and TFC; Q = 2,000. Get P from Q and TR, P = $5.00. P<MC; therefore decrease output. Answer: 5.

   c. P = MC, but MC is falling. Therefore output should be increased. Answer: 4.

   d. Get Q from TVC and AVC; Q = 6000. Get P from Q and TR; P = $1.00. Get AC from Q and TC; AC = $1.00. Get MC from the fact that AC is at a minimum; MC = $1.00. P = MC and there is no loss; therefore the current position is fine. Answer: 1.

e. $P = MC$, but check for possible loss. $P<AVC$, and therefore loss exceeds TFC; shut down. Answer: 6.

f. Get Q from TC and AC; $Q = 5,000$. Get P from Q and TR; $P = \$4.00$. $P = MC$, and there is no loss; therefore the current position is fine. Answer: 1.

g. MC is falling; therefore output should be increased. But AC is at its minimum level, through which MC should be rising. This indicates an impossible case. Answer: 7.

h. Get TC from TFC and TVC; $TC = \$21,000$. Get Q from TC and AC; $Q = 4,000$. Get AVC from Q and TVC; $AVC = \$3.00$. Get MC from the fact that AVC is at a minimum; $MC = \$3.00$. $P>MC$; therefore increase output. Answer: 4.

i. Get P from Q and TR; $P = \$3.00$. $P = MC$ and MC is rising, but check for possible loss. Compare P and AVC. The fact that $P<AVC$ indicates not only that there is a loss, but one of such magnitude that the firm should shut down. Answer: 6.

j. Get P from Q and TR; $P = \$8.00$. $P = MC$, and MC is rising, but check for possible loss. Get TVC from Q and AVC; $TVC = \$14,000$. Get TC from TVC and TFC; $TC = \$17,000$. Since TR is $16,000$, the loss is $1,000$. This is less than TFC of $3,000$, so the firm should continue to operate. Answer: 1.

6. $15.00; 450.

7. a. Demand shifts to the left, decrease, decrease, decrease

b. Supply shifts to the left, the same as, lower than

8. increase, increase

a. I

b. E

c. 1. U, I

   2. E, U

   3. U

9. a. See Figure 8-13. The equilibrium price is $1,000, quantity is 200 units.

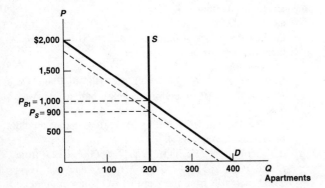

Figure 8-13

b. Pure economic rent is the return to this factor, which is fixed in total supply.

c. This tax will be paid by sellers out of economic rent. Buyers' price and quantity exchanged remain fixed.

d. See Figure 8-14. Supply shifts up by $100. This tax is split equally between buyers and sellers because the supply and demand curves are neither particularly elastic nor inelastic relative to one another.

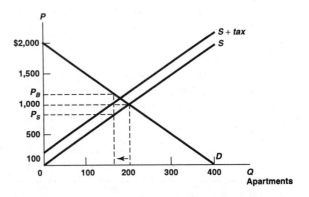

Figure 8-14

e. In part **c**, the supply cure was perfectly inelastic. This means that the tax will be paid by the suppliers, who cannot alter their quantity supplied in responses to changes in the market. In part **d**, the supply curve was more elastic. Thus, the tax was shared by the buyers and sellers. Each displays some ability to change behavior when price changes.

10. The demand curve should be a straight line, with a price-axis intercept of $9 and a quantity-axis intercept of 16. The supply curve should be a straight line with a price-axis intercept of $2.

TABLE 8-5

	Price	Quantity Demanded (units)	Quantity Supplied (units)	Marginal Utility/ Marginal Cost
Market	$5.00	8	8	MU = MC= $5.00
Individual A		3		MU = $5.00
Individual B		5		MU = $5.00
Firm I			5	MC = $5.00
Firm II			3	MC = $5.00

a. is, $16.

b. $5, 8 units. The planner would mimic the market.

VIII. Discussion Questions

1. See diagrams.

2. Since firms are price-takers, the increase in costs will initially cause no change in output. Costs rise, but marginal

cost and price remain constant, so the profit-maximizing level of output remains the same. Profits fall. The industry supply curve responds when firms exit the industry. Supply shifts left, the market price rises, and the total quantity of output exchanged in the market falls.

3. When economic profits are zero, firms are earning normal profits. This means that they are earning just enough to cover their opportunity costs.

4. As a result of the flood, supply shifted to the left, price rose, and the remaining farms saw their profits increase. In the future we would expect to see these economic profits attract new entrants. (See diagrams on page 115.)

5. Markets for computer chips.

6. Markets for professional sports stars.

7. If supply and demand are both downward-sloping, there may be no equilibrium in the market. (See diagram on page 115.)

8. Individual worker preferences determine whether or not the curve will be backward-bending. How do individuals feel about their jobs? How important is marginal income to workers?

9. Mine would bend backward at around $500 per hour! Yours may be different.

10. This might contradict the law of supply for this individual at high prices. However, note that as incomes for doctors have increased, more people have become interested in getting into the industry as suppliers. This has led to an increase in quantity supplied at higher prices across the market, even if many individuals in the market are on the backward-bending portions of their individual supply curves.

11. *Efficiency* deals with making the most out of the resources available. *Equity* deals with fairness in the distribution and use of resources. These terms are sometimes consistent with one another, but at other times they are not.

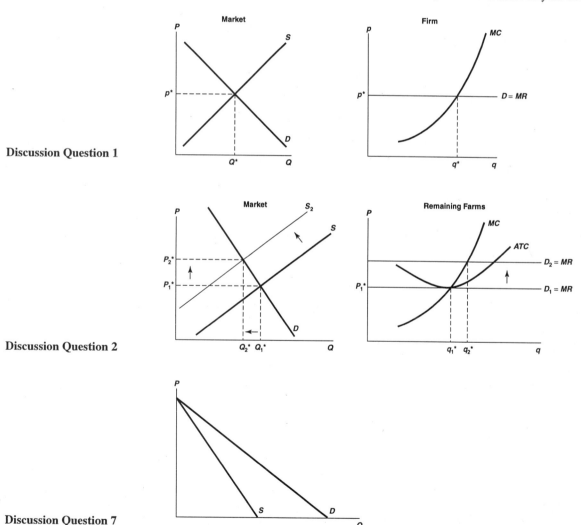

Discussion Question 1

Discussion Question 2

Discussion Question 7

CHAPTER 9

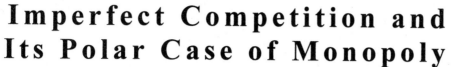

Imperfect Competition and Its Polar Case of Monopoly

I. CHAPTER OVERVIEW

The perfectly competitive market model described in Chapter 8 is important because it gives us a benchmark from which to compare markets as they are observed in the "real world." In fact, there are very few examples of perfect competition that exist; farming and textiles are close, but myriad government polices exist, from acreage restrictions to import quotas, that alter the behavior of firms.

This chapter presents the sources and patterns of imperfect competition, as well as a theoretical discussion of monopoly (the polar opposite of perfect competition) based upon the notions of *marginal cost* and *marginal revenue*. The main theme is illustrated in the quotation from Adam Smith's *Wealth of Nations* that precedes the text chapter: "The monopolists, by keeping the market constantly understocked, . . . sell their commodities much above the natural price, and raise their emoluments, whether they consist of wages or profit . . . ." In other words, the loss of perfect competition occurs when firms differentiate their products and gain control over price; the resulting concentration of industry, at any level, leads to lower output and higher prices for consumers as well as market and political power for monopolists.

II. LEARNING OBJECTIVES

After you have read Chapter 9 in your text and completed the exercises in this *Study Guide* chapter, you should be able to:

1. Define and describe the patterns of **imperfect competition**.
2. Compare the three varieties of imperfect competitors: **monopoly, oligopoly**, and **monopolistic competition**.
3. Discuss the sources of imperfect competition, namely, **cost conditions** and **barriers to entry**.
4. Explain the concept of **marginal revenue** as it applies to the monopolist. Calculate marginal revenue given data on market demand.
5. Define and illustrate the process of determining the profit-maximizing level of output for the monopolist.
6. Contrast the profit-maximizing rule for a perfect

competitor with the profit-maximizing rule for a monopolist, and show that perfect competition can be described as a special case of the general $MC = MR$ rule.
7. Recognize the importance of the **marginal principle**, and apply it to the decision-making process.

III. REVIEW OF KEY CONCEPTS

Match the following terms from column A with their definitions in column B.

A	B
__ Imperfect competition	1. Allow a firm to maintain monopoly in production for a period of 17 years as a return to development of a new product.
__ Monopoly	2. Occurs when firms in an industry try to make their products look or seem different from the products of rivals.
__ Oligopoly	3. Factors that make it hard for new firms to enter an industry.
__ Monopolistic competition	4. An industry in which a single seller has complete control over output and price.
__ Product differentiation	5. Entry barriers which protect domestic producers from foreign producers.
__ Economies of scale	6. People will maximize their incomes, profits, or satisfaction by counting only the marginal costs and benefits of a decision.
__ Barriers to entry	7. A firm gets an exclusive right to provide a service, and in return the firm agrees to limit its profits and to provide service for all customers.
__ Natural monopoly	8. An industry in which a few sellers control the market, recognizing their mutual interdependence.
__ Patents	9. Past costs that should not be considered when making a current decision.

119

___ Franchise
monopoly

___ Import
restrictions

___ Marginal
revenue

___ The marginal
principle

___ Sunk costs

10. Occur when the per unit costs of production decline as output increases.

11. The increment in total revenue that comes when output increases by one unit.

12. Occurs when a production function displays perpetual increasing returns to scale.

13. An industry in which many firms compete fiercely by differentiating their products.

14. Any market structure which varies from the perfectly competitive case.

IV. SUMMARY AND CHAPTER OUTLINE

This section summarizes the key concepts from the chapter.

A. Patterns of Imperfect Competition

1. *Imperfect competition* exists in a market when firms have been able to gain some control over the price of output. Recall that, in a perfectly competitive industry, firms produce a standardized product. This, combined with the fact that they are all very small, means that firms are *price-takers*. Imperfect competition describes any market setting in which firms have a degree of price-setting ability. This means that instead of the perfectly elastic demand curve, imperfect competitors face a downward-sloping demand curve for their products, which have been differentiated in some way.

2. Imperfect competition takes many forms, which can be placed roughly in the following three categories:

    a. A *monopoly is* a single seller of a unique product.

    b. An *oligopoly* includes a relatively small number of sellers of a similar product; because there are just a few competitors in the industry, mutual interdependence is a critically important factor in describing the behavior of competitors.

    c. A *monopolistically competitive industry* has many sellers of close substitutes. Firms take their market power from downward-sloping demand curves which allow them to choose *both* a profit-maximizing price *and* quantity of output to produce.

3. Firms differentiate their products in many different ways. Some physically change the characteristics or outward appearance of their products. For example, automakers produce cars in every conceivable color, size, shape, and style, and frequently introduce new lines. Others try to change the image of their products in the minds of consumers. For example, producers of soft drinks spend millions of dollars each year to convince consumers that Coke and Pepsi taste significantly different.

There are other ways a firm can make its product different from competitors' and create a market "niche." Sometimes location, quality, special services, and so on, can allow firms to have greater control over price.

4. There are two primary sources of market imperfections. First, production costs and *economies of scale* can help to determine the size of firms in an industry. Economies of scale exist when a firm's per unit production costs fall as output increases; this means that larger firms will have a cost advantage over smaller ones. The extent of concentration in an industry will be determined by the significance of economies of scale.

Second, in many industries *barriers to entry* exist that limit the ability of new firms to compete. Legal restrictions, such as *patents, franchises,* and *import restrictions* all provide some amount of monopoly power to producers. In other cases, high entry costs exist due to the importance of advertising and the significance of reputation effects. Brand proliferation on the part of existing firms can leave little room for a new rival to further differentiate the product. All of these factors make it much more difficult for rivals to enter a market, and limit the amount of competition that exists.

B. Marginal Revenue and Monopoly

1. Because the monopolist is the only producer of a unique product, the relevant demand curve for the firm is the entire market demand curve. The position of the firm relative to the market is very different from a situation of perfect competition, where the firm is so small that it perceives its demand as being perfectly elastic.

2. *Marginal revenue is* defined as the addition to total revenue that comes when a firm sells an additional unit of output. Because the demand curve slopes downward for the monopolist, the market price at which *all units are traded* must fall in order for the firm to sell additional units of output. This means that the sale of a marginal unit increases revenues by the amount of the sale; this increase is offset to some extent because prices on all previous units must also fall. Remember that in our discussion thus far, there is a single price in the market at which all units are traded.

3. A clear relationship exists between marginal revenue, demand, and elasticity. Remember from chapter 4 that a linear, downward-sloping demand curve is elastic at the top, unit-elastic at the midpoint, and inelastic at the bottom. When demand is elastic, total revenue *increases* as prices fall, but at a decreasing rate. This means that marginal revenue is positive, but declining. When demand is unit-elastic, total revenue *remains constant* as prices fall. This means that marginal revenue is zero; the increase in revenue due to the marginal sale are exactly offset by the decrease in revenue due to the price cut on previous units produced. Finally, when demand is inelastic, total revenue decreases as

prices fall. This means that marginal revenue is negative. Now, the increases in revenue due to the marginal sale are more than offset by the decreases in revenue due to the price cut on previous units produced. The marginal revenue curve will lie *below* the demand curve, and marginal revenue is always *less than* price.

4. The monopolist will choose the profit-maximizing level of output where marginal revenue is equal to marginal cost. This means that the firm should expand output as long as the addition to revenue is greater than the addition to costs. Given an upward-sloping marginal cost curve and a downward-sloping marginal revenue curve, once the equality is reached, further increases in output will result in costs that exceed revenues at the margin. This would not be smart!

5. Since the monopolist is a price-setter, we must also determine a profit-maximizing strategy for price. The monopolist will seek to set the highest price that the market will "bear." This price will be found by looking to the demand curve. Remember that the demand curve describes the maximum price that buyers are willing and able to pay for a particular quantity of output.

6. The perfectly competitive example can be thought of as a polar case of imperfect competition. With imperfect competition, the profit-maximizing level of output for the firm occurs where $MR = MC$. We learned in Chapter 8 that the profit-maximizing level of output for the perfectly competitive firm occurs where $P = MC$. However, notice that with perfect competition, $P = MR$. The perfect competitor is a price-taker. Once the market determines the price, the firm can sell all the units it has for that price. Each time the firm sells another unit, revenues change by the market price. Thus, a general rule has been established: *Any profit-maximizing firm will choose its optimal level of output where* MC = MR.

7. The marginal analysis presented in this chapter generalizes to many decision-making scenarios. The *marginal principle* states that people will maximize their incomes or profits or satisfactions by counting only the marginal costs and benefits of a decision. Past, or sunk, costs can be ignored if they do not have an impact on marginal costs or benefits.

V. HELPFUL HINTS

1. Three important characteristics help to define the type of market in which a firm operates. First is the number of firms; second is the degree of product differentiation; and third is ease of entry and exit. Perfect competition and monopoly define the polar cases in each of these characteristics; other cases of imperfect competition lie somewhere between these two extremes.

2. Notice that increased international trade has increased the level and significance of competition in many markets over the past decade, even in industries whose production processes are characterized by significant economies of scale. The U.S. domestic auto industry consists of three major players, Ford, General Motors, and Chrysler. Competitive pressure from Honda, Toyota, and BMW, to name a few, has moved the industry away from the tight oligopoly structure of the mid-century and toward monopolistic competition.

3. Some students seem to feel that a monopolist can set price "anywhere," because there are no substitutes for the product that the monopolist sells. This may seem to be the case, but note that there are very few *perfectly* inelastic demand curves out there. This means that quantity demanded falls when price increases, even if by just a small amount. Firms have to be sensitive to consumer demand; if consumers become too alienated, they will try harder to find substitutes or will refuse to buy altogether. Most of us consider electricity a necessity, and we purchase it from a local monopolist, albeit at a higher price than we would pay in a perfectly competitive industry. However, we can all imagine a price so high that we would use candles to light our homes, install wood-burning stoves for heat, and warm our water over our gas or wood stoves.

4. Imperfect competition does not imply the absence of competition. Rather, it implies that the extreme example of perfect competition is no longer valid. In fact, monopolistic competition describes the sorts of behaviors that most of us have come to recognize as highly competitive: lots of advertising and fierce product differentiation.

5. Next time you go to the cold cereal aisle in a U.S. supermarket, think carefully about the concept of brand proliferation. You will notice that cereal is made primarily by four producers: Kellogg, General Mills, Post, and Quaker. In fact, most stores have items grouped by *brand* rather than *product type*. That is, rather than grouping all the brands of raisin bran together on the shelf, for example, all cereals of a certain brand are shelved together. Look at the tremendous number of products made by each firm! Think about how hard this would make entry by a firm with two or three varieties of cereal, regardless of their uniqueness.

6. Tables 9-3 and 9-5 from your text illustrate the calculation of marginal revenue. Reading these tables can be tricky because marginal revenue is calculated *between* two points. To explain this, look at Table 9-5, which is reproduced here as Table 9-1. Notice that total revenue changes from 320 to 420 when quantity changes from 2 to 3 units (column 3); hence, marginal revenue *between* 2 and 3 units is 100 (column 6). Marginal revenue *between* 3 and 4 units is 60; hence, marginal revenue *at* 3 units is 80, splitting the difference between these two midpoints.

VI. MULTIPLE CHOICE QUESTIONS

These questions are organized by topic from the chapter outline. Choose the best answer from the options available.

TABLE 9-1 Summary of Firm's Maximum Profit

(1) Quantity q	(2) Price P ($)	(3) Total Revenue TR ($)	(4) Total Cost TC ($)	(5) Total Profit TP ($)	(6) Marginal Revenue MR ($)	(7) Marginal Cost MC ($)	
0	200	0	145	- 145			
					+180	30	MR>MC
1	180	180	175	+5			
					+140	25	
2	160	320	200	+120			
					+100	20	
3	140	420	220	+200			
					+ 60	30	
4*	120	480	250	+230	+40	40	MR = MC
					+20	50	
5	100	500	300	+200			
					- 20	70	
6	80	480	370	+110			
					- 60	90	
7	60	420	460	- 40			
					-100	110	MR < MC
8	40	320	570	- 250			

*Maximum-profit equilibrium

A. Patterns of Imperfect Competition

1. The essential characteristic of any imperfectly competitive market is that the single firm's:
   a. demand curve is downward-sloping.
   b. marginal revenue exceeds the price it charges.
   c. average cost curve falls over a substantial or large range of outputs.
   d. product is standardized from one firm to the next.
   e. average cost curve rises over a substantial or large range of outputs.

2. Which of the following are possible sources of imperfectly competitive markets?
   a. Declining average costs over the range of possible quantities demanded.
   b. Legal barriers to entry.
   c. Perceived product differentiation.
   d. Tariff protection from foreign competition.
   e. All of the above.

3. A firm operating in a perfectly competitive market is different from a monopolist because, among other reasons:
   a. a competitive firm can sell as much as it wishes at some given price, whereas a monopoly must lower its price if it wishes to increase the volume of its sales by any significant amount.
   b. a monopoly can always charge a price that yields a profit, whereas a competitive firm can never earn such a profit.
   c. the price elasticity of supply offered by a monopolist is higher than that offered by a competitive firm.

   d. a monopolist seeks to maximize profit, whereas a competitive firm's output decision rule equates price and average cost.
   e. a monopolist deliberately seeks to operate at the minimum level of average cost, but a competitive firm does not.

4. The term *oligopoly* refers to:
   a. general rubric for imperfect competition.
   b. a situation in which the number of competing firms is large but the products differ slightly.
   c. a situation in which the number of competing firms is small but greater than one.
   d. the form of imperfect competition in which firms act like a monopoly, regardless of the number of firms or type of product.
   e. none of these.

5. Monopoly exists whenever:
   a. there is only one seller of a particular product.
   b. a seller has at least some degree of control over the price he or she can charge.
   c. the profit earned by the seller exceeds the amount that should properly be earned as interest on money invested, plus an allowance for the risk undertaken.
   d. a seller manages to maintain his or her position through successful advertising.
   e. in none of these situations, necessarily.

6. Economies of scale occur whenever a firm's:
   a. marginal cost curve shifts.
   b. total costs are rising.
   c. patents are about to run out.
   d. diminishing marginal returns have set in.
   e. per unit production costs are falling in the long run.

B. Marginal Revenue and Monopoly

7. The term *marginal revenue* refers to:
   a. the price that can be obtained for the very last unit sold.
   b. total revenue divided by the total number of units sold.
   c. total revenue minus the price received for the very last unit sold.
   d. the difference between the increase in total revenue generated by the sale of the last unit and the increase in total cost generated by the production of that unit.
   e. the difference between the increase in total revenue generated by the sale of the last unit sold and the reduction in total revenue caused by selling all the other units at a lower price.

   Use Figure 9-1, which shows the current cost and demand information for a monopolist selling widgets, to answer questions 8 through 10.

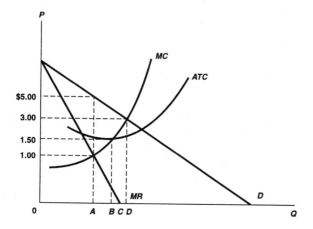

Figure 9-1

8. The profit-maximizing output level for this monopolist is:
   a. 0A.
   b. 0B.
   c. 0C.
   d. 0D.
   e. 0.
9. The profit-maximizing price for the monopolist to charge is:
   a. $1.00 per widget.
   b. $1.50 per widget.
   c. $3.00 per widget.
   d. $5.00 per widget.
   e. none of the above.
10. At the optimal level of output and price, the firm will:

a. earn economic profits.
b. break even, in an economic sense.
c. make losses, but continue producing in the short run.
d. be right at the shutdown point.
e. shut down in the short run.

11. If a firm's marginal revenue exceeds its marginal cost, maximum-profit rules require that the firm:
   a. increase its output in both perfect and imperfect competition.
   b. increase its output in perfect but not necessarily in imperfect competition.
   c. increase its output in imperfect but not necessarily in perfect competition.
   d. decrease its output in both perfect and imperfect competition.
   e. increase price, not output, in both perfect and imperfect competition.

12. Whenever the demand curve facing a given firm is perfectly elastic:
   a. the firm cannot be operating under conditions of perfect competition.
   b. the profit-maximizing rule which sets marginal cost equal to marginal revenue does not apply.
   c. price and marginal revenue are equal for every unit of output.
   d. price and marginal cost are equal for every unit of output.
   e. none of these conclusions is necessarily correct.

13. If a profit-maximizing monopoly has reached its equilibrium position, then price:
   a. must be less than marginal cost.
   b. must be equal to marginal cost.
   c. must be greater than marginal cost.
   d. may be equal to or below marginal cost, but not above it.
   e. none of the above is necessarily correct, since equilibrium does not require any particular relation between price and marginal cost.

14. Marginal revenue could equal price for a profit-maximizing firm:
   a. only when an industry is an oligopoly.
   b. only when an industry is a monopoly.
   c. if increased sales are associated with higher prices along a demand curve.
   d. whenever firms are able to differentiate their products and gain some control over price.
   e. only when an industry is perfectly competitive.

15. A monopolist has determined that marginal revenue is $2.00 and average cost is $1.75. It has also observed that $1.75 is the lowest sustainable average cost given current technology and input prices. To maximize profit, this firm should:
   a. increase price.

b.   decrease price.

c.   decrease output and sales.

d.   leave price and output unchanged.

e.   perhaps do any of these things; the information given is insufficient to tell.

16.   Which alternative in question 15 would be correct had it specified that price rather than marginal revenue is $2.00?

a.

b.

c.

d.

e.

Consider the following hypothetical short-run data for Pepe's Pizza, a local monopolist in Somewhere, USA. Pepe's sells 8-inch cheese pies only. Please use the daily data given in Table 9-2 to answer questions 17 through 20.

TABLE 9-2

Quantity Demanded	Price	Total Cost
0	$10	$15
1	9	20
2	8	25
3	7	30
4	6	35
5	5	40

17.   The profit-maximizing output for Pepe's is:

a.   0.

b.   1.

c.   2.

d.   3.

e.   none of the above.

18.   The profit-maximizing price for Pepe's is

a. $5.

b. $6.

c. $7.

d. $8.

e.   none of the above.

19.   Pepe's fixed costs are:

a. $5.

b. $8.

c. $10.

d. $15.

e.   none of the above.

20.   At the profit-maximizing level of output and price, Pepe's will earn:

a.   economic profits of $21.

b.   economic profits of 0; total revenues will equal total costs.

c.   losses of $9, but Pepe's will stay in business.

d.   losses equal to his fixed costs.

e.   none of the above; Pepe's will be out of business, even in the short run.

21.   If the price a firm obtains for its output is higher than the marginal cost associated with that particular output, then maximum-profit rules require that the firm:

a.   increase its output in both perfect and imperfect competition.

b.   increase its output in perfect but not necessarily in imperfect competition.

c.   increase its output in imperfect but not necessarily in perfect competition.

d.   decrease its output in both perfect and imperfect competition.

e.   increase price, not output, in both perfect and imperfect competition.

22.   A correct statement of the relationship between marginal revenue (*MR*) and price elasticity of demand holds that *MR* is:

a.   negative when demand is inelastic.

b.   zero when demand is inelastic.

c.   positive when demand is inelastic.

d.   negative when demand displays unitary elasticity.

e.   negative when demand is perfectly elastic.

23.   Jim and Tish are trying to decide whether or not to go skiing tomorrow. They have season tickets to a local ski mountain. Jim and Tish should:

a.   definitely go skiing, since they have already spent money on the season pass.

b.   ski only if the price of the pass is less than the benefit they will receive from the additional day of skiing.

c.   ski only if the marginal benefit of the day will be greater than the marginal costs of the day.

d.   not ski, since the pass has already been paid for.

e.   not ski, unless they can get a free ride and a free lunch.

VII. PROBLEM SOLVING

The following problems are designed to help you apply the concepts that you learned in this chapter.

A. Patterns of Imperfect Competition

1.   There are two major sources of market imperfection.

a.   One, listed under the general rubric of "cost conditions," can be represented graphically. Figure 9-2 illustrates three different firm cost curves along with industry demand curves. Which of the panels in Figure 9-2 illustrates relative cost circumstances that might lead to imperfectly competitive market structures? ____.

The existence of "natural monopoly" (**does / does not**) fall under this classification of cost conditions; if it does, which panel illustrates natural monopoly? ____ What name should be attached to the structure suggested by panel (*b*)? _____

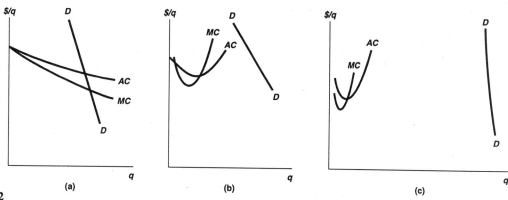

Figure 9-2

b. The second rubric is entitled "barriers to entry" and incorporates a variety of situations. Indicate with (B) in the blanks provided those items in the following list that can reasonably be included in this second category:

___ (1) 17-year patents for new products

___ (2) regulated entry into an industry

___ (3) tariff protection from foreign competitors

___ (4) imaginary product differentiation

___ (5) deliberate overinvestment in capacity to threaten new entrants with impossibly low price competition

c. In the case of product differentiation, the distinction between products (whether real or perceived) generates market power by moving the demand curve that the firm faces (**to the left / nowhere / to the right**) relative to the market demand curve for the general class of product. The result is that panel (**a / b / c**) of Figure 9-2 can become an appropriate representation of the firm's individual market situation.

B. Marginal Revenue and Monopoly

2. Columns (1) and (2) in Table 9-3 represent a demand schedule. Assume that a firm has done its market research accurately so that it knows all about this schedule and can thereby identify the quantities that it can sell at various prices. This firm must operate under conditions of (**perfect / imperfect**) competition, since as the output to be sold increases, price (**remains constant / must be reduced**). In fact, assume that this firm is a monopolist, and use these data to answer the following questions:

a. Column (3) of Table 9-3 shows total revenue. Complete the four blanks in this column. Use the figures in columns (2) and (3) to illustrate total revenue in the upper panel of Figure 9-3; i.e., show the total revenue associated with various output quantities. Join the points with a smooth curve.

b. Notice that the demand schedule becomes price-inelastic when price is sufficiently low—specifically,

when price falls below (**$6.00 / $5.50 / $5-00 / $4.50 / $4.00**).

TABLE 9-3

(1)	(2)	(3)	(4)	(5)	(6)
			Extra:		
		Total			Marginal
Price	Quantity	Revenue	Quantity	Revenue	Revenue
$14.00	10	$140			
			7	$64	$9.14
12.00	17	204			
			8	46	5.75
10.00	25	—			
			—	29	—
9.00	31	279			
			8	33	4.13
8.00	39	312			
			11	—	3.45
7.00	50	—			
			—	14	—
6.50	56	364			
			7	14	2.00
6.00	63	378			
			8	13	1.63
5.50	71	391			
5.00	80	—	—	—	—
			10	5	0 50
4.50	90	405			
			11	—	-0.09
4.00	101	—			
			—	-5	-0.38
3.50	114	399			

c. Table 9-4 shows the firm's total cost and marginal cost for production of the commodity whose demand curve is detailed in Table 9-3. Complete the four blanks in columns (3) and (4) of Table 9-4 with the proper figures.

d. The graph of columns (1) and (2) of Table 9-4 has already been drawn in the top panel of Figure 9-3 as a total cost curve (*TC*). Mark the curve that you drew earlier with "*TR*" to distinguish it from the cost curve. Now plot the marginal cost curve (denote it "*MC*") in

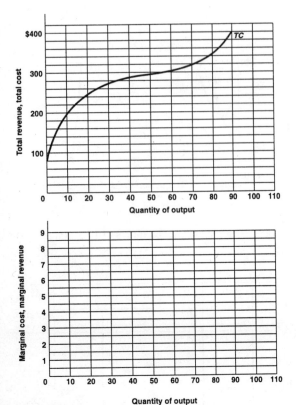

Figure 9-3

revenue curve (denote it *"MR"*) in the lower panel of Figure 9-3.

TABLE 9-4

(1) Output	(2) Total Cost	(3) Extra Cost	(4) MC per Unit
0	$90		
		$60	$12.00
5	150		
		35	7.00
10	185		
		30	6.00
15	215		
20	235	—	—
		15	3.00
25	250		
		12	2.40
30	262		
		10	2.00
35	272		
		8	1.60
40	280		
		6	1.20
45	286		
		5	1.00
50	291		
		4	0.80
55	295		
		5	1.00
60	300		
65	308	—	—
		10	2.00
70	318		
		12	2.40
75	330		
		15	3.00
80	345		
		20	4.00
85	365		
		35	7.00
90	400		

the bottom panel of Figure 9-3.

e. Figure 9-3 is too small to indicate the precise maximum-profit position, but it is sufficient to indicate that this best possible position is approximately (**45 / 65 / 85**) units of output.

f. Firms often consider the impact of a marginal change in production. If the firm were to find itself operating where *MR* (marginal revenue) falls short of *MC* (marginal costs), then it should (**increase / decrease**) its level of production and sales. The position where *MR* is (**less than / equal to / greater than**) *MC* represents a balance of marginal increments; it characterizes maximum profitability.

g. Column (4) in Table 9-3 shows the extra number of units sold as prices are reduced. Column (5) shows the extra revenue (positive or negative) that results from each price reduction. Complete the blanks in these two columns.

h. Although column (5) in Table 9-3 carries extra revenue figures, these are not *marginal* revenue figures, since *MR* is a per unit concept. The top figure in column (5), for example, is $64, but it came from an increase of 7 units sold. The $64 must be divided by 7 to get the *MR* figure of $9.14 in column (6). Complete the missing MR figures in column (6). Plot the marginal

i. The general profit-maximizing rule holds that firms expand their output until they reach the level where marginal cost equals marginal revenue. The approximate profit-maximizing level of output, using your diagram of marginal revenue and marginal cost, is ___.

j. To sell this output, the firm would charge a price of about (**$7.00 / $5.75 / $4.00 / $1.60**). Its total revenue would be roughly (**$380 / $580 / $780**). Total cost would be roughly (**$310 / $510 / $710**), leaving profit per period of about $70.

3. Figure 9-4 shows the per unit cost and revenue measures confronting a monopolist. The *DD* line is the market demand curve. *MR* is the corresponding market marginal revenue curve. *AC* is the firm's average cost curve, and *MC* represents the corresponding marginal cost schedule.

a. If output is 4, what must price be? ___.
b. What is marginal revenue at 4 units of output? ___.
c. At what level of output does average cost fall to its minimum level? ___.
d. What price would clear the market if output were set at this minimum AC level? ___.
e. What would total cost be at this level? ___.
f. What would total revenue be? ___.
g. What would profit be? ___.
h. At what output would profit be maximized? ___.
i. What is marginal revenue at this output? ___.
j. What is marginal cost at this output? ___.
k. What is average cost at this output? (Assume it is 20 cents above minimum level.) ___.
l. What is price at this output? ___.
m. What is total profit at this output? ___.

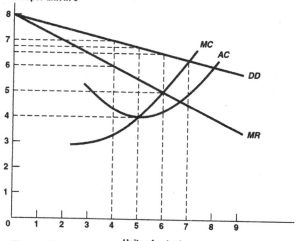

Figure 9-4

4. Consider another profit-maximizing-consultant problem, like the one you completed in Chapter 8. What would you recommend in each of the seven cases listed in Table 9-5? In each case, the firm in question is a monopoly and wants to maximize its profits (or minimize its losses). Enough information is supplied in each case, though you may have to fill in some of the blank spaces in the table to do your job. *Hint:* There is at least one "nonsense case," in which the figures are inconsistent and cannot be correct. Ferreting out such a circumstance could lead you to tell your client to do a better job in picturing either his or her market or cost structure.

Answer for each case by putting one of the numbers 1 through 5 from the code list below into the extreme right-hand column of the table. (The same number may of course be used for more than one question.)

1 = Firm is now at correct position.
2 = Firm should increase price and reduce quantity produced and sold.
3 = Firm should reduce price and increase quantity produced and sold.
4 = Firm should shut down operations because loss at best possible operating position exceeds fixed cost.
5 = A nonsense case—the figures supplied are inconsistent and could not all be correct.

5. In the section of the text headed "Let Bygones Be Bygones," it is emphasized that a firm, in setting output and price according to MR = MC, will disregard fixed cost. This does not mean that fixed cost can be ignored completely; maximum profits could be negative, for example, if fixed costs were too large. Nonetheless, in the determination of the profit-maximizing production/sales point, marginal revenue and marginal cost are the critical parameters.

a. Suppose that a monopolist's fixed costs increase, perhaps because a flat tax is levied against the firm's property. Would this tax raise the firm's AC curve? (**yes / no**)
b. Would the tax affect the monopolist's variable cost, or the AVC curve? (**yes / no**)
c. Would the tax affect the monopolist's marginal cost curve? (**yes / no**)
d. If the MC curve were unaffected, should such a flat tax change the maximum-profit output? (Presumably the tax would not affect output demand, so it would have no effect on marginal revenue.) (**yes / no / no, unless the firm is forced out of business**)
e. If the tax did not affect MC, MR, or maximum-profit output, would the price be changed? (**yes / no**)

TABLE 9-5

Case	Price	Marginal Revenue	Quantity of Output	Total Revenue	Total Cost	Fixed Cost	Average Cost	Marginal Cost	Answer
a.	$8.00	$4.00	2,000			$2,000	$4.00	$3.00	
b.	5.00	4.00	1,000		$4,000	1,000	At minimum level		
c.			4,000	$8,000			1.80	2.00	
d.	8.00	zero		32,000		5,000		4.00	
e.	1.00	2.00	10,000			2,000	2.00	2.00	
f.	3.00		2,000		6,000		At minimum level		
g.	2.50	2.00	10,000			4,000	3.00	2.00	

VIII. DISCUSSION QUESTIONS

Answer the following questions, making sure that you can explain the work you did to arrive at the answers.

1. List the continuum of industrial structures from perfectly competitive at one extreme to monopoly at the other. List examples of industries in the "real world" that you believe fit into these categories, and support your categorizations with evidence from the chapter. (Use examples other than those cited in your textbook.)

2. Table 9-2 in your textbook cites beer brewing as an industry in which significant economies of scale affect the production process and cost structure. Given these data, how can you explain the tremendous success of "microbreweries" (small, regional breweries) in the past decade? What has changed to allow these smaller firms to flourish?

3. Explain in your own words why the marginal revenue curve is downward-sloping, and why marginal revenue is less than price for each quantity of output.

4. Mr. Jones says, "If a firm does not produce at minimum average total cost in the long run, it will go out of business." Is this true for a monopolist? What factors exist to dampen the ability of a monopolist to extract ever higher profits?

5. OPEC, the international oil cartel, had a near monopoly on the world supply of oil in 1972. What demand-side factors led to the dissolution of this monopoly position? What supply-side factors led to the dissolution of this monopoly position?

IX. ANSWERS TO STUDY GUIDE QUESTIONS

III. Review of Key Concepts

14	Imperfect competition
4	Monopoly
8	Oligopoly
13	Monopolistic competition
2	Product differentiation
10	Economies of scale
3	Barriers to entry
12	Natural monopoly
1	Patents
7	Franchise monopoly
5	Import restrictions
11	Marginal revenue
6	The marginal principle
9	Sunk costs

VI. Multiple Choice Questions

1. A   2. E   3. A   4. C   5. A   6. E
7. E   8. A   9. D   10. A   11. A   12. C
13. C   14. E   15. B   16. E   17. D   18. C
19. D   20. C   21. B   22. A   23. C

VII. Problem Solving

1. a. A, does, A, oligopoly
   b. (1) B
      (2) B
      (3) B
      (4) B
      (5) B
   c. to the right, A

2. imperfect, must be reduced
   a. column 3 = $250, $350, $400, $404. See top panel of Figure 9-3.
   b. $4.50
   c. column 3 = $20, $8 column 4 = $4, $1.60
   d. See bottom panel of Figure 9-3.
   e. 65
   f. decrease, equal to
   g. column 4 = 6, 6, 9, 13
      column 5 = $38, $9, -$1.
   h. column 6 = $4.56, $2.33, $1.00. See bottom panel of Figure 9-3.
   i. 65
   j. $5.75, $380, $310

3. a. $7.00
   b. $6.00
   c. 5 units
   d. $6.75
   e. $20.00
   f. $33.75
   g. $13.75
   h. 6 units
   i. $5.00
   j. $5.00
   k. $4.20
   l. $6.50
   m. $13.80

4. a. $MR>MC$ means output should be increased; price will have to be reduced. Answer: 3.
   b. AC at a minimum means that $AC = MC$, in this case $AC = \$4.00$, and is equal to MR. Answer: 1.
   c. Price = TR/Q = $2.00. Since $MR<P$, output should be reduced to make MR equal to MC. Answer: 2.
   d. $MC>MR$, so output should be reduced. This firm is now maximizing revenue, not profit. Answer: 2.
   e. MR cannot exceed price. Answer: 5.
   f. $AC = TC/Q$ = $3.00. Since $\$3.00 = P>MR$, it must be that $MR<MC$. Answer: 2.
   g. $MR = MC$, so profit is maximum, but it is negative. $TR = \$2.50 \times 10,000 = \$25.000 < TC = AC \times Q = \$30,000$. Answer: 4.

5. a. yes
   b. no
   c. no
   d. no, unless the firm is forced out of business
   e. no

VIII. Discussion Questions

1.   Perfect competition > monopolistic competition > oligopoly > monopoly. Industries like agriculture and textiles might be perfectly competitive (without the government policies that affect these markets); industries like fast food and retail might be monopolistically competitive; industries like autos and steel might be oligopolistic; and industries like natural gas and electricity might be monopolistic.

2.   These small firms have been able to significantly differentiate their products and to convince consumers that their products are better than those produced by large firms. Changes in tastes and preferences among consumers have led to the success of these small breweries.

3.   The marginal revenue curve is downward-sloping because firms with monopoly power must lower price in order to sell additional units of output. Since there is a single market price, the monopolist must decrease price on all preceding units sold in order to lure additional buyers into the market. Thus, marginal revenue is always less than price.

4.   No this is not true for a monopolist. There are no competitive factors, or competitive pressures from potential entrants, that force the firm to produce with minimum average costs, even in the long run.

5.   Demand decreased due to changes in consumer behavior in many countries. Demand also became more elastic, as consumers had time to search for and develop suitable substitutes for oil-based products. On the supply side, the existence of economic profits for OPEC lured entrants into the market. Oil was discovered in the North Sea, in Mexico, and in Alaska; these new discoveries increased the worldwide supply of oil and eroded OPEC's monopoly power.

CHAPTER 10

Oligopoly and Monopolistic Competition

I. CHAPTER OVERVIEW

Chapter 10 explores various sources of monopoly power and the effect of imperfect competition on the marketplace. Although the measured degree of industrial concentration has declined in the United States in recent years, the ability of firms to differentiate their products produces monopoly power that has an important impact on market participants. Perfect competition provides consumers with the lowest prices and the highest levels of output, but concentration may lead to increases in research and innovation. Thus, evaluating the impact of imperfect competition is not an easy task.

As you work through this chapter, you will find that analysis of imperfect competition requires a solid understanding of both the perfectly competitive model and the monopoly model. Depending upon the nature of the firms in the industry, behavior may more closely follow one model than the other. For example, the market for personal computers is more like a perfectly competitive environment, while the market for automobiles is more like a monopoly environment. In any case, most "real world" markets can be placed somewhere along a continuum between the perfectly competitive and monopoly extremes.

Over the past century, policymakers in the United States have protected and served the interests of competition in most instances. A major question that must be considered as you work through this chapter is as follows: Do the benefits to competitive markets outweigh the costs of protecting and preserving them? Later chapters in the text will help you to develop a complete answer to this question.

II. LEARNING OBJECTIVES

After you have read Chapter 10 in your text and completed the exercises in this *Study Guide* chapter, you should be able to:

1. List the determinants of market power, and understand how cost structure, barriers to entry, and the potential for collusion influence the translation of that market power into a particular market structure of imperfect competition.

2. Understand the spectrum of imperfect competition, stretching from perfect competition at one extreme to monopoly at the other, and identify examples of industries which appear at various spots along the length of this spectrum.

3. Understand the potential risks and gains involved when a few firms collude to determine industry price and/or output. Use the model of cartel behavior to illustrate the effects of **tacit collusion** on markets.

4. Describe the importance of **game theory** for modeling firm behavior in noncollusive imperfectly competitive markets.

5. Conceptualize how profit-maximizing behavior in large firms might be compromised by the divorce of ownership from control. Translate profit-maximizing behavior from the theoretical models to the "real world" using **rules of thumb** like **cost-plus markup**, or using price discrimination.

6. Evaluate to your own satisfaction the **Schumpeterian hypothesis** that significant market power leads to extensive and socially desirable programs of research and development that would otherwise not be forthcoming.

7. Understand how imperfect competition leads to prices which exceed marginal cost, and use **deadweight loss** to evaluate the associated welfare cost.

8. Compare and contrast alternative intervention strategies that governments might pursue in order either to promote the emergence of competitive markets or to manage big business where it must exist due to the importance of economies of scale in production.

III. REVIEW OF KEY CONCEPTS

Match the following terms from column A with their definitions in column B.

A	B
__ Market power	1. The analysis of situations involving two or more decision makers who have conflicting objectives.

___ Concentration-
ratio

___ Herfindahl-
Hirschman Index

___ Strategic
interaction

___ Tacit collusion

___ Game theory

___ Price
discrimination

___ Separation of
ownership from
control

___ Markup
pricing

___ Schumpeterian
hypothesis

___ Inappropriability

___ Deadweight loss

___ Regulation

___ Antiturst policy

___ Collusive
oligopoly

2.   Pricing strategy in which firms take the expected average cost of a product and mark it up by a percentage.

3.   The loss in real income to both buyers and sellers that arises due to the existence of monopoly, tariffs, taxes, or other distortions.

4.   The percent of total industry output that is accounted for by the four (or eight) largest firms.

5.   Denotes a situation in which two or more firms jointly set their prices or outputs, divide the market among them, or make other business decisions jointly.

6.   Laws that prohibit certain kinds of anticompetitive behavior or restrict the emergence of highly concentrated industries.

7.   Occurs in large businesses in which the owners have given decision-making authority over to managers.

8.   Refers to the ability of a firm to control price and dominate other competitors in a market.

9.   General term that describes how each firm's business strategy depends upon its rivals' business behaviors.

10.   The inability of firms to capture the full monetary value of their inventions.

11.   Argues that the innovation produced by large firms more than offsets the losses brought about by too high prices.

12.   Allows specialized agencies to oversee the prices, outputs, entry, and exit of firms in certain industries.

13.   Occurs when firms refrain from competition without explicit agreements.

14.   The sum of the squares of the percentage market shares of all participants in a market.

15.   Occurs when the same product is sold to different consumers for different prices.

IV. SUMMARY AND CHAPTER OUTLINE

This section summarizes the key concepts from the chapter.

A. Behavior of Imperfect Competitors

1.   Declining costs and artificial or collusive barriers to entry can give firms operating in a particular market some degree of market power and thus some discretion over *both* quantity and price. One possible result is monopoly—a single seller of a particular commodity. Another possibility is oligopoly—a few sellers of the same product. Oligopolists need to be aware of the actions and reactions of other firms when they contemplate changes in their behavior. Monopolistic competition is a third possible structure, involving many sellers of close substitutes; long-run equilibrium here presents zero pure economic profit but inefficient cost allocations.

Market power can also be measured by the Herfindahl-Hirschman Index. The index is the sum of the squared market shares of all participants in the market. It differs from the concentration ratio in that it better reflects the existence of a single dominant firm in an industry with many smaller, or "fringe", producers. As this index approaches 10,000, the industry approaches monopoly. Both the CR and the HHI can be useful if one is trying to understand the degree of monopoly power that exists in an industry.

2.   Market power in an industry can be measured by *concentration ratios,* which define the percentage of total industry output that is controlled by the largest firms. (Concentration ratios are usually based on the largest four or eight firms, but can be calculated based upon any number of competitors.) As this percentage gets larger, the industry moves away from competition and toward monopoly.

3.   Oligopolists can try to collude in a way that mimics a monopoly supplier, but there are risks. Collusion is illegal in the United States, and in many other countries. Collusion presents circumstances in which it is profitable to cheat, but if all partners cheat, then every firm can end up worse off. *Cartels,* such as DeBeers in the diamond industry and OPEC in the oil industry, are collusive oligopoly arrangements that exist in international markets.

4.   Colluding oligopolists maximize their joint profits by producing where the marginal cost of each firm is set equal to the marginal revenue of market demand.

5.   Monopolistic competitors maximize profits where marginal cost equals the marginal revenue for their specific variant of product. Product differentiation occurs as each firm tries to design a product that has some unique characteristics, guaranteeing it some degree of monopoly power. Free entry and exit drive long-run equilibrium profits to zero, but because the monopolistic competitors' demand curves are downward-sloping, production will not occur at minimum average cost.

6. Rivalry exists in oligopolistic industries due to mutual interdependence. Modeling this rivalry is very difficult; industries tend to develop their own standards of behavior depending on the particular nature of the production and distribution process and on the demand for the product itself. *Game theory* is a method of analysis that is used in situations involving two or more decision makers who have conflicting objectives. Game theory can help us to understand and even to predict, in some cases, the behavior of rivals in an industry.

7. Price discrimination is a technique used by firms with monopoly power to extract additional consumer surplus. Price discrimination schemes occur when firms charge different consumers different prices for the same product. Firms want to charge higher prices to consumers whose demand is more inelastic.

B. Innovation and Information

1. In large firms, ownership is often divorced from control. This means that the owners of the firm have given decision-making authority over to a group of managers, who may or may not be operating in the best interest of the owners. Managers might be more interested in increasing their own salaries or improving their own working conditions than maximizing profits. Managers have less incentive to pay dividends; often it is in their own best interest to plow retained earnings back into the firm rather than to distribute them to owners.

2. Because of the difficulty in assessing actual market demand and cost structures a priori, firms approximate the profit-maximizing strategies that we have developed in theory by using *rules of thumb*. For example, *markup pricing rules* are strategies that set price at a percentage over estimated average production costs. This may land us exactly on the demand curve; the rules can be adjusted with experience to converge toward profit-maximizing pricing behavior in a world where managers do not operate with perfect information or certainty.

3. The Schumpeterian hypothesis suggests that large firms support valuable research and development that would not otherwise be forthcoming. However, in recent years small businesses have forged ahead, increasing their share of R&D advances. The real issue involves incentives for firms to innovate and to take risks. If firms believe that they will be unable to appropriate a significant portion of the benefits to R&D, they will be unwilling to make sufficient investments. Because information is costly to produce but cheap to reproduce, markets in information are subject to severe market failure. For example, markets for "bootlegged" computer programs exist in most countries around the world, making it more difficult for firms to justify large investments in new software.

C. The Balance Sheet on Imperfect Competition

1. Imperfect competitors generally produce too little and charge prices in excess of marginal cost. The welfare cost of their approach can be measured in terms of diminished consumer surplus—the *deadweight loss* that results from their exploiting whatever market power is available. The notion that big business exploits consumers is pervasive and so governments and policy-makers in the United States are encouraged to support competitive behavior.

2. Intervention strategies are used by governments as they attempt to preserve competitive markets. These include antitrust laws, regulation, government ownership or nationalization, price controls, and taxation. Regardless of their form, these actions all indicate a desire on the part of governments to encourage the efficiencies brought about by competition.

V. HELPFUL HINTS

1. As you learned in Chapter 9, entry barriers are important to the emergence of imperfect competition. However, notice that these barriers evolve over time. For example, IBM had a near monopoly in the market for computers throughout the 1960s and 1970s. Their economic profits encouraged entry by competitors; "Big Blue" was able to hold them at bay for years due to the fact that it was heavily invested in research and development. This led to large numbers of patents on new products. However, with the emergence of the personal computer around 1980, rivals burst into the market with a passion. Economic profits were soon eroded by fierce competition among firms in the industry, and IBM now sees itself fighting for market share.

2. Oligopoly behavior is very difficult to model, posing great challenges for economists. In oligopolistic industries, firms must explicitly recognize and react to their competitors. This mutual interdependence is one of the factors that makes modeling difficult. If you think about big industries in the U.S. economy, you can imagine why. Domestic airlines have a system of pricing that is mystifying to even the most knowledgeable travelers, auto producers use a complex and ever-changing system of rebates and financing incentives, and producers of breakfast cereals have an endless variety of products on the grocery store shelves. All of these industries are dominated by domestic oligopolies, requiring that firms be aware of the responses of competitors to changes in prices and output. Because of this mutual interdependence, economists have a wide class of models from which they can pick and choose when describing oligopoly behavior. There is no single model that can accurately generalize the actions and reactions of rivals.

3. Figure 10-6 in your textbook compares the long-run perfectly competitive market equilibrium with the long-run monopoly solution using the simplifying assumption that

marginal costs are fixed and constant. The result in no way depends upon this assumption. If marginal costs are upward-sloping, there is still a deadweight loss to monopoly. The assumption simply makes the illustration more clear.

VI. MULTIPLE CHOICE QUESTIONS

These questions are organized by topic from the chapter outline. Choose the best answer from the options available.

A. Behavior of Imperfect Competitors

1. Which of the following characteristics tends to prevail in highly concentrated markets?
    a.   Slightly higher than normal profits.
    b.   Above-average advertising expenditure.
    c.   Above-average research-and-development expenditure.
    d.   Below-average price flexibility.
    e.   All the above.

2. A concentration ratio describes the:
    a.   percentage of total industry sales accounted for by the largest four to eight firms.
    b.   percentage of total industry sales accounted for by the smallest four to eight firms.
    c.   degree of regulatory power that government policy-makers have over an industry.
    d.   degree of decision-making power that the owners of a firm have.
    e.   significance of antitrust policy in a particular industry.

Please use the following data to answer questions 3 and 4. Suppose the market for toy trains is composed of seven competitors with the following market shares;

Little Toot Toys	55%	Trains R Us	3%
I Think I can	25%	Thomas Trains	3%
Engines Inc.	8%	The Fastest Trains	2%
Silver Streak	4%		

3. In this industry, the four-firm concentration ratio is:
    a.   .12
    b.   .92
    c.   3730
    d.   3752
    e.   none of the above

4. In this industry, the Herfindahl-Hirschman Index is:
    a.   .12
    b.   .92
    c.   3730
    d.   3752
    e.   none of the above

5. Which of the following represents a contrived but nonetheless legal barrier to entry that might support an oligopolistic market structure?
    a.   Price setting below the lowest price which a potential new entrant could afford to charge.

b.   A tariff that keeps all but a trickle of foreign products off the domestic market.
    c.   Product differentiation among a few producers.
    d.   Average cost curves that reach their minima at roughly 30 percent of market demand.
    e.   All the above.

6. Which alternative to question 5 would have been correct if the barrier to entry were a cost barrier?
    a.
    b.
    c.
    d.
    e.

7. Which alternative to question 5 represents an illegal barrier to entry that might support an oligopolistic structure?
    a.
    b.
    c.
    d.
    e.

8. OPEC represents a market structure most accurately represented by:
    a.   the pure monopoly model.
    b.   a collusive oligopoly model with incomplete market coverage.
    c.   the monopolistic competition model.
    d.   the duopoly model.
    e.   perfect competition.

9. Which alternative to question 8 would have been correct if the market in question had been the market for soybeans?
    a.
    b.
    c.
    d.
    e.

10. If we consider an industry composed of many sellers of differentiated products, and if entry into this industry is free, then we should expect the long-run equilibrium position of the typical firm in this industry to have which of the following properties?
    a.   Average cost (AC) would be at its minimum possible level, and the price charged (P) would be equal to that AC.
    b. AC would be at its minimum level, and P would be above that AC.
    c. AC would be above its minimum level, and P would be above that AC.
    d. AC would be above its minimum level, and P would be equal to that AC.
    e. AC would be above its minimum level, but P would equal that minimum.

11. Suppose Figure 10-1 (top of next page) represents the demand and cost conditions for an industry operating as

an international cartel. The profit-maximizing price and output for this industry are:
a. $5 and 10 units.
b. $2 and 10 units.
c. $4 and 20 units.
d. $4 and 15 units.

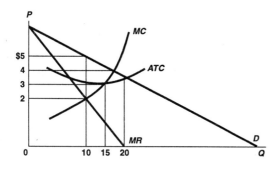

Figure 10-1

e. none of the above.
12. A firm in the industry described in question 11 is a:
a. monopolistic competitor.
b. collusive oligopolist.
c. noncollusive oligopolist.
d. perfect competitor.
e. single monopolist.
13. Price discrimination is a technique used by firms who want to:
a. capture the deadweight loss to monopoly.
b. capture additional consumer surplus by charging different prices to different consumers.
c. relinquish producer surplus by charging different prices to different consumers.
d. increase producer surplus by buying their inputs from the lowest-price provider.
c. none of the above

B. Innovation and Information

14. Ownership and control are sometimes divorced in a large corporation. Which of the following problems might arise as a result?
a. Managers might try to increase their own salaries and benefits rather than to maximize the profits of the firm.
b. Managers tend to be less likely to distribute profits as dividends rather than reinvest in the company.
c. Managers are often more risk-seeking than owners, leading to a greater degree of uncertainty than owners would prefer.
d. Both A and B are true.
e. None of the above.

15. One reason why a firm operating under conditions of imperfect competition is likely to want to use an administered or markup price is:
a. a lack of sufficient knowledge of marginal revenue at various levels of output.
b. a lack of sufficient knowledge of marginal cost at various levels of output.
c. the desire to have a break-even point occurring at a high level of output.
d. the fear that charging a higher price would attract new competition into the field.
e. the notion that this price corresponds to the most efficient plant output level.
16. The Schumpeterian hypothesis is:
a. big business is not necessarily bad business.
b. firms never really have any power to set prices, since demand curves must be considered.
c. research and development is more efficiently supported by a consortium of government, small business, and big business.
d. innovation would be accelerated if *managers* of large firms were required to be *owners* of large firms.
e. all the above.
17. In the past few years, the banking industry in the United States has experienced increasing concentration, as new banking regulations have allowed mergers across state lines. According to the Schumpeterian hypothesis, this increased concentration is:
a. good, because it leads to a redistribution of income from the wealthy to the poor.
b. good, because increased concentration creates external benefits in the area of innovation.
c. bad, because the banks involved are more likely to go bankrupt.
d. bad, because banks should be governed by local banking laws.
e. possibly good or bad, depending upon the profitability of the banks that are merging.

C. The Balance Sheet on Imperfect Competition

18. In light of the pros and cons of imperfect competition, policy could be directed at:
a. keeping the barriers to competition low.
b. attacking anticompetitive business conduct.
c. tolerating bigness if it is founded in technology.
d. encouraging the research-and-development efforts of large and small firms.
e. all the above.
Use Figure 10-2 (top of next page) to answer questions 19 through 23.
19. A profit-maximizing monopolist facing demand curve *DD* would maximize profits by selling:

a. 4 units at a price of $2.
b. 4 units at a price of $6.
c. 8 units at a price of $2.
d. 10 units at a price of $2.
e. 5 units at a price of $5.

20. Which answer to question 19 would have been the correct description of the competitive equilibrium?

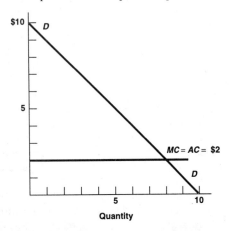

Figure 10-2

   a.
   b.
   c.
   d.
   e.

21. Which answer to question 19 would have been correct if the monopolist were trying to maximize revenue?
   a.
   b.
   c.
   d.
   e.

22. The monopolist of question 19 creates distortions whose welfare cost, measured in terms of consumer surplus, equals:
   a. $2.
   b. $4.
   c. $6.
   d. $8.
   e. $10.

23. Unlike antitrust laws, regulation:
   a. allows monopolies and near-monopolies to exist under the watchful eye of a government agency.
   b. breaks monopolized industries into many small firms which then operate competitively.
   c. places heavy taxes on firms to provide them with incentives to do the right thing.
   d. encourages government ownership, or nationalization, of industries that have been monopolized.

   e. provides firms with the capital that they need to pursue research and development of new products.

VII. PROBLEM SOLVING

The following problems are designed to help you apply the concepts that you learned in this chapter.

A. Behavior of Imperfect Competitors

1. Empirical research has uncovered patterns of correlation between the degree of concentration displayed by various industries and nonproduction activities such as research and development, advertising, and price administration.

Using the letters given, indicate in the blanks below whether the following descriptions most likely apply to a:
   a. High-concentration industry (H) like motor vehicles
   b. Moderate-concentration industry (M) like chemicals
   c. Low-concentration industry (L) like printing
   d. Perfectly competitive industry (P) like farming

___ a. Industry A shows a normal profit rate, high expenditure on research and development as well as advertising (each around 1.7 percent of total sales), and a moderate level of price administration.

___ b. Industry B shows negligible expenditure on research and development (measured as a percentage of total sales), negligible expenditure on advertising, and no price administration.

___ c. Industry C shows no economic profits in the long run, small expenditure on research and development as well as advertising (each less than 1 percent of total sales), but the highest level of price administration.

___ d. Industry D shows a normal profit rate, the highest expenditure on research and development, expenditure on advertising that is comparable to that of industry C, and a high degree of price administration.

2. Consider the hypothetical data in Table 10-1. This represents the market share of the top eight firms in this industry in 1995 and again in 2000.

TABLE 10-1

Firm	1995 Market Share	2000 Market Share
A	10%	30%
B	8	6
C	12	12
D	20	30
E	21	10
F	2	1
G	5	3
H	6	1

   a. Calculate the four-firm concentration ratios for 1995 and 2000. What happened in this industry over this time period?

b.   Calculate the eight-firm concentration ratios for 1995 and 2000. Do these calculations give you a different notion of developments in this industry over this time period?

c.   Calculate the Herfindahl-Hirschman Indexes for 1995 and 2000. What does this index tell you about changes in concentration in this industry over this time period?

3.   As stated above, oligopoly behavior is characterized by mutual interdependence; that is, rivals in an oligopolistic market must be constantly aware of one another's behavior. In Figure 10-3, *DD* represents the effective demand curve facing some oligopolist who abides by a collusive agreement with a few competitors. It could, for example, be the result of a consistent 30 percent share of total sales for any price along a market demand curve. Notice that every reduction of $1 in the price produces, for the firm when all other firms conform, an increase in sales of 10 units. Marginal revenue is given by *MR*. Average cost and marginal cost are assumed, for simplicity only, to be constant at $4 per unit regardless of output level.

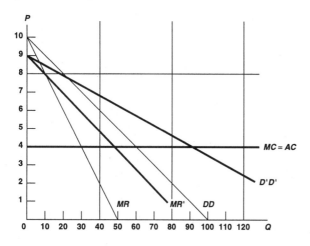

Figure 10-3

a.   On the basis of the assumption of perfect collusion, the firm will maximize profits along *DD* by agreeing to a price of $___, therefore selling ___ units and earning profits of $___.

b.   Now suppose that the firm could, by lowering its price relative to that of its colluding partners (i.e., by cheating on its collusive agreement), pick up an extra 20 units of sales for every $1 reduction in price. It could, in other words, increase its market share at the expense of other firms by lowering its price alone. The resulting demand and marginal revenue curves are represented in Figure 10-3 by *D'D'* and *MR'*, respectively. The firm could, in this case, move to a new profit-maximizing

position by (**reducing / maintaining / increasing**) its price to $___ and selling ___ units. The result would be $___ in profits.

c.   It is, of course, highly unlikely that the other firms would not catch on. Suppose, in response to the cheating of the first firm, that all the other firms changed their prices to the cheater's new price. DD would again be relevant, and the cheating firm's profits would fall to $___ as sales declined to ___ units.

d.   It is clear, therefore, that successful cheating is better for a single firm than is successful collusion, but cheating entails the risk of reducing profitability if all firms catch on and follow the behavior of cheaters to protect themselves. Were the process to continue, in fact, the firms would, collectively, end up producing the (**competitive / monopoly**) output and selling it at the (**competitive / monopoly**) price. In terms of Figure 10-3, price would converge to $___, output would converge to ___ units, and pure economic profit would converge to $___.

B. Innovation and Information

4.   a.   For a monopoly firm facing demand curve *DD* in Figure 10-4, profits would be maximized by setting a price equal to $___ and expecting to sell ___ units. Relative to average cost, that price amounts to a ___ percent markup over cost.

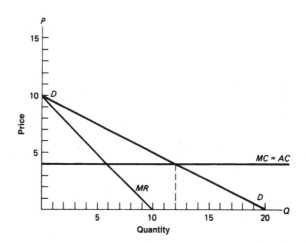

Figure 10-4

b.   Now complete Table 10-2 to convince yourself that a sequence of trial markup percentages could lead a careful manager to the profit-maximizing intersection of *MR* and *MC* without computing either schedule.

5.   The Schumpeterian hypothesis about the large firms which dominate imperfectly competitive markets postulates that "big business may have had more to do with creating our (high) standard of life than (with) keeping it down." This

hypothesis is based, at least in part, upon the notion that (**research-and-development expenditure / purchasing power / real competition**) seems to be concentrated most heavily in the largest firms on the American scene. Since Edwin Mansfield has argued that the social return to invention is (**3 / 0.5 / 5**) times the private gain, it can certainly be argued that research and development is (**overfunded / properly funded / underfunded**). However, the extent of underfunding depends critically upon the nature of innovation and the ability of firms to appropriate the gains to expensive research and development projects. Particularly when the (**average / total / marginal**) costs of reproducing an idea or product approach zero, high fixed costs of innovation may pay slim rewards to the deserving firm or individual.

TABLE 10-2

Percentage Markup over Cost	Price	(units)	Output Profit
60	$___	___	$___
80	___	___	___
100	___	___	___
120	___	___	___
110	___	___	___
105	___	___	___

C. The Balance Sheet on Imperfect Competition

6. It has been shown throughout Chapters 9 and 10 that $P > MR$ along a downward-sloping demand curve, and $MR = MC$ at the profit-maximizing output.

　　a. As a result, the price which a monopolist charges is (**higher than / lower than / equal to**) the competitive price.

　　b. Since monopolistic firms face downward-sloping demand curves, the monopolist must therefore produce (**less output than / more output than / the same output as**) the competitive industry would produce.

　　c. On the basis of the efficiency properties of the perfectly competitive market, it is thus clear that the marginal utility derived from consuming the monopolist's product is (**greater than / less than / equal to**) the marginal cost of producing the good in question.

　　d. Consult Figure 10-5. If the illustrated cost structure were representative of a *competitive market,* the long-run equilibrium output and price must equal ___ units and $___, respectively. A profit-maximizing monopolist would, meanwhile, sell ___ units at a price of $___. The result would be a reduction in consumer surplus from $___ to $___. Of that reduction, $___ would go to the monopolist in the form of excess economic profit, and $___ would represent deadweight loss.

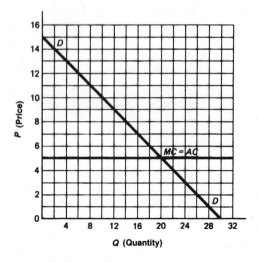

Figure 10-5

VIII. DISCUSSION QUESTIONS

Answer the following questions, making sure that you can explain the work you did to arrive at the answers.

1. Studies show that the measured degree of concentration in U.S. industry has been decreasing in recent years. What do you think Schumpeter would say about this trend?

2. In a monopolistically competitive market, the long-run position occurs where firms are earning no economic profits. However, firms are not at the minimum of their long-run average cost curves. How can this be? Why do some people charge that monopolistic competition leads to waste and inefficiency? What, if anything, do consumers gain when they purchase products from monopolistically competitive industries?

3. The DeBeers diamond syndicate is an example of a highly successful international cartel. Using the theory developed in the text, illustrate the profit-maximizing decision of competitors in this industry. Why might competitors decide to cheat? What impact might the emergence of Russia as an international competitor, but nonmember of the cartel, have on the stability of agreements?

4. What is the difference between collusive and noncollusive oligopoly in the United States? Why is collusive oligopoly illegal?

5. List and explain the alternative government policies that might be used to encourage competition in U.S. industry. If Schumpeter is correct, should these policies be adopted? Why or why not?

IX. ANSWERS TO STUDY GUIDE QUESTIONS

III. Review of Key Concepts

8	Market power
4	Concentration ratio
14	Herfindahl-Hirschman Index
1	Strategic interaction
13	Tacit collusion
9	Game theory
15	Price discrimination
7	Separation of ownership from control
2	Markup policy
11	Schumpeterian hypothesis
10	Inappropriability
3	Deadweight loss
12	Regulation
6	Antitrust policy
5	Collusive oligopoly

VI. Multiple Choice Questions

1. E   2. A   3. B   4. D   5. C   6. D
7. A   8. B   9. E   10. D   11. A   12. B
13. B   14. D   15. A   16. A   17. B   18. E
19. B   20. C   21. E   22. B   23. A

VII. Problem Solving

1. a. M
   b. P
   c. L
   d. H
2. a. 4-firm ratios: 63% in 1995, 82% in 2000. These numbers indicate that the industry has become more heavily concentrated during this time period.
   b. 8-firm ratios: 84% in 1995, 93% in 2000. These numbers again indicate that the industry has become more heavily concentrated during this time period. However, the change in the 8-firm ratio is not as dramatic, indicating that the degree of concentration has not changed as much as is indicated by the 4-firm ratio.
   c. 1995 HHI = 1214, 2000 HHI = 2091. Using the HHI, market concentration has increased over this time period.
3. a. $7, 30 units, $90
   b. reducing, $6.25, 45 units, $101.25
   c. $78.75, 35 units
   d. competitive, competitive, $4, 90 units, $0
4. a. $8, 6 units, 100%
   b. Table answers:
   Row 1 = $ 8, 14 units, $42 profits
   Row 2 = $ 9, 12 units, $48 profits
   Row 3 = $10, 10 units, $50 profits
   Row 4 = $11, 8 units, $48 profits

Row 5 = $10.50, 9 units, $49.50 profits
Row 6 = $10.25, 9.5 units, $48.88 profits
5. research-and-development expenditure, 3, underfunded, marginal
6. a. higher than
   b. less output than
   c. greater than
   d. 20 units, $5, 10 units, $10, $100, $25, $50, $25.

VIII. Discussion Questions

1. Schumpeter might be concerned about this trend. In his view, the existence of "big business" allows for greater amounts of research and innovation in an economy. He might fear that excessive levels of competition would lead to even less basic research than exists in the U.S. today.
2. All firms in a monopolistically competitive industry operate with *excess capacity*; this means that each firm reaches the profit-maximizing level of output before average total costs are minimized, in the long run. This leads to the charge that firms are wasteful and inefficient. There are many firms, each producing a slightly different version of the product. This product differentiation leads to costs of production that are higher than would be generated by a perfectly competitive industry. Consumers gain product variety and a wider range of choice in these markets.
3. See diagram.

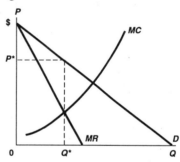

The cartel will produce Q^* units of output and sell it at P^* per unit. Competitors might decide to cheat if they think that they can lower price and increase sales without attracting the attention of other cartel members. As Russia enters this market as a competitor, the DeBeers cartel will suffer, unless it can pull Russia into the cartel. Successful cartels must maintain control over the supply of the product.
4. In a collusive oligopoly, members make agreements concerning market strategy and share information. In a non-collusive oligopoly, members consider the behavior of rivals, but they do not actually discuss strategy. Collusive oligopoly is illegal because it severely limits competition among rivals.
5. To encourage competition, the government might make all monopolies illegal. The government might break up large firms into several small firms. The government might refuse

to allow mergers when the merging firms operate in the same markets. According to Schumpeter, these actions all limit the size and scope of firms, and hence limit their incentives to be innovative.

CHAPTER 11

Uncertainty and Game Theory

I. CHAPTER OVERVIEW

In our discussions up to this point, firms and households have approached their decisions armed with complete and perfect information; actors in the economic play, in short, have been blessed with a clear picture of their economic circumstance and an equally clear portrait of the ramifications of their decisions. It is, however, never that easy. In real life, imprecise and fuzzy perceptions of economic circumstance complicate every decision, and economists have begun to consider seriously the effects of these complications. Chapter 11 introduces you to two major avenues of analysis.

Section A looks into decisions made under circumstances of uncertainty from two sources. The first is derived from the fact that the future is unknown. The best information available is frequently no better than a collection of possible futures with no prospect of resolution before a decision must be made. The second is derived from the potential that sudden and unforeseen events might dramatically alter even the basic components of an actor's economic condition. Hedging, speculation, and insurance all come into play in this arena.

Section B takes explicit note of the interdependence of decisions taken by more than one actor. The range of outcomes that one person must consider as he or she makes a specific decision can easily depend not only upon prior decisions by other people but also upon their response to the very decision being considered. Economists have long applied game-theoretic constructs to the analysis of strategic interaction among decisions, and those applications are now being assimilated into mainstream economic theory even as they grow significantly in number.

II. LEARNING OBJECTIVES

After you have read Chapter 11 in your text and completed the exercises in this *Study Guide* chapter, you should be able to:

1. Define a role in the economy for **speculators, arbitrage**, and **hedging.**
2. Illustrate the relationship between **risk aversion** and **diminishing marginal utility of income,** and apply

these concepts to the notion of **risk spreading** in insurance and capital markets.
3. Understand the importance of **moral hazard** and **adverse selection** in establishing insurance markets that function properly.
4. Define and interpret the basic terms used in **game theory: players, strategies, payoffs,** and **payoff tables.**
5. Use payoff tables to describe optimal strategies for players in a game. Find a **dominant strategy** for a firm, if one exists.
6. Use payoff tables to describe the concept of **Nash equilibrium** as a noncooperative solution to a game. Apply these concepts to "real world" scenarios in which unregulated markets may or may not lead to efficient equilibria.

III. REVIEW OF KEY CONCEPTS

Match the following terms from column A with their definitions in column B.

A	B
__ Speculation	1. Implies that the displeasure from losing a given amount of income is greater than the pleasure from gaining the same amount of income.
__ Arbitrage	2. The profits (or losses) earned when a particular set of strategies are pursued.
__ Hedging	3. Arises when the people with the highest risk are the most likely ones to buy insurance.
__ Risk aversion	4. Occurs when each player in a game chooses his or her own strategy without collusion or cooperation.
__ Diminishing marginal utility of income	5. Actions or sets of actions that a player follows.
__ Risk spreading	6. Each additional dollar that an individual earns brings less additional utility.

141

___ Moral hazard

___ Adverse selection

___ Players

___ Strategies

___ Payoffs

___ Nash equilibrium

___ Dominant
     strategy

___ Noncooperative
     equilibrium

___ Cooperative
     equilibrium

___ Winner-take-all
     games

___ Credibility

7.   Involves making profits from the fluctuations in prices.

8.   Occurs when no player can improve his or her payoff given the other player's strategy.

9.   Economic agents, or actors, who are engaged in strategic behavior.

10. Implies that individuals who own insurance engage in riskier behavior than they would engage in without insurance.

11. The purchase of a good or asset in one market for immediate resale in another market.

12. Takes risks that would be large for one person and spreads them around so that they are small risks for a large number of people.

13. The activity of avoiding a risk by making a counteracting sale or investment.

14. Arises when one player has a best strategy no matter what strategy the other player follows.

15. Situations in which the payoffs are determined primarily by relative merit.

16. Exists when players are expected to keep promises and carry out threats.

17. Comes when players act in unison to find strategies that will maximize their joint payoffs.

IV. SUMMARY AND CHAPTER OUTLINE

This section summarizes the key concepts from the chapter.

A. Economics of Risk and Uncertainty

1. In the "real world" life is filled with uncertainty and risks. Some of these risks are more important than others, to be sure, but almost every decision that we make as economists involves some degree of uncertainty about the course of future events. Uncertainty means that we do not know for sure what the future holds, while risk implies that there is some probability that an unfavorable event will occur in the future.

2. Due to the existence of uncertainty, *speculators* look to buy low and sell high across geographically defined markets, across time, and across states of nature. Speculators often exchange goods without taking possession of them; the point is not to buy what they need to use but rather to buy what can fetch a higher price in the future.

3. Speculators have three important functions. First, they buy goods in regions in which they are abundant and sell them in regions in which they are relatively scarce. For example, a speculator might buy apples from small farmers in Washington State and sell them to grocers in Arizona. This redistributes goods from areas in which oversupply would drive prices down to areas in which undersupply would drive prices up, and thus helps to equalize prices across markets.

Second, speculators buy goods when they are in abundance and commanding relatively low prices and sell them later when they are more scarce and commanding relatively high prices. This lowers supply in times of abundance, raises the supply in times of scarcity, and smoothes prices over time, providing greater stability in markets. For example, a speculator might buy the same apples from small farmers in Washington State during the month of September when apples are plentiful; after storing them for six months, the speculator might then resell the apples to an applesauce company, when apples are much less plentiful. This helps to smooth prices over the product's life cycle. This behavior is referred to as *arbitrage*.

Third, speculators engage in *hedging*. This involves the speculator in absorbing risks that others do not want to bear. For example, if the small orchard owners are afraid that the price of apples will fall precipitously before they get their crops to market, they might decide to sell the future crop to the speculator in June for a fixed price. The speculator actually purchases the crop in September for the agreed-upon price, hoping to immediately resell for a profit. Thus, the farmer is able to limit his or her uncertainty, and the speculator is left with the potential profits or losses on the sale of the apples.

4. The self motivated actions of speculators and arbitragers tend to moderate price and consumption instability in a wide variety of markets. Acting in their own individual best interest, these people generate an improvement in social welfare above and beyond the level of their individual gains. The source of this gain can be found in the principle of diminishing marginal utility, because it is diminishing marginal utility that leads to the conclusion that stable consumption is economically beneficial. The underlying point is simply put: Starting at some average level of consumption, *diminishing marginal utility* means that an increase in utility generated by the next unit of consumption is *smaller than* the increase in utility generated by the previous unit of consumption. When a product is abundant, marginal utility and prices are low; when a product is scarce, marginal utility and prices are high. By smoothing consumption over time and space, speculators are able to dampen these price swings, leading to greater economic efficiency.

5. A person is *risk-averse* when the displeasure from losing a given amount of income is greater than the pleasure from gaining the same amount of income. Simpler put, a risk-

averse individual experiences *diminishing marginal utility of income* due to the fact that an additional dollar will bring less utility than the previous dollar. The individual will lose more utility with the loss of a dollar than he or she would gain from acquiring a dollar. Therefore, a person who is risk-averse prefers a sure thing, or a "dollar in hand," to uncertain levels of consumption, other things equal.

6. Insurance companies are involved in *risk spreading*. This means that they take what would be a large risk for any single person and "pool" it, or spread it across a large number of people so that each individual's share is relatively small. For example, most people who own cars buy auto insurance. In fact, some states require owners to purchase insurance. There is some probability that any single driver will have an accident on any given day; that probability is higher for some people and in some areas. Insurance companies spread this risk over a larger number of people and across a wider area. Risk-averse individuals are willing to pay premiums, at least to some degree, to avoid the risk of an uncertain future. Private insurance markets can exist when there are many independent events and when there is little chance of moral hazard and/or adverse selection. Social insurance is sometimes provided in situations which cannot support private insurance markets.

In capital markets, this same principle holds. Oftentimes, a new venture is too risky for a single investor, but a group of investors working together may each be willing to accept a smaller share of the total risk.

7. Sometimes markets fail because people do not have perfect information about the uncertainty and risks that they face. *Moral hazard* occurs when ownership of insurance reduces an individual's incentive to avoid risky behavior. For example, knowing he has insurance, a particular motorist might drive faster than he otherwise would. *Adverse selection* occurs because the people who buy insurance are often those most likely to need it. The example in your text on health insurance is a good one. In the United States, most people who own health insurance are relatively wealthy and/or sick. Hence, the pool of insured people is not representative of the entire population; those who consider themselves relatively healthy may use their money on other things and forgo insurance. This drives rates up for those in the pool, and limits the gains to insurance.

8. In summary, efficient insurance markets can operate (a) when there exist many independent events or states of nature and (b) when there is little chance of moral hazard and/or adverse selection. Governments sometimes intervene by providing social insurance when private markets fail to operate.

B. Game Theory

1. Economic life is full of circumstances in which competition among a few individuals, firms, or even nations degenerates into a process of jockeying for positions of strategic dominance. *Game theory* has been applied by economists to provide the structure for systematic analysis of these sorts of situations. The basic structure involves (a) identifying the *players,* (b) specifying the various actions or *strategies* available to each player, and (c) completing a *payoff table* which records the outcomes of each combination of players' strategies.

2. Underlying this structure is the notion that all players (a) identify their individual goals, (b) recognize the goals of the other player(s), and (c) think through all the possible outcomes for each and every possible strategy. Players then pick the strategy with the highest payoff relative to their goals, assuming that the other players do likewise. (Note that in some situations, there may only be two players in the game.)

3. There sometimes exists a *dominant strategy* for a given player—a strategy which provides the best outcome regardless of what the other players do. If all players have a dominant strategy, then the game is solved by a dominant equilibrium.

4. Equilibria are more frequently *Nash* in character—that is, no player can make himself or herself better off by switching strategies, given the actions of the other players. Cooperative and noncooperative equilibria can then exist; with cooperative equilibrium, firms collude to determine the best strategies to pursue, while with noncooperative equilibrium, each firm pursues its optimal strategy without accounting for the welfare of rivals.

5. Perfect competition in the absence of externalities supports a noncooperative Nash equilibrium which is efficient. In many other situations, however, a cooperative equilibrium, which must be supported by some sort of intervention, can be socially superior to the noncooperative Nash equilibrium.

V. HELPFUL HINTS

1. Some people claim that speculators and arbitragers perform no productive function in an economy because, rather than producing any good or service, they simply buy and sell existing products. However, it is important not to understate the importance of the service that they provide to a market economy. Large supply fluctuations over time would lead to price volatility and to much greater uncertainty in markets. This in turn could lead to higher prices for consumers and to fewer consumers in general. The stability provided by these economic agents provides benefits to all agents in the market.

2. The term *expected value is* used throughout this chapter. You will learn more about it in a later chapter. For now, note that the expected value of an event is the weighted average of the possible outcomes where the probabilities of occurrence serve as weights. For example, when you toss a

coin, there are two possible outcomes: heads or tails. Each of these outcomes has a 50 percent chance of occurring. With the $1000 bet described in your textbook, you will win $1000 if the coin turns up heads and lose $1000 if the coin turns up tails. The expected value of the event is:

$$.5 (\$1000) + .5 (- \$1000) = 0$$

Expected utility can be calculated in the same way. The challenge, as always with utility, is to find some acceptable measure of utility to use in the calculation.

3.   Game theory is an exciting and relatively new area of economic analysis. It allows us to consider the kind of mutual interdependence that is pervasive in economic life. Most often, individual decisions about resource allocation are dependent upon the decisions made by others; most often, firm decisions concerning price and output are affected by the behavior of rivals or potential rivals. Hence game-theoretic concepts have been applied in a wide range of areas, from union-management bargaining, to household and family behavior, to international trade wars, to public policy and optimal taxation.

4.   Students sometimes have trouble differentiating between a Nash equilibrium and a dominant strategy for players. The key here is that a Nash equilibrium occurs when no player can improve his or her payoff *given the other player's strategy*. A dominant strategy occurs when one player has a best strategy *no matter what strategy the other player follows*. With Nash, we are saying that a firm is doing the best it can based upon what rivals are doing. With a dominant strategy, we are saying that a firm is doing the best it can.

VI. MULTIPLE CHOICE QUESTIONS

These questions are organized by topic from the chapter outline. Choose the best answer from the options available.

A. Economics Risk and of Uncertainty

1.   Speculation involves:

a.   buying inputs that your firm will use to produce final goods and services.
b.   knowledge of future events with certainty.
c.   riskless activities.
d.   making profits from the fluctuations in prices.

2.   Speculative activity tends to:
a.   spread consumption more evenly over time.
b.   concentrate consumption in particular regions in which production is most abundant.
c.   spread consumption more evenly across regions or areas.
d.   increase volatility of prices.
e.   both **a** and **c**.

3.   The welfare gain associated with smoothing consumption is derived from:
a.   diminishing income effects.
b.   increasing returns to scale.
c.   the law of comparative advantage.
d.   diminishing marginal utility.
e.   increasing marginal productivity.

Panels (*a*) and (*b*) of Figure 11-1 show the demand for some good *Y* in two separate regions of the country—regions A and B. There are 4 units of *Y* supplied initially to region A and 5 units supplied to region B. Use Figure 11-1 to answer questions 4 through 6.

4.   The welfare-maximizing transfer of *Y* would, in this case, without any transportation cost, involve moving:
a.   2 units of *Y* from A to B.
b.   2 units of *Y* from B to A.
c.   1 unit of *Y* from B to A.
d.   1 unit of *Y* from A to B.
e.   all the *Y* units to region A.

5.   The increase in total welfare generated by the maximally efficient transfer of *Y* identified in question 4 is equal to:
a. $1.
b. $2.
c. $3.
d. $4
e. $5.

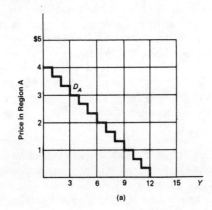
(a)

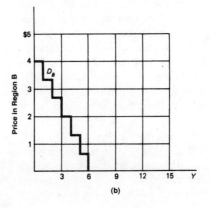
(b)

Figure 11-1

6. The transfer of no units of Y would be welfare-maximiz-
    ing if the cost of transporting each unit from one region
    to the other were greater than:
    a. $0.67.
    b. $1.00.
    c. $1.33.
    d. $1.67.
    e. $2.00.
7. In general, total welfare is maximized across space,
    time, or states of nature in the absence of transfer costs
    when the:
    a. marginal utilities of consumption are equal every-
        where.
    b. level of consumption is equal everywhere.
    c. total utility derived from consumption is equal
        everywhere.
    d. total value added in production is equal everywhere.
    e. slopes of the demand curves are equal everywhere.
    Suppose that Table 11-1 describes Janet's utility func-
    tion for income. Use it to answer questions 8 and 9.

TABLE 11-1

	Income	Total Utility
	$ 5,000	100
	10,000	250
	15,000	450
	20,000	600
	25,000	700
	30,000	750

8. The marginal utility of the 20,000th dollar is:
    a. .03 utils.
    b. 33.33 utils.
    c. 150 utils.
    d. 5000 utils.
    e. none of the above.
9. Janet is:
    a. indifferent to risk.
    b. risk seeking.
    c. risk averse.
    d. uncertain about risk.
    e. satiated with money.
    An individual has an income of $1000 and possesses the
    utility schedule shown in Figure 11-2. Use this schedule to
    answer questions 10 through 12.
10. Suppose this person faces a 50 percent chance of losing
    $100. Her expected utility would equal:
    a. 50 utils.
    b. 45 utils.
    c. 40 utils.
    d. 35 utils.
    e. 30 utils.

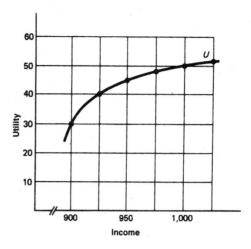

Figure 11-2

11. Which answer to question 10 correctly identifies her
    level of utility if she could arrange to receive her expect-
    ed level of income with certainty?
    a.
    b.
    c.
    d.
    e.
12. How much would the individual described in question
    10 be willing to pay as an insurance premium to guaran-
    tee an invariant income (prior to paying the premium) of
    $950—her expected income?
    a. $100.
    b. $75.
    c. $50.
    d. $25.
    e. It is impossible to tell from the information
        provided.
13. In 1994, as part of their transition to a market economy,
    the Russians decided to outlaw bankruptcy. This meant
    that regardless of the productivity or behavior of the
    owners and managers, firms were not allowed to go out
    of business. This would be most likely to create a(n):
    a. adverse selection problem.
    b. moral hazard problem.
    c. Nash equilibrium.
    d. hedging opportunity.
    e. dominant strategy.
14. Adverse selection occurs when:
    a. insurance reduces a person's incentive to avoid or
        prevent the risky event.

b. both players in a payoff matrix have a dominant strategy.

c. speculators engage in hedging.

d. the people with the highest risk are the most likely ones to buy insurance.

e. the people that are most risk-averse and most careful are the most likely to buy insurance.

B. Game Theory

15. Game theory is most useful for analyzing:
   a. the results of the Super Bowl.
   b. the ways that two or more players choose strategies that jointly affect each participant.
   c. uncertainty in economic analysis.
   d. equilibrium in a perfectly competitive market.
   e. adverse selection in markets for insurance.

16. In a game-theoretic model, a dominant strategy exists when:
   a. a player has a best strategy no matter what strategy the other player follows.
   b. no better strategy exists given the behavior of the other player.
   c. players cooperate and coordinate their behavior in order to maximize joint profits.
   d. players engage in a rivalry game involving price.
   e. the payoffs to the players are equal.

Figure 11-3 shows a payoff table for two firms, A and B. Each firm must choose to play one of two strategies. The payoffs to the players depend not only on the strategies they choose individually but also on the strategy that the rival plays. The numbers inside the cells show the payoffs to the two firms depending upon their choice of strategy. For example, if Firm A chooses strategy I and Firm B chooses strategy III, Firm A gets $20 and Firm B gets $50. Use Figure 11-3 to answer questions 17 through 20.

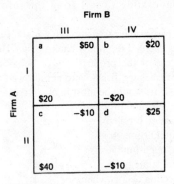

Figure 11-3

17. Which strategy is a dominant strategy for firm A?
   a. Strategy I.

b. Strategy II.
c. Strategy III.
d. Strategy IV.
e. None of the strategies available to firm A is a dominant strategy.

18. Which strategy is a dominant strategy for firm B?
   a. Strategy I.
   b. Strategy II.
   c. Strategy III.
   d. Strategy IV.
   e. None of the strategies available to firm B is a dominant strategy.

19. Which cell is a dominant equilibrium?
   a. Cell a.
   b. Cell b.
   c. Cell c.
   d. Cell d.
   e. None of the cells is a dominant equilibrium.

20. Which cell is a Nash equilibrium?
   a. Cell a.
   b. Cell b.
   c. Cell c.
   d. Cell d.
   e. None of the cells is a Nash equilibrium.

21. A cooperative equilibrium:
   a. occurs when the parties act in unison to find strategies that will benefit their joint payoffs.
   b. occurs when firms form a cartel.
   c. is unstable because firms have an incentive to cheat on agreements.
   d. all the above.
   e. none of the above.

22. Which of the following is an example of a "winner-take-all" game?
   a. UPS workers end a strike by securing a 5% wage increase for all workers.
   b. Russia and the United States end the cold war.
   c. A merit pay scheme awards a $50,000 bonus to the top salesperson of the year.
   d. Schools award tenure to all professors who are recommended by a faculty committee.
   e. All of the above are examples of winner-take-all games.

VII. PROBLEM SOLVING

The following problems are designed to help you apply the concepts that you learned in this chapter.

A. Economics of Risk and Uncertainty

1. Assume that the demand curve for some good Q drawn in Figure 11-4 applies equally well to two different regions of the country, region A and region B. Suppose, additionally,

that 10 units of Q are available initially in region A, while only 6 units are available in region B.

    a. Given this demand curve, the marginal utility of the last unit supplied in A would equal $___, while the marginal utility of the next unit which could be supplied in B would equal $___. Without any transportation cost, the transfer of 1 unit from A to B would cause utility in A to (**rise / fall**) by $___ and utility in B to (**rise / fall**) by $___ for a net gain in welfare of $___. The transfer of a second unit of Q from A to B would similarly (**increase / decrease**) total welfare, this time by $___. Total welfare across the two regions would, in fact, be maximized when the supply available in A equaled ___ units and the supply, available in B equaled ___ units. In that circumstance, the marginal utility of the last unit supplied to A would be $___ and the last unit supplied to B would be $___. The total transfer of ___ units from A to B would, in fact, maximally (**increase / reduce**) total welfare by $___. In general, total welfare is maximized where (**the marginal utilities of the last unit supplied are equal across regions / the total utilities of consumption are equal across regions / the quantities supplied across regions are equal**).

Figure 11-4

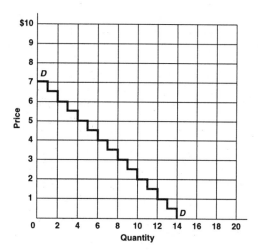

    b. Now suppose that it costs 75 cents per unit to transport Q from one region to the other. The first unit transferred (**from A to B / from B to A**) would again improve total welfare, this time by $___ . The next unit transferred would see (**another increase / a reduction**) in total welfare of $___. The advent of transportation costs would (**increase / reduce**) the gain in total welfare by ___ percent, from $___ to $___. There would exist no beneficial transfers of supply if transportation costs were greater than $___ per unit.

2.   Consider Figure 11-5. It shows the demand for some good X in every period of a three-period supply cycle. Assume that 30 units of X are supplied in the first period of the cycle and then nothing is supplied in either period 2 or period 3.

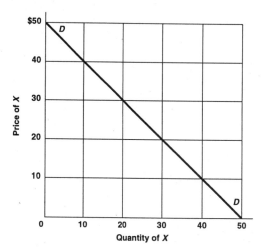

Figure 11-5

    a. If every unit of X were consumed in the first period, then consumption in periods 2 and 3 would be ___ units, and total welfare (the sum of consumer and producer surplus) over the entire cycle would equal ___ the (**area under the demand curve to the left of 30 units on the horizontal axis / value assumed by the demand curve above 30 units on the horizontal axis / total area under the demand curve**).

    b. Now assume that consumption is smoothed over the three periods so that consumption is 10 units in each. Without any carrying costs, the price in each period would equal $___. Total welfare in each period would equal $___, for a total over the three periods of $___. Total welfare (**would / would not**) be maximized in this case because (**the marginal utility of consumption in each period would be equalized / the total utility of consumption in each period would be equalized**). This is true despite the fact that the price of X would be ___ percent higher in period 1 than it was before.

    c. (advanced concept) Assume, as an additional complication, that it costs $5 in interest and storage fees to hold 1 unit of X for one period and $10 to hold 1 unit for two periods. As a result, the price of X would be $___ (**higher / lower**) in period 2 than in period 1 and $___ (**higher / lower**) in period 3 than in period 1. The only distribution of consumption over the three periods which would (1) support this price pattern and (2) exhaust total supply over the three period cycle would have consumption equal to ___ units, ___ units, and ___ units in periods 1, 2, and 3, respectively. [*Hint:* The holding fees suggest that $P_2 = P_1 + \$5$ and $P_3 = P_1 + \$10$. The slope of the demand curve is -1 so $X_2 = X_1 - \$5$ and $X_3 = X_1 - \$10$. The solution must then satisfy the condition that $(X_1 + (X_1 - \$5) + (X_1 - \$10)) = 30$.] The price of X would therefore be $___ in period 1, $___ in period 2, and $___ in period 3. Welfare in period 1 would then amount to $___; in period 2, $___; and in period 3, $___. Total welfare over the cycle would then be $___ (**higher / lower**) than the lumpy consumption pattern of part a and (**higher / lower**) than the costless-storage situation described in part **b**. In comparing the costless-storage case with the costly storage case described in part **c**, however, welfare falls by $___, an amount which is (**greater than / less than**) the total storage fees of $___ .

d.   Draw the price pattern for several cycles in Figure 11-6 and confirm that it corresponds to the pattern suggested in Figure 11-1 in the text.

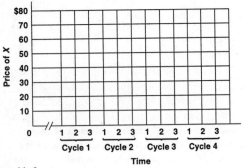

Figure 11-6

3.   Consult Figure 11-7. A cardinal utility schedule dependent upon the level of income is drawn there; it displays a (**diminishing / constant / increasing**) marginal utility of income.

a.   Suppose that income is $50,000 per year; in terms of utility measured on the vertical axis in utils, this $50,000 would produce utility equal to ___ utils.

b.   Now suppose that we consider a "lottery" that has an expected payoff of $0 but which will return a gain of $10,000 with a probability of 50 percent or a loss of $10,000 with a probability of 50 percent. Would playing this lottery improve welfare? ____ To see why or why not, notice that $60,000 would produce ___ utils—a gain of ___ utils over $50,000. An income of $40,000 would, meanwhile, produce ___ utils—a reduction of ___ utils from $50,000. Losing $10,000 therefore produces a (**larger / equal / smaller**) change in utility than gaining an extra $10,000 because marginal utility is (**increasing / constant / decreasing**).

c.   To put this another way, the average level of utility that could be expected if the lottery were played would be ____. This level could be achieved with a fixed income of $___. The risk involved in the lottery therefore costs, in terms of constant-income alternatives, $___, the difference between $50,000 without the lottery and the $___ value of taking the lottery.

d.   (advanced concept) Finally, assume that the lottery is not optional. Assume, instead, that it necessarily faces an individual with the utility schedule graphed in Figure 11-7. How much would this person pay to get out of the uncertainty of receiving $40,000 with a 50 percent probability or $60,000 with a 50 percent probability? The lottery yields the same average utility as a constant income of $___. The person would, therefore,

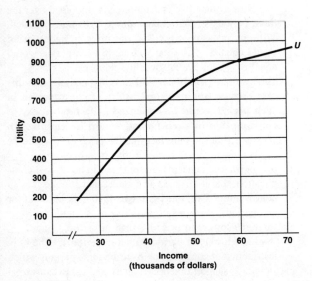

Figure 11-7

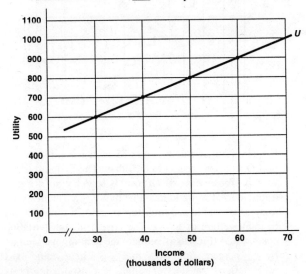

Figure 11-8

pay $\$$___ for an insurance policy that would remove the risk of the lottery—thereby guaranteeing an income of $\$$___ even though the lottery produces an average income of $\$$___.

4. Now suppose that the utility schedule is given by the straight line drawn in Figure 11-8. To avoid any lottery (e.g., the case in question 3 with $10,000 on either side of $50,000) with an expected return of $0, an individual with this schedule would be willing to pay $\$$___. Why?

_____
_____
_____
_____

5. a. Efficient insurance markets can exist if there are (**many / only a few**) independent events and if there is little chance of ___ or ___.

   b. Indicate whether each of the following circumstances illustrates a problem of (a) moral hazard, (b) adverse selection, or (c) too few independent events.

   ___ (1) The existence of some cataclismic event can cause enormous damage in a small but populated area.

   ___ (2) The purchase of insurance against automobile theft makes owners less cautious about where they park their cars.

   ___ (3) High premium charges drive careful car owners to forgo theft insurance in lieu of "self-insurance."

   ___ (4) The existence of the FDIC makes bankers more risk-seeking than they would otherwise be.

   c. Failure of private insurance markets frequently leads to government financed programs of ___. List a few examples:

   (1) _____
   (2) _____
   (3) _____

B. Game Theory

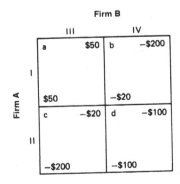

Firm B

Figure 11-9

6. Consult Figure 11-9. It is constructed just like the pay-off matrices discussed in the text, with two firms (A and B) and four strategies (I and II for firm A and III and IV for firm B). The numbers in the boxes indicate outcomes: the number in the upper right corner applies to firm B, while the number in the lower left corner applies to A. Cell c, for example, corresponds with firm A playing strategy II and firm B playing strategy III; note, in this case, that firm A would lose $200 while firm B would lose only $20.

The payoff matrix in Figure 11-9 shows that strategy I (**is / is not**) a dominant strategy for firm A. If A were to choose strategy I over II when B chooses III, then A would (**earn $50 / lose $200 / lose $20 / lose $100**) instead of (**earning $50 / losing $200 / losing $20 / losing $100**); on the other hand, if A were to choose strategy I over II when B chooses IV, then A would (**earn $50 / lose $200 / lose $20 / lose $100**) instead of (**earning $50 / losing** $200 / **losing $20 / losing $100**).

Strategy III (**is / is not**) a dominant strategy for firm B, as well, so cell (**a / b / c / d**) is a dominant equilibrium. It (**is / is not**) a Nash equilibrium because:

_____
_____
_____
_____

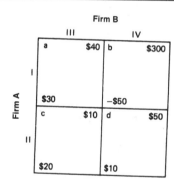

Firm B

Figure 11-10

7. Figure 11-10 displays a different payoff matrix for two firms, A and B. (**Firm A has / Firm B has / Both firms have / Neither firm has**) a dominant strategy; it is strategy ___ for firm A and strategy ___ for B. The Nash equilibrium is indicated by cell (**a / b / c / d**) because firm B will (**always / sometimes / never**) choose ___ strategy and firm A will certainly choose strategy ___ as soon as it realizes that B will play strategy ___.

8. Figures 11-11 through 11-14 display four more payoff matrices for firms A and B. Complete Table 11-2 by identifying A's dominant strategy, B's dominant strategy, the cell indicating a dominant equilibrium, the cell indicating a Nash equilibrium, and the cell indicating a cooperative equilibrium. If any of these categories is not exhibited by any figure, write "n/a" in the corresponding blank.

9. Pollution abatement can cost any firm money, raising its products' prices and damaging its market share (if it acts alone). The key to effective abatement regulation is therefore frequently seen to be one of getting all the polluting firms to act together to reduce pollution from all sources simultaneously. Figure 11-15 displays a payoff matrix which illustrates this point.

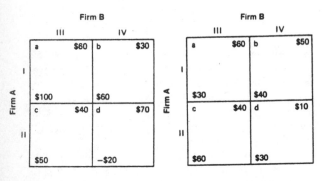

Figure 11-11   Figure 11-12

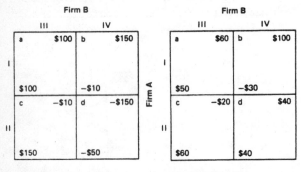

Figure 11-13   Figure 11-14

TABLE 11-2

	Fig. 11-11	Fig. 11-12	Fig. 11-13	Fig. 11-14
A's dominant strategy	___	___	___	___
B's dominant strategy	___	___	___	___
Dominant equilibrium	___	___	___	___
Nash equilibrium	___	___	___	___
Cooperative equilibrium	___	___	___	___

The two firms can choose to control their emissions or not. If they both choose to control their emissions, they each make $___ in profits; this is the situation of cell (a / b / c / d). This (is / is not), however, a Nash equilibrium. Each firm has an incentive (not to control emissions / to control emissions) if it knows that the other will be acting to control emissions; it would then earn $___ at the expense of the other firm, whose profits fall to $___. The Nash equilibrium, therefore, is indicated by cell (a / b / c / d) where each firm earns $___. Only a (noncooperative / cooperative) equilib-

rium supports the socially desirable control-control outcome of cell a. (This is socially optimal as long as we assume that the society desires low levels of pollution.)

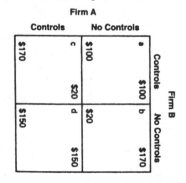

Figure 11-15

VIII. DISCUSSION QUESTIONS

Answer the following questions, making sure that you can explain the work you did to arrive at the answers.
1. Discuss the important functions of speculators. Why might it be efficient to support the efforts of these people, even though they produce no output in the economy?
2. Define hedging, and describe a situation in which this service might be useful for some risk-averse people.
3. Explain why adverse selection might cause problems in the markets for auto insurance.
4. Define the term *moral hazard*. Why might the savings and loan crisis of the 1990s have been initiated by moral hazard problems?
5. What is the difference between a game that has an equilibrium in dominant strategies and a game that has a Nash equilibrium?
6. Explain why the perfectly competitive equilibrium is a Nash equilibrium.

IX. ANSWERS TO STUDY GUIDE QUESTIONS

III. Review of Key Concepts

7   Speculation
11   Arbitrage
13   Hedging
1   Risk aversion
6   Diminishing marginal utility of income
12   Risk spreading
10   Moral hazard
3   Adverse selection
9   Players
5   Strategies

2	Payoffs
8	Nash equilibrium
14	Dominant strategy
4	Noncooperative equilibrium
17	Cooperative equilibrium
15	Winner-take-all games
16	Credibility

VI. Multiple Choice Questions

1. D 2. E 3. D 4. B 5. B 6. B
7. A 8. A 9. C 10. B 11. B 12. C
13. B 14. D 15. B 16. A 17. B 18. E
19. E 20. D 21. D 22. C

VII. Problem Solving

1. a. $2.50, $4.50, fall, $2.50, rise, $4.50, $2.00, increase, $1.00, 8 units, 8 units, $3.50, $3.50, 2, increase, $3.00, the marginal utilities of the last unit supplied were equal across regions
   b. from A to B, $1.25, another increase, 25 cents, reduce, 50%, $3.00, $1.50, $1.50

2. a. 0, $1050, area under the demand curve to the left of 30 units on the horizontal axis
   b. $40, $450, $1350, would, the marginal utility of consumption in each period would be equalized, 100 percent
   c. $5, higher, $10, higher, 15, 10, 5, $35, $40, $45, $637.50, $450.00, $237.50, $1325, higher, lower, $25, $100

3. diminishing
   a. 800
   b. no, 900, 100, 600, 200, larger, decreasing
   c. 750, $46,500 (approximately, the following answers are based on this estimate), $3500, $46,500
   d. $46,500, $3500, $46,500, $50,000

4. $0. Since total utility is linear, the individual is risk neutral, or indifferent to risk. Therefore he or she is not willing to pay anything to avoid risk.

5. a. many, adverse selection, moral hazard
   b. (1) too few independent events
      (2) moral hazard
      (3) adverse selection
      (4) moral hazard
   c. social insurance
      (1) social security
      (2) Medicaid, health care for the poor
      (3) systems of national health care, such as the Canadian system

6. is, earn $50, losing $200, lose $20, losing $100, is, a, is, any dominant equilibrium is a Nash equilibrium because neither player would have an incentive to switch strategies,

given what the other player is doing.
7. Firm B has, neither I nor II, IV, d, always choose strategy IV, II, IV.
8. See Table 11-2.
9. $100, a, is not, not to control emissions, $170, $20, d, $150, cooperative.

TABLE 11-2

	Fig. 11-11	Fig. 11-12	Fig. 11-13	Fig. 11-14
A's dominant strategy	I	n/a	n/a	II
B's dominant strategy	n/a	III	n/a	IV
Dominant equilibrium	n/a	n/a	n/a	cell d
Nash equilibrium	cell a	cell c	cell d	cell d
Cooperative equilibrium	cell a	cell c	cell a	cell d

VIII. Discussion Questions

1. Speculators help to smooth consumption across time, space, or uncertain states of nature.
2. Hedging is the activity of avoiding a risk by making a counteracting sale or investment. This service might be useful for an individual who will have goods to sell in the future, but who is worried about uncertain market events that might erode prices between now and the point of sale.
3. Adverse selection might cause problems in the markets for auto insurance if those who are most likely to get in an auto accident are most likely to get insurance. This would mean that rates are higher for everyone in the insured pool because there will be more accidents occurring among people with insurance.
4. Moral hazard occurs when insurance reduces an individual's incentive to avoid or prevent risky events. The savings and loan crisis might have been initiated by moral hazard problems if bank directors were following investment strategies that were more risky than they would have been without government deposit insurance provided by the FDIC.
5. A dominant strategy occurs for a player when there is a best strategy for him or her no matter what strategy the other player follows. A dominant equilibrium occurs when both players have and follow their dominant strategies. A Nash equilibrium occurs when both players follow their best strategies *given the strategy of their opponent*.
6. The perfectly competitive equilibrium is a Nash equilibrium because no buyer or seller has a better strategy to follow given the behavior of all other market participants. Firms set marginal cost equal to marginal revenue, given prices dictated by the market. Consumers set the ratios of marginal utilities to price equal for all goods in their market baskets. In a noncooperative setting, there is no strategy for any firm that will increase profits, and no strategy for consumers that will increase utility.

CHAPTER

How Markets
Determine Incomes

I. CHAPTER OVERVIEW

Now that you have studied how pricing and production decisions are made in *output* markets, it is time to consider how pricing and employment decisions are made in *input* markets. You will recall that relative scarcity and need were seen to determine why it costs more to buy some goods than it does to buy others; but what accounts for the large differences in the wages and salaries offered to people engaged in various occupations? Scarcity? Need? Or something else?

Even casual consideration of any productive enterprise reveals that all inputs work interdependently to produce a given product or service. Given this complex interdependence, how can one compute levels of compensation that reflect accurately the importance of their respective contributions? How, more specifically, are wage rates determined? And interest rates? And land rents? And so on?

This begins a series of chapters that focus on the distribution of income. Critical in determining the nature of the distribution must be, of course, the ownership of the factors of production and the prices that they command. Chapter 12 begins, therefore, with a brief introduction to what economists mean when they speak of income and wealth, and where they look to find the sources of income and wealth in a modern economy.

There is, however, more to the distribution of income than simply cataloguing who owns what. There is, more specifically, the question of what determines how much each factor is worth. We can find an answer to this question using the familiar tools of supply-and-demand analysis. The fundamental differences between product markets and factor markets lie in the *sources* of supply and demand components. In a product market demand materializes because the good being produced and sold generates some utility for the consumer; the consumer is willing to pay some positive price for the privilege of owning the good in question. In an input market factors of production are demanded only because they can be employed to produce an item of value. The demand for inputs is therefore a *derived demand* based not upon the immediate, innate value of the input to a firm, but upon the *value of some other good that it can be employed to produce.*

Our examination of these issues begins with the demand side of an input market. Because a firm must hire labor, buy raw materials, and invest in machinery, it is the demander of productive inputs. Its demand is not, however, unlimited. It makes its employment decisions on the basis of least-cost combinations of inputs defined by its production function and the prices of those inputs. The derived demand for any input will therefore result from (1) the cost-minimizing behavior of profit-maximizing firms and (2) a marginal-productivity theory of income distribution.

The final section of Chapter 12 will show how this notion of derived demand can be used in a market context. It will, in particular, play derived demand against alternative input supply schedules.

II. LEARNING OBJECTIVES

After you have read Chapter 12 in your text and completed the exercises in this *Study Guide* chapter, you should be able to:

1. Compile a list of questions concerning the **distribution of income** and the factors that help to determine the shape of this distribution. Differentiate between the terms **income** and **wealth** as they are used in economics.
2. Recognize the major sources of income and the major reservoirs of wealth in the United States. Describe who owns the factors of production which generate this income and wealth.
3. Establish a role for government in redistributing income and wealth using **taxation** and **transfer payments**.
4. Define the notion of a **derived demand** for a factor of production, and explain why the demands for factors are interdependent. That is, explain why the demand for any single factor depends on the level of use of other inputs in the production process.
5. Show how the demand curve for an input is represented by its **marginal revenue product** schedule, i.e., explain why the derived demand for any input can be found by multiplying the marginal product of that input by the marginal revenue of output.

151

6. Show precisely why, in cases of perfect competition, the marginal revenue product of any input is equal to the competitive price of output multiplied by its marginal product. Then show how the imperfectly competitive case differs from this.

7. Demonstrate why the **least-cost rule** describes an optimal combination of factors for firms to use. Further demonstrate that the firm that hires all inputs up to the point at which their prices equal their marginal revenue products will guarantee that (1) it is producing the profit-maximizing output and (2) it is incurring the least cost; i.e. (1) the marginal revenue of its sales will equal the marginal cost of its production, and (2) the least-cost rule will be satisfied.

8. Show how the market derived-demand curve for any input is equal to the horizontal sum of the marginal revenue product curves of all the firms which employ that input. Recall that a market supply curve for any good, and so for any factor, is equal to the horizontal sum of the individual factor owner's supply curves.

9. Illustrate how interaction between the supply and the demand for factors of production determines their market prices. Explain why the distribution of income is the result of the workings of supply and demand in an economy's input markets.

III. REVIEW OF KEY CONCEPTS

Match the following terms from column A with their definition in column B.

A
__ Income distribution
__ Income
__ Wealth
__ Transfer payments
__ Personal income
__ Marginal product
__ Law of diminishing returns
__ Marginal revenue product
__ Derived demand
__ Least-cost rule

B
1. Means that the demand for a factor of production depends upon the demand for the final product.
2. The firm will choose an optimal combination of inputs such that the ratios of the marginal products to the prices of the inputs are equal for all inputs.
3. Direct payments from government to individuals that are not in return for current goods and services.
4. Refers to the flow of wages or things of value earned by a person or household during a given time period.
5. Consists of the net dollar value of assets owned at a point in time.
6. Equal to market income plus transfer payments.
7. The addition to total output when the firm hires an additional unit of a single factor of production.
8. Examines the determination of income in a society.
9. States that as the firm hires additional units of an input, eventually the marginal product of that input will fall.
10. The product of marginal revenue and marginal product.

IV. SUMMARY AND CHAPTER OUTLINE

This section summarizes the key concepts from the chapter.

A. Income and Wealth

1. The *theory of the distribution of income* is concerned with (1) the *determination* of income, and (2) the *allocation* of total product among factors of production. Both these questions are important; we need to understand how income is generated in an economy, and then how these wages, rent, interest, and profits are distributed across the owners of labor, land, capital, and entrepreneurial ability.

2. *Income* is a *flow* of money; *wealth* is a *stock* of accumulated economic assets. Remember that a stock measure of any economic variable describes the total quantity of the variable *at a particular point in time;* a flow measure describes the accumulation of an economic variable *over a period of time.* Both of these measures are important in describing how the returns to factors are distributed across a society.

3. Sometimes, governments take actions to *redistribute* income and wealth in a society. This decision is a normative one and usually occurs when policymakers have determined that there is significant inequity in the distribution of income and wealth, or when some market failure has occurred. The two most popular tools used to achieve this redistribution are *taxes* and *transfer payments.* Governments collect money as taxes and return it to people in the form of direct payments that are not in return for current goods and services.

B. Input Pricing by Marginal Productivity

1. The demand for any factor of production is a *derived demand*, which means that the demand for the factor depends upon, or is derived from, the demand for the final product that it helps to produce. For example, the demand for coal miners depends upon the demand for coal. Increased concern over acid rain and other ecological problems has decreased the demand for coal, and hence decreased the

demand for coal miners. The demand for computer chips depends upon the demand for computers. The explosion in the popularity and use of personal computers in the past decades has increased the demand for computers, and hence increased the demand for computer chips.

2. The demand for any input depends directly, and most importantly, upon the productivity of that factor. Take a moment to review some of the production theory from Chapter 6: A production function describes how inputs are transformed into output. Production can be measured in several ways, but the key to our analysis is marginal product, which is defined as the addition to total output that occurs when a firm hires an additional unit of an input. Remember that the law of diminishing returns states that as additional units of an input are added to a production process in the short run, eventually marginal product will fall. This means that the marginal product schedule is downward-sloping, at least over some levels of output.

Given this description of the production process, the demand for an input will be defined by its *marginal revenue product* (*MRP*). Marginal revenue product measures the addition to total *revenue* that occurs when a firm hires an additional unit of an input. *MRP* translates marginal product, which is measured in output units, to a meaningful dollar figure. To calculate *MRP*, multiply the marginal product of the input by the marginal revenue.

3. The derived demand for any factor in a perfectly competitive industry is the (multiplicative) product of the price of output and the marginal product at each level of factor employment; this is simply a consequence of the horizontal demand curve faced by perfect competitors, which guarantees that price equals marginal revenue. However, in an imperfectly competitive industry, $P > MR$ because the firm must lower the price of all units sold in order to sell additional units of output. (Remember that the imperfect competitor is able to charge the maximum price that the market will bear at the optimal level of output.)

4. The *least-cost rule* states that a firm will hire its optimal combination of inputs when each input's marginal revenue product is equal to its price. This means that the last dollar spent on each input will yield the same marginal productivity. Suppose input A is used to produce output X. Then,

$$MRP_A = P_A ==> MR_X \times MP_A = P_A ==> MP_A / P_A = 1 / MR_X$$

The same expression can be written for each of the other inputs used to produce X; thus the ratio of the marginal product of each input to its price must be equal to the inverse of the marginal revenue of good X. Under these conditions the firm will (a) be producing the profit-maximizing output and (b) be operating at least cost.

Suppose that you are producing widgets using labor and capital. Suppose further that the marginal product of the last worker was 100 widgets, and you pay workers $50 per day. The marginal product of capital was 300 widgets, and you

pay $100 per day for each unit of capital. Finally, suppose at this point you have exhausted your budget on these two inputs.

Note the problem here: Capital is three times as productive as labor but only costs twice as much! The least-cost rule is violated; you could have produced the same output with lower costs by using less labor and more capital. Or, you could have produced more output with the same total expenditure by using less labor and more capital. When the least-cost rule does not hold, any firm can reallocate its resources to lower costs and increase profits.

5. The market demand curve for any input is the horizontal sum of the derived demand curves of all firms employing that input. Likewise, the market supply curve for any input is the horizontal sum of the supply curves of all factor owners selling that input.

6. As in any other market we have discussed, given demand and supply curves, we can describe an equilibrium price and quantity exchanged in the market for a factor of production. Thus, the distribution of income in an economy is at least in part determined by market forces. Individuals and households sell the factors that they own in input markets; relative scarcity in these input markets combines with need to determine the returns to resource owners.

7. In spite of the importance of this analysis, other questions surrounding the distribution of income and wealth remain unanswered. For instance, how is the initial distribution of factors determined? How does government policy interact with market forces? These issues will be discussed in greater detail in the next two chapters.

V. HELPFUL HINTS

1. Income and wealth are both important concepts in economics. They both measure the value of resources available to individuals and households in an economy. However, income is a flow concept. It measures the amount of money that accrues to a resource over a period of time. Wealth is a stock concept. It measures the value of resources at a particular point in time. It is critical that you see the difference between these measures and use each when appropriate.

2. Your text authors point out the importance of the interdependence that exists among factors of production, but it bears repeating here. This interdependence occurs because most inputs in a production process are *complements,* at least to some extent. This means that the inputs are used together to produce output. Although there is often some substitutability across factors, it is rare that inputs are perfect substitutes. That is, it is rare that a firm could use all land and no labor, or all labor and no land, for example, to produce a product. Farmers are able to marginally reduce acreage and increase the number of farmhands hired, or vice versa, and hold output fixed. However, all land and no labor, or all labor and no land, will yield zero output.

This is an important concept to consider, because it affects the way we think about a factor's productivity and value to the firm. When the North American Free Trade Agreement (NAFTA) was being debated in the United States, many opponents lamented the fact that workers in Mexico and the Caribbean earn much lower wages than workers in the United States and predicted the wholesale movement of many industries upon passage of the agreement. What they failed to realize was that workers in these regions are paid less because they are much less productive than their U.S. counterparts. An important reason for this lower productivity involves the notion of factor interdependence. Workers in other countries have much less capital equipment and technology to work with; their productivity will tend to remain lower as long as this is the case.

3. The decision rule for input employment is parallel to the firm's profit-maximizing output rule. If we think about marginal revenue as the amount of money that flows *into* the firm when it sells an additional unit of output and marginal cost as the amount of money that flows *out* of the firm when it sells an additional unit of output, then the general decision rule says produce until the amount coming in is equal to the amount going out on the margin. Likewise, if we think about marginal revenue product as the amount of money that flows *into* the firm when it hires an additional unit of input and factor price as the amount of money that flows *out* of the firm when it hires an additional unit of input, then this decision rule also says to hire inputs until the amount coming in is equal to the amount going out on the margin. This very general rule can be applied to many economic decisions.

4. For a more extensive discussion of the alternative shapes of supply curves in factor markets, return to Chapter 8 in your textbook, which describes perfectly elastic, perfectly inelastic, and backward-bending supply curves.

VI. MULTIPLE CHOICE QUESTIONS

These questions are organized by topic from the chapter outline. Choose the best answer from the options available.

A. Income and Wealth

1. Income refers to:
   a. total cash expenditures made by households over the course of a year.
   b. the net dollar value of assets owned at a point in time.
   c. payments from households to governments.
   d. the total value of a stock portfolio owned by an investor.
   e. total flow of wages or other things of value earned by a person or household over the course of a year.

2. Wealth refers to:
   a. total cash expenditures made by households over

the course of a year.
   b. the net dollar value of assets owned at a point in time.
   c. payments from households to governments.
   d. the total value of a stock portfolio owned by an investor.
   e. total receipts or cash earned by a person or household over the course of a year.

3. The single most important asset of most households in the U.S. is:
   a. a home.
   b. a stock portfolio.
   c. a car.
   d. savings account balances.
   e. expected social security payments.

4. Severe recession in the northeast coupled with a decline in the defense-oriented manufacturing base led to a severe decrease in the demand for housing in Connecticut in the early 1990s. This meant that homeowners':
   a. wealth declined due to the decreased price of housing.
   b. income declined due to the decreased price of housing.
   c. wealth increased as the price of housing returned to a more normal level.
   d. transfer payments from the state increased.
   e. income declined due to the decreased supply of housing available.

B. Input Pricing by Marginal Productivity

5. During the 1960s and 1970s, as the baby boom generation flowed through grade school, high school, and college, the demand for teachers increased. This describes:
   a. a derived supply of teachers.
   b. a derived demand for teachers.
   c. an increase in the supply curve of teachers.
   d. a decrease in the demand curve for teachers.
   e. none of the above.

6. Which of the following examples illustrates the law of diminishing returns at a fish packing plant?
   a. The firm expands its plant facility in order to take advantage of economies of scale.
   b. The firm hires additional workers for the third shift but finds that marginal product falls with each additional worker.
   c. An increase in interest rates increases the fixed costs of the firm's operations.
   d. The firm starts using cod instead of halibut for its frozen fish filets.
   e. All the above describe diminishing returns.

7. If inputs A, B, and C are used together to produce product X, then the marginal product of input A is the:

a.   extra output of X resulting from the employment of 1 extra unit of A, inputs B and C being increased proportionately.

b.   amount of input A required to produce 1 extra unit of X, the amounts of inputs B and C being held constant.

c.   extra output of X resulting from the employment of 1 extra unit of A, the amounts of inputs B and C being held constant.

d.   amount of input A required to produce 1 extra unit of X, the amounts of inputs B and C being increased proportionately.

e.   none of the above.

8. The marginal revenue product of input A used to produce output X is the:

a.   marginal product of A multiplied by the price of A.

b.   average product of A multiplied by the price of X.

c.   marginal product of A multiplied by the quantity of X produced.

d.   average product of A multiplied by the marginal revenue of X.

e.   none of the above.

The production function in Table 12-1 describes the relationship between the number of workers employed in a widget factory per day and total product. Widgets are sold in a perfectly competitive market. Use Table 12-1 to answer questions 9 through 11.

TABLE 12-1

Quantity of Labor	Total Product
0	0
3	60
4	75
5	80
6	80
7	76
8	70

9. Diminishing returns set in after the:
a.   second worker.
b.   third worker.
c.   fourth worker.
d.   fifth worker.
e.   sixth worker.

10. If the price of labor is $150 per day and the price of widgets is $10, how many workers should this firm hire?
a.   0.
b.   2.
c.   3.
d.   4.
e.   5.

11. If the price of labor falls to $50 per day while the price of a widget remains fixed, how many workers should this firm hire?

a.   0.
b.   2.
c.   3.
d.   4.
e.   5.

12. A firm operates in conditions of imperfect competition. The price of one of the factors of production, input A, is $10; its marginal product is 5. If this firm were operating at its profit-maximizing output, then the marginal revenue from the sale of X must be equal to:
a. $1.00.
b. $1.50.
c. $2.00.
d. $5.00.
e. $10.00.

13. Given the information provided in question 12, the marginal revenue product of input A must have been:
a. $1.00.
b. $1.50.
c. $2.00.
d. $5.00.
e. $10.00.

14. The firm from question 12 also uses input B, whose marginal product is 100 at the current usage level. The price of input B must be equal to:
a. $1.
b. $2.
c. $5.
d. $100.
e. $200.

15. Consider a monopoly. The price of one of its inputs, input A, is $10, and the marginal product of A is 5. The price of its output is $2. The firm has satisfied the least-cost rule for input employment. This firm is:

a.   not producing its maximum-profit output and should contract production.

b.   not producing its maximum-profit output and should expand production.

c.   producing its maximum-profit output at least cost.

d.   producing its maximum-profit output but could reduce its costs by employing less of input A and more of its other inputs.

e.   producing its maximum-profit output but could reduce its costs by employing more of input A and less of its other inputs.

16. Return to the data provided in question 15. If you were told that marginal revenue must be one of the five following dollar amounts, then you would know that marginal revenue must be equal to:
a. $1.
b. $2.
c. $3.
d. $4.
e. $5.

17. Now alter the information provided in question 15 in one respect only: assume that the firm operates in a perfectly competitive industry. Which alternative in question 16 would now be correct;
a.
b.
c.
d.
e.

18. The least-cost rule for a firm making an optimal input employment decision using inputs A and B states:
a. $MP_A / P_A = MP_B / P_B$
b. $MP_A \times P_A = MP_B \times P_B$.
c. $MU_A / P_A = MU_B / P_B$.
d. $MRP_A = MRP_B$.
e. none of the above.

19. The market demand curve for labor in an economy is the:
a. vertical summation of the individual firms' marginal product curves.
b. horizontal summation of the individual firms' marginal revenue product curves.
c. horizontal summation of the individual firms' marginal cost curves.
d. inverse of the marginal revenue curve.
e. perfectly elastic demand curve at the market price.

20. Consider a simple, one-good economy with two factors of production—one of fixed supply and one of variable supply. If production in this economy were to display constant returns to scale, then:
a. each factor should earn a return based on average productivity.
b. the returns to both factors sum to a total which exceeds total output.
c. the sum of the factor shares equals total product.
d. the area under the total product curve is total output.
e. both factors should receive the same return.

21. According to John B. Clark's theory of income distribution, if 10 units of a particular input were employed, then the price paid to each of those units should be equal to the value of:
a. the average of the marginal products of each of the 10 units.
b. its own marginal product.
c. the marginal product of the tenth unit.
d. the average product of the 10 units.
e. none of the above.

VII. PROBLEM SOLVING

The following problems are designed to help you apply the concepts that you learned in this chapter.

A. Income and Wealth

1. a. **Income** is defined as the amount of money received from all sources during a given period of time (a year, a month, etc.). In the spaces provided below, list the major sources of income in the United States (labor income, rent, dividends, interest, and transfer payments) in the order of their importance.
(1) _____
(2) _____
(3) _____
(4) _____
(5) _____

b. **Wealth** consists of the net dollar value of assets owned at any particular time. In the spaces provided below, list three major tangible assets and three major financial assets that comprise wealth in the United States in the order of their importance.
Tangible assets:
(1) _____
(2) _____
(3) _____
Financial assets:
(1) _____
(2) _____
(3) _____

B. Input Pricing by Marginal Productivity

2. Suppose that good X is produced from three inputs, A, B, and C; a very small portion of the production function is recorded in Table 12-2.

TABLE 12-2

| | | Employment Levels | |
Output	A	B	C
200	10	30	20
203	10	31	20

a. We can infer from Table 12-2 that (**the MP of X is 3 / the MP of A is 3 / the MP of B is 3 / the MP of C is 3**). If the employment of some input such as B were gradually to increase, then we should expect that the marginal product of B would gradually (**increase / decline**) because of the (**law of diminishing returns / relative scarcity of B that would result in the production process**). Similarly, if the quantity of B employed were to decline, then we should expect that the marginal product of B would (**increase / decline**) because of the (**law of diminishing returns / relative scarcity of B that would result in the production process**).

c. If the employment of some input such as B were gradually to increase, with the employment of inputs A and C held constant, then we should expect to see the marginal products of A and C (**increase / decrease**) because of the (**law of diminishing returns / relative scarcity of A and C that would result in the production process**). This exercise helps to illustrate the (**independence / interdependence**) of input productivities.

3. Suppose that a firm is satisfying the least-cost rule with respect to inputs A, B, and C and that it wants to find out if it is at its maximum-profit output level. To do this, it can look at any one of its inputs—say, input A. A's price might be $4 per unit, for example, and its *MP* might be 3. Assume that the firm knows that the marginal revenue from the sale of X is $1.

a. Under these conditions, A's *MRP* is (**$1 / $2 / $3 / $4 / $7 / $12**). Since it costs (**$1 / $2 / $3 / $4 / $7 / $12**) to buy that last unit of A, its employment (**added $1 to / subtracted $1 from / did not change**) total profit. The firm, remember, is satisfying the least-cost rule in making its employment decisions. It follows, therefore, that the same conclusion would have been reached had we looked at input B or input C. Hence, in the given circumstances, the firm (**definitely is / definitely is not / may or may not be**) earning maximum possible profit. In order for it to move toward higher profit, in fact, it should (**reduce / increase**) its output by (**reducing / increasing**) its employment of all inputs.

b. Now try a different example to illustrate the point more fully. Suppose that the *MP*s of A, B, and C are, respectively 12, 8, and 2. Let their prices be, respectively, $6, $4, and $1. The firm (**is / is not**), therefore, producing its current output at minimum cost.

c. Continue this second illustration by assuming that the marginal revenue from the sale of X is equal to $1. Input A's *MRP* would therefore equal (**$12 / $10 / $8 / $6 / $4 / $2**). Input B's *MRP* would meanwhile equal (**$12 / $10 / $8 / $6 / $4 / $2**). The *MRP* for input C would be (**$12 / $10 / $8 / $6 / $4 / $2**). This firm (**is / is not**) producing the profit-maximizing output. To achieve this maximum, it should (**increase / decrease**) its output by (**increasing / decreasing**) its employment of (**input A only / input B only / input C only / all inputs simultaneously**).

d. As the firm makes these adjustments in employment, the marginal revenue products of all inputs (**fall / rise**). The increase in the employment of each input should be halted when each *MRP* has (**fallen below / reached equality with / risen above**) the price of the (**input / finished product**).

4. Consult Table 12-3. The outputs of identical fields of corn are recorded there for a variety of levels of employment of labor. Let there be 10 workers in an economy defined by the two cornfields, and let the world determine the price of corn at $2.

TABLE 12-3

Labor Employed	Corn Output (bu)	Marginal Product of Labor	Marginal Revenue Product of Labor
0	0	n/a	n/a
1	10	___	$___
2	19	___	___
3	27	___	___
4	34	___	___
5	40	___	___
6	45	___	___
7	49	___	___
8	52	___	___
9	54	___	___
10	55	___	___

a. Fill in the "Marginal Product" and "Marginal Revenue Product" columns of the table. The numbers that you record there will be used to demonstrate that paying labor (the only input here) its marginal revenue product will result in a level of output that maximizes the value of the corn crop in terms of the world price.

b. Suppose, initially, that seven workers toil in one field (field A) and three toil in the other (field B). The output of field A would be ___ bushels worth $___; each worker, if paid his or her marginal revenue product, would receive $___. The output of field B would meanwhile be ___ bushels worth $___; each worker there would receive $___ . In response to the wages that you computed, you should expect that workers would want to move (**from A to B / from B to A**).

c. Suppose that the workers do indeed move so that four workers remain to work field A while six work field B. Output of field A would fall to ___ bushels with a value of $___, and output of field B would climb to ___ units worth $___ on the world market. The total value of output would climb from $___ to $___.

d. To equalize the wages paid to workers in both fields so that there will be no incentive for workers to want to switch from one to the other, ___ workers would have to work each field. Were that the case, total output would climb to ___ bushels worth $___ and each worker would earn $___. There (**exists another / does not exist any other**) distribution of workers that would increase the output of corn and thus increase the value of the economy's production on the world market.

5. You are once again a consultant on profit maximization. What would you recommend in each of the five cases listed in Table 12-4?

In each case, the production of some good X depends only upon the employment of inputs A and B. Assume for each case that the marginal product of input A is constant and equal to 3 and that the marginal product of B is constant and equal to 9. The heading "*MR* from Sale of X" in Table 12-4 refers to marginal revenue at the current level of output and sales. Similarly, the headings "Price of A" and "Price of B" denote the prices which the firm must pay for inputs A and B.

Indicate, for each case, whether or not the firm has achieved a position of maximum profit. Write "yes" or "no" in the column provided. Use the following numerical codes to indicate, in the last column, what is wrong with the firm's present position.

1 = Present position is the correct one.
2 = For present output, employment of A is too high, employment of B too low.
3 = For present output, employment of A is too low, employment of B too high.
4 = Reduce output by employing less of both A and B.
5 = Increase output by employing more of both A and B.

TABLE 12-4

Case	MR from Sale of X	Price of A	Price of B	At Maximum Profit?	Answer
A	$1	$2	$10	___	___
B	2	6	18	___	___
C	3	12	18	___	___
D	4	9	18	___	___
E	5	21	54	___	___

6.   The market demand for any input is the (**vertical / geometric / horizontal**) sum of the individual demand schedules of all the firms interested in employing that input; i.e., the sum of their (**marginal product / marginal revenue product / marginal utility**) schedules.

More specifically, suppose that there are only three firms interested in employing input A, and that these firms sell their output, X, in a perfectly competitive market. (There should be more firms in a perfectly competitive market, but for the sake of illustration here we will keep things simple.) The firms' production functions are given in Table 12-5.

TABLE 12-5

Quantity of Input A	Total Product Firm 1	Total Product Firm 2	Total Product Firm 3
1	15	5	2
2	29	15	7
3	42	30	17
4	54	50	25
5	65	65	30
6	75	75	30

a.   If the price of input A is $10, and the price of X is $1, what is the optimal quantity of input A for each firm to hire?

Firm 1 = ___; Firm 2 = ___; Firm 3 = ___.

b.   If the price of input A rises to $15, and the price of X remains at $1, what is the optimal quantity of input A for each firm to hire?

Firm 1 = ___; Firm 2 = ___; Firm 3 = ___.

c.   Using this information, draw a market demand curve for input A in Figure 12-1.

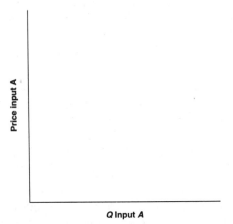

Figure 12-1

d.   Suppose that the market supply of input A is fixed at 15 units. Draw the market supply curve in Figure 12-1. The equilibrium price in the market for input A is $___ and the quantity exchanged will be ___.

e.   The market supply curve for input A is (**perfectly elastic / perfectly inelastic**). This means that

_____

_____

_____

_____

VIII. DISCUSSION QUESTIONS

Answer the following questions, making sure that you can explain the work you did to arrive at the answers.

1.   List and explain two factors that help to determine the distribution of income in an economy.

2.   Which factor of production receives the greatest portion of national income in the United States? Given the small number of people who control land, capital, and entrepreneurship, why might the government step in to redistribute this income? What methods might the government use?

3.   Explain in your own words how declining interest rates affect the incomes and wealth of (1) many older, retired people and (2) younger families with children. Who benefits from lower interest rates and who loses?

4. Why do we say that there is a derived demand for factors of production?

5. Consider the Happy Firm, which produces baseball caps using labor and capital. Presently, $MP_L / P_L > MP_C / P_C$. Carefully explain why this is not optimal for the firm. That is, why should the firm change its mix of labor and capital?

6. Reconsider Figure 12-7 from your textbook. Your authors explain that "it is the amount of wealth rather than the rate of return that makes the rectangle of the top wealth-holders so large." Use this idea to explain the adage, "Shirt sleeves to shirt sleeves in three generations."

IX. ANSWERS TO STUDY GUIDE QUESTIONS

III. Review of Key Concepts

8	Income distribution
4	Income
5	Wealth
3	Transfer payments
6	Personal income
7	Marginal product
9	Law of diminishing returns
10	Marginal revenue product
1	Derived demand
2	Least-cost rule

VI. Multiple Choice Questions

1. E   2. B   3. A   4. A   5. B   6. B
7. C   8. E   9. A   10. D   11. E   12. C
13. E   14. E   15. A   16. A   17. C   18. A
19. B   20. C   21. C

VII. Problem Solving

1. a. (1) Labor income
      (2) Transfer payments
      (3) Interest
      (4) Dividends
      (5) Rent
   b. (1) Own home
      (2) Rental property
      (3) Motor vehicle
      (1) Interest-earning accounts
      (2) Equity in business
      (3) Stocks and mutual funds
2. a. the MP of B is 3
   b. decline, law of diminishing returns, increase, law of diminishing returns
   c. increase, relative scarcity of A and C that would result in the production process, interdependence
3. a. $3, $4, subtracted $1 from, definitely is not, reduce, reducing
   b. is

c. $12, $8, $2, is not, increase, increasing, all inputs simultaneously
   d. fall, reached equality with, input
4. a. See Table 12-3.

TABLE 12-3

Labor Employed	Corn Output (bu)	Mrp of Labor
0	0	n/a
1	10	$20
2	19	18
3	27	16
4	34	14
5	40	12
6	45	10
7	49	8
8	52	6
9	54	4
10	55	2

   b. 49, $98, $8, 27, $54, $16, from A to B
   c. 34, $68, 45, $90, $152, $158
   d. 5, 80, $160, $12, does not exist any other
5. a. no, 3
   b. yes, 1
   c. no, 2
   d. no, 5
   e. no, 4
6. horizontal, marginal revenue product
   a. 6, 6, 3
   b. 1, 5, 0
   c. See Figure 12-1.
   d. See Figure 12- 1. $10, 15 workers
   e. perfectly inelastic. This means that workers shrill supply the same quantity of labor at any wage; workers will not respond to changes in the wage rate.

VIII. Discussion Questions

1. Market supply and demand and government redistribution policies.
2. Labor receives the greatest portion of national income. To redistribute income accruing to land, capital, and entrepreneurship, the government might place higher taxes on this income, to be used for government welfare programs.
3. Declining interest rates hurt many people who are elderly or retired by lowering income earned on savings. Declining interest rates help younger families with children by making borrowing (particularly mortgage borrowing for home purchases) less costly. Borrowers benefit from lower interest rates but savers suffer.
4. We say there is a derived demand for factors of production because the demand for the factors is dependent upon the demand for the final product. Without a demand for the good that the factor is used to produce, there would be no demand for the factor.

5.   This situation is not optimal for the firm because the last dollar spent on labor was more productive than the last dollar spent on capital. If the firm shifted some resources from capital to labor, total output would increase without any increase in expenditure.

6.   This adage implies that it is difficult to move from the middle to the upper class. Because people in the upper class have more capital assets, and because they are willing to undertake more risky investment projects, they are able to build on their wealth much more quickly than someone in the middle class. Because people in the middle class have a smaller pool of wealth to begin with, and because they invest more conservatively, they may be unable to hurdle class boundaries.

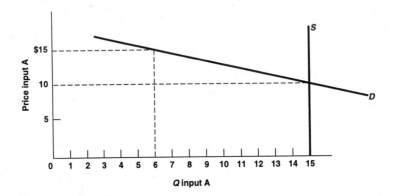

Figure 12-1

CHAPTER

The Labor Market

I. CHAPTER OVERVIEW

Whether you have experience waiting on tables, running a cash register, selling clothing, cutting hair, or managing a Subway franchise, most of you have experience in labor markets. Many of you have worked in exchange for a wage, to earn money for school or to support yourselves and your families. This experience should give you an edge in this chapter, since you can apply what you know to the theoretical models described here.

Wages and salaries account for approximately 75 percent of the national income of the United States. Despite their importance, wages are just prices. You learned in earlier chapters that prices are determined by the interaction between demand and supply, and labor markets follow these same basic rules. We will explain how wages and salaries are determined, and why wages and salaries differ across countries, across populations of particular countries, and across occupations. Demand and supply factors will both have roles to play in these explanations.

We will also see that labor markets are unlike markets for final products in interesting ways. Labor is a "special" commodity; we cannot separate the work from the worker and so issues particular to individuals sometimes get in the way of market solutions. Thus we must also explore the roles of other important labor market institutions, unions and discrimination.

II. LEARNING OBJECTIVES

After you have read Chapter 13 in your text and completed the exercises in this *Study Guide* chapter, you should be able to:

1. Discuss the determinants of the shape and position of the labor demand curve.
2. Use these determinants, along with the perfectly competitive market model, to illustrate wage dispersion across countries.
3. Describe **hours worked, labor force participation,** and **immigration** as important determinants of labor supply
4. Explain how **differences in jobs, differences in people,** and a **lack of competition** can produce wage differentials across groups.

5. Trace the history of the labor movement in the United States, and show how unions operate to raise wages and restrict labor supply.
6. Use economic analysis to describe **discrimination** in labor markets. Apply this analysis to discrimination against women and against minorities in U.S. labor markets.
7. Review the empirical evidence which documents the significance of labor market discrimination, and discuss the laws and policies that have been developed to eliminate discrimination from the marketplace.

III. REVIEW OF KEY CONCEPTS

Match the following terms from column A with their definitions in column B.

A	B
__ Real wages	1. When wages rise, workers experience an increase in income. They feel "richer" and can buy more of all goods, including leisure.
__ Perfectly competitive labor markets	2. Education and training that make a worker more productive.
__ Compensating differentials	3. The process of negotiation between representatives for firms and workers for the purpose of establishing mutually agreeable conditions of employment.
__ Labor supply	4. Wages accruing to Michael Jordan, famous basketball star, that are in excess of what he could earn at his next-best available occupation.
__ Substitution effect	5. Unions in which workers are grouped on the basis of a particular skill.
__ Income effect	6 A market in which there are large numbers of workers and employers, none of which has the power to affect wage rates.

__ Human capital

__ Pure economic rent

__ Noncompeting groups

__ Craft unions

__ Industrial unions

__ Collective bargaining

__ National Labor Relations Act

__ Bilateral monopoly

__ Lump-of-labor fallacy

__ Discrimination

__ Statistical discrimination

7. Occurs when there are but one buyer and one seller, particularly of labor.

8. Occurs when individuals are treated on the basis of the average behavior of members of the group to which they belong.

9. Find it difficult and costly for a member of one profession to enter into the other.

10. States that "Employees shall have the right to join labor organizations, to bargain collectively, and to engage in concerted activities."

11. Wage differentials that serve to compensate for the relative attractiveness or nonmonetary differences among jobs.

12. Refers to the number of hours that people desire to work in exchange for a wage.

13. The view that the amount of work to be done in an economy is fixed.

14. When wages rise, workers are tempted to work longer hours. Each hour is now better paid, making the "price" of taking an hour of leisure higher.

15. Occurs when a difference in earnings arises because of an irrelevant personal characteristic, such as race, gender, age, or religion.

16. Union in which workers are grouped around the entire industry in which they are employed.

17. The purchasing power of an hour's work.

IV. SUMMARY AND CHAPTER OUTLINE

This section summarizes the key concepts from the chapter.

A. Fundamentals of Wage Determination

1. Average wages have increased in the United States over the past century. This does not mean that all workers in the economy have experienced the same good fortune or that all occupations have experienced continual wage growth. However, a rising trend in the average wage is indicative of an increase in labor productivity and a general improvement in economic well-being.

2. Remember that the market demand curve for any input is the horizontal summation of the individual firm marginal revenue product curves. (Marginal revenue product = MRP = marginal revenue × marginal product.) This function is downward-sloping because of the law of diminishing returns and, in imperfectly competitive markets, also because marginal revenue is declining. Given this scenario, the demand for labor increases when the marginal product of labor increases.

In this century, the marginal products of many types of labor have increased tremendously due to increases in capital that allow workers to be more productive on the job, and also due to improvements in education that have increased literacy rates in the United States. Increased labor productivity has pushed the demand for labor to the right and pulled wages up for many workers. We can test this theory by looking across countries and noting that where education, literacy, and capital bases are low, wages also tend to be low.

3. *Labor supply* refers to the number of hours that a particular population desires to work in exchange for wages. Three key elements help to determine the shape and position of the supply curve in any particular labor market. First, the *number of hours worked* determines the individual labor supply curve. Although many people have no control over standard workdays or workweeks, the number of hours worked over the course of a lifetime is something that most people can choose. Remember that the market supply curve is the horizontal summation of the individual supply curves.

The opposing forces of *income* and *substitution effects* on labor supply create the possibility of a backward-bending labor supply curve. As wages climb, the supply curve will display its usual positive slope only if the substitution effect (which pushes people toward working more) dominates the income effect (which tempts people to work less). The substitution effect says that higher wages lead to higher "opportunity costs" of leisure; that is, when wages increase the "cost" of not working increases. This encourages workers to substitute *away from leisure*. The income effect says that higher wages lead to higher worker income. With more income, people can afford to *buy more of all goods, including leisure*. If the substitution effect dominates, an increase in wages inspires an increase in the quantity of labor supplied and thus an upward-sloping labor supply curve. If the income effect dominates, as it may for high wages, then an increase in wages might actually inspire a reduction in the quantity of labor supplied.

Second, *labor force participation* helps to determine the shape and position of the market supply curve. Some people may choose not to participate in the labor force but may instead become homemakers or do volunteer work. Due to technical problems surrounding measurement, economists only count as employed those who work in exchange for a wage or salary, and only count in the work force those who

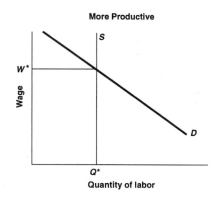

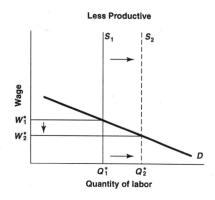

Figure 13-1

are employed or actively seeking work. As the labor force participation rate changes, the shape and position of the market labor supply curve will change as well.

Third, *immigration* can have an impact on the market labor supply curve. As people from other countries have moved into the United States over the course of the century, the labor supply curve has shifted to the right. Many of these people enter into markets as noncompeting groups; that is, they enter low-skill, low-wage jobs in neighborhoods populated by people from their home countries. As their job skills and English skills improve, they have the opportunity to enter a wider range of job markets. Figure 13-1 illustrates the initial impact of the entry of large numbers of immigrants into two different labor markets. Notice that the supply curve in the less productive labor market shifts to the right, further widening the wage differentials that exist.

4. In spite of the fact that the average wage is increasing in the United States, wide wage differentials exist across groups of workers. This runs counter to the predictions of perfect competition, which describes markets in which perfect information and a homogeneous product drive all prices in a market to equilibrium.

5. According to economists, wage differentials have three important sources. First, *jobs differ in their attributes and in their attractiveness.* Jobs that are particularly unpleasant earn *compensating differentials.* This means that supply and demand reflect the utility or "disutility" that workers get from doing particular tasks. For example, because workers in a nuclear facility have to experience more risk than do workers in many other jobs, the supply of these workers is lower and wages tend to be higher. This wage differential compensates individuals for experiencing relatively unpleasant circumstances.

Differences across people also lead to wage dispersion. Innate physical and mental abilities, education and training, and experience are but a few characteristics that make workers heterogeneous, that is, different from one another. Labor quality depends upon *human capital,* the stock of useful and productive knowledge that workers accumulate during their lifetimes. All of these factors help to explain why some

workers earn more than other workers. For example, the average salary for professional baseball players in the major leagues is less than $1 million. However, players with star quality sign multimillion-dollar contracts as a return to the amount of human capital that they have been able to amass.

Finally, *the absence of competition in markets can lead to wage dispersion.* By "absence of competition" we mean that markets are often divided into *noncompeting groups* meaning that it is difficult and costly for a member of one profession to enter another. For example, although a college economics professor might be a "doctor of philosophy," he or she cannot costlessly begin a medical practice tomorrow! As labor markets have become more and more sophisticated, workers have increasingly specialized in particular production tasks; this has created large numbers of noncompeting groups due to the fact that it is difficult and expensive, and often requires lots of training and education, to enter any particular field as a practitioner.

B. Economics of Labor Unions

1. In spite of the fact that only one-seventh, or about 15 percent, of the work force in the United States remained unionized in 1995, the labor movement has had, and continues to have, a significant impact on the appearance and operation of labor markets. Samuel Gompers was the father of this movement and was the founder of the American Federation of Labor (AFL), a large group of craft unions. Today, the AFL-CIO (Congress of Industrial Organizations) exists as a large coalition of craft and industry unions.

2. The main task of unions is to engage employers in *collective bargaining,* the negotiation process that can take place between representatives of firms and workers for the purpose of establishing mutually agreeable conditions of employment. Unions negotiate over compensation issues and also over work rules (job assignments, tasks, job security, etc.) and procedural features(seniority, layoff policy, dispute resolution, etc.) of the workplace. Workers were guaranteed the right to collective bargaining in 1935 by the National Labor Relations Act. This basic right allows employees to work together to improve the conditions of

their employment; without this right, a single worker is often at a disadvantage in bargaining with his or her employer.

3. Empirical evidence shows that unions have been somewhat successful at increasing the wages of members. They have achieved this goal most successfully by monopolizing labor supply and controlling entry into particular occupations.

C. Discrimination by Race and Gender

1. Labor market *discrimination* occurs when a difference in earnings arises simply because of an irrelevant personal characteristic, such as race, gender, religion, age, or sexual orientation. These characteristics are difficult, if not impossible, for the worker to change, and there is no reason for the worker to desire changes in these characteristics.

2. In economic terms, competitive forces should eliminate discrimination from markets. Employers who discriminate are hiring from a smaller pool of potential applicants or failing to take advantage of the productive talents of those already employed. This type of inefficiency should eventually drive them out of business. However, discrimination based upon prejudice can become so integrated into social behavior that minority groups with particular characteristics are often discriminated against in education and training programs, making them unable to compete for certain jobs. Empirical evidence shows that differentials across gender and racial groups are not entirely due to discrimination but that a significant portion of the differential cannot be explained by human capital or other market-based factors.

3. Public policy to reduce discrimination in labor markets has taken several different forms. The Equal Pay Act of 1963 requires employers to pay men and women equal wages for the same work. The Civil Rights Act of 1964 outlaws discrimination in hiring, firing, and employment. Both of these pieces of legislation have laid a legal foundation for eliminating discrimination.

V. HELPFUL HINTS

1. Notice that the substitution and income effects that influence the labor supply curve are similar to the substitution and income effects that occur as consumers move along a demand curve. Substitution effects occur when the price of a product or of leisure rises; consumers substitute toward relatively cheaper goods or work time. Income effects occur when a consumer has more purchasing power; consumers can buy more of all goods, including leisure. With both applications, the effects may support one another or may contradict one another.

2. Human capital is a specific type of productive capital. Workers pursue education and training in order to raise their value to employers; hence, there are costs and benefits to making an investment in human capital.

Think of this investment in this same way you would think of any other type of capital investments. As long as the marginal benefit outweighs the marginal cost, the investment project should be undertaken. The benefits include the extra wages that you will earn over the life of the investment, while the costs include the payments that you make for tuition, books, fees, etc. Of course, education and training programs bring utility to workers in ways that cannot always be measured in dollars and cents. However, this dollars-and-cents type of analysis can be useful in making decisions about human capital investments.

3. Table 13-4 in your textbook is somewhat complex, so it is reproduced here as Table 13-1. As this table reveals, market wage structures show a great variety of patterns.

Notice that the labor situations have been defined based on two characteristics. First, in a particular market are workers all alike (homogeneous), or do workers differ in some important ways (heterogeneous)? Second, in a particular market are jobs all alike, or do they differ based upon some general characteristic of the market?

In *case 1*, people are homogeneous and jobs are all alike. This is the extreme perfectly competitive situation, and wages will be equal across all jobs and all workers. In *case 2*, people are still homogeneous, but jobs differ in their attractiveness. To make jobs "equal" those jobs that are more unpleasant receive higher wage compensation, while those that are more pleasant receive lower wage compensation. The idea here is that wages adjust until the total utility a worker receives from each job will be about equal, once all job characteristics are accounted for. *Case 3* deals with heterogeneous people separated into noncompeting groups based upon skill, experience, education, training, or other factors that make an occupation difficult to enter. In this case, wage differentials are referred to as *pure economic rent*, which is defined as the excess of wages above the workers' best available incomes in other occupations. For example, the difference between what Oprah earns as an entertainer and her wages as, say, an accountant, would be termed pure economic rent. Finally, *case 4* deals with heterogeneous people divided into *partially* competing groups. This means that there is some limited mobility between groups, so groups have less monopoly power over occupations. High-wage occupations are slowly flooded with job applicants, leading to an increase in supply, and thus lower wages. By contrast, low-wage occupations are slowly abandoned by workers, leading to a decrease in supply, and thus, higher wages. Once mobility of workers is allowed, even partially, wages have a tendency to move toward some general-equilibrium level.

4. Your authors state, "The largest group to suffer from economic discrimination is women." While this may be true in the United States, and in some particular occupations, discrimination is often based on prejudice, and so it is generally

TABLE 13-1 Summary of Competitive Wage Determination

Labor Situation	Wage Result
1. People all alike—jobs all alike.	No wage differentials.
2. People all alike—jobs differ in attractiveness.	Compensating wage differentials.
3. People differ, but each type of labor is in unchangeable supply ("noncompeting groups").	Wage differentials that are "pure economic rents."
4. People differ, but there is some mobility among groups ("partially competing groups").	General-equilibrium pattern of wage differentials as determined by general demand and supply (includes situations 1-3 as special cases.

culturally and socially determined. Therefore, it differs across countries. Think about the extreme anti-Moslem sentiments displayed in Serbia and Bosnia, and consider the degree of anti-Semitism that has existed around the world. Both examples describe discrimination based on religious affiliation. Discrimination against African Americans in the United States has also been significant and is racially motivated. Age discrimination suits have become more prevalent of late, as the elimination of mandatory retirement has allowed people to work far beyond age 65. The point is that economic discrimination has targeted different groups at different times, and it would be wrong to ignore the impact of any of these instances.

VI. MULTIPLE CHOICE QUESTIONS

These questions are organized by topic from the chapter outline. Choose the best answer from the options available.

A. Fundamentals of Wage Determination

1. Average wages have increased in the United States over the past 100 years because:
   a.   people have been working longer and longer hours.
   b.   as the capital base expands, workers have more equipment and technology to work with. This makes them more productive.
   c.   as the capital base expands, firms substitute capital for labor. This drives the marginal product of labor down.
   d.   increased educational and training opportunities have made workers more productive.
   e.   both **b** and **d** are correct.

2. A perfectly competitive labor market is one in which:
   a.   there are large numbers of workers and employers, none of which has the power to affect wage rates appreciably.
   b.   there are large numbers of workers who are all union members bargaining with a single large employer.
   c.   training is difficult and time-consuming, so few workers enter the occupation although there are many potential employers.
   d.   monopoly power is used to determine wages and employment levels.
   e.   a single employer purchases labor in a small town in which workers have other employment options.

3. Imperfect competition in a labor market could be indicated by a situation in which:
   a.   one firm makes wage determinations for an entire industry.
   b.   different wages are paid for different jobs in order to compensate for differences in risk.
   c.   different wages are paid for different jobs because the jobs have different requirements.
   d.   the wages paid for certain jobs are really payments of economic rent.
   e.   the excess of one wage rate over another is a compensating differential.

4. Wage differentials exist across countries primarily because of:
   a.   the existence of international trade agreements between countries.
   b.   the amount of capital that workers have available to them differs across countries.
   c.   the amount of education and training that workers receive is different across countries.
   d.   firms try to discriminate against workers in less-developed countries.
   e.   both **b** and **c** are correct.

5. Determinants of the supply of labor for a given economy include:
   a.   the size of its population.
   b.   the rate of participation of its population in the labor force.
   c.   the standard or legislated length of the workweek.
   d.   the quality and level of skill embodied in the work force.
   e.   all the above.

6. The substitution effect, applied to a worker's decision to change the number of hours worked daily when offered a different hourly wage, refers specifically to which of the following statements?
   a.   If the wage offered to workers rises, workers will want to buy better and more costly goods, so each worker must work longer hours.
   b.   A general increase in wages tends to produce a general rise in consumer prices that cancels out any real-income gain for workers.
   c.   Leisure (nonwork) time is desirable, so a worker's normal inclination is to choose more leisure in response to any rise in real income.

d. The cost of working is leisure (nonwork) time sacrificed; hence, if the wage offered to workers falls, then leisure will become relatively less expensive.

e. Any labor cost increase prompts employers to try to substitute capital for labor in production.

7. Which alternative in question 6 would have been correct had that question referred to the income effect rather than the substitution effect?

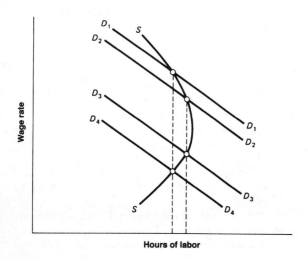

Figure 13-2

a.

b.

c.

d.

e.

Figure 13-2 illustrates a backward-bending labor supply curve and four possible demand curves. Use the diagram to answer questions 8 through 11.

8. If the demand curve changes from position 1 to position 2, then the:

a. substitution effect dominates the income effect.

b. substitution effect and income effect cancel one another out.

c. income effect dominates the substitution effect.

d. income effect and the substitution effect work in the same direction.

e. none of these statements is correct.

9. If the demand curve moves from position 2 to position 3, which alternative in question 8 would be correct?

a.

b.

c.

d.

e.

10. If the demand curve moves from position 3 to position 4, which alternative in question 8 would be correct?

a.

b.

c.

d.

e.

11. If the demand curve moves from position 4 to position 3, which alternative in question 8 would be correct?

a.

b.

c.

d.

e.

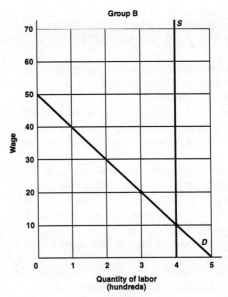

Figure 13-3

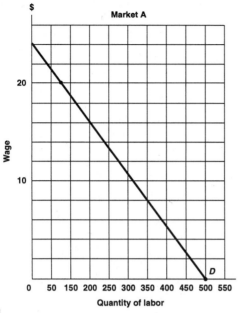

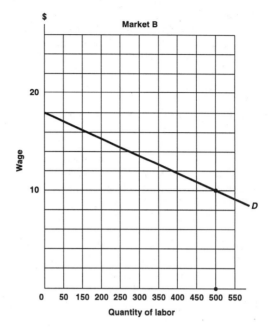

Figure13-4

12. Empirical evidence on labor supply decisions has shown that the:
    a. labor supply curve for adult males is slightly backward-bending.
    b. labor supply curve for adult women is slightly backward-bending.
    c. labor supply curves for all groups are upward-sloping.
    d. wage elasticity of supply for all groups is greater than 1.
    e. wage elasticity of supply for all groups is negative.

13. The diagrams in Figure 13-3 show the labor markets of two noncompeting groups. Suppose antidiscrimination laws lead to the movement of 100 workers from group B to group A. This would cause:
    a. daily wages in group A to increase to $50 and daily wages in group B to decrease to $20.
    b. daily wages in group A to decrease to $40 and daily wages in group B to increase to $20.
    c. daily wages in group B to decrease to $40 while wages in group B remain constant.
    d. wages in both groups to remain constant.
    e. equalization of wages across these two groups.

14. The concept of noncompeting groups in the labor market is considered useful in explaining:
    a. structural unemployment.
    b. wage differentials among different categories of labor.
    c. the lack of mobility among older workers.
    d. the impact on nonunionized sectors of wage increases in unionized sectors of the economy.

    e. why wage rates in certain industries have risen faster than the average.

15. The diagrams in Figure 13-4 describe the labor demand curves for two noncompeting groups in the labor market. If there are 100 workers in market A and 500 workers in market B, daily wages will be:
    a. $25 in market A and $5 in market B.
    b. $10 in market A and $10 in market B.
    c. $20 in market A and $0 in market B.
    d. $20 in market A and $10 in market B.
    e. none of the above.

16. To say that there is an economic-rent element in a person's income means that:
    a. this income comes at least in part from property ownership rather than from the labor supply.
    b. this income exceeds what it would be were the labor market perfectly competitive.
    c. if the price offered for this person's labor were increased, then he or she would want to reduce the number of daily hours worked.
    d. this income is much above average but is the result of some relatively unique natural talent.
    e. this person's labor supply curve is perfectly inelastic with respect to price, at least within some range of prices, because he or she is somewhat unique.

B. Economics of Labor Unions

17. Collective bargaining contracts:
    a. allow individual workers to bargain more effectively with their employers to improve only their own con-

ditions of employment.

b.   involve representatives of firms and workers in a process of negotiating conditions of employment.

c.   enforce conditions of employment that are determined solely by employers.

d.   can only be negotiated by members of the AFL-CIO.

e.   involve negotiation between firms and workers over only the economic package.

18. A labor union which wants simultaneously to raise wages for its members and to maintain as much employment as possible for them will be helped most by:

a.   an elastic derived demand for labor.

b.   an elastic supply of labor.

c.   an inelastic demand for the finished product.

d.   a perfectly competitive labor market.

e.   a perfectly competitive product market.

Figure 13-5 shows the supply and demand for labor in a market in which a union represents worker interests in a collective bargaining process. Use the diagram to answer questions 19 and 20.

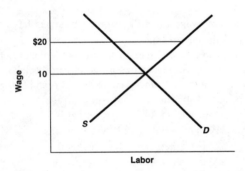

Figure 13-5

19. If the union negotiates a $10 wage:

a.   employment will increase.

b.   employment will decrease.

c.   wages will rise but employment will remain constant.

d.   wages will fall but employment will remain constant.

e.   wages and employment will remain at the perfectly competitive level.

20. If the union negotiates a $20 wage:

a.   employment will increase.

b.   employment will decrease.

c.   wages will rise but employment will remain constant.

d.   wages will fall but employment will remain constant.

e.   wages and employment will remain at the perfectly competitive level.

21. Some people argue that the high unemployment in Europe in the early 1990s reflected the fact that a fixed amount of labor demand was spread over too few people. Thus, they recommended that the number of work hours per person be reduced. This view is referred to as the:

a.   law of comparative advantage.

b.   fallacy of composition.

c.   law of diminishing returns.

d.   principle of Ocam's razor.

e.   lump-of-labor fallacy.

C. Discrimination by Race and Gender

22. If everyone in the labor force were exactly alike (i.e., no difference in skills or competence), and if the labor market were perfectly competitive, then:

a.   any wage-rate differences would have to be explained as qualitative differentials.

b.   there would still be a considerable range of different wage rates explained only in terms of perceived differences in skill.

c.   any wage-rate differences could nonetheless be explained as compensating differentials.

d.   any wage-rate differences would have to be explained in terms of the differing wage policies adopted by different firms.

e.   there would necessarily be only one wage rate.

23. Economists would expect to see discrimination disappear from labor markets because:

a.   government has enacted laws against it.

b.   competitive forces will drive inefficient firms out of business.

c.   the marginal cost of hiring an additional minority job candidate is higher than the marginal benefit.

d.   firms must hire the best candidate for each position in order to satisfy affirmative action requirements.

e.   none of the above.

24. In order to reduce labor market discrimination:

a.   the U.S. government now hires only minorities.

b.   the Civil Rights Act of 1964 and the Equal Pay Act of 1963 were passed.

c.   firms formed a coalition and agreed to provide equal employment opportunities for all.

d.   the Clayton Act of 1914 and the National Labor Relations Act of 1935 were passed.

e.   labor unions agreed to admit more women and minorities.

25. Which of the following is the best example of statistical discrimination?

a.   Ben hires no women as accountants because they are more likely than men to take time off to care for children.

b.   Alice hires no African-Americans at her firm because she believes that black and white workers can-

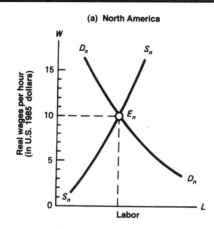

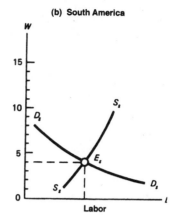

Figure 13-6

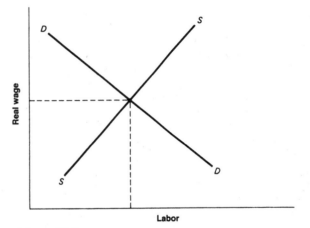

Figure 13-7

not work productively together.

c.   Ralph places all workers over the age of 60 into less demanding positions within his firm.

d.   A union only allows white males as members.

e.   Betty is determined to hire a little girl with red hair to play Annie in her new stage production of the hit musical "Annie."

VII. PROBLEM SOLVING

The following problems are designed to help you apply the concepts that you learned in this chapter.

A. Fundamentals of Wage Determination

1.   Figure 13-6 provides some insight into why real wages in North America are so much higher than they are in South America. From the units on the graph, in fact, it would appear that the real wage in North America is (**2 / 2.5 / 3**) times larger. One key to this difference is that (**the supply-of-labor curve is much higher in the South America panel / the demand-for-labor curve is much higher in the North America panel / the demand-for-labor curve is much higher in the South America panel**). Inasmuch as the demand-for-labor curve is a (**potential / derived / product**) demand curve, there are at least *two* reasons why it should be so positioned in panel (*a*) relative to panel (*b*). List them below:
      (1)
      (2)

2.   a.   The supply of labor has at least three major determinants. List them below:
      (1) _____
      (2) _____
      (3) _____
     b.   On the basis of the supply and demand curves depicted in Figure 13-7, indicate in the blanks provided the likely effect on the real wage of each of the following economic adjustments. Denote an increase by (+), a reduction by (-), and no change by (0).

____ (1) An increase in the working population

____ (2) A move toward shorter workweeks

____ (3) An increase in labor force participation by women

____ (4) Passage of stronger child labor laws

____ (5) Restriction of certain types of people from employment

____ (6) A large wave of immigrants who all want to work

Buried in your answers to these wage questions are the answers to questions like: Why do labor unions push for shorter workweeks? Why does labor fear opening U.S. borders to anyone who wants to come? Why do some drag their feet in the fight against discrimination on personal economic grounds?

3.   Suppose that the hourly wage offered to you rises. Assume that you have some freedom over the number of hours you choose to work per day or per week. In these circumstances, economic theory predicts that you might choose to work more, fewer, or the same number of hours per day.

     This indicates the opposite and conflicting pulls of the *substitution effect* and the *income effect*.

a.   When you are offered a higher wage for each hour worked, you are then sacrificing more money income than before for each hour you do not work; i.e., the opportunity cost of leisure is climbing. The higher hourly wage is thus an inducement to work (**more / fewer**) hours per day or week because leisure has become more expensive. This by itself is the substitution effect. It encourages a worker to give up some (**working hours in favor of leisure / leisure hours in favor of work**).

b.   Leisure time is (for most people) a desirable thing; as real incomes rise, most folks want more of it. The offer of a higher hourly wage makes more leisure possible (**with / without**) the sacrifice of some income. The pull of the income effect is toward (**fewer / more**) working hours and correspondingly (**fewer / more**) hours of leisure.

c.   For example, suppose that you are working 40 hours weekly given a $6 hourly wage, for a weekly income of $240. If your wage rises to $10, you could choose to earn $350 per week by working (**35 / 40 / 45**) hours. If this is the case, the (**substitution / income**) effect has dominated.

4.   There are four panels in Figure 13-8, one for each of the four parts to this question. For each part listed below, draw a new supply and/or demand curve in the corresponding panel to represent the effect of the change indicated, and predict the direction that the change will push the real wage and employment. For example, if one of the parts stated that there is an increase in the supply of labor, then you would draw a new supply curve to the right of the existing one and predict that wages would fall (-) and employment would climb (+). Record your predictions in Table 13-2.

a.   The job becomes more onerous than usual, and people demand compensation for its additional burdens.

b.   The job becomes extremely specialized, and only 10 people can accomplish the task that it requires.

e.   Education and training improve the quality of the labor employed.

d.   The job market is suddenly cut in half because of noncompeting discrimination.

TABLE 13-2

Part	Effect on Employment	Effect on Wages
a.	—	—
b.	—	—
c.	—	—
d.	—	—

B. Economics of Labor Unions

5.   a.   The union movement in the United States has had an important impact on the development of labor markets in this century. (**Industrial / Craft**) unions were the first to emerge, organized by Samuel Gompers around particular workplace skills. (**Industrial / Craft**) unions were organized later around entire industries, such as coal, steel, and autos.

b.   Collective bargaining is the process of negotiations between representatives of firms and workers for the purpose of establishing mutually agreeable conditions of employment. Suppose Figure 13-9 describes labor market conditions in the newly organized widget industry. Initially, the equilibrium wage rate is $___ per day and ___ workers are employed in the industry. Suppose the

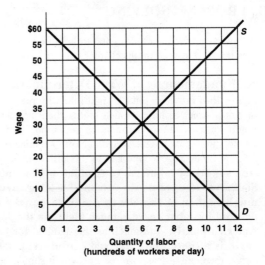

Figure 13-9

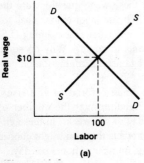
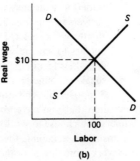
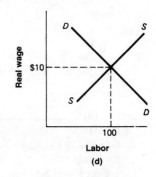

Figure 13-8

union targets a wage of $45 per day. This will limit employment to ___ workers and will lead to an excess (**demand / supply**) of ___ workers in the market.

c. In reality the union may or may not be able to achieve its wage target. A bilateral monopoly situation arises when (**a single union / a group of unions**) and (**a single buyer / a group of buyers**) of labor negotiate with one another. The result is a topic for game-theoretic research and modeling techniques.

C. Discrimination by Race and Gender

6. a. Consult Figure 13-10, which shows two labor markets separated by discrimination. Demand curves in both are indicated with *DD* notation; both have the same slopes. The supply curves are vertical at 10 and 5, respectively. If the discrimination were to lapse, then the demand curve in panel (*a*) would apply to everyone. The result would be (**an increase / a reduction**) in the wage paid to those initially alone in market A, from $___ to $___. This change would be caused by (**diminishing marginal productivity / diminishing labor utility / increasing productivity**). At the same time, those who were initially confined to market B would see their wage (**climb / fall**), a change that can be attributed to (**diminishing marginal productivity / increased productivity / increased labor utility**). The net effect would be an increase in the dollar value of output (GDP, if this were a macro model) of (**$10 / $15 / $20**). Illustrate these changes in the diagrams in Figure 13-10.

b. If the derived demand curve in market A were extremely inelastic, how would your answers to the qualitative parts of paragraph **a** change?

VIII. DISCUSSION QUESTIONS

Answer the following questions, making sure that you can explain the work you did to arrive at the answers.

1. Table 13-1 in your text lists wages and fringe benefits in Mexico at $1.75 per hour (1997). What kinds of actions might be taken to shift the labor demand curve to the right in Mexico?

2. Table 13-3 in your text lists average wages per full-time employee in the farming industry at $18,709 (1999). List and explain two factors that might explain low relative wages in this industry.

3. Think about the investment in human capital that you are making by taking this course in economics. List all of the direct costs, all of the opportunity costs, and then think about what you expect to gain. Is this investment a profitable one? Explain.

4. Since the mid-1960s, the labor force participation rate of women has risen dramatically, from 40 percent to almost 60 percent of the population. Your authors state, "A change of this magnitude cannot be explained by economic factors alone. To understand such a significant alteration in working patterns, one must look outside the narrow scope of economics—to changing social attitudes toward the role of women as mothers, homemakers, and workers."

List and explain three such changes that have occurred over this time period that may have had an impact on the labor force participation rates of women in the U.S. economy.

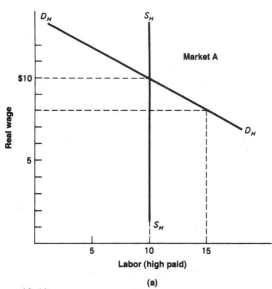 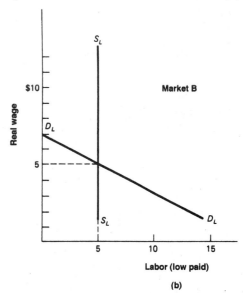

Figure 13-10

5. Immigration policy in the United States has been alive with controversy over the past few years, as people in border states like California and Florida have become inundated with both legal and illegal immigrants. Use market models to illustrate the impact of these immigrants on local labor markets. Who gains and who loses when large numbers of immigrants enter a labor market? On what does this depend?

6. We can use the concept of *price elasticity* (Chapter 4 in your text and in this *Study Guide*) to gain some insights into labor markets and the effects of unionization.

   a. Define the concept of price elasticity of demand in labor markets. Suppose you hear that the elasticity of demand for a particular type of labor is -2.5. How would you interpret this?

   b. Define the concept of price elasticity of supply in labor markets. Suppose you hear that the elasticity of supply for a particular type of labor is .4. How would you interpret this?

   c. We learned in this chapter that unions work to increase wages for the workers they represent. Will this be an easier or less easy task to accomplish if the demand curve for the final product is relatively elastic? Use a diagram to illustrate your answer.

IX. ANSWERS TO STUDY GUIDE QUESTIONS

III. Review of Key Concepts

17	Real wages
6	Perfectly competitive labor markets
11	Compensating differentials
12	Labor supply
14	Substitution effect
1	Income effect
2	Human capital
4	Pure economic rent
9	Noncompeting groups
5	Craft unions
16	Industrial unions
3	Collective bargaining
10	National Labor Relations Act
7	Bilateral monopoly
13	Lump-of-labor fallacy
15	Discrimination
7	Statistical discrimination

VI. Multiple Choice Questions

1. E   2. A   3. A   4. E   5. E   6. D
7. C   8. C   9. B   10. A   11. A   12. A
13. B   14. B   15. D   16. E   17. B   18. C
19. E   20. B   21. E   22. C   23. B   24. B
25. A

VII. Problem Solving

1. 2.5, the demand-for-labor curve is much higher in the North America panel, derived
   (1) more resources in North America
   (2) more technology in North America

2. a. (1) population
      (2) labor force participation
      (3) hours worked per week

   b. (1) -, because the supply curve shifts right
      (2) +, because the supply curve shifts left
      (3) -, because the supply curve shifts right
      (4) +, because the supply curve shifts left
      (5) +, because the supply curve shifts left
      (6) -, because the supply curve shifts right

3. a. more, leisure hours in favor of work
   b. without, fewer, more
   c. 35, income

4. See Table 13-2.

TABLE 13-2

Part	Effect on Employment	Effect on Wages	Graph
a.	-	+	Supply shifts left
b.	≈	+	Supply vertical at 10
c.	+	+	Demand shifts right
d.	-	+	Supply shifts left

5. a. Craft, Industrial
   b. $30, 600, 300, supply, 600
   c. a single union, a single buyer

6. a. a reduction, $10, $8, diminishing marginal productivity, climb, increased productivity, $15
   b. If the curve $D_H D_H$ were sufficiently inelastic, then the addition of five workers from market B could lower the wage below $5. All five workers would not move, if that were the case, and the equilibrium wage in both markets would still exceed $5.

VIII. Discussion Questions

1. Workers might obtain more training and education, increasing their productivity. Firms might find new markets for their final products, increasing demand for final products and the workers needed to produce output.

2. Markets for farm labor are nearly perfectly competitive. Farm employees often need little formal education and hence have not invested large sums of money in human capital development.

3. Direct costs include the costs of tuition, books, tutoring, childcare expense if you have a family that must be cared for, and travel to and from school. Opportunity costs account for what you could be earning at the next-best use of your time. This might be overtime pay if you worked additional hours in the market or it might be measured by the value of tasks that you would be completing at home, such as laundry, a freshly painted room, or bedtime stories. You

hope to gain increased productivity so that you earn more money in the marketplace or take more value into any task that you might undertake over the course of your lifetime.

4 a. Improved technology in the household, allowing greater productivity per hour spent.

b. Many Women now have better control over their reproductive lives.

c. Government legislation has provided better access to education and jobs for women.

5. See diagram. Immigrants gain because they often have better job opportunities and higher wages in the U.S. Employers gain because the price of labor is now lower. Workers who were already in the market lose because their wages are now lower. Local taxpayers lose if they have to bear the burden of higher welfare costs brought on by these immigrants.

6. a. Price elasticity of demand in labor markets measures the responsiveness of employers to changes in wage rates. If the wage elasticity of demand is -2.5, we would say that if wages increase by 10 percent, then the quantity of labor demanded would fall by 25 percent.

b. Price elasticity of supply in labor markets measures the responsiveness of workers to changes in wage rates. If the wage elasticity of supply for labor is .4, we would say that if wages increased by 10 percent, then the quantity of labor supplied would increase by 4 percent.

c. The more inelastic the demand curve for the final product, the easier it is for firms to raise wages. The more inelastic the demand for the final product, the smaller the buyer response to any change in the price of the product. Firms can pass cost increases on to consumers more easily.

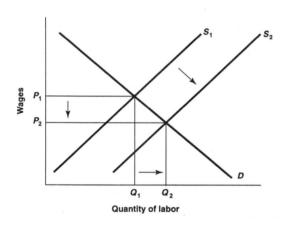

CHAPTER 14

Land and Capital

I. CHAPTER OVERVIEW

Preceding chapters have outlined how input prices are determined, with special emphasis on the wages paid to labor. It is now time to extend the analysis to include the determination of the economic rents and the return to capital.

Economic rent, strictly interpreted, is the return paid to an input which is available in fixed supply and which has only one possible occupation. Economic rent is, as a result, perhaps the simplest input price to analyze because it emerges immediately from markets characterized by perfectly inelastic supply. Rents are, nonetheless, critical to the accurate calculation of the economic and social costs of production. They also provide a convenient benchmark against which to measure the relative (in)efficiency of various taxation schemes.

Market determination of the return to capital is, by way of contrast, an extremely complicated process. The return to capital depends upon many factors, economic and psychological, that lie well beyond the straightforward intersection of a derived demand curve and a simple supply curve. It depends upon the willingness of people to forgo present consumption to finance increased consumption in the future. It depends upon the uncertainties inherent in forecasting the future, and the aversion of people to the risks that those uncertainties create. It even depends upon policies enacted on a macroeconomic and sometimes international level. For present purposes, however, only the simplest of theories will be explored. Brief mention of the many possible complications will be made, but the focus of the chapter will be a simple but appropriate description of the workings of the capital market. This rather extreme caveat notwithstanding, your work in Chapter 14 will produce substantial insight into one of the most critical topics of contemporary research.

II. LEARNING OBJECTIVES

After you have read Chapter 14 in your text and completed the exercises in this *Study Guide* chapter, you should be able to:

1. Explain the concept of **economic rent**, the circumstances under which it applies, and the inferences which can be drawn from those circumstances regarding the theory of efficient taxation.

2. Define precisely what economists mean when they speak of physical capital, and understand why **capital** is not a primary factor of production.

3. Define the **rate of return on capital** and describe how it relates to an interest rate.

4. Explain **present value** and its importance in evaluating the potential profitability of a capital project. Record a formula for the present value of a perpetual asset which generates a constant return and of a more general asset which generates an arbitrary stream of returns into the future. Trace the sensitivity of the present value in either circumstance to changes in the interest rate.

5. Define **profit** in a statistical sense, and explain the roles of (a) implicit rents, interest payments, and wages; (b) rewards for risk taking; and (c) monopoly rents in determining profit.

6. Explain the major factors that determine (a) the derived demand for capital and (b) the supply of capital in the classical theory. Relate the theory to some of its major qualifications: (a) technological change, (b) uncertainty and risk, (c) present and future inflation, and (d) macroeconomic shocks and policies.

7. State the relationship between the **real** rate of interest, the **nominal** rate of interest, and the rate of **inflation**. Explain why the **classical theory of capital investment** uses the real rate of interest as its price variable.

III. REVIEW OF KEY CONCEPTS

Match the following terms from column A with their definitions in column B.

A	B
___ Rent	1. Measures the increase in output when the firm hires an additional unit of capital, all else fixed.
___ Henry George	2. The value today of an asset that yields a stream of income over time.

__ Capital

__ Rentals

__ Rate of return
on capital

__ Profits

__ Real interest
rates

__ Nominal interest
rates

__ Present value

__ Roundaboutness

__ Marginal product
of capital

__ Risk premium

__ Implicit returns

3.   The difference between total revenues and total costs.

4.   The opportunity costs of factors owned by firms.

5.   Interest rates that measure the quantity of goods we get tomorrow for goods forgone today.

6.   The price of using a piece of land for a period of time.

7.   Describes the fact that investment in capital goods involves forgoing present consumption to increase future consumption.

8.   Consists of those durable produced goods that are in turn used as productive inputs for further production.

9.   Denotes the net dollar return per year for every dollar of invested capital.

10. Return to investors that covers uninsurable risk of investment.

11. Interest rates that are measured in dollar terms.

12. Payments for the temporary use of capital goods.

13. Believed that government should be financed primarily through property taxes on land.

IV. SUMMARY AND CHAPTER OUTLINE

This section summarizes the key concepts from the chapter.

A. Land and Rent

1.   *Economic rent is* the return paid to a specialized factor available in fixed supply. In this chapter, *land* is the specialized factor of interest. The market equilibrium price of land is determined mainly by the demand for it, relative to the fixed supply available. We call the price of using a piece of land for a period of time *rent*.

2.   Efficient taxation occurs in markets for land due to the presence of the perfectly inelastic supply curve. This means that a tax will cause no distortion in either the quantity supplied or the price paid *by the employer*; only the supplier bears the burden.

3.   Because of this efficiency property when taxes are placed on markets for land, Henry George recommended financing government principally through property taxes on land. Although this idea has not served as a foundation for tax policy in the United States, it filters to the forefront of debates surrounding taxation from time to time.

B. Capital and Interest

1.   *Physical capital* consists of structures, equipment, and inventories of inputs and outputs that are in turn used as productive inputs for further production. Payments for the temporary use of capital goods are called *rentals*.

2.   Capital is the result of deferred consumption which yields a positive return by adding to future production potential. The *rate of return to capital is* a percentage computed from the ratio of net annual receipts and the dollar value of capital. For example, suppose you buy an ounce of gold today for $350 and sell it a *year* from now for $400. Your rate of return on that investment is $50/$350 = 14 percent.

3.   The supply of funds necessary to finance investment in physical capital is generated by deferred-consumption saving. However, when people save, they expect a return; *interest rates* are annual returns on borrowed funds. The *real* rate of interest is equal to the *nominal* rate reduced by the *rate of inflation*.

4.   *Present value* is the value today of a stream of future returns. If these (net) returns are indexed by N_t, with t representing the time period, and i represents an interest rate, then:

$$V = \frac{N_1}{(1+i)} + \frac{N_2}{(1+i)^2} + ... + \frac{N_t}{(1+i)^t}$$

For example, consider an investment opportunity with a two-year life. In the first year the investment will bring in $30,000, and in the second year, $40,000. The relevant market interest rate is 10 percent. If the investment costs $50,000 today, What is its present value?

Given this information, N_1 = $30,000, N_2 = $40,000, and i = 10 percent. The present value can be found as follows:

$$V = \frac{\$30,000}{(1+.1)} + \frac{\$40,000}{(1+.1)^2} - \$50,000 = \$10,330.55$$

If an asset has perpetual life, and if $N_t = N$ = *permanent* annual receipts, then the equation simplifies to:

$$V = \frac{\$N}{i}$$

The higher the interest rate i, the lower the present value V in any case.

5.   Very simply put, *profits* are revenues less costs. They accrue to many owned, nonlabor factors of production in the form of *implicit rents*. They can also represent rewards for risk taking and monopoly rents derived from continued scarcity. Empirical studies show that over the past 30 years, U.S. corporations have earned a modest rate of return on their investments—only about 6 percent after taxes.

6.   Investment in capital goods involves indirect *roundaboutness*. This means that forgoing consumption today in

order to increase investment leads indirectly to even greater consumption in the future.

7. The *derived demand for capital* comes from its marginal product. Remember that the law of diminishing returns applies to capital, too. That is, as a firm continues to invest in capital, the rate of return on marginal dollars will eventually fall. This causes the demand for capital to be downward-sloping. High interest rates reduce the number of capital investment projects with positive present values and thus the demand for (new) capital. Low interest rates do the opposite, thereby encouraging capital-intensive investment.

8. In short-run equilibrium, a fixed amount of capital is rationed such that the rate of return on capital exactly equals the market interest rate. In the short run, the supply of capital is fixed, based on past investments; thus, its price is determined by the position of the demand curve.

9. In long-run equilibrium, the supply of capital is upward-sloping, which means that as interest rates rise, savers are willing to supply more funds to the market. Thus, in the long run, the equilibrium is found where the demand for capital crosses the supply of capital.

10. Acceptance of the supply-and-demand structure of classical capital theory is subject to qualifications which relate to technological change, uncertainty and risk, inflation, and macroeconomic fluctuations. Taxes and inflation can alter the behavior of investors because they lower the *real* return on investments. Technological changes usually increase the return on investments by increasing the productivity of resources. Finally, we must remember that all investments carry risk and uncertainty. Any decision is based upon *best estimates* of the future. Since the future is rarely certain, there are few absolute guarantees that the return for a given investment will be as predicted.

V. HELPFUL HINTS

1. The perfectly inelastic supply curve, applicable in the case of land, should be familiar to you. It was introduced in Chapter 4, with elasticities, reviewed in Chapter 8, and applied to the general case of factors of production in Chapter 12. Look back to those sources if you need a review.

2. Economists' interest in the case of the single-occupation input with perfectly inelastic supply led them to ask another question: Does the payment made to such an input constitute a cost of production? At first, this may seem to be an odd question. Each separate user of that input must pay the price, high or low, for the quantity of that input which he or she employs, and that outlay certainly is a cost of production. On the other hand, production costs are supposed to reflect social costs. Chapter 2 used the production-possibilities frontier to point out that the way to get more of some good A is to transfer some of the inputs used in the production of some other good B into the production of A, i.e., to sacrifice some

consumption of B for the potential of increasing the production of A. This sort of substitution is possible, of course, only for inputs which can be used to produce either A or B.

Economic rents are, by definition, paid only to inputs which have just one possible occupation; they apply, therefore, only to inputs whose employment cannot be transferred from the production of one good to the production of another. Their employment does *not* entail a cost to society. When these inputs are put to work, their employment does not impose any sacrifice of any other commodity.

3. There are several different ways to define and measure profits. Footnote 8 from your text reviews these, but the concept is important and bears repeating here. Remember that accountants measure profits as revenues less explicit costs. If profits are positive, a firm pays all its bills and has something left over. Economists measure profits as revenues less explicit costs *less implicit costs*. Implicit costs are the opportunity costs of doing business, or what the firm could earn if it put resources to their next-best alternative use. If *economic* profits are positive, then a firm is not only earning something after paying bills, but also its earnings are greater than they would be if resources were put to their next-best alternative use. This is a very important distinction.

4. The present-value formula can be run in reverse to yield *future value*. Suppose we have $10 to put in an investment that is expected to yield 10 percent per year for three years. How much money will we have at the end of the life of the investment? Note that each year, the interest will become part of the *new* principal that is carried into the following year. So:

> Year 1: $10.00 + ($10.00 × .1) = $11.00
> Year 2: $11.00 + ($11.00 × .1) = $12.10
> Year 3: $12.10 + ($12.10 × .1) = $13.31

At the end of each year we have what we started with *plus* interest on what we started with.

5. Capital is one of those terms that economists use in a very specific way. *Physical capital* includes structures, like factories and warehouses; equipment, like drills and hammers; and inventories of inputs and outputs, like finished automobiles and shirts. People sometimes use the term to refer to *financial* capital, or money used to save or to invest. *Beware!* This is *not* what an economist means by the term *capital*.

VI. MULTIPLE CHOICE QUESTIONS

These questions are organized by topic from the chapter outline. Choose the best answer from the options available.

A. Land and Rent

1. *Rent* is defined by economists as:
   a. a payment for the use of factors of production that are infinitely abundant in supply.

b.   structures, equipment, or inventories that can be used to produce other things.

c.   the payment for the use of factors of production that are fixed in supply.

d.   the interest rate paid for the use of land.

e.   all of the above.

2.   If supply were perfectly inelastic with respect to price, and if total demand were to decline, then the quantity supplied would:

a.   not fall, and price would fall more than it otherwise would.

b.   not fall, and price would fall less than it otherwise would.

c.   fall, and price would fall more than it otherwise would.

d.   fall, and price would fall less than it otherwise would.

e.   none of these results would necessarily occur .

3.   If a productive input had only one opportunity for employment (i.e., if there were only one commodity it could help to produce), then the price paid to it:

a.   would tend to fall below the normal competitive level, because of the absence of competitive bidding.

b.   would be a cost to each of its separate users but not a cost to the whole community or society.

c.   should not be counted as a cost by each of its separate users, although it would still be a cost to the whole community or society.

d.   would be a cost both to its separate users and to the whole community or society.

e.   would not be a cost either to its separate users or to the whole community.

4.   Suppose that land is fixed in total supply but has many alternative uses (one of which is tobacco production). A 50 percent tax on the rental price of any land used for tobacco production would result in:

a.   a 50 percent increase in the rent which tobacco producers must pay.

b.   a 50 percent decrease in the rent paid by users of tobacco land.

c.   a 50 percent decrease in the rent received (net) by owners of such land.

d.   no change in the amount of rent paid or received.

e.   none of these consequences.

5.   It would be correct to say that economic rent is not a cost of production because:

a.   it is not a payment to a factor of production that actually makes a contribution to the output of finished goods.

b.   the suppliers of the input in question can receive the same price for employment in one occupation as they can in another

c.   the rent payment in question is really a payment for buildings or improvements to the land, not for the use of the land itself.

d.   when this factor is used for the production of good A, its employment does not entail any sacrifice of any other good B.

e.   competition among the suppliers will continually tend to push the price of this factor toward zero.

6.   Economic analysis suggests that:

a.   society's resources cannot be allocated properly into employment unless competitive rent payments are made.

b.   rental payments to factors with relatively price elastic supply should be taxed more heavily.

c.   economic rent does not enter into the cost of production .

d.   the allocation of resources can be distorted if certain input supplies are inelastic with respect to price.

e.   rental payments to factors with relatively price-elastic supply should be taxed more heavily.

7.   Suppose Figure 14-1 represents the market for land in Connecticut. A tax of $100 per acre will:

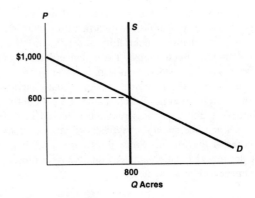

Figure 14-1

a.   be shared equally between buyers and sellers.

b.   cause the buyers' price to increase by $75 and the sellers' price to fall by $25.

c.   have no effect on the market, since supply is perfectly inelastic.

d.   cause no change in the buyers' price but will reduce the sellers' price by the full $100.

e.   cause no change in the sellers' price but will reduce the buyers' price by the full $100.

B. Capital and Interest

8.   Capital consists of:

a.   structures, such as factories and homes.

b.   equipment, such as machine, tools and computers.

c.   inventories of final products and inputs.

d.   all of the above.

e.   money that people are willing to lend.

9. If the rate of return on any capital asset were to be computed, several items of information would be needed. Which among the following would *not* be required?
   a. The original cost of purchasing or constructing the asset.
   b. The means of financing the original purchase.
   c. The estimated maintenance or operating cost that must be paid in order to keep the asset in satisfactory operating (revenue-earning) condition throughout its life.
   d. The estimated revenue that the asset will produce throughout its lifetime.
   e. The degree of "riskiness" surrounding estimated revenue, i.e., the degree of uncertainty about future revenues.

10. An asset's present value is:
   a. its original cost plus an estimate of maintenance expense throughout its lifetime.
   b. the same thing as its original cost.
   c. the sum of all its discounted net earnings.
   d. the sum of all its net earnings, without discounting.
   e. the rate of interest at which the asset would just become worth buying or building.

11. According to the classical theory, which of the following accurately describes the role played by the law of diminishing returns in the determination of interest rates?
   a. As capital goods accumulate relative to the supplies of land and labor, the rate of return of new additions to the capital stock must fall.
   b. The cost of producing additional capital goods must necessarily increase (in the absence of innovation).
   c. A steady increase in output must lower the price of a consumer good and thus lower the return to capital.
   d. Innovation cannot continually check the long-run tendency of the interest rate to fall.
   e. None of the above.

12. In classical investment theory, the rate of interest is determined by the:
   a. estimated rate of return to various capital projects.
   b. extent to which the public wishes to use the income it receives for consumption.
   c. estimated rate of return to various capital projects and the extent to which the public wishes to use the income it receives for consumption.
   d. estimated rate of return to various capital projects and the size of the capital stock.
   e. estimated rate of return to various capital projects and the rate of technological development.

13. Classical investment theory holds that there should be:
   a. a tendency toward a long-run equilibrium in which the market interest rate would be zero.
   b. a tendency toward a long-run equilibrium in which gross investment would be constantly falling.
   c. a tendency toward a long-run equilibrium in which

net investment would be maintained at a steady and nonzero rate.
   d. a tendency toward a long-run equilibrium in which saving out of income would be zero.
   e. no tendency toward any sort of long-run equilibrium.

14. The classical theory described in question 13 neglected the fact that:
   a. the amount saved out of income might be influenced by the interest rate.
   b. it is necessary to discount future items of income in order to establish their present value.
   c. while the interest rate may approach zero, it cannot actually reach zero.
   d. technological change might continually increase the rate of return to capital.
   e. people are typically impatient to consume now, rather than accumulate for future consumption.

15. A certain asset is expected to yield a steady net income (i.e., after allowing for all costs or expenses) of $100 annually from now until eternity. If the market rate of interest were 8 percent per year, then the market value of this asset should be:
   a. $800.
   b. $1250.
   c. $8000.
   d. $10,000.
   e. infinity.

16. If the market rate of interest rises, other things equal, then the present value of any given capital asset should:
   a. rise; and the more the asset's expected revenues extend far into the future, the more it will rise.
   b. rise; and the more the asset's expected revenues accrue in the immediate rather than the remote future, the more it will rise.
   c. fall; and the more the asset's expected revenues extend far into the future, the more it will fall.
   d. fall; and the more the asset's expected revenues accrue in the immediate rather than the remote future, the more it will fall.
   e. not be changed at all.

17. The present discounted value of $500 payable 1 year from now, at a market interest rate of 9 percent annually, is:
   a. $459.
   b. $559.
   c. $263.
   d. $545.
   e. none of the above.

18. Implicit in any discussion of capital and interest is a rule for the proper method of determining the worth, or value, of any asset. This rule instructs us to:
   a. value assets according to the original cost of construction or purchase, deducting from this cost figure an

appropriate depreciation figure to arrive at present value.

b. value assets according to the net revenue they are expected to yield in the future.

c. value assets according to the discounted sum of the net revenue that they are expected to yield in the future.

d. determine the dollar figure which represents the net productivity of the asset and then discount that net productivity figure by means of the interest rate.

e. do none of the above.

19. If market interest rates generally fall, then the present value of any capital asset should:

a. fall, since lower interest rates indicate that revenue amounts accruing at any future date are now given a higher present value.

b. fall, since lower interest rates indicate that revenue amounts accruing at any future date are now given a lower present value.

c. remain unchanged, unless relevant cost or revenue factors thereby changed.

d. rise, because lower interest rates indicate that revenue amounts accruing at any future date are now given a lower present value.

e. rise, because lower interest rates indicate that revenue amounts accruing at any future date are now given a higher present value.

20. Which alternative in question 19 would be correct had the question referred to the asset's rate of return instead of its present value?

a.

b.

c.

d.

e.

21. In a period of deflation (i.e., of generally falling prices), the "real" rate of interest obtained by any lender will:

a. exceed the nominal rate.

b. become a negative figure.

c. fall below the stated rate, although not to the extent of becoming a negative figure.

d. become a meaningless, incalculable figure.

e. exceed the rate of unemployment.

22. The rate of return to any capital good could reasonably be described as the:

a. rate of interest at which the capital good could just be worth buying or building, i.e., the rate of interest for which the present value of anticipated revenues would exactly match the present value of anticipated costs.

b. dollar amount of profit that would accrue if that capital good were bought or built.

c. same thing as the market rate of interest.

d. physical increase in output (as distinct from the money value) that would accrue if that capital good were bought or built.

e. percentage figure obtained by adding up all net revenues that would accrue from the capital good and dividing this total by its cost.

23. If business firms generally became more optimistic regarding the revenues that should accrue from the investment projects that they are planning, then the computed rate of return to that capital:

a. would increase, since revenues enter into the computation of the rate of return.

b. would decrease, since the rate of return is an interest rate, and the interest rate varies inversely with the value of the investment project.

c. would not change, since the rate of return is governed by technical considerations, not by expected revenues.

d. would probably fall, although there is a special case in which it would rise.

e. may do any of the above since the effect of a change in expected revenues upon the rate of return is unpredictable.

24. Profits are defined as the:

a. difference between total revenues and total costs.

b. difference between marginal revenue and marginal cost at equilibrium.

c. total revenues a firm earns from the sale of its product.

d. amount of money that is distributed to shareholders as dividends.

e. amount of money that the firm reinvests in its plant and equipment.

25. A firm's rate of profit is determined by:

a. implicit returns on factors of production that the firm owns.

b. the level of risk in which the firm is engaged.

c. the level of innovation that the firm is able to undertake.

d. all of the above.

e. none of the above.

VII. PROBLEM SOLVING

The following problems are designed to help you apply the concepts that you learned in this chapter.

A. Land and Rent

1. When an input has only a single employment, its supply curve will be perfectly inelastic with respect to price, because the suppliers have no alternative to which to turn should price be low. They must supply the same quantity, if necessary, even at a very low price.

a. If the market for this input is competitive, will the price necessarily be low? (Circle one.)

(1) Yes, if competitive forces are operating.

(2) It is impossible to tell. The price will be set where the demand curve crosses this perfectly inelastic supply curve; if demand for this limited supply is sufficiently large, the equilibrium price will be very high.

b. The single-occupation case illustrates how fallacious a "cost of production" theory of price can be. Suppose that the input in question is cows and that cows are useful only for giving milk. Now suppose, as well, that the demand for milk has driven its price to an extremely high level. The resulting derived demand for cows would certainly support a correspondingly high price for cows. It would, in such a situation, be *incorrect* to assert that (circle one):

(1) the price of cows is high because the price of milk is high.

(2) the price of milk is high because the price of cows is high.

In short, you (**could / could not**), in this case, give a meaningful explanation of the price of milk in terms of the costs involved in producing milk.

2. Modern tax theory has generalized the notion of taxing inputs whose supply is perfectly inelastic into what are called "Ramsey taxes." The observation which supports this generalization notes simply that taxes are more efficient in (a) raising revenue and (b) minimizing the loss in consumer surplus if they are imposed on goods with either (relatively) inelastic demand or inelastic supply. Figure 14-2 will help you explore the rationale behind this.

a. In panel (*a*), a demand curve *DD* is drawn through point E to indicate, given supply curve *SS* an equilibrium price and quantity pair of (price = $5, quantity = 9). Demand curve *D'D'* has also been drawn to reflect the effect of a $2-per-unit tax on the sale of good X. Since $5 is required by suppliers to produce X, the new, after-tax equilibrium quantity must be ___ units, for which

people would spend $___ per unit and suppliers would receive $___ per unit. Before the tax, consumer surplus was $___; after the tax it will have (**risen / fallen**) to $___. Tax revenue would, moreover, equal $___.

b. Panel (*b*) repeats the process for a demand curve *DD* that, through the (price = $5, quantity = 9) equilibrium, is relatively (**more elastic / more inelastic**). *D'D'* again represents effective demand after a $2 per-unit tax has been imposed. The after-tax equilibrium would, in this second case, be ___ units selling at a price of $___, of which $___ per unit would show up in the hands of the supplier. Consumer surplus would, in this case, (**rise / fall**) from $___ before the tax to $___ after the tax. Total revenue generated by the tax would, meanwhile, equal $___. Note that the relative inelasticity of demand in panel (*b*) has allowed more revenue to be generated

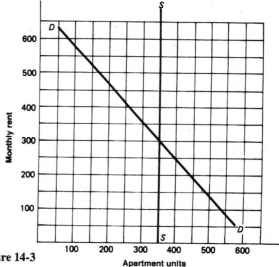

Figure 14-3

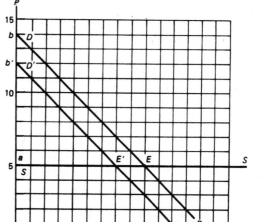

Figure 14-2

(a)

(b)

by the same per unit tax with a smaller loss in consumer surplus.

3. Consult Figure 14-3; *DD* there represents a demand curve for rental housing, while *SS* represents a short-run supply curve. The equilibrium rent for housing would be $___.

  a. Suppose the rent-control authorities have determined that rents should be lowered and have imposed a (**ceiling / floor**) equal to 80 percent of the equilibrium price. The quantity of rental housing provided would, in the short run illustrated in Figure 14-3 (**increase / remain the same / decline**), while the quantity demanded would (**increase / remain the same / decline**) . Additionally, the ceiling would (**provide incentives for / remove incentives for**) landlords to increase the supply.

  b. Now consider a 20 percent tax on rents collected by landlords. This policy would produce (**the same / a different**) equilibrium in the rental market in terms of quantity supplied in the short run. The rent paid would, meanwhile (**climb / remain the same / fall**), and a shortage of rental housing (**would / would not**) materialize. In the long run, though, the quantity supplied could fall along a sloped supply curve, and a shortage could thereby materialize.

B. Capital and Interest

4. Consider an asset that will cost you $100, right now, to construct. If you construct it, there will be no payoff for two years, but this asset will pay you $121 two years from now—nothing before that, and nothing after. This $121 is free of any incidental costs or expenses; it is the net return on your $100 outlay. The $121 return is safe; there is no uncertainty about its arrival. This capital asset has an annual rate of return of ___ percent. The principal amount of $100 would earn $10 interest over the course of the first year. Left in the account as "extra principal," this interest would also earn interest so that $11 in total interest would be earned in the second year. The total value of the initial $100, measured at the end of year 2, would be $121—$100 principal plus $21 (= $10 + $11) in interest.

  a. Two different dollar figures are involved in this example: a cost figure of $100 today and a revenue figure of $121 two years from today. An interest rate matches the two differing dollar figures, so the rate of return of a capital asset is best expressed as (**a dollar figure / an interest rate**).

  b. If you had to borrow $100 to construct the asset of part **a** and could borrower this money at a cost of 5 percent annually, would you do so? (**yes / no**)

  c. Would you borrow the money at 9 percent annually? (**yes / no**) At 11 percent annually? (**yes / no**).

5. Suppose you have money available to lend or to use in the purchase of some revenue-yielding asset. The market interest rate is 10 percent annually, but the borrowers in this market are of such good credit standing that the risk of any borrowers' defaulting on his or her loan is virtually nonexistent. The owner of an asset such as the one described in question 4 (i.e., one guaranteeing a single return of $121 at the end of 2 years) offers to sell it to you.

  a. If this asset were available for $90, would you buy it? (**yes / no**) If you did, then the interest rate that you would be earning on your outlay would be (**less than / more than**) 10 percent.

  b. If the asset were available for $100, then it would be (**an unusually good buy / an unusually poor buy / as good as, but no better than, other available alternatives**) .

  c. Would you pay $102 for this asset? (**yes / no**) If you did, then the interest rates that you would be earning on your outlay would be (**less than / equal to / more than**) 10 percent.

6. a. Suppose that you own a piece of land which brings you net rental income (after allowing for maintenance cost, etc.) of $5000 yearly and that you expect this annual rental to continue well into the future. The present value of this land would be (circle one):

    (1) $5000.

    (2) the sum of all expected future receipts of $5000.

    (3) the sum of all expected future annual receipts, each discounted to the present by means of the market interest rate.

  b. Suppose the asset in part a is expected to yield $5000 each year into the indefinite future and thus represents a "perpetual-income stream." What principal would have to be involved if its interest yield were $5000 annually and the interest rate were 4 percent annually? $___.

  c. There is a simple formula for computing the capitalized value of such perpetual-income assets. Write it down, and make sure the formula works for the case of part **b**.

---

7. You must decide whether asset A or asset B has the higher present value. Asset A promises to make four income payments of $1225 each at the end of years 1, 2, 3, and 4. Asset B promises to make five payments of $1000 each at the end of years 1, 2, 3, 4, and 5. The confidence with which payments can be expected is the same for both. The market interest rate is 10%.

  Calculate the present values of A and B: Asset A = ___ and asset B = ___. You decide to invest in (**asset A / asset B**).

8. The panels of Figure 14-4 show demand and supply curves for capital. The demand curves describe the behavior of business firms in the economy, who are borrowing money

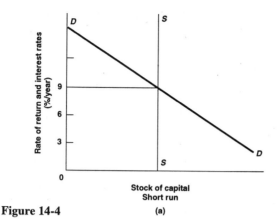

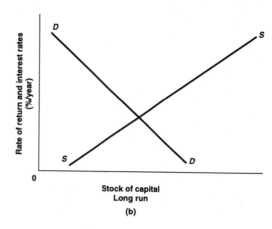

Figure 14-4

(a)   (b)

in order to pursue investment projects. The supply curves describe the stock of capital that is available to these business firms at alternative interest rates. Panel (a) describes these relationships in the short run and panel (b) describes these relationships in the long run.

    a.   The demand curves in both these panels are downward-sloping. What accounts for this?

_____

_____

    b.   Given the stock of capital indicated in panel (a) of Figure 14-4, the equilibrium short-run interest rate in this economy is ____.

    c.   As time goes by, the stock of capital goods will (**fall / remain constant / increase**) because the short-term interest rate is (**high / low**) compared to long run equilibrium. In terms of panel (*a*), the vertical *SS* curve will (**shift to the left / remain constant / shift to the right**) and the market interest rate will (**rise / remain constant / fall**). Show this shift in panel (*a*) of Figure 14-4.

    d.   The supply curve in panel (*b*) is upward-sloping. What accounts for this? What is the difference between the short-run and the long-run supply of capital?

_____

_____

_____

    e.   The short-run supply of capital curve will adjust until the short-run interest rate is equal to (**0 / the inflation rate / the long run equilibrium interest rate**). Show this in the panels of Figure 14-4.

VIII. DISCUSSION QUESTIONS

Answer the following questions, making sure that you can explain the work you did to arrive at the answers.
1.   Explain, in your own words, why a tax on land is efficient. Would you agree with Henry George that government

operations might be financed through land taxation only? Do you think this would be equitable?
2.   True or false: "The real interest rate is the sum of the nominal interest rate and the inflation rate."
3.   As interest rates rise, the present value of any stream of income will fall. Explain this in your own words, using the present value equation for illustration.
4.   What does "roundaboutness" mean? Why is it important to consider when making investment decisions?
5.   Why is the short-run capital supply curve perfectly inelastic, while the long-run capital supply curve is upward-sloping?
6.   Suppose that you run a roadside fruit and vegetable stand, situated on your own land. You would, typically, describe your net income as "profit." Would this be correct? What role might implicit rents and wages play in your definition of profits?
7.   Three important sources of profits have been identified in this chapter. What are these?
8.   If there are some parts of profit which cannot be converted into implicit wages, implicit rent, or implicit interest in situations other than perfect competition, then it is necessary to answer another question: What useful function is performed or undertaken by the individual who receives a profit? Profit is the reward for doing what? How should you answer these questions?
9.   Innovation, in the Schumpeterian view, is a risky and uncertain business. The majority of would-be innovators fail. Why does Schumpeter describe market dynamics as "the process of creative destruction"? Explain.

IX. ANSWERS TO STUDY GUIDE QUESTIONS

III. Review of Key Concepts
  6   Rent
  13   Henry George
  8   Capital

12	Rentals
9	Rate of return on capital
3	Profits
5	Real interest rates
11	Nominal interest rates
2	Present value
7	Roundaboutness
1	Marginal product of capital
10	Risk premium
4	Implicit returns

VI. Multiple Choice Questions

1. C   2. A   3. B   4. A   5. D   6. A
7. D   8. D   9. B   10. C   11. A   12. C
13. D   14. D   15. B   16. C   17. A   18. C
19. E   20. C   21. A   22. A   23. A   24. A
25. D

VII. Problem Solving

1. a. (2)
   b. (2), could not
2. a. 3, $7, $5, $13.50, fallen, $1.50, $6
   b. more inelastic, 7, $7, $5, fall, $40.50, $24.50, $14
3. $300
   a. ceiling, remain the same, increase, remove incentives for
   b. the same, remain the same, should not
4. 10, a. an interest rate
   b. yes
   c. yes, no
5. a. yes, more than
   b. as good as, but no better than, other available alternatives
   c. no, less than
6. a. (3)
   b. $125,000
   c. $PV = N / i$, sphere N is the regular payment and i is the interest rate.
7. Assets A = $3790, Asset B = $3882, Asset B.
8. a. In both the short run and long run, there is an inverse relationship between the quantity of capital demanded and the interest rate. As the capital stock increases, the rate of return on capital falls. Hence, the market interest rate must be lower in order to make these projects profitable.
   b. 9 percent
   c. increase, high, shift to the right, fall
   d. In the short run, capital is a fixed input. However, in the long run the supply of capital can adjust to changes in demand.
   e. the long-run equilibrium interest rate

VIII. Discussion Questions

1. A tax on land is considered to be efficient because the tax will not alter the behavior of buyers or sellers in the market. This sort of tax system may or may not be considered equitable, depending upon who the initial owners of land are.
2. False. The nominal interest rate is the sum of the real interest rate and the rate of inflation.
3. As interest rates rise, the present value of any stream of income will fall. From the equation, it can be seen that the denominator will get larger; this means that the value will be smaller in present value. As interest rates rise, the opportunity cost of any sum of money received in the future will rise. This means that the value today of the income stream must be smaller
4. Roundaboutness refers to the fact that capital goods are used to create final goods and services. Production of capital goods requires forgoing present consumption so that consumption in the future can be even greater.
5. The short-run capital supply curve is perfectly inelastic because the capital stock is fixed in the short run. In the long run all inputs become variable, and the capital stock can be adjusted as interest rates change.
6. Net income, or revenues less explicit costs is one definition of profits, but it may ignore the value placed on inputs that you own. For example, the land and fruit stand you own may have no alternative use, but it should earn a rent.
7. Profits are the implicit returns to factors of production owned by the firm. Profits are a reward for risk-taking and innovation. Profits are a return to monopoly power.
8. Profits are a return to entrepreneurship, that is, profits are a return to the risk-taking, innovative activities that any capitalist must undertake in order to produce in a market economy.
9. Schumpeter would argue that monopoly and innovation are inextricably linked. A firm may be in a monopoly position, but that position may have resulted entirely from successful innovation. Schumpeter worried about too much government interference in big industry, fearing that this intervention would take away the incentive firms have to develop new products or methods of production. He might be particularly wary of the recent decisions against Microsoft, arguing that this kind of government will eliminate the profit incentives that are the result of successful research and development.

APPENDIX TO CHAPTER

Markets and Economic Efficiency

I. APPENDIX OVERVIEW

Previous chapters have shown that individual competitive markets lead to efficient solutions to allocation problems when these markets are allowed to operate without interference and without any influence from beyond their boundaries, i.e., under the partial equilibrium assumption that all other prices and quantities in the surrounding economy are *fixed* and *unchanging*. This appendix addresses a general-equilibrium system in which production decisions in one market have an impact upon pricing and production decisions in another market, which in turn act as feedback to the original decision. This introduces the much more realistic notion of an economy in which all prices and wages are determined simultaneously. How can we characterize such a system?

II. LEARNING OBJECTIVES

After you have read this appendix in your text and completed the exercises in this *Study Guide* chapter, you should be able to:

1. Define the term **allocative efficiency** and explain how it relates to Adam Smith's invisible hand theory.

2. Review the seven **partial-equilibrium** results, covered in previous chapters, with which competitive markets solve the simultaneous questions of *what, how,* and *for whom.*

3. Describe what is meant by the term **general equilibrium**. Use a circular-flow diagram to illustrate the interdependent nature of agents and markets in an economy.

4. List the assumptions and basic principles that underlie the definition of a general-equilibrium solution to a resource allocation problem. Trace the path from these assumptions to the consumer and producer conditions that must exist in input and output markets for general equilibrium to exist.

5. Describe in detail how the myopic actions of individuals and firms in a perfectly competitive economy would lead to the equality of marginal (social) cost, marginal utility, and price for every good at every firm

and for even individual. Illustrate the resulting efficiency in terms of a **utility-possibility frontier**.

III. REVIEW OF KEY CONCEPTS

Match the following terms from column A with their definitions in column B.

A	B
__ Allocative efficiency	1. Shows the outer limit of utilities or satisfactions that an economy can attain.
__ Partial-equilibrium analysis	2. Occurs when there is no way to reorganize production or consumption so as to increase the satisfaction of one person without reducing the satisfaction of another person.
__ General-equilibrium analysis	3. Involves the behavior of a single market, household, or firm, taking the behavior of the rest of the economy as given.
__ Utility-possibility frontier	4. Examines how the simultaneous interaction of all households, firms, and markets solves the questions of *how, what,* and for *whom.*

IV. SUMMARY AND CHAPTER OUTLINE

This section summarizes the key concepts from the appendix.

1. Before discussing the efficiency properties of any economy, we need to know what we mean by the term *efficiency*. Economists have several definitions, but for the purpose of this discussion, we will use *allocative efficiency*, which occurs when there is no way to reorganize production or consumption so that the satisfaction of one person will increase without the satisfaction of another person decreasing.

2. Microeconomic analysis is, in its simplest form, conducted in partial equilibrium. Consumers maximize utility given limited income, product prices, and a pattern of tastes.

Firms maximize profits given technology, some type of demand structure, and input prices. To move toward generalization is to allow all individuals and firms to interact and thereby *jointly* determine an entire set of prices and quantities which clear a multitude of markets simultaneously. This move will help us to understand the *interdependence* of markets of all sorts (input markets interact with other input markets, product markets interact with other product markets, and input markets interact with product markets).

3.   Competitive markets work despite the myopic actions of individuals. Utility-maximizing consumers generate individual demand curves that are summed horizontally to generate market demand for final products. Profit-maximizing firms face marginal cost schedules that are summed horizontally to generate market supply for final products. In a similar fashion, marginal revenue product schedules support the demand side of input markets. All of these partial equilibrium processes are going on simultaneously! Each market is comprised of individual maximizers, whose behavior in aggregate brings about an efficient outcome

4.   A *circular-flow* diagram can be used to describe the interaction between markets and agents. Figure 14A-1 from your text is reproduced here, also as Figure 14A-1.

The top half of this diagram shows interaction between firms and households in the market for final products. You can see that households buy goods and services from firms; consumers optimize by setting the ratios of their marginal utilities equal to the ratios of market prices. Firms optimize by setting marginal cost equal to market price. Thus the "invisible hand," i.e., the price system, is coordinating the behavior of households and firms.

The bottom half of this diagram shows interaction between firms and households in the market for factors of production. Here, you can see that households sell factors to firms; households optimize by setting the marginal utility of the factor, determined by their own preferences, equal to its market price. Firms optimize by setting the ratios of the marginal products of inputs equal to the ratios of market prices. Once again, the invisible hand is coordinating the behavior of households and firms.

5.   The assumptions that underlie the definition of a competitive general equilibrium are as follows:

a.   All markets are perfectly competitive and are subject to the relentless competition of many buyers and sellers.

b.   Prices are perfectly flexible, rising or falling as supply and demand shift.

c.   Firms are profit maximizers.

d.   Households are utility maximizers.

e.   There are no natural monopolies (i.e., no tremendous economies of scale).

f.   No externalities, entry-limiting regulations, or monopolistic labor unions exist.

These assumptions guarantee the most extreme form of perfect competition. They allow us to say, "*If* these conditions hold, then a general equilibrium will look like X." We know that in the "real world" these conditions do not hold. However, by understanding this extreme example, we can begin to add back the complexity needed to make the model realistic and, in so doing, gain some insights into the workings of a large and complicated economic system.

6.   Given these assumptions, we can establish some conditions for a competitive equilibrium:

a.   *Consumer equilibrium* occurs when the ratio of the marginal utilities for any two goods is equal to the ratio of their prices. That is,

$$\frac{MU_A}{MU_B} = \frac{P_A}{P_B}$$

This means that at the utility-maximizing consumption bundle, the consumer's *subjective* tradeoff between two goods, A and B, is equal to the *market* tradeoff defined by the price ratio.

b.   *Producer equilibrium* occurs when, first, the ratio of the marginal costs for any two outputs is equal to their price ratio, and second, the ratio of the marginal products for any two inputs is equal to their price ratio. That is,

$$\frac{MC_A}{MC_B} = \frac{P_A}{P_B} \qquad\qquad \frac{MP_L}{MP_K} = \frac{P_L}{P_K}$$

This means that at the profit-maximizing level of output, marginal cost is equal to marginal revenue, which equals price. Further, this means that the ratio of the marginal costs must equal the ratio of the market prices. Finally, the firm is choosing the minimum cost bundle of inputs, L and K, for producing the optimal level of output.

When these conditions hold, the economy as a whole is efficient and no one can be made better off without making someone else worse off.

7.   This result can be illustrated using a utility-possibility frontier. A utility-possibility frontier shows the maximum possible utility that an economy can attain. Consider Figure 14A-2.

This frontier shows the combinations of utilities for two parties, Dave and Mary, that are allocatively efficient. (Assume Dave and Mary are the only agents in an economy.) Once they arrive at any point on the frontier, they can make no further reallocations that will make one better off without hurting the other. Notice that if Dave and Mary are at a point like B, they can <u>both</u> be <u>made</u> better off by moving to point C. Point D is not attainable; this society's resources are insufficient to provide more utility, or Dave and Mary's preferences are such that they simply cannot experience greater utility.

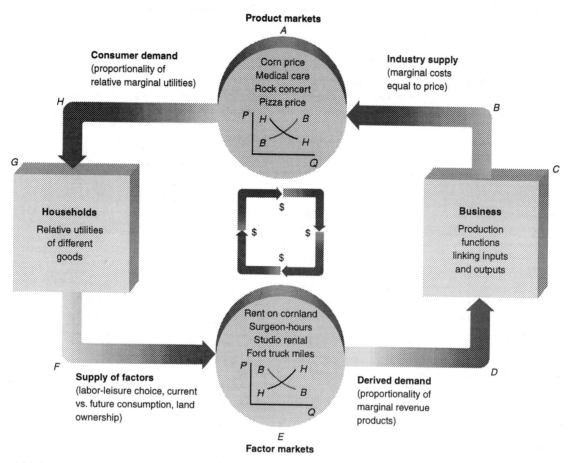

Figure 14A-1

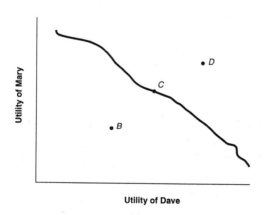

Figure 14A-2

V. HELPFUL HINTS

1. Economists often refer to the topics of this chapter as *welfare economics;* however, we have said nothing about improving the status of the poor. We are referring instead to that branch of economics in which the words "better" and "worse" are used, i.e., in which it is said that some situation A is more desirable than some alternative situation B.

The statement "A is preferable to B" requires that its author apply some sort of evaluative metric or scale. Since individual preferences differ, welfare economics is a difficult area of study. Nonetheless, the following statement seems fair: "Situation A is preferable to B if, in the course of a change from B to A, some people would be made better off while nobody would be made worse off." In the vernacular of economics, A would then be a *Pareto improvement* over B. (Vilfredo Pareto was a nineteenth-century economist who developed much of the efficiency theory that economists use today. Many people prefer to use the term *Pareto efficiency* rather than *allocative efficiency,* although they mean the same thing.)

Very few of these convenient "nobody-worse-off changes" exist in reality. Notice that most tax policies designed to improve the equality of the income distribution would not meet Pareto's standards; any tax will help some people only at the expense of others. The next step in welfare economics is to find situations in which the predicted gain of the gainers exceeds the predicted loss of the losers. In such a circumstance, the gainers could "bribe" the losers to make the change, or the gainers could be taxed by a sufficient amount to compensate the losers fully and still have some part of their gains left. A Pareto improvement is therefore possible even if it requires some extraordinary administration.

2. Remember from Chapter 12 that efficient solutions are not necessarily *equitable,* where equity implies that a solution is "fair" based on individual value judgments. Equity is an important characteristic of an economic system, more important in some systems than in others. It tends to be defined by each system individually, based on cultural norms and values. Some people believe that equity means equal, that each household or firm has an equal share of society's resources. Other societies believe that equity is achieved when resources are distributed based upon the needs of households or firms. Still others believe that equal access to resources is enough to provide for equity. In any case, the efficient solution outlined in this chapter may or may not be equitable, and so the general equilibrium in competitive markets defined here may or may not be a desirable goal for an economy.

3. The utility-possibility frontier shows a set of equally efficient points, given two individuals' utility functions. A natural next question is, which point on the frontier is best? As with the production-possibilities frontier discussed in chapter 1, we cannot choose an optimal solution given the frontier alone. To determine which point is "best" we would have to have more information about the society and its preferences.

VI. MULTIPLE CHOICE QUESTIONS

Choose the best answer to the following questions from the options available.

1. Economists use the term *allocative efficiency* to describe an efficient allocation of resources in an economy. This means that:
    a.   the economy has determined that there is no reallocation of resources that would be more equitable.
    b.   there is no way that resources could be reallocated without harming someone.
    c.   firms in the economy are all earning economic profits, which are being redistributed to households.
    d.   all firms in the economy are producing with mini-

mum marginal costs.
    e.   none of the above.

2. Adam Smith developed the "invisible hand" doctrine. This describes the fact that:
    a.   a central planner determines the optimal employment of resources.
    b.   an economy can only run smoothly if government directs resources using tax policy.
    e.   people pursuing their own best interests will effectively promote the public welfare.
    d.   market competition results in wasted resources.
    e.   monopolistic sellers will exploit economies of scale, so all industries should consist of large firms.

3. Partial-equilibrium analysis, unlike general-equilibrium analysis:
    a.   focuses on the interdependent nature of markets and agents in the economy.
    b.   involves the behavior of a single market, household, or firm, taking the behavior of the rest of the economy as fixed.
    c.   examines how the simultaneous interaction of all households, firms, and markets solves basic economic questions.
    d.   all the above.
    e.   none of the above.

4. Any characterization of the general-equilibrium properties of perfect competition must include statements which imply that the:
    a.   ratio of the marginal utilities of any two goods must, for all individuals, equal the corresponding ratio of their marginal costs.
    b.   marginal utilities of all goods consumed must be proportional but not equal to the marginal costs of those goods for each consumer.
    c.   marginal physical product of each input is equal to the price of that input.
    d.   marginal revenue product of each input is equal to the price of the finished good it produces.
    e.   ratio of total expenditure on any good to its price equals marginal utility

5. The profit-maximizing motive in perfect competition differs from the profit-maximizing motive in imperfect competition in which of the following respects?
    a.   The perfect competitor tries to equate price and average cost, which does *not* lead to maximum profit.
    b.   The perfect competitor tries to equate price and marginal cost, which does *not* lead to maximum profit.
    c.   The perfect competitor tries to equate marginal revenue and marginal cost, which does *not* lead to maximum profit.
    d.   The imperfect competitor tries to equate price and marginal cost, which leads to a larger profit than the equating of marginal revenue and marginal cost.
    e.   They differ in none of these ways, because the firms

in both situations are equally interested in earning as much profit as possible.

6. The theory of perfect competition, according to most economists:

a. gives a reasonably accurate description of "real world" performance, even though it cannot be used to evaluate the efficiency of that performance.

b. roughly describes "real-world" performance, despite competitive imperfections, and is most important for appraising the efficiency of that performance.

c. is most important for appraising the efficiency of "real world" performance, even though it is not even approximately correct in describing that performance.

d. bears almost no resemblance to "real world" performance and cannot be used to evaluate its efficiency, but is most important because its material is a lead into the theory of imperfect competition.

e. with relatively minor monopoly exceptions, gives an accurate outline of "real-world" performance and can be used to identify the monopoly exceptions.

7. *Four* of the following *five* alternatives state conditions which must be satisfied if the equilibrium conditions of perfect competition are to be satisfied. One alternative states a condition that is not required; i.e., one should not necessarily be the result of perfect competition. Which one?

a. Price is equal to average cost.

b. For each individual and for each good he or she consumes, the ratio of the marginal utility to the price is the same for all such goods.

c. Price is equal to marginal cost.

d. There is no significant inequality in the distribution of income among individuals.

e. Price is equal to minimum average cost.

8. One of the following alternatives states a condition which must be satisfied to meet the requirements of perfect competition. Which one?

a. Market prices are unresponsive to short-run changes in demand or in supply.

b. Price is equal to average cost but not marginal cost.

c. Different wage rates are paid in different geographical locations for work whose requirements are exactly the same in alternative locations.

d. Product differentiation yields a price that equals average cost but not minimum-attainable average cost.

e. Marginal cost is equal to average cost.

9. Consider an economy consuming two goods A and B. Currently, the marginal utility of A is 100 and the marginal utility of B is 28. The price of A is $25 while the price of B is $7. In this case, the consumer equilibrium condition is:

a. satisfied, since the marginal utility of A is greater than the marginal utility of B.

b. not satisfied, since the marginal utilities of A and B are not equal.

c. not satisfied, since the prices of A and B are not equal

d. satisfied, since the ratios of the marginal utilities to the prices are equal for each good.

e. satisfied, since the last dollar's worth of good A brings more utility than the last dollar's worth of good B.

10. A utility-possibility frontier shows:

a. the combinations of two goods that the economy can afford to trade.

b. maximum quantities of two goods that an economy can produce, given a fixed resource base, stable technology, full employment, and full efficiency.

c. combinations of two goods that bring equal utility to the consumers.

d. the outer limit of utilities that an economy can attain.

e. none of the above.

Figure 14A-3 shows a utility-possibility frontier for a very small economy, consisting of only Al and Barbara. Use the diagram to answer questions 11, 12, and 13.

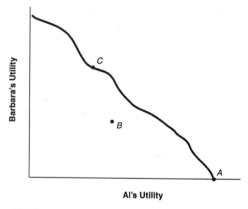

Figure14A-3

11. At point *A*:

a. Barbara could be made better off without hurting Al.

b. Al could be made better off without hurting Barbara.

c. neither Al nor Barbara could be made better off without hurting the other person.

d. Al and Barbara would be beyond the possibilities available to this economy.

e. Barbara has all of the utility and Al has none.

12. At point *B*.:

a. Barbara could be made better off without hurting Al.

b. Al could be made better off without hurting Barbara.

c. neither Al nor Barbara could be made better off

without hurting the other person.

    d.   Al and Barbara would be beyond the possibilities available to this economy.

    e.   a and b are both possible.

13. At point *C*:

    a.   Barbara could be made better off without hurting Al.

    b.   Al could be made better off without hurting Barbara.

    c.   neither Al nor Barbara could be made better off without hurting the other person.

    d.   Al and Barbara would be beyond the possibilities available to this economy.

    e.   Al has all of the utility and Barbara has none.

14. Many economies around the world are organized around socialist principles. In these economies:

    a.   efficient allocations of resources are not possible.

    b.   equitable allocations of resources are not possible.

    c.   efficiency conditions can hold just as in competitive market economies.

    d.   efficiency conditions can hold only if prices are directed by central planners.

    e.   none of the above.

VII. PROBLEM SOLVING

The following problems are designed to help you apply the concepts that you learned in this appendix.

1. a. In the spaces provided, list the seven partial-equilibrium conditions that you have learned in previous chapters.

    (1) _____

    (2) _____

    (3) _____

    (4) _____

    (5) _____

    (6) _____

    (7) _____

These conditions, all involving the behavior of single markets, households, or firms, have all been subjected to partial-equilibrium analysis. They have, thus far, been explored under the assumption that (**all people are equal / all other things are equal / all government policies are equal**).

  b. It is not possible simply to build a general-equilibrium model of an entire economy by "tacking" partial-equilibrium models of individual sectors or markets together. Consider a specific illustration with two commodities: butter and margarine. Suppose that the markets for both are initially in equilibrium. Now let a technical development sharply reduce the cost of producing margarine. What would happen? In terms of supply and demand we should expect to see the supply curve for margarine

shift (**left / right**), thereby establishing a new and (**higher / lower**) equilibrium price for margarine. Since the two goods are substitutes, though, the adjustment in the price of margarine just noted should make the demand curve for butter shift (**to the left / to the right**), thereby producing a new and (**higher / lower**) price for butter. This process would continue until some final, mutually compatible pair of prices was achieved.

2. a. Table 14A-1 is intended to illustrate the meaning of "efficient resource allocation." It assumes that the economy produces only three goods, X, Y, and Z. A general equilibrium has been reached with the quantities recorded on line 1 being supplied in that equilibrium by the prices recorded on line 3.

TABLE 14A-1

		X	Y	Z
1.	Total quantities of goods produced and bought	3,000	4,000	5,000
2.	Marginal utilities of goods for a typical consumes	100	50	200
3.	Price of good	$2	$1	$4
4.	Marginal cost of good	$2	$1	$4

Given the X, Y, and Z prices on line 3, the "typical consumer" (**has / has not / may or may not have**) reached his or her maximum-satisfaction position. How do you know this?

_____

_____

_____

The ratios of marginal utility to price are all equal to ____ (a numerical answer is possible). If supplying firms operate under conditions of perfect competition, then, with prices as on line 3 and marginal costs as on line 4, they (**have / have not**) reached maximum-profit positions. How do you know this?

_____

_____

  b. Compute the marginal rate of substitution (*MRS*) and marginal rate of transformation (*MRT*) for each of the three possible pairings of X, Y, and Z. (Remember that *MRS* is a ratio of appropriate marginal utilities and *MRT* is a ratio of appropriate marginal costs. An "X" marked in the table indicates that the information is not necessary for calculations in its row.) Record your answers in Table 14A-2. Explain the equilibrium conditions that you find in this table:

_____

_____

_____

Note the general-equilibrium quality of this situation. Consumers reach maximum-satisfaction positions by juggling their X, Y, and Z purchases. Producers adjust the levels of their marginal costs by varying the quantities of X, Y, and Z that they produce and sell. The quantities on line 1 and the prices on line 3 must be such that they simultaneously satisfy *both* consumers and producers. The situation must be one in which neither consumers nor producers can see any advantage in any change of position.

3. Figure 14A-4 displays several points relative to a utility-possibility frontier for a simple, two-person economy. Record in the spaces below which point(s) illustrate the effects of the following circumstances relative to a Pareto efficient allocation indicated by point *E*:

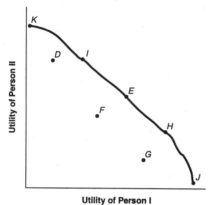

Figure 14A-4

    a. Unemployed resources: ___.
    b. Wage discrimination against person I: ___.
    c. Unrestrained pollution in the production of a good consumed exclusively by II that hurts only I: ___.

4. Kenneth Arrow and Gerard Debreu, both of whom have won Nobel Prizes in economics, were among the first to prove the existence of competitive general equilibrium. Their proof depended upon a long list of qualifications, or assumptions. List at least five in the spaces provided; after each qualification, state *in parentheses* which competitive condition would have been violated if the qualification had been ignored.

    a. _____

    b. _____

    c. _____

    d. _____

    e. _____

VIII. DISCUSSION QUESTIONS

Answer the following questions, making sure that you can explain the work you did to arrive at the answers.
1. What is the difference between partial-equilibrium and general-equilibrium analysis. Why is it important to consider equilibrium in all markets at the same time?
2. Bob says, "General equilibrium is easy! Just calculate a partial equilibrium in all markets, and you are finished!" Do you agree with this? Why or why not?
3. Use a cricular-flow diagram to trace the impact of the following events:
    a. General Motors hires an additional shift of assembly line workers.
    b. United Parcel Service (UPS) is shut down by a strike of its unionized workforce, many of whom drive trucks and deliver packages for the company.
In each case, what are the partial-equilibrium effects? What are the general-equilibrium effects?
4. Why do we have to make so many assumptions before we can build a general-equilibrium model? What purpose do these assumptions serve?
5. All this talk about Adam Smith and the invisible hand! What does it mean; what, exactly, did he mean by an "invisible hand?"

IX. ANSWERS TO STUDY GUIDE QUESTIONS

III. Review of Key Concepts
2   Allocative efficiency
3   Partial-equilibrium analysis
4   General-equilibrium analysis
1   Utility—possibility frontier

VI. Multiple Choice Questions
1. B 2. C 3. B 4. A 5. E 6. B
7. D 8. E 9. D 10. D 11. C 12. E
13. C 14. C

TABLE 14A-2	MU_x	MU_y	MU_z	MRS	MC_x	MC_y	MC_z	MRT
1. X and Y	100	50	X	—	$2	$1	X	—
2. Y and Z	X	50	200	—	X	$1	$4	—
3. X and Z	100	X	200	—	$2	X	$4	—

VII. Problem Solving

1. a. (1) competitive supply and demand determine prices and quantities in individual markets.

(2) Market demand curves are derived from the marginal utilities experienced by consumers for different goods.

(3) Competitive supply curves are derived from the marginal costs of different goods.

(4) Firms calculate marginal costs of products and marginal revenue products of factors, and then choose profit-maximizing output levels and input usage.

(5) These marginal revenue products, summed for all firms, provide the derived demands for the factors of production.

(6) These derived demands for land, labor, or capital goods interact with their market supplies to determine factor prices.

(7) The factor prices and quantities determine incomes. all other things are equal

b. right, lower, to the left, lower

2. a. has. The ratio of marginal utility to price for each input is equal to the ratio of marginal utility to price for each other input. $50, have. Marginal cost is equal to price for each good.

b. See table.
The marginal rate of substitution is equal to the marginal rate of transformation for each pair of goods.

3. a. D, F, G
   b. G
   c. G

4. a. no increasing returns to scale. (Otherwise positive profits and price in excess of marginal cost would emerge.)

b. no externalities. (Otherwise the prices of some goods would not match their true social costs.)

c. flexible wages and prices. (Otherwise unemployed resources would be possible.)

d. no uninsurable risk. (Otherwise inefficient losses might occur.)

e. no monopolies or other types of imperfect competi-

tion. (Otherwise prices in excess of marginal cost would be forthcoming.)

VIII. Discussion Questions

1. Partial-equilibrium analysis focuses on a single market and assumes that conditions in all other markets remain fixed. General-equilibrium analysis takes into account the interaction between markets. General-equilibrium is important because it allows us to consider the impact of an event on all markets as well as the feedback effects of an event.

2. This is not accurate. Simply considering the partial-equilibrium solutions in each market ignores the feedback effects that occur between markets.

3. a. The initial impact of this event occurs in the resource market, where a household sells additional labor hours in exchange for a wage. This causes the output in the auto industry to increase, leading to an additional sale of an automobile to the household sector.

b. The initial impact of this strike is felt in the input markets. There is a sharp reduction in the supply of transportation services, increasing the costs of moving all sorts of goods and packages. This puts upward pressure on output prices, which depend upon the resource costs; as marginal production costs rise, firms tend to contract output. This could lead to decreases in the level of employment, as well as substitution across alternative transportation carriers.

4. Because the economy is so complex, we have to make simplifying assumptions before we can begin to generate general-equilibrium results for an economy. The assumptions strip away some of the complexity and allow us to focus on particular aspects of the economy that are of interest.

5. The invisible hand refers to the price mechanism which shuttles signals between buyers and sellers. If there is excess supply of commodities, prices are lowered until the market clears. If there is excess demand for commodities, prices are increased until the market clears. Thus, the price mechanism operates like an "invisible hand," delivering signals to buyers and sellers so that markets reach equilibrium.

	MU_x	MU_y	MU_z	MRS	MC_x	MC_y	MC_z	MRT
1. X and Y	100	50	X	2	$2	$1	X	2
2. Y and Z	X	50	200	.25	X	$1	$4	.25
3. X and Z	100	X	200	.50	$2	X	$4	.50

CHAPTER

15

Comparative Advantage
and Protectionism

I. CHAPTER OVERVIEW

In this chapter, Samuelson and Nordhaus present the basic economic model of trade. The fundamental point is that foreign trade can improve welfare (i.e., the standard of living) of most nations, even if they already are the most productive in producing everything. Part of David Ricardo's great contribution to the study of international trade was to show that inefficiency in all lines of production would make a country poor, but it would not cause its trading opportunities to totally evaporate. Relatively efficient and inefficient countries can still trade to mutual advantage, provided there are some differences in their relative costs of production. The first part of the chapter explains Ricardo's innovative view of trade.

Once the case for free trade is made, Samuelson and Nordhaus turn the coin over to look at its opposite side—protectionism. If free trade is so beneficial, why do we see so many barriers to free trade in the real world? To answer this question, it is essential to see how trade barriers work. Only then can their effects be delineated and their merits evaluated. The second section of Chapter 15 tends to this task. With the effects of protectionism firmly in hand, the various arguments for and against protection are then critically reviewed.

II. LEARNING OBJECTIVES

After you have read Chapter 15 in your text and completed the exercises in this *Study Guide* chapter, you should be able to:

1. Discuss some of the recent trends in foreign trade and understand the economic factors that lie behind international trade patterns.
2. Distinguish between **absolute advantage** and **comparative advantage**.
3. Explain, using a simple two-commodity model, how a country can increase its real income by specializing (for the purpose of export) in the commodity in which it has a comparative advantage and importing the commodity in which it has a comparative disadvantage.

4. Understand that the Ricardo model is easily extended to include multinational trading arrangements.
5. Use supply-and-demand analysis to outline the economic effects of protection. Show that opening trade in a good drives its domestic price toward equality with its world price. Show that a tariff can be expected to generate welfare losses.
6. Outline the economic as well as the noneconomic arguments for trade restriction and evaluate their validity.
7. List a few nontariff barriers to trade that have been employed by the United States in the past few years and explain how they work.

III. REVIEW OF KEY CONCEPTS

Match the following terms from column A with their definitions in column B.

A	B
__ Principle of comparative advantage	1 Occurs when a firm from Country B sells its product in Country A at a price beneath its average cost, or at a price lower than the existing domestic price in Country B.
__ Absolute advantage	2. Illustrates pre- and post-trade production and consumption, and trade alternatives for a country.
__ Comparative advantage	3. Program or policy which protects the domestic economy at the expense of other countries.
__ Terms of trade	4. Tariff that maximizes a country's domestic real income by shifting the terms of trade in its favor.
__ Consumption-possibility curve	5. Each country will specialize in the production and export of those goods that it can produce at *relatively* low cost and import those which it produces at *relatively* high cost.

__ Multilateral trade

__ Tariff

__ Quota

__ Mercantilism

__ Dumping

__ Optimal tariff

__ Infant industry tariff

__ "Beggar thy neighbor" policy

6.   Tariff which is used to protect a new domestic industry from powerful fully developed international competitors.

7.   Exists when a country can produce a commodity at lower *relative* cost.

8.   Exists when a country can produce a commodity with greater *absolute* efficiency or lower resource cost.

9.   The exchange of goods and services among a multitude of nations.

10.   A ratio of export prices to import prices which defines the upper and lower price boundaries for goods traded between countries.

11.   Pre-Ricardian economic philosophy that espoused the benefits of trade surpluses and the acquisition of gold.

12.   A tax on imported goods and services.

13.   A limit on the quantity of imports.

IV. SUMMARY AND CHAPTER OUTLINE

This section summarizes the key concepts from the chapter.

A. The Nature of International Trade

1.   The fundamental point of this chapter is that foreign trade can improve the welfare (i.e., the standard of living) of most nations, even if they are the most productive in producing everything.

2.   There are several differences between international trade and domestic trade. When a country moves into the international arena, it:

   a.   enjoys a much richer menu of products to choose from.

   b.   must deal with the laws and regulations of another sovereign nation.

   c.   must trade its currency in foreign exchange markets.

3.   While there are numerous reasons why nations may find it beneficial to engage in international trade, there are three main economic considerations:

   a.   diversity in conditions of production.

   b.   economies of scale and decreasing average costs.

   c.   differences in tastes

B. Comparative Advantage Among Nations

1.   If the United States had no domestic sources of tin, then it would surely have to import the tin it needed. What is not so obvious is why the United States, or any other country for that matter, should import a commodity which it could and does produce. The basic message of this chapter is that a nation should import some goods which it is capable of producing at home if it wants to use its resources to the best advantage. Each country should move toward specializing in the production of those commodities it is best equipped to make, given its own resources and those available to other countries. It should export part of what it has produced, receiving in exchange other goods (imports) which it is less equipped to make.

2.   Before trying to understand why certain frequently held notions about international trade are incorrect, you must first grasp the basic notion of **comparative advantage**; it alone explains why, in terms of real income, it pays each nation to move toward specializing in the production of a specific good or goods, to export those goods, and to use the proceeds of that export trade to finance the import of other goods. A country has an **absolute advantage** in the production of any good X if it can produce X at a smaller cost than a potential trading partner. It has a **comparative advantage** in the production of X if it can produce X *relatively* less expensively than it can produce some other tradable commodity.

3.   The potential gains from trade are derived from comparative advantage. A country can collect these gains by concentrating its production efforts on goods in which it has a comparative advantage, exporting some or all of its output in exchange for goods in which it has a comparative disadvantage. A country with absolute advantages in the production of all goods can therefore still improve its welfare through trade if it concentrates on the production of goods in which its absolute advantage is largest.

4.   The Ricardo model, which first described comparative advantage and the potential gains from trade, is a classical, full-employment model. Adjustment in the product mix designed to take full advantage of the potential can, however, be marked painfully by the short- to medium-term unemployment of displaced factors of production. Even when long-run equilibrium has been achieved with full employment, moreover, some people may be worse off than before. The idea is only that *aggregate* welfare has been improved.

5.   The *mercantilist* philosophy was that a nation ought to apply the same principles of prudence appropriate for a family. It is prudent for a family to try to save part of its income. The nation, mercantilists said, is just the family on a larger scale. And they equated saving, at the national level, with the accumulation of gold.

   The argument is not totally fallacious. Any nation will find it desirable to have reserves of gold (or foreign exchange) to cope with changing events which may produce balance-of-payments deficits. Even at the family level, though, the argument for "prudence" is wrong if interpreted as meaning that all families must hoard their money. Saving which is not allowed to flow into investment spending leads only to depression and to a fall in saving.

C. Protectionism

1. Three principal reasons, often working together, explain the rationale behind most of the actual or proposed restraints of foreign trade:

    a. A country fears unemployment and regards import competition as a potential source of that unemployment.

    b. A country is short of foreign exchange reserves and sees increased tariffs as a potential source of new revenue.

    c. The groups within a country who would benefit most directly from protection bring political pressure to bear for its imposition.

2. In a period of heavy unemployment, it is hard to preach comparative advantage and free trade to legislators and business people. They will argue that a reduction in imports would raise domestic employment at the expense of lower aggregate demand and correspondingly higher unemployment abroad, and so they might advocate an increase in protective tariffs. Such an attempt to "export unemployment" could, of course, be negated when other countries retaliate with similar tariff increases.

3. It would be wrong to insist that import restrictions can never reduce unemployment. The proper objection is that fiscal and monetary policies can be far more effective. Moreover, these policies avoid the dubious ethics of trying to foist off domestic unemployment onto other nations, and they do not incur the danger of retaliation.

4. Given reasonable assurance that unemployment can be handled by methods other than protection, many people in developed countries find it fairly easy to accept the free-trade principle; but people living in less developed countries tend to be more hesitant. They look at the world's most prosperous nations and hope that their own country might someday enjoy equally high standards of production and income. They wonder if some restriction on imports may be needed in order to widen production and employment opportunities and to foster their nation's industrial growth.

5. Simple supply-and-demand analysis can be employed to show that protection strategies increase domestic prices and generate welfare losses by (a) promoting inefficient domestic production and (b) reducing consumption.

6. Unless the protection is prohibitive, it can generate revenue for the government (tariff collections or import license auctions can be equivalent in this regard).

7. Noneconomic arguments for protection are sometimes made: national interest and/or security, cultural and/or regional integrity, and so on. Domestic subsidies can be more effective in these instances.

8. Other economic arguments are false: protecting domestic employment, special-interest protection, and mercantilistic pursuit of favorable terms of trade. Alternative domestic policies can be more effective in these instances.

9. Dynamic arguments for protection are more attractive, but they can be risky. Optimal tariff barriers and infant-industry protection run the risk of retaliation, for example.

V. HELPFUL HINTS

1 *Absolute advantage* means lower resource cost, or more efficient use of resources. *Comparative advantage* means lower relative cost, that is, relative to what has to be given up.

Consider the following example. There are two countries: Annastasia and Bobbyland, or A and B. Prior to trade, they each produce two goods: robots (R) and xylophones (X). Table 15-1 shows the labor cost (assuming labor is the only factor of production) of producing a unit of each good.

TABLE 15-1 Labor Hours Needed to Produce One Unit

	A	B
R	1 hour	10 hours
X	3 hours	20 hours

Annastasia has an absolute advantage in the production of *both* goods. It can produce them with fewer resources. To evaluate comparative advantage, we need to measure the *relative* cost of producing each commodity within each country.

In Annastasia, the relative cost of producing one robot is 0.33 xylophones. Here is why: When Annastasia decides to produce robots, it costs 1 hour of labor for each one. If that hour of labor had been used in the manufacture of xylophones, it could have produced *one-third* of a xylophone instead.

In Bobbyland, the relative cost of R is 0.50X. Relatively speaking, or relative to what each country has to give up, Annastasia has a comparative advantage in the production of R.

In A, the relative cost of producing one X is 3R. In B, the relative cost of producing one X is 2R. So, B has a comparative advantage in the production of X. Relatively speaking, B gives up less to produce X.

2. In a two-good world, it is definitionally impossible for a country to have a comparative advantage in the production of both goods. However, in a many-good world, one country will *always* have a comparative advantage in something.

3. Prices do not need to be measured in money terms—they can be measured in terms of the other good.

VI. MULTIPLE CHOICE QUESTIONS

These questions are organized by topic from the chapter outline. Choose the best answer from the options available.

A. The Nature of International Trade

1. Countries engage in international trade to:
   a. take advantage of economies of scale.
   b. acquire additional resources.
   c. satisfy the tastes of their citizens.
   d. all of the above.
   e. **a** and **b** only.

2. One of the big differences between domestic trade and international trade is that:
   a. the distances, and hence the transportation costs, are greater.
   b. foreigners are harder to deal with.
   c. currencies must be exchanged.
   d. all of the above.
   e. none of the above.

B. Comparative Advantage Among Nations

3. In terms of comparative advantage, the *most correct* explanation of why bananas are imported instead of being grown commercially in the United States is that:
   a. bananas cannot be produced in the temperate zones.
   b. it would take a great deal of effort to produce bananas in the United States.
   c. bananas can be produced with less effort in other countries than they can in the United States.
   d. U.S. resources are better employed in producing other commodities, and tropical-country resources are better employed in banana production than in other things.
   e. the U.S. climate does not lend itself to banana production.

4. Before international trade begins, a country will have an equilibrium ratio of prices (determined by relative production costs in the classical Ricardo model) between any two commodities. If trade involving these commodities begins with another country, then this price ratio will ordinarily be altered:
   a. only if a change in production costs results within the country.
   b. in all cases (except when the volume of international trade proves to be too small to affect it).
   c. only in cases where the volume of international trade is small.
   d. not at all, since it is an equilibrium relationship.
   e. only in cases where the volume of international trade is exceedingly large.
   Use Table 15-2 to answer questions 3 through 7. The table records the output of labor (assumed to be the only input involved) in the production of wine and cloth in two countries, A and B.

TABLE 15-2

Production per Hour	Country A	Country B
Yards of cloth	5	15
Liters of wine	10	20

5. Comparing the two countries and contemplating trade between them on the basis of production advantages, it would be correct to say that Country A has:
   a. an absolute advantage in cloth production.
   b. an absolute advantage in wine production.
   c. a comparative advantage in cloth production.
   d. a comparative advantage in wine production.
   e. a comparative advantage in neither commodity.

6. Suppose that initially there is no trade between these two countries. In Country A, the currency unit is the "donaro;" in Country B. it is the "gelt." The prices of cloth in A and B in their pretrade situations are, respectively, 20 donaros and 60 gelts. For an equilibrium in which each country continues to produce both commodities, the corresponding wine prices would have to be:
   a. 5 donaros, 20 gelts.
   b. 40 donaros, 45 gelts.
   c. 10 donaros, 45 gelts.
   d. 10 donaros, 80 gelts.
   e. 40 donaros, 80 gelts.

7. If trading opportunities were to open (international transport costs assumed to be zero or negligible), then we should expect Country B to:
   a. import wine.
   b. export wine.
   c. import both commodities.
   d. export both commodities.
   e. neither export nor import, since its productive situation is such that there is no prospect of profitable trade with Country A.

8. Before the trading opportunity of question 5 emerged, each country had its own price ratio, reflecting domestic production costs. If trade develops between Countries A and B. this ratio—specifically, the ratio of the price of wine to the price of cloth—should:
   a. rise in Country A, fall in Country B.
   b. fall in Country A, rise in Country B.
   c. rise in both.
   d. fall in both.
   e. not change in either country, except perhaps during a short transitional period before equilibrium is reestablished.

9. Once international trade has been established and a new equilibrium has been reached, then the ratio of cloth price to wine price (transport costs still assumed to be

zero) might reasonably be:
a.　1.2 in both countries.
b.　1.6 in both countries.
c.　1.3 in A, 2.1 in B.
d.　2.1 in A, 1.3 in B.
e.　2.3 in both countries.

10. Differences in comparative production costs are usually cited as the principal basis for international trade. Another (and different) possible source of international exchange is:
a.　differences in climates.
b.　fixed foreign exchange rates.
c.　differences in transport costs.
d.　differences in labor skills.
e.　economies of mass production.

11. Trade between countries of comparable size but with different standards of living will be:
a.　profitable to the country with lower living standards at the expense of the one with higher standards.
b.　profitable to both as long as price ratios differ in the two countries, but of no profit to either once a common price ratio has been established.
c.　profitable in some degree to both, even after a common price ratio has been established.
d.　unprofitable to both because one country would be at an absolute disadvantage in all products.
e.　profitable to the country with higher living standards at the expense of the one with lower living standards.

C. Protectionism

12. One argument for tariffs contends that they should be imposed to help a domestic producer to compete when the level of foreign wages is significantly below the level of domestic wages. This argument:
a.　is conceded by most economists to be correct, although sometimes exaggerated in order to justify some level of tariff protection.
b.　is fallacious because there are almost no instances in which there is any real difference between the levels of foreign and domestic wages.
c.　ignores the fact that differences in relative costs constitute the principal basis for international trade.
d.　may be correct with respect to money wages at home and abroad but is not correct with respect to real wages.
e.　is not correctly described by any of the preceding.

13. Country A imposes a new tariff on Country B's products. Country B is considering a retaliatory tariff on A's goods. On economic grounds, B should:
a.　reject the idea of a tariff increase.
b.　make the retaliatory tariff less than A's tariff.
c.　make the retaliatory tariff more than A's tariff.

d.　impose the retaliatory tariff only if B is in a situation of full employment.
e.　adjust the price of its currency relative to A's currency.

14. The policy of the mercantilists with respect to foreign trade held that:
a.　imports should exceed exports—i.e., the country should "get more than it gives"—in order to increase real income at home as much as possible.
b.　exports should exceed imports in order to bring in gold.
c.　since this trade represented commerce, it should be encouraged to the greatest possible degree—i.e., there should be free trade.
d.　exports should be kept in balance with imports and at the lowest possible level of both.
e.　trade in agricultural products was more important than trade in industrial goods.

15. The principal reason high-wage American labor should not require tariff protection from lower-paid foreign labor is:
a.　no American labor would be thrown out of work even if there were no tariffs.
b.　the high per-worker-hour productivity of American labor in many industries is an offset to the lower cost of foreign labor.
c.　American consumers tend to buy American-made goods in preference to foreign-made goods.
d.　a high-wage American industry can be presumed to have a comparative advantage over foreign competitors.
e.　none of the preceding reasons.

16. The argument by workers in a protected industry in the United States that free trade would worsen the income position of American labor is:
a.　not valid even for workers in that industry after allowance is made for the improvement in real income afforded by cheaper imports.
b.　not valid even for workers in that industry after allowance is made for the employment effect of increased exports.
c.　valid for workers in that industry but probably not valid for American labor as a whole.
d.　valid for workers in that industry and probably valid for American labor as a whole.
e.　probably valid for workers in that industry but unquestionably invalid for American labor as a whole.

17. From a purely economic point of view, the best level at which to set a tariff (under static assumptions) is:
a.　the prohibitive point.
b.　the amount needed to bring the level of foreign costs up to the level of domestic costs.
c.　zero.
d.　a level sufficiently low so that it is not likely to invite retaliation by other countries.
e.　the level at which revenues from the tariff will be at

a maximum.

18. One argument for tariff protection contends that a tariff would improve the terms of trade in dealing with other nations. This argument:
    a. is a refinement of the mercantilist argument that a nation's exports should exceed its imports.
    b. may be valid if the tariff-imposing country is a relatively large one and the tariffs a relatively small one.
    c. is a refined version of the infant-industry argument and hence has no validity.
    d. may be valid if the tariff-imposing country is unimportant in world trade for the commodity or commodities involved.
    e. may be valid if it is applied to all the country's imports, without or almost without exception.

19. It may be argued that a tariff should be imposed on a commodity if that commodity is considered essential to material well-being and/or if it is suspected that the foreign suppliers thereof might use their supply control for purposes of political blackmail. Most economists hold that:
    a. the tariff is justified if the commodity is deemed really essential.
    b. subsidy would be preferable to a tariff if the commodity is deemed really essential.
    c. the best remedy for threats of political blackmail is to insist on all-around free trade.
    d. although the imposition of a tariff might be used as a threat, political moves should be met by political countermoves (even to the threat of war), not by economic moves.
    e. its domestic production should be nationalized if the commodity is deemed really essential.

20. If we reduce the flow of import goods by imposing heavy tariffs, our exports are likely to be affected in which of the following ways?
    a. They will likely be reduced when other countries retaliate by imposing tariffs against those exports (as is likely), but not otherwise.
    b. There is little reason to expect that they will be affected at all, since retaliatory tariffs have usually proved ineffective.
    c. They will likely be increased, since other countries will find it necessary to buy more from us to compensate for the higher cost of the goods they sell us.
    d. They will likely be increased if the tariff raises the level of employment and national product at home, but not otherwise.
    e. They are likely to be reduced in all or almost all circumstances.

21. A valid counter to the argument that a tariff results in increased money wages in the protected industry is that:
    a. workers in that industry will in all probability suffer a loss in real wages.

b. workers in other industries will suffer a loss in real wages.
    c. the increase in money wages in the protected industry will cause unemployment.
    d. tariffs cannot increase money wages in any industry.
    e. any increase in real wages is likely to lead to inflation.

22. Arguments cited in favor of a protective tariff frequently note that tariffs (a) protect domestic industry against foreign competition and (b) bring revenue to the government. In response to these arguments, it may be said that:
    a. the tariff reduces rather than increases the sales of the domestic industry.
    b. if the industry in question enjoys an absolute advantage in production, it stands in no need of such a tariff.
    c. the emphasis on government revenue may lead to a tariff per unit much higher than the domestic industry needs for protection.
    d. an effective tariff will actually bring in no government revenue at all.
    e. none of these statements is correct.

23. A difference between a tariff on an imported good and a quota on the same good is that:
    a. a quota can never be made to yield revenue for the government, whereas a tariff can.
    b. a tariff can never be made to yield revenue for the government, whereas a quota can.
    c. a quota can be used to shut off all, or virtually all, the inflow of the imported good, whereas a tariff cannot.
    d. a tariff can be used to shut off all, or virtually all, the inflow of the imported good, whereas a quota cannot.
    e. a quantity-equivalent quota will generate the same revenue only if import rights are auctioned.

24. A prohibitive tariff:
    a. was used during the Prohibition.
    b. effectively chokes off all imports.
    c. prohibits placing a tariff on certain commodities.
    d. is less restrictive than a nonprohibitive tariff.
    e. is none of the above.

VII. PROBLEM SOLVING

The following problems are designed to help you apply the concepts that you learned in the chapter.

A. The Nature of International Trade

1. a. As shown in Figure 15-2, the trend in the United States over the past half-century has been to (**open / close**) its economy to foreign trade.
   b. The usual measure of openness, the ratio of ___

and/or ___ to GDP has, in fact, **(risen / fallen)** over time.

c. The percentage of U.S. GDP that is related to trade is **(higher / lower)** than the percent which characterizes most of the economies of Europe.

Figure 15-1

B. Comparative Advantage Among Nations

The questions which follow build toward an examination of the theory of comparative advantage by looking at economic conditions before trade begins. The idea is to start by identifying a country's before-trade position and standard of living and then to show how the initiation of foreign trade can increase real income.

The same simplifying assumptions employed in the text are employed here. There are only two regions: "America" and "Europe." Only two commodities are involved: food (F) and clothing (C). All the costs of producing either F or C can be measured in hours of labor. For some reason, however, the yields from an hour of labor, in the making of both F and C, differ across international boundaries.

TABLE 15-3

Yield of 1 Labor-Hour	Units of F	Units of C
In America	20	6
In Europe	10	8

TABLE 15-4

	Minutes of Labor Required to Produce:	
	1 Unit of F	1 Unit of C
In America	3	10
In Europe	6	7.5

2 The quantities of F and of C resulting from 1 hour of labor in America and in Europe are given in Table 15-3. These data translate into the input requirements recorded in Table 15-4.

a. Assuming that "1 hour of labor" means the same thing in both countries, the figures indicate that America is more productive in **(F / both F and C / C / neither F**

nor C).

b. Europe is, meanwhile, more productive in **(F / both F and C / C / neither F nor C)**.

c. In an 8-hour day, therefore, a worker in America can produce either 8 x 20 = 160 units of F or **(10 / 48 / 64 / 80)** units of C.

d. In Europe a worker can produce either 64 units of C or **(10 / 48 / 64 / 80)** units of F.

3. This chapter assumes that all the costs of producing either commodity in either region are labor costs and that all revenue from sale of the commodity goes to that labor.

a. If the market price of a unit of F in America were $1, then the hourly wage earned by an American worker producing F would be **($0.05 / $0.10 / $1.00 / $10.00 / $20.00)**.

b. If, instead, F's price in America were $0.05 (5 cents), then the corresponding hourly wage for an F worker would be **($0.05 / $0.10 / $1.00 / $10.00 / $20.00)**.

c. Similarly, if C's price per unit in America were $2, then the hourly wage of a C worker would be **($0.30 / $0.60 / $2.00 / $10.00 / $12.00)**.

d. If the price per unit of F were £1 (1 pound) in Europe, then the hourly wage of an F worker there would be **(£1 / £4 / £6 / £8 / £10)**.

e. If C's price in Europe were £1, on the other hand, then the corresponding hourly C wage would be **(£1 / £4 / £6 / £8 / £10)**.

4. Suppose that the prices of F and C in America are both $1.

a. A worker, free to choose an occupation in either industry, would earn more by going to work in the production of **(F / C)**. Specifically, earnings per hour would be **($1 / $6 / $8 / $10 / $20)** in the production of F and **($1 / $6 / $8 / $10 / $20)** in the production of C.

Given freedom of labor to enter either occupation (and with no other preference between them), the prices noted above (both $1) **(could / could not)** characterize an "equilibrium" situation in America. If these prices did prevail—say, because the government tried to enforce them by law—then **(only F / only C / both F and C)** would be produced.

b. If the prices of both F and C were somehow £10 in Europe, then (again assuming no barrier to movement between occupations) **(all the workers would move into production of F / all the workers would move into production of C / there would be no change in the production mix of F and C)**.

c. The point is that the supply of resources (here, the entire labor force) would shift away from production of the "underpriced" commodity unless the prices of F and C stand in the proper relation to one another, i.e., unless they reflect relative marginal costs. If the price of F were $3 in America, then the price of C would have to be **($1 / $3 / $8 / $10 / $12)**, if both F and C are to be produced.

If the price of C were $2 in America, then the price of F should be (**$0.30 / $0.60 / $1.00 / $1.50 / $2.00**).

Prices of $2.40 for F and $9 for C (**would / would not**) support an equilibrium.

d.   It is relative prices that matter here. In America, the ratio between p_F and p_C must be (**1:1 / 3:10 / 5:10 / 10:3**) because only that ratio matches the underlying ratio of production costs, measured in labor time needed to produce 1 unit of each commodity.

The absolute level of prices would be governed by such factors as the quantity of money circulating within the country.

e.   If prices of F and C somehow got stuck at $2.40 and $9, respectively, workers would move away from the production of (**F / C**) and into the production of (**F / C**).

In Europe, the same requirement holds, except that the relationship must match productive conditions there.

f.   If the price of F in Europe were £4, then the price of C would have to be (**£1 / £2 / £3 / £4 / £5**) to support an equilibrium in which both commodities were produced. More generally, Europe's price ratio (F to C) must be (**3:10 / 5:10 / 4:5 / 5:4**).

The questions thus far have assumed that there is no international trade between America and Europe. Now assume that the opportunity for trade between the two regions suddenly materializes. Assume, for simplicity, that the costs of shipping goods from one region to the other are so small that they can be considered zero. The prices of F and of C in America are, respectively, 60 cents and $2.

5.   In America (and in Europe), opening trade would disrupt the pretrade domestic "equilibrium." For example, in the United States, trade supplements domestic supplies of C.

a.   The price of C should therefore (**rise / remain unchanged / fall**). This in turn means that the ratio of the price of F to the price of C (i.e., p_F/p_C) should (**rise / remain unchanged / fall**).

b.   We know that workers would leave the "under-priced" occupation if America's price ratio p_F/p_C were anything other than 3:10 (or 0.3). In this case, workers would move from the production of (**F / C**) to the production of (**F / C**) as the price ratio rose, and that would be good.

Why? Because America's new export trade means that more workers are needed in the production of American exports—commodity F.

c.   In Europe, which imports what America exports, there would (**be a / not be any**) corresponding change in domestic prices. There, the ratio p_F/p_C would (**rise / remain unchanged / fall**).

The price of F would fall as imports arrived from America. The price of C would rise, meanwhile, since there would now be a new and increased demand for European C in America.

d.   Workers would leave the production of (**C / F**), moving instead to production of Europe's export—com-

modity C.

6.   The points of these questions can be illustrated graphically. Take the input requirements listed in question 1 as given, and suppose that Europe and America are both endowed with 10 hours of labor (not very realistic, to be sure, but a convenient number around which to build some illustrative geometry). Suppose further that both regions start, in the absence of any trade, by dividing their labor resources equally between F and C.

a.   In panel (*a*) of Figure 15-2, draw the production possibility frontier for America, and identify the initial production mix as point A. Draw the corresponding frontier for Europe in panel (*b*), and identify the initial production mix as point *B*.

b.   The slope of the American frontier, equaling ___ in magnitude, represents the relative domestic price ratio of food to clothing in America. The corresponding slope of the European frontier, equaling in ___ magnitude, is similarly the relative domestic price ratio in Europe.

c.   Start with America, which produces ___ units of F and ___ units of C; Europe begins producing ___ units of F and ___ units of C. Total "world" production of C is ___ units; total production of F is ___ units.

7.   Suppose now, for the sake of argument, that America chooses to specialize in F in trade with Europe at the European domestic price ratio.

a.   In panel (*a*) draw a budget constraint (a consumption frontier based upon specializing in the production of F and trading to get C) indicating the possible points of consumption given this strategy. If America were to continue to consume the original 30 units of C, then it could increase its consumption of F from 100 units to ___ units by selling ___ units of F for 30 units of C. Welfare in America, assuming a smooth transition from a 50-50 labor split to 100 percent concentration in the production of F, would therefore necessarily (**fall / stay the same / rise**).

Now play the same game from the other side of the Atlantic. Assume that Europe decides to specialize completely in the production of C and buys as much F as it wants given the American price ratio.

b.   Draw the appropriate budget constraint in panel (*b*).

c.   If Europe were still interested in consuming 40 units of C, it could increase its consumption of F from 50 units to ___ units by selling 40 units of C for ___ units of F. European welfare would, in this second case, also (**climb / remain the same / fall**), again making the same assumption of continued full employment during the transition.

8.   The world production frontier can now be constructed.

a.   Suppose, first of all, that both countries specialize in F; production of F would equal __ units in America and __ units in Europe, for a total of __ units; total production of C would then equal __ units.

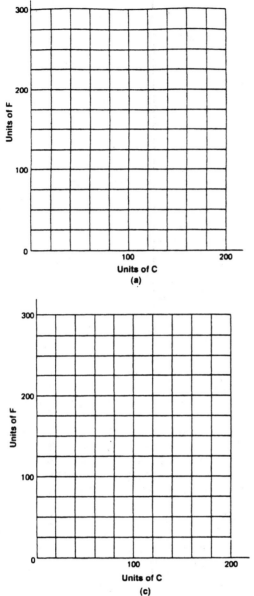

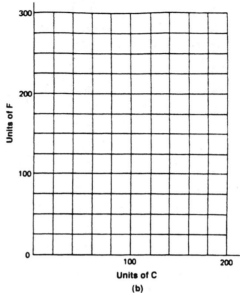

Figure 15-2

b.   Plot this combination in panel (c) and label it point *D*.

Now reverse the specializations of both countries.

c.   Total production of F would then equal __ units, with the production of C climbing to a maximum of __ units.

d.   Plot this second point in panel (c) and label it *E*.

Halfway between these extremes are two intermediate cases of mixed specialization.

e.   If Europe specialized in C and America specialized in F, then __ units of F would be produced along with __ units of C.

f.   Denote this point *G* and plot it in panel (c), as well.

g.   If the specializations were reversed, though, __ units of F would be produced in Europe and __ units of C would be produced in America.

h.   This point, plotted and labeled *H* in panel (c), (**would / would not**) be on the frontier because the production level(s) of (**F is / C is / neither F nor C is / both F and C are**) lower at *H* than at *G*.

The world frontier is now at hand.

i.   A straight line connecting points *D* and *G* would correspond to specialization by (**America / Europe**) in the production of (**F / C**) and some intermediate combination of F and C produced in (**America / Europe**). Similarly, points along a line connecting points *G* and *E* would correspond to specialization in (**America / Europe**) in the production of (**F / C**) and some intermediate combination in (**America / Europe**).

(*Note: The frontier you just drew should look like the frontier shown in the text.*)

j.   Finally, plot the pretrade initial production point in panel (c) and label it *I*; it (**is / is not**) on the frontier. The point chosen by free trade outlined above would be (**D / E / G / H**). It (**would / would not**) be on the frontier, and it would, for both countries, be superior to the initial, pretrade position.

C. Protectionism

9. Consult Figure 15-3. Curve *SS* represents a domestic supply curve for some good X; if X is a competitive industry, then *SS* represents the horizontal sum of the marginal cost curves of many firms. Curse *DD* represents domestic demand for the same good. It is implicitly assumed that consumers do not care where the good was made; they simply want to buy the indicated quantities at the indicated prices.

    a. The market-clearing price in the absence of trade is $\$\_\_$, and ___ units of X would be demanded and supplied domestically at that price. If the world price of \$5 were allowed to prevail, though, then ___ units of X would be demanded, ___ units would be supplied domestically, and ___ units would be imported.

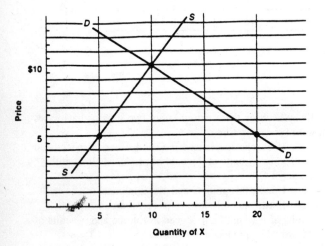

Figure 15-3

Now suppose that the domestic government has been convinced somehow to restrict imports by 50 percent.

    b. A tariff of $\$\_\_$ per unit imported would do the trick, but it would raise the domestic price to $\$\_\_$. At that price, __ units would be demanded, __ units would be supplied domestically, and __ units would be imported. The effect of the tariff, therefore, is to (**raise / lower**) the price of X, (**raise / lower**) domestic production and employment, and (**raise / lower**) imports.

    c. Given the tariff of part *b*, the government would collect $\$\_\_$ in revenue; this is revenue that would be collected above and beyond the revenue that it collected from its domestic tax base. *(Hint:* To see the tax on your diagram, construct a box underneath the supply and demand curves. The length is the 7.5 units that are imported, and the height is the \$2.50 tariff.)

The higher domestic price would, however, promote (**less /**

more) efficient production at home, and thereby produce an efficiency (**loss / gain**) of $\$\_\_$.

The marginal cost of producing X at home would, quite simply, increase to a level 50 percent higher than the marginal cost incurred by the rest of the world. The domestic economy would, in other words, be wasting resources in the production of X that would have been employed more efficiently somewhere else.

    d. If the government chose to impose a quota rather than a tariff, then it would award licenses to import up to __ units of X.

    e. If there were no tariff, but if it cost \$2.50 per unit to transport X from the world marketplace into the domestic economy, then your answers to part **b** (**would / would not**) be altered. The revenue in part *c* identified as going to the government (**would / would not**) simply go to the transport company.

10. a. The mercantilist approach to international trade argued that a nation should try to have (**exports / imports**) in excess of (**exports / import**)—hence the phrase "favorable balance of trade." Any surplus so obtained would be used to acquire (**merchandise / gold**).

    b. The mercantilist position was thus strongly disposed toward (**protectionism / free trade**). It was a convenient argument for many (**producer / consumer**) groups seeking protection against foreign competition.

    c. It would be (**possible / impossible**) for every nation to practice mercantilism successfully, since it is (**possible / impossible**) for every nation to have a surplus of exports. A general attempt to practice this philosophy, by trying to expand exports and restrict imports, would lead to a major (**rise / fall**) in (**exports alone / imports alone / both exports and imports**).

VIII. DISCUSSION QUESTIONS

Answer the following questions, making sure that you can explain the work you did to arrive at the answers.

1. Look back at the very beginning of the chapter and the quote from F. Bastiat. Would David Ricardo agree or disagree with the Candle Makers?

2. Explain, in words, how two countries mutually benefit from trade.

3. Precisely who are the winners and who are the losers when countries place tariffs and/or quotas on imported goods?

4. It has been argued that raising tariffs generates more revenue for the government. Do you agree?

5. List two noneconomic arguments that have been advanced for protection. Are there any alternates to tariffs and quotas?

IX. ANSWERS TO STUDY GUIDE QUESTIONS

III. Review of Key Concepts

5   Principle of comparative advantage
8   Absolute advantage
7   Comparative advantage
10   Terms of trade
2   Consumption-possibility curve
9   Multilateral trade
12   Tariff
13   Quota
11   Mercantilism
1   Dumping
4   Optimal tariff
6   Infant industry tariff
3   "Beggar thy neighbor" policy

VI. Multiple Choice Questions

1. D   2. C   3. D   4. B   5. D   6. C
7. A   8. A   9. B   10. E   11. C   12. C
13. A   14. B   15. B   16. C   17. C   18. B
19. B   20. E   21. B   22. C   23. E   24. B

VII. Problem solving

1. a. open
   b. imports, exports, risen
   c. lower
2. a. F
   b. C
   c. 48
   d. 80
3. a. $20.00 ($1.00 × 20)
   b. $1.00 ($0.05 × 20)
   c. $12.00 ($2.00 × 6)
   d. £10
   e. £8
4. a. F. $20, $6, could not, only F
   b. all the workers would move into production of F
   c. $10 ($3.00 × 3.33), $0.60 ($2.00/3.33), would not
   d. 3:10
   e. F, C
   f. £5, 4:5
5. a. fall, rise
   b. C, F
   c. be a, fall
   d. F
6. a. See dashed lines in Figure 15-1, panels (a) and (b).
   b. -3.33, -1.25
   c. 100, 30, 50, 40, 70, 150
7. a. See Figure 15-1, panel (a), 162.5, 37.5 (37.5/30 = 1.25), rise

   b. See Figure 15-1 (top of next page), panel (b).
   c. 133.33, 133.33 (40 x 3.33), climb
8. a. 200, 100, 300, 0
   b. See Figure 15-1, panel (c).
   c. 0,140
   d. See Figure 15-1, panel (c).
   e. 200, 80
   f. See Figure USA, panel (c) .
   g. 100, 60
   h. See Figure 15-1, panel (c), would not, both F and C
   i. America, F. Europe, Europe, C, America
   j. See Figure 15-1, panel (c), is not, G. would
9. a. $10, 10, 20, 5, 15
   b. $2.50, $7.50, 15, 7.5, 7.5, raise, raise, lower
   c. $18.75 (2.50 × 7.5), rectangle CEFG in Figure 15-2; less, loss, $3.125 (2.5 × 2.5 × 0.5), triangle ABC in Figure 15-2 (bottom on next page)
   d. 7.5
   e. would not, would
10. a. exports, imports, gold
    b. protectionism, producer
    c. impossible, impossible, fall, both exports and imports

VIII. Discussion Questions

1. David Ricardo would vehemently disagree with the Candle Makers. Ricardo's principle of comparative advantage points out that both countries can gain and be made wealthier by trade, even if one nation is much wealthier than the other.
2. When countries trade, each country specializes in the production of the commodity that it can produce relatively cheaper than the other. So in each country, resources are moved into the industry where productivity is highest. As a result, total combined output is greater. Besides, countries would not trade if trading made them worse off.
3. The winners are the domestic industry that gets protected and the government that brings in the tariff revenue. The losers are everyone else: domestic consumers who pay more, efficient foreign firms that export less, and efficient domestic industries that now will export less if the foreign government retaliates with a tariff of its own.
4. Tariffs do indeed raise money for the government. However, there are efficiency losses and losses in consumer surplus that must be taken into consideration as well.
5. Noneconomic arguments for tariffs include national security, protection of the environment, and the preservation of culture or tradition. Some of the alternatives to tariffs and quotas are voluntary export restrictions and nontariff barriers such as licensing restrictions and bureaucratic red tape.

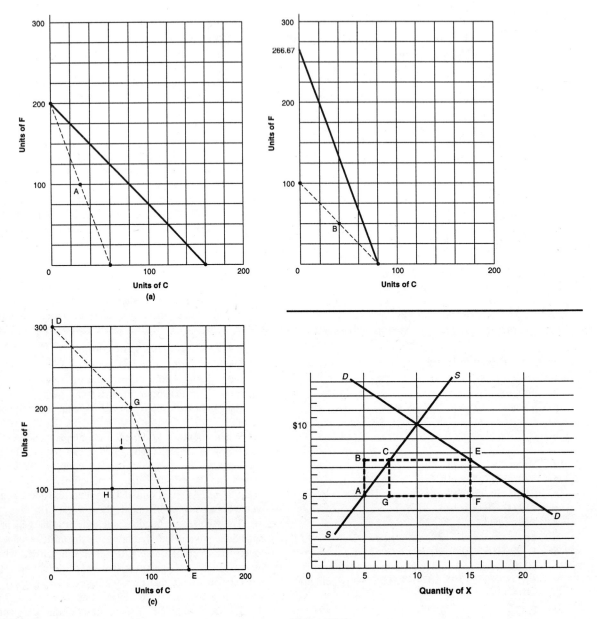

Figure 15-2

Figure 15-3

CHAPTER 16

Government Taxation and Expenditure

I. CHAPTER OVERVIEW

Government has, in most industrial countries, grown tremendously over the course of this century. In response to two world wars, a deep and severe depression, a cold war, and a myriad of other social and economic concerns, governments have taken on the burdens of providing for an increasingly complex society. Government spending has increased. Taxation, income-support programs, and regulatory intervention have increased.

This growth in the size and scope of government has not come without controversy. Those opposed to big government in the United States believe that "Uncle Sam" has overstepped his bounds and needs to be reigned in. It must be admitted before we even begin our discussion that "government failure" is as much of a possibility as "market failure;" that is, government programs can fail to distribute resources in an efficient or equitable manner. However, in order to make this assessment, we need to develop some analytical tools.

It is our goal in the chapter to, first, learn about the types of roles that a government could play in a mixed economy. Second, we will turn our attention to the roles actually assumed by government at all levels in the U.S. economy. We will consider the major expenditure patterns of government at all levels that help to define a system of fiscal federalism that distributes responsibilities across local, state, and federal authorities. Finally we will address issues of taxation and develop some alternative strategies that might be used to collect revenues that must be used to finance all this spending.

II. LEARNING OBJECTIVES

After you have read Chapter 16 in your text and completed the exercises in this *Study Guide* chapter, you should be able to:

1. Describe the path that **fiscal federalism** has followed in the United States this century.
2. List, explain, and provide examples of the four major functions that government must consider: (a) improving economic efficiency, (b) reducing economic inequality, (c) stabilizing the economy through macroe-

conomic policies, and (d) conducting international economic policy.
3. Discuss the construction of an efficient system of fiscal federalism and the blurring of responsibilities that necessarily occurs along the boundaries of the different levels of government. List the most important types of expenditures made at each level.
4. Describe the conflicting principles of taxation—the **benefit approach** and the **ability-to-pay approach**—and the compromise between the two that has been accomplished in the United States. Relate these principles to the notions of **horizontal** and **vertical equity**.
5. Categorize alternative tax schemes as **progressive, proportional** or **regressive** and as involving **direct** or **indirect** taxation.
6. Understand the principles around which the federal, state, and local tax system are organized.
7. Discuss efficiency as an issue in the design of a tax system
8. Define the term **tax incidence** and explain why and how a tax might not be "paid" by the economic agent identified in the tax code.

III. REVIEW OF KEY CONCEPTS

Match the following terms from column A with their definitions in column B.

A	B
__ Economic regulation	1. Tax that takes a larger fraction of income in taxes from poor families than from rich families.
__ Social regulation	2. States that the government should levy the heaviest taxes on those inputs and outputs that are most price-inelastic in supply or demand.
__ Laissez-faire	3. Concerns the tax treatment of people with different levels of income.
__ Income redistribution	4. The view that government should interfere as little as possible in economic activity and

205

__ Public-choice
theory

__ Fiscal federalism

__ Entitlement
programs

__ Benefit principle

__ Ability-to-pay
principle

__ Horizontal equity

__ Vertical equity

__ Progressive taxes

__ Regressive taxes

__ Direct taxes

__ Indirect taxes

__ Effective tax rate

__ Marginal tax rate

__ Value-added tax

__ Ramsey tax rule

leave decisions to the market-place.

5.   Collects taxes at each stage of the production process.

6.   Taxes designed to help the environment as well as to raise revenues.

7.   Implies a division of fiscal responsibilities among the different levels of government.

8.   Government policies designed to protect public health and safety.

9.   Government policies designed to enforce price controls, establish conditions of exit and entry, and set safety standards for markets.

10. Equal to total taxes divided by total income.

11. States that those who are essentially equal should be taxed equally.

12. Claimed that the disincentive effects of high marginal tax rates were responsible for many of the nation's ills—low savings, recession, etc.

13. Government policies designed to devote more resources to providing services for poor people.

14. The branch of economics that studies the way that governments make decisions.

15. The way that the burden of a tax is ultimately borne and its total effects on the behavior of economic agents.

16. Holds that different individuals should be taxed in proportion to the benefit that they receive from government programs.

17. Taxes that are levied on goods and services, and thus only "indirectly" on individuals.

18. Programs that provide benefits or payments to any person who meets eligibility requirements set down by law.

19. States that the amount of taxes people pay should relate to their income or wealth.

__ Supply-side
economics

__ Green taxes

__ Tax incidence

20. Tax that takes a larger fraction of income from rich families than from poor families.

21. The extra tax that is paid per dollar of extra income.

22. Taxes that are levied directly upon individuals or firms.

IV. SUMMARY AND CHAPTER OUTLINE

This section summarizes the key concepts from the chapter.

A. Government Control of the Economy

1.   Governments use primarily three tools to influence private economic activity: *taxes, expenditures and transfer payments*, and *regulations*. Taxing and spending are often referred to as fiscal tools; the government is operating as a consumer or is attempting to redistribute income. Regulations establish rules which limit the ability of firms to operate in their own best interest.

2.   The economic role of government has grown dramatically at all levels and across many countries over the last half-century. *Economic regulation* has involved government in price setting, in monitoring and encouraging competition, and in establishing safety standards in many industries. Examples of actions in this area include the recent decision against Microsoft in the software industry, and the development of the Occupational Safety and Health Administration (OSHA), which oversees the welfare of employees at work. *Social regulation* has involved government in the area of public health and safety. Examples of actions in this area include the institution of seat belt laws in many states and the Clean Air Act, which established clear targets for diminishing the amount of pollution in the air we breathe.

3.   There are four primary functions of government in a mixed economy. *First*, government can take actions to improve *economic efficiency*. Although the invisible hand can bring about efficient solutions to economic problems, there are times when the market fails. A legal system is needed to enforce contracts and to establish rules for agents operating in the economy. Some sort of antitrust policy is needed to limit the extremes of imperfect competition and the emergence of monopoly power. Government is needed to improve the quality of information in an economy and to negotiate efficient solutions to problems involving externalities and public goods. In short, the government can help to move the economy toward the efficiency represented by the competitive ideal.

Second, government can take actions to make the *distribution of income less unequal*. Remember that efficiency and equity do not necessarily go hand in hand. There is no reason to believe that an efficient economy will provide an equitable distribution of income and resources. When society becomes concerned about inequalities, government can step in and redistribute income and wealth, usually by means of taxing and spending policies.

Third, government can take actions to *stabilize the economy*. From its earliest days, capitalist societies have gone through expansionary times, in which the level of economic activity was high and growing, as well as contractionary times, in which the level of economic activity was low and sinking. Inflation and unemployment have, from time to time, caused problems in the economy and led to instability. The role for government in this case is to develop policy initiatives that will counteract these natural tendencies of a capitalist economy and smooth out these swings over the course of the business cycle.

Fourth, government plays an important role in *representing the country in the international economy*. In recent years this has meant that government tries to facilitate international trade by limiting tariff and quota barriers. Wealthy nations have developed programs to aid poorer countries, particularly in times of crisis. Also, macroeconomic policies are coordinated across governments in order to make them more effective.

B. Government Expenditures

1. The United States has adopted a system of *fiscal federalism* that assigns various expenditure programs to the levels of government whose jurisdictions most closely match the geographical boundaries of their spillover effects. As a result, we see the federal government providing and managing programs like national defense, space exploration, and foreign affairs. We see local governments taking care of things like police protection, fire protection, public education, and other "local public goods." Finally, we see state governments administering highway, port, and welfare programs, as well as health care and criminal justice systems. Frequently the money required to support the programs at state and local levels flows down from the federal government, but the administration of the programs is conducted at the lowest possible level.

It should be noted, of course, that this structure is in a *constant state of flux*. The boundaries between governments and the spillover effects of programs are typically hard to define, and programs are forever being transferred from one level of government to another.

2. Government taxation and spending at all levels account for roughly one-third of GDP, with 70 percent of that total spent at the federal level. The largest federal spending category is national security and international affairs, but the fastest growing category is *entitlement programs* which provide benefits or payments to any person who meets certain eligibility requirements set down by law. Examples of entitlement programs include social security, Medicare, and unemployment insurance.

C. Economic Aspects of Taxation

1. Tax policy is informed by two opposing points of view—the *benefits approach* and the *ability-to-pay approach*. The underlying question here is, who should pay, and who should pay the largest amount, for collective goods? Following the benefits approach, we would tax people in proportion to the benefit they receive from government programs. This may work well for things like state parks; those who use the parks might pay a larger share of their upkeep. However, for various entitlement programs, this criterion falls a bit short. For example, if welfare recipients could afford to pay for the welfare program, they would not need to take advantage of it.

Following the ability-to-pay approach, we would tax people in proportion to their income or wealth. The higher the income or wealth, the higher the taxes. Some individuals would be paying for programs and services that they would never need to take advantage of; the notion of fairness involves redistribution of resources within the system.

2. Further issues of fairness are reflected in the notions of *horizontal* and *vertical* equity. *Horizontal equity* implies that people who are viewed as equal should he taxed equally. *Vertical equity* relates to the tax treatment of people with different levels of income. The bottom line here is that equity is very difficult to define in absolute terms.

A tax system must carefully balance these alternative notions in order to result in a fair distribution of resources.

3. Taxes are *progressive* if they take *larger* proportions of higher incomes and *regressive* if they take *smaller* portions of higher incomes. Income taxes tend to be progressive by design; sales and excise taxes tend to be regressive by conduct. A tax is not, however, progressive simply because it collects more money from a rich individual than from a poor one. To establish whether a tax is regressive or progressive, you must (1) find the amount of tax typically paid at various income levels within the population and (2) express this tax paid as a percentage of income. If these percentage figures rise as income rises—that is, if the percentage of income paid in tax rises as income rises—then the tax is progressive. If the percentage figures go down as you move to higher income levels, on the other hand, then the tax is regressive. If the percentage figure is pretty much the same at all income levels, then the tax is neither progressive nor regressive; rather, it is *proportional*.

Taxes can further be classified as *direct* (levied directly upon individuals or firms) or *indirect* (levied on goods and services, and hence only indirectly on individuals or firms who consume those goods and services). An example of a direct tax is the personal income tax; an example of an indirect tax is a gasoline tax.

4. The federal government raises most of its revenue from individual and corporate income taxes. Other federal taxes include sales and excise taxes, payroll taxes, and corporate profits taxes. Sales and excise taxes are levied as a percent-

age of sales or per unit of an item purchased; these are controversial because they appear to be regressive. Because poorer people tend to spend larger portions of their income on consumption goods, they tend to pay a larger portion of their income as sales taxes. Payroll taxes are collected to pay for social insurance programs. Corporations must pay corporate profits taxes; these are controversial in the sense that they provide disincentives for corporate investment.

5. Local governments employ property taxes most heavily. In fact, approximately 30 percent of the total revenues of state and local government are raised through property taxes. (Henry George would he pleased to hear this!) States rely on sales taxes and, in some cases, income taxes.

6. Given this overview of taxes in the United States, it is worth wondering whether or not this group of policies provides an efficient use of resources. Taxes certainly have incentive effects and hence alter the behavior of market agents. For example, higher income tax rates effectively lower wage rates for workers. We know that decreases in wages are accompanied by both substitution effects, which encourage workers to supply *fewer* hours, and income effects, which may encourage workers to supply *more* hours. In either case, individual behavior may be modified in response to changes in tax policy. Exemptions in the tax rate exist for home mortgage interest, giving people an incentive to invest in housing markets. Knowing that tax rates are scheduled to change encourages people to alter the timing of their receipts. All of these factors are important to consider when investigating the efficiency of taxation.

In addition to these incentive effects, we must also ask which goods and services can be taxed most efficiently. The *Ramsey tax rule* states that the government should levy the heaviest taxes on those inputs and outputs that are most price-inelastic in supply or demand. This will result in the *smallest* change in quantity exchanged across the market and will generate the *greatest* amount of revenue for the government. However, remember that the types of goods that tend to have the most inelastic demands are necessities; increasing taxes on food, fuel, water, etc. might be worrisome on the grounds of equity.

7. Questions of incidence ask who pays specific taxes in the form of decreased purchasing power. They are related to questions about the degree to which various taxes create disincentives for people to work harder and/or save more. The benefit or transfer portrait of expenditure programs tends to offset regressive treatment of low-income taxpayers.

V. HELPFUL HINTS

1. A more complete analysis of government *fiscal* policies (taxing and spending), along with models of their effects on the economy, can be found in a course on macroeconomics. Take one!

2. Even the most extreme advocates of laissez-faire would agree that the government has a role to play in establishing and maintaining a legal system in an economy. Without some set of rules and regulations and without some ultimate arbitrator of disagreements, contracts would be very difficult to enforce, and uncertainty would increase dramatically. Take Russia as an example. The dismantling of the socialist structure has led to the introduction, for the first time in 80 years, of private property. Without a strong legal system, problems arise as agents attempt to understand both ownership and responsibility to contractual obligations. This has been a huge hurdle for the Russians; until the legal system is accepted as part of the system endless disputes will occur, and foreign investors will be less willing to enter into contracts with Russian businesses.

3. The term *business cycles* was used in this chapter. This term refers to the natural expansions and contractions that occur in the level of economic activity over time. Consider Figure 16-l. The *trend line* shows a stable and steady growth path for the macroeconomy. It indicates that the level of economic activity tends to increase steadily over time. However, in reality, the growth path of the macroeconomy is not so stable and smooth. In fact, the level of economic activity follows the business cycle: periodic peaks and troughs that occur naturally. In its role as provider of stability the government takes actions which serve to *dampen* these business cycles and move the economy closer to the trend line.

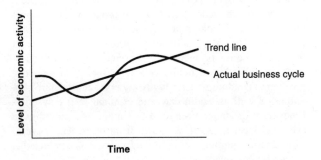

Figure 16-1

4. It is sometimes difficult to understand why sales taxes are regressive. Since everyone in a particular state pays the same tax *percentage* on purchases, it can sometimes appear as though sales taxes are proportional. However, remember that to establish whether a tax is regressive or progressive, you must find the amount of tax typically paid at various income levels within the population and express this tax paid as a percentage of income. The regressive aspect of sales taxes occurs because at low income levels, the actual amount of tax paid as a percentage of income is *higher* than it is at high income levels.

5. Two questions dominate any discussion of taxation: *"Who should pay?" and "How do we know if the person who should pay is, in fact, actually paying?"* These questions are very difficult to answer; as someone once said, "Don't tax you, don't tax me, tax the man behind that tree." Simply put, few people actually *like* to pay taxes.

Suppose, for example, that the benefits to be derived from some public project will accrue entirely to an identifiable group of people from within the population. It might then be reasonable to assert that the tax revenues required to finance that project should be collected from the people who benefit; e.g., taxes for the construction of roads might be collected solely from the people who use the roads. However, life is rarely this simple.

In most cases of public finance, policymakers must wrestle with the question of fairness and equity: How can society define a fair and equitable basis for distributing the burden of taxation? The debate on these issues is a never-ending one. One side argues that the rich should carry most or all of the burden simply because they are rich and can afford it, while the poor cannot. The opposition insists that "making money" is at least one of the incentives for personal initiative and effort. According to this argument, accepting a "soak-the-rich" philosophy may create a tax system that undermines incentive and encourages the most talented and inventive members of the population to move someplace where the tax laws are less severe. There are no magic policies that will satisfy everyone at the same time.

6. The burden of taxation was explored and illustrated in Chapter 4; it bears repeating here. Remember we found that the more *in*elastic side of the market will pay the larger portion of any new tax. Consider Figure 16-2. Panel (*a*) shows the division of the tax when the *supply curve is more inelastic* than the demand curve, while panel (*b*) shows the division of the tax when the *demand curve is more inelastic* than the supply curve.

VI. MULTIPLE CHOICE QUESTIONS

These questions are organized by topic from the chapter outline. Choose the best answer from the options available.

A. Government and Control of the Economy

1. Which of the following is a tool that the government can use to manage the economy?
   a. Taxes.
   b. Direct expenditures.
   c. Transfer payments.
   d. Regulation.
   e. All the above.

2. Which of the following statements is an accurate description of the history of government spending in the United States?
   a. The cost of government at all levels climbed from nearly 10 percent of GDP in 1913 to around 15 percent in the early 1990s.
   b. The cost of government at all levels climbed from 25 percent of GDP in 1913 to 35 percent in the early 1990s.
   c. The cost of government at all levels climbed from approximately 10 percent of GDP in 1913 to nearly 35 percent in the early 1990s.
   d. The cost of the federal government in the United States has remained relatively constant, at around 10 percent of GDP since 1913.
   e. None of the above.

3. Taxation in the United States:
   a. has grown during the twentieth century at a rate that far exceeds the rate of growth of government spending.
   b. has grown at a rate that, until 1981, roughly matched the rate of growth of government spending.
   c. has fallen in size in terms of fraction of GDP since 1939, but has climbed in absolute terms.

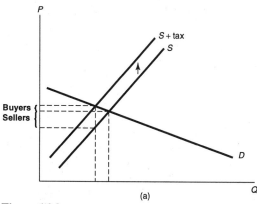

(a)

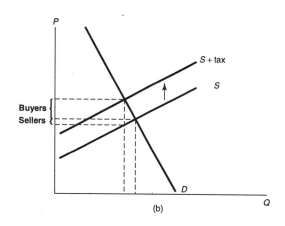

(b)

Figure 16-2

d. rose dramatically in the 1980s in an effort to balance the federal budget.

e. none of the above.

4. Regulatory activity in the United States:

a. is composed of only economic regulations, which involve price controls, entry and exit standards, and safety standards.

b. is composed of only social regulations, which involve public health and safety.

c. includes both economic and social regulations.

d. was eliminated in the 1930s in response to the depression.

e. was increased in the 1980s, as policymakers ignored the costs and benefits of policies and assumed that any regulation is better than no regulation.

5. Regulation grew in the United States as it became clear that a laissez-faire policy was vulnerable to:

a. pockets of poverty that are exploited by the more fortunate.

b. the business cycle, which buffets the economic lives of nearly every citizen.

c. inefficient and unfair discrimination on the basis of sex, race, and other factors.

d. the flagrant abuse of the environment.

e. all the above.

6. Government can play a number of roles in a mixed economy. These potential roles include:

a. prescribing a legal framework that defines "the rules of the game."

b. reallocating resources to accomplish greater efficiency in the face of, say, monopoly or pollution.

c. effecting macrostabilization by prudent exercise of fiscal, monetary, and other policies.

d. reallocating resources to accomplish greater equity.

e. all the above.

B. Government Expenditures

7. The largest single money item in the U.S. federal government budget is currently:

a. energy, science, and environment.

b. national defense and international affairs.

c. interest on the public debt.

d. general government (including justice) .

e. social security.

8. Any highway that is built by the government and made available toll-free to the public represents an example of:

a. private consumption.

b. a transfer expenditure.

c. a welfare expenditure.

d. monetary policy.

e. none of the above.

9. A government might reasonably introduce a widespread program of transfer payments in order to:

a. create a surplus in its budget.

b. effect some change in the social decision on the question of *for whom* goods are to be produced.

c. provide more collective consumption.

d. move the economy's production-possibility curve outward and to the right.

e. reduce inflation.

10. Entitlement programs include:

a. social security.

b. national defense.

c. international monetary activity.

d. the space program.

e. all the above.

11. In the late 1980s and early 1990s, the American public began to worry about the increasing size of the federal budget deficit. The feeling was that:

a. legislators are maximizing the government's profits by running increasingly larger budget deficits.

b. without the discipline of competition, government has no incentive to spend money efficiently.

c. government budget deficits lead to an efficient allocation of society's resources.

d. government budget deficits lead to an equitable allocation of society's resources.

e. none of the above.

C. Economic Aspects of Taxation

12. Suppose the town of Somewhere, USA, decides to build a new ice skating rink. The town government decides to finance the building of this rink by raising every one's income taxes by 1 percent. This tax scheme is based on the:

a. benefit principle of taxation.

b. indirect principle of taxation.

c. ability-to-pay principle of taxation.

d. value-added principle of taxation.

e. Ramsey tax rule.

13. If the town government from question 12 had decided instead to finance the building of this rink by levying a tax on electricity, the scheme would be based on the:

a. benefit principle of taxation.

b. direct principle of taxation.

c. ability-to-pay principle of taxation.

d. value-added principle of taxation.

e. Ramsey tax rule.

14. The corporation income (profits) tax is defined as a tax levied on:

a. only the dividends paid to stockholders.

b. the value added to production by each corporation.

c. the corporation's total net sales.

d. additions to corporate retained earnings.

e. dividends paid plus undistributed profits.

15. One type of income not subject to taxation at all under U.S. income tax law is:

a.   income in the form of dividends from stock owned.

b.   income in the form of interest on corporation bonds owned.

c.   firm-provided medical insurance.

d.   real income adjusted for the most recent year's inflation.

e.   income in the form of capital gains.

16. An argument made in favor of the corporation income tax is that:

a.   it taxes only earnings above the normal return on invested capital.

b.   without it, some fraction of corporation income may not be currently taxed at all.

c.   on balance, it is a regressive tax.

d.   it taxes the income received by bondholders.

e.   it means double taxation (at least in part) of corporation earnings.

17. Which alternative in question 16 would be correct had it referred to an argument *against* the corporation income tax?

a.

b.

c.

d.

e.

18. The tax yielding the largest annual revenue for the federal government (disregarding social security withholdings from wages and salaries) is the:

a.   personal income tax.

b.   corporation income tax.

c.   value-added tax.

d.   excise tax on liquor and tobacco.

e.   property tax.

19. Suppose that the tax on an income of $20,000 is equal to $4000. Assume, as well, that the tax would rise to $4800 if this income were to rise to $22,000. The marginal rate of tax implicit in these figures is:

a.   20 percent.

b.   about (but not more than) 21 percent.

c.   more than 21 percent, but just under 22 percent.

d.   40 percent.

e.   none of the above.

20. A general sales tax, without any exempted commodities, is considered to be a:

a.   progressive tax because it applies to luxuries as well as necessities.

b.   regressive tax because wealthy people spend a smaller percentage of their total incomes on taxed commodities, and hence the proportion of tax payments to income is greater for poor people.

c.   progressive tax because wealthy people spend more than poor people.

d.   regressive tax because more money is collected from a poor person than from a rich one.

e.   proportional tax because everybody pays the same tax percentage on each purchase.

21. A proportional tax is correctly defined as one in which (taking the taxpaying population overall, or in terms of the typical taxpayer):

a.   the ratio of tax collected to income received is the same at all income levels.

b.   about the same amount of tax is collected per taxpayer, regardless of taxpayer incomes.

c.   the percentage of income taken in tax falls as income climbs.

d.   the amount of money taken in tax rises as income falls.

e.   the preceding descriptions do not apply (because none of them is correct).

22. Which alternative in question 21 would be correct had that question referred to the correct definition of a progressive tax?

a.

b.

c.

d.

e.

23. Which alternative in question 21 would be correct had that question referred to the correct definition of a regressive tax?

a.

b.

c.

d.

e.

24. The incidence of a tax is:

a.   its tendency to fluctuate in total amount collected as the economy moves from boom to recession and back.

b.   its relative importance in the budget of the government involved.

c.   extent to which payment can be avoided through one or more "loopholes."

d.   its burden, in the sense of identifying the people whose real incomes are actually reduced by that tax.

e.   the effect to which its imposition is likely to induce those who must pay it to work less, in an effort to avoid part of such payment.

VII. PROBLEM SOLVING

The following problems are designed to help you apply the concepts that you learned in this chapter.

A. Government Control of the Economy

1. a.   Since World War I, the size of government, measured in terms of expenditures, taxation, and/or regulation, has (**remained remarkably stable / fallen slightly since World War II after growing rapidly between**

wars / grown dramatically). Compared with spending amounting to slightly more than 10 percent of GDP prior to World War I, the sum of budgets across all levels of government in the United States had, by the 1980s (**fallen back to 10 percent of GDP after peaking during the Carter administration at 21 percent / grown steadily to nearly 25 percent of GDP / stabilized at approximately 35 percent of GDP**).

Over the same period of time, tax revenues collected by all levels of government have (**kept pace with / grown at a slightly slower pace than / grown at a slightly faster pace than**) expenditures, with enormous shortfalls coming during (**the Great Depression / World War II / the Reagan years**). Nonetheless, tax revenues are still perhaps (**5 / 50 / 500**) percent larger now than their were at the turn of the century.

b. The ability of the U.S. government to regulate some of the activities of some of its citizens is justified by reference to the U.S. Constitution. In the spaces below, list at least four industries which have faced significant regulation over the past half-century.

(1) _____
(2) _____
(3) _____
(4) _____

2. It is interesting to note that the size of the government in a nation's economy seems to depend upon the size of that economy; measured as a proportion of GDP, poor, less developing countries show a tendency to tax and spend (**less than / more than / about the same as**) advanced countries. Using Figure 16-2 from your text, reproduced here as Figure 16-3, circle the country in each of the following pairs whose government spends more as a fraction of GDP:

    a. United States / Philippines
    b. United States / United Kingdom
    e. United States / France
    d. United States / Japan
    e. United States / Sweden
    f. South Korea / Sierra Leone
    g. Iran / Japan

Notice that the United States, despite all the political furor about the size of the American government, ranks far from the top among developed countries in this ordering. In absolute terms, the size of the American government is enormous, of course; but relative to GDP, its size is considerable more modest.

3. a. Government can serve four distinct functions in a mixed economy. List them in the spaces provided:

    (1) _____
    (2) _____
    (3) _____
    (4) _____

    b. Each of the following activities falls into at least

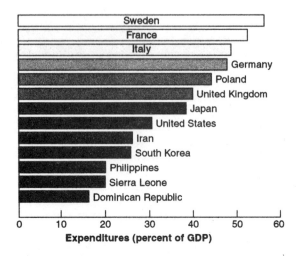

Figure 16-3

one of the four categories that you just identified; indicate which in the spaces provided.

(1) Cutting taxes to reduce unemployment:

_____

(2) Specifying that the manufacturer is liable for any harm caused by his or her product:

_____

(3) Placing a tax on a steel producer's pollution:

_____

(4) Legislating that it is illegal to discriminate on the basis of sex:

_____

(5) Enacting an income policy that penalizes larger than specified wage increases:

_____

(6) Enacting a program of aid to families with dependent children:

_____

(7) Enacting day-care help to allow women to work outside the home:

_____

(8) Writing laws that allow triple damages to be awarded in cases of gross and wanton negligence:

_____

B. Government Expenditures

4. For the fiscal year 2001, the budget for the U.S. federal government is projected to be approximately (**$.5 / $1.0 / $1.8 / $2.0**) trillion. This total exceeds the 1980 level of expenditure by over $575 billion. The largest single item within this total for 2001 is (**interest on the public debt / national defense, veterans, and international affairs / education, labor, and development / social security**) . The expenditure for this item amounts to approximately (**$426 / $437 / $337**) billion. (**National defense / Energy / Space and technology / Entitlement**) programs have grown more quickly than any other programs in the federal budget. Spending on these items increased from (**10 / 28 / 40**) percent of the budget in 1960 to (**22 / 47 / 58**) percent of the budget in 1994.

C. Economic Aspects of Taxation

5. a. The *benefit* approach to taxation argues that the distribution of tax levied between citizen A and citizen B should be proportional to the benefit each receives from the expenditures of government—a "pay for what you get" principle. Which of the following (one or both) may be considered a valid criticism of this principle?

   (1) It assumes the particular tax in question can be linked to a particular type of expenditure. If a government's expenditures are large and varied, this link is often difficult to determine.

   (2) Even if a particular tax can somehow be linked to a particular type of spending (e.g., federal government spending on national defense), it is difficult to decide, in quantity terms, how much benefit rich citizen A derives from it in comparison with poor citizen B.

   b. An alternative principle is that tax payments constitute a sacrifice by citizens and that the distribution of sacrifices should match people's *ability to pay*. It isn't altogether easy to establish what "ability to pay" really means, but one interpretation is that (pick one):

   (1) every citizen should pay an equal amount of money in taxes, thus equalizing sacrifices.

   (2) taxes should be levied and collected in strict proportion to the amount of income received by citizens.

   (3) the tax system should be constructed so that the government collects its revenue from those who have the money.

   c. The ability-to-pay approach raises two distinct issues of equity. The first asserts that equals should pay equal taxes. This approach is identified by economists as (**horizontal / vertical / reasonable**) equity. As simple as that assertion appears, it buries the fundamental question of how to determine when two people are equal. For example, are two people earning $30,000 per year equal if one of them has incurred $8000 in medical expenses? The tax codes say no. Medical expenses above 3 percent of adjusted gross income were deductible in 1991 (unless the taxpayer took the standard deduction).

The second equity issue involves the taxation of unequals; it is captured under the general rubric of (**horizontal / vertical / redistributive**) equity. This is the more controversial issue because of the (dis)incentive effects of income taxation. No hard-and-fast rules have been generalized to describe vertical equity.

6. a. In order to know whether a tax is progressive or regressive, it is (**essential / not strictly essential**) to know how much money it typically collects from individuals at different levels of income.

   b. One existing U.S. tax is easily classified within this progressive-regressive distinction; namely the ____ tax. This tax is (**progressive / regressive**).

   c. A tax levied as 1 percent on the first $5000 of income, 2 percent on the next $5000, 3 percent on the next $5000, and so on, would be (**progressive / proportional / regressive**).

   d. A tax of 10 percent on all income except the first $1000—that $1000 being exempt from tax—around be (**progressive / proportional / regressive**).

   e. If it is true that among cigarette smokers people with a yearly income of $8000 typically buy four packs of cigarettes per week, whereas those with an income of $16,000 typically buy six packs per week, then an excise tax of 10 cents per pack would be a (**progressive / proportional / regressive**) tax.

7. Suppose that the federal tax schedule given in Table 16-1 is being proposed for the next tax year.

TABLE 16-1

Income	Tax Payment	Effective Tax Rate
$ 5,000	$ 50	____
10,000	200	____
15,000	750	____
20,000	2,000	____
25,000	3,750	____
30,000	7,500	____

Calculate the effective tax rate at each level of income in the third column of Table 16-1.

Using Figure 16-4, plot the relationship between income earned and the percentage of income paid in taxes. This tax is (**regressive / proportional / progressive**). How can you tell?

8. a. Disregarding social security taxes, the two taxes which yield the most revenue for the federal government, ranked in order of their revenue importance, are:

   (1) _____

   (2) _____

   b. The most important tax at the level of state govern-

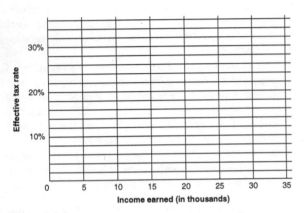

Figure 16-4

ment is the ____ tax; the most important tax at the level of local government is the ____ tax.

c.   The single biggest expenditure items at the state and local government level are for ____.

9.   A *value-added tax* is computed on the basis of the value added to goods by various firms at various stages of production. If a textile firm were to pay $4000 for the yarn, material, and labor required to weave cloth which it sells for $10,000, then the value which it would add to these materials would equal (**$4000 / $6000 / $10,000 / $14,000**); a value-added tax would be levied on this amount.

Suppose another firm—a garment manufacturing firm—bought all this cloth and paid the full $10,000 for it. Suppose, as well, that it paid another $2000 for all its other raw materials, such as thread, and sold the resulting output of garments for $20,000. The value added by this firm would be (**$2000 / $4000 / $6000 / $8000 / $10,000 / $20,000**).

VIII. DISCUSSION QUESTIONS

Answer the following questions, making sure that you can explain the work you did to arrive at the answers.

1.   List three industries or countries in which markets are reemerging as the primary determinant of resource allocation. Why are markets replacing governments as the primary allocators of the world's resources?

2.   The Food and Drug Administration has recently established new guidelines for product labels. The purpose of this policy is to standardize the labeling across products so that consumers can more easily make comparisons. What sort of market failure is this policy designed to attack?

3.   Explain what is meant by the term *fiscal federalism*. List the three levels of government spending that this term implies in the United States and describe some of the functions that occur at each level.

4.   Why do governments have little incentive to spend money efficiently? Given the large federal budget deficits that resulted from the Reagan and Bush era, would you encourage policies that impose some constraints on federal spending?

5.   List the pros and cons of the benefits principle and the pros and cons of the ability-to-pay principle of taxation. Which approach do you find most appealing?

6.   State the Ramsey tax rule. Think of four goods that might be subject to taxation if this rule is imposed. Why might you worry about equity when considering the Ramsey tax rule?

IX. ANSWERS TO STUDY GUIDE QUESTIONS

III. Reviews of Key Concepts

9	Economic regulation
8	Social regulation
4	Laissez-faire
13	Income redistribution
14	Public-choice theory
7	Fiscal federalism
18	Entitlement programs
16	Benefit principle
19	Ability-to-pay principle
11	Horizontal equity
3	Vertical equity
20	Progressive taxes
1	Regressive taxes
22	Direct taxes
17	Indirect taxes
10	Effective tax rate
21	Marginal tax rate
5	Value-added tax
2	Ramsey tax rule
12	Supply-side economics
6	Green taxes
15	Tax incidence

VI. Multiple Choice Questions

1. E   2. C   3. B   4. C   5. E   6. E
7. E   8. E   9. B   10. A 11. B   12. C
13. E 14. E   15. C   16. B 17. E   18. A
19. D 20. B   21. A   22. C 23. Dg

VII. Problem Solving

1. a.   grown dramatically, stabilized at approximately 35 percent of GDP, grown at a slightly slower pace than, all three, 500

b.   Airlines, trucking, utilities of all sorts, banking, cable television, to name a few

2. less than

    a.   United States
    b.   United Kingdom
    c.   France
    d.   Japan
    e.   Sweden
    f.   South Korea
    g.   Japan

3. a. (1) Redistribute income
        (2) Work toward macroeconomic stability
        (3) Allocate resources efficiency and provide a legal framework
        (4) Allocate resources equitably
    b. (1) Macro stabilization
        (2) Legal framework
        (3) Promote efficiency
        (4) Legal, efficiency, and equity issues
        (5) Macro stabilization
        (6) Promote equity
        (7) Promote equity and efficiency
        (8) Legal framework

4. $1.8; social security; $426; Entitlement; 28; 58.

5. a. both (1) and (2)
    b. (3)
    c. horizontal, vertical

6. a. essential
    b. Federal income, progressive
    c. progressive
    d. progressive
    e. regressive

7. a. The effective tax rate is the total tax divided be total income. Entries for the column are .01, .02, .05, .10, .15, .25.
    b. Plot the data from part a.
    c. progressive. The effective tax rate increases as income increases.

8. a. (1) personal income tax
        (2) corporate income tax
    b. sales, property
    c. local public goods, particularly education

9. $6000, $8000

VIII. Discussion Questions

1. Russia, China, (East) Germany. The market seems to be winning the day because governments have not been very successful at allocating resources across these economies.

2. This policy is designed to help correct asymmetric information between buyers and sellers.

3. Fiscal federalism refers to the practice of dividing government responsibilities among federal, state, and local authorities. The federal government handles national defense and international policies. The state government handles many transfer policies and welfare benefits. Local governments collect property taxes and take great responsibility for public education for grades K-12.

4. Governments have little incentive to spend money efficiently because there is no profit motive involved in decisions. Elected officials must worry about reelection, but they do not have to worry about competitive pressures that exist to provide private industry with incentives to be efficient. Policies that constrain federal spending might be good if they provided legislators with constraints; however, these policies might he counterproductive during a recession, when the government's ability to run deficits helps to smooth out business-cycle effects.

5. The benefits principle forces those who use services to pay for them; however, it ignores the fact that, in many cases, those who use services do so because they have limited income. The ability-to-pay principle taxes people based on their ability to pays, so that people with higher income or wealth contribute more to the tax system. However, it ignores the fact that many of the people who are able to pay do not take advantage of government services.

6. The Ramsey tax rule states that the most efficient taxes are placed on goods whose demand is most inelastic. Goods like electricity, medications, food, and gasoline might fit this definition. Equity issues come into play here, since these goods are necessities. We might want to make sure that we hold prices on these goods as low as possible.

CHAPTER 17

Promoting More Efficient Markets

I. CHAPTER OVERVIEW

Government has three major roles to play in supporting a modern domestic economy: maintain efficiency, promote macroeconomic stability and growth, and establish a fair distribution of income. This chapter concentrates on one of government's primary challenges in exercising its efficiency role—performing a watchdog function to prevent excessive abuse of market power. Also, the chapter focuses your attention on the two major tools employed by the U.S. government to put some "teeth" into its careful monitoring of business activity: regulation and antitrust activity.

Regulation is often employed when economies of scale are so significant in a production process that a monopoly is the only efficient solution. Government agencies are organized to monitor the behavior of the monopolist and to protect the interests of consumers. Antitrust legislation is designed to prevent monopolies from forming and to attack anticompetitive abuses. The Sherman Antitrust Act and the Clayton Act form the backbone of antitrust policies; the Federal Trade Commission Act established the FTC as the agency in charge of monitoring and enforcing the legislation. Of course, as with any laws, the courts ultimately interpret their meaning, and a century of legal precedent defines the meaning of these statutes.

II. LEARNING OBJECTIVES

After you have read Chapter 17 in your text and completed the exercises in this *Study Guide* chapter, you should be able to:

1. Distinguish between two brands of regulation: **economic** and **social**. List examples of each.
2. List and explain three major **public-interest** justifications for regulation. Understand the difference betwen these and **interest-group** theories of regulation.
3. Describe the process of regulating natural monopolies, particularly in the provision of public utilities.
4. Review the history of regulated industries in the U.S. in the past several decades.

5. Summarize the major pieces of antitrust legislation in the U.S. and explain their historical signifcance.
6. Review recent antitrust cases and explain the importance of these decisions in establishing a new industrial landscape in the U.S.
7. Understand the difference between **horizontal** and **vertical** mergers, and the merger guidelines that are used by the antitrust authorities.

III. REVIEW OF KEY CONCEPTS

Match the following terms from column A with their definitions in column B.

A	B
__ Command and control	1. Join together unrelated businesses.
__ Market incentives	2. Established a regulatory agency to prohibit unfair methods of competition and to warn against anticompetitive mergers.
__ Natural monopoly	3. Regulatory strategy in which price is set such that a firm's total costs are distributed to each product sold.
__ Economies of scope	4. A group of firms, usually in the same industry, that combine together by a legal agreement to regulate production, prices, or other industrial conditions.
__ Average-cost pricing	5. Government commands people to undertake or desist from certain activities through government regulation.
__ Marginal-cost pricing	6. Means that only unreason able restraints of trade come within the scope of the Sherman Act and are considered illegal.
__ Two-part tariff	7. Involves charging different prices to different customers when there is no difference in the cost of delivering the product.

__ Trust

__ Sherman
Antitrust Act

__ Clayton Act

__ FTC Act

__ Per se
prohibitions

__ Rule of reason

__ Predatory pricing

__ Tying contracts

__ Price
discrimination

__ Bell doctrine

__ Vertical
mergers

__ Horizontal
mergers

__ Conglomerate
mergers

8. Harnessing of market forces to achieve regulatory goals.

9. Occurs when companies in the same industry combine.

10. Means that there is no defense that will justify a set of actions.

11. Arrangements whereby a firm will sell product A only if the purchaser also buys product B.

12. Occurs when the most efficient way of organizing production in an industry is through a single firm.

13. Regulatory strategy in which the firm's price is set equal to its marginal cost.

14. Establishes the fact that monopolies are illegal and that the attempt to monopolize is illegal.

15. Occur when two firms at different stages of the production process come together.

16. Pricing strategy in which a firm charges a fixed fee to cover the overhead costs and then adds a variable cost to cover the marginal costs.

17. Occurs when a firm sells its output for a price that is less than the costs of production, presumably to drive competitors out of business.

18. Passed to clarify and strengthen the Sherman Act by detailing specific illegal behavior.

19. Arise when a number of different products can more efficiently be produced by a single firm than by separate firms.

20. Stated that regulated monopoly and competition should not be mixed.

IV. SUMMARY AND CHAPTER OUTLINE

This section summarizes the key concepts from the chapter.

A. Business Regulation: Theory and Practice

1. In the United States, regulation is the most popular mechanism with which governments at all levels protect their citizens from potential abuses of market power, particularly when a natural monopoly is under scrutiny. Regulation, in its broadest context, includes all rules and laws designed to change or control the operation of an economic enterprise. There are, in fact, two major categories within that context: economic and social. *Economic regulation* can be accomplished by controlling prices, production, standards, and exit and entry conditions. *Social regulation* is directed at correcting (negative) externalities.

2. There are several reasons to regulate industry. First, government may want to contain market power and encourage competition in markets. However, when natural monopolies exist, regulatory agencies are established to protect consumer interests while allowing the monopoly to operate. Second, information failures may need to be remedied. In some cases, consumers may have insufficient information on products. Before the government began to take on this task, the markets cried out, "Let the buyer beware!"—implying that it was the consumer's responsibility to make sure that products were safe and effective. Now the government protects consumers by overseeing the production and distribution of many products, from food to infant car seats. Third, government may want to diminish the severity of externalities. For example, the Environmental Protection Agency is a regulator whose main activity is to design and enforce pollution control strategies. Finally, government may choose to step into an industry when the regulators have been "captured" by the regulated. This happens when the regulators actually begin to protect the firm's best interest rather than the consumer's.

3. The next logical question is, how do regulators set industrial standard? Several alternative strategies exist. With *average-cost pricing*, regulated firms are allowed to set price equal to the average total costs of production; that is, the firm takes all its costs and distributes them to each product sold. This brings them to a solution that is similar to the long-run perfectly competitive solution that has firms producing at minimum average total costs.

With *marginal-cost pricing*, the firm is restricted to setting price equal to marginal cost. This again brings them to a solution that is similar to perfect competition; however, particularly when economies of scale are significant, this may lead to losses for the firm. For example, many municipal transportation systems exist as regulated natural monopolies. (Running several subway systems in the same city hardly seems practical.) Equity considerations imply that these companies hold their prices to a bare minimum as a service to commuters and working people. Because these firms cannot generate enough revenues to cover costs at this price, they are often subsidized by the city government.

4. For the past two decades, a significant trend toward deregulation has been spreading across the economy. From airlines to trucking to banking to electricity, many industries have shed the yoke of regulation and entered the world of free competition. Most of these industries have emerged stronger and more competitive than they were under regulation.

B. Antitrust Policy

1. Antitrust policy exists to limit the excesses of imperfect competition. *Unregulated* monopoly power allows firms to operate at socially inefficient levels, charging too much for too little product. Monopolists charge a price that is greater than marginal cost, and often greater than average costs, allowing them to earn economic profits into the long run. This means that the monopoly solution yields a distribution of resources that is not allocatively efficient.

Imperfect competition can emerge due to the existence of economies of scale; if the technology in an industry is such that output can be produced efficiently only when a single firm exists, we have a natural monopoly.

2. Of course, antitrust policy is written with full knowledge that imperfect competition has both a good and a bad side. Unbridled exploitation of market power can, on the one hand, depress output and generate excessive prices and profits. On the other hand, however, there do exist economies of scale that should not be sacrificed simply for the sake of having many firms instead of few. There is, moreover, a demonstrable correlation between market concentration and research into discovery and development of new products and new processes. In light of this dichotomy of properties, it is the primary lesson of this chapter that antitrust activity should (1) keep the barriers to competition low, (2) tolerate bigness when size is determined by technology, and (3) be vigilant against anticompetitive practices whenever they occur.

3. The three most significant pieces of antitrust legislation in the United States are the *Sherman Antitrust Act*, the *Clayton Act*, and the *Federal Trade Commission Act*. The Sherman Act declares contracts, combinations, and conspiracies in restraint of trade illegal and further states that attempting to monopolize is illegal. The Clayton Act outlines specific anticompetitive behaviors that are illegal, such as price discrimination, tying contracts, and interlocking directorates. The Clayton Act also limits corporate mergers which would lessen competition; horizontal mergers are the most troublesome in this regard. The FTC Act established a commission whose duty is to prohibit "unfair methods of competition" and to warn against anticompetitive activity.

4. The application of these antitrust laws is not an easy task. It is often difficult to know if any illegal behavior exists or to determine exactly what a firm's intent might be. Thus, on the basis of *conduct*, it is hard to know whether or not firms are behaving illegally. In addition, it is often difficult to know exactly how to define a *market* or how to define *competitors*. For example, consider the automobile industry. Is it oligopolistic, consisting of just three big firms (Ford, Chrysler, GM) in the United States, or is it really perfectly competitive, consisting not only of Ford, Chrysler, and GM but also of Honda, Toyota, BMW, Mazda, etc.? How do we define markets, and, once we define them, how can we describe the behavior of firms relative to one another? On the basis of *structure*, it is hard to know whether or not firms

are operating in an illegal fashion.

5. Recent antitrust activity has, in fact, focused on promoting efficiency in business practices and not on attacking "bigness" per se. The notion underlying this concentration on conduct rather than structure in an economy that is facing increasing competition from around the world is that collusive agreements which try to fix prices are the most troublesome source of inefficiency. Large firms which can exploit decreasing costs as they compete internationally can be a source of economic strength as long as they do indeed compete.

V. HELPFUL HINTS

1. Figure 17-2 in your text is complicated, so we have reproduced it here as Figure 17-1. First, notice the shape and position of the average and marginal cost curves. Because they are everywhere downward-sloping, this looks like a natural monopoly. The larger the firm gets, the lower its per unit costs. Given a market demand and marginal revenue curve, the profit-maximizing firm will produce where marginal cost is equal to marginal revenue and set the highest price it possibly can. This leads to P_M and Q_M as industry price and output.

Notice further the inefficiencies inherent in this solution. At Q_M price is greater than average costs, and it is greater than marginal costs. This opens the door to regulators, who would like to make some adjustments. Remember that regulators, in theory, are charged with the duty of protecting *consumer* interests. This means they should be fighting to establish prices and output levels that come closer to the competitive ideal. Average-cost pricing moves in that direction by setting price equal to average costs, allowing the firm to cover its opportunity costs (*R*). Marginal-cost pricing often pushes prices below the firm's average costs, forcing the firm to incur a loss (*I*). No monopolist will remain in business given this sort of price, unless they are subsidized by another government agency.

2. When an industry is deregulated, several events may occur. First, supply might increase as the number of competing firms increases. (Examples include telephone service and airlines.) This increase in supply should lower prices for consumers. Along with this increase in supply comes increased competition, which often takes the form of advertising. Advertising may increase consumer demand, expanding the size of the market for all competitors. This chain of events seems to reflect both the market for telephone service and the market for airline travel. Deregulation led to tremendous increases in supply, followed by a barrage of advertising as competitors scrambled for market share. The resulting increase in demand has enlarged opportunities for all firms.

3. There are many reasons for firms to pursue conglomerate mergers. One of the most appealing has to do with risk and uncertainty. A firm that acquires subsidiaries in other

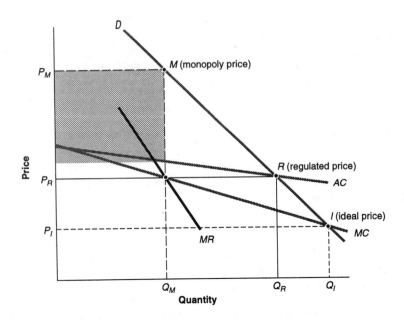

Figure 17-1

industries is able to spread its risk across a greater number of options, limiting the uncertainty it faces in the marketplace. For example, Philip Morris, a large producer of cigarettes, purchased the Kraft food chain several years ago. As the market for cigarettes became increasingly risky, the firm began searching for ways to *diversify* its holdings. It achieved this diversification, in part, by purchasing relatively safe product lines.

VII. MULTIPLE CHOICE QUESTIONS

These questions are organized by topic from the chapter outline. Choose the best answer from the options available.

A. Business Regulation: Theory and Practice

1. Which of the following would be considered a form of economic regulation?
    a. OSHA regulations designed to ensure safety in the workplace.
    b. EPA regulations designed to improve air quality.
    c. Public utility regulations designed to promote efficient and equitable pricing of electricity.
    d. FDA regulations designed to ensure the safety of new drugs.
    e. All the above.
2. Which of the following would be considered a form of social regulation?
    a. Product quality standards designed to protect consumers.

b. Public utility regulations designed to promote efficient and equitable pricing of cable television.
c. NRC regulations designed to ensure the safe operation of nuclear power plants.
d. Insurance regulations designed to promote premiums which are fair and economically justifiable.
e. All the above.

3. Rather than command firms to comply with regulatory standards, government agencies have recently begun to use market incentives. These types of programs:
    a. allow the market to operate freely, with no regulation.
    b. bribe firms to behave in the proper manner by offering rewards for good behavior.
    c. harness the forces of supply and demand to achieve regulatory goals.
    d. encourage firms to capture regulators.
    e. none of the above.
4. Which of the following represents a reason for suspecting that a natural monopoly might best serve a particular market?
    a. A tariff structure which allows domestic pricing above the world price.
    b. The presence of increasing returns to scale throughout a range of output which covers the entire market.
    c. The invention of a new product which is covered by a 17-year patent.
    d. The creation of monopoly power by an act of government which restricts market entry
    e. All the above.

The diagram in Figure 17-2 describes cost and demand conditions in the market for a product. Use it to answer questions 5 through 10.

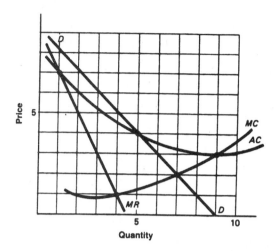

Figure 17-2

5. An unregulated monopolist would operate by producing an amount which would clear the market at what price?
   a. $1.
   b. $2.
   c. $3.
   d. $4.
   e. $5.
6. Which price would be the ideal regulated price for the monopolist represented above?
   a. $1.
   b. $2.
   c. $3.
   d. $4.
   e. $5.
7. How much output would the monopolist in Figure 17-2 produce if regulated by average-cost pricing?
   a. 9 units.
   b. 7 units.
   c. 5 units.
   d. 4 units.
   e. 1 unit.
8. If the monopolist whose cost and demand conditions are given in Figure 17-2 were to face an ideal price regulation, how much of a subsidy would be required, per unit, to sustain his or her activity?
   a. Exactly $5 per unit.
   b. Exactly $4 per unit.
   c. More than $2 per unit but less than $4 per unit.
   d. More than $1 per unit but less than $2 per unit.
   e. Exactly $1 per unit.

9. Net of the subsidy (judged to be $1.25 per unit), how much consumer surplus would be gained over the unregulated case if the monopolist in Figure 17-2 were to face ideal price regulation?
   a. $16.00.
   b. $10.00.
   c. $7.75.
   d. $4.50.
   e. Zero? since the subsidy exhausts the entire gain.
10. Which answers to question 7 should have been correct if that question had referred to marginal-cost price regulation?
    a.
    b.
    c.
    d.
    e.

B. Antitrust Policy

11. Imperfect competition is inefficient because it yields:
    a. less output than a perfectly competitive industry.
    b. higher prices than a perfectly competitive industry.
    c. lower output and lower profits than a perfectly competitive industry.
    d. lower prices and lower profits than a perfectly competitive industry
    e. **a** and **b**.
12. The Sherman Antitrust Act:
    a. outlaws contracts, combinations, and conspiracies in restraint of trade.
    b. specifies that price discrimination is illegal.
    c. established the FTC to oversee competitive behavior in markets.
    d. encourages firms to exploit economies of scale to their fullest.
    e. **a** and **d**.
13. Which of the following made price discrimination not based on cost differentials illegal?
    a. The Sherman Antitrust Act.
    b. The Humphrey-Hawkins Act.
    c. The Clayton Antitrust Act.
    d. The Gramm-Rudman Act.
    e. The Federal Trade Commission Act.
14. Which answer to question 13 would have been correct if that question had referred to making the formation of a monopoly a felony?
    a.
    b.
    c.
    d.
    e.
15. Which answer to question 13 would have been correct if that question had referred to making unfair and deceptive business practices unlawful?

a.

b.

c.

d.

e.

16. Current thinking about the application of antitrust legislation looks most critically upon:

    a. horizontal mergers.

    b. multinational mergers.

    c. vertical mergers.

    d. conglomerate mergers.

    e. mergers of any kind.

17. Firms which exercise market power charge prices above marginal cost because:

    a. profits are maximized where marginal revenue equals marginal cost, and downward-sloping demand places marginal revenue below price.

    b. such firms never operate in the elastic region of demand where marginal revenue is negative.

    c. the effective demand curve which they face is horizontal, indicating an ability to charge prices which exceed the market-clearing level.

    d. profits are maximized where price equals marginal cost, and downward-sloping demand places marginal revenue above price.

    e. increasing returns to scale and their associated declining average costs mean that marginal cost and price always exceed average cost.

VII. PROBLEM SOLVING

The following problems are designed to help you apply the concepts that you learned in this chapter.

A. Business Regulation: Theory and Practice

1. Place (**E**) or (**S**) in the blanks provided to indicate whether each of the following regulatory activities is an example of an economic regulation or a social regulation:

    ___ a. Restraints on price-setting practices among firms

    ___ b. Clean air policy

    ___ c. Limits on the rates of return earned by utilities

    ___ d. Drug testing by the FDA

    ___ e. Requirement to provide electricity to every one who asks for it

    ___ f. Constraints on entry into and exit from given markets

2. Price controls are frequently mentioned as a possible means of controlling the potential abuses of monopoly power. Pervasive use of price controls to limit monopoly power can, however, cause a plethora of economic problems. In the blanks provided, check off those effects which might appear in a list of possible difficulties existing with price controls:

    ___ a. Alienation of business and government

    ___ b. International trade problems

    ___ e. Shortages and surpluses

    ___ d. Absence of necessary flexibility in relative prices

    ___ e. Increased unemployment

3. Consult Figure 17-3.

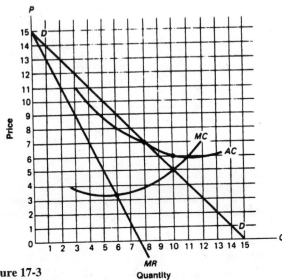

Figure 17-3

a. For the indicated demand and cost curves, it is clear that the unregulated monopolist would produce ___ units of output for sale at a price of $___. Excess pure economic profits of $___ would then be earned.

b. Regulation to the point of zero profits would meanwhile require a price specification of $___, at which ___ units of output would be expected. Consumer surplus would, in this case, increase from the unregulated monopoly level of $18 to $___.

c. Ideal price regulation to the point where efficiency conditions were satisfied would, meanwhile, require a price specification of $___, with ___ units of output expected only if the monopolist's losses in the amount of $___ were covered. Consumer surplus would rise further to $___ but would actually equal $___ if the subsidy to cover the losses just noted were deducted. This (**would / would not**) represent an improvement over the average-cost pricing alternative.

B. Antitrust Policy

4. a. Imperfect competition is undesirable from an economic standpoint mainly because of the (**excess profits generated by the exploitation of price and quantity /**

distortions that it produces in the allocation of resources).

b. For a monopolist, the equality of marginal benefit and marginal cost does not result from self-motivated profit maximization. Since price is always (**greater than / equal to / less than**) marginal revenue, profit maximization requires that marginal cost be maintained at a level that is (**higher than / equal to / lower than**) the going price. Why? Because profits are maximized where marginal cost equals marginal revenue, and marginal revenue is less than price. Price ratios still reflect ratios of marginal utility, though, so monopoly power yields marginal cost that is (**higher than / equal to / lower than**) marginal benefit. Total welfare (**cannot / can**) then be improved by rearranging resources. How? In a way which (**brings resources into / moves resources out of**) the monopolists' markets to (**increase / decrease**) their output. Based on the efficiency properties of the perfectly competitive market, it is clear that the marginal utility derived from consuming the monopolist's product is (**greater than / less than / equal to**) the marginal cost of producing the good in question.

5. Consult Figure 17-4. The long-run competitive output and price for a market with the indicated cost structure must equal __ units and $__, respectively. If this market is monopolized, an unregulated, profit-maximizing monopolist would sell ___ units at a price of $___. The result would be a reduction in consumer surplus from $___ to $___. Of that reduction, $___ would go to the monopolist in the form of excess profit, and $___ would represent lost welfare that would disappear (deadweight loss).

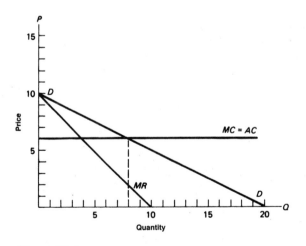

Figure 17-4

6. a. Suppose that the monopolist depicted in Figure 17-4 faces a lump-sum tax on profits of $8. The unregulated, profit-maximizing monopolist would then (**increase**

the price above $8 / decrease the price below $8 / maintain the price at $8**) to support a (**larger / smaller / constant**) level of production and sales.

b. Suppose, instead, that government taxes the monopolist's implicit return to capital and that the effective (constant) marginal cost of production thereby increases from $6 to $8 per unit. Output should (**fall to / rise to / continue to remain fixed at**) ___ units; price would (**climb to / fall to / remain at**) $___, representing an increase in price (**equal to / less than / greater than**) the $___ increase in unit costs.

7. The text notes three important pieces of antitrust legislation which laid the groundwork for subsequent antitrust activity:

1. The Sherman Antitrust Act (1890) (SA)
2. The Clayton Antitrust Act (1914) (CA)
3. The Federal Trade Commission Act (1914) (FTCA)

Match each of the following provisions to its landmark legislation by recording SA, CA, or FTCA in the blanks provided; if none applies, write "none":

___ a. Price discrimination that is not based upon cost differentials and is designed to lessen competition is declared illegal.

___ b. Unfair and deceptive business activities and practices are declared illegal.

___ c. No corporation can acquire another if such an acquisition would substantially reduce competition.

___ d. Forming a monopoly is declared a felony.

___ e. Lobbying for tariff protection against foreign competition is declared illegal.

___ f. Restraint of trade or commerce among states is declared illegal.

___ g. Restraint of trade or commerce with foreign nations is declared illegal.

___ h. Imposing a contract which prohibits the purchase of a competitor's product is illegal.

8. One significant change in the way that the legal system of the United States deals with the potential problems of imperfect competition is found in the judicial attention paid to how business is actually conducted. According to this new view of how the law should be enforced, it is more important to attack *behavior* that signifies the abuse of market power than it is to concentrate on markets that display offensive industrial organization. These abusive methods of conducting business, including (a) price fixing, (b) output restraint, (c) market division, (d) predatory pricing, and (e) price discrimination, are not necessarily confined to the concentrated industries with extreme and potentially profitable market power. Some of them can appear in competitive markets as well.

The following list contains examples of the five types of conduct just noted. Identify each example with the conduct that it represents, and record your answer in the space provided.

a. An agreement between retailers and the manufacturer not to sell a certain doll for less than $25:.

_____

b. The pricing of computers below production costs to prevent entry by potential competitors:

_____

c. An agreement among suppliers of oil not to sell more than 1 million barrels per day:

_____

d. A policy in which a particular firm sells hammers to hardware stores for $8.99 each and to the Defense Department for $410.22 each:

_____

e. An agreement among sugar retailers to sell only in specified geographical regions of the United States:

_____

f. An agreement among airlines to increase fares 20 percent over the weekend:

_____

g. The destruction of thousands of pounds of coffee beans before they get to market:

_____

VIII. DISCUSSION QUESTIONS

Answer the following questions, making sure that you can explain the work you did to arrive at the answers.

1. Why might regulation using market incentives be more efficient than regulation using command-and-control orders?

2. What major factors must be considered when deciding whether to regulate a monopolistic industry or break it up? What basic criteria might you establish to help make this decision?

3. What are economies of scope? How do they differ from economies of scale?

4. Why might a regulator choose to impose marginal-cost pricing for a monopoly? List and explain two different scenarios in which marginal-cost pricing might be appropriate. What will the effect be on the firm?

5. Review the three main pieces of antitrust legislation in the United States. What does each add to extend or clarify the nature of antitrust policy?

6. Review the path of antitrust policy as it has been interpreted by the courts during this century.

7. Around the world today, many countries have different attitudes toward antitrust. In Japan, for example, companies are encouraged to work together to gain a competitive edge over international competitors. The government maintains a careful process of subsidization of industry that helps to germinate young businesses and cushion the blows dealt by the business cycle. Given the nature of antitrust policy in the United States, can our firms expect to compete in the global economy? Has the Sherman Antitrust Act outlived its usefulness?

8. Do you think that the Bell doctrine, along with the recent decision against Microsoft, will discourage firms from innovation?

IX. ANSWERS TO STUDY GUIDE QUESTIONS

III. Review of Key Concepts

5	Command and control
8	Economic incentives
12	Natural monopoly
19	Economies of scope
3	Average-cost pricing
13	Marginal-cost pricing
16	Two-part tariff
4	Trust
14	Sherman Antitrust Act
18	Clayton Act
2	FTC Act
10	Per se prohibitions
6	Rule of reason
17	Predatory pricing
11	Tying contracts
7	Price discrimination
20	Bell doctrine
15	Vertical mergers
9	Horizontal mergers
1	Conglomerate mergers

VI. Multiple Choice Questions

1. C 2. C 3. C 4. B 5. E 6. B
7. C 8. D 9. C 10. B 11. E 12. A
13. C 14. A 15. E 16. A 17. A

VII. Problem Solving

1. a. E
   b. S
   e. E
   d. S
   e. E or S
   f. E

2. All these effects indicate difficulties with price controls.

3. a. 6, $9, $6
   b. $7, 8, $32
   c. $5, 10, $10, $50, $40, would nonetheless

4. a. distortions that it produces in the allocation of resources
   b. greater than, lower than, lower than, can, brings resources into, increase, greater than

5. 8, $6, 4, $8, $16, $4, $8, $4

6. a. maintain the price at $8, constant
   b. fall to, 2, climb to, $9, less than, $2

7. a. CA
   b. FTCA
   e. CA
   d. SA

   e. none
   f. SA
   g. SA
   h. CA
8. a. Price fixing
   b. Predatory pricing
   c. Output restraint
   d. Price discrimination
   e. Market division
   f. Price fixing
   g. Output restraint

VIII. Discussion Questions

1. Market incentives encourage firms to change their behavior as part of their own profit-maximizing strategy. Command-and-control orders require firms to make decisions in order to avoid penalty. Thus, market incentives may be more efficient.

2. Is the monopoly reasonable? Does the monopolist use unfair tactics to maintain monopoly power? Criteria might include the difference between price and marginal cost, and the difference between price and average costs. This would help us to determine how far the monopolist is from the competitive ideal.

3. Economies of scope exist when several products can be produced more efficiently by a single firm than by separate firms. Economies of scale exist when a firm's long-run average costs decline as output increases.

4. A regulator might choose marginal-cost pricing for a monopoly if it desires an outcome that mirrors the competitive ideal. This holds prices low for customers. Marginal-cost pricing might be appropriate for a public transportation company or for public housing. In both these cases, regulators want to keep prices for consumers as low as possible. Firms would have to receive subsidies if they are to stay in business.

5. The three important pieces of legislation are the Sherman Antitrust Act, the Clayton Act, and the Federal Trade Commission Act. Sherman is antimonopoly legislation, Clayton details illegal practices, and the FTC Act established a regulatory agency to oversee antitrust activity.

6. Key points include swings between the rule of reason and per se illegality during this century, as well as the existence of "merger mania" during the 1980s.

7. We may find that in order to compete internationally, U.S. firms must be allowed to work together in some ways. However, this runs counter to the path of antitrust policy as it has been enforced over the past 100 years. The Sherman Act will have outlived its usefulness if we are willing to admit that decreased competition among domestic producers is in the best interest of international competitiveness and consumer welfare.

8. Only time will tell. The returns to innovation are economic profits; profitability is greater the longer the firm can hang onto its monopoly power. If the FTC seems intent on prosecuting firms that are monopolists, then the returns to innovation will fall!

CHAPTER 18
Protecting the Environment

I. CHAPTER OVERVIEW

Farmers in the rain forests of South America daily cut down vast stands of trees; workers on oil rigs pump thousands of gallons of oil per day out of the North Sea; and coal miners in Russia take the long ride into the earth each morning. All of these people are involved in harvesting the world's natural resources, which bring wealth and prosperity to many countries.

This chapter applies the microeconomic theory that we have developed throughout the text to a "real-world" problem: How does an economy decide how to use its natural resources? Societies have addressed this question for centuries, some deciding that nature is wild and in need of taming through technology, and others fearing the inherent power of nature and its mysterious forces. In either case, the situation calls for allocation of scarce resources, so *economists* should be able to provide some answers!

This chapter begins with a brief description of alternative types of natural resources and the severity of the scarcity problem. The second section addresses a market allocation of natural resources and investigates issues which make the questions more complex than they might seem at first glance. How quickly should exhaustible resources be depleted? How do differences in ownership rights affect these decisions? The final section addresses the problem of externalities, which occur when production imposes costs on outside individuals or on society at large. When externalities occur, the market has failed because demand or supply cannot capture the true costs and benefits of actions; as we learned in the last two chapters, this tends to lead to a role for government in the marketplace.

II. LEARNING OBJECTIVES

After you have read Chapter 18 in your text and completed the exercises in this *Study Guide* chapter, you should be able to:
1. Discuss why the theory on overpopulation growth developed by Malthus had such a great impact on the way people think about resource use. Explain why Malthus's somewhat gloomy predictions have not come about.

2. Describe the relationship between the economy and the environment, as well as the relationship between economic development, and the environment.
3. Differentiate between **appropriable** and **inappropriable** resources, and between **renewable** and **nonrenewable** resources. Explain how decisions concerning the optimal use of environmental resources differ depending upon the category in which they fall.
4. Review the path of resource prices over the past several decades. Respond to the notion that resource prices should tend to increase as population increases and demand for many goods and services shifts to the right.
5. Define the term **externality**. Describe the mechanism by which inefficiencies develop in markets when external costs and benefits are present.
6. Use cost-benefit analysis to find the socially efficient quantity of pollution that will occur. Construct a diagram that illustrates this decision-making process.
7. Review alternative policies that are designed to correct externalities, such as **emissions fees, markets for pollution permits, private contracts**, and **liability rules**. Compare the pros and cons of these alternatives.

III. REVIEW OF KEY CONCEPTS

Match the following terms from column A with their definitions in column B.

A	B
__ Malthusian population theory	1. Method by which efficient environmental standards are set by balancing the marginal costs of abatement against the marginal benefits of pollution reduction.
__ Exponential growth	2. Posits that voluntary negotiations among parties affected by an externality will, under some circumstances, lead to an efficient market outcome.
__ Rule of 70	3. A good which can be provided to everyone as easily as it can be provided to one person.

___ Appropriable
resources

___ Inappropriable
resources

___ Externalities

___ Public goods

___ Private goods

___ Cost-benefit
analysis

___ Contingent
valuation

___ Coase theorem

___ Tradable
emissions
permits

4.   Argued that the universal tendency for population to grow exponentially but for agriculture to grow arithmetically leads to periodic famine.

5.   Allow firms to settle on the optimal method and allocation of pollution abatement once the regulators determine the allowable level of pollution.

6.   A commodity whose full economic value can be captured by firms or consumers.

7.   Occurs when a variable increases at a constant proportional rate from period to period.

8.   Involves asking people how much they would be willing to pay in a hypothetical situation to keep some natural resource undamaged.

9.   States that a magnitude growing at a rate of r per year will double in $(70 / r)$ years.

10.   A commodity whose costs and benefits do not accrue to their owners.

11.   A good that can be divided up and provided separately to different individuals, with no external benefits or costs to others.

12.   Occur when costs or benefits of a market transaction "spill over" onto other people.

IV. SUMMARY AND CHAPTER OUTLINE

This section summarizes the key concepts from the chapter.

A. Population and Resource Limitations

1.   Resources are limited, but society's wants are unlimited. Thomas Malthus was one of the first people to address this basic economic "fact of life" as it relates to land and natural resources. Malthus hypothesized that the overpopulation of the earth would be its ultimate downfall; because population grows exponentially, but agriculture grows only arithmetically, periodic famines are inevitable. As the population grows, it becomes increasingly difficult to feed everyone. Therefore, some people will starve, causing the population to fall back down to a sustainable level.

Although this theory opened an important debate, it was inherently flawed. Malthus failed to consider the importance of technology, which has led to tremendous increases in the

ability of people around the globe to feed themselves. In spite of these flaws, the ideas had a tremendous impact on the nature of public policy in the British Empire, and they generated an extreme lack of sympathy for the poor.

2.   Some simple correlations can be found between groups of people and environmental factors. First, pollution trends tend to follow an inverse U-shaped curve across different stages of economic development. Early stages of development tend to generate increases in pollution as subsistence farming is replaced by manufacturing; later stages of development tend to generate decreases in pollution as increased incomes and standards of living change preferences in favor of a cleaner natural environment. Second, human health is very positively correlated with per capita incomes, leading many to conclude that the only way for a society to generate a clean environment is to become wealthy enough to "buy" it.

B. Natural-Resource Economics

1.   A commodity is *appropriable* when firms or consumers can capture its full economic value. This means that owners can expect some sort of return from use of the resource. *Inappropriable* commodities are those whose costs and benefits do not accrue to their owners. Thus, a 40-acre plot of land is appropriable; the owner can allow a farmer to use it in exchange for a rent payment. However, Lake Michigan is inappropriable, since I could freely dump all my garbage into it, making the water less pleasant for all others who use it.

2.   A *nonrenewable resource* is one whose services are essentially fixed in supply and not regenerated quickly enough to be economically relevant. Oil is essentially nonrenewable. The earth produces more of it but it takes thousands of years. *Renewable resources* are those whose services can be replenished regularly. Notice that people may choose *not* to replenish those resources. For example, for years timber companies cut acres and acres of timber without replanting. The trees would eventually replenish themselves, but not for hundreds of years.

3.   Natural resources play a critical role in production and consumption activities in the U.S. economy. Without these resources, we would not be able to play our stereos, drive our cars, or heat our homes. Why, then, is there no concerted strategy on the part of nations and governments to conserve what seem to be the sources of our prosperity—that is, fossil fuels and other natural resources?

The answer to this question is difficult. Some economists might argue that the resources are not truly *essential*, because they are not needed to sustain life in most regions of the world. Air is essential, oil is not. In a world of technological development and innovation, increasingly short supplies of one resource will be replaced by some substitute resource.

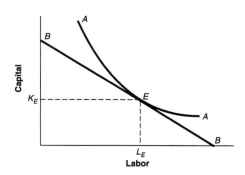

Figure 18-1

4. The following illustration involves concepts presented in the Appendix to chapter 7. The *isoquant AA* in Figure 18-1 shows combinations of capital and labor that can be used in a production process to generate the same quantity of output. The *isocost BB* shows combinations of capital and labor that cost the same amount of money. This firm will choose optimal levels of labor and capital usage such that the desired output level is produced with least cost (point *E*). Notice that as the price of labor rises, the firm will have an incentive to *substitute* capital for labor in the production process. It is this sort of substitutability that makes few resources truly essential.

5. Although the world's population has increased over the past several decades, resource prices have been dropping rather than rising. This means that new technology as well as newfound reserves have allowed supply increases to outstrip demand increases.

C. Environmental Economics

1. An *externality* is present when the benefits (in the case of a positive externality) or the costs (in the case of a negative externality) of an activity spill over into the lives of other people without their paying or being compensated. *Public goods* represent the extreme case of externality on the positive side; pollution, on the negative side.

2. Consider the economic consequences of a negative externality—for example, the emission of heavy toxic smoke from a factory chimney. No matter how disagreeable it might be to those who work or live nearby, the factory's owners might feel no obligation to clean up their act until public pressure, usually in the form of legislation, forces them to do so. A more recent example is acid rain. Many utilities and manufacturers, especially those involved in metal processing, emit sulfur dioxide and nitrogen oxide from their smokestacks. These chemicals combine with moisture in the atmosphere to form sulfuric acid and nitric acid. The acidity of falling rain and snow is thereby increased, creating a more acidic environment in lakes and rivers, in which fish cannot reproduce. Moreover, there may

be long-term impacts on human health from these and other chemical emissions.

3. Externalities lead to economic inefficiency. The above mentioned factory may have some incentive to clean its emissions; for example, better health for the workers might be promoted, or more efficient burning of fuel. These *private benefits* will be reflected in the market demand curve. The firm will clean its smoke until the marginal benefits of additional abatement just equal the marginal cost of cleanup. However, the market demand curve will fail to account for the *public benefit* that would derive from cleanup. Hence, unless the market supply and demand can somehow account for these public benefits and costs, there will be an *oversupply* of those goods that bring external costs and an *undersupply* of those goods that bring external benefits.

4. The discussion above can be illustrated graphically. Figure 18-2 shows the *marginal cost of abatement (MC)* and *marginal private benefit (MPB)* in the market for pollution abatement. Note that the marginal benefit curve is downward-sloping; as the most significant problems are eliminated, the benefit received from an additional unit of abatement will get smaller. The marginal cost curve is upward-sloping, indicating that as the area gets cleaner and cleaner, it becomes increasingly costly to produce an additional unit of abatement.

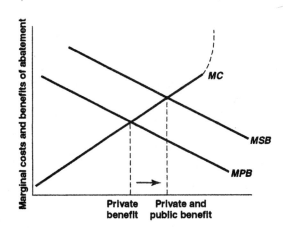

Figure 18-2

If the private demand curve could reflect the total *public* demand—not just the demand by a single firm— for pollution abatement, it would look something like *MSB*. In this case, the quantity of abatement would be higher and there would be less pollution.

5. Several policies exist to correct externalities. Governments can use direct controls, or social regulation, to impose standards and guidelines on markets. The regulator simply sets standards, expects compliance, and punishes or imposes sanctions on those who do not comply. In other

cases, the government has used market solutions to limit pollution. The regulators establish a total amount of pollution to
be tolerated, issue permits for the "right to pollute" to this
extreme, and then let the market determine how the permits
are to be distributed among firms, how the pollution is to be
eliminated, and, thus, what the ultimate distribution of pollution will be. We would expect that firms who can most easily (and cheaply) eliminate pollution will *sell* their permits to
firms who find it more difficult (and costly) to reduce pollution. Critics of this system argue that permits will be distributed such that firms with high pollution-abatement costs
will buy up all the permits and continue to pollute, maybe
even to a greater extent.

6. Private approaches also exist to correct externalities.
Ronald Coase, a Nobel Prize-winning economist, argued that
as long as property rights are well defined and negotiation
costs are low, voluntary negotiations among the parties
affected by an externality will lead to the efficient outcome.
Return to our smoking factory above. Coase would argue
that the local townspeople have a powerful incentive to get
together with the firm owner and agree on an optimal level
of pollution. Coase would further argue that this requires no
government antipollution program!

Liability rules and litigation can also lead to the elimination of externalities without direct government intervention.
As you can imagine, the game-theoretic analysis introduced
in Chapter 12 can help to illustrate these negotiation
processes.

7. Global "greenhouse" warming poses a true challenge to
formulators of environmental policy. Because the solution to
the problem involves an international public good, it is very
difficult to imagine any individual firm, or country, spending
the resources necessary to solve the problem.

V. HELPFUL HINTS

1. The prevalence of severe environmental problems in
socialist economies seems odd. At first glance, it seems like
government ownership and direction of resources would lead
to a decrease in the severity of these sorts of problems.
However, in the absence of private property rights, no single
individual has responsibility for resources. In this setting,
many resources become "public goods," available for free
use and abuse by all. This appears to be a real flaw in the
allocative system.

2. Figure 18-3 in your text describes an *isoquant* and *isocost* map; a similar diagram is shown here in Figure 18-3.

This material was covered in the appendix to Chapter 7.
Remember that an isoquant shows combinations of two
inputs (labor and capital) that can be used to produce a given
level of output. This gives us information about the production process; for example, between points A and B, 2 units of
capital can be substituted for 1 unit of labor, and output will
remain unchanged. This notion of input substitutability is

important when determining whether or not a particular
resource is essential.

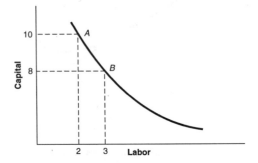

Figure 18-3

3. The oil embargo of 1972-1973 brought the reality of
scarcity home to the American people. The oil supply
decreased dramatically as OPEC's policies took hold, and oil
prices soared. Energy policy was at the top of all politicians'
lists of priorities, and people talked endlessly of their conservation efforts. It seemed as though we would have to face
the fact that our oil reserves are not unlimited.

Almost 30 years later, oil prices (adjusted for inflation)
have fallen and supplies again seem plentiful. Most people
have returned to their old consumption habits, warming
homes above 72°F in winter and cooling below 65°F in summer. What happened? In two words, *market forces*. The
extra-normal profits earned by OPEC encouraged further
exploration. As a result, significant reserves were found in
Alaska, in Mexico, and in the North Sea. When these new,
nonOPEC reserves hit the market, supply swung back out to
the right and has generally kept moving. However, in the
spring of 2000, OPEC again seemed to exercise some market
muscle, restricting supply. Market prices shot up once again.

This example helps to illustrate the difficulty inherent in
questions of resource allocation. What is the actual supply?
How can we measure it? How can we possibly anticipate the
technological developments that will allow us to gather and
to use our resources more efficiently in the future? How
does imperfect competition lead to market power for producers? These types of questions make the study of natural
resources and environmental economics challenging and
fascinating.

VI. MULTIPLE CHOICE QUESTIONS

These questions are organized by topic from the chapter outline. Choose the best answer from the options available.

A. Population and Resource Limitations

1. Malthus believed that:

    a. population increases geometrically while agricultural production remains fixed.

    b. overpopulation is not a worry, since the resources available to the world are infinite.

    c. population increases geometrically while agricultural production increases only arithmetically.

    d. total population tends to remain fixed over time, while agriculture increases arithmetically.

    e. poor relief must be improved, so that famine, war, and disease would not destroy the work force.

2. The major flaw in Malthus's argument was that he failed to account for:

    a. increased government intervention in the economy.

    b. the tremendous impact of improvements in technology.

    c. the redistribution efforts of government that occur through taxing and spending.

    d. diminishing returns to a fixed supply of land.

    e. all the above.

3. Which of the following hypotheses has generally been found to be true?

    a. Human health is highly correlated with per capita incomes.

    b. Pollution tends to decrease in the early stages of development.

    c. Pollution tends to increase in the later stages of development.

    d. Human health tends to be unaffected by development.

    e. The best way for a society to maintain a decent environment is to avoid development and remain poor.

B. Natural-Resource Economics

4. Inappropriable resources are:

    a. free to the individual and the society.

    b. goods whose costs and benefits do not accrue to their owners.

    c. expensive for an individual to produce but can be provided efficiently by government.

    d. efficiently priced and allocated by a market economy.

    e. the side-products of externalities.

5. Appropriable resources are:

    a. free to the individual and the society.

    b. free to the individual but costly to the society.

    c. expensive for an individual to produce but can be provided efficiently by government.

    d. efficiently priced and allocated by a market economy.

    e. the side-products of externalities.

6. All of the following resources are nonrenewable *except*:

    a. oil.

    b. fisheries.

    c. copper.

    d. diamonds.

    e. coal.

    Use the isoquant diagram in Figure 18-4 to answer question 7.

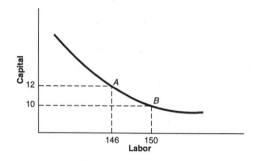

Figure 18-4

7. Between points *A* and *B*, output will remain constant when ___ labor units are substituted for ___ capital units.

    a. 2 for 4.

    b. 4 for 2.

    c. 0 for 4.

    d. 2 for 6.

    e. 5 for 5.

8. If the isoquants for capital and labor are L-shaped, we can say:

    a. that capital is nonrenewable.

    b. that capital is appropriable.

    c. that capital is essential.

    d. there are no other products left to produce.

    e. all the above.

9. Over the past several decades, the prices of resources have actually been:

    a. rising.

    b. falling.

    c. remaining constant.

    d. falling proportionally.

    e. doubling.

10. Which of the general diagrams in Figure 18-5 explains your answer to question 9?

    a.

    b.

    c.

    d.

    e.

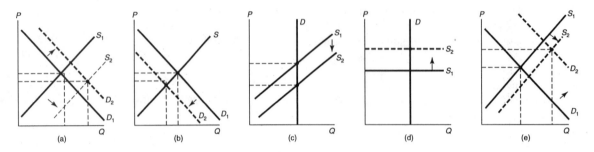

Figure 18-5

C. Environmental Economics

11. Which of the following cannot be called a public good?
    a. national defense.
    b. a dam that protects a region from flooding.
    c. a measles vaccine.
    d. a public concert.
    e. a ham sandwich.

12. In the course of production, a firm with a constant marginal cost of $125 per unit of output emits a pollutant that causes a harm of $5 per unit. What will be the market price if the economy is perfectly efficient?
    a. $125.
    b. $130.
    c. $5.
    d. $120.
    e. The firm will go out of business.

The diagram in Figure 18-6 indicates the private costs and benefits accruing from pollution abatement in a particular firm. Use it to answer questions 13 and 14.

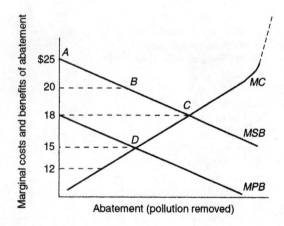

Figure 18-6

13. The efficient level of pollution abatement when only private benefits are considered is indicated by:
    a. *A.*
    b. *B.*

    c. *C.*
    d. *D.*
    e. none of the above.

14. If there is a $3 social benefit per unit of pollution abatement and the market is perfectly competitive, the price will be:
    a. $25.
    b. $20.
    c. $18.
    d. $15.
    e. $12.

15. The Coase result states that:
    a. negotiation would always solve an externality problem if only government would get out of the way.
    b. the potential exists for negotiation to diminish the magnitude of an externality if property rights are well defined and negotiation costs are not too severe.
    c. negotiation must be forgone in lieu of direct governmental intervention whenever an externality problem becomes too severe.
    d. negotiation will always generate an efficient solution as long as negotiation costs are not too high and property rights are clearly defined.
    e. none of the above.

16. Liability laws help to eliminate externalities because:
    a. the FTC can use them to establish absolute levels of pollution to allow.
    b. expensive lawsuits will eliminate the need for public goods.
    c. the difference between the marginal social benefit and the marginal private benefit of pollution abatement will be redistributed in the courts.
    d. individuals are no longer legally liable for the damage they cause others.
    e. none of the above.

VII. PROBLEM SOLVING

The following problems are designed to help you apply the concepts that you learned in this chapter.

A. Population and Resource Limitations

1. Overpopulation was a serious issue in the early 1960s, when Rachel Carson's book *Silent Spring* opened environmental concerns to public debate in 1963. Although population growth has slowed in recent years in industrialized countries, in many less developed countries in Africa and South America the population explosion is still a matter of grave concern.

   a. (**Adam Smith / Thomas Malthus / Rachel Carson**) developed some of the earliest views on population growth in the book *An Essay on the Principle of Population*, written in (**1745 / 1798 / 1876 / 1945**). This text presented the theory that there is a universal tendency for population to increase (**arithmetically / geometrically / exponentially**) while the food supply grows only (**arithmetically / geometrically / exponentially**). Because of the (**laws of supply and demand / equality of marginal utilities / law of diminishing returns**), as society continues to increase production of agricultural goods, it becomes increasingly harder to produce additional units of those goods. Malthus overlooked the fact that this is a (**short-run / long-run**) phenomenon, and that over time, changes in resource availability and technology will allow society to overcome these problems.

   b. Very few general conclusions can be drawn concerning the relationship between populations and their environments. It seems pollution tends to follow (**a U-shaped curve / an inverse U-shaped curve**) as economic development increases. Also, it seems as though human health is (**positively / negatively**) correlated with per capita income.

2. As stated in your text, "Exponential growth and compound interest are important tools in economics." You learned some of the basic concepts surrounding these tools in Chapter 14; let's put them to work in the area of natural resource economics.

   a. Suppose a resource such as labor is growing at 5 percent per year. If there are 100 people in the labor force today, there will be ___ people in the labor force in five years.

   b. Notice that your answer to part *a* (**is / is not**) 125. The notion of compound interest implies that the increase each year is 5 percent over the labor force *base* that existed at the close of the previous year.

   c. What growth rate per year would you need in your labor force if you must have 150 people at the end of the five-year time horizon? ___.

B. Natural-Resource Economics

3. Before we can talk about markets for resources, we have to distinguish between two broad categories for resources. A resource is (**appropriable / inappropriable**) if firms or consumers can capture its full economic value. A resource is (**appropriable / inappropriable**) if it is free to the individual but costly to society.

   a. Many markets exist for appropriable resources. Consider the hypothetical data on the market for oil given in Table 18-1. (Quantities are in barrels per day.)

TABLE 18-1

Price per Barrel	Quantity Supplied	Quantity Demanded
$50	150,000	0
40	120,000	20,000
30	90,000	40,000
20	60,000	60,000
10	30,000	80,000
0	0	100,000

Use Figure 18-7 to plot these supply and demand curves. The equilibrium price in the market will be $___ per barrel

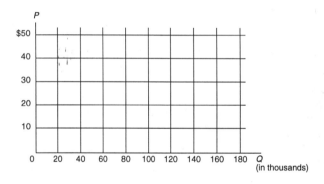

and the quantity exchanged will be ___ barrels.
Figure 18-7

   b. Suppose firms form a cartel and attempt to control the market supply and hence the market price. They manage to cut supply in *half*. Show this new supply curve in Figure 18-7 and show the new equilibrium. Price will (**rise / fall**) to $___ and quantity will (**rise / fall**) to ___.

C. Environmental Economics

4. Externalities occur when production or consumption inflicts involuntary costs or benefits on others. Pollution is one of the best examples of a *negative* externality, because many people have to pay the cost of the behavior of firms who dump trash into the air or water.

   We will employ *cost-benefit analysis* to determine how a private firm makes decisions concerning pollution abatement. Figure 18-8 shows the marginal cost and marginal benefits that firm A will incur if it chooses different levels of pollution abatement.

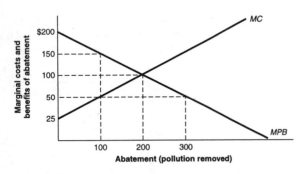

Figure 18-8

a. Suppose the government imposes a requirement that 200 units of pollution be removed. Describe the impact of this policy.

_____

_____

b. Suppose instead that the government charges a $100 emissions fee. Describe the impact of this policy.

_____

_____

c. Let's compare these two policy actions. The absolute requirement yields ___ units of pollution abatement. The emissions fee yields ___ units of pollution abatement and $___ collected by government. The fee leads to (**a greater / a lesser / an equal**) amount of pollution abatement.

5. Consider Figure 18-9, which depicts the marginal private and social benefits of pollution abatement, along with the marginal costs.

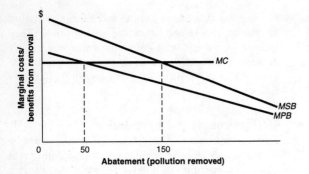

Figure 18-9

a. Given the curves defined in Figure 18-9, some government action is required because the privately determined level of pollution abatement would be ___ tons, at which the marginal cost of abatement equals (**the marginal social damage caused by the pollution /**

zero / **the marginal private benefit of the pollution abatement**). That quantity (**is greater than / is less than**) the efficient level of pollution abatement, ___ tons, defined by the equality of the marginal cost of abatement and (**the marginal social damage caused by the pollution / zero / the marginal social benefits of pollution abatement**).

b. Suppose that those hurt by the pollution offer to pay the polluter $4 for every unit of pollution not emitted. This would mean that the marginal private benefit of pollution abatement would (**climb by $4 / remain the same / fall by $4**) because each unit of pollution abated would mean an additional gain of $4 in compensation.

VIII. DISCUSSION QUESTIONS

Answer the following questions, making sure that you can explain the work you did to arrive at the answers.

1. Review Malthus's ideas concerning population growth. How did these ideas affect the attitudes of the British toward the poor? How might they continue to affect attitudes of some Americans toward immigrants?

2. Why might we expect the switch to a market economy lead to improvements in the environment in Russia?

3. During the Carter administration in the late 1970s, politicians and private citizens alike debated the proper formulation of an "energy policy" for the United States. However, as oil supplies again became more plentiful, this notion was forgotten by most people. Should we be concerned about creating a long-term strategy for resource use? Why or why not?

4. Use supply and demand curves to illustrate why the prices of natural resources have declined over the course of the century.

5. Explain why externalities lead to inefficiencies in the distribution of resources.

6. Compare and contrast command methods of regulation with market-oriented methods of regulation. Which methods tend to eliminate externalities most efficiently?

7. Why is the "greenhouse effect" referred to by the authors of your text as the "granddaddy of public goods problems?" What makes this problem so difficult to solve? How did the Kyoto Protocol attempt to solve this problem?

IX. ANSWERS TO STUDY GUIDE QUESTIONS

III. Review of Key Concepts

4	Malthusian population theory
7	Exponential growth
9	Rule of 70
11	Appropriable resources

10	Inappropriable resources
12	Externalities
3	Public goods
6	Private goods
1	Cost-benefit analysis
8	Contingent valuation
2	Coase theorem
5	Tradable emissions permits

VI. Multiple Choice Questions

1. C   2. B   3. A   4. B   5. D   6. B
7. B   8. C   9. B   10. A   11. E   12. B
13. D   14. C   15. B   16. C

VII. Problem Solving

1. a.   Thomas Malthus, 1798, exponentially, arithmetical-ly, law of diminishing returns, short-run
    b.   an inverse U-shaped curve, positively
2. a.   128
    b.   is
    c.   8.5 percent
3. appropriable, inappropriable
    a.   See Figure 18-7. $20, 60,000

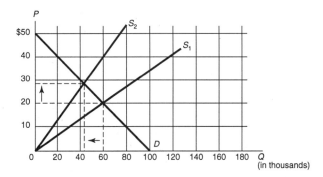

Figure 18-7

    b.   rise, $28.58, fall, 42.8
4. a.   The marginal cost of pollution abatement is equal to the marginal benefits of pollution abatement.
    b.   The firm will equate the fee with the marginal cost and choose abatement of 200 units.

c.   200, 200, $20,000, an equal
5. a.   50, the marginal private benefit of the pollution abatement, is less than, 150, the marginal social benefits of pollution abatement.
    b.   climb by $4

VIII. Discussion Questions

1. Malthus was concerned about the fact that population was growing much too fast for production in agriculture to keep up. Thus, he thought that many poor people would starve, serving as a natural check on overpopulation. These ideas hardened the attitudes of the British toward the poor in nineteenth-century Britain. Many middle-class merchants became more willing to allow the poor to starve based on the Malthusian theory that this was just part of a natural adjust-ment process.
2. A switch to a market economy in Russia might improve the environment by distributing private ownership rights to natural resources.
3. Given the fact that oil is a nonrenewable resource, some sort of energy policy seems to be in order.
4. Supply has increased more dramatically than demand.
5. Externalities lead to inefficiencies in the distribution of resources. This is because private demand and supply curves cannot account for all of the costs and benefits that occur as a result of production and consumption.
6. Command methods involve regulators in establishing standards with which the firms must comply. Regulators give firms detailed instructions on the type of controls to use and the technology involved. Market-oriented methods allow each firm to determine its own best solutions to pollu-tion problems. Markets tend to work most efficiently because each firm is allowed to make its own decisions with respect to the best methods to employ.
7. The "greenhouse effect" is a particularly difficult prob-lem to solve because the solution will provide benefits to many people; once the solution is available, it will be impos-sible to exclude anyone from enjoying the benefits. Hence, few are willing to pay to implement the solutions to the problem. The Kyoto Protocol was an agreement among countries to limit emissions of greenhouse gases by 2010. The agreement allowed countries to purchase emissions trad-ing rights from other countries, harnessing market forces to solve a problem generated by market failure!

CHAPTER 19

Efficiency vs. Equity:
The Big Tradeoff

I. CHAPTER OVERVIEW

Many countries around the world are driven by two distinct motives as they define their economic systems. Most people desire, on the one hand, to have a chance to work hard and to have that hard work rewarded. They want the opportunity to improve their standard of living and to provide economic advantages for their children. These sorts of goals often lead to a limited economic role for government.

On the other hand, many people also want to provide some measure of equity across their societies. As we have seen in earlier chapters, each economic system must define equity for itself by combining social and cultural characteristics with historical reality. Regardless of the particular definition chosen, government must step in to administer these collective decisions.

As noble as these two goals are, one of the lessons of economics is that these goals frequently get in each other's way. The very programs that provide some measure of protection for the disadvantaged cost money to run; they therefore require tax revenues to operate, and taxation reallocates society's resources from those who have achieved some measure of economic success to those who have not. Welfare programs themselves are often accused of generating disincentives among the disadvantaged, discouraging them from working to provide better lives for themselves. Arthur Okun, a famous economist, termed this whole business the big tradeoff—the classic tradeoff between equity and efficiency that all societies must struggle with.

These objectives make it clear that the debate hinges on the theoretical tradeoff between equity and efficiency, but the fundamental lesson of this chapter is that the debate must be conducted in the context of the practical, political world of interdependent government decision making. This chapter investigates the sources of inequality found in the distributions of income and wealth. Given this inequality, alternative antipoverty policies are considered. Finally, the issue of health care reform is considered and at the close of this microeconomic section of your textbook you are left to ponder the appropriate role for government in the market for health care services.

II. LEARNING OBJECTIVES

After you have read Chapter 19 in your text and completed the exercises in this *Study Guide* chapter, you should be able to:

1. Understand the difference between the terms **income** and **wealth** as economists use them, and recognize the major sources of income and the major reservoirs of wealth in the United States.

2. Use the **Lorenz curve** as a tool to investigate relative (in)equality in the distribution of income and/or wealth. Outline (a) the information that these curves are intended to convey, (b) the link between that intention and their construction, and (c) the interpretation of the bulges that they usually portray. Compare the distribution of income across countries or regions using Lorenz curves.

3. Outline and explain potential sources of inequality in the distribution of income both across the United States and elsewhere around the globe.

4. Define the term **poverty** and characterize the group of people that tends to be poor. Trace historical trends in poverty.

5. Contrast three notions of equity (equality of political rights, opportunity, and outcome), and use Arthur Okun's notion of a leaky bucket to delineate the costs of providing increased equity.

6. Use an **income-possibility curve** to illustrate efficiency-equity tradeoffs that must occur when income is redistributed. Discuss the inefficiency that is created by redistribution.

7. List the major welfare programs still in place in the United States (food stamps and child nutrition; aid to the needy aged, blind, and disabled; Medicaid; housing assistance; etc.). Note the comparative expense of running each. Understand how qualifying standards might impose very high effective marginal tax rates on the working poor.

8. Define two views of poverty, and trace the implications of both for government activity.

237

9. Critically analyze the notion of substituting a negative income tax for the plethora of welfare programs currently in place. Describe the pros and cons of income supplements for the poor.

10. Discuss the nature of the 1996 welfare reform program and list its positive and negative aspects.

11. Provide an overview of the health care system as it developed in the United States over the past four decades. Establish a role for government in the system to provide **public goods**, lessen the severity of **imperfect information**, and improve **equity**.

12. Outline the pros and cons of alternative approaches to health care reform.

III. REVIEW OF KEY CONCEPTS

Match the following terms from column A with their definitions in column B.

A	B
__ Personal income	1. Shows incomes available to different groups when government programs redistribute income.
__ Disposable income	2. Program that would provide an income supplement, rather than impose an income tax, to those who earn below a certain income level.
__ Wealth	3. Diagram that shows the degree of inequality in the income distribution.
__ Distribution of income	4. Goods whose benefits are indivisibly spread among the entire community, whether or not individuals choose to purchase them.
__ Lorenz curve	5. Total income or receipts earned by a person or household in a given year.
__ Subsistence cost	6. Wage supplement applied to labor income.
__ Poverty line	7. Combination of public and private solutions to health care issues.
__ Income-possibility curve	8. Shows the dispersion of incomes.
__ Welfare state	9. Occurs when people with the highest risk are the most likely ones to purchase insurance.
__ Negative income tax	10. Personal income less any taxes paid.
__ Earned income credit	11. Line of demarcation between those the government labels "poor" and "nonpoor."

__ Public goods	12. Found by multiplying the minimum family food budget by three.
__ Private goods	13. Individuals share the cost of care with an insurer.
__ Adverse selection	14. Situation in which the government modifies market forces guarantee people a minimum standard of living.
__ Moral hazard	15. Goods with no external costs or benefits.
__ Non-Price rationing	16. Often takes the form of waiting for services.
__ Coinsurance	17. Dollar value of financial and tangible assets minus the amount of money owed to banks or other creditors.
__ Managed care	18. Occurs when insurance reduces the incentives for individuals to avoid risk and expense through prudent behavior.

IV. SUMMARY AND CHAPTER OUTLINE

This section summarizes the key concepts from the chapter.

A. The Sources of Inequality

1. *Income* is measured as the *flow* of money to an individual during a specified period of time; major sources include labor earnings, rental payments, dividends, interest payments, and transfer payments. *Wealth* is a measure of the net dollar value *at a given point in time* of tangible and intangible assets, including homes, rental properties, other real estate, and motor vehicles, on the one hand, and cash holdings, bank accounts, business equity, and stocks and bonds, on the other.

2. The *Lorenz Curve* plots the percentage of income earned or wealth accumulated by x percent of the population, reflecting the equality of income or wealth distributions. Comparing the positions of Lorenz curves over time or across countries can suggest trends in equality or allow for intercountry comparisons of levels of equality.

3. Labor earnings vary because of differences in ability, differences in work intensity, and differences in occupations across workers. Property incomes vary because of differences in wealth and inheritance. Only a small fraction of America's wealth can be accounted for by life-cycle saving; entrepreneurship is a dominant source of wealth for the richest Americans.

4. *Poverty* is a condition in which people have inadequate incomes. In order to define poverty numerically, government determines a "poverty line," which is a minimum level of income that families need to maintain a subsistence level of consumption. In the United States, this level has been

determined to be three times the amount of money needed to purchase a subsistence level of food for a family for a single month; this was $16,800 in 1998. Poverty affects some groups more significantly than others. Minorities and single women with children have experienced particularly high poverty rates in the United States, possibly because these groups have received relatively low levels of education and training, resulting in their being ineligible for many high-paying jobs. Also, discrimination in hiring and promotion may be responsible for lower wages and fewer opportunities for women and minorities.

5. Interesting trends in inequality and poverty have occurred over this century in the United States. Between 1930 and 1975, inequality in the distribution of income fell and poverty rates dropped dramatically. The Depression era policies of President Roosevelt during the 1930s led to the development and resulting refinement of a welfare "safety net;" programs like social security and Medicare have particularly led to significant declines in poverty among the elderly. Another significant wave of welfare programs came into being during the Great Society era of Presidents Kennedy and Johnson. Over the same time period, increases in productivity and improvements in technology made workers more valuable to firms and hence led to increases in income.

Between 1975 and 1998, this trend has reversed, and the distribution has in fact become increasingly unequal. This trend has been caused in part by changes in government policy; many welfare programs have been eliminated or cut. Additionally, the college/high school wage premium has increased as jobs in manufacturing become more scarce and returns to training and education increase. Increases in the compensation of top executives and professionals have ballooned the most extreme incomes in the top quintile. All of these factors have played a role in the increasing inequality in the United States over the past two decades.

6. The notion that industrialization would help only the rich has not been borne out by experience. Enormous inequality is displayed by the industrializing countries, and the distribution of wealth throughout most of the world is extremely concentrated at the top. Nonetheless, most of the economies in the industrialized world display distributions of income without a large, thoroughly impoverished underclass.

B. Antipoverty Policies

1. Three important notions of equity dominate our thinking. First, political equality includes the right to vote, trial by jury, and other constitutional liberties. Equality of economic opportunity implies that there should be some sort of level playing field defined for economic agents, administered by the legal system. Equality of economic outcome is the most contentious; it would provide the same consumption for all people, regardless of their contributions to the economic system.

2. Economists have recognized that movement toward equity generally involves efficiency losses—Okun's analysis of a *leaky bucket* of disincentives and administrative costs illuminates this idea. How big are the leaks? What are their sources? First, there are the administrative costs of running welfare and tax redistribution programs. Second, there is the potential for welfare programs to create disincentives to work. Third, there is the potential for progressive taxation to retard saving and investment and thus growth. Finally, there are potentially harmful changes in attitude and behavior that might be fostered by a progressive tax and welfare state. More people might cheat on their taxes, or lie around and not work, and so on. All these leaks are hard to measure, and the jury is still out.

The opposite side of the argument can lead to the suggestion that the tradeoff between equity and efficiency is overstated to the extreme. What if the drive toward equality opened opportunities to extraordinarily productive people who would have otherwise been shut out? What if programs that provide health care and nutrition for poor families actually broke the cycle of poverty, thereby increasing productivity and efficiency? Would not, then, operating the welfare state and incurring its expense be an investment in expanded human capital for the future?

3. An *income-possibility curve* can help to illustrate the inefficiencies involved in redistribution. Figure 19-5 from your text is reproduced here as Figure 19-1.

The population is divided into two equal-size groups based on income. The lower income group is measured on the Y axis and the higher income group is measured on the X axis. Point A shows the distribution of income when there is no redistribution and each group consumes its own income. If markets are perfectly competitive, this point will be efficient, but it may be considered inequitable because the high-income group consumes a significantly greater amount of income than the low-income group.

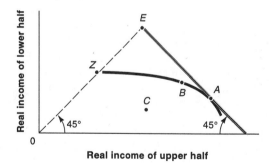

Figure 19-1

Suppose this society decides to institute a redistribution program. The move from A to E would describe an efficient program, with each dollar transferred from the high-income group resulting in a dollar increase in the low-income pool.

Due to the existence of the inefficiencies described above, most redistributions would cause a move along the *ABZ* curve, showing that a dollar transferred from the high-income group results in *less than a dollar* increase in the low-income pool.

4.   The United States offers a wide array of programs designed to alleviate poverty (welfare, food stamps, Medicaid, Aid to Families with Dependent Children, etc.). These programs are frequently criticized for necessitating high effective marginal tax rates on income. However, all federal poverty programs in place today amount to only approximately 10 percent of the total federal budget.

5.   Two general views of poverty can be described as follows. Some social scientists would argue that poverty is the result of social and economic conditions over which the poor have no control. Basic inequality of opportunities within the economy create insurmountable barriers for large communities of people. Other social scientists claim that poverty is created by maladaptive individual behavior. This theory describes the poor as being lazy, shiftless, and unconcerned about their own productivity. Most people believe that elements of both of these theories characterize the nature of poverty.

6.   Many economists believe that the current set of welfare programs in the United States generates disincentives for the poor. For example, in order to maintain welfare benefits for their children, single mothers must not live with the fathers of their children. This stipulation leads to the dissolution of families, something that no one would in fact want to encourage.

In order to remedy this situation, a welfare reform program was put in place in 1996. It primarily targeted the old Aid to Families with Dependent Children (AFDC) program, revising many of the entitlements that it had contained. States are given block grants to distribute as they see fit. Each family is now limited to 5 years of lifetime benefits. Adults in the program must now engage in market work activities after 2 years on the program. Legal immigrants may now be excluded from the program.

Although designed to eliminate some of the disincentive effects generated by the old program, many economists fear that these changes will have a tremendous impact on the number of women and children living in poverty. Table 19-4 in your textbook reports that in 1998, 18.9 percent of children under 18 years of age live in poverty. This startling statistic may skyrocket when AFDC benefits are revoked from those families that have exhausted their five years on the new program.

7.   In order to reverse these disincentives, the *negative income tax* is advocated by many as an alternative means of coping with poverty. This program would provide a cash supplement, or "negative tax," to people whose income falls below a particular threshold. Families with incomes above this level will pay a positive tax. The *earned income tax*

credit is a derivative of this program that has been instituted in the United States. This wage supplement accrues to those families whose income is below $13,000 per year.

C. Health Care: The Problem that Won't Go Away

1.   Enormous increases in health care costs over the past decade have brought the issue of the health care delivery system in the United States to the front burner. Cost increases might be blamed on the fact that the income elasticity is very high for health care services. This tells us that as income increases by some percentage, the quantity of health care demanded increases bet an even larger percentage. As incomes have increased, so has the demand for health care, putting upward pressure on prices. Technological developments have, counterintuitively, led to *increases* in costs as many hospitals and doctors have spent large amounts of money on sophisticated machinery and equipment. Finally cost increases have been blamed on the fact that the U.S. system often involves payment by a "third party." This means that the government or an insurance company actually pays the seller for health care services on behalf of a client. For example, if you have insurance and you go to your doctor for the flu, you may not pay for the visit; rather, you submit a bill to your insurance company, which then pays some or all of the bill. This distances the consumer from the payment process and encourages him or her to discount the importance of price when choosing a health care provider

2.   Although for some people the system provides the best care found anywhere in the world, for others it is prohibitively expensive and inefficient—hence, the public debate. The ultimate question: How much of a role should government have in delivering health care to citizens? Using terms introduced in this chapter, is health care really a "public good," and can it be delivered more efficiently when government acts to pool the interests of the collective?

3.   There are several potential roles for government in the health care system. First, health care might be termed a *public good,* meaning that its benefits are spread significantly across the entire community. If this is the case, a private system will provide too little of the good to satisfy society's true demand. For example, it is important for expectant mothers to receive good prenatal care. This leads to healthier babies and eventually to healthier, more productive workers; thus, prenatal care is beneficial not only to the mother and child but also to the wider community. Private markets for prenatal care cannot reflect the social benefits generated by the provision of such care, and they cannot incorporate the "social demand" for the good. In situations such as these, private demand will consistently *underestimate* the true demand for the good or service.

There is also a large amount of *asymmetrical information* in markets for health care. It is often quite difficult for a patient to have enough knowledge to carefully assess his or her own condition. Thus buyers must trust the expertise of sellers; this can lead to inefficiencies. *Adverse selection* occurs in insurance markets because people know more about their own health and well-being than insurers. This means that the people who buy insurance will tend to be those who most need it, leading to a generally more risky pool of insured individuals and to higher costs for all. *Moral hazard* occurs due to the fact that insurance may induce people to take greater risks than they would without insurance. For example, knowing that I have insurance allows me to ski more recklessly than I would otherwise. I know that the insurance company will pay a large portion of the costs I might incur due to injury.

Finally, governments may play a role in creating a more equitable distribution of health care services. As stated earlier, health care in the United States is very good for many people, but also very expensive. Wealthy people can afford the best care in the world, but poorer people have to deal with significant rationing. Private markets simply will not provide for equity.

4. Several alternatives exist for improving health care delivery. The *pure market alternative* suggests that each family should pay 100 percent of the costs of any procedure. This helps to solve some problems of information asymmetries but fails to recognize and enhance the public good properties that exist. A *nationalized health service* would place health care delivery in the hands of government, introducing a single-payer system. This solves some of the above problems but suggests an extreme case of moral hazard and leads us to expect excess demand across the market. A compromise policy, *managed competition*, has been introduced in the hope that it will capture the strengths of the two extremes. The bottom line here is that there are no easy answers and that designing policies that are both efficient and in the collective best interest is very difficult.

V. HELPFUL HINTS

1. Throughout this chapter we have referred to *median* family income. A median is one way of defining the *average* in a set of data; it is the observation that is exactly in the middle of a distribution, with half of the observations below it and half of the observations above it. There are other ways to describe the average. Oftentimes people refer to the *mean* family income; the mean is the sum of the observations divided by the number of observations. People also might refer to the *mode* of family incomes; this is the income that occurs most frequently. All these definitions help to describe the distribution of income.

2. Your text mentions a *Gini coefficient*, which can be calculated using a Lorenz curve. This coefficient allows us to quickly and easily compare income distributions across time or across regions. Without it, we are left trying to eyeball the

differences using diagrams.

To find a Gini coefficient, calculate the area between the actual Lorenz curve and the curve of perfect income equality. In Figure 19-2, this is the gray shaded area. Multiply this area by two and you have your Gini! This quantifies the notion of inequality so that we can make comparisons.

3. Many critics have opposed national health insurance and managed competition because both plans provide explicit rules as to how care is to be *rationed*. We might point out that care is rationed under the current system! Those who have the money to pay for insurance are able to afford and obtain care. Those who are very poor or old have the government as provider and are able to obtain care at taxpayer expense. All other people are effectively rationed out of the system.

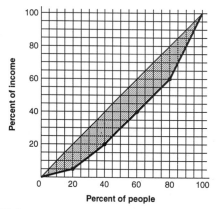

Figure 19-2

VII. MULTIPLE CHOICE QUESTIONS

These questions are organized by topic from the chapter outline. Choose the best answer from the options available.

A. The Sources of Inequality

1. A Lorenz curve is a graph whose axes measure the:
   a. total amount of income in dollars on one axis and the total number of individuals or families receiving that income or a lower one on the other.
   b. percentage of people (10 percent, 20 percent, etc.) on one axis and the percentage of total income received by the lowest 10 percent, the lowest 20 percent, etc., on the other.
   c. number of individuals or families receiving a certain income on one axis and the percentage of the total population represented by that number on the other.
   d. number of individuals or families in different occupations on one axis and the median income received in that occupation on the other.

e. income classes (e.g., $0 to $1999 and $2000 to $3999) on one axis and the percentage of individuals or families in each such income class on the other.

2. Absolute or total equality in an income distribution would appear on a Lorenz-curve chart as a:
   a. curved line well bowed out from the diagonal.
   b. curved line close to the diagonal.
   c. right-angled line.
   d. 45° diagonal line.
   e. none of the preceding.

3. Which alternative in question 2 would have been correct had that question referred to absolute inequality in income—i.e., a situation in which one individual or family gets all the income and the others receive no income at all?
   a.
   b.
   c.
   d.
   e.

4. From the mid-1970s to the mid 1990s in the United States:
   a. the lowest 20 percent and the highest 20 percent of the income distribution became poorer relative to the middle 60 percent.
   b. the highest 20 percent became relatively poorer and the lowest 20 percent became relatively richer.
   c. the highest 20 percent became relatively richer and the lowest 20 percent became relatively poorer.
   d. both the highest and the lowest 20 percent of the income distribution became richer at the expense of the middle class.
   e. none of the above.

5. The *median* family income is the:
   a. figure obtained by listing all incomes from lowest to highest and taking the one exactly in the middle of the ranking.
   b. income figure that would result if the total incomes received by all families were divided equally among those families.
   c. income it is estimated a family must have in order to reach the "minimum comfort" level of consumption.
   d. level of income found at the exact midpoint of a Lorenz curve.
   e. none of the preceding.

6. Which alternative in question 5 would be correct had that question referred to the *mean* rather than to the *median* family income?
   a.
   b.
   c.
   d.
   e.

7. If there were any inequality at all in the distribution of income, which of the following would be true of the group making up the lowest 20 percent in the income ranking?
   a. It is just as likely as not that it will receive more than 20 percent of this total income.
   b. It must receive exactly 20 percent of this total income.
   c. It will usually, but not always, receive less than 20 percent of this total income.
   d. It must have received less than 20 percent of the total income of all groups together.
   e. None of the above is necessarily true.

8. The poverty line, computed to reflect a minimum-subsistence income:
   a. was $16,800 for a family of four in 1998.
   b. includes only cash payments, ignoring in-kind benefits received from government and other sources.
   c. is roughly three times the minimum-subsistence food budget.
   d. does not include an adjustment for improvements in other aspects of the quality of life that have occurred over time.
   e. all the above.

9. The average income of the lowest 20 percent of the population has increased by more than 130 percent since 1929:
   a. so the need for antipoverty programs is a myth.
   b. but the percentage of total income that growth represents has held steady at around 5 percent.
   c. but almost all that growth is explained by growth in total GDP.
   d. choices **b** and **c** only.
   e. none of the above.

10. Differences in ability are commonly cited to explain differences in income. This explanation:
    a. covers only part of the reason, because there are so many more instances of skewness in ability than there are of skewness in income.
    b. covers only part of the reason, because the shape of the income distribution is significantly different from that of the ability distribution.
    c. covers only part of the reasons because the measured range of individual ability differences is much wider than the range of income differences.
    d. gives a reasonably complete interpretation of income differences.
    e. is almost meaningless because there is no suitable way of comparing ability differences against income differences.

11. Which of the following is *not* a reason that might explain the incidence of poverty in contemporary America?
    a. Differences in education and training.
    b. The existence of noncompeting groups.

c. Differences in economic environment, including the distribution of wealth.

d. The asymmetric effect of recession on demographic groups.

e. Differences in ability among all people.

B. Antipoverty Policies

12. A poor family's employment earnings are supplemented by a negative income tax—in the amount, say, of $4000. Under this tax proposal, if family employment earnings were to rise by $1000, the income received from the negative tax would typically:

    a. fall by $1000.

    b. fall by more than $1000.

    c. fall by some amount less than $1000.

    d. fall by $4000.

    e. rise by some amount such as $500.

Use the diagram in Figure 19-3 to answer questions 14 and 15.

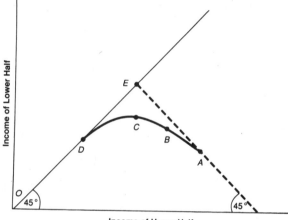

Figure 19-3

13. Let point A represent some initial distribution of income between the indicated upper half and the lower half. Which point would represent the equal distribution of income if there were no leaks in the bucket?

    a. *A*.

    b. *B*.

    c. *C*.

    d. *D*.

    e. *E*.

14. Which answer to question 14 would have been correct if it had asked for the point that would represent equality given the leaks that produce curve *ABCD*?

    a.

    b.

    c.

    d.

    e.

15. Which of the following is not likely to be a significant source of leaks in the equity-efficiency tradeoff?

    a. The administrative costs of running a welfare income redistribution program.

    b. The work disincentives of the progressive income tax.

    c. The disincentives against saving and investment that are produced by the progressive income tax.

    d. A change in attitude that makes cheating on taxes more acceptable.

    e. All the above could be significant, though there is little evidence to support choice **c**.

16. In the 2000 budget, which of the following was the largest item targeted directly at helping the poor?

    a. Medicaid.

    b. Aid to Families with Dependent Children.

    c. Food stamps and child nutrition.

    d. Aid to the aged, blind, and disabled.

    e. Housing assistance.

17. Despite the fact that many people complain about the number of programs for the poor funded by the federal government, these programs comprise:

    a. less than 1 percent of the budget.

    b. about 5 percent of the budget.

    c. nearly 8 percent of the budget.

    d. about 15 percent of the budget.

    e. more than 25 percent of the budget.

18. "Inefficiency" in income redistribution means the:

    a. reduction in total output caused by those unfavorably affected by redistribution and by their decision to pay less in income tax by working less.

    b. administrative costs of redistribution and the burden it places on federal workers.

    c. lesser skills of the gainers from redistribution.

    d. total amount of income transferred from upper income groups to lower income groups.

    e. resulting reduction in total taxes collected by the government.

19. The earned-income tax credit:

    a. acts as a wage supplement.

    b. is a supplement to earned income of up to 40 percent.

    c. can simultaneously support the poorest families and maintain incentives for the working poor.

    d. all of the above.

    e. none of the above.

20. In 1996, Congress passed a welfare reform package that changed the nature and incentives provided by the old Aid for Families with Dependent Children program. Which of the following goals or guidelines was included as part of the reform package?

    a. Families no longer receive aid as an entitlement.

    b. The Federal government took on responsibility for paying for and administering the program.

    c. Legal and illegal immigrants are now eligible for

benefits.

d.   Adults in the program are encouraged to work, but are not required to find employment outside the home.

e.   Children living in poverty are to receive additional in-kind benefits.

C. Health Care: The Problem that Won't Go Away

21. The health care debate has become quite heated in recent years primarily because:

a.   the quality of health care in the United States is poor for the majority of people.

b.   the cost of health care has skyrocketed.

c.   government can no longer afford to provide single payer services.

d.   a majority of people would prefer the Canadian system to the U.S. system.

e.   money for research and development in private markets has dried up.

22. A public good is one in which the cost of exclusion is:

a.   low, and the marginal cost of one more consumer is low.

b.   high, and the marginal cost of one more consumer is low.

e.   low, and the marginal cost of one more consumer is high.

d.   high, and the marginal cost of one more consumer is high.

e.   irrelevant, as is the marginal cost of consumption.

23. The cost of health care has increased dramatically because:

a.   income elasticity for it is high.

b.   technological advantages have lowered the cost of doing business, allowing for increased profits for practitioners.

c.   consumers pay 100 percent of their health care expenses, eliminating the need for third-part payers.

d.   doctors earn an extra-normal return on their investment in human capital that government chooses not to eliminate.

e.   none of the above.

24. Wilma graduated from college and got a new full-time job which provides health insurance. Because of this, she decided to take skydiving lessons. This is an example of:

a.   adverse selection.

b.   moral hazard.

c.   asymmetric information.

d.   government failure.

e.   managed competition.

25. Many proponents of markets have hailed the superiority of a pure market solution to the health care dilemma. Which of the following problems does this program leave unsolved?

a.   Adverse selection.

b.   Moral hazard.

c.   Insufficient funds for research and development.

d.   Excess demand.

e.   None of the above.

26. Some politicians claim that price controls would help to hold down the costs of medical care. What problem would these controls create, according to economists?

a.   Patients would face delays in obtaining adequate care.

b.   There would be an excess demand for care.

c.   Medical care would be of lower quality.

d.   Medical innovation would be reduced.

e.   All the above.

VII. PROBLEM SOLVING

The following problems are designed to help you to apply the concepts that you learned in this chapter.

A. The Sources of Inequality

1.   a.   Consider a group consisting of 10 individuals. The first receives a weekly income of $1, the second $2, and so on, with the tenth receiving $10. The first individual is low on the income totem pole, representing the bottom 10 percent (ranked in terms of income) of this particular population. The $1 received by this poverty-stricken person is about 2 percent of the total weekly income received by all, which totals $55. Complete Table 19-1 by computing the requisite percentages. For example, the lowest 20 percent of the population consists of the $1 individual plus the $2 individual. Their combined income total of $3 is about 5-1/2 percent of the combined incomes of all 10; i.e., $3 is about 5-1/2 percent of $55. So 5-1/2 should go in the first blank box of Table 19-1.

TABLE 19-1

Percent of Income Received by Lowest:									
10%	20%	30%	40%	50%	60%	70%	80%	90%	100%
2	—	—	—	—	—	—	—	—	100

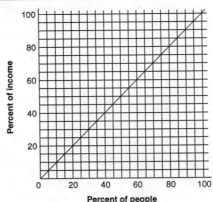

Figure 19-4

b. Draw the Lorenz curve illustrating this distribution of income in Figure 19-4.

c. If the distribution of income were more unequal than that indicated at the beginning of this question, then the Lorenz curve would (**bulge closer to the lower right-hand corner / be drawn nearer to the 45° diagonal**); if it were less unequal, the curve would (**bulge closer to the lower right-hand corner / be drawn nearer to the 45° diagonal**).

2. Suppose, using the data provided in question 1, that a 20 percent income tax is imposed by the government.

Such a tax would collect, assuming no disincentive effects, $11 in revenue. Assume further that it costs $1 to administer the tax and that the remaining $10 is distributed to everyone as equal $1 "social" payments. Fill in the blanks in Table 19-2 and draw a new Lorenz curve in Figure 19-4 to illustrate the resulting after-tax-and-payment distribution of income; use a different color pencil or pen for clarity.

3. The following list records changes in a Lorenz curve that might be expected in response to some change in economic circumstance:

1. Movement up toward the 45° line.
2. Movement away from the 45° line.
3. No movement at all.

Using the numbers from the list above, indicate in the blanks provided the likely effect of the following changes in economic condition on a Lorenz curve illustrating a distribution of income:

a. A 5 percent proportional income tax whose revenues are not redistributed.

b. A 5 percent proportional income tax whose revenues are redistributed equally to everyone.

c. A progressive income tax (which taxes higher incomes at a higher rate) whose revenues are not redistributed.

d. A progressive income tax (which taxes higher incomes at a higher rate) whose revenues are redistributed equally to everyone.

e. A 5 percent sales tax whose revenues are not redistributed.

f. A deep recession that reduces employment for the working-class poor.

4. Table 19-3 records data that describe the distribution of income in the United States in 1984.

TABLE 19-3

Cumulative Percentage of People	Cumulative Percentage of Income
20	4.7
40	15.7
60	32.7
80	57.1
100	100.0

a. Plot the corresponding Lorenz curve in Figure 19-5.

b. For each of the following, record in the blanks provided whether the corresponding Lorenz curve would be much further away from the 45° line (MF), slightly further away from the 45° line (SF), slightly closer to the 45° line (SC), or much closer to the 45° line (MC) than the curve you just drew:

___ (1) A Lorenz curve depicting the distribution of income in the United States in 1972.

___ (2) A Lorenz curve depicting the distribution of income in the United States in 1929.

___ (3) A Lorenz curve depicting the distribution of income in an "industrializing" nation in 1984.

___ (4) A Lorenz curve depicting the distribution of wealth in the United States in 1984.

___ (5) A Lorenz curve depicting the distribution of income in the United Kingdom in 1996.

___ (6) A Lorenz curve depicting the distribution of income in the United States in 1996.

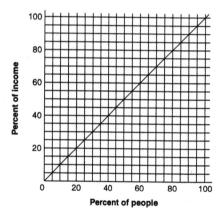

Figure 19-5

TABLE 19-2

Person	10%	20%	30%	40%	50%	60%	70%	80%	90%	100%
Income	$1.00	$2.00	$3.00	$4.00	$5.00	$6.00	$7.00	$8.00	$9.00	$10.00
Taxes paid	$0.20	___	___	___	___	___	___	___	___	___
Income after taxes	$0.80	___	___	___	___	___	___	___	___	___
Income after taxes and payment	$1.80	___	___	___	___	___	___	___	___	___
Percent of total income after the program received by the lowest indicated %	33.%	___	___	___	___	___	___	___	___	100%

5. The poverty line is determined by computing (**a maximum poverty index / a minimum-subsistence income / an average American's food budget**). Social workers provide some information for the computation, and their numbers are corroborated by multiplying a subsistence food budget by (**2 / 3 / 4**). Why? Because families at the lower end of the income scale typically spend (**one-quarter / one-third / one-half**) of their incomes on food. In 1962, the poverty line income for a family of four was $3100; in 1998, the same benchmark income was (**$7800 / $9675 / $10,625 / $16,800**).

6. Table 19-4 records the incidence of poverty in some of the major demographic groups of the United States in 1982 and 1995.

TABLE 19-4

Population Group	Percent of Group in Poverty	
	1982	1998
White	12.0	10.5
Black	35.6	26.2
Hispanic	29.9	25.6
Elderly	14.6	10.5
Married couples	7.6	5.3
Families headed by women	40.6	29.9
Total population	15.0	12.7

a. Families headed by women ranked (**first / second / third**) on the list, with ___ percent of their numbers falling below the poverty line in 1998. Blacks ranked (**second / first / fourth**), with ___ percent in 1998.

b. Referring now to Figure 19-6, note that the average income of the bottom one-fifth of the population (ranked by income) has climbed ___ percent since 1930, from $___ (real 1989 dollars) to $___.

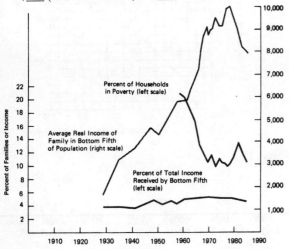

Figure 19-6

c. As a percentage of national income, however, the income earned by the lowest 20 percent of the popula-

tion (**fell / remained roughly the same / rose**), to stand at about (**4 / 5 / 10**) percent in 1996. For the lowest 20 percent, therefore, 60 years of history has (**shifted the Lorenz curve in toward the 45° line / done little to the Lorenz curve / shifted the Lorenz curve away from the 45° line**), indicating (**a trend toward greater equality / no significant trend toward greater equality / a trend toward less equality**) in the lower incomes. Put another way, the average income of the lowest 20 percent of the population has climbed only because (**total income has fallen / total income has remained the same / total income has risen**).

7. The very concept of equality is at best a controversial issue. Most people would agree that equal opportunity, equal access to adequate education, and equal access to the electoral process are essential elements of American democracy. But what about a (more) equal distribution of income? More specifically, should a progressive income tax system be used to redistribute income? There is no definitive response to this question. There are too many potential sources of inequity in the distribution of income that would exist regardless of the economic policy of the U.S. government. List at least five of these sources in the spaces provided below:

a. _____

b. _____

c. _____

d. _____

e. _____

B. Antipoverty Policies

8. Figure 19-7 can be used to illustrate the *disincentive* or *leaky-bucket* consequence of income redistribution. The horizontal and vertical axes measure, respectively (to the same scale), the incomes of the upper half and the lower half of the population. This diagram has a 45° line emerging from the origin. If there were complete equality in income distribution (if each individual received exactly the same income as every other individual), then the words "upper half" and "lower half" would be meaningless. Alternatively, the so-called upper half (*any half*) of the population would receive exactly the same total income as the so-called lower half. The distribution between them would have to be represented by some point (such as *E*) on this 45° line. (Remember, the scales on the two axes are the same.)

a. In fact, incomes are not equally distributed. On this diagram, then, the point indicating the distribution between the two halves must lie (**to the right of and below / to the left of and above**) the 45° line.

Suppose that total income received by both halves is *0H*, divided between an upper-half total of *0G* and a lower-half total of *GH*. A 45° line is drawn from point *H* extending up to the other 45° line. Point *E* is where the two lines meet.

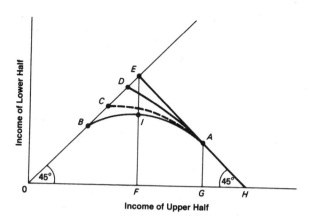

Figure 19-7

On *EH*, point *A* is chosen such that *AG* is equal to *GH*.

Now we have things sorted out as they should be. *OG* (measured horizontally) is the upper-half income total; *AG* (measured vertically) is the lower-half total. Point *A* indicates the distribution of income between the two halves. Any movement toward greater equality of income distribution would mean a move away from *A* (**toward / and also away from**) *E*. Suppose there is such a movement, with absolutely no disincentive, or leaky-bucket, effect. That is, suppose that the population's entire income total is (**reduced / not reduced at all**). On the diagram, this redistribution movement will follow the straight line *EH* from *A* toward *E*.

b. It is usually argued that any movement directed toward greater equality of income distribution would have at least some disincentive consequences. Suppose this redistribution is tackled by means of heavier progressive income taxation. The extra taxes thus collected from higher income people would be passed on to lower income groups. Insofar as people try to avoid heavier taxation by working shorter hours or in other ways earning less money income, the total of real GDP would (**fall / rise**). The path of redistribution will no longer run along the straight line *EH*. Starting at *A*, it will drift (**above / below**) *EH*. The total of real income will become (**less / more**) than it was at point *A*. The more sweeping the intended income redistribution, the (**less / more**) pronounced this disincentive effect is likely to be.

c. The three curved lines in Figure 19-8, *DA*, *CA*, and *BA*, show three possible sets of disincentive consequences. Among them, the smallest disincentive effect is indicated by (**DA / CA / BA**).

Notice that line *CA* is approximately flat in the region close to point *C*. This means that if redistribution toward complete equality were pressed hard enough, the resulting drop in total GDP would be sufficient for the real income of the lower half, in absolute terms, to

(**increase only slightly / not increase at all / decrease**). In relative terms, though, the share of the lower half would (**still increase / remain constant / decrease**).

9. a. List the following welfare-transfer programs in the order of their importance in the federal budget of 1998: Medicare; Medicaid; social security; unemployment compensation, food stamps and child nutrition; housing (Table 19-5 in the text).

   (1) _____
   (2) _____
   (3) _____
   (4) _____
   (5) _____
   (6) _____

   b. The total amount budgeted for these programs in 1998 was $___ billion. This is a large amount of money, but it should be noted that only $___ billion (___ percent of the total budget) is spent on programs designed to benefit the poor directly, with $___ billion devoted to all income security programs.

10. Consider a welfare system organized around the following rules of qualification:

   1. Basic welfare support is $4000; 50 cents is deducted from that amount for every dollar earned up to $8000.
   2. $3000 in food stamps is available for $1000, provided outside earnings do not exceed $2500.
   3. $2500 in housing subsidy is granted, but that amount is reduced by 50 cents for every dollar earned over $2000.
   4. $1000 per child in supplemental income is available to families with dependent children and outside incomes that do not exceed $3999.

   Fill in the blanks of Table 19-5 to reflect the benefits received by each of four different families according to these rules. Assume that each family takes advantage of all four programs to the fullest extent possible (not, in reality, a good assumption).

   Family A has one child and no private outside income.
   Family B has no children and a private income of $2000.
   Family C has two children and an outside income of $2500.
   Family D has two children and an outside income of $4000.

TABLE 19-5

	Family A	Family B	Family C	Family D
1. Basic Welfare	—	—	—	—
2. Food stamps	—	—	—	—
3. Housing subsidy	—	—	—	—
4. AFDC	—	—	—	—
5. Outside income	—	—	—	—
6. Total	—	—	—	—
7. Marginal tax rates:				
Last dollar earned	—	—	—	—
Next dollar earned	—	—	—	—

C. Health Care: The Problem that Won't Go Away

11. Recalling that public goods are enjoyed by everyone, consider the two demand curves for some public good G represented in the two panels of Figure 19-8.

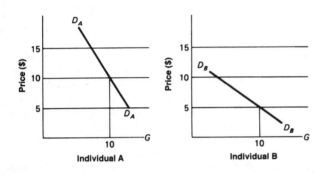

Figure 19-8

If 10 units of G were offered, then the two people represented here would *together* be willing to pay $___, consisting of $___ from individual A and $___ from individual B. This suggests that each person should (**necessarily pay an equal proportion / pay according to the marginal benefit that he or she would receive as indicated by the individual demand curves / pay according to how much he or she earns in income and how much property he or she owns**).

12. The health care system in the United States has been the subject of much controversy in the past several years.

    a. Although the quality of health care in the United States is very high for many people, approximately (**5 percent / 15 percent / 25 percent**) are without insurance coverage and hence must pay extremely high prices for care.

    b. Health care costs rose from (**2 percent / 4 percent / 10 percent**) of GDP in 1940 to (**15 percent / 24 percent / 35 percent**) of GDP in 1999. Three principal reasons for this tremendous increase are cited. These are:

        (1) _____

        (2) _____

        (3) _____

    c. Because of the existence of market failures in the health care delivery system, there may be a role for government in its provision. Three main types of market failure are most prevalent; write definitions for these below.

        (1) Asymmetrical information (AI):

        _____

        _____

        (2) Adverse selection (AS):

        _____

        _____

        (3) Moral hazard (MH):

        _____

        _____

    d. For each of the scenarios below, determine the source of the market failure (AI, AS, or MH).

        ___ (1) An individual applying for health insurance knows that he has a history of stomach ulcers but withholds this information from the insurance company.

        ___ (2) An individual goes in for a routine checkup and is informed that she needs a root canal. She cannot decide what to do, because she is not sure that she really needs the surgery.

        ___ (3) A 25 year-old male, after retiring from a career in minor league baseball, decides not to purchase health insurance because he believes that his probability of illness or injury is small.

        ___ (4) An individual purchases health insurance and then pursues her life's dream, to become a race car driver.

VIII. DISCUSSION QUESTIONS

Answer the following questions, making sure that you can explain the work you did to arrive at the answers.

1. Carefully distinguish between *income* and *wealth*. What different notions of well-being do these quantities embody? How does inequality in the distribution of income compare with inequality in the distribution of wealth?

2. Table 19-1 in your text, reproduced here as Table 19-6, shows the income distribution in the United States for 1995. What are the three most important observations that you can make about these data?

TABLE 19-6

(1) Income Class of Households	(2) Income Range	(3) Percentage of All Households in This Class	(4) Percentage of Total Income Received in This Class
Lowest fifth	Under $12,664	20.0	3.8
Second fifth	$12,664-$24,229	20.0	9.4
Third fifth	$24,300-$37,999	20.0	15.8
Fourth fifth	$38,000-$58,199	20.0	24.2
Highest fifth	$58,200 and over	20.0	46.8
Top 5 percent	$99,372 and over	5.0	18.6

Source: U.S. *Bureau of the Census, Money Income of Households, Families, and Persons in the United States:* 1992, Current Population Report, Series P60, No. 184, September 1993.

3. Figure 19-2(*a*) from your text, reproduced here as Figure 19-9, shows Lorenz curves for several different countries. It is apparent that the United States has decidedly greater income inequality than several other developed coun-

tries. Why is this? List and explain two possible explanations for this outcome.

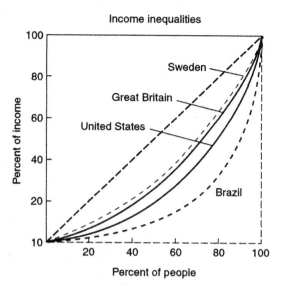

Figure 19-9

4. What does Table 19-4 from your text, reproduced here as Table 19-7, tell you about the incidence of poverty among different population groups in the United States? What might be some causes of these differentials?

TABLE 19-7.

Poverty in Major Groups, 1992

Population Group	Percent of Group in Poverty
Total population	14.5
By racial group:	
White	11.6
Black	33.3
Hispanic	29.3
Other	17.0
By age:	
Under 18 years	21.9
18 to 64 years	11.7
65 years and over	12.9
By type of family:	
Married couple	7.5
Female householder, no spouse present	38.5
Unrelated subfamilies	54.8
By education:	
No high school diploma	25.6
High school diploma, no college	10.4
Some college	7.0
Bachelor's degree or more	3.0

Source: U.S. Bureau of the Census, *Poverty Status in the United States: 1992, Current Population Repo,"* Series P-60, No. 185, September 1993.

5. Review the trends of income inequality in the United States in this century. How might a negative income tax be used to reverse the recent rising trend of income inequality?
6. Ed states: 'The answer to the problem of skyrocketing health care costs is simple! The government needs to impose a set of price controls that will, by definition, hold costs down." Do you agree with Ed?
7. Explain the difference between public goods and private goods. Why does the government step in to provide public goods, in many cases?
8. Review the alternative health care reform strategies: pure markets, nationalized health service, and managed care. Based upon this limited information on the alternatives, which plan would you favor? Why?
9. End-of-chapter question 8 in your text describes a health care rationing system that would focus on those medical treatments that show the greatest increase in the number of "disability adjusted life years" per dollar of expenditure. Carefully explain this system and relate it to firm and consumer optimization problems. Why does health care have to be rationed at all?

IX. ANSWERS TO STUDY GUIDE QUESTIONS

III. Review of Key Concepts

5	Personal income
10	Disposable income
17	Wealth
8	Distribution of income
3	Lorenz curve
12	Subsistence cost
11	Poverty line
1	Income-possibility curve
14	Welfare state
2	Negative income tax
6	Earned income tax credit
4	Public goods
15	Private goods
9	Adverse selection
18	Moral hazard
16	Non-price rationing
13	Coinsurance
7	Managed care

VI. Multiple Choice Questions

1. B   2. D   3. C   4. C   5. A   6. B
7. C   8. E   9. D   10. B   11. D   12. C
13. E   14. D   15. E   16. A   17. D   18. A
19. D   20. A   21. B   22. B   23. E   24. B
25. C   26. E

VII. Problem Solving

1. a. Table row: 5.5, 11, 18, 27.25, 38, 51, 65.5, 81.75
    b. See Figure 19-4.

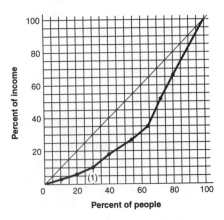

Figure 19-4

    c. bulge closer to the lower right-hand corner, be drawn nearer to the 45° diagonal
2. Table rows:
    Taxes paid = $.40, $.60, $.80, $1.00, $1.20, $1.40, $1.60, $1.80, $2.00
    Income after taxes = $1.60, $2.40, $3.20, $4.00, $4.80, $5.60, $6.40, $7.20, $8.00,
    Income after taxes and payment = $2.60, $3.40, $4.20, $5.00, $5.80, $6.60, $7.40, $8.20, $9.00
    Percent of total income = 8.1, 14.4, 22.2, 31.5, 42.2, 54.4, 68.1, 83.3
    The Lorenz curve should be closer to the 45° line, indicating a more equal distribution of income.

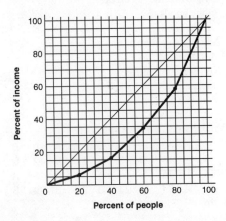

Figure 19-5

3. a. 3
    b. 1
    c. 1
    d. 1
    e. 2
    f. 2
4. a.
    b. (1) SC
        (2) SF
        (3) MF
        (4) MF
        (5) SC or MC, depending upon your perspective.
        (6) SF
5. a minimum-subsistence income, 3, one-third, $15,569
6. a. second, 36.5, first, 39.3
    b. 400 percent, $2000, $8000
    c. remained roughly the same, 4 percent, done little to the Lorenz curve, no significant trend toward greater equality, total income has risen
7. Ability, education, occupation, work effort, property ownership, inheritance, and discrimination are all possible sources.
8. a. to the right of and below, toward, not reduced at all
    b. fall, below, less, more
    c. *DA*, not increase at all, still increase
    d. increase, decrease
9. a. (1) Social Security
        (2) Medicare
        (3) Medicaid
        (4) food stamps and child nutrition
        (5) housing
        (6) unemployment insurance
    b. $804.4, $277.9, 15.5, $911.1
10. See Table 19-5.

TABLE 19-5

	Family A	Family B	Family C	Family D
Basic welfare	$4,000	$3,000	$2,750	$2,000
Food stamps	2,000	2,000	2,000	0
Housing sub.	2,500	2,500	2,250	1,500
AFDC	1,000	0	2,000	0
Outside income	0	2,000	2,500	4,000
Total	9,500	9,500	11,500	7,500
Marginal tax rates:				
Last dollar earned	NA	50%	100%	200,100%
Next dollar earned	50%	100%	200,100%	100%

11. $15, $10, $5, pay according to the marginal benefit that he or she would receive as indicated by the individual demand curves.
12. a. 15 percent
    b. 4 percent, 15 percent
        (1) high income elasticities for demanders
        (2) technological advances in medical care
        (3) insulation of consumers from prices

c.   (1) Parties participating in the health care system must depend on doctors for information, which only the doctors fully understand in most cases.

(2) Faced with premium fees that are most often based on average costs of insuring health, low-risk individuals may choose not to purchase insurance.

(3) Occurs when insurance reduces the incentives for individuals to avoid risk and expense through prudent behavior.

d.   (1) AI

(2) AI

(3) AS

(4) MH

VIII. Discussion Questions

1.   *Income* refers to total receipts or cash earned by a person or household. *Wealth* is a broader term that includes the dollar value of financial and other tangible assets, less any money owed to creditors. These terms incorporate very different notions of economic well-being. Wealth indicates an accumulation of personal property that often comes from the sale of factors that are particularly lucrative or that comes from luck or inheritance. The distribution of wealth in the United States is far more unequal than the distribution of income. In fact, 33 percent of the wealth is owned by 1 percent of the population.

2.   The top fifth of the income distribution claims over 15 times the income of the bottom fifth. The lowest fifth of the income distribution claims a very small share of the total income earned.

3.   The United States has a much more unequal distribution of income than many other developed countries. The United States government has limited the extent of redistribution via taxes and transfers. Access to education and training has not been equal for all.

4.   Minority populations in the United States experience higher rates of poverty. Some causes of these differentials might relate to discriminatory practices in education and in hiring.

5.   Inequality in the distribution of income decreased in the United States between 1930 and 1975. However, between 1975 and 1992, inequality in fact increased. A negative income tax could be used if individuals living in poverty received a tax rebate rather than a tax bill. This might reverse the recent trend by redistributing income from the rich to the poor.

6.   This might not be a wise idea. Price controls lead to excess demand in markets. With prices held artificially below equilibrium levels, there exists no mechanism that will eliminate excess demand; hence, health services will have to be rationed using some mechanism other than the invisible hand.

7.   Private goods have no external costs or benefits. Public goods have benefits that are indivisibly spread among the entire community, whether or not individuals choose to purchase the public good. The government tends to provide public goods. Since it is difficult to exclude people from consuming the good once it is available, producers have no incentive to produce it.

8.   Pure markets require each family to pay 100 percent of all health care bills, with no government support of programs for the elderly or the poor. Nationalized health services provide health care to all on an equal basis. Managed competition uses government regulatory power to place constraints on the free operation of the price system. All of these programs have costs and benefits.

9.   This type of rationing system is based on a "triage" system developed to maximize efficiency in the use of scarce resources available to treat wounded soldiers during wartime. The idea is that resources are directed toward those who are most likely to survive. Health care must be rationed in any case because there are limited wants but unlimited resources. This method would employ a cost-benefit approach to resource allocation.

CHAPTER 20

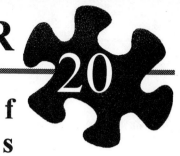

Overview of Macroeconomics

I. CHAPTER OVERVIEW

The study of macroeconomics is the study of the "big picture." It is the study of how entire economies make decisions about using resources. It ponders the sources of growth, inflation, unemployment, and business cycles. It ponders the ability of governments to help (or hinder) their economies by manipulating a wide variety of policy instruments. It asks why some policies work and why some fail.

Applied macroeconomists who study the impact of economic policy on the economy as a whole have found that certain policy objectives, and the instruments used to achieve them, may at times be incompatible. While a particular policy objective may be admirable when considered at face value, strenuous pursuit of that policy may be damaging to other objectives of arguably equal importance. For example, policies which produce low unemployment rates may also generate increased inflation.

Once you complete your work on this overview, you will not have many answers. You will, instead, have collected a multitude of questions whose answers will be addressed over the course of the next 16 chapters. Your work on this list of questions will not, however, be an exercise in futility. In noting the significance and the context of each question, you will build a strong foundation which can support your acquisition of greater macroeconomic knowledge.

II. LEARNING OBJECTIVES

After you have read Chapter 20 in your text and completed the exercises in this *Study Guide* chapter, you should be able to:

1. Explain the difference between microeconomics and macroeconomics.
2. Identify the major goals of macroeconomic policy.
3. Identify the major macroeconomic policy instruments used to achieve these goals.
4. Understand some of the major economic events and the related governmental policies that influenced the United States during this century.
5. Appreciate the contribution of John Maynard

Keynes to the development of governmental macroeconomic policy.
6. Recognize the potential for tradeoffs between two or more policy objectives (e.g., price stability versus high employment, rapid growth versus high current consumption, etc.).
7. Understand how **policy instruments** and **exogenous variables** affect **induced** (or endogenous) **variables**.
8. Appreciate the importance of the international economy and a nation's connection to it.
9. Develop the fundamentals of aggregate supply, aggregate demand, and macroeconomic equilibrium.
10. Use aggregate supply and aggregate demand analysis to illustrate how *policy instruments* and *external variables* can influence either the demand or the supply side of the macroeconomy.

Note to Students *As you begin the macro section of the text there are many new terms and concepts to learn. A little extra time and effort on your part to learn them now will pay off later!*

III. REVIEW OF KEY CONCEPTS

Match the following terms from column A with their definitions in column B.

A	B
__ Employment Act of 1946	1. A sudden change in conditions of cost or productivity that shifts **aggregate supply** sharply.
__ Business cycle	2. Total quantity of goods and services that the nation's businesses are willing to produce and sell in a given period.
__ Fiscal policy	3. Short term decline in an economy's real output.
__ Monetary policy	4. Monitors the cost of a fixed basket of goods and services bought by the typical urban consumer.

253

__ Incomes policies

__ Gross domestic product (GDP)

__ Nominal

__ Real

__ Potential GDP

__ GDP gap

__ Unemployment rate

__ Consumer Price Index

__ Net exports

__ Trade policies

__ Aggregate supply

__ Aggregate demand

__ International financial management

__ Supply shock

__ Recession

__ Inflation

5. Numerical value of the difference between the value of exports and imports.

6. Percent of the labor force that is unemployed.

7. Pattern of expansion and contraction of economic activity.

8. The central bank's management of the nation's money, credit, and banking system to affect macroeconomic activity.

9. Rate of growth or decline of the price level from one year to the next.

10. Governmental policies used to control wages and prices.

11. Total amount that different sectors of the economy willingly spend on goods and services in a given period.

12. Maximum level of output that is also compatible with stable prices.

13. Measurements at current market prices.

14. Manner in which a country establishes the price of its own currency in terms of the currency of other nations.

15. With this, the federal government declared its responsibility to promote maximum employment, production, and purchasing power.

16. Use of government expenditure and taxes to affect macroeconomic variables.

17. The difference between potential and actual GDP.

18. Measurements at constant market prices.

19. Tariffs, quotas, and other regulations that restrict or encourage imports and exports.

20. Market value of all final goods and services produced in a country during a year.

IV. SUMMARY AND CHAPTER OUTLINE

This section summarizes the key concepts from the chapter.

A. Key Concepts of Macroeconomics

1. **Macroeconomics** is the study of the behavior of the economy *as a whole*. It examines the overall level of a nation's output, employment, and prices. **Microeconomics**, on the other hand, studies *individual* prices, quantities, and markets.

2. As a result of the Great Depression, many economists and policymakers alike recognized that the government had to be more involved in stabilizing the nation's economic health. *The General Theory of Employment Interest and Money*, written by John Maynard Keynes, revolutionized macroeconomics. Keynes pointed out that (a) market economies may not, by themselves, be able to achieve a position of full employment and economic prosperity, but could instead be stuck in a position of high unemployment and underutilized production capacity; and (b) the government could use **fiscal** and **monetary policies** to reduce unemployment and shorten economic downturns.

3. In broad terms, a healthy economy is characterized as one with a high and steady level of economic growth, a high level of employment and low *un*employment, and stable (or gently rising) prices. In an attempt to achieve these objectives, most governments use a combination of **fiscal** and **monetary policy**. **Incomes policies** are used less frequently to control wages and prices in an economy.

4. Economic growth is subject to erratic upturns and downturns referred to as **business cycles**. The government uses its **policy instruments** to lessen these swings in economic activity and strives to keep GDP at or close to its potential.

5. The labor force is divided into two groups: those individuals who are working and those who are seeking work. The **unemployment rate** measures the percent of the labor force that is seeking work. Individuals who are neither working nor seeking work are not in the labor force. These individuals include young children, full-time students, retirees, and full-time household caregivers. These individuals are *not* counted by economists as being unemployed, because they are not seeking employment. Individuals who would like to work full-time but are currently stuck in part-time jobs are counted as employed.

6. Stable prices are a critically important component of economic health. Rapid price changes distort the economic decisions of both companies and individuals. The most common measure of the overall price level is the **consumer price index (CPI)**.

7. Our economy is tied very closely with the rest of the world through trade and finance. Political leaders and central bankers around the globe increasingly attempt to coordinate their macroeconomic policies, for a nation's fiscal and monetary policies can spill over to affect its neighbors.

B. Aggregate Supply and Demand

1. A nation's **aggregate supply (AS)** depends on the price level that businesses can charge, as well as the economy's

capacity or potential output. **Potential output** (or **GDP**) is itself determined by the availability of productive inputs and the managerial and technical efficiency with which those inputs are combined.

2. **Aggregate demand (AD)** refers to the total amount that different sectors in the economy willingly spend on goods and services in a given period. Aggregate demand is the sum of spending by consumers, businesses, and governments. *AD* is influenced by the level of prices, as well as monetary policy, fiscal policy, and other factors.

3. The interaction of the downward-sloping **aggregate demand schedule** and the upward-sloping **aggregate supply schedule** determines the total output of the economy. National output and the price level settle at that level where demanders willingly buy what businesses willingly sell. The resulting output and price level determine employment, unemployment, and net exports.

4. The *AS* and *AD* schedules can be used to analyze some of the major economic events that have influenced the U.S. economy this century: (a) the economic expansion during the Vietnam war, (b) the stagflation caused by the supply shocks of the 1970s, (c) the deep recession caused by the monetary contraction of the 1980s, and (d) the phenomenal record of economic growth for this century.

5. The major task of macroeconomic policy is to diagnose the condition of the economy and to prescribe the right medicine. For sure, there is not always agreement among economists or even among fiscal and monetary policymakers in the administration as to what should be done. Nevertheless, the influence of government policy on economic activity can be very large.

V. HELPFUL HINTS

1. When calculating the **unemployment rate** make sure that you include only those individuals who are *actively looking for work*. Remember, the **labor force** includes the unemployed and those who are working in the marketplace.

2. Economic growth is *always* measured in **real** or inflation-adjusted terms. If nominal GDP increases from one year to the next by 8 percent, and if inflation during that year also increases by 8 percent, then there has been *no* growth in the economy. Prices have simply increased by 8 percent, and that is why (nominal) GDP is 8 percent higher than it was the year before. There is no such thing as **nominal** economic **growth**!

3. In order to make comparisons in GDP over time, or across countries, *real* numbers should be used. (Economists love to measure data in real terms.)

4. Economic growth is often measured in percentage terms. Percentage changes are fairly easy to calculate. Any percentage change is simply the change in some variable, divided by some base or initial value, multiplied by 100. For

example, if you have two apples and you give one to a friend, we could say that your holding of apples has been reduced by 50 percent. The change is 1, and the base value is 2; we multiplied by 100 to get 50 (percent). It is that simple. In footnote number 2 in this chapter of your text, Samuelson and Nordhaus use the following expression to calculate the rate of inflation in the CPI:

$$\text{Rate of inflation of consumer prices} = \frac{\text{CPI (this year)} - \text{CPI (last year)}}{\text{CPI (last year)}} \times 100$$

This expression is clearly recognizable as a *percentage change*.

5. The warning from the text on *AS* and *AD* curves is worth repeating. Do not confuse the macroeconomic *AD* or *AS* curves with the microeconomic demand and supply curves. In *micro*, the demand and supply curves show the quantities and prices of commodities in *individual markets*, with such things as national income and other goods' prices held constant. In *macro*, however, the *aggregate* supply and *aggregate* demand curves show the determination of *total* output and the *overall* price level, with such things as the money supply, fiscal policy, and the capital stock held constant. The two sets of curves have a family resemblance, but they explain very different phenomena.

6. When analyzing *AS* and *AD* diagrams, watch for movements *along* the curves as compared to *shifts* in the curves. If the price level changes, the curves will *not* shift. Remember, since the price level is measured along the vertical axis, changes in it can be explained by movements along the curves—this was how the two schedules were constructed in the first place. If any other relevant variable changes (e.g., fiscal policy, monetary policy, or even the weather), then (at least) one of the curves will shift. Review the appendix to Chapter 1 if you need to work on this concept.

7. Like the production-possibility frontier, the aggregate supply and aggregate demand diagram is a model of the economy. We make some simplifying assumptions and hold other variables constant in order to better understand and explain some economic issue.

8. As you continue your study of *macro*economics, relate these new concepts back to issues of scarcity and the production-possibility frontier presented in Chapter 1. Note, too, the relationship to such *micro*economic issues as businesses, markets, and individuals.

VI. MULTIPLE CHOICE QUESTIONS

These questions are organized by topic from the chapter outline. Choose the best answer from the options available.

A. Key Concepts of Macroeconomics

1. The study of macroeconomics includes, among other topics, which of the following?
   a. the sources of inflation, unemployment, and growth.
   b. the microeconomic foundations of aggregate behavior.
   c. the reasons why some economies succeed and some fail.
   d. policies that can be enacted to improve the likelihood of success in achieving macroeconomic objectives.
   e. all the above.

2. The practice of directing government policy to support the macroeconomic health of the United States was initiated formally in:
   a. the Humphrey-Hawkins Act of 1978.
   b. the Tax Reform Act of 1986.
   c. the Full Employment and Balanced Growth Act of 1946.
   d. Balanced Budget Act of 1985.
   e. none of the above.

3. The objective of stable prices can, in the view of at least some economists, be tackled by adjustments in:
   a. fiscal policy.
   b. monetary policy.
   c. incomes policies.
   d. all the above.
   e. none of the above.

4. The main difference between nominal and real GDP is that:
   a. real GDP is adjusted for price changes while nominal is not.
   b. nominal GDP is adjusted for price changes while real is not.
   c. nominal GDP is better for comparing output across several years.
   d. real GDP increases more during periods of inflation.
   e. Keynes argued that nominal GDP was calculated incorrectly during the Great Depression.

5. The main difference between a recession and a depression is that:
   a. depressions usually precede recessions.
   b. unemployment is higher and lasts longer during a depression.
   c. recessions tend to be caused by inappropriate fiscal policy, while depressions are usually caused by poor monetary policy.
   d. recessions are considered part of the business cycle, while depressions are not.
   e. economic forecasters do a better job of predicting depressions.

6. If *potential GDP* is greater than *actual GDP* then:
   a. exports must be greater than imports.
   b. inflation has increased from the year before.
   c. there is probably some unemployment in the economy.
   d. comparisons should be made in *nominal* terms.
   e. *both* **a** and **b**.

7. Policies directed at stimulating exports can influence:
   a. the domestic employment picture.
   b. price stability.
   c. the growth of actual GDP relative to potential GDP.
   d. the foreign trade balance.
   e. all of the above.

8. John Maynard Keynes is probably *best* remembered for his:
   a. marriage to a Russian ballerina.
   b. shrewd investments on behalf of King's College.
   c. advice to the British treasury.
   d. collection of modern art and rare books.
   e. new way of looking at macroeconomics and macroeconomic policy.

9. Which of the following pairs of objectives seems to be mutually contradictory?
   a. low inflation and low unemployment.
   b. low unemployment and high rates of growth in actual GDP.
   c. high rates of growth in actual GDP and balance in foreign trade.
   d. price stability and balance in foreign trade.
   e. price stability and rapid growth in potential GDP.

10. Unemployment, inflation, and the rate of growth of actual GDP are all examples of:
    a. policy variables.
    b. external variables.
    c. international variables.
    d. variables determined by the economy.
    e. none of the above.

11. Which of the following is a determinant of potential output in the long run?
    a. taxes.
    b. money.
    c. technology.
    d. capital investment.
    e. *both* **c** and **d**.

B. Aggregate Supply and Demand

12. The aggregate supply curve is positively sloped in the short run because of:
    a. increasing costs of production.
    b. decreasing returns to scale.
    c. output prices generally rising more quickly than input prices.
    d. the potential for high unemployment.
    e. none of the above.

13. In a macroeconomic model of the economy, which of the following is most likely to be considered as an exogenous variable?

a. Foreign exports to the United States.
b. Domestic exports.
c. Interest rates.
d. Taxes.
e. Monetary policy.

14. In a macroeconomic model of the economy, which of the following is most likely to be considered as an induced variable?
a. Supply shocks.
b. Foreign exports.
c. Population growth.
d. World War II.
e. National output.

15. The short-run effect of increased defense spending that is not accommodated by increased taxation could be:
a. higher prices and higher GDP.
b. higher prices and lower GDP.
c. lower prices and lower GDP.
d. lower prices and higher GDP.
e. lower prices and the same GDP.

16. If the AD schedule had shifted to the right in order to accommodate the OPEC oil shock, then:

a. both prices and GDP would have remained stable.
b. output would have remained the same, albeit with higher prices.
c. output would have increased and prices decreased.
d. domestic oil prices would have fallen.
e. none of the above.

17. The effect of the orchestrated increase in interest rates in the United States in the early 1980s can be best illustrated in an AS-AD graph by:
a. a shift left in the AS curve.
b. a shift right in the AS curve.
c. a shift left in the AD curve.
d. a shift right in the AD curve.
e. no shift in either the AD or the AS curve.

18. 1973 has been referred to as the "year of the seven plagues" because:
a. of the repeated cover-ups of the Watergate break-in.
b. of numerous antiwar protests around the country.
c. severe supply shocks and turmoil in markets that disrupted the world economy.
d. the return of the seven plagues to Egypt.
e. none of the above.

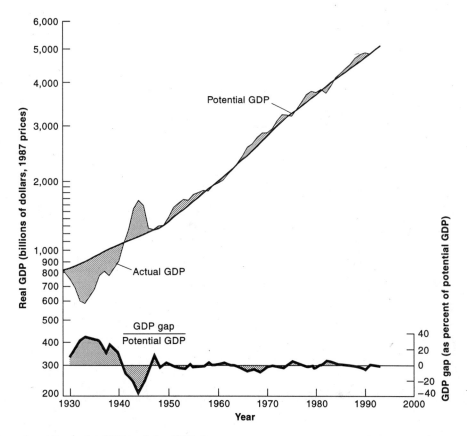

Figure 20-1 Actual and Potential GDP and the GDP Gap

VII. PROBLEM SOLVING

The following problems are designed to help you apply the concepts that you learned in the chapter.

A. Key Concepts of Macroeconomics

1. Output is usually measured in terms of gross domestic product, its most comprehensive yardstick. Figure 20-2 from the text is reproduced here as Figure 20-1 (see page 249). Use it to answer parts **e, f, g,** and **h** of this question.

   a. GDP is the (**market / discounted / stable**) value of all goods and services produced during any given year.

   b. When measured at current prices, this measure is termed (**nominal / real / potential**) GDP.

   c. When measured after correcting for inflation, it is termed (**nominal / real / potential**) GDP.

   d. When measured in terms of maximum sustainable output, it is termed (**nominal / real / potential**) GDP.

   e. During the late 1970s, periods of high inflation caused real GDP to (**match potential GDP / exceed nominal GDP / fall short of nominal GDP**).

   f. Periods of high unemployment during the early 1980s caused nominal GDP to (**exceed potential GDP / fall short of potential GDP / fall short of real GDP**) .

   g. During what time period was the GDP gap largest?

   ____

   Historically, what occurred during this time period?

   h. When the GDP gap as a percent of GDP is negative, what can you say about the relationship between *actual* and *potential* GDP?

   Historically, what occurred during this (these) time period (s)?

2. Price stability, as a goal of macroeconomic policy, does not mean absolute stability of all prices. Absolute stability would eliminate the natural role of changes in relative prices in allocating goods and services. Figure 20-4 from the text is reproduced here as Figure 20-2. Use it to answer parts **c, d, e,** and **f** of this question.

   a. Price stability is, instead, an objective stated in terms of a price index like the CPI that (**ignores price movements across goods and services / averages price movements across goods and services / includes only price increases across goods and services**) .

   b. Inflation, then, is measured as (**the rate of change in the index / the absolute value of the price index / the absolute price levels of a representative number of goods**).

   c. In what year was inflation the highest? ____.

   d. In the last 25 years, inflation peaked in the (**mid-1970s and early 1980s / mid-1980s and early 1990s / mid-1970s and mid-1980s**).

   e. How would you explain the dramatic fall in prices during the first years depicted in Figure 20-2?

   f. Between 1929 and 1988, the average rate of inflation measured by the CPI was about (**8.7 / 1.2 / 3.4**) percent.

3. The policy tools available to the policymaker are varied. They fall under three general rubrics: fiscal policy (FP), monetary policy (MP), and incomes policy (IP). Match each of the following more specific policies with its general classification by recording the appropriate abbreviation in the space provided:

   a. A change in federal income tax rates. ____

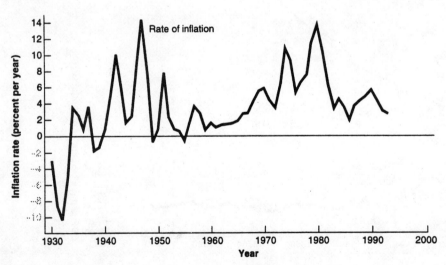

Figure 20-2 The Rising Trend of Consumer Price Inflation, 1929-1994

b. An increase in the money supply. ___

c. A tax penalty on high wage settlements. ___

d. An increase in defense spending. ___

e. The elimination of the interest rate deduction against taxable income. ___

f. A change in the rate of interest that banks pay when *they* borrow money. ___

g. A presidential order limiting the price increase that manufacturers can charge for newly produced goods.

___

4. Which of the following are policy instruments (PI), and which are external variables (EV) that may shock the economy from beyond its boundaries? Identify each by recording the appropriate abbreviation in the space provided:

a. Money supply ___

b. Wars ___

c. Expanding grain sales to the Soviet Union ___

d. Government spending ___

e. Sunspots ___

f. Population growth ___

g. Import tariffs ___

h. Tax deductions ___

i. Changes in the weather ___

j. Public employment programs ___

k. OPEC oil embargo ___

5. Suppose the population of the country is 200 million people. Suppose further that there are 96 million people working at jobs in the marketplace and there are 4 million people looking for work.

a. How large is the labor force? ___

b. What is the unemployment rate? ___

c. For each of the statements below determine what will happen to the *labor force* and the *unemployment rate*.

1. A student graduates from college and starts to search for a job.

The labor force will (**increase / decrease / remain the same**), and the unemployment rate will (**go up / go down / remain unchanged**).

2. A student graduates from college and is immediately hired by her mother's business.

The labor force will (**increase / decrease / remain the same**), and the unemployment rate will (**go up / go down / remain unchanged**).

3. Jane Jones quits her job and starts looking for a better one.

The labor force will (**increase / decrease / remain the same**), and the unemployment rate will (**go up / go down / remain unchanged**).

4. John Jones quits his job to spend more time with his kids.

The labor force will (**increase / decrease / remain the same**), and the unemployment rate will (**go up / go down / remain unchanged**).

5. Sam Smith is unhappy at his current job. He starts looking for a new job but does not quit his current job.

The labor force will (**increase / decrease / remain the same**), and the unemployment rate will (**go up / go down / remain unchanged**).

6. Question 8 at the end of the chapter ("Discussion Questions") mentions a price index known as the *GDP deflator*. This price index is similar to the *CPI* in that it is an overall measure of inflation or price increases in the country. One of the key differences between the two indexes is that the *CPI* includes a sample of typical *consumer goods and services* while the *GDP deflator* includes *all* goods and services produced in the economy. (There are some other differences, too, but we can postpone a discussion of those until we have a more detailed discussion about inflation in Chapter 30.)

One year is chosen as the base year for the price index. In the base year the price index has a value of 100. Since prices generally rise over time, the price index will usually be less than 100 in years prior to the base year and greater than 100 in years after the base year.

To calculate real GDP from nominal GDP we would divide by the price index, or GDP deflator, and then multiply by 100. Or we can write:

$$\text{Real GDP} = \frac{\text{nominal GDP}}{\text{GDP deflator}} \times 100$$

Similarly, nominal GDP could be calculated from real GDP with the following formula:

$$\text{Nominal GDP} = \frac{\text{real GDP} \times \text{GDP deflator}}{100}$$

Table 20-1 includes hypothetical numbers for GDP in five different years.

TABLE 20-1

Year	Nominal GDP	Real GDP	GDP Deflator	Percent Change In Real GDP
1	___	3690	84	------
2	3800	___	91	___
3	4000	___	100	___
4	4240	___	106	___
5	___	4800	110	___

a. Calculate real GDP in years 2, 3, and 4.

b. Calculate nominal GDP in years 1 and 5.

c. Explain the relationship between nominal and real GDP in year 3.

d. Calculate the percentage change in real GDP from year to year.

e. According to your calculations, which year was the best? Explain.

f.   Explain the growth rate in GDP from year 3 to year 4.

g.   According to your calculations, which year was the worst? Explain.

h.   Can you think of a historical example in the United States when the GDP deflator actually decreased from one year to the next? (*Hint*: Look back at Figure 20-2.)

B. Aggregate Supply and Demand

7.   Figure 20-3 uses aggregate supply and demand to illustrate four possible reactions to changes in the macroeconomic environment. In each panel, *AD* and *AS* represent initial positions of aggregate demand and aggregate supply, respectively In panels (*a*) and (*b*), *AS'* represents a new position for the aggregate supply curve; in panels (*c*) and (*d*), *AD'* represents a new position for aggregate demand.

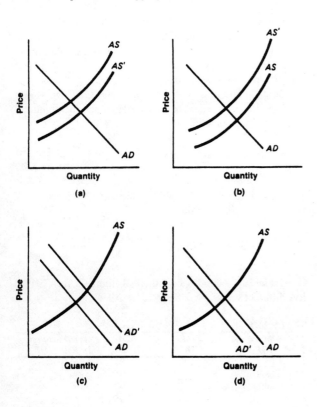

Figure 20-3

Table 20-2 lists six possible changes in the macroeconomic environment.

a.   Use column 2 to identify which panel in Figure 20-3 best illustrates each change.

b.   Use columns 3 and 4 to indicate the direction of the change in price and output. Use a "+" sign for increases and a "-" sign for decreases.

TABLE 20-2 Changes In the Macroeconomic Environment

(1) Condition	(2) Panel	(3) Price	(4) Output
1. Increase in defense spending	___	___	___
2. Weather-related crop failure	___	___	___
3. Large cut in personal taxes	___	___	___
4. Increase in interest rates	___	___	___
5. Reduction in government taxation of inputs	___	___	___
6. Reduction in money supply by the central bank	___	___	___

8.   Suppose that Figure 20-4 illustrates the effect of a sudden negative energy shock.

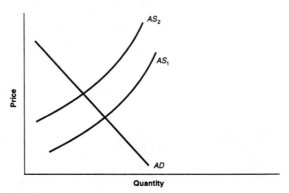

Figure 20-4

a.   *AD* would represent the preshock aggregate demand curve, (*AS$_1$* / *AS$_2$*) would represent the preshock aggregate supply curve, and (*AS$_1$* / *AS$_2$*) would represent the postshock aggregate supply curve.

b.   (**An increase / A decrease / No change**) in aggregate demand would be required in the short run to accommodate the shock and keep output at its preshock level.

c.   As a result of the change in **b**, (**prices / output**) would be even (**smaller / greater**) than after the initial energy shock.

VIII. DISCUSSION QUESTIONS

Answer the following questions, making sure that you can explain the work you did to arrive at the answers.

1.` Briefly explain Keynes's main contribution to macroeconomics.

2.   In what ways did the Employment Act of 1946 indicate a change in federal government policy?

3.   Describe the primary policy instruments that the government uses to influence the economy. Indicate which part or branch of the government controls each instrument.

4.   What is meant by a "tight money" policy? What effect did this policy have on the United States from 1979 to 1982?

5. How should the United States respond if a major oil price shock were to occur today? Describe how the policy instruments that are used may be incompatible.

IX. ANSWERS TO STUDY GUIDE QUESTIONS

III. Review of Key Concepts

15	Employment Act of 1946
7	Business cycle
16	Fiscal policy
8	Monetary policy
10	Incomes policies
20	Gross domestic product (GDP)
13	Nominal
18	Real
12	Potential GDP
17	GDP gap
6	Unemployment rate
4	Consumer Price Index
5	Net exports
19	Trade policies
2	Aggregate supply
11	Aggregate demand
14	Exchange-market management
1	Supply shock
3	Recession
9	Inflation

VI. Multiple Choice Questions

1. E   2. C   3. D   4. A   5. B   6. C
7. E   8. E   9. A   10. D   11. E   12. C
13. B   14. E   15. A   16. B   17. C   18. C

VII. Problem Solving

1.
   a. market
   b. nominal
   c. real
   d. potential
   e. fall short of nominal GDP
   f. fall short of potential GDP
   g. 1930s, the Great Depression
   h. actual GDP exceeds potential GDP, World War II and the Vietnam war
2.
   a. averages price movements across goods and services
   b. the rate of change in the index
   c. 1947
   d. mid-1970s and early 1980s
   e. The dramatic fall in prices accompanied the decline in output and widespread unemployment during the Great Depression.

f. 3.4
3.
   a. FP
   b. MP
   c. IP
   d. FP
   e. FP
   f. MP
   g. IP
4.
   a. PI
   b. EV
   c. PI
   d. PI
   e. EV
   f. EV
   g. PI
   h. PI
   i. EN
   j. PI
   k. EV
5.
   a. 100 million
   b. $(4/100) \times 100 = 4$ percent
   c. 1. increase, go up
      2. increase, go down
      3. remain the same, go up
      4. decrease, go up
      5. remain the same, remain unchanged
6.
   a. $(3800/91) \times 100 = 4175.82$, 4000, $(4240/106) \times 100 = 4000.00$
   b. $(3690 \times 91)/100 = 3099.60$, $(4800 \times 110)/100 = 5280.00$
   c. Year 3 is the base year since the GDP deflator equals 100. In that year nominal and real GDP will be the same.
   d. $[(4175.82 - 3690.00)/3690] \times 100 = 13.17$
      $[(4000.00 - 4175.82)/4175.82] \times 100 = -4.21$
      $[(4000.00 - 4000.00)/4000] \times 100 = 0$
      $[(4800.00 - 4000.00)/4000] \times 100 = 20$
   e. Year 5 was the best in terms of real GDP growth. From looking at the numbers for the GDP deflator, it also appears that year 5 had the smallest increase in inflation.
   f. From year 3 to year 4, real GDP was unchanged so there was no growth.
   g. Year 3 was the worst since real GDP fell. The economy was in a recession. To make matters worse, inflation increased by $(9/91) \times 100 = 9.89$ percent, more than any other year.
   h. If prices fall from one year to the next, the GDP deflator will fall. This happened during the Great Depression.

7.

TABLE 20-2 Changes in the Macroeconomic Environment

(1) Condition	(2) Panel	(3) Price	(4) Output
1. Increase in defense spending	c	+	+
2. Weather-related crop failure	b	+	-
3. Large cut in personal taxes	c	+	+
4. Increase in interest rates	d	-	-
5. Reduction in government taxation of inputs	a	-	+
6. Reduction in money supply by the central bank	d	-	-

8.   a. AS_1, AS_2
     b.   An increase
     c.   prices, greater

VIII. Discussion Questions

1.   In 1936, Keynes challenged the current views on economic theory and policy. He argued for a much wider role of the government in fighting the Depression and establishing economic policy.

2.   For the first time the federal government affirmed its role in promoting economic growth, full employment, and price stability.

3.   The two main policy instruments of the government are monetary policy and fiscal policy. Monetary policy is controlled by the Federal Reserve System, and fiscal policy is determined by the executive and legislative branches of the government. Monetary policy relies primarily on changes in interest rates and the money supply, while fiscal policy refers to government spending and taxes.

4.   A "tight money" policy occurs when the Federal Reserve reduces the growth rate of the money supply. In 1979, the Fed was very concerned about the high rate of inflation in the United States. The tight money policy which it pursued slowed the economy down and reduced inflation, but it also contributed to the subsequent recession.

5.   As a result of the oil-price shock, prices will increase and output will fall. If the government tries to limit the price increases with tight monetary policy or restrictive fiscal policy, it will make the output and unemployment problem worse. If, instead, the government tries to maintain employment and output, prices will go even higher. Ideally, the government could enact some sort of supply-side change to shift the aggregate supply curve back to the right.

CHAPTER 21

Measuring Economic Activity

I. CHAPTER OVERVIEW

This important chapter must be approached carefully and patiently. You will, however, discover that there is really only one basic idea being presented here. It is surrounded by complication, to be sure, but the point of this chapter is singular: *The accounting procedure with which a nation measures its total output in any one year simply adds up the market value of all the goods and services that it produces.* Every nation uses its limited stock of labor, machines, and materials to produce commodities and services.

There are many difficulties associated with computing the output for an entire nation. Your job is not to do the counting. Your job, instead, is to understand the rules that govern the counting. Having completed your work in this chapter, you will have achieved the objectives listed below. Without this achievement, you will find it very difficult to understand what economists mean when they talk about growth, unemployment, and inflation.

II. LEARNING OBJECTIVES

After you have read Chapter 21 in your text and completed the exercises in this *Study Guide* chapter, you should be able to:

1. Describe what **gross domestic product (GDP)** is and why it is so important to have an accurate measurement of the nation's output.

2. Define the **flow-of-product** approach and the **earnings** or **cost** approach to computing GDP.

3. Understand **intermediate products** and the **value-added** approach to computing GDP.

4. Explain how focusing on either final product in the product approach or value added in the earnings approach helps statisticians avoid **double counting** in the computation of GDP.

5. Explain the difference between **nominal** and **real** GDP, paying close attention to the role of the GDP deflator.

6. Divide GDP into its major component parts in the flow-of-product approach: consumption (C), gross private domestic investment (I), government purchases of goods and services (G), and net exports (X) . That is, explain why:

$$GDP = C + I + G + X.$$

7. Understand the differences between **gross domestic** product, **net domestic** product, and **gross national** product.

8. Understand the process by which GDP is related to the **disposable income** of households.

9. Argue why, in general, total gross national investment (I_T) must equal the sum of all private saving (S^P), and government surplus (S^G).

10. Understand what GDP does and does not measure, and appreciate why economists have begun developing "augmented national accounts."

11. Distinguish between the three different price indexes, the CPI, the GDP deflator, and the PPI, and understand how they are used to adjust for inflation.

III. REVIEW OF KEY CONCEPTS

Match the following terms from column A with their definitions in column B.

A	B
__ Final product	1. Gross investment minus capital depreciation.
__ Real GDP	2. Exports minus imports of goods and services.
__ Nominal GDP	3. Household income minus personal taxes.
__ GDP deflator	4. The difference between a firm's sales and its purchases of materials and services from other firms.
__ Intermediate good	5. Adjusts for rapid shifts in relative prices by changing the base period for constructing prices and quantities more quickly.
__ Value added	6. Good or service that is produced and sold for consumption or investment.

263

__ Net exports

__ Net domestic
product

__ Government
transfer payments

__ Disposable
income

__ Gross national
investment

__ Net investment

__ National income

__ Chain weights

__ Consumer Price
Index

__ Producer Price
Index

7.   GDP evaluated at the actual market prices of the current year.

8.   Government payments to individuals that are not made in exchange for goods and services.

9.   Gross domestic investment plus net foreign investment.

10. Good used to produce other goods.

11. Measures the cost of buying a standard basket of consumer goods and services at different time periods.

12. GDP minus capital depreciation.

13. Price index used to convert nominal GDP to real GDP.

14. GDP evaluated at a set of constant prices.

15. Based on approximately 3400 commodity prices and measures the level of prices at the wholesale or producer stage.

16. Total factor incomes received by labor, capital, and land.

IV. SUMMARY AND CHAPTER OUTLINE

This section summarizes the key concepts from the chapter.

1.   The gross domestic product (or **GDP**) is the most comprehensive measure of a nation's total output of goods and services. It enables the President, the Congress, and the Federal Reserve to judge whether the economy is contracting or expanding, whether the economy needs a boost or should be reined in a bit, and whether a severe recession or inflation threatens. Without measures of economic aggregates like GDP, policymakers would be adrift in a sea of unorganized data. In addition, macroeconomic theory would be impossible to understand without GDP and other indicators of national output.

2.   There are two different ways of measuring GDP: a **flow-of-product** approach and an **earnings or cost** approach. In a world of perfectly precise measurement, these two methods would arrive at the exact same number for GDP. In reality, the two approaches provide a useful check for one another.

3.   In the **flow-of-product** approach, GDP is measured by how much is spent on products (or goods and services) in the economy. In the macroeconomy there are four main areas of spending:

   a.   purchases by households or consumers (C)
   b.   investment spending by businesses (I)
   c.   purchases of goods and services by the government

(G)

   d.   *net* exports, which is the difference between the value of our exports to other countries and the value of the products that we import from abroad (X)

The inclusion of *net* exports in GDP may seem a little confusing. If foreigners purchase some of the goods and services that are produced in this country, we would want to include that spending in our calculation of GDP. However, if some of our spending is used to purchase products that were produced in other countries, we need to subtract that figure from GDP since it does not reflect production at home.

4.   The **earnings or cost** approach is used to calculate GDP by summing up all the costs of doing business. These costs include the wages paid to labor, the rents paid to land, and the profits paid to capital. Since households ultimately provide the land and the money used to acquire capital, these business costs also represent the earnings that households receive. When we include the wearing out of capital equipment (**depreciation**) and the influence of the government (i.e., **taxes** and **transfer payments**), the analysis becomes somewhat more complicated, but the basic thrust of the analysis remains the same: *the total dollar value of all spending must equal the total value of all earnings.*

5.   GDP is measured as the total production of *final* goods and services during a year. A *final product* is one that is sold for consumption purposes or is an investment good. The point here is that the product is not changed or modified and sold again to someone else. The product has reached its final stage and is now being used either as a consumption good or a piece of capital equipment. When a car manufacturer orders glass from a glass company to use in its automobiles, the glass is considered an *intermediate good* The value of this glass should *not* be measured as part of GDP, because when the car (i.e., the final product) is sold, the purchase price will include the value of the glass. If we counted the glass when the car manufacturer purchased it, we would have counted the glass twice. This is the *double-counting problem* that GDP statisticians try to avoid.

To adjust for this problem in the *earnings or cost* approach, statisticians measure only the *value added* by businesses at each stage of production. The value added is calculated as the difference between a firm's sales and its purchases of materials and services from other firms.

6.   When we evaluate the nation's current output at current market prices, we measure *nominal GDP*. This is equivalent to multiplying output by price, for all units of every commodity that is produced, and then adding all these numbers up. So, nominal GDP is a huge sum of prices times quantities (PQ). Therefore, if nominal GDP changes from one year to the next it could be due to a change in P, or Q, or both. Since we are very interested in the growth of the economy over time, we need to know which component(s) of GDP is (are) changing.

Suppose, for example, that prices increase from one year to the next, and output decreases such that the result of multiplying P times Q remains exactly the same. Nominal GDP will be unchanged, and looking only at GDP, it will appear as if the economy is in the same spot it was a year ago. In fact, this economy has a couple of new problems. Prices are higher, so there is an increase in inflation. Output is lower, so there is probably an increase in unemployment, too. When both inflation and unemployment increase together, economists refer to this situation as **stagflation**. (The economy slows down or *stagnates* at the same time that prices increase.)

In order to accurately assess the **real** growth of the economy over time, we need to measure output with a constant set of prices. One year is chosen as the base year and then every year's output is evaluated in terms of the prices in the base year. (The base year that the United States uses to calculate real GDP is 1987.) Finally, if we divide nominal GDP by real GDP (and multiply by 100), we get the overall price index which we call the **GDP deflator**.

$$\frac{\text{Nominal GDP}}{\text{Real GDP}} =$$

$$\frac{(\text{current } P \text{ times current } Q)}{(\text{base year } P \text{ times current } Q)} = \text{GDP deflator}$$

7.   Until a few years ago (1991), the United States relied primarily on gross *national* product, rather than GDP, as its primary measure of output. GNP focuses on the ownership of resources, while GDP is concerned with where the production takes place. For example, Fords produced in Britain with U.S.-owned capital would be included in U.S. GNP but excluded from U.S. GDP. For a nation like the United States, which owns a great number of production facilities abroad but also has a large number of foreign firms producing goods and services within its domestic economy, the two measures are nearly identical. There are two main reasons for making the switch. First, most other countries were already using GDP as their measure of aggregate output, so changing to GDP made it somewhat easier to make comparisons with other countries. Second, GDP probably gives us a more reliable picture of the health of the domestic economy, which is critically important in setting macroeconomic policy.

8.   The relationship between savings and investment in an economy is important. Consider first a simple economy with no government, no foreign sector, and no business savings. In the *earnings or cost approach*, GDP equals *total* household income. Households spend most of their income (C), but some household income is saved (S) as well. In the *flow-of-product* approach to GDP, total spending in the economy consists of household consumption spending (C) and investment spending by firms (I). Therefore, we can calculate GDP in either of the two following ways:

$$\text{Earnings or cost GDP} = \text{total household incom} = C + S$$
$$\text{Flow-of-product GDP} = C + I$$

The linkage between S and I should be apparent; and there is a logical explanation for the relationship between these two variables. When households save, they are sending a signal to the market economy. Households are saying to producers, "We are not interested in purchasing goods and services today. We are putting some of our income aside so that we will have more to spend in the future." On the other hand, when firms invest, they are using some of their (scarce) resources to acquire or build capital equipment. They produce fewer goods and services today so that they will have greater production capabilities in the future—just at the time consumers want them if all goes well. It should also be pointed out that firms usually finance their investment projects by borrowing the funds from the credit market. The primary source of funds flowing into the credit market is household *savings*.

In a sense, savings can be viewed as a *leakage* from the economy—it represents money which is not spent directly by the household. If we consider consumption spending as the primary source of spending in the economy, investment spending by firms can be considered as a supplement or *injection* which adds to total spending. In our circular-flow analysis, all leakages should match all injections.

In an expanded economy which includes foreign trade and the government, we should include net exports (X) as another injection of spending, and the government surplus (S^G), if there is any, as a leakage. In the case where private savings (S^P) includes both personal saving and business saving, an injection-leakage identity can be written as:

$$I + X = S^P + S^G$$

9.   The essence of *investment* in all its various forms is that it is production for future benefit. A newly finished machine tool yields no direct consumer satisfaction whatsoever. It is built to yield future benefit; it is expected to contribute to consumer-goods production in the future, throughout its coming 5-year or 10-year life. A *new* house counts within the investment category in a similar way; it is expected to contribute to consumer satisfaction over a long number of years.

A manufacturer's additional inventory at the end of the year must receive the same treatment. Suppose a shirt company made $1000 worth of shirts in 1994 which it did not sell in that year. The shirts it did sell count as part of consumption. The shirts it made but did not sell must also go into GDP (because they were made in 1994), but because they weren't sold they do not go into consumption. They are included in investment because they will be consumed in the future, presumably *next* year.

This inventory rule works both ways. Had the shirt company's beginning inventory been $4000 and its closing inventory $3000, then we would include a figure of *minus* $1000 within *investment*.

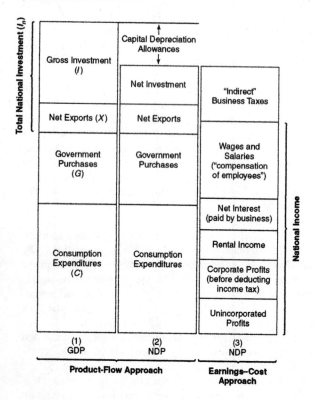

Figure 21-1

10. Figure 21-1 can be used to review the basics of national income accounting and illustrate the equivalence of the *flow-of-product* and *earnings or cost* approaches. The flow-of-product approach is illustrated in columns 1 and 2 as the sum of government purchases (*G*), consumption expenditures (*C*), net exports (*X*), and investment (*I*). The difference between GDP and NDP is clearly shown as depreciation. Total national investment (investment plus net exports) appears at the top of both—*gross* in column 1 and *net of depreciation* in column 2. The third column depicts the earnings or cost approach to the same accounting problem. Note that there are essentially five fundamental categories represented there:
  a. Wages and salaries
  b. Interest earned (by people lending money to firms)
  c. Rentals and other property income (paid to people who supply property)
  d. Corporate and unincorporated profits
  e. Indirect business taxes (levied on businesses)
The profits noted in item **d** above are, by definition, the

difference between the value of outputs and the cost of inputs. They are, in other words, the residual values that guarantee that the earnings or cost approach generates the same result as the flow-of-product approach.

11. GDP is at best an accurate measure of a nation's output. It is not, nor is it intended to be, a measure of overall well-being or satisfaction. Economists have begun developing "augmented national accounts" that include estimates of the *underground economy* and subtract the costs of pollution.

12. Inflation is measured as a rate of change in a price index from one period (e.g., 1 year) to the next. If P_1 represents the price index recorded in year 1 and P_2 represents the index recorded in year 2, then inflation between years 1 and 2 would be:

$$\frac{P_2 - P_1}{P_1} \times 100\%$$

When an economy experiences inflation it does not necessarily mean that *all* prices have increased. Rather, inflation indicates an increase in the *general* level of prices and costs.

13. Different price indexes are used to measure inflation in the economy. One commonly quoted price index, based on the prices of the things that a typical consumer buys, is the *Consumer Price Index* (CPI). It is based on the cost of a market basket of goods and services computed across 364 classes of commodities. The weights given to the categories in the CPI represent the share of income devoted to purchases in the indicated category observed in a survey conducted between 1982 and 1984.

A second widely used price index is the *Producer Price Index* (PPI). It is based on the wholesale prices of approximately 3400 products.

The GDP deflator, discussed above, can be viewed as a price index for all the components of GDP. Since the GDP deflator is based on current output, the weights, in essence, change every year. This makes the GDP deflator somewhat more difficult to calculate. The weights used in both the CPI and PPI are based on previous years, so the only current information needed to calculate these indexes are current prices. To calculate the GDP deflator data are needed on both current output and prices.

V. HELPFUL HINTS

1. In macroeconomics, the term *simple economy* is usually used to describe an economy with just a household and a business sector. Once the model is developed for this narrowly defined economy, it can then be expanded to include the government and international trade.

2. *Investment* is another one of those terms that has special meaning to economists (and to students of economics). Investment spending is undertaken by firms to acquire or

build new capital equipment and buildings which then add to the firms' productive capability in the future. Investment, to an economist, is *not* money. Investments represent additions to the (physical) stock of durable capital goods.

3. Capital goods, like everything else, wear out or *depreciate* over time. Consequently, a portion of each year's investment is used to replace worn out plant and equipment. This replacement of "used up" capital does not really add to economic growth—it helps prevent the economy from slipping backward but does not push the economy forward. Ideally, *net domestic product (NDP)* which equals *GDP minus depreciation*, would give a better picture of the nation's economic health. However, depreciation is difficult to measure, so GDP is the universally accepted measure of output.

4. The linkage between savings and investment is very important. The additional linkage between investment and economic growth is also very important. Look for this in the chapters that follow.

5. Be careful to distinguish between government spending on goods and services and government *transfer payments*. The G in C + I + G + X includes the government's purchases of final goods and services (medicines for V.A. hospitals, books for schools, airplanes for the Air Force) . It does not (and should not) include transfer payments like veterans' benefits and social security payments. These transfer payments are a very large part of the government's budget but should not be included in the *flow-of-product* calculation of GDP. Note that these transfer payments would be shown as a flow from government to households, *not* to firms. The government's budget includes *both* what it spends for goods and services and the transfer payments that it makes to its citizens.

6. In the national income accounts the term *capital consumption allowance* is often used for *depreciation*. The two terms mean the same thing and thus are interchangeable.

7. Taxes that are paid out of income include personal and corporate income taxes. These are *direct taxes*. Other taxes that firms collect, and then send to the government, like sales taxes and excise taxes, are considered as *indirect taxes*.

8. Take another look at Figure 21-4, "From GDP to National Income to Disposable Income," in your text. It should be clear that the numbers in the first bar of the chart (GDP) are calculated from the *product approach* and that the second bar (NI) is found using the *earnings or cost approach*.

9. Price indexes suffer from two main deficiencies. They do not, for one thing, take quality changes in account. Better products that cost more would cause any price index to rise. This should not be measured as inflation. Second, price indexes with fixed weights fail to reflect the consumer's substitution out of more expensive items and into cheaper products as prices rise. This pattern of behavior diminishes the impact of product-specific inflation.

10. Remember, economic growth is *always* measured in real

terms. There is no way to make meaningful comparisons between years if price changes are not controlled for. Stay away from people who talk about nominal growth.

VI. MULTIPLE CHOICE QUESTIONS

These questions are organized by topic from the chapter outline. Choose the best answer from the options available.

1. The *flow-of-product* and *earnings or cost* approaches to GDP:
   a. measure two different aspects of GDP and are therefore unrelated to each other.
   b. are two different ways of measuring the same thing.
   c. should both arrive at the same number if GDP is measured in real terms, but not if GDP is measured nominally.
   d. have nothing to do with the circular-flow diagram.
   e. none of the above.

2. The double-counting problem refers to:
   a. the inclusion of both intermediate and final products in the calculation of GDP.
   b. the nominally higher value for GDP when prices double.
   c. the equivalence of the *flow-of-product* and *earnings or cost* approaches.
   d. the problems caused by using value-added measures in the lower loop.
   e. all the above.

3. There would be double counting in the computation of GDP if statisticians were to sum the:
   a. net value added by the iron-mining industry and the net value added by the steel manufacturing industry.
   b. net increase in inventories of flour mills and the net increase in inventories of bakeries.
   c. total output of iron ore and the total output of iron.
   d. value added by bakers and the value of flour mills.
   e. total of consumer services purchased and the total of investment goods produced.

4. To compute a firm's contribution to GDP on a value added basis, the value at market price of the goods that it has produced must be diminished by:
   a. all indirect business taxes paid.
   b. any undistributed profits.
   c. depreciation.
   d. all sales to other business firms.
   e. none of the above.

5. Economic growth is always measured in real terms because:
   a. output changes from year to year.
   b. the *flow-of-product* approach does not always yield the same figure as the *earnings or cost* approach.
   c. the differences in nominal GDP from year to year

are too large.

   d. the price level changes from year to year.

   e. all the above.

6. In GDP statistics, investment includes:

   a. any product produced for the government during the year in question.

   b. any purchase of common stock issued during the year in question.

   c. any increase in the amount of year-end inventories over inventories held at the beginning of the year in question.

   d. any commodity bought by a consumer but not fully consumed by the end of the year in question.

   e. none of these items.

7. In GDP statistics, a negative gross investment figure:

   a. could never occur.

   b. could appear if the total of depreciation on buildings and equipment was sufficiently large.

   c. would automatically occur if there was no production of buildings or equipment during the year.

   d. could be caused by a sufficiently large reduction in inventories during the year.

   e. would mean that the economy had produced more than it had consumed.

8. In NDP statistics, a negative investment figure:

   a. could never occur.

   b. could appear if the total of depreciation on buildings and equipment was sufficiently large.

   c. would automatically occur if there was no production of buildings or equipment during the year.

   d. could be caused by a sufficiently large increase in inventories during the year.

   e. would mean that the economy had produced more than it had consumed.

9. In GDP statistics, the value of housing services, in which the houses are occupied by their owners, is:

   a. not counted, since property services are not considered production.

   b. not counted, since such property services are included in the value of the house itself.

   c. not counted in GDP, but it does appear in NDP using an arbitrary estimate of rental value.

   d. counted in GDP using an arbitrary estimate of rental value.

   e. counted in NDP, but not in GDP.

10. One of the five items listed below is *not* in the same class as the other four for purposes of national income accounting. Which one?

   a. corporation income (or profits).

   b. government transfer payments.

   c. net interest payments by business.

   d. rental income.

   e. wages and salaries.

11. If you want to compute disposable personal income from NDP, then one thing you must *not* do is:

   a. deduct depreciation.

   b. add government transfer payments.

   c. deduct indirect business taxes.

   d. deduct social security levies.

   e. deduct undistributed corporation profits.

12. In computing the size of the government spending component of GDP, all government:

   a. expenditures on commodities and services are counted.

   b. expenditures on commodities are counted; those on services are not.

   c. expenditures on final commodities and services are counted as well as all government transfer payments.

   d. transfer payments are counted, but not expenditures on commodities or services.

   e. none of the above is correct.

13. The term *national income (NI)* as used in the national product and national income statistics means:

   a. NDP plus all taxes that are not considered taxes paid out of income—i.e., NDP plus indirect business taxes.

   b. NDP minus all taxes that are considered taxes paid out of income, such as the personal and corporation income taxes.

   c. NDP plus all taxes that are considered taxes paid out of income, such as the personal and corporation income taxes.

   d. NDP minus all taxes that are not considered taxes paid out of income—i.e., NDP minus indirect business taxes.

   e. none of the above.

14. If nominal GDP was $360 (billion) in 1992 and if the price level rose by 20 percent from 1990 to 1992, then the 1992 GDP, measured in 1990 prices, was (in billions):

   a. $300.

   b. $320.

   c. $340.

   d. $360.

   e. $432.

15. In computing the national income and national product accounts, it would be incorrect to add together which of the following two items?

   a. consumption expenditures and personal saving.

   b. net investment and consumption expenditures.

   c. corporate profits and net interest paid by business.

   d. government purchases and consumption expenditures.

   e. government purchases and wages and salaries.

16. Statisticians use chain weights:

   a. to connect the weights of products together.

   b. when constructing price indexes for the metal industries.

   c. when nominal GDP is increasing faster than real

GDP.

    d.   when real GDP is increasing faster than nominal GDP.

    e.   when relative prices of products are shifting rapidly.

17. The consumer price index is in part based upon the share of income devoted to which of the following major categories?

    a.   shelter.

    b.   food.

    c.   medical expenses.

    d.   transportation expenses.

    e.   all of the above.

18. Inflation measured in terms of annual changes in the CPI using a single year's spending weights might overestimate the impact of inflation on individual purchasing power because it:

    a.   ignores the likely substitution out of relatively expensive categories.

    b.   ignores the depressing effect of world prices on American goods.

    c.   ignores the effects of unemployment on aggregate demand.

    d.   inaccurately includes the price effects of improved production technology.

    e.   does all of the above.

19. The 1983 price index for the medical care component of the CPI was 357. It must therefore be true that the 1983 value of the CPI:

    a.   must have been greater than 357.

    b.   must have been less than 357.

    c.   must have been exactly equal to 357.

    d.   could have been anything because medical expenses are really not included in the CPI.

    e.   was none of the above.

VII. PROBLEM SOLVING

The following problems are designed to help you apply the concepts that you learned in the chapter.

1. Suppose, in a simple economy, that national output consists of only two commodities: X, a consumer good, and Y, a capital good (some form of machine or tool needed in production). In 1994, just 500 units of X were produced and sold to consumers at a price of $2 each. Twenty units of Y were produced and sold to business firms, at a price of $10 each.

    a.   The total output for 1994 was (**$500 / $800 / $1000 / $1200 / $1500 / $2000**).

The figure computed above is the *gross* domestic product. To produce this total output, however, the nation's existing stock of capital goods must have been, to some extent, used up or worn out; that is to say, the capital stock must have depreciated. Suppose that the nation began the year

with a stock of 100 Y machines (assuming, for simplicity, that there is just one kind of capital good involved). By the year's end, a few of these machines, the oldest, will have become completely worn out, and all the others will have moved just a little closer to the scrap heap.

Suppose, now, that the best possible estimate of this depreciation for 1994 is $50. There is no cash expenditure in a depreciation figure; it is just an estimate of the extent of "wearing out" during the year. With the price of a new Y machine being $10, it is *as though* five Y machines, brand new at the year's beginning, had been completely worn out by the year's end in the production of the national product for 1994.

The gross domestic product figure of $1200 included the value of the 20 new Y machines produced. But in making these machines and also in making the 500 units of consumer good X, the *equivalent* of five new Y machines were totally used up.

    b.   The available capital stock had not, therefore, *grown* by 20 machines by year's end; it had, instead, increased by only (**5 / 10 / 15**) machines.

    c.   With "gross" meaning "no allowance for depreciation" and "net" meaning "after allowance for depreciation," this nation's gross domestic product (GDP) for 1994 was $1200, and its net domestic product (NDP) was (**$1000 / $1050 / $1100 / $1150 / $1200**).

There are certain distinctions that are made among the goods that comprise either GDP or NDP. The most basic of these distinctions is the division between (a) goods that were produced to be consumed during the year in question and (b) goods that were produced during the year not to be consumed but to be added to the existing stock of capital. This is precisely the difference noted above, with X representing a consumption good and Y representing an investment good.

The *consumption* goods total is the same figure in both GDP and NDP. The *investment* goods figure in GDP is gross investment: total production of new capital goods without depreciation allowance. The investment figure in NDP is net investment: value of new capital goods produced after a deduction for depreciation.

    d.   In the example above, the GDP of $1200 would divide between consumption of (**$200 / $800 / $1000 / $1150 / $1200**) and gross investment of (**$0 / $100 / $150 / $200 / $250 / $300**).

    e.   The NDP of $1150 would divide between consumption of (**$200 / $800 / $1000 / $1200 / $1500**) and net investment of (**$0 / $100 / $150 / $200 / $250 / $300**).

2. Government statisticians use *value-added* measurements when using the cost or earnings approach to GDP. Table 21-1 shows the (hypothetical) steps and costs involved in producing a ton of steel. In our simplified example, the miner purchases no intermediate products or goods. We can assume that the miner's family has owned the iron ore mine for years and that the miner works the mine and trucks the

ore away. We are also assuming that all the relevant costs of production are included in the table below.

TABLE 21-1

Stage of Production	(1) Sales Receipts		Cost of Intermediate Materials		(3) Value Added
1. Miner	$4	-	$0	=	$4
2. Iron manufacturer	9	-	___	=	___
3. Steel manufacturer	16	-	___	=	___
4. Steel retailer	20	-	___	=	___

a. Fill in columns (2) and (3) in the table.

b. Which firm adds the most value to the final product? ___

c. What is the total of all sales receipts? ___

d. What is the total of all the value addeds? ___

e. Which figure belongs in GDP? ___ Briefly explain why.

f. Compare the steel retailer's sales receipts with the sum of the value addeds. Explain the relationship between these two numbers.

3. The country of Easyliving produces just three goods: apples, T-shirts, and bicycles. The prices of each good and the outputs for three years are listed in Table 21-2.

TABLE 21-2

Product	Year 1 P_1	Year 1 Q_1	Year 2 P_2	Year 2 Q_2	Year 3 P_3	Year 3 Q_3
Apples	$1	50	$3	60	$4	70
T-shirts	6	100	8	140	7	160
Bicycles	80	90	100	100	90	110

a. Calculate nominal GDP for each year.
   1. nominal $GDP_1 =$
   2. nominal $GDP_2 =$
   3. nominal $GDP_3 =$

b. Assume that the first year is used as the base year. Calculate real GDP for each year.
   1. real $GDP_1 =$
   2. real $GDP_2 =$
   3. real $GDP_3 =$

c. Calculate the value of the GDP deflator for each year.
   1. GDP deflator$_1 =$
   2. GDP deflator$_2 =$
   3. GDP deflator$_3 =$

d. Measure the rate of inflation from:
   1. year 1 to year 2.
   2. year 2 to year 3.

(**Hint**: These are percentage changes in the GDP deflator.)

e. By how much did the economy of Easyliving grow from:

1. year 1 to year 2?
2. year 2 to year 3?

(**Remember**: Economic growth is always measured in real terms.)

f. Suppose year 2 is used as the base year instead of year 1. Recompute your figures for real GDP, the GDP deflator, and the change in inflation.

real $GDP_1 =$ ____ GDP deflator$_1 =$ ____

real $GDP_2 =$ ____ GDP deflator$_2 =$ ____ % change = ____

real $GDP_3 =$ ____ GDP deflator$_3 =$ ____ % change = ____

(**Note**: The percentage changes in inflation should be comparable to part **d** above!)

4. A nation's GDP was $260 billion in 1980 and $325 billion in 1990. Both figures were computed as usual in terms of market prices for the year involved. The price index rose from 100 in 1980 to 130 in 1990.

a. Real output (**increased / decreased**) from 1980 through 1990.

b. In terms of 1990 prices, the 1980 GDP would be $___.

c. In terms of 1980 prices, the 1990 GDP would be $___.

d. The overall rate of inflation during the ten years is about ___.

5. A firm's income statement begins with the value of its sales for a given period. Say, for example, that a given firm's 1994 sales amount to $800. All costs incurred in making and selling these goods are then listed: depreciation, wages, interest paid, rents paid. Suppose depreciation was $25 and the other three items summed to $650. Profit could then be computed as the revenue that remains after deducting all such costs.

a. In this instance, profit would be (**$0 / $25 / $50 / $75 / $100 / $125 / $150**).

b. The initial sales figure of $800 would be this firm's contribution to the flow-of-product computation of GDP. Deduct depreciation, and its NDP contribution would be (**$700 / $725 / $750 / $775**).

c. Its earnings or cost figure would meanwhile equal the total of wages, interest paid, rent paid, and profit: (**$700 / $725 / $750 / $775**). This earnings or cost figure would therefore be (**less than / equal to / greater than**) the (net) flow-of-product figure.

d. Profit is the residual item which makes things come out even. Had our firm paid out wages, interest, and rents totaling $775, its profit (allowing for depreciation) would have been (**$0 / $25 / $50 / $70 / $100**). The earnings or cost figure would (**still / no longer**) be $775, so it would (**still / no longer**) match the (net) product flow estimate.

6. Suppose that a house built in the first half of 1994 is sold as a rental property for $90,000 in the same year. Let total rental income for the 6 months be $6000, and estimate $600 of depreciation for this same period. In the 1994 statistics, the proper entries for this house would be:

    a. gross investment of (**$0 / $600 / $6000 / $89,400 / $90,000**),

    b. net investment of (**$0 / $600 / $6000 / $89,400 / $90,000**), and

    c. consumption expenditures of (**$0 / $600 / $6000 / $89,400 / $90,000**).

    The construction and use of this house would therefore appear in the 1994 GDP and NDP statistics as follows:

    d. GDP (**$89,400 / $90,000 / $95,400 / $96,000**);

    e. NDP (**$89,400 / $90,000 / $95,400 / $96,000**).

7. Table 21-3 includes data for the economy of Simple economy. These figures are complete—there are no government or foreign sectors.

    a. The difference, in year 1, between 110 consumer goods produced and 90 consumer goods consumed is explained by (**an increase / a decrease**) in inventories on hand at the (**beginning / end**) of the year.

TABLE 21-3

	Year 1	Year 2
New buildings produced	5	5
New equipment produced	10	10
Consumer goods produced	110	90
Consumer goods consumed	90	110
Estimated depreciation on existing buildings during year	10	10
Estimated depreciation on existing equipment during year	10	10
Inventories of consumer goods at beginning of year	30	50
Inventories of consumer goods at close of year	50	30

TABLE 21-4

	Year 1	Year 2
Gross domestic product	(1) ___	(7) ___
Breakup of GDP into:		
Consumption	(2) ___	(8) ___
Gross investment	(3) ___	(9) ___
Net domestic product	(4) ___	(10) ___
Breakup of NDP into:		
Consumption	(5) ___	(11) ___
Net investment	(6) ___	(12) ___

    b. The difference, in year 2, between 90 consumer goods produced and 110 consumer goods consumed is explained by (**an increase / a decrease**) in inventories on hand at the (**beginning / end**) of the year.

    c. Complete Table 21-4 for the years 1 and 2.

    d. A negative *net* investment figure (**could / could not**) appear in the national product statistics if *total depreciation* exceeded the total value of new buildings and equipment produced. A negative *gross* investment figure (**could / could not**) appear if the value of *inventory* reduction exceeded the total value of new buildings and equipment produced.

8. Columns (1) and (2) in Table 21-5 record hypothetical price indexes for the five major categories in the CPI for two successive years. Columns (3) and (4) indicate the proportions of income allocated to the five categories in the two years. The information in columns (3) and (4) are used to weight the relative importance of the various categories.

    a. Based upon the CPI formula using year 1 weights, the price index for year 1 would be _____ .

    b. Again based upon the CPI formula using year 1 weights, the price index for year 2 would be _____ .

    c. On the basis of this calculation, the rate of inflation would be calculated as _____ %.

    Now suppose that the year 2 price index is computed on the basis of year 2 weights.

    d. The index would then equal _____ , with the resulting inflation rate (**rising / falling**) to _____ %.

    e. If year 2 weights were used to compute the index for year 1, then the year 1 index would equal _____ , and the inflation rate would instead equal _____ %.

    The point of this exercise is not that one index is correct and others are wrong. It is, instead, that the selection of weights can be critical in the computation of inflation.

    f. However, on the basis of the substitution that occurred, it can be said that the computation that used year 1 weights for both years probably (**overestimated / underestimated / correctly estimated**) the effect of inflation on the real well-being of the population.

TABLE 21-5

	Underlying Price Indexes		Underlying Income Shares	
	(1)	(2)	(3)	(4)
Category	Year 1	Year 2	Year 1 (%)	Year 2 (%)
Food	100	110	20	20
Clothing	100	150	20	5
Fuel	100	100	20	35
Medical	100	110	20	15
Transport	100	105	20	25

VIII. DISCUSSION QUESTIONS

Answer the following questions, making sure that you can explain the work you did to arrive at the answers.

1. Explain, in your own words, why measuring GDP in real terms is important.

2. Explain the use of value-added measurements in the earnings or cost approach to GDP.

3. Explain the linkage between savings and investment in an economy.

4. Figures 21-2 and 21-3 from the text are reproduced here

(also as Figures 21-2 and 21-3).

a. What has happened to the ratio of net investment to GDP since the late 1970s?

b. What can you say about the growth in (real!) GDP since the late 1970s?

c. What could possibly account for the change in the ratio of net investment to GDP?

d. Does this have any implications for the economy's future growth?

5. Briefly explain the difference between GDP and GNP. Why did the United States switch to the use of GDP as its main measurement value for the macroeconomy?

6. Briefly explain why GDP may not be a good measure of overall well-being or happiness.

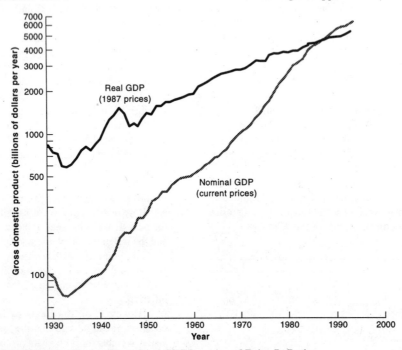

Figure 21-2 Nominal GDP Grows Faster Than Real GDP because of Price Inflation

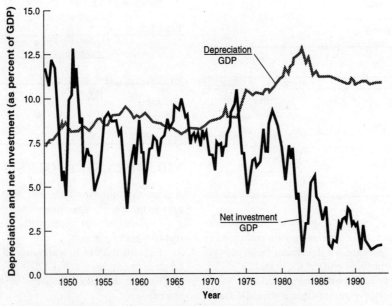

Figure 21-3 Fraction of National Output Devoted to Net Investment Has Plummeted

IX. ANSWERS TO STUDY GUIDE QUESTIONS

III. Review of Key Concepts

6	Final product
14	Real GDP
7	Nominal GDP
13	GDP deflator
10	Intermediate good
4	Value added
2	Net exports
12	Net domestic product
8	Government transfer payments
3	Disposable income
9	Gross national investment
1	Net investment
16	National income
5	Chain weights
11	Consumer Price Index
15	Producer Price Index

VI. Multiple Choice Questions

1. B 2. A 3. C 4. E 5. D 6. C
7. D 8. B 9. D 10. B 11. A 12. A
13. D 14. A 15. E 16. E 17. E 18. A
19. E

VII. Problem Solving

1. a. $1200
   b. 15
   c. $1150
   d. $1000, $200
   e. $1000, $150
2. a.

TABLE 21-1

Stage of Production	(1) Sales Receipts	(2) Cost of Intermediate Materials		(3) Value Added
1. Miner	$4	— $0	=	$4
2. Iron manufacturer	9	— 4	=	5
3. Steel manufacturer	16	— 9	=	7
4. Steel retailer	20	— 16	=	4

b. The steel manufacturer
c. $49
d. $20
e. $20. If you add up all the sales receipts, all of the intermediate products would be counted twice.
f. The steel retailer sells the finished steel. It is that value that belongs in GDP. When value addeds can be measured accurately, they will always add up to the price of the finished product.

3. a. 1. $50 + $600 + $7200 = $7850
      2. $180 + $1120 + $10,000 = $11,300
      3. $280 + $1120 + $ 9900 = $11,300
   b. 1. $ 7850
      2. $(60 \times \$1) + (140 \times \$6) + (100 \times \$80) = \$8900$
      3. $(70 \times \$1) + (160 \times \$6) + (110 \times \$80) = \$9830$
   c. 1. 100.00
      2. 126.97
      3. 114.95
   d. 1. $[(126.97 - 100.00)/100.00] \times 100 = 26.97\%$
      2. $[(114.95 - 126.97)/126.97] \times 100 = -9.47\%$
   e. 1. $[(8900 - 7850)/7850] \times 100 = 13.38\%$
      2. $[(9830 - 8900)/8900] \times 100 = 10.45\%$
   f. real $GDP_1 = \underline{\$9950}$ GDP deflator$_1$ = $\underline{78.89}$
      real $GDP_2 = \underline{\$11,300}$ CDP deflator$_2$ = $\underline{100}$ change = $\underline{+26.76}$
      real $GDP_3 = \underline{\$12,490}$ GDP deflator$_3$ = $\underline{90.47}$ to change = $\underline{-9.53}$

4. a. decreased
   b. $260 \times 1.30 = $338 billion
   c. $325/1.30 = $250 billion
   d. 30 percent

5. a. $800 - $675 = $125
   b. $775
   c. $650 + $125 = $775, equal to
   d. $0, still, still

6. a. $90,000
   b. $89,400
   c. $6,000
   d. $96,000
   e. $95,400

7. a. an increase, end
   b. a decrease, end
   c. (1) 125, (2) 90, (3) 35, (4) 105, (5) 90, (6) 15, (7) 105, (8) 110, (9) -5, (10) 85, (11) 110, (12) -25
   d. could, could

8. a. 100
   b. 115
   c. 15 %
   d. 107.25 ($[110 \times .2] + [150 \times .05] + [100 \times .35] + [110 \times .15] + [105 \times .25]$), falling to 7.25%
   e. 100, 7.25%
   f. overestimated

VIII. Discussion Questions

1. Measurement in real terms is important to get an accurate picture of changes in GDP from year to year. Unless you adjust for price changes, you may get the impression that the economy has experienced a growth in output, when in fact it may have suffered from inflation.

2. Most products pass through different stages of production. At each step in the production process, we should consider just what changes are made at that particular step. If we do not, the value of someone's work will be counted

again, and we will wind up overstating the value of the product. The value-added approach provides a useful check on the expenditures approach to GDP measurement.

3. There are (at least) two important signals that an increase in savings sends to the economy. First, when households save they spend less, so firms get a signal that consumers do not, at least in the present, want to purchase as many goods and services as firms perhaps thought they would. Second, the increase in savings increases the availability of loanable funds from the credit market. Interest rates are pushed lower, and firms are more likely to increase investment spending. Since consumption spending is lower, firms are encouraged to use their investment spending to add to their productive capability in the future, rather than increase current production of goods and services.

4.   a.   The ratio of net investment to GDP has fallen since the late 1970s.

b.   Real GDP has grown since the late 1970s, but since the real GDP line is rather flat, the rate of growth has been low.

c.   A number of factors could account for the decrease in the net investment to GDP ratio. The savings rate could have fallen, the economy could be in a prolonged recession, or government budget deficits could have increased which would drain more funds from the credit market.

d.   Lower rates of investment in the present suggest that the economy's rate of growth in the future will be lower.

5.   GDP is a geographic measure of output. It measures output that takes place within the borders of a country, regardless of who owns the resources. GNP measures output according to who owns the resources. When Nissan produces cars in Tennessee, that output is part of U.S. GDP because the production takes place within the United States. However, if we were measuring GNP, the value of those automobiles would be part of Japan's GNP since Nissan is a Japanese corporation. Many foreign corporations currently produce goods and services in the United States, but many U.S. corporations produce goods and services abroad. So for the United States, these two measures of aggregate output are nearly equal.

Most of the other nations in the world use GDP as their measure of output, so it is convenient that the United States does too. GDP also tends to give a more accurate assessment of the current economic health of the domestic economy. This is important when determining economic policy.

6.   Economists recognize that GDP is a measure of output; it is not a measure of economic well-being, or satisfaction, or happiness. Many things we value currently go unmeasured. Examples include work done in the home, leisure time, and unreported economic transactions. Some items that most people do not like go unmeasured as well. These things include crime, pollution, and the fear and psychic costs of armed conflict. Currently, data are not available to measure these things accurately. We are left with a measure of output, not a measure of well-being.

CHAPTER 22

Consumption and Investment

I. CHAPTER OVERVIEW

In this chapter we begin to build a new model of the macro-economy. Remember, economists use models to get a better understanding of some economic issue. We used the *production-possibility frontier* model to explain scarcity and the allocation of resources. We used the *circular-flow* model to better understand the flow of resources, products, and money in the economy. The circular-flow model also proved to be very useful in the last chapter in explaining the *flow-of-product* and *earnings or cost* approaches to GDP accounting.

The focus of this new model is on the main building blocks of the macroeconomy (**C, I, G,** and **X**) and the use of policy instruments to implement change in the economy. This work will take us several chapters. In this chapter we focus on the two main components of the private-market economy, consumption and investment spending. The tools described in these pages were outlined by Keynes more than 60 years ago in *The General Theory.* Even though their application in macroeconomics has been debated and changed over the intervening years, the impact of their development is still felt today. Therefore, it is useful to study the basic Keynesian construction of the major components of aggregate demand for at least two reasons.

First, a careful review of the Keynesian foundations builds an understanding of the antecedents of modern macroeconomic theory. Without such an understanding, contemporary macro theory can often appear isolated and impenetrable; students find it hard to understand why certain questions were ever raised, much less fathom their proposed answers.

Second, it is equally important to view the evolutionary process which brought us to our current state of economic awareness. To do this, particularly in macroeconomic analysis, we need a point of departure—a historical benchmark against which the reasons behind changes in viewpoint can be cast. The original Keynesian construction is an excellent starting point in this effort, and the integration of monetary policy into that model is an equally good example of the type of change that has occurred.

II. LEARNING OBJECTIVES

After you have read Chapter 22 in your text and completed the exercises in this *Study Guide,* you should be able to:

1. Understand the deterministic relationship between income and consumption (household spending on food, clothing, etc.). Understand, too, that saving, the mirror image of consumption, is also determined in large part by income.

2. Define (a) the consumption function, (b) the savings function, (c) the marginal propensity to consume, and (d) the marginal propensity to save.

3. Follow the aggregation of *individual* consumption functions into a *national* consumption function determined by disposable income, wealth, **permanent income**, and the life-cycle hypothesis.

4. Recognize that the U.S. savings rate has declined sharply over the last decade, and discuss some of the reasons behind the decline.

5. Recognize investment spending as a second major component of total spending. Understand that the level of investment spending in an economy depends upon anticipated revenues, costs, and expectations about the future.

6. Formalize the relationship between the interest rate and the level of investment in the investment demand schedule.

7. Visualize consumption and investment as two of the key components of *aggregate demand* in the economy.

III. REVIEW OF KEY CONCEPTS

Match the following terms from column A with their definitions in column B.

A	B
__ Disposable income	1. Assumes that people save in order to smooth their consumption spending over their lifetime.
__ Dissave	2. Shows the relationship between interest rates and investment spending.

__ Break-even point

__ Consumption function

__ Savings function

__ Marginal

__ Marginal Propensity to consume

__ Marginal propensity to save

__ Permanent income

__ Life-cycle hypothesis

__ Wealth effect

__ Accelerator principle

__ Investment demand curve

3. Level of income that households receive when all temporary influences are removed.

4. Used throughout the study of economics to mean extra or additional.

5. The rate of investment will be primarily determined by the rate of change of output in the economy.

6. The level of household income, after taxes have been paid, that is left for consumption spending and saving.

7. The fraction of an extra dollar of income that goes into saving.

8. Where a household neither saves nor dissaves, but consumes all its income.

9. The relationship between higher levels of wealth and higher levels of consumption spending.

10. The extra amount that people consume when they receive an extra dollar of income.

11. Shows the relationship between the level of consumption expenditures and disposable income.

12. Shows the relationship between the level of savings and income.

13. To draw down on wealth, or borrow.

IV. SUMMARY AND CHAPTER OUTLINE

This section summarizes the key concepts from the chapter.

A. Consumption and Saving

1. Consumption (C) is determined primarily by disposable income (DI); a *consumption function* therefore relates consumption to disposable income. Saving (S) is the amount of disposable income not devoted to consumption. The *savings function* is the mirror image of the consumption function because saving plus consumption always exhausts disposable income.

2. The marginal propensity to consume (MPC) is the ratio of a change in consumption to the underlying change in disposable income. The marginal propensity to save (MPS) is the corresponding ratio of a change in saving with respect to a change in disposable income. $MPC + MPS = 1$ because $C + S = DI$.

3. *Individual* consumption functions can be aggregated to estimate a *national* consumption function. It, too, depends upon disposable income. Trends in national consumption spending are important for two reasons:

a. Consumption is the largest component of spending in our economy, and our task in this chapter, and those that follow, is to understand the determination of aggregate demand.

b. Whatever portion of income is not consumed (i.e., saved) is available to the nation for investment, and investment serves as a driving force behind long-term economic growth.

4. The consumption function diagram is plotted with consumption expenditure on the vertical axis and disposable income on the horizontal axis. As is *always* the case, if some other relevant variable changes, like *wealth* or *permanent income*, the consumption function (and the corresponding saving function) will shift up or down.

5. The decrease in the personal savings rate in the United States has been significant. The savings rate is critically linked to the long-term health of the economy. The level of national savings determines the rate of capital formation. The capital stock, in turn, determines the level of economic growth and potential output. When a nation's savings rate is low, its equipment and factories become obsolete and its infrastructure begins to rot away.

6. The reasons behind the decline in the personal savings rate in the United States have been the subject of much debate. Some of the possible explanations include:

a. The social security system, which guarantees (at least a minimal level of) income for retirees and thereby encourages less personal saving.

b. The improvement of capital and credit markets, which has made it easier for households to borrow.

c. The rapid growth in personal wealth, due primarily to increases in stock market prices, may have lowered the personal savings rate. The authors make an important distinction between two measures of personal savings: that contained in the national income and product accounts, and individual balance sheets. The national accounts measure of savings excludes (stock market) capital gains, but individual balance sheets include this money. This explains, at least in part, why the national savings rate appears so low, while the personal savings rate seems much higher. Look again at Figure 22-8 in your text.

B. The Determinants of Investment

1. Investment—spending on new housing, plants and equipment, and additions to inventories is the second major component of aggregate demand. It is important not only for its role in determining aggregate demand but also for its relationship to the stock of capital, the long-term growth of the economy, and aggregate supply.

2. An important determinant of investment is the overall level of output or GDP in the economy. Firms are more likely to invest in new plant and equipment if managers believe there is a strong market for their products. Hence if the economy is growing and sales are rising, firms are more likely to invest. This relationship between the rate of change of output and the rate of investment is known as the **accelerator principle**.

3. A second important determinant of investment is cost. Because capital equipment usually lasts a number of years and is expensive, firms typically finance investment projects by borrowing. Therefore, *interest rates* are an important cost associated with investment. An additional cost factor related to investment is the corporate *tax* levied on firms by the government. Taxes decrease profits, thereby decreasing the attractiveness of investment projects. Alternatively, investment tax credits, given by the government, may encourage firms to expand investment.

4. Investment is the most *volatile* component of aggregate demand. One of the reasons behind the volatility of investment is the importance of *expectations* in determining the level of investment spending. Since investment projects, by their very nature, depend upon the future, corporate leaders spend a great deal of time and effort trying to establish accurate forecasts of the business climate and the economy.

5. The investment demand curve relates the interest rate to the level of investments It is downward-sloping and can shift up or down as the level of output in the economy, tax rates, and expectations about the future change.

6. Figures 22-7 and 22-9 from the text are reproduced here as Figures 22-1 and 22-2. Note how the pattern of consumption spending is fairly stable and predictable. As disposable income in the economy increases, so does consumption spending. It almost looks like a one to one relationship. In fact, if the savings rate in the economy is five percent, the slope would be 0.95. Investment spending, on the other hand, is indeed more volatile. As the rate of growth – of course, you remember that growth is always measured in *real* terms – in GDP increases, so does the rate of change in real investment. However, the relationship is not as stable as the one between consumption and disposable income. When the rate of growth in GDP varies between two and four percent, the rate of change in investment varies from slightly less than zero to over ten percent!

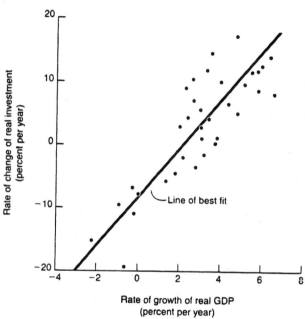

Figure 22-2

V. HELPFUL HINTS

1. If you are unfamiliar with graphs, slopes, and plotted lines, head back immediately to the appendix to Chapter 1.

2. There is a precise accounting relationship between *disposable income, consumption*, and *saving*. After taxes have been paid, households are left with disposable income. This money is either consumed or saved—there are no other choices. Any two of these three terms will always, by definition, determine the value of the third.

3. Economists are very fond of marginal analysis and *margin means change* (especially small change). Change, you should recall, is also how we measure a line's slope (*change*

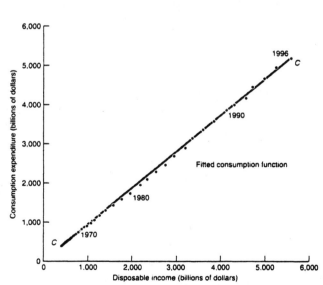

Consumption Relates to Income

Figure 22-1

in Y axis over *change* in X axis between two points) . So margin is the same thing as slope. This concept is very useful for economists. For example, from microeconomics: the *slope* of total cost is *marginal* cost, and the *slope* of total revenue is *marginal* revenue; and from macroeconomics: the *slope* of the consumption function is the *marginal* propensity to consume, and the *slope* of the savings function is the *marginal* propensity to save. The sooner you learn this, the easier your time as a student of economics will be!

4. The 45° line plays an important part in several economic diagrams. As long as the same scale of measurement applies to both axes, the 45° line will provide a direct and equivalent mapping from the numbers on one axis to the same numbers on the other axis. In our consumption function diagram, points along the 45° line illustrate observations where consumption equals disposable income, the break-even level of income. (Note that the slope of the 45° line is 1.)

5. As you work with the consumption function and the investment demand schedule remember how to distinguish between movements along the curve and shifts in the curve. If a variable measured along the axis changes, like disposable income in the consumption function, you move along the curve to determine the new point of observation. On the other hand, if a variable changes that is not measured on the graph, and it is relevant to the analysis, like expectations in the investment demand schedule, then the curve will shift to illustrate the change.

VI. MULTIPLE CHOICE QUESTIONS

These questions are organized by topic from the chapter outline. Choose the best answer from the options available.

A. Consumption and Saving

1. The marginal propensity to consume is:
    a. the ratio of total consumption to total income at any income level.
    b. the change in income caused by a change (increase or decrease) in consumption spending.
    c. a schedule showing the amount of consumption spending for each income level.
    d. the ratio of a change in consumption to a change in income level at any income level.
    e. none of these things.
2. At the **break-even** level of income:
    a. the *MPC* is equal to the *MPS*.
    b. the *MPS* is equal to 0.
    c. consumption is equal to saving.
    d. saving is equal to 0.
    e. households are borrowing more than they are saving.
3. The break-even point on a family's consumption function is the point at which:

a. its saving equals its income.
b. its income equals its consumption.
c. its saving equals its consumption.
d. its consumption equals its investment.
e. the marginal propensity to consume equals 1.

4. The relationship between the marginal propensities to consume and to save holds that:
    a. their sum must equal 1, since some fraction of marginal income must go to extra consumption spending and the remaining fraction to extra saving.
    b. the ratio between them must indicate the average propensity to consume.
    c. their total must indicate the current total of disposable income received, since *DI* must divide between consumption and saving.
    d. the point at which they are equal must be the break-even level of income.
    e. their total must equal 0.

5. *Personal saving*, as the term is used in this chapter in connection with national income and national product analysis, reflects:
    a. the total of all assets held by families.
    b. income received within the period in question but not spent on consumption.
    c. the total of all assets held by families minus the total of their liabilities.
    d. income received within the period in question and either used only to buy a security or deposited in a bank.
    e. income received within the period in question but not spent on consumption or used to buy a security or deposited in a bank.

6. If people do not consume all their incomes and if they put the unspent amount into a bank, they are, in national income and product terms:
    a. saving but not investing.
    b. investing but not saving.
    c. both saving and investing.
    d. neither saving nor investing.
    e. saving, but investing only to the extent that they buy securities.

Use Figure 22-3 to answer questions 7 through 10.

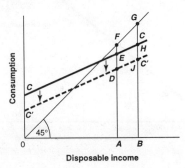

Figure 22-3

7. The solid line *CC* is the consumption function for some family or community. If the total amount of consumption expenditure were *EA*, then the amount of disposable income must be:
   a. *AB*.
   b. *FD*.
   c. *FA*.
   d. *DA*.
   e. none of the above.

8. Equivalently, given the same total amount of consumption expenditure *EA* in the diagram, then the amount of disposable income must also be:
   a. *EA*.
   b. *GB*.
   c. *ED*.
   d. *0A*.
   e. none of the preceding.

9. If the consumption function is given as line *C'C'*, and disposable income is equal to *GB*, then savings must be equal to:
   a. *GJ*.
   b. *HJ*.
   c. *FG*.
   d. *DJ*.
   e. *FE*.

10. A change in consumption expenditure from *HB* to *EA* could be the result of:
   a. a decision to spend more and save less at each level of income.
   b. a decrease in disposable income from *0B* to *0A*.
   c. a decision to spend less and save more at each level of income.
   d. an increase in disposable income from *0A* to *0B*.
   e. none of the preceding.

Use Figure 22-4 to answer questions 11 through 13.

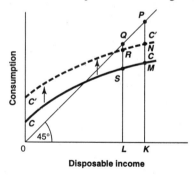

Figure 22-4

11. A shift in the consumption function from the solid line *CC* upward to the broken line *C'C'* would illustrate:
   a. an increase in consumption expenditure resulting from a rise in disposable income.

   b. a decision on the part of the family or community involved to consume more and save less at any given level of disposable income.
   c. a decrease in consumption expenditure resulting from a fall in disposable income.
   d. a decision on the part of the family or community involved to consume less and save more at any given level of disposable income.
   e. none of these events.

12. If the consumption function were indicated by the solid line *CC* and the amount of disposable income were *0K* then the amount of saving out of disposable income *0K* must be:
   a. *PK*
   b. *MK*.
   c. *PM*.
   d. *NM*.
   e. none of the preceding.

13. If the amount of disposable income were to change from *0K* to *0L*—the solid *CC* line still indicating the consumption function—then the amount of saving out of income would become:
   a. *SM*.
   b. *QR*
   c. *PQ*.
   d. *RS*.
   e. *QS*.

14. With regard to *both* of the consumption function diagrams (Figures 22-3 and 22-4), the primary difference between them is that:
   a. the *MPC* (marginal propensity to consume) is constant in Figure 22-3, and the *MPC* decreases as income increases in Figure 22-4.
   b. the *MPC* decreases as income increases in Figure 22-3, and the *MPC* is constant in Figure 22-4.
   c. the *MPC* increases as income increases in Figure 22-3, and the *MPC* is constant in Figure 22-4.
   d. the *MPC* is constant in Figure 22-3, and the *MPC* increases as income increases in Figure 22-4.
   e. in both instances, the *MPC* falls as income increases, but it falls more rapidly in Figure 22-4.

15. The consumption function refers to:
   a. the level of income at which consumption spending just equals income.
   b. the inclination on the part of some consumers to "keep up with the Joneses" in their consumer spending.
   c. the fraction of extra income that will be spent on consumption.
   d. a schedule showing the amount a family (or community) will spend on consumption at different levels of income.
   e. the fact that, at low incomes, families spend more on consumption than the amount of their incomes.

16. According to the statistical evidence, which of the following characterizes the typical American family's behavior with respect to consumption?

 a. An increasing proportion of income is spent on consumption as income increases.

 b. The same proportion of income is spent on consumption at all except very low income levels.

 c. The same proportion of income is spent on consumption at all income levels.

 d. A decreasing proportion of income is spent on consumption as income increases.

 e. The same proportion of income is spent on consumption at all except very high income levels.

17. A family spends $2000 on consumption when its income is 0, and $6000 on consumption when its income is $6000. Assume that its consumption function is a straight line. This family's marginal propensity to consume is:

 a. 2/3.

 b. 3/4.

 c. 4/5.

 d. 1.

 e. greater than 1.

18. The family from question 17 has a marginal propensity to save equal to:

 a. 1/3.

 b. 2/3.

 c. 3/4.

 d. 1/4.

 e. $2000.

19. **Permanent income** can be best described as:

 a. money which has been saved for years and not likely to be spent by the household.

 b. income left for the household after all taxes have been paid.

 c. the sum of consumption and saving over the long run.

 d. the long-run trend in household income.

 e. none of the above.

20. Which of the statements below about savings is *false*?

 a. One of the possible reasons for the decline in the personal savings rate is social security.

 b. The improvement of capital and credit markets may have contributed to the decline in the savings rate.

 c. Saving can be viewed as a residual of what is left over after households spend their income.

 d. The savings rate is higher in the United States than in Japan.

 e. All of the statements above are *true*.

21. The difference between the national income account measure of savings and savings figures obtained from individual balance sheets is due to:

 a. different measures of inflation.

 b. the exclusion of capital gains in the national income accounts.

 c. the exclusion of capital gains in individual balance sheets.

 d. the difference between individual and aggregated data.

 e. none of the above, the two measures of saving are the same.

B. The Determinants of Investment

22. Which of the following would be regarded as investment by an economist?

 a. any purchase of a corporate bond.

 b. any amount saved out of income and not hoarded.

 c. any purchase of a *new* corporate bond.

 d. any productive activity resulting in present consumption.

 e. none of the preceding.

23. Investment spending does *not* include:

 a. purchases of new housing.

 b. purchases of new factories.

 c. additions to a firm's inventory of finished goods.

 d. the issuing of new stock.

 e. *All* of the above are considered as part of investment.

24. Which of the following best describes the relationship between interest rates and the level of investment spending?

 a. They are directly related to each other.

 b. They are inversely related to each other.

 c. They move together but in no discernible relationship.

 d. They are unrelated.

 e. None of the above.

25. The *accelerator principle* states that:

 a. as the economy heats up, inflation increases.

 b. as the pace of economic growth quickens, investment will increase.

 c. as government spending increases, investment increases as well.

 d. an increasing supply of money accelerates the growth of investment.

 e. it is very difficult to slow down a rapidly growing economy.

26. We would move along the *demand-for-investment* schedule to a new level of investment spending if:

 a   corporate profits taxes increased.

 b. Congress passed an investment tax credit.

 c. business managers became more optimistic about the future.

 d. interest rates changed.

 e. all the above.

27. Which statement below best describes the terms *investment and consumption*?

 a. Both activities are undertaken by the same group

(i.e., households), although not always for the same reasons.

b. Both are demands calling for the current use, or employment, of the economy's stock of productive inputs.

c. Both are components of disposable income.

d. In both cases, the only factor of major consequence which governs them is the level of national product or disposable income.

e. None of the preceding.

VII. PROBLEM SOLVING

The following problems are designed to help you apply the concepts that you learned in the chapter.

A. Consumption and Saving

1. Suppose that a certain family's weekly expenditure on consumption (C) is governed by this rule: Spend $100 plus one-half of weekly DI. Its consumption and saving at various income levels could then be represented in tabular form.

a. Fill in the blanks in Table 22-1. (*Remember*: S must be the difference between DI and C; at low income levels, therefore, S will be a negative amount.)

TABLE 22-1

DI	C	S
$ 0	$___	$___
100	___	___
200	___	___
300	___	___
400	___	___
500	___	___

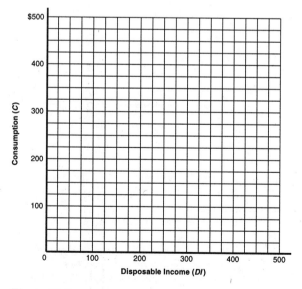

Figure 22-5

b. Use the grid in Figure 22-5 to plot the points relating consumption (C) to disposable income for the six DI values in your table. Join these points with a line.

c. Now draw a diagonal line from the bottom left corner to the top right corner of your diagram. (If possible, use a different color to distinguish this line from the consumption function.)

You have just drawn a 45° line running through all the points for which C = DI. The 45° line runs through the point marking off $100 of DI and $100 of C, through the point marking $200 DI and $200 C, through $300 DI and $300 C, and so on. In fact, the 45° line can be represented algebraically by C = DI (consumption equals disposable income) .

It should be clear, at this point, that the 45° line can be used to identify the particular DI level at which the family just "breaks even," spending on consumption an amount exactly covered by its disposable income. The *break even point* appears on the 45° line where that line intersects the consumption schedule.

d. For the family depicted in your diagram, this intersection occurs where DI equals (**$100 / $200 / $300 / $400**). To the left of this intersection, the consumption function lies (**above / below**) the 45° line, and the family spends on C (**more / less**) than its DI. To the right of the intersection, the consumption function lies (**above / below**) the 45° line, and the family spends (**more / less**) than its DI. Given an income in excess of $200, therefore, the family would save part of its DI.

e. When DI equals $400, the vertical distance up to the 45° line from the X axis is (**$500 / $400 / $300**). At this point, the vertical distance up to the consumption function from the horizontal axis is (**$500 / $400 / $300**); this is the amount of C spending. The difference of (**$0 / $100 / $200**), or the vertical distance between the two lines, is the amount of saving (S).

f. Your diagram also indicates that if the family's DI were $300, it would (**save / dissave**) (**$0 / $50 / $100 / $150**). If DI were $100, then it would (**save / dissave**) (**$0 / $50 / $100 / $150**).

The family will, in fact, dissave for any DI for which the consumption function lies above the 45° line. This means simply that the family would draw on past savings or borrow in order to supplement DI currently received for C spending should its income ever fall (temporarily) below the break-even DI level of $200.

g. The amount of saving can be plotted directly on a saving-DI graph. Use the DI and S data from Table 22-1 to plot the savings schedule on the grid in Figure 22-6.

2. It follows from the construction of a consumption function that any change in DI is likely to produce some *changes* in both consumption spending (C) and saving (S). When economists talk about change, they are really talking about

marginal analysis—in this case, the marginal propensity to consume (*MPC*) and the marginal propensity to save (*MPS*).

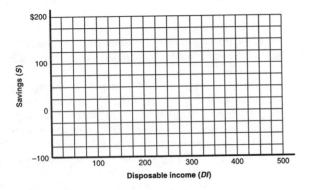

Figure 22-6

a.   Use the data from the last question to fill in the blanks below:
   1.   *MPC* = ___.
   2.   Slope of consumption schedule = ___.
   3.   *MPS* = ___.
   4.   Slope of savings schedule = ___.

Now consider another (individual) consumption function which is defined in Table 22-2.

TABLE 22-2

Yearly DI	Yearly C	Increase in C
$12,000	$11,600	
		$640
13,000	12,240	
		590
14,000	12,830	

b.   Use the data from Table 22-2 to fill in the blanks below:
   1.   For a change in yearly *DI* from $12,000 to $13,000, *MPC* = ___ and *MPS* = ___.
   2.   For a change in yearly *DI* from $13,000 to $14,000, *MPC* = ___ and *MPS* = ___.

3.   Assume that a family has a weekly disposable income of $450. Like the household in the first question, its consumption spending equals $100 plus one-half of weekly *DI*.
   a.   Consumption spending equals ___.
   b.   One family member now leaves home, so the consumption function changes. It now becomes one-half of *DI*, plus $75. If family *DI* were unaffected by the change, then its weekly *C* spending would now be (**$300 / $325 / $350 / $375**).
   c.   On a consumption function graph this change would be represented as (pick one):
      1.   a movement downward along the existing curve.
      2.   a movement upward along the existing curve.

   3.   a shift of the entire consumption function upward to a new position.
   4.   a shift of the entire consumption function downward to a new position.
   d.   Has the value of the marginal propensity to consume changed? (**No. / Yes, it has risen. / Yes, it has fallen.**)

Suppose, finally, that a new consumption function is established such that consumption spending becomes two-fifths of *DI*, plus $75.
   e.   The value of the *MPC* would then have (**fallen / remained unchanged / risen**).
   f.   The value of the *MPS* would now equal
   g.   Write an equation that describes this consumption function.

---

4.   The solid line *CC* in the diagram in Figure 22-7 illustrates a community's consumption function. One possible level of total *DI* is indicated by the horizontal measure 0*A*; the corresponding level of consumption expenditure is measured by the vertical distance 0*D*.

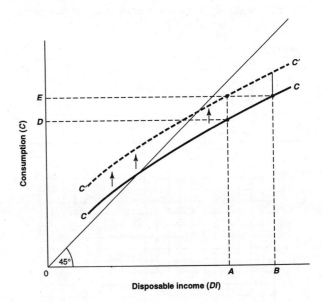

Figure 22-7

a.   Suppose we observe an increase in the community's *C* expenditure from 0*D* to 0*E*. This increase could be the consequence of:
   1.   only an increase in *DI* from level 0*A* to level 0*B*.
   2.   only some factor other than a *DI* increase—a factor causing the consumption function to shift upward to a new position indicated by the broken line *C'C'*.
   3.   either of the above—an increase in *DI* or a

decision to spend more prompted by some factor other than an increase in *DI*.

b. A respected economic authority predicts a coming recession. His prediction is influential, and people decide that they should spend less and save more as a precaution against coming hard times (even though *DI* has not fallen—not yet, at any rate) . If this decision were to be illustrated in Figure 22-7, it would imply (pick one):

    1. a movement downward and to the left along a given consumption function, say, the solid *CC* one, to indicate the reduced *C* spending caused by reduced disposable income.

    2. an upward movement of the entire consumption function, say, from the position indicated by the solid *CC*: line upward to the broken *C'C'* line.

    3. a downward movement of the entire consumption function, say, from the position indicated by the broken *C'C'* line downward to the solid *CC* line.

5. Which of the following events would cause the consumption function to shift up (**U**), shift down (**D**), or not shift at all (**NS**) ?

a. An anticipated down-turn in business conditions that leads people to worry that they might lose their jobs. (**U / D / NS**)

b. A reduction in the interest rate paid by banks that makes saving less attractive to everyone. (**U / D / NS**)

c. A reduction in taxes that enables people to retain more of their incomes after taxes. (**U / D / NS**)

d. An actual contraction in the economy that causes a reduction in the availability of outside or overtime employment. (**U / D / NS**)

B. The Determinants of Investment

6. *Investment*, as the term is used in economics, generates employment while the investment item in question is being built, and thereby generates income for those people employed in the item's construction. In this sense, do the following, by themselves, constitute investment?

a. Having a contractor build a new house for you. (**yes / no**)

b. Buying a house built a year ago. (**yes / no**)

c. Buying duPont stock on the stock market. (**yes / no**)

d. Buying stock in a newly formed corporation. (**yes / no**)

e. Using money obtained from the bond or stock issue of item **d** to build a new factory building. (**yes / no**)

7. Indicate whether each of the following is true (**T**) or false (**F**):

a. A firm is considering building a new plant to add to its output capacity. To do this sensibly, it must try to evaluate the future market for its product to be sure there is likely to be sufficient demand to justify the resulting increase in production. This evaluation requires that the firm estimate, among other things, the likely degree of competition from rival firms and the coming "general business conditions"—i.e., the probable future course of GDP. (**T / F**)

b. This means, then, that the flow of investment expenditure is governed by many considerations frequently having to do with forecasts about the future. (**T / F**)

c. A large corporation which has been steadily adding new plant and equipment may stop doing so because it feels it has caught up with probable demand for its product for the time being. If it stops, the investment flow will be correspondingly reduced even though the stock of capital is maintained net of depreciation. (**T / F**)

d. Such investment plans may be postponed or canceled because the firm is fearful of a recession, that is, a drop or pause in GDP. This would again mean a drop in the flow of investment spending. (**T / F**)

e. If any such reduction in the investment-spending flow were to occur, then it would be reasonable to assume that there would be an immediate and matching reduction in the flow of personal saving. (**T / F**)

f. Suppose that the economy goes through a period of high interest rates caused by a variety of internal and external factors. The result should be a reduction in both the investment financed through borrowing and the investment financed through retained earnings. (**T / F**)

8. Table 22-3 highlights the characteristics of four separate investment projects. Suppose that the annual cost of investment is based on market interest rates. Four different possible values of interest rates are given in the table: 3, 6, 10, and 15 percent, respectively. Assuming that the interest rate is the only cost of each investment, we can compare the annual revenue of each $1000 invested (found in column 3) with the annual interest cost per $1000 borrowed. For example, at 3 percent the cost of borrowing $1000 is $30 per year.

a. At 6 percent the cost of borrowing $1000 is $___

TABLE 22-3

(1) Project	(2) Total Investment (millions)	(3) Annual Revenue per $1000	Annual Profit per $1000 at:			
			3%	6%	10%	15%
A	$10	$1000	$970	940	900	850
B	6	250	___	___	___	___
C	14	100	___	___	___	___
D	5	50	___	___	___	___

per year.

At 10 percent the cost of borrowing $1000 is $___ per year.

At 15 percent the cost of borrowing $1000 is $___ per year.

As long as the annual revenue per $1000 exceeds the annual cost, the investment project will add to the firm's profit and should be undertaken.

b.   Now you are ready to complete the annual profit columns in the table. The numbers for project A are already filled in. Fill in the blanks for projects B, C, and D.

c.   Given these rates of interest, will the firm ever *not* invest in project A? ___ What about project B?

d.   At what rate of interest will this firm stop investing in project C? In project D?

The firm's total demand for investment is the total of all the investment projects that the firm is willing to fund at various rates of interest. For example, at 3 percent all the investment projects are profitable and the firm would spend $35 million on investment (10 + 6 + 14 + 5).

e.   Fill in the blanks in Table 22-4 and then use these numbers to plot this firm's demand-for-investment schedule in Figure 22-8.

TABLE 22-4

Rate of Interest	Demand for Investment
3%	$35
6%	___
10%	___
15%	___

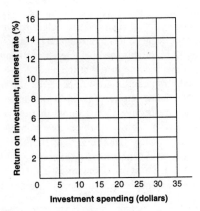

Figure 22-8

f.   Now suppose that expectations of future business activity take a turn for the worse and that the annual revenue per $1000 for each project is cut in half. Plot a second curve in Figure 22-8 which reflects the new investment demand schedule.

1.   The demand curve has (**shifted left / shifted right / remained in the same place**) as a result of the perceived change in economic climate.

2.   Had expectations *improved* and expected revenues doubled, on the other hand, the curve would have (**shifted left / shifted right / remained in the same place**).

9.   This last question explores the relationship between saving and investment. Indicate whether each of the following is true (**T**) or false (**F**):

a.   Money saved by a family and hidden in a mattress in the family's home is money withdrawn from the income stream; it creates no income or jobs for anyone as long as it remains in the mattress. (**T / F**)

b.   Money saved by a family and promptly used to buy a new house is money put right back into the income stream. The family's actions would count as both saving and investment. (**T / F**)

c.   Money saved by a family and promptly used to buy existing or newly issued General Motors stock would count as both saving and investment. (**T / F**)

d.   Money saved and deposited in a savings account in a bank counts as saving. This is not investment in the economic sense. As long as this money stays deposited, it can potentially be used for investment spending if the bank lends it to a borrower who will use it for investment purposes. (**T / F**)

e.   Much investment spending is financed by using other people's money, i.e., by borrowing from a bank or by selling bond or stock issues. (**T / F**)

f.   If business conditions seem particularly uncertain, people with money to spare may hesitate to lend it, feeling that would-be borrowers are likely to get into trouble and be unable to make repayment. Thus, even though there are mechanisms for converting saving into investment, this does not mean that all saved money is automatically transformed into investment. (**T / F**)

VIII. DISCUSSION QUESTIONS

Answer the following questions, making sure that you can explain the work you did to arrive at the answers.

1.   Assume that there are 200 families in a community. Each of these families spends exactly $100 plus one-half its total income each week on consumption. Half (100) of these families are "poor;" they each receive weekly incomes of $200. The other 100 families are "rich;" they receive $400 apiece weekly.

An increase in total consumption spending is desired in this community. To achieve the increase, it is proposed that rich families be taxed $100 apiece weekly and that the tax proceeds be given to poor families to spend. Thus, each and every family would have a net weekly income of $300.

The following justification is given for the tax: Poor families spend 100 percent of their incomes on consumption; they receive $200 in income, and they spend a total of $200. Rich families spend only 75 percent of their incomes; they receive $400, but they spend only $300. So the total consumption spending would be increased by redistribution of income.

   a. Would such a proposal, if adopted, increase total consumption spending? Explain your answer in terms of the marginal propensity to consume.

   b. Are there any different circumstances in which such a redistribution-of-income proposal would increase consumption spending? Again answer in terms of the *MPC*.

   c. Explain two circumstances in which a redistribution of income through this tax scheme might actually lower consumption spending. (This is a hard question; think beyond the *MPC* notion that was sufficient for answering part **b**.)

2. Explain why, for most households, the *MPC* decreases with income.

3. Why does it not make sense for the national *MPC* to be greater than 1?

4. Briefly discuss the main determinants of investment spending in the economy.

5. Explain the relationship between saving and economic growth.

IX. ANSWERS TO STUDY GUIDE QUESTIONS

III. Review of Key Concepts

6	Disposable income
13	Dissave
8	Break-even point
11	Consumption function
12	Savings function
4	Marginal
10	Marginal propensity to consume
7	Marginal propensity to save
3	Permanent income
1	Life-cycle hypothesis
9	Wealth effect
5	Accelerator principle
2	Investment demand curve

VI. Multiple Choice Questions

1. D 2. D 3. B 4. A 5. B 6. A
7. C 8. D 9. A 10. B 11. B 12. C
13. E 14. A 15. D 16. D 17. A 18. A
19. D 20. D 21. B 22. E 23. D 24. B
25. B 26. D 27. B

VII. Problem Solving

1. a.

TABLE 22-1

DI	C	S
$ 0	$100	$-100
100	150	-50
200	200	0
300	250	50
400	300	100
500	350	150

b. and c.

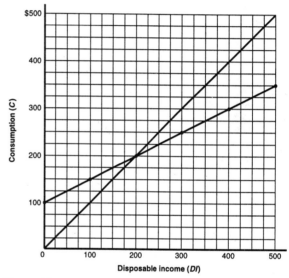

Figure 22-5

   d. $200, above, more, below, less
   e. $400, $300, $100
   f. save, $50, dissave, $50
   g.

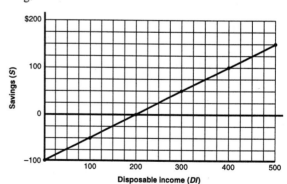

Figure 22-6

2. a. 1. 0.50
        2. 0.50
        3. 0.50
        4. 0.50
    b. 1. 0.64, 0.36
        2. 0.59, 0.41
3. a. $325
    b. $300
    c. 4
    d. No.
    e. fallen
    f. 0.60
    g. $C = 75 + (0.4) DI$
4. a. 3
    b. 3
5. a. D
    b. U
    c. NS
    d. NS
6. a. yes
    b. no
    c. no
    d. no
    e. yes
7. a   T
    b. T
    c. T
    d. T
    e. F
    f. T
8. a. 60, 100, 150
    b.

TABLE 22-3

Annual *Profit per $1000 at:*			
	3%	6%	10%	15%
Project B	$220	$190	$150	$100
Project C	$ 70	$ 40	$ 0	-$ 50
Project D	$ 20	-$ 10	-$ 50	-$100

    c. No. No.
    d. any interest rate above 10 percent, any interest rate above 5 percent
    e. $30, $16, $16. See Figure 22-8.
    f. See Figure 22-8.
        1. shifted left
        2. shifted right
9. a. T
    b. T
    c. F
    d. T

e. T
f. T

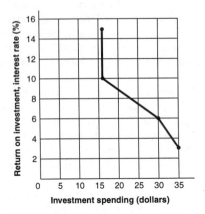

Figure 22-8

VIII. Discussion Questions

1. a. Total consumption spending would remain unchanged. Since each group has the exact same *MPC*, the transfer of income would probably help the "poor" families provide for themselves, but total spending would not be affected.

    b. If the poorer families had a higher *MPC* than the rich families, the transfer of income would increase consumption spending.

    c. First, if poorer families had a lower *MPC* than the rich, total consumption spending could fall. Second, if the tax on the rich reduces their incentive to work, incomes and thereby consumption spending could decrease.

2. The basic necessities of life—food, clothing, and shelter—must be met by all households, regardless of their income. As incomes increase, households can afford nicer commodities, but once necessities have been met, there is more of an opportunity to think about the future and save.

3. It is impossible for the nation, as a whole, to spend more than it produces. If the change in spending is greater than the change in income, there must be dissaving or borrowing. When there is borrowing, there must be some saving in the economy. If the *MPC* is greater than 1, there would not be any saving.

4. Investment spending is determined by interest rates, business expectations, and the level of GDP itself.

5. Saving can be viewed as the postponement of consumption. This encourages firms to produce less and invest more. Investment leads to greater productive capacity and economic growth.

CHAPTER 23

Business Fluctuations and the Theory of Aggregate Demand

I. CHAPTER OVERVIEW

Chapter 23 explores business cycles and one of the main economic variables that they influence—aggregate demand. Throughout its economic history the United States and other nations have been subject to fluctuations—upturns and downturns—in economic growth. One of the critical issues facing the economics profession is whether economic policy can be designed to adequately control the adverse effects of the business cycle. Or should policy makers be satisfied with being able to simply dampen the amplitude of cyclical swings?

Aggregate Demand, which can be influenced greatly by business cycle activity, can also have a powerful impact on output, employment, and prices—especially in the short run. This chapter reviews the components of aggregate demand and discusses the overall shape of the aggregate demand curve. In addition, there is a discussion of the factors that can cause the aggregate demand curve to shift. As always, be careful to distinguish between movements *along* the curve and *shifts* in the curve.

II. LEARNING OBJECTIVES

After you have read Chapter 23 in your text and completed the exercises in this *Study Guide* chapter, you should be able to:

1. Outline the business-cycle experience of the United States and the causes behind it.
2. Understand the successive phases of the business cycle.
3. Describe the business-cycle theories that lie behind aggregate supply and aggregate demand.
4. Appreciate the use of econometric modeling in forecasting business-cycle behavior.
5. Explain why the economy's aggregate demand curve is downward-sloping.
6. Understand the differences between *micro*economic and *macro*economic demand.
7. Provide reasons for shifts in the aggregate demand curve.

III. REVIEW OF KEY CONCEPTS

Match the following terms from column A with their definitions in column B.

A	B
__ Business cycle	1. Rapid output growth stimulates investment which in turn, stimulates further economic growth.
__ Recession	2. Variables outside the AS-AD framework.
__ Depression	3. Nominal money supply divided by the price level.
__ Business-cycle phases	4. Swings in total national output usually lasting between 2 and 10 years and marked by widespread expansion or contraction in the economy.
__ Expansion	5. Rooted in the Keynesian tradition, but is more pragmatic in its explanation of movements in aggregate supply and demand.
__ Multiplier-accelerator theory	6. Fiscal and monetary decisionsmade by the government to shift aggregate demand.
__ Demand-induced cycles	7. Phase of the business cycle characterized by economic growth.
__ Aggregate demand	8. A decline in real GDP for at least two consecutive quarters.
__ Real money supply	9 Concentrate primarily on monetary forces in analyzing movements in AD and AS in the economy.
__ Policy variables	10. Business cycles caused by shocks to AD.
__ Exogenous variables	11. Prolonged, cumulative slump in real GDP.
__ Monetarists	12. Total quantity of output that is willingly bought at a given level of prices, other things held constant.

287

___ Keynesian
macroeconomics

13. Peak, trough, expansion, and
contraction.

IV. SUMMARY AND CHAPTER OUTLINE

This section summarizes the key concepts from the chapter.

A. Business Fluctuations

1.   Business cycles are all different—and all the same. Each one has its own cause, its own length of time, its own degree of severity, and its own trajectory. Despite all these differences, though, they all seem to follow the same general pattern: decline into recession (**contraction**); bottom out (**trough**); climb into recovery and continue into boom (**expansion**); reach an apex (**peak**); and start all over. The differences are confounding, but the similarities suggest the possibility that some general pattern of policy might reduce the severity of the cycle.

2.   There are many possible explanations for the sources of business cycles, but it may be helpful to classify them into two categories: external and internal. External sources include changes that occur outside the economic system. There are many possibilities here: natural disasters, wars, new discoveries. Internal mechanisms include the *multiplier-accelerator theory* and *demand-induced cycles*. Recall from Chapter 22 that the accelerator theory describes a relationship between the rate of (real) GDP growth and investment spending. The multiplier-accelerator theory adds to the accelerator the relationship between investment and GDP. In a nutshell, GDP growth generates investment (accelerator), which in turn, contributes to further GDP growth (multiplier). As Samuelson and Nordhaus indicate, the multiplier will be explained in greater detail in the next chapter. Hang in there! The main point behind demand-induced business cycles is to realize that economic growth or decline can be caused by rightward and leftward shifts in the aggregate demand curve.

3.   Economists do not fully understand the roots and causes of business cycles. Appropriately, many different theories have been developed. Some work better than others; some work better under different circumstances. Samuelson and Nordhaus review six different theories. Problem number 6 in section VII. below, reviews these theories.

B. Analytical Foundations of Aggregate Demand

1.   Aggregate demand (*AD*) includes all the desired spending by the different sectors in the economy: consumption (*C*), private domestic investment (*I*), government purchases of goods and services (*G*), and net exports (*X*).

2.   The primary reason for the downward slope of the *AD* curve is the **money-supply effect**. As prices in the economy increase, other things held constant, the **real money supply**

decreases. The real money supply is defined as the *nominal money supply* divided by the price level. The supply of *real* money becomes relatively scarce or tight, and therefore, the price of obtaining money, or the rate of interest, goes up. All types of spending that rely on borrowed funds—consumption items, investment, even net exports—decline. Hence, we observe that higher price levels lead to a decrease in the aggregate demand for goods and services, or a movement up and along the aggregate demand curve.

3.   There are some important differences between microeconomic and macroeconomic demand curves. In *micro*, the focus is on a particular market for a particular good. When we construct the demand curve, we allow the price of the good to vary, while *all other prices and consumer incomes are held constant*. In *macro*, we attempt to get a picture of the entire economy, not just one market. The general price level varies along the vertical axis, and *total output and real incomes change* as we move along the aggregate demand curve. The primary reason for the negative slope of the aggregate demand curve is the money-supply effect; the main reason for the downward slope of the single market demand curve is the substitution effect.

4.   There are numerous reasons why the aggregate demand curve might shift. The two main categories of shift variables are policy variables and exogenous variables. *Policy* variables include changes in either monetary or fiscal policy.

Exogenous variables are variables determined outside the framework of the model, or beyond the control of policymakers. Examples of exogenous variables include changes in foreign countries (oil-production decisions, growth rates abroad), advances in technology, and movements in the stock market. We are not implying here that the economy and government policies have no bearing on these "outside" variables, only that it is possible for changes to originate in these areas and that such changes can have an effect on the level of spending (i.e., aggregate demand) in the economy.

Whether change is due to policy variables or exogenous variables, the aggregate demand curve will shift (right or left) in response to these "shocks." There is not universal agreement among economists about the relative importance of these factors. Those economists who stress the importance of the role of the money supply are called *monetarists*. Other economists focus more on the influence of exogenous variables and fiscal policy. The mainstream of economic thinking today includes aspects of both the Keynesian and monetarist points of view.

V. HELPFUL HINTS

1.   Several different theories of business cycles are presented in this chapter. You should realize that there are many unsolved economic problems, and economics cannot *always* provide exact and clearly defined answers or solutions.

What economic analysis does provide in these circumstances, is a structure and framework for investigating and learning about the economic problem at hand. Once informed, you can argue for, or against, particular theories.

2. Do not forget: The **G** in aggregate demand measures the government's purchases of goods and services. This is not the same thing as the government's budget expenditures which also include transfer payments and interest on the debt.

3. The phrase "other things held constant" is important. In order to clarify specific economic relationships it is desirable to change just one variable at a time. When two or more variables change at once (which in reality happens all the time), it becomes very difficult to isolate causes from effects. For example, when we construct the aggregate demand curve, we vary the price level and hold all other things—including the money supply—constant. And when we analyze the effect of policy or exogenous variables on AD, we change just one variable at a time and hold everything else constant.

4. Models that explain simple economic relationships may teach us a great deal, but may at times, seem removed from the helter-skelter activity of the real world. The price we pay for realism in economic models is complication. Recall Samuelson's and Nordhaus's discussion of business-cycle models that contain systems of equations and thousands of variables.

5. Remember, we use models to understand and explain how the economy functions. You should always be aware of the simplifying assumptions being made.

VI. MULTIPLE CHOICE QUESTIONS

These questions are organized by topic from the chapter outline. Choose the best answer from the options available.

A. Business Fluctuations

1. Business cycles seem to be caused:
   a. exclusively by external factors.
   b. exclusively by internal factors.
   c. by factors of any type that mostly influence aggregate demand.
   d. by factors that only influence aggregate supply.
   e. all the above.

2. Which of the following would you *not* expect to see during a period of recession?
   a. Lower business investment in durable equipment.
   b. Lower stock prices and lower demand for labor.
   c. Lower tax receipts from corporations and individuals.
   d. Lower corporate profits.
   e. Lower unemployment compensation payments.

3. Which of the following time frames was marked by the most severe period of recession?

a. 1969-1970.
b. 1982-1983.
c. 1974-1975.
d. 1960-1961.
e. 1953-1954.

4. Which of the following time frames was marked by the most energetic period of economic boom?
   a. 1983-1984.
   b. 1973-1974.
   c. 1938-1939.
   d. 1955-1956.
   e. 1967-1968.

5. The implication of the theory of political business cycles is that:
   a. anti-inflationary medicine is generally administered early in an administration.
   b. the year after an election is frequently a year of austerity.
   c. the year of an election is frequently a year of growth and prosperity.
   d. the timing of elections can dictate the timing of the business cycle.
   e. all the above are correct.

6. If we look to any particular kind of spending as a key factor in accounting for the business cycle, we find it in:
   a. net investment, specifically spending on inventories.
   b. net investment, specifically spending on durable goods.
   c. consumer spending.
   d. variations in spending by state and local governments.
   e. none of the above, the point stressed being that no single type of spending plays any key role.

7. The role of consumer spending in the business cycle, according to U.S. experience, is best understood by noting that:
   a. changes in consumer durable purchases may occasionally set off an upswing or downturn, and changes in consumer spending will intensify the effect of any disturbance originating outside the consumer sphere, via the multiplier.
   b. consumer spending and investment seem to have approximately equal parts to play in the cycle, although the two are so intermixed that it is difficult to separate one from the other and to analyze the role of either.
   c. changes in consumer spending on nondurables most commonly initiate the downturn in a major business cycle, whereas increases in consumer durable purchases are most likely to start the upturn as replacement of worn-out durable items becomes necessary.
   d. changes in consumer spending are most often the initial disturbing factor, and the impact then spreads to investment, thus intensifying the original disturbance.

e. consumer spending has no part to play in the cycle, which (except for wartime disturbances) is almost entirely due to changes in investment.

8. Statistically, the widest swings between peak and bottom of the business cycle are to be found in:
   a. the supply of consumer services.
   b. the production of inventories.
   c. the production of durables and capital goods.
   d. wholesale rather than retail goods.
   e. export and import goods.

9. The multiplier-accelerator theory focuses on the relationship between:
   a. taxes, consumer spending, and GDP.
   b. monetary policy, interest rates, and investment.
   c. GDP and investment spending.
   d. GDP and any component of aggregate demand.
   e. exogenous and policy variables.

10. Which of the following would be considered as a *supply shock* to the economy?
   a. a sharp increase in foreign oil prices.
   b. weather-related crop failures.
   c. a reorganization of the domestic health care industry.
   d. all of the above.
   e. none of the above.

11. The index of leading indicators is best described as:
   a. combination of several statistics that generally give an accurate indication of the direction of economic growth ahead..
   b. a combination of data on boxcar loadings and steel production.
   c. a type of econometric forecasting model.
   d. all of the above.
   e. choices **a.** and **c.** only.

B. Analytical Foundations of Aggregate Demand

12. Which of the terms below is *not* a component of aggregate demand?
   a. consumption expenditure.
   b. government expenditure.
   c. net exports.
   d. investment expenditure.
   e. all of the above terms are part of AD.

13. Which of the following expressions best describes the money-supply effect?
   a. As the money supply increases, so does inflation.
   b. As the economy grows, the central bank increases the supply of money.
   c. Aggregate demand and the money supply are positively related.
   d. As prices increase, the decline in the real money supply will affect aggregate demand.

e. Money makes the world go round.

14. Which of the following is a reason why the aggregate demand curve should be drawn downward-sloping?
   a. Higher prices reduce potential GDP by reducing labor force participation.
   b. Higher prices cause interest rates to fall, thereby depressing investment.
   c. Higher prices cause interest rates to rise, thereby depressing investment.
   d. Higher prices inspire increased labor force participation and therefore increase consumption expenditures.
   e. None of the above makes any sense in explaining the negative slope of an aggregate demand curve.

15. One of the similarities between microeconomic and macroeconomic demand is that both:
   a. hold income constant.
   b. rely on the substitution effect to explain demand.
   c. rely on the money-supply effect to explain demand.
   d. vary inversely with price.
   e. hold the prices of all other goods constant.

16. Which of the following should be expected to shift the aggregate demand curve to the left?
   a. an increase in government spending.
   b. a reduction in net exports.
   c. a reduction in labor force participation.
   d. the adoption of an improved production technology.
   e. a reduction in the value of the dollar.

17. Which of the following should be expected to shift the aggregate demand curve to the right?
   a. an increase in government spending.
   b. a reduction in net exports.
   c. a reduction in labor force participation.
   d. an increase in taxes.
   e. a decrease in the money supply.

18. According to the money-supply effect, which produces a downward-sloping aggregate demand curve, lower prices in the context of a fixed real money supply should:
   a. make credit more difficult to obtain.
   b. increase interest rates and thereby reduce investment.
   c. depress stock market values and thereby reduce consumption.
   d. all the above.
   e. none of the above.

19. According to *monetarists*, the primary determinant of the total dollar of spending in the economy is:
   a. interest rates.
   b. the money supply.
   c. taxes.
   d. transfer payments.
   e. the government debt.

VII. PROBLEM SOLVING

The following problems are designed to help you apply the concepts that you learned in the chapter.

A. Business Fluctuations

1. Record in the spaces provided the business-cycle phase during which you would expect to observe the indicated events; denote contraction by (**C**) and expansion by (**E**):

    ___ a. Business investment increasing
    ___ b. Profits falling
    ___ c. Tax receipts climbing
    ___ d. Demand for labor rising
    ___ e. Stock prices falling
    ___ f. Inflation accelerating
    ___ g. Unemployment-insurance payments increasing
    ___ h. Interest rates falling

2. a. Recessions (or depressions) most commonly arise from a (**drop / rise**) in (**consumption / investment / government spending**).

    b. This initial (**drop / rise**) has magnified consequences because of the multiplier effect; i.e., total spending drops (**even more / somewhat less**) than the initial drop in (**C / I / G**) .

    c. Among the following economic variables, the greatest cyclical fluctuation is typically found in (**wholesale prices / production of capital goods / production of basic materials such as petroleum / expenditures on consumer goods**).

3. Play a "what if" game to test your understanding of a few definitions.

    a. If you were to believe that changes in the population were never caused by changes in economic circumstance, then a theory that held that changes in total population caused the business cycle would be (**an external / an internal / a political**) theory of the cycle.

    b. Were you to go to the other extreme, holding that changes in population were exclusively the result of changes in economic circumstance (e.g., you might think that depression increases the number of poor people who cannot have children because they cannot support them), then a theory that proposed a causal relationship between changes in total population and the business cycle would be (**an external / an internal / a political**) theory of the cycle.

    c. The notion that incumbent political parties use the policy tools at their disposal to time recovery and boom for election years and recession and trough for off-election years is (**an external / an internal / a political**) business-cycle theory.

4. Consider Figure 23-1. Suppose that an economic downturn is caused by a shift in aggregate demand.

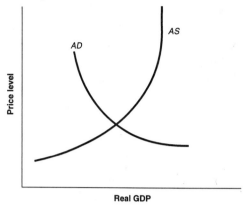

Figure 23-1

a. Illustrate this on the diagram.
b. Give an example of a particular *AD* change that could cause this shift.
c. What sort of policy change would you recommend to move the economy out of this slump?

5. Now look at Figure 23-2, which is identical to Figure 23-1. Suppose, this time, that an economic downturn is caused by a shift in aggregate supply.

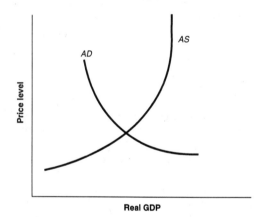

Figure 23-2

a. Illustrate this on the diagram in Figure 23-2.
b. Give an example of a particular *AS* change that could cause this shift.
c. What sort of policy change would you recommend to move the economy out of this slump?
d. Which type of economic downturn is worse, one caused by a shift in *AD* or one caused by a shift in *AS*? Briefly justify your answer.

6. Samuelson and Nordhaus describe six different theories of the business cycle in this chapter. For each of the theories listed below, match it with the number of its description and the letter of the economist(s) who support it.

___ Monetary theories

___ Multiplier-accelerator model

___ Political Theories

___ Equilibrium-business-cycle theories

___ Real business cycle

___ Supply shocks

1. Business cycles caused by shifts in aggregate supply.

2. Innovations and changes in productivity in one sector can spread to the rest of the economy.

3. Misperceptions about prices and wages lead people to supply little or too much labor. This leads to cycles in output.

4. Output growth stimulates investment which generates further growth in output.

5. Cyclical swings caused by changes in the money supply and the availability of credit.

6. Fluctuations in the business cycle attributed to politically-motivated changes in fiscal and monetary policy.

a. W .Nordhaus and E. Tufte

b. R. Lucas, R. Barro, and T. Sargent

c. J. Schumpeter, E. Prescott, P. Long, and C. Plosser

d. M. Friedman

e. R. J. Gordon

f. P. Samuelson

B. Foundations of Aggregate Demand

7. a. Aggregate demand is generally downward-sloping when drawn against a price index due, in large part, to the (**substitution effect / money-supply effect / income effect**).

b. Higher prices, given a constant real money supply, can be expected to cause interest rates to (**rise / fall / stay the same**), cause stock market prices to (**rise / fall / stay the same**), (**reduce / increase / have no effect on**) the international value of the dollar, and generally make credit (**more difficult / easier**) to obtain.

c. In light of these effects, use the spaces provided below to explain how the values of the components of aggregate demand would change if prices were to fall:

   1. Consumption:

   2. Investment:

   3. Government:

   4. Net exports:

8. The first column of Table 23-1 records a series of changes in economic circumstance.

a. Indicate in column (2) the component of aggregate demand (*C, I, G,* or *X*) that would be most directly affected by each change; then note the direction of the effect in column (3) (use + to designate an increase and - to signify a reduction).

b. In column (4) identify whether panel (*a*), (*b*), or (*c*) of Figure 23-3 best illustrates the result graphically as a shift from *AD* to *AD'*.

c. Use column (5) to explain your reasoning. The first row has been completed for you.

d. Look back at column (1) in the table. Circle the letter of those changes in which the effect was generated by a change in a *policy* variable; place a star next to the changes in which the effect was generated by a change in an *exogenous* variable.

9. There is a critical difference between the microeconomic construction of a demand curve for a specific product and the macroeconomic construction of an aggregate demand curve. Indicate whether each of the statements recorded below accurately describes a microeconomic demand curve for a specific product or a macroeconomic aggregate demand curve; use the terms "micro" and "macro."

a. The curve is drawn under the assumption that income is held constant.

b. Total incomes and output vary along this curve.

c. The curve is downward-sloping because consumers can substitute into and out of the consumption of various goods.

d. The curve is downward-sloping because the nominal money supply is fixed.

e. The curve is drawn against a price index even though relative prices may change within that index.

f. The curve is derived from individuals' responses to changes in one price, other prices assumed constant.

TABLE 23-1

(1) Change	(2) AD Component	(3) Direction	(4) Panel	(5) Explanation
a. Increased population	Consumption	+	(b)	More people mean enlarged consumption.
b. Reduced money supply	___	___	___	_____
c. Increased personal income taxes	___	___	___	_____
d. Severe recession abroad	___	___	___	_____
e. Anticipated recession at home	___	___	___	_____
f. Anticipated recession abroad	___	___	___	_____
g. Rapid escalation in house prices	___	___	___	_____
h. An October stock market crash	___	___	___	_____
i. Diminished defense spending	___	___	___	_____
j. Higher prices abroad	___	___	___	_____

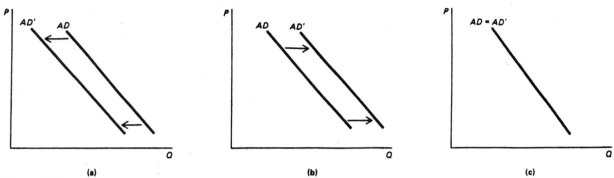

Figure 23-3

VIII. DISCUSSION QUESTIONS

Answer the following questions, making sure that you can explain the work you did to arrive at the answers.

1. Figure 23-4 illustrates how different sectors of the economy were affected by three recessions in the United States. Use the bar chart to discuss how the recessions affected different sectors of the economy in different ways.

2. Figure 23-4 from the text is reproduced here on page __ as Figure 23-5. Discuss several reasons why the aggregate demand curve in the economy might shift to the left. For what reasons might policy makers want aggregate demand to shift in this direction?

IX. ANSWERS TO STUDY GUIDE QUESTIONS

III. Review of Key Concepts

4	Business cycle
8	Recession
11	Depression
13	Business-cycle phases
7	Expansion
1	Multiplier-accelerator theory
10	Demand-induced cycles
12	Aggregate demand
3	Real money supply
6	Policy variables
2	Exogenous variables
9	Monetarists
5	Keynesian macroeconomics

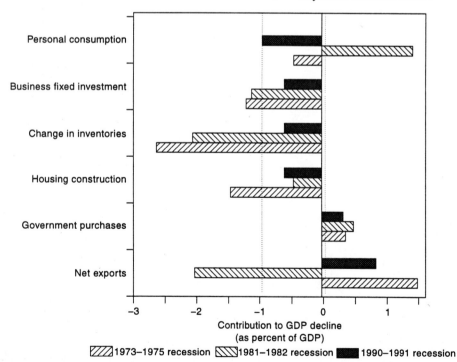

Figure 23-4

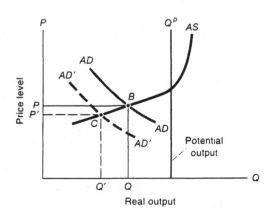

Figure 23-5

VI. Multiple Choice Questions

1. C   2. E   3. B   4. E   5. E   6. B
7. A   8. C   9. C   10. D   11. A   12. E
13. D   14. C   15. D   16. B   17. A   18. E
19. B

VII. Problem Solving

1.   a.   E
    b.   C
    c.   E
    d.   E
    e.   C
    f.   E
    g.   C
    h.   C
2.   a.   drop, investment
    b.   drop, even more, I
    c.   production of capital goods
3.   a.   an external
    b.   an internal
    c.   a political
4.   a.

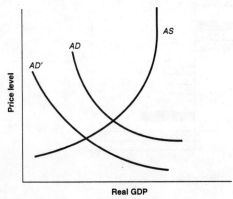

Figure 23-1

b. This shift could be caused by a reduction in consumption, investment, government spending, or net exports. In reality, investment spending is the most volatile of these four possibilities.

c. Stimulative fiscal policy, either a tax cut or an increase in government spending, could be used to get the economy out of the slump. Alternatively, the Fed could pursue an easy monetary policy.

5.   a.

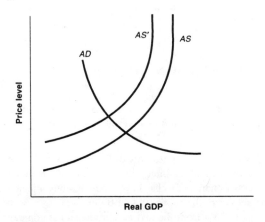

Figure 23-2

b. The AS could shift to the left due to an increase in input prices or due to some external shock that raises the price of a commodity that is vital to production in the economy. (The OPEC oil embargo comes to mind.)

c. Usual fiscal or monetary policy measures would have to focus on either the inflation problem or the unemployment problem. It is not possible to alleviate both problems at once. Ideally, the government could use a supply-side policy to shift the aggregate supply curve back to the right.

d. The AS shift is worse since it creates both inflation and unemployment problems.

6.   5   d   Monetary theories
    4   f   Multiplier-accelerator model
    6   a   Political theories
    3   b   Equilibrium-business-cycle theories
    2   c   Real business cycle
    1   e   Supply shocks
7.   a.   money-supply effect
    b.   rise, fall, reduce, more difficult
    c.   1. Spending would increase due to the increase in the real money supply. Consumers would be able to purchase more goods and services with the same income.

      2. Lower interest rates would increase investment spending.

      3. Lower prices would allow the government to purchase more real goods and services with its budget.

4. Lower prices would attract more foreign customers. Net exports would increase.

8.   a., b., c.

TABLE 23-1

(2)	(3)	(4)	(5)
b. Investment	-	(a)	Higher interest rates lower investment.
c. Consumption	-	(a)	Higher taxes reduce disposable income.
d. Net exports	-	(a)	Recession abroad means less foreign demand for goods and services.
e. Investment or Consumption	-	(a)	The fear of lower profits or income reduces spending.
f. Investment	-	(a)	The fear of lower profits in export markets lowers investment.
g. Consumption	+	(b)	Increase in consumer wealth increases spending.
h. Consumption or Investment	-	(a)	Reduced consumer wealth and/or increased cost of raising funds lowers aggregate demand.
i. Government	-	(a)	Reduced government spending lowers aggregate demand.
j. Net exports	+	(b)	Imports are reduced, domestic spending increases.

d.   Place a circle around b, c, and i.
     Place a star next to the remaining changes.

9.   a.   micro
     b.   macro
     c.   micro
     d.   macro
     e.   macro
     f.   micro

VIII. Discussion Questions

1.   The recession of 1973-1975 was the most severe for home construction, inventories, and investment. The decline in inventories suggests that firms depleted their inventories rather than produce more products.

The 1981-1982 recession was also felt in the same three sectors, but to a lesser extent. Net foreign trade declined more during this recession than during either of the other two recessions, and consumer spending actually increased. The increased consumer spending may have contributed to the trade deficit. This was not a bad recession for the consumer.

The 1990-1991 recession seems to have been less severe than the other two recessions, but it was the worst one for consumers. It was also more evenly spread throughout the economy.

2.   Aggregate demand will shift to the left whenever any of the components *AD* decrease. A decrease in investment spending, an increase in taxes which causes a reduction in consumption spending, or a decrease in net exports would all cause aggregate demand to shift to the left.

If the economy is growing too fast, policy makers, fearing inflation, may want to slow it down. In general, policy makers may want *AD* to shift to the left when inflation is viewed as a problem in the economy.

CHAPTER 24

The Multiplier Model

I. CHAPTER OVERVIEW

In the previous four chapters you were introduced to many of the fundamental concepts of macroeconomic analysis: aggregate supply, aggregate demand, GDP, price indexes, consumption, saving, and investment. In this chapter we put the pieces of the puzzle together. The tools and concepts developed here are the essential building blocks for what follows. The completed picture will give you a better understanding of how the macroeconomy works and will enable you to evaluate various governmental economic policy proposals. You will also be ready to formulate your own ideas for economic policies to deal with such problems as high levels of inflation, sluggish periods of high unemployment, or stagnant times marked by unacceptably high levels of both maladies.

In the first section of this chapter, the **multiplier model** is discussed. The multiplier is one of the key building blocks that we will use over and over again. The time you spend now to learn it thoroughly will pay large dividends later.

In the second portion of the chapter, the government sector is added into the analysis. We are especially interested in the relationship between fiscal policy, i.e. government spending and taxes, and the multiplier.

The chapter closes with a review of empirical estimates of the multiplier, and you should not be surprised by the wide range in these estimates. Economists who estimate multipliers face not only the uncertainties of dealing with an enormously complex economy but also the ramifications of different academic and philosophical traditions.

When you have worked through this chapter, you will have a better understanding of the complex interdependencies that frame the contemporary world economy.

II. LEARNING OBJECTIVES

After you have read Chapter 24 in your text and completed the exercises in this *Study Guide* chapter, you should be able to:

1. Understand the equivalence of the S and I and $C + I$ approaches to equilibrium in a *simple* economy.
2. Explain the process by which a simple economy moves toward equilibrium if it is not initially at an equilibrium position.

3. Explain the difference between *planned* and *actual* spending and investment.
4. Derive the value of the *multiplier* from the marginal propensity to consume (*MPC*) and explain how the multiplier is used to determine a new equilibrium position in a simple economy when investment spending changes.
5. Understand how the multiplier model fits into the AS-AD model of the economy.
6. Understand how governmental fiscal policy affects output in the multiplier model.
7. Explain the different effects of taxes and government spending on aggregate demand.
8. Understand how the **tax multiplier** differs from the **expenditure multiplier**.
9. Calculate the equilibrium level of GDP in an economy with government and trade.
10. Relate the multiplier model developed here to the real world and appreciate the complexity of economic research which attempts to measure the value of the multiplier.

III. REVIEW OF KEY CONCEPTS

Match the following terms from column A with their definitions in column B.

A	B
__ Closed economy	1. Used to show how a dollar change in investment or government spending affects the economy.
__ Actual investment	2. The change in spending on goods and services when disposable income changes by a dollar.
__ Lump-sum taxes	3. Government programs involving spending, transfer payments and taxes.
__ Expenditure multiplier	4. Economy without foreign trade or finance.
__ Tax multiplier	5. Occurs when all *planned* spending in the economy equals what is *actually* spent.
__ Fiscal policy	6. Country which participates in the world economy and is linked

__ Equilibrium

__ Marginal
  propensity to
  consume

__ Open economy

with other countries through trade
and finance.

7.   Is calculated by multiplying
the expenditure multiplier by the
MPC.

8.   Money paid to the
government which is a constant
fixed dollar value and not related
to GDP.

9.   Planned investment spending
plus any unanticipated changes in
inventories.

IV. SUMMARY AND CHAPTER OUTLINE

This section summarizes the key concepts from the chapter.

A. The Basic Multiplier Model

1.   In a simple, closed economy the intersection of the
desired savings and investment schedules will determine the
equilibrium value of GDP. In order to simplify the analysis,
Samuelson and Nordhaus (and for that matter, most other
principles text authors) make the assumption that investment
spending is exogenous. In other words, they treat investment
spending as a given that is not determined by GDP. This
allows us to plot the investment schedule against GDP as a
horizontal line. This is not to say that investment spending
cannot change. If investment changes, say, due to a change
in interest rates (or any other factor), the investment schedule
will simply shift up or down. (Since the investment schedule
here is horizontal, we cannot really talk about right and left
shifts.) Investment is independent of GDP.

Note to Students *Be sure to note how the axes on diagrams
are labeled. We are talking here about the relationship
between investment spending and GDP. Investment is plotted on the vertical axis and GDP on the horizontal axis.
This presentation and discussion in no way violates or
changes the investment demand schedule that we developed
Chapter 22. Please refer to Figure 24-1.*

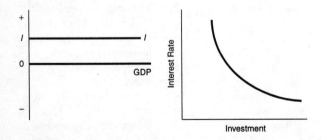

Figure 24-1

When the economy is at equilibrium the *desired* spending
and savings of households is equal to the *desired* production
and investment of firms. However, if households spend too
little, or less than firms thought they would, businesses are
left with unsold goods. These unsold goods are added to
business inventories and count as part of investment. In this
case, *desired* investment will be less than *actual* investment
and the economy will not be at an equilibrium position. In
subsequent production periods, firms will produce less and
lay off workers. GDP falls and the economy moves toward a
position where *desired* saving equals *desired* investment.

2.   The equilibrium position in the economy can also be
found by comparing the total demand for goods and services
(*C* + *I*) with total output. Figure 24-3 from the text is reproduced here as Figure 24-2. As above, if households spend
too little, firms will be left with unplanned additions to their
inventories and the economy will contract.
Diagrammatically, this approach compares total spending
with total output (GDP) and the 45° line is extremely useful
in comparing the two terms. When the *C* + *I* schedule crosses the 45° line, total spending equals total output, and the
economy is at equilibrium. Here, our assumption of fixed or
exogenous investment is very helpful. The *C* + *I* schedule
will have the same slope as the *C* schedule. The fixed difference between the two lines is the constant level of investment spending. The horizontal investment line has no slope
of its own, so the slope of the *C* + *I* line is due entirely to the
slope of *C*! Consumption is critically important in this
model. This is as it should be—consumption spending
accounts for approximately two-thirds of the U.S. aggregate
demand.

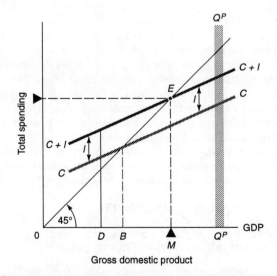

**Figure 24-2 In the Expenditure Approach, Equilibrium GDP
Level Is Found at the Intersection of the C+I Schedule with 45°
Line.**

3. The *multiplier* is also critically linked to consumption. When firms invest more, the workers employed on the investment project will earn more income. The *MPC* determines how much of their extra income they will spend. The recipients of this spending will then turn around and spend more based on the *MPC*. The analysis is simplified by assuming that the same *MPC* applies at all levels of income. Fortunately, in each round marginal spending gets a little smaller (because some of the extra income is saved), and the process converges. The result, however, is that GDP changes by some *multiple* of the initial investment project. The more households spend, the larger that multiple will be. The following formula can be used to calculate the expenditure multiplier:

$$\text{Expenditure multiplier} = \frac{1}{1 - MPC} = \frac{1}{MPS}$$

4. The effectiveness of the multiplier in generating real changes in output depends upon how close the economy is to full employment or potential GDP. If an economy is operating at close to full employment, it will be difficult for a new investment project to generate more employment or output since the economy is close to full employment already. At this point, higher levels of spending will add to the general level of prices (inflation) and comparatively little to real output.

The multiplier model that we are working through can be traced back to Keynes. The focus of Keynes's attention in *The General Theory* (1936) was the Great Depression. Perhaps his development and discussion of the multiplier was not overly concerned with changes in the price level, because inflation, at that point, was hardly a concern for anyone.

5. In the simple model which we consider in the first part of the chapter, only two things could throw an economy out of equilibrium: a decision to change the level of investment up or down and/or a decision to change the level of consumption up or down. Either the *I* line must shift or the *C* line must shift. Without one or the other of these shifts, a Keynesian equilibrium is, in this simple model, eternally durable.

Investment is, of course, inherently volatile. T h a t was one of the lessons of the last chapter. Disturbances to equilibria in simple models like ours are therefore usually cast in terms of sudden, unanticipated changes in *I*, and that is the approach taken here. The consumption function can also shift, to be sure, but the effects of such a shift are similar to the effects of a change in investment, and their coverage is postponed until later.

B. Fiscal Policy in the Multiplier Model

1. The multiplier applies to both external and internal variables that influence and buffet the economy. External

changes include wars, the weather, and OPEC oil price changes. Some examples of internal variables that affect the economy via the multiplier are government spending, taxes, and investment. Sometimes these changes are expected, sometimes they are not. Sometimes these changes are very beneficial and help stabilize the economy, and sometimes they do not. The main point here is that a solid understanding of what multipliers are and how they influence the economy is critical to your understanding of macroeconomics. Policymakers must have an appreciation for the working of the multiplier.

2. Economists have long recognized the role the government plays in providing collective or public goods and redistributing income. Keynesian macroeconomic theory further defined the role of government to include stabilizing the economy via active fiscal policy measures. Fiscal policy, when used appropriately, has a significant impact on output, employment, and prices.

3. The government finances its expenditures by taxing (and borrowing). *Lump-sum taxes* are introduced when a fixed sum of money is collected by the government as taxes, regardless of the level of output in the economy. In this case, *DI* is no longer equal to GDP. However, the relationship between the two terms is very direct:

$$DI + T = \text{GDP}$$

4. Government spending (*G*), like investment is treated as exogenous with respect to GDP. The government spending schedule has no slope of its own—it is a horizontal line when plotted against GDP. This is not to say that *G* cannot change. In fact, government spending will change frequently. This is precisely what fiscal policy is all about. A change in *G* means the total spending line will shift up or down. Total spending in the economy now equals *C* + *I* + *G*. (The only remaining term to be added is net exports.)

5. If total spending in the economy exceeds the level of output, the economy will expand. Alternatively, if *C* + *I* + *G* is less than the level of output, the economy will contract.

6. The effect of a change in G on GDP is *exactly* the same as a change in *I*. It represents a change in spending outside of, or beyond, the consumption function. Therefore, the same *expenditure multiplier* can be used: $1/(1 - MPC) = 1/MPS$.

7. *The tax multiplier equals the expenditure multiplier times MPC.* When the government changes taxes, there will also be a multiplied effect on the economy. However, the tax multiplier will always be smaller than the expenditure multiplier. Here is the reason: When the government raises taxes, households will not pay for the additional tax *entirely* by reducing *C*. They will pay *part* of the tax increase by drawing down *S*. Similarly, when taxes are reduced, households do not typically spend their entire tax cut. Part of the newfound income is saved. Most likely you can appreciate the

importance of the *MPC* in determining the allocation of the tax between *C* and *S*. When taxes change, disposable income changes. The *MPC* determines how much of the *DI* change is spent. This is the logic behind the tax multiplier formula above.

8. This last point should be helpful for those working through problem 9 in the Questions for Discussion section at the end of the chapter in the **textbook**.

Keynes pointed out that if everyone in an economy attempted to save more at the same time, spending in the economy would be reduced. This reduction in spending would cause a contraction in the economy, layoffs would occur, income would fall, and savings would actually decrease—the exact opposite of what people were trying to do.

Remember, Keynes was writing during the Depression. The last thing we needed, Keynes argued, was reduced spending—for whatever reason. During the Depression, firms were cutting back and going out of business. There was just no way businesses were willing or able to increase investment, even if savings had increased.

In a growing economy that is at, or close to, full employment, we can count on firms picking up the slack and investing more when savings increase. When the economy is fully employed, firms have a much greater incentive to add to their capital bases. So, one of the keys to resolving the **paradox of thrift** is knowing the economic health of the nation. The closer the economy is to full employment, the less we have to worry about the paradox.

V. HELPFUL HINTS

1. Do not forget: The *G* in aggregate demand measures the government's purchases of goods and services. This is not the same thing as the government's budget expenditures, which include transfer payments and interest on the debt.

2. The assumption of constant wages and prices when the multiplier model is first introduced allows us to measure its effect on output *only*. The closer the economy is to full employment, the smaller the real change will be and the larger the price increase will be.

3. When the economy is at full employment, we can say it is operating at its potential. *Full employment GDP equals potential GDP.*

4. In a simple economy, without government spending, taxes, trade, or international finance, GDP can be used interchangeably with disposable income (DI).

5. Stimulative fiscal policy works best when there are unemployed resources. The closer an economy is to full employment, the less *real* change there will be in output and the more inflation there will be as a result of stimulative fiscal policy.

6. The terms GDP and *Q* can be used interchangeably. They both represent the output of the economy.

7. Transfers to households are like *negative* taxes. When we talk about taxes we are really talking about *net taxes* or *taxes less transfers*. Taxes themselves are always greater than transfer payments because in addition to redistributing income, the government needs money to purchase goods and services.

8. When lump-sum taxes change, the *C* and hence the *C* + *I* + *G* + *X* lines will *shift*. These lines shift to the *right* by the amount of the tax *increase* and to the *left* the amount of the tax *decrease*. The magnitude of the vertical shift is equal to the change in tax multiplied by the *MPC*.

VI. MULTIPLE CHOICE QUESTIONS

These questions are organized by topic from the chapter outline. Choose the best answer from the options available.

A. The Basic Multiplier Model

1. Suppose that business firms change their plans and increase the total of their spending on new plant and equipment. The basic multiplier model would lead us to expect:
   a. no change in GDP.
   b. GDP and consumer spending to rise.
   c. GDP to rise but consumer spending to be unaffected.
   d. GDP to rise but consumer spending to fall.
   e. GDP to fall but consumer spending to rise.

2. In the simplest Keynesian model with only consumption and investment contributing to aggregate demand, if the value of the marginal propensity to consume is 0.8, then the value of the multiplier must be:
   a. 1.6.
   b. 2.5.
   c. 2.8.
   d. 4.0.
   e. 5.0.

3. If an equilibrium level of GDP were altered by a reduction in planned investment spending, then we would expect to see GDP:
   a. fall but saving (*S*) rise.
   b. fall but no change in *S*.
   c. fall and *S* fall also.
   d. remain unchanged but *S* fall.
   e. none of the preceding.

4. Assume that government spending and net exports are both zero. On a graph that plots spending against GDP, the intersection of the consumption function and a 45° line drawn up from the origin necessarily indicates:
   a. the GDP level at which net investment spending (*I*) first rises above zero.
   b. equality of consumption (*C*) and *I*.
   c. equilibrium GDP.
   d. equality of *C* and saving.

e. none of the above, unless *I* happens to be zero.

5. Consider a simple economy with no government or trade. Actual GDP would then be above its equilibrium level if:

a. the amount that consumers planned to save exceeded the amount that businesses and others planned to invest.

b. the total of planned consumption spending (*C*) exceeded the total of planned *I*.

c. there were no unscheduled or unplanned *I*.

d. GDP had moved temporarily above the break-even point on the consumption function.

e. the total of planned *I* plus the total of planned *C* exceeded the current level of GDP.

6. Which alternative in question 5 would have been correct had that question referred to a GDP below its equilibrium level?

a.

b.

c.

d.

e.

7. Suppose that the current level of GDP is $500 billion and that consumers wish to spend $390 billion of that $500 billion on consumption. Let the total amount of investment spending planned be $120 billion. These figures indicate that GDP is:

a. out of equilibrium and will fall in the future.

b. out of equilibrium and will rise in the future.

c. out of equilibrium, but whether it will rise, fall, or remain at its present level is indeterminate.

d. in equilibrium.

e. none of the above necessarily, since from the information given, GDP may be in equilibrium or out of it.

8. If GDP is in equilibrium, then:

a. consumption must be just equal to investment.

b. business receipts from consumption spending must just equal national income.

c. any increase in spending must result in an inflationary gap.

d. the overall budgets of federal, state, and local governments must be just balanced.

e. none of the above is necessarily correct.

9. Whenever total planned investment exceeds the total of planned saving, then:

a. GDP will fall below potential GDP.

b. GDP will rise above potential GDP.

c. GDP will rise if initially below potential GDP.

d. GDP will fall only if initially at potential GDP.

e. there is no reason to expect any change in GDP, either up or down, or to expect, as a necessary result, any change in potential GDP.

10. When we assume that planned investment spending is independent of GDP, then:

a. when investment is plotted against GDP, it will be a horizontal line.

b. the *C* + *I* spending line will be parallel to, and have the same slope as, the consumption schedule.

c. we assume that GDP has no direct influence on investment.

d. we are making a simplifying assumption about investment to get a better understanding of the basic multiplier model.

e. all the above.

11. When actual investment is greater than planned investment:

a. households are saving less than firms anticipated they would.

b. the economy could still be at an equilibrium position.

c. relative to household consumption plans, firms produced too many goods and services.

d. capital depreciation in the economy must be increasing.

e. the multiplier is getting larger.

12. The basic multiplier model does not work very well when the economy is close to full employment because:

a. it is difficult for the economy to produce more real output.

b. prices tend to become more inflexible as the economy gets closer to potential GDP.

c. potential GDP is a moving target which is nearly impossible to hit with precision.

d. it is not meaningful to talk about full employment in a simple economy.

e. none of the above.

13. According to Figure 24-3, the level of autonomous consumption spending in the economy is:

a. A.

b. B.

c. 0.

d. D.

e. E.

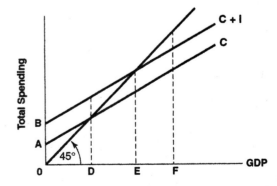

Figure 24-3

14. Assume that point F in Figure 24-3 represents potential GDP in the economy. According to the diagram, the economy is:
    a. at its potential.
    b. beneath its potential, but moving towards potential GDP.
    c. beneath its potential and without any changes will stay where it is.
    d. beyond its potential, but moving back towards potential GDP.
    e. beyond its potential and without any changes will stay where it is.

15. According to Figure 24-3 investment spending in the economy:
    a. is increasing.
    b. is decreasing.
    c. increases up to point E and then decreases.
    d. is constant and unchanging.
    e. is too low.

16. Assume that both axes in Figure 24-3 are drawn to the same scale. According to the diagram, the multiplier:
    a. is equal to 1.
    b. is greater than 1.
    c. is less than 1.
    d. changes with GDP.
    e. cannot be determined without additional information.

B. Fiscal Policy in the Multiplier Model

17. Lump-sum taxes:
    a. equate government spending and taxes.
    b. ensure that DI will equal GDP.
    c. are constant, regardless of GDP.
    d. are paid from savings.
    e. none of the above.

18. Government spending is plotted as a horizontal line with respect to GDP because:
    a. we assume, for simplicity, that G is independent of GDP.
    b. the tax multiplier is smaller than the expenditure multiplier.
    c. government spending has not changed in recent years.
    d. all the above.
    e. none of the above.

19. The stimulative effect of a tax cut is smaller than an equivalent dollar increase in government spending because:
    a. a portion of the tax cut will be saved.
    b. the MPC is less than 1.
    c. the vertical shift in the spending line is less for changes in T than for changes in G.
    d. all the above.
    e. none of the above.

20. When government spending changes, the effect on the economy is:
    a. the same as a change in taxes.
    b. smaller than a change in taxes.
    c. the same as a change in investment.
    d. larger than a change in investment.
    e. greater than a tax change, but smaller than a change in investment.

21. Which expression below best describes the relationship between the *tax multiplier* and the *expenditure multiplier*?
    a. expenditure multiplier = tax multiplier × MPC.
    b. tax multiplier = expenditure multiplier × MPC.
    c. expenditure multiplier + tax multiplier = 1.
    d. tax multiplier = expenditure multiplier × MPC.
    e. expenditure multiplier = tax multiplier / (1-MPC).

22. During the Reagan administration:
    a. fiscal policy was rarely used.
    b. the paradox of thrift was resolved.
    c. the economy experienced both recession and prosperity.
    d. exports exceeded imports.
    e. none of the above.

23. If GDP is in equilibrium in an economy with government, then:
    a. consumption must be just equal to investment.
    b. business receipts from consumption spending must just equal national income.
    c. any increase in spending must result in an inflationary gap.
    d. the overall budgets of federal, state, and local governments must be just balanced.
    e. none of the above is necessarily correct.

24. GDP is in equilibrium at its full-employment level. The federal government finds it necessary to increase its expenditures on goods and services by $10 billion. It wants to increase taxes sufficiently so that there will be no more serious threat of inflation; i.e., it wants the net change in the equilibrium level of GDP to be zero. The probable increase in tax collections needed will be:
    a. more than $10 billion.
    b. $10 billion.
    c. less than $10 billion, but not zero.
    d. zero.
    e. less than zero; i.e., tax collections can be reduced.

25. There is a small but significant difference between the multiplier effect of an increase of, say, $10 in government spending and that of a decrease of $10 in personal taxes levied. This is because:
    a. government spending, by increasing income earned, increases consumption spending.
    b. a $10 reduction in taxation has a significantly greater effect on the government surplus or deficit than does a $10 increase in government spending.
    c. a tax reduction affects consumer income and spending directly, whereas the effect of an increase in govern-

ment spending on consumers is only indirect.

    d.   a $10 reduction in personal taxes does not produce a $10 increase in consumer spending, since part of this reduction goes into extra saving.

    e.   none of the above reasons.

26. Whenever total planned investment exceeds the total of all planned saving in an economy with government, then:

    a.   GDP will fall below potential GDP.

    b.   GDP will rise above potential GDP.

    c.   GDP will rise if initially below potential GDP.

    d.   GDP will fall only if initially at potential GDP.

    e.   there is no reason to expect any change in GDP, either up or down, or to expect, as a necessary result, any change in potential GDP.

27. Assume that the following conditions hold:

    A.   GDP is initially in equilibrium.

    B.   The government then increases its total expenditure on goods and services by $2 billion.

    C.   There is no increase at all in tax collection.

    D.   The marginal propensity to consume is 0.75.

Assuming that there are no price-inflationary consequences in the new equilibrium thus produced, GDP will:

    a.   fall by $4 billion.

    b.   rise by $2 billion.

    c.   rise by $6 billion.

    d.   rise by $8 billion.

    e.   rise by $4 billion.

28. Which alternative in question 23 would be correct if that question referred to a total reduction of $2 billion in the government's income tax collections, with *no increase* at all in its expenditure on goods and services?

    a.

    b.

    c.

    d.

    e.

VII.   PROBLEM SOLVING

The following problems are designed to help you apply the concepts that you learned in the chapter.

A. The Basic Multiplier Model

1. Consider the consumption and investment diagrams in Figure 24-4.

    a., Look first at the solid investment line in the right-hand diagram To draw this line horizontally is to say that investment spending (**rises / remains unchanged / falls**) as GDP increases.

    b.   The left-hand diagram says that if GDP were equal to 0E, consumption spending would be (*HA / JA / ME / KE*). With GDP at 0E, saving would equal (*HA /JA /*

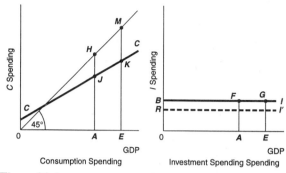

Figure 24-4

MK / KE).

    c.   If GDP were to fall to 0A, however, then C spending would equal (*HA /JA / ME / KE*), and S would equal (*HJ / JA / MK / KE*).

    d.   Saving (S) must equal investment (I) if GDP is to be in equilibrium. Assume that the same scale of measurement was used to construct both of the diagrams in Figure 24-4. Measure the two levels of saving in the left-hand diagram (*HJ* and *MK*), and compare them with the investment amount indicated along the solid I line on the right. The S value which would match this I value would be (*HJ / MK*). At this point, GDP is equal to (*0A / 0E*).

    e.   Now suppose that the level of investment spending decreases such that R0 rather than B0 indicates the level of investment spending in the economy. Again measuring S against I, it follows that saving would now be (*HJ/ MK*) and GDP would equal (*0A / 0E*).

    f.   When investment spending drops from B0 to R0, then C spending (**also drops / remains unchanged / increases**) in the new equilibrium.

2. By now, it should be clear that investment spending plays an important role in determining the level of GDP. We must, therefore, explore more fully what happens when the level of I spending changes. For this, we will use Figure 24-4. Assume that GDP is initially at equilibrium at a level of $100, with I spending at $30 and C spending at $70. Suppose investment spending then decreases, dropping from $30 to $20. The horizontal I line of Figure 24-5 drops to a new and lower position at I'. We can follow the move to a new equilibrium in a step-by-step manner, as outlined in the next several paragraphs.

    The flow of total spending directed toward producers drops immediately from $100 to $90 because the I spending component of this flow has dropped. It will take a little time before consumers begin to feel the impact of this drop. When business was paying out $100 in wages and salaries, interest, and dividend payments, it was simply passing on

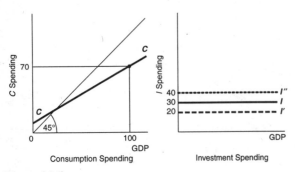

Figure 24-5

money it received from the buyers of consumption and investment goods. When (because of the drop in investment spending) this incoming flow drops to $90, the earnings flow (wages and salaries, dividend payments, etc.) must also drop correspondingly. There is no alternative source which could maintain the sum of those payments at the old $100 level. Some workers will be laid off or required to work part-time, and total profits earned by business will fall. Specifically, the flow of earned income reaching consumers must likewise drop from $100 to $90. Not great news, to be sure, but the news gets worse.

a. When income (measured here as GDP) drops, consumption will (**drop / restrain constant / rise**); this is what the consumption function tells us. The question is, by how much? To answer this, we must know the marginal propensity to consume. Suppose, for example, that the *MPC* is 0.6. This would mean that the reduction in consumption prompted by the initial $10 reduction in income would equal (**$0 / $6 / $10**). That is, consumption would equal (**$10 / $64 / $70 / $90 / $100**) instead of $70 if income fell from $100 to $90; saving, meanwhile, would equal (**$0 / $6 / $10 / $26 / $30 / $36**) instead of $30.

b. Investment has fallen to $20. Is *S* equal to *I* after the decrease in *C*? (**yes / no**) Is GDP at an equilibrium level? (**yes / no**)

We have now reached the point in the analysis at which the notion of "multiplier" must be considered. Although consumption has fallen from $70 to $64 in response to the $10 drop in GDP, we are still nowhere near a new equilibrium GDP level. The fact that GDP is still out of equilibrium is evident from the fact that *S* ($26) is still not equal to *I* ($20). The important point to note here is that the reduction in consumption spending has exactly the same effect on production and on income as the initial drop in investment. So, GDP will continue to fall.

c. When *I* first decreased, GDP fell by $10. Now, in response to the decrease in *C*, GDP will fall by an additional (**$3 / $6 / $10**). GDP, which first fell from $100 to $90, will now drop further, to (**$60 / $80 / $84 / $88**).

d. It is not necessary to pursue this repeated sequence of consumption and savings adjustments to its logical conclusion. It should be clear that it will gradually dampen, ending when (with investment at $20) (**GDP has fallen to zero / saving has fallen to zero / saving has fallen to $20**).

This question had two objectives. First, it exercised your understanding of equilibrium. Throughout, in fact, the economy was out of equilibrium. To cement your grasp of why, recall what happened when GDP first fell to $90. By the *S* = *I* test, *C* = $70 and *I* = $20 could not have been in equilibrium because saving was $30. But what of the consumption side of the analysis; did total spending match supply? When GDP fell to $90, *C* fell to $64, and *C* + *I* equaled $84—hardly an equilibrium position.

Second, there was an initial elaboration of the multiplier sequence. Mathematically, this kind of sequence is known as a "convergent geometric progression"—an elegant phrase, useful for impressing your friends (or some of them) on social occasions, if you can manage to work it into the conversation. All you need to know about such a progression is that its sum has a finite limit. That is, GDP does not keep dropping until it collapses to zero or below. The sequence involved here is as follows: 10 + 6 + 3.6 + etc. The sum of this sequence, fully extended, is 25, not infinity. The full GDP drop will be $25, and GDP, upon dropping from its original value of $100, will stop when it reaches a new equilibrium at $75.

How do we know that? A straight-line consumption function with an *MPC* of 0.6 (i.e., a slope of 0.6) which matches a GDP value of $100 with a consumption value of $70 (the original equilibrium position) must have the following equation:

$$C = \$10 + 0.6 \text{ (GDP)}$$

And this means that:

$$S = -\$10 + 0.4 \text{ (GDP)}$$

Try it! GDP = $100 means that *C* = $10 + $60 = $70. So what happens when GDP = $75? *C* = $10 + $45 = $55, and *S* = $75 - $55 = $20. Since *I* now equals $20, this must be in equilibrium. Also, *C* + *I* = $55 + $20 = $75 = GDP.

3. Saving equals investment in equilibrium, so we must be able to use a saving-investment diagram to illustrate equilibrium GDP. If we know the consumption function, then we can derive the savings schedule according to *S* = GDP - *C*. In Figure 24-6, the *SS* line is such a savings schedule; it corresponds to the consumption function in Figure 24-5. The solid *I* line is also replicated from Figure 24-5. The intersec-

tion of the *SS* and *I* curves, at GDP = $100, indicates the initial equilibrium GDP level, because it is the only GDP level at which *S* and *I* are equal.

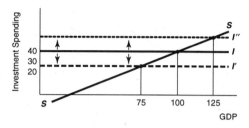

Figure 24-6

a. The dashed *I'* line shows what happens if *I* spending drops from $30 to $20. The new equilibrium GDP must be (**$20 / $30 / $60 / $75 / $90 / $100**), for the same reason as before. If *I* spending is to he $20, then *S* must be $20 also; $75 is the only GDP level at which *S* is $20.

b. Also shown in Figure 24-6 is a dotted *I"* line, at $40. If *I* spending were to rise to this level, the diagram indicates that the resulting GDP equilibrium level would be (**$75 / $100 / $110 / $125 / $150**).

4. In Figure 24-7, the line *CC* is the same consumption function we have used before. At the GDP level indicated by 0*G* in Figure 24-7, *C* spending would be *DG*.

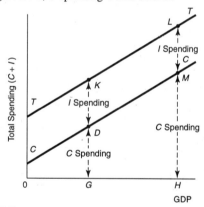

Figure 24-7

For purposes of considering GDP, of course, our interest is in total spending (consumption spending plus investment spending), and there is no reason why investment cannot be added to consumption on a standard diagram to reflect total spending. Simply draw the line *TT* above *CC*, and make the vertical distance between these two lines an immediate reflection of investment. The *TT* line thus reflects aggregate demand for any level of GDP.

a. The vertical distance from any point on *TT* down to the axis line now measures total spending, *C + I*. At

GDP level 0*G*, for example, investment would equal *KD*, consumption would equal *DG*, and total spending, *I + C*, would equal *KG*—i.e., *KD* plus *DG*. Similarly, if the GDP level were 0*H*, then investment would be indicated by (**LM / DG / MH**) and consumption spending would *equal* (**LM / DG / MH**). Total spending would be measured by (**LM / KG / MH / LH**).

Figure 24-8 is basically the same as Figure 24-7. The same *CC* and *TT* lines appear; in fact, only a 45° line has been added. The fundamental issue, now, is this: Pick any level of GDP at random. Given a consumption function and a level of investment, would that GDP represent an equilibrium?

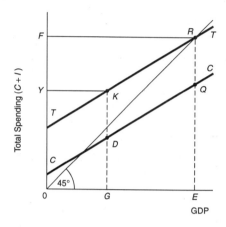

Figure 24-8

b. For example, take a GDP of 0*G* in Figure 24-8. Total spending, *C + I*, would then be *KG*, but point *K* is off the 45° line and *KG* is not equal to 0*G*. That is, GDP would not be equal to *C + I*. In fact, an equilibrium GDP level can occur only at the point where the total-spending line, *TT*, cuts across the 45° line. This is at point *R*, indicating a GDP of 0*E*. Here, total spending of *RE* (**is / is not**) equal to GDP of 0*E*.

c. At any GDP lower than (to the left of) 0*E*, *S* would be (**less than / equal to / greater than**) *I*. At any GDP higher than (to the right of) 0*E*, *S* would be (**less than / equal to / greater than**) *I*.

5. Any change in *I* spending has a magnified, or "multiplied," effect on the GDP level because it sets off a series of *C* changes (as outlined earlier).

a. If the multiplier equals 3 and investment increases by $10 billion, then GDP would (**rise / fall**) by (**$10 / $20 / $30 / $40 / $50**) billion.

b. If *I* spending rose by $10 billion with a multiplier of 4, then GDP would (**rise / fall**) by (**$10 / $20 / $30 / $40 / $50**) billion.

The multiplier formula in a simple Keynesian

model with only consumption (as a function of GDP) and investment is

$$\text{Expenditure multiplier} = \frac{1}{1 - MPC} = \frac{1}{MPS}$$

c.   This means that if the *MPC* is 0.6, the multiplier equals (**1 / 2 / 2.5 / 3 / 3.5 / 4**). If the *MPC* is 0.8, the multiplier equals (**1 / 2 / 2.5 / 3 / 3.5 / 4 / 5**).

d.   Suppose there is a change in investment (either a rise or a fall) of $10. If the *MPC* equals 0.6, then the resulting change in GDP (rise or fall) is (**$10 / $20 / $25 / $30 / $50**) . If the *MPC* equals 0.8, then the resulting change in GDP (rise or fall) is (**$10 / $20 / $25 / $30 / $50**).

(*Note*: The multiplier formula given above holds only in the simplified conditions specified. We will soon incorporate some complications, and the multiplier formula will be changed accordingly.)

6.   Table 24-1 describes a simple economy's consumption function.

TABLE 24-1

GDP	C
130	112
150	126
170	140
190	154
210	168
230	182
250	196
270	210
290	224
310	238

a.   If the amount of investment spending were $60, then equilibrium GDP would equal $_____.

b.   If investment fell to $30, equilibrium GDP would equal $_____.

7.   Consult Figure 24-9. The top panel illustrates equilibrium in the consumption-investment geometry of the Keynesian model; the bottom panel presents equilibrium using aggregate supply and aggregate demand. Remember

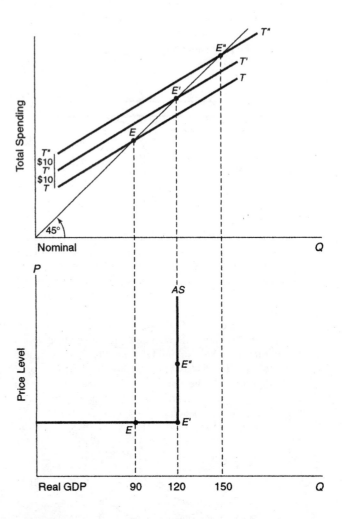

Figure 24-9

that the top diagram holds prices *fixed*, whereas the bottom diagram has price as a variable on the *Y* axis. Note also that the shape of the aggregate supply curve drawn there is an extreme representation of the shape identified previously.

TABLE 24-2 Equilibrium Output Can Be Found Arithmetically as the
Level Where Planned Spending Equals GDP
GDP Determination Where Output Equals Planned Spending
(billions of dollars)

(1) Levels of GDP and DI	(2) Planned Consumption	(3) Planned Saving (3) = (1) - (2)	(4) Planned Investment	(5) Level of GDP (5) = (1)	(6) Total Planned Spending and Investment (6) = (2) + (4)	(7) Resulting Tendency of Output
4,200	3 800	400	200	4,200 >	4,000	↓ Contraction
3,900	3 600	300	200	3,900 >	3,800	↓ Contraction
3,600	3,400	200	200	3,600 =		Equilibrium
3,300	3,200	100	200	3,300 <	3,400	↑ Expansion
3,000	3,000	0	200	3,000 <	3,200	↑ Expansion
2,700	2,800	-100	200	2,700 <	3,000	↑ Expansion

We are assuming here that the highest level of real output that this economy can achieve is $120. This point represents complete full employment of all resources: no more can be produced.

a.   Draw, first of all, an aggregate demand curve in the lower panel of Figure 24-9 that would support the same equilibrium level as curve *TT* in the upper panel.

b.   Now let investment increase to *I'* so that *T'T'* becomes the appropriate representation of total spending. Draw a second aggregate demand curve in the bottom panel to illustrate the same new equilibrium. Reading from the vertical and horizontal axes, it appears that the $10 increase in investment has produced a (**$5 / $10 / $15 / $30**) increase in GDP; the multiplier would, therefore, appear to be _____.

c.   Consider, finally, line *T"T"* in the upper panel. It would appear, given the geometry of the upper panel, that the second $10 increase in investment should, by producing *T"T"*, cause GDP to increase by another $_____.

d.   This will, however, not be the case, because *T'T'* has already brought GDP up to its maximum potential. The second increase in *I* will simply cause (**prices / employment / output**) to rise. Show this by drawing a third aggregate demand curve in the lower panel.

8.   Table 24-1 from your text is reproduced here as Table 24-2.

a.   Use the axes in Figures 24-10 and 24-11 to plot these data. In Figure 24-10, plot saving and investment. Indicate the level of equilibrium GDP in the economy.

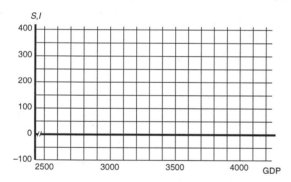

Figure 24-10

b.   In Figure 24-11, plot *C*, *C* + *I*, and the 45° line. The equilibrium levels of GDP should line up vertically in the two diagrams.

c.   What is the value of the *MPC*?

d.   What is the value of the *MPS* ?

e.   Write down an equation for the consumption schedule. (*Hint*: It should be in the form of:

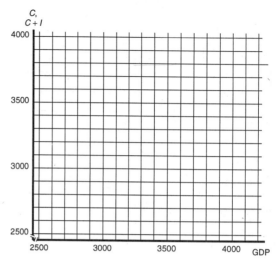

Figure 24-11

$$C = \text{intercept} + (MPC \times GDP).)$$

f.   What is the value of the multiplier?

g.   Assume that there are idle resources and room for expansion in the economy. If investment spending changes by $50, what will be the new equilibrium level of GDP?

h.   At the new equilibrium position, *C* = _____, and *S* = _____.

B.   Fiscal Policy in the Multiplier Model

9.   Consider Figure 24-12. The two consumption schedules illustrate the effect of a *lump-sum tax* on household spending. The solid line, *CC*, represents consumer spending before the tax; the dashed line, *C'C'*, shows consumption after the tax. (Note that the vertical distance between the two consumption schedules is $300 and the rightward shift is equal to $400.)

a.   What is the value of the *MPC*? ____

b.   How large is the (lump-sum) tax increase? ____

c.   When GDP is $4000, what is *DI*? ____

d.   What is the value of the *expenditure multiplier*? ____

e.   What is the value of the *tax multiplier*? ____

f.   What economic problem might the government have been trying to correct when it imposed the tax in the first place?

g.   Besides raising taxes, what other fiscal policy action could the government have taken to correct this problem?

10.   Needless to say, once we have taxes in our model, we need to include government spending as well. Figure 24-13 includes an after-tax consumption schedule for the economy. Investment is independent of GDP and is equal to $200. Government spending is also assumed to be independent of GDP and is equal to $300.

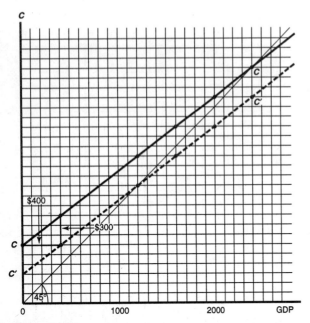

Figure 24-12

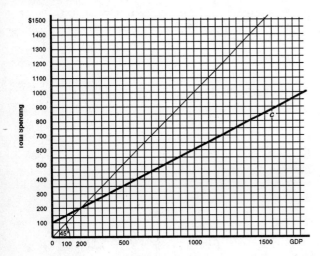

Figure 24-13

a. Plot the $C + I$ line on the diagram. What is the value of the intercept? ____

b. Plot the $C + I + G$ total-spending line on the diagram. What is the value of its intercept? ____

c. If government spending increases, the $C + I + G$ line will shift (**up / down / not at all**) due to the change in ($C / I / G$).

d. If lump-sum taxes increases, the $C + I + G$ line will shift (**up / down / not at all**) due to the change in ($C / I / G$).

e. If the changes in taxes and government spending from parts c and d are of equal magnitude, then (**both shifts will be of equal size / the shift in part c will be larger / the shift in part d will be larger**).

11. Table 24-3 represents an economy that has taxes and government spending but is not yet open to trade.

TABLE 24-3 Output Determination with Government

(1) GDP	(2) Taxes	(3) DI	(4) C	(5) I	(6) G	(7) C + I + G
1200	200	___	900	200	300	1400
1450	___	___	1100	___	___	___
1700	___	___	1300	___	___	___
1950	___	___	1500	___	___	___
2200	___	___	1700	___	___	___
2450	___	___	1900	___	___	___
2700	___	___	2100	___	___	___

a. Taxes in the economy are lump-sum, so you can easily complete the rest of column (2).

b. Investment and government spending are both independent of GDP, so you can fill in the rest of columns (5) and (6) as well.

c. Complete the disposable income entries in column (3).

d. Calculate total spending for the economy in column (7).

e. What is the equilibrium level of GDP in the economy?

f. When the economy is at equilibrium, what is the level of saving?

When the economy is at equilibrium, investment should equal saving. Now that the government is included, we have to allow for the possibility of government saving. Government saving is equal to $T - G$. (If the difference between T and G is negative, then the government is borrowing, or running a deficit.)

g. Determine if $I = S + (T - G)$ when the economy is at equilibrium.

h. What is the value of the MPC?

i. What is the value of the expenditure multiplier?

j. What is the value of the tax multiplier?

k. If the government increases spending by $100, what would be the new equilibrium value of GDP?

l. What economic problem might exist for the government to make this fiscal policy change?

m. If the government wanted to achieve the same change in GDP as in part **k** by cutting taxes instead, how large would the tax cut have to be?

VIII. DISCUSSION QUESTIONS

Answer the following questions, making sure that you can explain the work you did to arrive at the answers.

1. Figure 24-2 from the text is reproduced here as Figure 24-14. Explain why point *M* represents the equilibrium point in this simple economy and explain how this economy would move toward equilibrium if GDP were less than *M* and *I* was greater than *S*.

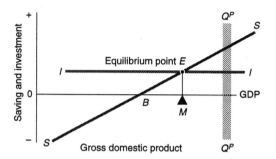

Figure 24-14

2. Figure 24-3 from the text is reproduced on page **XXX** as Figure 24-2. Explain why point *M* represents the equilibrium point in this simple economy and explain how this economy would move toward equilibrium if GDP were greater than *M* and the level of output was greater than *C + I*.

3. Explain, in your own words, how an increase in investment spending generates a multiplied effect on GDP.

4. Why is it that the multiplier model becomes less and less valid as an economy gets closer and closer to full employment?

5. Explain what the tax multiplier is and why it is less than the expenditure multiplier.

IX. ANSWERS TO STUDY GUIDE QUESTIONS

III. Review of Key Concepts
4 Closed economy
9 Actual investment
8 Lump-sum taxes
1 Expenditure multiplier
7 Tax multiplier
3 Fiscal policy
5 Equilibrium
2 Marginal propensity to consume
6 Open economy

VI. Multiple Choice Questions
1. B 2. E 3. C 4. E 5. A 6. E
7. B 8. E 9. C 10. E 11. C 12. A
13. A 14. C 15. D 16. B 17. C 18. A
19. D 20. C 21. B 22. C 23. E 24. A
25. D 26. C 27. D 28. C

VII. Problem Solving
1. a. remains unchanged
   b. *KE, MK*
   c. *JA, HJ*
   d. *MK, 0E*
   e. *HJ, 0A*
   f. also drops
2. a. drop, $6, $64, $26
   b. no, no
   c. $6, $84
   d. saving has fallen to $20
3. a. $75
   b. $125
4. a. *LM, MH, LH*
   b. is
   c. less than, greater than

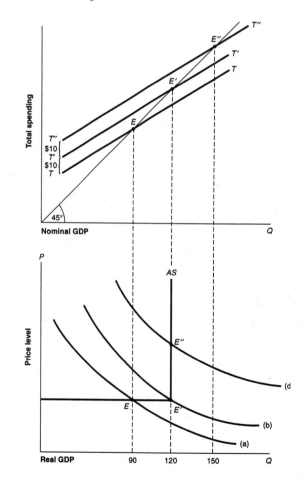

Figure 24-9

5. a.   rise, $30
    b.   rise, $40
    c.   2.5, 5
    d. $25, $50
6. a. $270
    b. $170
7. a.   See Figure 24-9.
    b. $30, 3
    c. $30
    d.   prices
8. a.   See Figure 24-10

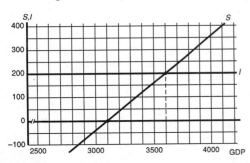

Figure 24-10

    b.   See Figure 24-11.
    c.   0.67
    d.   0.33
    e. $C = 1000 + (0.67 \times GDP)$
    f.   3
    g. $3,600 + $150 = $3,750
    h. $C = \$3,500, S = \$250$

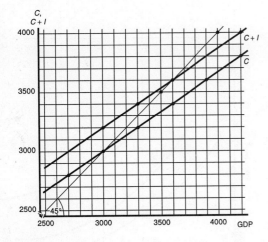

Figure 24-11

9. a. $MPC = 0.75$
    b. $400
    c. $3600

    d.   4
    e.   3
    f.   The government may have been trying to decrease inflation in the economy. Alternatively, it could be trying to balance its budget.
    g.   The government could decrease spending.
10. a.   See Figure 24-13. The intercept is 300.

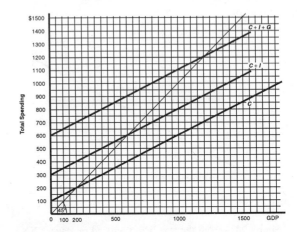

Figure 24-13

    b.   See Figure 24-13. The intercept is 600.
    c.   up, G
    d.   down, C
    e.   the shift in part c will be larger
11. a, b, c, d. See Table 24-3.

TABLE 24-3 Output Determination with Government

(1) GDP	(2) Taxes	(3) DI	(4) C	(5) I	(6) G	(7) C + I + G
1200	200	1000	900	200	300	1400
1450	200	1250	1100	200	300	1600
1700	200	1500	1300	200	300	1800
1950	200	1750	1500	200	300	2000
2200	200	2000	1700	200	300	2200
2450	200	2250	1900	200	300	2400
2700	200	2500	2100	200	300	2600

    e.   2200
    f. $DI - C = 300$
    g. $I = 200, S = 300, T - G = -100$. Yes, $I = S + (T - G)$.
    h. $MPC = 200/250 = 0.8$
    i.   5
    j.   4
    k.   The change in GDP equals $100 \times 5 = $500. The new equilibrium value for GDP is $2700.
    l.   Unemployment may be high and the economy may be in a recession.
    m.   If the government wants GDP to increase by $500 and the tax multiplier is 4, the tax cut would have to be $125.

VIII. Discussion Questions

1. Saving can be viewed as the portion of disposable income that is not spent. Planned investment spending by firms will exactly offset that reduction in spending when the simple economy is at equilibrium. If GDP is less than M and investment is greater than saving, then from the firms' perspective households are spending more and saving less than the firms anticipated. Firms see their inventories being drawn down lower than they would like. Firms respond to this situation by increasing employment and output. Hence, the economy moves toward M.

2. At point M total spending $(C + I)$ equals GDP or output. All the goods and services produced are purchased either by households or firms. If GDP is greater than M, total spending is less than output. Firms are left with unsold goods and services. In order to reduce their inventories, firms will lay off workers and produce fewer goods and services. The forces of the market will make GDP contract.

3. When investment spending increases, this creates additional employment opportunities for workers. The employees working on the investment project earn income. The MPC determines how much of that extra income, they will spend. As labor spends more money, the firms that sell goods and services to the workers earn more income, and they are encouraged to expand. This process continues, but at each subsequent step in the chain the additions to income and GDP get smaller and smaller.

4. As an economy gets closer and closer to full employment, it becomes more and more difficult to increase real output.

Once full employment is reached, the economy cannot produce any more. As certain industries experience an increased demand for their products, this will put upward pressure on prices. The only way an industry can expand is if it bids resources away from other sectors in the economy. The increase in output in one industry will be matched by a decrease in output in another industry, albeit at higher prices.

5. The tax multiplier is used to show the effect of a change in taxes on GDP. When the government raises taxes, households do not reduce their consumption spending by the full amount of the tax increase. Instead, they pay for part of the increase in taxes by reducing saving. Similarly, when taxes are cut, households save part of their increase in disposable income and do not spend it all. Therefore, a tax change has a smaller dollar for dollar impact on the economy than a change in government spending.

CHAPTER 25

Money, Banking, and Financial Markets

I. CHAPTER OVERVIEW

The determination of national output has, up until now, been described with little or no reference to money. It is now time to correct this omission; money is perhaps the most powerful tool of modern stabilization policy, and to continue to ignore its potential would be an enormous mistake. As you progress through the next chapters, it will become clear to you that the omission was a matter of exposition—a recognition that we could not do everything at once. The models that were constructed in earlier chapters can be expanded to include the monetary side of an economy. It therefore made sense to develop them fully before adding a second, *financial* dimension to their stories.

Chapter 25 begins with a discussion of the evolution of money and its associated financial institutions. It is perhaps surprising to note here at the beginning that there is no single, functional definition of "money." Since there are different "near-money" financial instruments available from across a wide spectrum of contemporary financial institutions, it is not possible to write a single all-encompassing definition of money. Economists offer, instead, a list of definitions, each one applying to a slightly different notion and/or application of "money" or "credit."

In this chapter you are also introduced to the demand for and the supply of money. You may begin to suspect that you will shortly see a money market evolve, which could be incorporated into our multiplier model; this will happen in the next chapter. Before that happens, though, we need to learn a little more about money and commercial banking.

The final section explores other types of financial assets. Included here is a discussion of assets that lie outside the technical definitions of M_1 and M_2, but nevertheless are held in great quantities by millions of Americans. There is a brief analysis of the workings of the stock market as well as an introduction to some of the strategies of financial investment.

II. LEARNING OBJECTIVES

After you have read Chapter 25 in your text and completed the exercises in this *Study Guide* chapter, you should be able to:

1. Outline the highlights of the evolution of the monetary system from **barter**, through **commodity money**, and into today's system of **fiat money**.
2. Understand the differences between M_1 and M_2.
3. Discuss the role of interest rates in determining the price of money, and understand the differences between *nominal* and *real* interest rate movements.
4. Describe the three *functions of money* and explain their role in supporting the **transactions demand** and the **assets demand** for money.
5. Outline briefly the evolution of the banking system from a collection of simple goldsmith depositories of wealth into an interconnected array of banks and other financial intermediaries.
6. Describe the process by which a banking system built on **fractional reserves** can create money. Understand the mathematics behind the resulting **money multiplier**, and define the two qualifications upon which its precise computation is dependent.
7. Understand the trade-off between risk and return on financial investments.
8. Discuss some of the historical trends in the U.S. stock market, including the great crash of 1929 and the fall in October, 1987.
9. Understand the basis of the **efficient-market** hypothesis and how it translates into a **random walk** theory of stock market prices.
10. Understand the economic concepts that lie behind the formulation of a rudimentary personal financial strategy.

III. REVIEW OF KEY CONCEPTS

Match the following terms from column A with their definitions in column B.

A	B
__ Money	1. Measures the ease with which an asset can be converted into cash.
__ Barter	2. Money which is used to purchase goods and services—M_1 is considered this.

__ Monetary economy

__ Commodity money

__ Bank money

__ Transactions money

__ Fiat money

__ Broad money

__ Riskless interest rate

__ Liquidity

__ Nominal interest rate

__ Portfolio theory

__ Financial intermediary

__ Reserves

__ Money-supply multiplier

__ Multiple expansion of bank deposits

3.   Process by which the banking system transforms reserves into a much larger amount of bank money.

4.   Interest rate on money, measured in money terms; also called the money interest rate.

5.   Anything that serves as a commonly accepted medium of exchange or means of payment.

6.   Sometimes called asset money or near money, it includes M_1 plus savings accounts in banks and similar assets.

7.   The exchange of goods for other goods.

8.   Value determined by reserve requirements, and measures the number of times each new dollar of deposits is expanded into new money by the banking system.

9.   Describes how investors diversify their wealth into different assets.

10. Bank assets held in the form of cash.

11. Checks written on funds deposited in a bank or other financial institution.

12. Particular physical good, with some intrinsic value, that also serves as a medium of exchange.

13. Rate of interest which is paid on loans that have virtually no chance of default or nonpayment.

14. Money that is recognized as the *legally* accepted medium of exchange.

15. Accepts deposits from one group of people and lends them to others.

16. Economic system in which trade takes place through a commonly accepted medium of exchange.

There are so many new terms and expressions in this chapter that we have included another section of matching. To help you keep the two sections separate, the expressions in this section are preceded with letters rather than numbers. Persistence now will pay off!

A

__ Amortization

B

a.   Borrowing money to buy stock, using the stock itself for collateral on the loan.

__ Inflation-indexed bonds

__ Transactions demand

__ Asset demand

__ Risk-averse

__ Balance sheet

__ Unit of account

__ Financial intermediary

__ Bank run

__ Bear market

__ Bull market

__ Margin purchases

__ Speculative bubble

__ Stock price index

__ Efficient-market theory

__ Random walk

b.   Market prices contain all the available information on the value of a stock.

c.   The use of money as a measure of current value or price.

d.   Movements of stock prices which, over time, are completely unpredictable.

e.   Repayment of the principal on a loan.

f.   Occurs when many depositors go to a bank and attempt to withdraw their funds.

g.   Price increases based on the market's expectation of further price increases, rather than on actual increases in firm profits or dividends.

h.   U.S. government financial asset with interest payments linked to the price level in the economy.

i.   Stock market with rising prices.

j.   Weighted average of the prices of a group or basket of company stocks.

k.   Institutions that take deposits from one group and lend the funds to other groups.

l.   Financial statement comparing a company's asset with its liabilities and net worth.

m.   The need for money to purchase goods and services.

n.   Stock market with falling prices.

o.   The desire to avoid taking gambles when making financial investments.

p.   The holding of money as a store of value or wealth.

IV. SUMMARY AND CHAPTER OUTLINE

This section summarizes the key concepts from the chapter.

A. Money and Interest Rates

1.   The money used in the U.S. economy (and for that matter in most developed economies) has no intrinsic value, but its supply has an enormous effect on the nation's output, employment, and price level. It would be difficult to overstate its importance.

2.   Economies based primarily on a **barter** system of transactions do not work very well. Individuals spend too many

precious (and scarce!) resources lining up trading partners and less time producing goods and services.

3. The primary measure of money that we will use in our model of the economy is **transactions money**, or M_1. M_1 includes coin and currency in circulation (i.e., not held by banks), plus demand and other checkable deposits. Our focus on money that is in circulation stems from our concern for money that can be used to facilitate economic transactions. Money held by banks has little influence on the pace of economic activity. The term *demand deposits* is used synonymously with *checking accounts* since you have access to this money anytime and anywhere you are, as long as you have your checkbook. The money is available upon (your) *demand*, as long as the recipient of the money is willing to accept your check. NOW accounts are an example of bother checkable deposits." The acronym stands for "*Negotiable Order of Withdrawal.*" These are interest-bearing accounts that allow depositors to write checks.

4. While M_1 is the most appropriate measure of money as a means of payment, a broader monetary aggregate, M_2, is also watched very closely. M_2 includes M_1 plus savings accounts and small time-deposits. Savings accounts and time deposits earn interest and are slightly less liquid than the components of M_1. Over the past 10 years, this broader definition of money has been a more stable indicator of money supply growth than has M_1. This is due, in part, to all the new kinds of checking instruments that have been created by banks.

5. Bonds pay a fixed amount of money, called a coupon payment, every year until they mature. (Actually, most bonds make coupon payments every six months, but we can safely assume here that the payment is made just once a year.) For example, if you purchase a ten-year $1000 bond that pays 6% interest, you would get paid $60 interest every year (the coupon payment) and at the end of ten years receive your $1000 (principle) back as well. Existing bonds can be traded, that is, bought and sold, in the bond market until they mature. If current market interest rates rise above $6, the market price of your bond would fall. Consider the last year of your ten-year bond. If current market rates of interest are 8%, why would anyone pay you full price for your 6% bond? They could earn 8% on some alternative financial investment. At the end of the tenth year the owner of the bond will get paid $1060. We need to find the amount of money, which when multiplied by 1.08 yields $1060. So the present value or current market price of your bond would = $1060/1.08 = $981.48.

6. Interest rates are the price of money. If you *save*, you may view the interest you earn as a payment, or return to saving. It can also be considered as the price others (usually banks) are willing to pay you for the use of your money. Similarly, if you *borrow*, you must pay interest to compensate the lender for giving up the opportunity to use the money (that you borrowed) in some alternative use.

There is no one rate of interest for the economy. Other things held constant, the rate of interest will be higher:

  a. The longer the time to maturity of the deposit or loan.

  b. The greater the risk associated with that particular loan or financial investment.

  c. The less liquid the asset is. Liquidity measures the ease with which an asset can be converted into cash.

  d. The higher the administrative costs associated with the loan.

U.S. government securities (or bonds) are among the safest loans a saver can make because the U.S. government is very unlikely to default on its loans. For this reason the U.S. government is able to borrow money at relatively low rates of interest. This rate of interest is often referred to as the "riskless interest rate."

7. Lenders and borrowers alike need to be concerned about the effect of inflation on the value of their financial assets and debt. As inflation increases, the real value, or purchasing power, of money decreases. Suppose you borrow $500 from a bank for one year at an interest rate of 6 percent. When the bank decides to give you a loan, it gives up the opportunity to use that $500 in other ways. In this particular case, let us assume that the bank gave up the opportunity to purchase a new $500 desk for one of its managers. At the end of the year, you must pay the bank back $530 ($500 × 1.06). Suppose further that during the year that you had your loan, inflation in the economy increased by 10 percent. The desk that the bank could have purchased last year now costs $550! When you pay back the loan, the bank cannot use your loan repayment—even with the interest—to purchase the desk. In real, or inflation-adjusted, terms, the bank lost money. *Nominally*, or in dollar terms, the bank earned 6 percent on its loan. However, in *real* terms it *lost* 4 percent! (The bank is now $20 short of the purchase price of the desk; $20 is 4 percent of $500.) You can calculate the real rate of interest very easily:

$$\text{Real rate} = \text{nominal rate} - \text{inflation rate}$$

In 1997 the government introduced *inflation-indexed bonds*. The interest rate on these 10-year bonds is indexed to the general price level. In addition, when the principal is repaid when the bond terminates, its value is also adjusted for inflation in the economy. You should realize that when the government (or any other organization) issues or sells bonds, it is really borrowing money. Buying bonds is a form of saving. Individuals buying government bonds get paid interest for their loan.

8. Money has no usefulness as a commodity. We cannot eat it or wear it or use it for shelter. We demand money so that we can use it to purchase the commodities we need or want. There are three basic functions that money performs. It serves as

a. a medium of exchange
b. a unit of account
c. a store of value

The *medium of exchange* function is the most basic. If people do not universally accept the money (at least within a country) as a means of payment, then we are back to barter. It is that simple.

Unit of account means that whatever we use as money should also be used to measure prices or value. It would be silly to have dollars as our money and then measure prices in terms of apples or donuts or Mexican pesos.

Money serves as a *store of value* in that it does not physically deteriorate over time (this was a problem with some forms of commodity money) or lose its acceptability. Rates of interest on cash are naturally nonexistent, but NOW accounts and the components of M_2 earn interest. While these rates of interest are relatively low, there is also virtually no risk associated with this form of wealth.

9. The cost of holding wealth or assets as money is the forgone opportunity to earn higher rates of return or interest on other financial investments.

10. There are two main reasons why people hold wealth as money: (a) transactions demand and (b) asset demand. The transactions demand goes hand in hand with the medium of exchange function of money, while the asset demand matches up with the store of value function. While other assets may pay higher rates of interest, most portfolio managers diversify their wealth among different types of assets.

B. Banking and the Supply of Money

1. Banks hold a portion of their assets in the form of non-interest-earning *reserves*. These reserves are held on hand in the form of cash or are deposited with the central bank. The reserves are held to meet legal reserve requirements and to meet the day-to-day cash needs of the bank.

2. The fractional-reserve banking system enables banks to expand (or contract) the money supply. A portion of each new deposit must be held in the form of idle reserves, but the rest can be loaned out. As the money that is lent out is deposited in other banks, they "pick up the ball" and create additional new loans (money).

Just as the *MPS* was a key component of the expenditure multiplier, the reserve requirement is the key component of the money-supply multiplier.

$$\text{Money-supply multiplier} = \frac{1}{\text{required reserve ratio}}$$

Note that in both cases, the denominator indicates an amount of money that is being withdrawn from the system each time it changes hands. Every time a new deposit is made, the bank must withdraw the required reserves before loaning the rest to a new borrower. Likewise, every time a marginal dollar of income is earned by a household, a portion is saved before the rest is spent on consumption. The multipliers are *not* the same, but their structure is quite similar.

3. In reality, the money creation process will be diminished if banks hold excess reserves or when all of the new money is not deposited in banks.

Banks make loans in order to make profits. If bankers are pessimistic about the economy or the creditworthiness of loan applicants, they will make fewer loans and hold excess reserves. It is preferable to make no money (on reserves) than to lose money on bad loans.

The money creation process assumes that at each step along the way, the newly created money is deposited in someone's checking account. If, instead, the money is held outside of banks (it could even leave the country), then the expansion process will slow down.

C. A Tour of Wall Street

1. *Financial economics* studies how rational investors should allocate their funds to attain their financial objectives. The word "rational" implies that individuals make use of all the available information in the market place. It does not mean that individuals are infallible or that mistakes never occur. After all, sometimes the information we receive is not entirely accurate. Besides money itself, and savings accounts, the main financial assets that households hold include government bonds and bills, stocks or equities, and pension funds. Generally, there is a trade-off between return and risk on financial assets. Assets with higher risk, or more volatility on their rate of return, usually offer the potential for greater earnings.

2. Millions of Americans have purchased stock in the **stock market**. In recent years, the U.S. stock market has reached one record high after another and new investors may not have learned that there is no guarantee that the market will always rise. While analysts seem to agree that current market increases have been fueled by a strong economy with low inflation and low unemployment, investors need to be wary of *speculative bubbles*. In this case, stock prices increase because people think they are going rise in the future. Such bubbles are not based on actual firm earnings or dividends and invariably pop.

In an **efficient market**, new information affects stock and commodity prices; predictable events have already been incorporated into market prices. Since the new information is unpredictable, prices in the market tend to follow a *random walk*.

V. HELPFUL HINTS

1. Money is like grease or oil for an engine; it makes the economy run more smoothly and efficiently.

2. "Small time-deposits" are savings deposits (at banks) of up to $100,000.

3. There is an example in Chapter 25 dealing with interest rates and monthly payments on a 30-year fixed-interest rate mortgage. If the *annual* rate of interest is 10 percent, you would have to pay one-twelfth of that every *month*. Each month your payment would include one-twelfth of 10 percent or 10/12 percent (or 0.833 percent) of the annual interest on the loan. Note that if the monthly payment is $877.58, over 30 years you would pay a total of $315,928.80, $215,928.80 of which is interest on the $100,000 loan!

4. Remember, bonds pay a fixed amount of interest during their life. There is an inverse relationship between current market interest rates and the market price of bonds.

5. Whether you lend or borrow, *always* make the effort to get an estimate of the (projected) rate of inflation in the economy. This is precisely why many banks now offer loans with rates of interest that vary over the life of the loan. They are protecting themselves against inflation.

6. There are other definitions of money beyond M_1 and M_2. As you move to "higher" definitions the additional components of money become less and less liquid. Each new broader definition of money includes the components of the lower-numbered definition that precedes it.

7. In recent years there have been many changes in the banking system. Many savings banks now offer checking or demand-deposit accounts, and commercial banks may offer savings-type accounts. While commercial banks are still the primary source of bank money (or checking accounts), the distinction between *commercial* banks and *savings* banks has become blurred.

8. When bankers and portfolio managers use the term *investment* they are probably not using it in our economic sense of the word. To avoid confusion, think of the assets these professionals work with as *financial investments*.

Remember, to economists *investment* means the purchase of something tangible that adds to the productivity capability of the economy. Companies may use the funds they receive from selling stocks and bonds to make investment purchases (new equipment, factories, etc.), but the stocks and bonds themselves are not considered investment. They are part of savings.

VI. MULTIPLE CHOICE QUESTIONS

These questions are organized by topic from the chapter outline. Choose the best answer from the options available.

A. Money and Interest Rates

1. Barter, the first step in the evolution of a monetary system above self-sufficiency, gave way to commodity money because:
   a. barter was an inefficient transaction mechanism involving high transaction cost incurred by the necessity of finding someone willing to trade what you have for what you want.
   b. barter was inconvenient at best.
   c. barter stood in the way of efficient division of labor unless the output was divisible.
   d. barter depended upon a double coincidence of wants that became increasingly unlikely as economies grew more diverse.
   e. all the above.

2. Commodity money was a step toward efficiency, but it was undermined frequently by:
   a. frequent relapse into barter.
   b. the vagaries of supply and demand for the commodity that altered the value of the money.
   c. the inability of communities to agree to one commodity.
   d. the inability of communities to find a commodity that was not perishable.
   e. none of the above.

3. Suppose that a one-year bond pays $100 of interest plus the original principal of $2000 when the bond matures. If market rates of interest are 8%, how much should you be willing to pay for this bond?
   a. $1888.88.
   b. $1944.44.
   c. $2000.20.
   d. $2160.50.
   e. $2268.68.

4. Suppose that a one-year bond pays $100 of interest plus the original principal of $2000 when the bond matures. If market rates of interest are 4%, how much should you be willing to pay for this bond?
   a. $1784.00.
   b. $1888.88.
   c. $2019.23.
   d. $2080.20.
   e. $2184.00.

5. The real rate of interest is equal to:
   a. the nominal rate minus the inflation rate.
   b. the inflation rate minus the nominal rate.
   c. the nominal rate plus the inflation rate.
   d. the inflation rate divided by the nominal rate.
   e. the nominal rate divided by the inflation rate.

6. The strictest definition of money, M_1, includes:
   a. coins, currency, and demand deposits.
   b. coins, currency, and time deposits.
   c. coins, currency, and all deposits in a bank.
   d. all currencies and near-monies.
   e. none of the above.

7. Financial intermediaries are institutions that:
   a. buy and sell all types of goods, including merchandise.
   b. include only international corporations that have large holdings of various types of currency.
   c. accept the deposits of some people and institutions

and use that money to support the borrowing needs of others.

   d.   are not really necessary in the United States because of the size of the federal debt.

   e.   all the above.

8.   Commercial banks are the largest category of financial intermediaries; others include:

   a.   life insurance companies.

   b.   pension funds.

   c.   savings and loan institutions.

   d.   money market funds.

   e.   all the above.

9.   The essential difference between money and near-money is that:

   a.   money is directly spendable, whereas near-money is not.

   b.   near-money includes all deposits in bank accounts, whereas money includes none of these.

   c.   the velocity of circulation of money is rapid, while that of near-money is slow.

   d.   near-money is fiat money, whereas money is not.

   e.   near-money is made up of any and all items that can be marketed for a money price.

10.   If you write a check on your bank account, that check:

   a   counts as part of M_1 provided it is a valid check, i.e., there are funds in the bank to support it.

   b.   counts as part of M_1 whether valid or not, provided the person to whom it is given accepts it.

   c.   counts as part of M_1 if used to buy goods and services, but not otherwise.

   d.   does not count as part of M_1, since no bank account is considered part of the money supply.

   e.   does not count as part of M_1; to count both it and the deposit account on which it is drawn would be double counting.

11.   When money has been deposited in any private financial institution (e.g., a commercial bank, a savings and loan association, etc.), the critical factor in deciding whether that deposit should count as part of M_1 is that:

   a.   checks can be freely written against the deposit by its owner.

   b.   the deposit has insurance or backing by the government or some public institution.

   c.   the institution maintains 100 percent backing or reserve for the deposit—whether the backing is provided by the government or not.

   d.   the institution has a legal franchise which permits its deposits to be counted as money.

   e.   as long as the money deposited consists of genuine bills or coins, then the deposit within any such institution must be counted as part of the money supply.

12.   Money serves as:

   a.   a medium of exchange.

   b.   a store of value.

   c.   a unit of account.

   d.   all the above.

   e.   none of the above.

13.   On the basis of the transactions demand component of the demand for money:

   a.   the demand for money climbs as the interest rate climbs.

   b.   the demand for money climbs as the interest rate falls.

   c.   the demand for money falls as nominal income rises.

   d.   the demand for money falls as nominal income falls.

   e.   none of the above.

14.   Which answer to question 10 would have been correct had that question referred to the assets demand component of the demand for money?

   a.

   b.

   c.

   d.

   e.

15.   The "demand for money" means:

   a.   the desire to hold securities which can readily be converted into money at a fixed or near-fixed price if necessary.

   b.   the amount which businesses will wish to borrow at any given interest rate.

   c.   the desire to save more money out of income as protection against the uncertainties of the future.

   d.   the same thing as "asset demand for money alone."

   e.   the same thing as the sum of "assets and transactions demand for money."

B. Banking and the Supply of Money

16.   In a fractional-reserve banking system, such as that of the United States, the required reserve ratios imposed on commercial banks:

   a.   are primarily intended to set a limit on the total money supply rather than to serve as adequate protection against bank runs.

   b.   are in excess of what is normally required but are sufficient to cover what would be needed if for any reason people became uneasy over the safety of bank deposits.

   c.   are essentially an average of the amounts needed to meet the public's demands in good times and bad.

   d.   are now obsolete, according to the text, and will shortly be replaced by a 100 percent reserve requirement.

   e.   are not correctly described by any of the above.

17.   The commercial banking system (all banks taken together) lends money to business firms and consumers, normally by setting up demand deposits which the borrow-

ers may spend. As a result, the money supply:

a. decreases by the total amount of all coins and bills deposited with the banking system for safe-keeping.

b. neither increases nor decreases.

c. increases by an amount somewhat less than the system's total coin-and-bill deposits, owing to the fraction it holds as reserves.

d. increases by an amount just equal to the system's total coin-and-bill deposits.

e. increases by an amount considerably greater than the system's total coin-and-bill deposits.

18. The economy's total money supply will increase whenever commercial banks:

a. increase their deposits with a Federal Reserve Bank.

b. increase their total loans to the public.

c. increase their demand deposit liabilities by receiving coins or bills from the public as deposits.

d. withdraw part of their deposits from a Federal Reserve Bank.

e. reduce their demand-deposit liabilities by paying out part of these accounts in the form of coins or paper bills.

19. I deposit, in bank X, $10,000 in paper currency which has for a long time been hidden and out of circulation. The legal minimum reserve requirement for banks is 25 percent of deposits. Bank X is one among many banks. Unless bank X is already short on reserves, this deposit would enable the bank, if it wished, to increase its loans by at least:

a. an undetermined amount.

b. $7500.

c. $10,000.

d. $30,000.

e. more than $30,000.

20. Assuming that the loan increase does not set off any increase of coins and paper currency in hand-to-hand circulation, the deposit described in question 16 would enable the banking system to increase its loans by a maximum of:

a. zero.

b. $7500.

c. $10,000.

d. $30,000.

e. more than $30,000.

21. In the circumstances of questions 16 and 17, if consideration were given to some small increase of coins and paper currency in hand-to-hand circulation, the most probable maximum amount (among the five alternatives listed below) by which the banking system as a whole could increase loans would be:

a. zero.

b. less than $5000.

c. between $20,000 and $30,000.

d. between $30,000 and $40,000.

e. more than $40,000.

22. Had bank X been a monopoly bank, with all other circumstances as in question 16 (including zero hand-to-hand circulation leakage), then the maximum amount by which this deposit would have enabled bank X to increase its loans, if so disposed, would be:

a. zero.

b. $7500.

c. $10,000.

d. $30,000.

e. more than $30,000.

23. If the required reserve ratio had been 20 percent rather than 25 percent, with all other circumstances as in question 16, the deposit would have enabled bank X to increase its loans, if so disposed, by:

a. zero.

b. $2000.

c. $8000.

d. $10,000.

e. $40,000.

24. If the deposit of question 16 (where the reserve requirement equaled 25 percent) had been a $10,000 check drawn on bank Y, then this deposit (considered in isolation from all other deposits or withdrawals) would have enabled bank X to increase its loans, if so disposed, by:

a. zero.

b. $7500.

c. $10,000.

d. $30,000.

e. more than $30,000.

25. The deposit of question 21 would enable the entire banking system to increase its loans, if so disposed, by:

a. zero.

b. $7500.

c. $10,000.

d. $30,000.

e. more than $30,000.

26. If the legal required reserve ratio is a minimum of 30 percent of the amount of demand deposits, and if the banking system now has excess reserves of $15 million, then (disregarding any resulting increase in hand-to-hand circulation) the banking system could increase demand deposits by a maximum of:

a. zero.

b. $10.5 million.

c. $15 million.

d. $35 million.

e. $50 million.

27. The "excess reserves" of a commercial bank consist of:

a. assets which, although not money, can be quickly converted into money by the bank should the need arise.

b. money and near-money assets possessed by the bank in excess of 100 percent of the amount of its demand deposits.

c.   cash which must be kept on hand, not because everyday bank needs require it but because of a legal requirement.

d.   money held by the bank in excess of that fraction of its deposits required by law.

e.   the difference between the amount of its money assets and the amount of its demand deposits.

28   The money multiplier is the multiplicative inverse of the required reserve ratio as long as:

a.   currency leakages into circulation and/or foreign markets do not occur.

b.   banks do not maintain excess reserves.

c.   the required reserve ratio is far in excess of the reserves that banks think are prudent given the deposits that they hold.

d.   all the above.

e.   none of the above.

C. Financial Economics

29. The Dow-Jones Industrial Average:

a.   is an example of a stock-price index.

b.   is used to follow trends in the stock market.

c.   includes some corporations whose stock is traded on the New York Stock Exchange.

d.   is all of the above.

e.   is none of the above.

30. The Standard and Poor 500:

a.   is a package of 500 basic stocks for lower income investors.

b.   includes the 500 most profitable stocks traded on the New York Stock Exchange.

c.   has, on average, been the most profitable Wall Street investment.

d.   was one of the few stock market indexes not to fall during the stock market drop of October 1987.

e.   is a weighted average of the stock prices of the largest 500 American corporations.

31. A speculative bubble:

a.   is compatible with the efficient-market theory.

b.   is more likely to occur during a bear market.

c.   was probably at least partly responsible for the stock market collapse in October 1987.

d.   is a theoretical concept and not likely to be observed in reality.

e.   is none of the above.

32. The essential property of margin buying of a stock is:

a.   participation in stock buying during a period of price rise by inexperienced investors.

b.   trading in a stock in quantities that do not really exist.

c.   any purchase of a stock in anticipation of a rise in its price, provided the stock is held for a short period only.

d.   a stock purchase financed in part by use of bor-

rowed money.

e.   none of the above.

33. The contribution of margin buying to the great stock market crash of 1929 was which of the following?

a.   Owners of stock were forced to sell that stock in order to raise the cash needed to buy the further stock which their margin commitment required them to buy.

b.   The small, or marginal, stock buyers grew panicky and dumped their stock for whatever price they could get.

c.   Margin buying had increased the volume of stock trading and thus intensified the fall in prices, but otherwise it played no special part in the crash.

d.   The lenders of money sold the stock they were holding as collateral security when stock prices began to fall substantially.

e.   Margin buyers made an unsuccessful attempt to stop the decline in stock prices by increasing the amount of their buying.

34. As the result of some favorable news regarding a company, the price of its stock rises. If we were to use supply and demand curves to illustrate the nature of that price rise, we would say that it resulted from:

a.   solely a rightward shift of the demand curve.

b.   solely a leftward shift of the supply curve.

c.   both a rightward demand-curve shift and a leftward supply-curve shift.

d.   principally a rightward shift of the supply curve.

e.   principally a rightward shift of both demand and supply curves.

35. "It is not possible to make profits by looking at old information or at patterns of past price changes. The price movements of a stock over time are completely unpredictable." This statement can best be described as:

a.   chaos theory.

b.   a speculative bubble.

c.   a random walk.

d.   "no news is good news."

e.   utter nonsense.

36. The efficient-market theory:

a.   states that all public information is reflected almost immediately in the price of a share of common stock.

b.   implies that "beating the market" involves predicting unforeseeable events.

c.   implies that stock market prices move in the short run as if they were random numbers.

d.   implies that diversification is a reasonable strategy for investing in the stock market.

e.   all the above.

37. One group of stock market investors buys and holds for the long pull, disregarding short-term price fluctuations. The overall effect that this type of investor has on the market is that he or she:

a.   destabilizes it in that his or her purchases keep tend-ing to push price upward.

b.   stabilizes it by refusing to sell on price declines but destabilizes it by making the market "thinner."

c.   stabilizes it by making it "thinner."

d.   destabilizes it by selling at times which have no relation to the current price of the stock.

e.   does none of these things, since his or her group is not of sufficient importance to have any impact.

VII. PROBLEM SOLVING

The following problems are designed to help you apply the concepts that you learned in the chapter.

A. Money and Interest Rates

1.   Money evolved because it was essential for large systems of exchange.

a.   It began as (**fiat money / commodity money / metal money**) when people started to measure the val-

ues of various goods and services in terms of so many units of one particular commodity.

b.   Today, all U.S. money is (**fiat money / commodity money / gold-based money**)—legal tender which must be accepted for (**all private and some public / some private and all public / some private and some public / all private and all public**) debts.

2.   It has become conventional, in tables listing the money supply, to make the distinction between M_1 and M_2. Items within M_1 are exclusively the three strictly defined money items. The M_2 category takes account of the "very close to being money" items.

a. M_2 consists of the total of (**these "very close" items alone / the "very close" items plus the M_1 items**).

A basic problem with the "very close to being money" idea is, how close is very close? The "official" definition of M_2 includes only time deposits in commercial banks and money market funds. Why not federal government bonds? The market for such bonds is so well organized that ordinari-

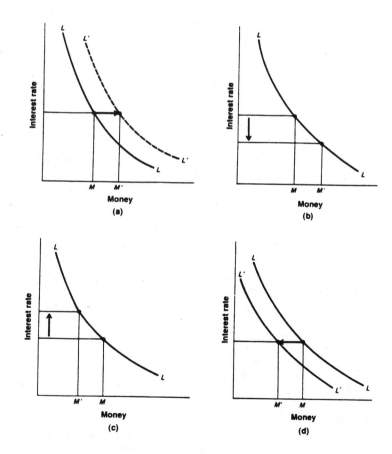

Figure 25-1

ly they can be converted into money very rapidly indeed. If such bonds were included, however, then why not other easily marketed securities? As in all such cases, the decision is necessarily an arbitrary one.

    b. Other time deposits and government bonds are lumped into a category called (**convertible money / non-money / near-money / high-grade money**).

    c. Consider the following list of financial "items":

        (1) Any deposit in a commercial bank on which checks may be issued

        (2) Reserves of a commercial bank

        (3) A deposit in a mutual savings account or in a credit union of $130,000

        (4) A high-grade corporation bond

        (5) A check drawn on a commercial-bank checking account

List the numbers of those items which would be included in M_1: _____

Now list those items which would be included in M_2:

_____

_____

3. People (and institutions) are willing to pay interest because borrowed funds allow them to satisfy consumption needs and/or make profitable investments. The rate of interest that is paid is dependent upon a number of factors. The changes listed below should cause the rate of interest paid to rise (R), fall (F), or stay the same (S). Put the appropriate letter in the blank preceding each of the following statements:

    ___ a. An increase in the term of the debt

    ___ b. A reduction in the risk associated with the debt

    ___ c. An increase in the degree of liquidity

    ___ d. A reduction in the cost of administering the debt

    ___ e. An increase in the rate of inflation

    ___ f. A decrease in long-term corporate profits

4. The demand for money is a result of both the transactions demand and the asset demand.

    a. The transactions demand for money means that the demand for money will (**increase / be unaffected / decrease**) as income climbs.

    b. As interest rates fall, the demand for money should, through its assets demand component, (**fall / remain the same / climb**).

5. The four panels in Figure 25-1 show the quantity of money demanded changing from M to M'. Record in the spaces provided the letter of the panel that best illustrates each of the following changes in economic conditions:

    a. An increase in nominal GDP that leaves interest rates fixed

    b. An increase in the rate of interest

    c. A reduction in prices that is not yet reflected in interest rates

    d. A reduction in interest rates that is not yet reflected in a change in aggregate demand

    e. A situation in which banks find themselves with excess idle reserves

    f. A decrease in the asset demand for money

    g. An increase in the transactions demand for money

B. Banking and the Supply of Money

6. In the spaces below, list five types of financial intermediaries:

    a. _____

    b. _____

    c. _____

    d. _____

    e. _____

7. The questions which follow begin with a situation in which there is no "bank money." They trace the development of such money through lending activity on the part of banks.

    These questions concern an isolated community which uses initially only gold coins as money. The local goldsmith has a storage vault for gold. She is prepared to store money for others in this vault, charging a small fee. She chooses to list such deposits as an asset on her balance sheet, matched by a "deposit liability" of equal amount. Her balance sheet, with respect to such deposits, is shown in Table 25-1.

TABLE 25-1

Assets	Liabilities
Gold coins in vault $10,000	Deposits payable to customers on demand $10,000

    a. Jones, a *customer* of the goldsmith, owes her neighbor, Bart, some gold. Bart needs to go shopping and asks if Jones can repay the loan. The goldsmith's shop has already closed for the day, so Jones gives Bart a note reading as follows:

    To: Ye Gold Shoppe / Pay Bart $5 from my deposit.
    (Signed) Jones

What is the name used today for such a note? ___

    b. Bart presents the note the next morning, but instead of taking gold coins, he asks the goldsmith to keep the money stored in his name. Is any change necessary in the goldsmith's balance sheet? If so, explain.

_____

_____

8. Observing how convenient it was to settle an account by check, the townspeople adjust their behavior and now handle many transactions by check. Occasionally a depositor withdraws gold to make a payment but the person receiving payment usually deposits it once again, since the vault is the safest place for gold storage and checks can always be drawn against such deposits.

    A responsible merchant now asks the goldsmith for a

loan of $2000. The goldsmith has no gold free of deposit claims, having only the $10,000 deposited with her. Is there any reason why she should nonetheless consider making the loan? Explain.

9. Assume that the loan is made, and the merchant is given $2000 in gold. Table 25-2 shows the goldsmith's balance sheet after these transactions have been completed.

TABLE 25-2

Assets	Liabilities
Gold $8,000	Demand deposits $10,000
Loans 2,000	

a. Assume that Ye Gold Shoppe is the only goldsmith in the community. When the merchant gets the loan, he initially deposits it in his account with the goldsmith. Fill in Table 25-3 showing what Ye Gold Shoppe's balance sheet would look like after the merchant makes the deposit.

TABLE 25-3

Assets	Liabilities
Gold ....$____	Demand deposits .....$____
Loans ....____	

b. Has the money supply increased? (**Yes / No**)
c. If so, by how much?

10. Now we are going to change things slightly. Assume that the community holds $2000 in gold for transactions, and the goldsmith has made $20,000 in loans. Table 25-4 reflects this new situation.

TABLE 25-4

Assets	Liabilities
Gold ....$ 8,000	Demand deposits ...$28,000
Loans 20,000	

a. The total money supply (M_1) is now $___, consisting of $___ in bank money (demand deposits) and $___ in gold held in circulation.
b. Should the $8000 in gold in the goldsmith's vault count as part of M_1? (**Yes / No**) Briefly explain why or why not.

Let us now add three aspects of contemporary realism to the scenario.

(1) Imagine that the institution of goldsmith has evolved into the institution of banker. The balance sheets that will be considered in the questions which follow therefore apply to banks.

(2) Suppose that the gold-based currency system of the previous questions has evolved into a system of fiat money.

(3) Presume that a central financial authority of the government requires that banks maintain reserve stores of currency equal to at least 20 percent of their total demand deposits.

For the time being, however, there is still only one bank (Bank A, grown up from Ye Gold Shoppe) in town.

11. a. Bank A has $8000 in reserve currency on deposit and is fully "loaned out" against the 20 percent legal reserve requirement. Assume that $2000 in cash and currency is held across the community in transactions demand. Show the bank's balance sheet in Table 25-5.

TABLE 25-5

Assets	Liabilities
Reserves ....$____	Demand deposits .....$____
Loans ....____	

b. Given only one bank, the community's total M_1 is at this point $____, consisting of $____ in bank money (again, demand deposits) and $____ in transactions currency.

12. a. A storekeeper brings $500 in cash into the bank for deposit. Use Table 25-6 to show Bank A's resulting balance sheet, before any new loans are issued.

TABLE 25-6

Assets	Liabilities
Reserves ....____	Demand deposits .....$____
Loans ....____	

b. With this deposit, the storekeeper now has enough money on deposit to repay a $1000 loan. His deposit is therefore reduced by $1000, and he is given back his note. Disregarding any interest on the loan, complete a revised balance sheet in Table 25-7.

TABLE 25-7

Assets	Liabilities
Reserves ....$____	Demand deposits .....$____
Loans ....____	

c. When the loan is paid off, is the community's M_1 affected? (**Yes / No**) If so, how? If not, why not?

We have assumed, thus far, that there is just one bank in town. Suppose, instead, that there are two banks: the original (Bank A) and a new one (Bank B).

13. a. The new bank (Bank B) attracts depositors away from Bank A. Perhaps it has a more convenient location or has friendlier tellers. In any event, things finally shake out such that each bank is of equal size and has $4000 in reserves. (The reserve requirement for both banks is still 20 percent.) The townspeople still hold $2000 in currency for transactions. Complete Table 25-

8 to show the balance sheet for either bank (remember they are, at this point, identical), assuming that each is fully loaded up against a 20 percent required reserve ratio.

TABLE 25-8 Bank A or Bank B

Assets	Liabilities
Reserves ....$____	Demand deposits .....$____
Loans ....____	

b.   The community's total M_1 is $____, with $____ in bank money and $____ in circulation.

14. Now suppose that a local woman who has been working abroad returns home with $3000 of new currency. She deposits the cash entirely with Bank B.

a.   Show the balance sheet for Bank B in Table 25-9, assuming that Bank B has not yet had a chance to issue new loans.

TABLE 25-9 Bank B

Assets	Liabilities
Reserves ....$____	Demand deposits ..$____
Loans ....____	

b.   Now assume that Bank B extends loans to the maximum extent allowed by the 20 percent required reserve ratio. Revise Bank B's balance sheet in Table 25-10, assuming that all the people who receive a loan from Bank B deposit their (new) money in demand deposits in Bank A.

TABLE 25-10 Bank B after It Makes the Loans

Assets	Liabilities
Reserves ....____	Demand deposits ..$____
Loans ....____	

c.   What is the resulting amount of new loans for Bank B? $____

15. a.   Use Table 25-11 to show the *immediate* change in Bank A when the loan recipients deposit their money.

TABLE 25-11

Assets	Liabilities
Reserves ....$____	Demand deposits ..$____
Loans ....____	

b.   Now use Table 25-12 to show the balance sheet for Bank A after it meets its reserve requirement.

TABLE 25-12

Assets	Liabilities
Reserves ....$____	Demand deposits ....$____
Loans ....____	

c   How much in new loans has Bank A loaned out?

$____
d.   What is the total amount of new loans in the community after these first two steps in the process have been completed? $____

e.   By how much has M_1 grown? $____

16. Suppose this process continues, back and forth, between the two banks.

a.   What will be the total increase in new loans? $____

b.   What will be the total increase in reserves? $____

c.   What will be the total increase in the money supply? $____

d.   What is the value of the money-supply multiplier? ____.

17. a.   Complete Table 25-13 by recording in column (1) the money multipliers that correspond to the required reserve ratios listed in the left-hand column.

TABLE 25-13

Required Reserve Ratio (%)	Money Multipliers	
	(1)	(2)
3	____	____
5	____	____
10	____	____
12	____	____
16	____	____

b.   Now complete column (2) under the assumption that banks hedge against the reserve requirement by holding 2 percentage points above and beyond the requirement in "extra reserve." (The notion here is that banks' hedging against being short can turn a required reserve ratio set by the monetary authorities into a functionally stricter requirement and that the actual money multiplier can fall as a result.) Required reserve ratios are, in practice, set higher than necessary so that banks are discouraged from doing too much of this sort of hedging. Why? Because it adds an element of unpredictability to the computation of the money multiplier that the monetary authorities would prefer to live without.

18. The combined balance sheet (billions of dollars) of all the commercial banks in Bancoland appears in Table 25-14. The legal reserve requirement is 10 percent of deposits.

TABLE 25-14

Assets	Liabilities
Reserves (deposits Federal Reserve and cash in vaults) $30	Demand deposits $100
Loans 70	

a.   These banks thus have excess reserves of (**$0 / $5 / $10 / $15 / $20 / $30**) billion.

b.   Show their balance sheet in Table 25-15 after they have taken full advantage of excess reserves to expand loans. Assume that all new money remains as demand deposits.

TABLE 25-15

Assets	Liabilities
Reserves ....$____	Demand deposits .....$____
Loans ....____	

19. The process of bank-money creation is most easily explained in terms of a deposit of cash in a bank. Bear in mind, though, that once the credit expansion process is completed and banks are fully loaned up, most deposits made with banks do not permit any further loan expansion at all.

Assume that the banking system is fully loaned up in both of the cases which follow. The reserve requirement is 10 percent.

a. I deposit $1000 in cash in my bank. Which description of this transaction is better?

(1) This $1000 will permit the banking system to expand loans by $9000.

(2) Unless the $1000 was a net addition to reserves, no loan expansion by the banking system is possible. The money may have been withdrawn from another bank (or even my bank) a day or two earlier.

b. I deposit a $1000 salary check in my bank. Again, pick the better description:

(1) This $1000 will permit the banking system to expand loans by $9000.

(2) My bank's reserves are increased but at the cost of the reserves of some other bank. There has been no net addition to the entire banking system's reserves.

C. Financial Economics

20. *Margin buying* on the stock market works as follows: You want to buy XYZ stock, currently selling at $40 per share; you think XYZ will rise to $50 or higher. You have $1000 in cash; this will buy only 25 shares (disregarding the broker's commission and other incidental buying costs) . But with a margin requirement of 25 percent, you can buy a larger number of shares. You do this by borrowing $3000 from your broker or, via the broker, from a bank or other lending agency.

a. The loan proceeds plus your own cash will buy (**25 / 50 / 100 / 200**) shares.

b. Of course, you must put up some security against your loan, but you can furnish XYZ stock worth (**$1000 / $3000 / $4000**). This is accepted as adequate security for your $3000 loan.

If XYZ does indeed go to 50, you sell your stock, pay off the principal and interest on your loan, and pocket the rest of your profit, happy at having taken an economics course. But if, instead, XYZ should drop below 40 say, to 35—you will get a call from your broker to report that the bank "wants more margin," because the value of the asset you have supplied as collateral is falling.

c. Specifically, if the market price of XYZ is $35, your investment will be worth (**$2500 / $3000 / $3500 / $3750**).

d. With a margin requirement of 25 percent, and assuming that you are still using the stock as collateral, the most you can now borrow is (**$2525 / $2625 / $2725 / $2825**).

e. You must put up some more security or else pay off part of the loan. You have to come up with an additional (**$375 / $400 / $425 / $450**).

If you fail to come across, the bank will sell your XYZ stock. If it sells at close to 30, the entire sale proceeds go to cover your loan, leaving you with the sad reminder that you should first have read beyond Chapter 1 in the text before venturing into the stock market.

f. Note the unstable quality of a market heavily involved with margin buying. If prices begin to fall, this sets off a (**further wave of selling / wave of buying**), as borrowers cannot furnish more margin and lenders sell to protect their loans. This pushes stock prices down even more.

21. a. A "bull" market is one in which most expectations are that stock prices are going to (**rise / fall**). Most people with cash are accordingly inclined to (**buy / refrain from buying**) stocks. Most people holding stocks are inclined to (**continue to hold / sell**) them. The consequence of such expectations is that stock prices general ly (**rise / fall**).

b. A "bear" market is one in which most expectations are that stock prices are going to (**rise / fall**). Most people with cash are accordingly inclined to (**buy / refrain from buying**) stocks. Most people holding stocks are inclined to (**continue to hold / sell**) them. The consequence of such expectations is that stock prices generally (**rise / fall**).

22. Suppose, for the sake of illustration, that you decide that you want to buy a few shares of stock in a firm that has suddenly become more profitable. The firm has just marketed a new product for which demand is unexpectedly high, or just developed a new technology that will dramatically lower its costs and improve its competitive position, or just discovered an enormous oil deposit under its Texas plant.

a. In any case, you are attracted to the stock because future earnings by that firm should be significantly (**higher / lower**) than had originally been expected.

b. You and other investors will want to (**buy / sell**) stock in that firm.

c. People who already own stock in that firm will, on the other hand, want to (**sell / hold onto**) their shares in the expectation that they will soon be worth (**less / more**) .

d. The result will be an immediate (**increase / reduc-**

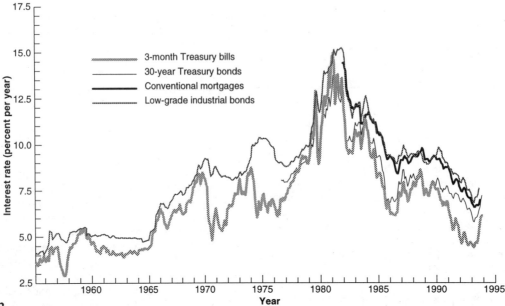

Figure 25-2

tion) in the price of that stock in response to (**higher /
lower / unchanged**) demand and (**higher / lower /
unchanged**) supply at the original market-clearing
price.

By the time you get to the market and find someone who
will be willing to sell you the shares that you want, therefore,
the price will already include the increment in value of the
newly announced profitability that you had hoped to cash in
on.

e.   The problem is that the efficient-market hypothesis
means that the effects of foreseeable events are already
included in the prices of stocks before you can get to
them. You are therefore left with trying to predict
unforeseeable events in your effort to "beat the market."
As a result, if you invest in the stock market and accept
the hypothesis, then you should (circle one or more):

(1) concentrate your purchases on a small number
of stocks.

(2) buy a widely diversified collection of stocks.

(3) keep altering your portfolio—i.e., trade frequently.

(4) stick to your portfolio—i.e., trade infrequently.

VIII. DISCUSSION QUESTIONS

Answer the following questions, making sure that you can
explain the work you did to arrive at the answers.

1.   Samuelson and Nordhaus write that the barter system
"operates under grave disadvantages." Briefly discuss the
advantages of a monetary economy.

2.   Figure 25-2 (on previous page) from the text is reproduced here (also as Figure 25-2) . Are the interest rates on
the vertical axis nominal or real? How do you know?

3.   Figure 25-4 from the text is reproduced here as Figure
25-3. Explain what would happen to the transactions
demand for money schedule under each of the following situations:

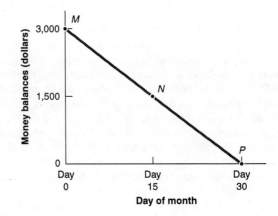

Figure 25-3

a.   All prices and incomes double.

b.   Real income doubles.

c.   Interest rates increase.

4.   Explain the difference between the transactions demand
and the asset demand for money.

5. What are financial intermediaries and what function do they perform?

6. What sorts of real-world considerations tend to slow down the money creation process and reduce the size of the money-supply multiplier?

7. Briefly explain the *efficient-market* theory. What are the objections to this view of markets?

8. Compare and contrast two significant U.S. stock market crashes this century. How has the banking system changed in the interim years?

9. Explain what is meant by the term *speculative bubble*. What sorts of dynamics does this create in the market?

10. Carefully explain what information is contained in a stock price index. What are the two most common indexes used in the United States?

IX. ANSWERS TO STUDY GUIDE QUESTIONS

III. Review of Key Concepts

5	Money
7	Barter
16	Monetary economy
12	Commodity money
11	Bank money
2	Transactions money
14	Fiat money
6	Broad money
13	Riskless interest rate
1	Liquidity
4	Nominal interest rate
9	Portfolio theory
15	Financial intermediary
10	Reserves
8	Money-supply multiplier
3	Multiple expansion of bank deposits

III. Review of Key Concepts (continued)

e	Amortization
h	Inflation-indexed bonds
m	Transactions demand
p	Asset demand
o	Risk-averse
l	Balance sheet
c	Unit of account
k	Financial intermediary
f	Bank run
n	Bear market
i	Bull market
a	Margin purchases
g	Speculative bubble
j	Stock price index

b Efficient-market theory
d Random walk

VI. Multiple Choice Questions

1. E   2. B   3. B   4. C   5. A   6. A
7. C   8. E   9. A   10. E   11. A   12. D
13. D   14. B   15. E   16. A   17. E   18. B
19. B   20. D   21. C   22. D   23. C   24. B
25. A   26. E   27. D   28. D   29. D   30. E
31. C   32. D   33. D   34. C   35. C   36. E
37. B

VII. Problem Solving

1. a. commodity money
   b. fiat money, all private and all public

2. a. the "very close" items plus the M_1 items
   b. near-money
   c. M_1: only (1). (We cannot count (5) because that would be double counting the money in the checking account.) M_2: (1), (3) would count if it were less than $100,000.

3. a. R
   b. F
   c. F
   d. F
   e. R
   f. S

4. a. increase
   b. climb

5. a. (a)
   b. (c)
   c. (d) (due to the decrease in nominal GDP)
   d. (b)
   e. (b)
   f. (d)
   g. (d)

6. a. commercial banks
   b. savings and loans
   c. life insurance funds
   d. pension funds and credit unions
   e. money market funds

7. a. This is a check.
   b. Total deposits in the goldsmith's vault are unchanged. Only the ownership of those deposits has changed. The goldsmith will want to make a record of that.

8. The goldsmith should make the loan. Only a few of the depositors withdraw their gold at any one time. Besides, the gold that is withdrawn is likely to be paid to someone in the community and then redeposited with the goldsmith.

9. a.

TABLE 25-3

Assets		Liabilities	
Gold	$10,000	Demand deposits	$12,000
Loans	2,000		

    b.   Yes

    c. $2,000

10. a. $30,000, $28,000, $2,000

    b.   No, The gold must be withdrawn before it can be spent. If and when it is withdrawn, bank liabilities would decrease as well.

11. a.

TABLE 25-5

Assets		Liabilities	
Reserves	$8,000	Demand deposits	$40,000
Loans	32,000		

    b. $42,000, $40,000, $2,000

12. a.

TABLE 25-6

Assets		Liabilities	
Reserves	$8,500	Demand deposits	$40,500
Loans	32,000		

    b.

TABLE 25-7

Assets		Liabilities	
Reserves	$8,500	Demand deposits	$39,500
Loans	31,000		

    c.   Yes. Assuming no other changes, M_1 falls by $1000. However, the bank can now loan that money to someone else.

13. a

TABLE 25-8 Bank A or Bank B

Assets		Liabilities	
Reserves	$4,000	Demand deposits	$20,000
Loans	16,000		

    b. $42,000, $40,000, $2,000

14. a.

TABLE 25-9 Bank B

Assets		Liabilities	
Reserves	$7,000	Demand deposits	$23,000
Loans	16,000		

    b.

TABLE 25-10 Bank B after it Makes the Loans

Assets		Liabilities	
Reserves	$4,600	Demand deposits	$23,000
Loans	18,400		

    c. $2,400

15. a.

TABLE 25-11

Assets		Liabilities	
Reserves	$6,400	Demand deposits	$22,400
Loans	16,000		

    b.

TABLE 25-12

Assets		Liabilities	
Reserves	$4,480	Demand deposits	$22,400
Loans	17,920		

    c. $1920

    d. $4320

    e. $4320 + 3000 = $7320

16. a. $12,000

    b. $3,000

    c. $15,000

    d. $5

17. a, b.

TABLE 25-13

Required Reserve Ratio (%)	Money Multipliers	
	(1)	(2)
3	33.33	20.00
5	20.00	14.29
10	10.00	8.33
12	8.33	7.14
16	6.25	5.56

18. a. $20

    b.

TABLE 25-15

Assets		Liabilities	
Reserves	$30	Demand deposits	$300
Loans	270		

19. a.   (2)

    b.   (2)

20. a.   100

    b. $3000

    c. $3500

    d. $2625

    e. $375

f. further wave of selling
21. a. rise, buy, continue to hold, rise
    b. fall, refrain from buying, sell, fall
22. a. higher
    b. buy
    c. hold onto, more
    d. increase, higher, lower
    e. (2) and (4)

VIII. Discussion Questions

1. In a monetary economy the pace of economic activity increases dramatically. Once there is a universally accepted currency, people can spend more time producing and far less time looking for trading partners.

2. The interest rates in the diagram must be nominal. Remember, the real rate equals the nominal rate minus the rate of inflation. The U.S. economy experienced relatively high rates of inflation in the early 1980s. The increase in nominal interest rates reflects this. Besides, real rates of interest of 10 percent or more would be incredibly high.

3. a. If all prices and incomes double, the transactions demand for money would double. The curve would look the same, but the entries on the vertical axis would be doubled as well. The household would have $6000 in money balances on day 0 and, as before, have $0 left on day 30.

    b. If real income doubles, the transactions demand for money will increase but will not double. Most households would spend part, but not all, of the increase in real income.

    c. If interest rates increase, households (and especially businesses) become more concerned with cash management. At high rates of interest, it is worthwhile for the household to make more frequent trips to the bank for withdrawals to pay for transactions. Spending patterns may not change. What will change is the amount of cash that the household keeps on hand. The transactions demand schedule will shift to the left.

4. When people hold some of their wealth in the form of money in order to buy goods and services, this is referred to as the transactions demand for money. Alternatively, most financial analysts suggest that individuals should diversify their wealth into different types of assets with varying degrees of risk. While wealth held in the form of cash earns relatively little or no interest, it is also a good store of value and is relatively risk-free. Wealth held in the form of money is very liquid and enables individuals to respond quickly to changes in the financial marketplace. As the market improves or as new investment possibilities develop, those individuals with liquid assets will be best able to take advantage of new opportunities.

5. An intermediary is like a middle man. Financial intermediaries (FI) use the money from depositors and then loan it or invest it. Either way, someone else gets to use the money, and they pay interest back to the FI. The FI keeps part of the interest to cover expenses and (hopefully) make a profit, and the rest is paid back to the depositor. For example, banks use deposits to make loans, and pension funds use deposits for long-term, low-risk investments.

6. When money is created, some of the new money is usually held in the form of cash for transactions purposes. Banks create money when they receive new deposits. If more money is held for transactions and is not deposited in banks, this will slow down the money creation process. Also, if people hoard money, i.e., do not spend it and do not deposit it, the money creation process will slow down. Finally, if money leaves the domestic economy through foreign travel or trade, the process will again slow down.

7. The efficient-market theory states that the price of a stock reflects all the information the market has about that stock.

All new information is quickly understood by market participants and becomes immediately incorporated into market prices. The market does respond to news and surprises, but these are unpredictable events.

Samuelson and Nordhaus discuss four criticisms of the efficient-market theory. (a) If everyone believes the theory and assumes the market automatically adjusts to changes, there will be little or no incentive to trade. If everyone behaved this way, the market would be inefficient.. (b) Those who are quicker, and smarter or who have better advisers may make more money than others. (c) The efficient-market theory does a poor job of explaining why the value of stocks fell so dramatically during the crash of 1987. (d) The efficient-market theory works best when applied to individual stocks. It does a poorer job of explaining fluctuations in the entire market.

8. The crash in 1929 was much longer and more severe. The market eventually lost 85 percent of its value as opposed to 25 percent in 1987. The recovery in 1987 was very quick. Many analysts believe the recovery was due, in large part, to the quick reaction by the Fed. The banking system is much more proactive than in 1929 and has established margin requirements which are much higher.

9. A speculative bubble occurs when stock prices increase based on hopes and dreams and not on any concrete information about the increased profitability of firms. As long as other investors observe the rising prices and purchase stock in an attempt to benefit from the increase in prices, the market will continue to inflate. At some point, investors realize the market and their stocks are way overvalued, so they rush to sell to avoid the plunge. The bubble has just popped!

10. Stock price indexes are weighted averages of the prices of a group of stocks. These indexes are used to track trends in the stock market. The Dow-Jones Industrial Average follows the stocks of 30 large industrial corporations, and the Standard and Poor 500 tracks the 500 largest American firms.

CHAPTER 26

Central Banking and Monetary Policy

I. CHAPTER OVERVIEW

This chapter completes a critical link in our picture of the macroeconomy. The real-world functions of the United States central bank, the Federal Reserve System, are discussed, and the role of money is incorporated into the Keynesian multiplier model of Chapter 24. This chapter builds on the discussion of fractional reserve banking from the last chapter and presents an initial discussion of how changes in the money supply can influence real economic variables Changes in aggregate demand must be translated into increases or decreases in real GDP, prices, and employment.

We begin the chapter by considering how a central-banking system works—first in a domestic and then in an international environment. With particular reference to the Federal Reserve System of the United States, we will see how a variety of tools can be used to adjust monetary policy. Since monetary policy is arguably the most important factor in modern macroeconomic stabilization policy, especially in the short and medium runs, it is essential that you understand not only how each control mechanism works in theory but also how each is managed in the real world of policy-making. This understanding is then expanded by relating changes in these control mechanisms to changes in the real economy.

II. LEARNING OBJECTIVES

After you have read Chapter 26 in your text and completed the exercises in this *Study Guide* chapter, you should be able to:

1. Describe the operating structure of the Federal Reserve System of the United States (the "Fed"), paying close attention to the role of the Board of Governors and the Federal Open Market Committee.
2. Explain precisely how **open-market operations**, changes in the discount rate, and changes in the reserve ratio requirements affect the money supply.
3. Describe the differences between monetary policy variables, intermediate target variables for that policy, and objective variables that help define the intermediate targets.

4. Outline the changes in targets that occurred in October 1979 and after August 1982; show the evolution through those changes to the current policy philosophy of the Fed.
5. Explain the effects of deregulation on the Fed and the banking system.
6. Define "sterilization" of international capital movement, and explain why it is necessary.
7. Describe the link between changes in the supply of money and changes in the nominal interest rate in the money market supply-and-demand diagram.
8. Describe the transmission mechanism link between changes in bank reserves (R) and changes in nominal GDP that works through the money supply (M), the nominal interest rate (i), investment (I) and other spending, and the resulting changes in aggregate demand (AD).
9. Explain how a reduction in the supply of money might cause nominal interest rates to climb in the short run but fall in the (very) long run; and correspondingly, how the long-run effect on real interest rates may be ambiguous.

III. REVIEW OF KEY CONCEPTS

Match the following terms from column A with their definitions in column B.

A	B
__ Board of Governors	1. Asset whose primary purpose is to put funds aside for the future.
__ Federal Open Market Committee	2. Markets where short-term funds are lent and borrowed.
__ Open-market operation	3. A monetary variable that is influenced directly by Federal Reserve policy in its attempt to achieve its ultimate objectives.
__ Discount-rate policy	4. These include open-market operations, the discount rate, and reserve requirements.
__ Reserve requirements policy	5. Seven-member core group of people who control the Fed.

__ Intermediate
targets

__ Ultimate
objectives

__ Transactions
account

__ Non-transactions
account

__ Sterilization

__ Monetary
transmission
mechanism

__ Money markets

__ Neutrality of
money

__ Policy
instruments of
the Fed

6.   Route by which changes in monetary policy bring about changes in output, employment, and prices.

7.   Actions by a central bank that insulate the domestic money supply from international reserve flows.

8.   The inability of money to affect real or inflation-adjusted variables in the long run.

9.   Twelve-member group at the Fed which, among other things, controls the Fed's decision to buy and sell bonds.

10. Changing the legal reserve ratio requirement on deposits with banks and other financial institutions.

11. Goals of monetary policy to achieve steady growth, low unemployment, and low inflation.

12. Setting the interest rate at which banks can borrow reserves from the Fed.

13. Asset whose primary purpose is to serve as a means of payment.

14. Fed purchase or sale of government bonds—the single most important and frequently used tool of modern monetary policy.

IV. SUMMARY AND CHAPTER OUTLINE

This section summarizes the key concepts from the chapter.

A. Central Banking and the Federal Reserve System

1.   Monetary policy in the United States is set by the Board of Governors of the Federal Reserve System. The Fed, through decisions made by the board, controls the discount rate (the rate charged by the Fed to banks which borrow from its discount window), open-market operations (through the Open Market Committee), and the reserve requirement (which specifies the maximum benchmark for the money multiplier).

Changes in the discount rate work by clarifying the stance of the Fed; higher (lower) rates suggest tighter (looser) monetary policy. Open-market purchases (sales) of government securities by the Fed transfer funds to (from) the banking system from (to) the Fed, increase (reduce) reserves, and set the wheels in motion to affect aggregate demand.

2.   Monetary policy, in essence, is policy designed to make the borrowing of money easier or more difficult, as conditions require. Those who borrow money do so in order to spend it. Consequently, if the amount of borrowing can be increased or decreased, so too can the total volume of spending; and as spending goes, so goes GDP. The total of borrowing can be manipulated by the Federal Reserve System—the central bank of the United States. The Fed can significantly influence total borrowing because of the power it can exercise over the reserves of the commercial banks.

3.   Commercial banks do not keep a deposit with the Fed just to demonstrate their faith in the banking system. They do so because they are legally required to keep a reserve against their own customer deposit accounts, and a deposit with the Fed is the most convenient way of keeping most of it. This is particularly true because there are continually accounts to be settled with other banks, and this can be done at a Federal Reserve Bank. Cash on the bank's own premises "vault cash," or "till money"—may also be counted as part of this reserve, but the reserve must take one of these two forms: either a deposit with the Fed or cash on hand.

4.   Should the commercial banks happen to have excess reserves when the Fed begins a tighter-money open-market operation, then this operation would simply soak up part of the excess; banks would be under no pressure to reduce their loans and deposits because of a shortage of reserves. The Fed must continue its operation until the banks do come under pressure. The point of specifying high reserve requirements is to see that this won't happen, because the Fed can assume that banks will operate close to the reserve requirement.

5.   The U.S. dollar has become something of an international currency. It is widely held by foreign central banks, financial institutions, and business firms. Any flow of these foreign held dollars back to the United States may increase commercial-bank reserves—and hence the U.S. domestic money supply. An outflow of dollars (caused, say, by an excess of U.S. imports over U.S. exports) may have the reverse effect. This movement of dollars into and out of the United States can look just like a change in the money supply. The Fed sometimes *sterilizes* these flows by enacting changes in its policies to negate their effect.

6.   Today, central banks everywhere seem to be acutely sensitive to the charge that they have caused (or contributed significantly to) past inflation by excessive expansion of the money supply. Central-bank presidents and monetary officials from around the world have responded to this sensitivity by becoming strongly inclined toward tight money. In 1980, the remarkably high interest rates began to reflect this attitude. Blame for the subsequent worldwide recession of 1982 has been laid by many observers squarely on those high interest rates. It is especially revealing to note that most policy officials at the Western economic summit conferences have called on the United States to *lower* its interest rates, not by expanding the money supply but by reducing the size

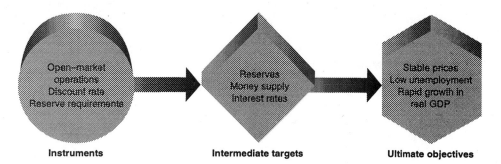

Instruments   Intermediate targets   Ultimate objectives

Figure 26-1

of the federal deficit—but that is a story for another chapter!

B. The Effects of Money on Output and Prices

1. The money supply can change as business firms and families seek to borrow more or to borrow less. The Federal Reserve seeks to control this money supply (and interest rates), having as its goal the maintenance of a reasonably stable price level, the avoidance of recession, and steady economic growth. The money supply can also change with movement in international reserves. While the transactions involved can be exceedingly complex, the elements that need to be grasped for present purposes are relatively simple.

2. The process by which changes in monetary policy affect output, employment, growth, and prices is called the **monetary transmission mechanism**. The steps in the process are summarized as follows:

    a. The Fed takes steps (using one of its three instruments) to change bank reserves.

    b. Each dollar change in bank reserves produces a multiple (via the money-supply multiplier) change in bank deposits and, hence, in the money supply.

    c. The change in the money supply will tend to change interest rates and credit conditions.

    d. Changes in the interest rate affect investment most significantly, but they can also affect consumption behavior, purchases of consumer durables, government spending, and net exports. All of these are components of aggregate demand.

    e. The changes in aggregate demand will ultimately affect output and income, employment, economic growth, and inflation.

Figure 26-3 from the text, reproduced here as Figure 26-1, provides us with a neat summary of this process.

3. The actual link between changes in the money supply and the real economy depends upon two downward-sloping schedules. The first, the demand for money, is downward-sloping because of the assets demand for money. The sec-

ond, the demand for investment, is downward-sloping because lower (higher) interest rates make more (fewer) investment projects attractive. The process is illustrated in Figure 26-2.

   a. The quantity of money in an economy affects the nominal interest rate and thus the availability of credit. Specifically, the greater the quantity of money available, the lower the interest rate. This relationship is portrayed

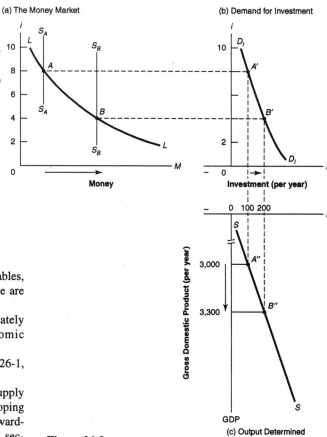

Figure 26-2

in panel (*a*) of Figure 26-2 by movement along curve *LL*—the demand-for-money curve—as the money supply climbs from S_AS_A to S_BS_B.

b   The interest rate influences investment spending in a similar fashion. The lower the interest rate, the more attractive is physical investment in, say, plant and equipment. This is one of the lessons of Chapter 23, and it is portrayed in panel (*b*) of Figure 26-2 by movement along D_ID_I the demand-for-investment curve—from *A'* to *B'* as the interest rate falls from 8 percent to 4 percent.

c.   The level of investment is one of the major determinants of GDP. The saving-investment equality that characterized equilibrium GDP in Chapter 22 is portrayed in panel (*c*) of Figure 26-2. The change in the money supply moves equilibrium out along curve *SS* from *A"* to *B"*.

Should the money supply climb from S_AS_A to S_BS_B, the interest rate would fall from 8 percent to 4 percent, investment would climb from $100 to $200, and nominal GDP would climb from $3000 to $3300. We need to adjust for (possible) changes in the price level to determine the change in *real* GDP.

4.   It is possible that in the long run changes in the money supply lead to proportionate changes in all nominal values but no changes in the real variables of output and employment. This is the so-called **neutrality of money**. It should not be considered as a universal law (like the law of demand) and may be altered by subsequent events in the economy.

V. HELPFUL HINTS

1.   The central bank of the United States, or the Federal Reserve System, is commonly referred to as simply **the Fed**. It would be very difficult to overstate the Fed's importance in the U.S. economy. Few people outside of the fields of economics or finance appreciate the significance of the Fed.

2.   Several times in this chapter Samuelson and Nordhaus refer to the Fed's attempts to influence "real" variables or the "real side" of the economy. The word "real," in this sense, refers to inflation-adjusted measures of output, employment, and growth. (You may recall that economic growth is always measured in real terms.)

3.   The Fed is a bank for banks. It holds their deposits (called *bank reserves)* and lends them money (at the discount rate). Unlike consumers, who may apply for a loan at a bank whenever they like, banks should ask the Fed for loans only when they are in serious financial trouble. The Fed is often called "the lender of last resort."

4.   An open-market *purchase* means that the Fed is *buying bonds* and injecting reserves. The *money supply* should *grow*. An open-market *sale* means that the Fed is *selling bonds* and withdrawing reserves. The *money supply* should *shrink* or at least its rate of growth should slow down.

5.   The terms *treasury bills, government bonds,* and *government securities* can, for our purposes, all be used interchangeably. They are all instruments that the Fed owns, buys, and sells in its attempt to control the money supply. The Fed uses these government bonds because there is a huge supply of them and because they are relatively risk free. The Fed and most other financial institutions hold large portfolios of these bonds.

6.   The Fed does not change reserve requirements often. It is not because this instrument is ineffective, but precisely the opposite! Reserve requirement changes are very powerful, especially when they are increased. If the Fed suddenly increased reserve requirements, many banks would be short reserves. Banks typically lend excess reserves to one another, but in this situation very few banks, if any, would have excess reserves available to lend—they would all be looking to borrow. Interest rates would tend to rise. The Fed also prefers to control the money supply in much more *subtle* ways. The Fed buys and sells securities all the time with a group of different government bond dealers. Most of these transactions are done in order to steady the money supply; only rarely does the Fed undertake policy actions. It is nearly impossible, on any given day, to determine what the Fed's position in the bond market is. Nevertheless, a great deal of people spend a great deal of time and effort "Fed watching" to try to get advance or inside knowledge of changes in monetary policy.

7.   The Fed sets a target for what it thinks the appropriate level of the money supply should be. This target is based on the health of the economy and projections or forecasts of where the economy is headed. Over any given six-month or year-long period the Fed may or may not hit this target precisely; the Fed, after all, cannot control the entire economy and all the possible changes that may occur. Nevertheless, the Fed decides what it thinks the appropriate level of the money supply should be. This is why the money supply curve is drawn as a nearly vertical line. It is not interest rates that determine monetary policy, but the health of the economy.

VI. MULTIPLE CHOICE QUESTIONS

These questions are organized by topic from the chapter outline. Choose the best answer from the options available.

A. Central Banking and the Federal Reserve System

1.   The phrase "open-market operations" refers specifically to:

a.   commercial banks' lending to business firms and to consumers.

b.   the Federal Reserve's making loans to commercial banks.

c. changes in interest rates caused by an increase or a decrease in the total of commercial-bank loans.

d. the operations of the Federal Reserve designed to increase or to decrease the total of member-bank demand deposits.

e. the Federal Reserve's buying or selling government securities.

2. The principal assets on a Federal Reserve balance sheet are:

a. gold certificates and cash, deposits by banks, and deposits by government.

b. Federal Reserve notes, government securities, and loans.

c. gold certificates and cash, bank deposits, and loans.

d. gold certificates and cash, loans, and government securities.

e. Federal Reserve notes, gold certificates and cash, and member-bank deposits.

3. Which among the following combinations constitutes the tools of monetary policy used by the Federal Reserve in its routine operations (i.e., excluding tools that might be employed in exceptional situations)?

a. discount-rate policy, control over stock-buying margin requirements, and moral suasion.

b. moral suasion and legal reserve-requirement changes.

c. open-market operations and discount-rate changes.

d. discount-rate policy and legal reserve-requirement changes.

e. open-market operations, legal reserve-requirement changes, and selective controls over consumer and mortgage credit.

4. The total of Federal Reserve notes held by business and the public appears on the Federal Reserve balance sheet:

a. as a liability, because these notes are IOUs of the Fed.

b. as an asset, since these notes constitute part of the money supply; i.e., they are cash.

c. as a liability, because these notes are part of reserves; i.e., they represent deposits made by commercial banks.

d. within the capital accounts section, since this represents the money by means of which the Federal Reserve is financed.

e. not at all—only notes not held by business or the public appear on this balance sheet.

5. If the Federal Reserve System raises the discount rate, this act should be interpreted as part of a general policy intended primarily to:

a. reduce the total of commercial-bank reserves.

b. increase the amount saved out of income by the public.

c. encourage increased borrowing from the Fed by commercial banks.

d. increase the total of commercial-bank reserves.

e. do none of the preceding.

6. Suppose the Federal Reserve System conducts a large-scale open-market purchase of government securities from the public. Which alternative in question 5 would have correctly identified its primary objective?

a.

b.

c.

d.

e.

7. If a commercial bank deposits a $20 Federal Reserve note with the Federal Reserve, how will the Federal Reserve balance sheet be affected?

a. The asset "discounts and loans" will rise.

b. The liability "commercial-bank demand deposits" will fall.

c. The asset "U.S. government securities" will rise.

d. The liability "Federal Reserve notes" will rise.

e. None of the preceding is correct.

8. One reason why a reduction in the discount rate might have limited effectiveness as a tool of monetary policy is the fact that:

a. the Fed, although it can increase the quantity of money held by the public, cannot force the public to spend that money, which is what is needed to increase GDP.

b. the Fed no longer has the same statutory power it once had to change the discount rate.

c. the Fed cannot control the quantity of discount borrowing, since banks seek to borrow only if and when they choose.

d. such a reduction is likely to be offset by an increase in member-bank reserves.

e. such a reduction is likely to drive down the prices of stocks and bonds.

9. If the Federal Reserve sells a large quantity of U.S. government securities to the public, it would be reasonable to conclude that this action is intended to:

a. increase the total of personal saving.

b. decrease the total of loans made by commercial banks to their customers.

c. increase the total of deposits of member banks with the Federal Reserve.

d. decrease the general level of interest rates.

e. increase the volume of Federal Reserve notes in circulation.

10. If the Federal Reserve buys a large quantity of U.S. government securities from the public, then:

a. the Federal Reserve liability in the form of bank reserve deposits will go up.

b. the commercial-bank liability "demand deposits" will go down.

c. the total quantity of money held by the public will

go down.

d. the Federal Reserve asset "discounts, loans, and acceptances" will go up.

e. the commercial-bank asset "loans and discounts will go down.

11. If the Federal Reserve wants to restrict the growth of the total money supply, its task is made more difficult if:

a. it lacks legal power to reduce the reserve requirements of commercial banks.

b. commercial banks are holding large excess reserves.

c. the amount of personal saving out of income is very high.

d. gold is being exported to other countries in large quantities.

e. business firms and the public are anxious to buy more government bonds than they now hold.

12. The *discount rate,* as this term is used in monetary-policy discussion, means:

a. the degree of reduction in price required by the Federal Reserve when it purchases any government security.

b. the degree of pressure exerted by the Federal Reserve upon commercial banks to reduce their loans to customers.

c. the interest rate charged by the Federal Reserve on loans made to commercial banks.

d. the extent to which the Federal Reserve is acting so as to increase the money supply and the level of GDP.

e. none of the preceding.

13. A large-scale "easier credit" operation conducted by the Federal Reserve through open-market operations will:

a. raise the price of government securities.

b. reduce the total of commercial-bank reserves.

c. lower the level of prices generally.

d. lower the price of government securities.

e. raise the legal reserve requirements imposed upon commercial banks.

14. The Federal Reserve System of the United States is part of:

a. the judicial branch of government.

b. the administrative branch of government.

c. the legislative branch of government.

d. the regulative branch of government.

e. none of the above.

15. The Federal Reserve's objectives include:

a. economic growth.

b. a high level of employment.

c. stable prices.

d. moderate long-term interest rates.

e. all of the above.

16. In which of the following foreign-market activities is the Fed involved?

a. Sterilization.

b. Foreign-exchange-rate intervention.

c. Helping alleviate international financial crises.

d. All of the above.

e. Choices **b**. and **c**. only.

17. The Glass-Steagall Act:

a. was passed during the Great Depression.

b. prohibited banks from selling insurance or brokerage services.

c. was passed to increase the stability of banks.

d. was repealed in 1999.

e. is all of the above.

B. The Effects of Money on Output and Prices

18. If the Fed seeks to increase GDP, which of the following is *not* among the steps that link the Fed's action to GDP?

a. Increase investment to raise the level of total spending.

b. Increase interest rates to make lending more attractive to holders of cash.

c. Increase bank reserves to encourage the banks to increase their non-cash assets.

d. Increase demand deposits.

e. Increase the availability of credit.

19. In the "monetarist experiment" of 1979 the Fed decided to:

a. reorganize the operations of the foreign desk.

b. focus primarily on interest rate movements rather than bank reserves and the money supply.

c. focus primarily on bank reserves and the money supply rather than interest rate movements.

d. direct the Treasury to print more money.

e. do none of the above.

20. The bank deregulation of the early 1980s has:

a. reduced the ability of the Fed to control the money supply.

b. begun a process to lift interest rate ceilings from accounts in financial institutions

c. preserved the reserve requirement on transactions accounts.

d. done nothing to undermine the legislative mandate to the Fed that it announce its policy objectives.

e. done all the above.

21. On the basis of the transactions demand component of the demand for money:

a. the demand for money shifts right as the nominal interest rate rises.

b. the demand for money shifts right as the nominal interest rate falls.

c. the demand for money falls as nominal income rises.

d. the demand for money falls as nominal income falls.

e. none of the above occurs.

22. Which answer to question 20 would have been correct

had that question referred to the assets demand component of the demand for money?

a.

b.

c.

d.

e.

23. The demand curve for investment:

a. parallels the demand curve for money in that high interest rates reduce demand.

b. most precisely plots the real rate of interest against quantity of investment funds demanded.

c. is negatively sloped because high real interest rates cause marginal investment projects to be rejected.

d. is a vital link between changes in the money supply and nominal GDP.

e. is described by all the above.

24. A reduction in interest rates engineered by the Federal Reserve can reasonably be expected to:

a. encourage investment because it makes the lending of money more profitable to bankers.

b. discourage investment because it makes the borrowing of money less attractive.

c. have little or no effect on investment, since that is not its purpose—interest rate changes are intended to alter security prices, not investment.

d. discourage investment because it makes the lending of money less attractive.

e. encourage investment because it makes the borrowing of money more attractive.

25. Monetary policy is made somewhat *less* effective in restraining a period of excessive spending whenever:

a. the demand-for-investment schedule is highly elastic.

b. dollars held abroad are attracted to higher interest rates in the United States.

c. the money demand schedule is highly elastic.

d. changes in interest rates tend to bring with them changes in the market value of securities.

e. investment spending responds more to changes in credit availability than to changes in interest rates.

26. Because the difference between real and nominal interest rates is the rate of inflation:

a. nominal rates can fall, in the long run, in response to tight monetary policy.

b. nominal rates must rise, in both the short and the long runs, in response to tight monetary policy.

c. there is no difference between the demand for money and the demand for investment.

d. the paradox of thrift is less of a concern.

e. none of the above is correct.

VII. PROBLEM SOLVING

The following problems are designed to help you apply the concepts that you learned in the chapter.

A. Central Banking and the Federal Reserve System

1. Suppose, for the sake of illustration, that an open-market operation designed to lower inflation is orchestrated by reducing the level of reserves available to the entire banking system.

a. The result would be (**an expansion / a contraction**) in the quantity of bank money supplied to the economy. It should be expected, therefore, that interest rates would (**climb / fall**) and the supply of credit would (**contract / expand**).

b. Businesses would therefore find it (**easier / more difficult**) to finance new investment. Individuals would feel (**richer / poorer**) and would therefore (**increase / reduce**) their consumption expenditures. And so on.

c. Aggregate demand would, in general, (**climb / fall**) and thus put pressure on GDP to (**climb / fall**), prices to (**climb / fall**), and/or unemployment to (**climb / fall**).

2. Consider the $247.4 billion liability that appeared on the 1991 Federal Reserve balance sheet under "Federal Reserve notes." Identify which of the following statements are correct by circling the appropriate letters:

a. This liability represents the bulk of the paper money circulating in the United States. It is, in fact, all such money except for a few bills of various types (silver certificates, U.S. notes) which date back to earlier generations. (These are still held in small amounts by the public, but they are being withdrawn whenever they come out of hiding and reappear in circulation.)

b. This figure of $247.4 billion represents the total of all such Federal Reserve paper money existing outside the Fed itself, i.e., held by commercial banks and by the public.

c. This total of paper money is listed as a liability by the Federal Reserve because, in the last analysis, such bills are simply IOUs of the Fed and must be listed on its balance sheet as any such IOU must be.

d. If any member commercial bank deposits a $10 Federal Reserve note with the Fed, then on the Fed's balance sheet the liability bank reserves rise by $10 and the liability Federal Reserve notes fall by $10 (since this particular IOU is no longer outstanding).

e. If a Federal Reserve employee receives a brand-new $10 Federal Reserve note as part of his or her salary, the Fed's liability Federal Reserve notes must rise by $10.

f. If any commercial bank withdraws $10 from its deposit with its Federal Reserve Bank and takes this withdrawal in the form of a $10 Federal Reserve note, then the Fed's liability bank reserves must fall by $10, and its liability Federal Reserve notes must rise by $10.

g. Federal Reserve notes held by a commercial bank in its own vaults may be counted as part of its legal reserve.

h. The public can increase its holding of Federal Reserve notes simply by withdrawing part of its demand-deposit accounts. This action would decrease the deposit-money total and increase the total of paper money held by the public.

Questions 3 through 7 deal with the operation of monetary policy in terms of Federal Reserve and commercial-bank balance sheets. In these questions, assume that each bank is required to keep a bank reserve of at least 10 percent of its own total demand deposits (owned by its customers). Assume, as well, that the bank tries to keep this reserve as follows: 7.5 percent as a deposit with the Fed and 2.5 percent as cash on its own premises—vault cash.

We start with the balance sheets (in billions of dollars) in Tables 26-1 and 26-2 for the Federal Reserve and the combined commercial banks.

TABLE 26-1 Federal Reserve

Assets		Liabilities	
Gold certificates	$10	Federal Reserve notes	$15
Gov't. securities	35	Deposits:	
Loans	5	U.S. Treasury	5
		Bank reserves	30

TABLE 26-2 Combined Commercial Banks

Assets		Liabilities	
Federal Reserve deposits	$ 30	Demand deposits	$400
Vault cash	10		
Loans	360		

3. This question outlines the working of the principal instrument which the Federal Reserve uses in conducting its monetary policy: *open-market operations.* Suppose that the Fed decides (for reasons that will shortly be evident) to buy government securities (i.e., government bonds) from the public. It enters the bond market and buys $10 (billion) of short-term government securities (bidding up the prices of these securities somewhat, if necessary, in order to obtain them). The Fed pays for these bonds by drawing checks on itself. As a consequence of this bond purchase by the Fed, two significant account totals have increased:

a. The public now has an additional $10 in its total demand deposits with commercial banks.

b. The commercial banks likewise have an additional $10 in their deposits With the Federal Reserve.

Write out new balance sheets in Table 26-3 for the Fed and the banks, corresponding to those in Tables 26-1 and 26-

2 but showing the changes just described. (As yet, the banks have changed neither their vault cash nor their loans.)

TABLE 26-3 Federal Reserve

Assets		Liabilities	
Gold certs.	$_____	FR notes	$_____
		Deposits:	
Gov't. securities	_____	U.S. Treasury	_____
Loans	_____	Bank reserves	_____

Combined Commercial Banks

Assets		Liabilities	
FR deposits	$_____	Demand deposits	$_____
Vault cash	_____		
Loans	_____		

4. a. Commercial banks now (**have excess reserves / are just fully loaned up / are deficient in their total reserve requirement**). This means that they (**will want to increase / must decrease**) their total loans in order to increase their earnings.

b. Specifically, their total reserves are now (**$10 / $20 / $30 / $40 / $50**), and this is sufficient to maintain demand deposits totaling a maximum of (**$300 / $350 / $400 / $450 / $500 / $550 / $600**).

5. In Table 26-4, show balance sheets for both the Fed and the combined banks after the banks have taken full advantage of this opportunity to increase their loans. Remember that both Fed deposits and vault cash count as reserves and that, by assumption, banks want to keep them in a 3-to-1 ratio. Vault cash is increased by withdrawing part of their Fed deposit. Assume that the withdrawal is made in Federal Reserve notes.

TABLE 26-4 Federal Reserve

Assets		Liabilities	
Gold certs.	$_____	FR notes	$_____
		Deposits:	
Gov't. securities	_____	U.S. Treasury	_____
Loans	_____	Bank reserves	_____

Combined Commercial Banks

Assets		Liabilities	
FR deposits	$_____	Demand deposits	$_____
Vault cash	_____		
Loans	_____		

6. a. Assuming that the banks do increase their loans to the maximum allowed by the reserve requirement, then the money supply will (**increase / decrease**), altogether by (**$0 / $20 / $40 / $60 / $80 / $100**).

b. How would you expect this to affect the level of GDP? Explain briefly. —————————

c. In sum, if the Federal Reserve enters the securities market as a buyer, its objective would be to (**raise / restrain**) GDP by making credit (**easier / more difficult**) to obtain.

d. This would be an *easy-money policy*. Interest rates, those on bank loans in particular, should (**rise / fall**) .

7. If the Federal Reserve wanted to reduce credit and to restrain GDP, then it would pursue a *tight-money policy*. It would work the open-market process of the previous questions in reverse.

a. That is, the Fed would enter the securities markets as a (**buyer / seller**) . If necessary, it would accept a price somewhat (**higher / lower**) than the previously existing market level in order to bring about its (**purchases / sales**) of government securities.

b. The buyers of these securities (insurance companies, other financial institutions, business corporations, even individuals) would pay for them by means of checks drawn on their commercial bank accounts. The Fed would return these checks to the banks involved and require settlement by (**increasing / reducing**) the reserve deposit which these banks kept at the Fed.

c. When the reserves of commercial banks decline, then the banks (unless they have excess reserves) must (**increase / decrease**) their loans to customers. The effect of this tighter-money open-market operation is that the totals of commercial bank loans and demand deposits go (**up / down**).

(If you wish, you can work all this out in detail, starting with the same pair of balance sheets in Table 26-4 and with a sale by the Fed of $10 of its government securities. Remember that if a bank has more Federal Reserve notes than needed to cover the 2.5 percent vault-cash requirement, it can return the excess to the Fed, thereby increasing the amount of its reserve deposit.)

8. a. Notice a difference between easy- and tight-money policies. When an easy-money policy gives them more reserves, the banks (**must / may or may not**) then increase their loans to the fullest possible extent.

If they do not like the credit prospects of the would-be borrowers standing in line, they may decide not to become fully loaned up. The Fed can do nothing to force them to change this decision. Conversely, the Fed can always push a tight-money operation until any excess reserves have been mopped up.

b. Thereafter, the banks (**do not have any / still have some**) choice. They (**need not necessarily / must**) reduce their loans outstanding.

9. In a tight-money period, interest rates are generally going to move (**up / down**). In such a period (circle all that apply):

a. borrowed money is harder to obtain because the total of loans granted may be going down.

b. the total supply of borrowable money may be smaller.

c. the total of loans granted may actually be increasing, but not as fast as the demand for such loans; to any borrower, money therefore seems harder to obtain.

10. a. Consider how an inflow of foreign-held dollars increases U.S. commercial-bank reserves. The effect is the same as it would be if the Federal Reserve had conducted an open-market (**purchase / sale**) of securities. However, the Fed did not initiate this action, and it may decide to undertake offsetting action; i.e., it can *sterilize* the increase in reserves by means of an open-market (**purchase / sale**).

To illustrate this matter of international reserve movements more fully, consider a different example, one arising out of foreign trade. Suppose that the Bavarian Motor Works and Audi-Volkswagen have sold $100 million worth of their automobiles in the United States. These sales are not matched by U.S. sales abroad, so the United States has imported $100 million more than it has exported. The two German companies accordingly have $100 million in deposits in U.S. commercial banks. These companies, being German-based, want to convert their dollars into deutsche marks, so they sell their dollar accounts to the West German central bank, the Bundesbank, receiving the marks that they want in exchange.

The Bundesbank in turn sells these dollar accounts to the Federal Reserve. It doesn't matter here how the Fed makes payment to the Bundesbank; that is a matter of international settlements, a topic discussed later in the text. The point is that the Fed now owns the U.S. commercial-bank deposit accounts worth $100 million.

b. In this respect, it is in exactly the same position as it would have been if it had conducted an open-market operation, (**buying / selling**) U.S. government securities. It has an increased claim on these banks.

c. If the Fed wishes, it can ask the banks to settle up. This will cause them to (**lose / gain**) reserves. In effect, the Fed would have conducted a (**tight- / easy-**) money operation.

d. Of course, if the Fed considers that policy undesirable in the light of domestic conditions, it can keep the commercial-bank deposit accounts or it can conduct a sterilizing, or offsetting, (**tight- / easy-**) money operation.

11. The political independence of the Federal Reserve is an issue of enormous importance. As it stands now, the Fed belongs to (**the administrative / the legislative / the judicial / no single**) branch of government. It reports directly to (**Congress / the President**), hears advice and criticism from (**Congress / the President / everyone**), but makes up its own mind about the direction of policy actions. This may or may not be consistent with fiscal policy.

12. Another issue of potentially extreme consequence is the effect of recent deregulation on the ability of the Fed to control the money supply. Two significant acts of Congress in 1980 and 1982 greatly diminished the Fed's power.

a.   Non-transactions accounts were (**totally / partially**) deregulated, and thus, by 1986, there were (**no / higher / lower**) interest rate ceilings and (**higher and substantial / lower and minimal**) reserve requirements applied to those accounts. These non-transactions accounts include (**savings / checking / store-based credit**) accounts.

b.   Transactions accounts were (**totally / partially**) deregulated, as well, with interest rate ceilings (**lapsing / being raised / being lowered**) by 1986, but with substantial reserve requirements remaining.

B. The Effects of Money on Output and Prices

13. The *LL* curve drawn as it is in panel (*a*) of Figure 26-3 suggests that if the interest rate were to go up, some people would decide they ought to (**use some of their "idle" money to buy securities / sell some of their securities and hold money as an asset instead**). Alternatively, the total quantity of money which people would want to hold as an *asset* would (**increase / decrease**) if the interest rate were to fall.

In sum, interest is the reward paid to you for parting with money (parting with liquidity). If the interest rate falls, that reward is less, and the attractiveness of parting with money decreases; i.e., the demand to hold money becomes a stronger force.

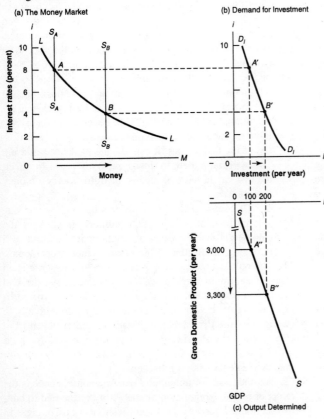

Figure 26-3

14. Figure 26-3 shows how the Fed would try to use an increase in the money supply to push an economy out of a recession; i.e., the ultimate policy goal here is to increase nominal GDP. Start at point *A*. The policy step is to increase the money supply from S_AS_A to S_BS_B; it can be accomplished by a large open-market operation.

The Fed would simply enter the securities market and (**buy / sell**) government securities—bidding (**up / down**) their prices to the extent necessary to make supply and demand match. Equilibrium in the money market therefore moves from point *A* to point *B*. with the nominal rate of interest lower than before. Therefore, with (**lower / higher**) interest rates and easier credit conditions, borrowers with real investment projects in mind are (**discouraged / encouraged**) to undertake them.

15. a.   Look once again at the *LL* curve in Figure 26-3 Suppose it was much steeper (closer to being vertical). Compared with the one drawn, a steeper curve would mean that any given change in interest rates—say, the indicated reduction from 8 percent to 4 percent—would produce a (**larger / smaller**) change in the demand for money. Starting from point *A* but with a steeper *LL* curve than the one shown, the Fed would have to pump a (**smaller / larger**) amount of extra money into the economy to get the interest rate down from 8 to 4 percent.

b.   Conversely, if the *LL* curve were flatter (closer to being horizontal), then the Fed's task (for any desired reduction in interest rates) would be (**easier / more difficult**). If the *LL* curve were flatter, it would mean that asset holders were highly sensitive to interest rate changes. Even a fairly modest reduction in interest rates would "turn them off" to securities; they would want to sell securities in large quantities and to hold money instead.

16. Figure 26-3 depends, in its final panel, on our multiplier model that determines GDP by the equality of saving and investment. Figure 26-4 portrays the increase in investment that was depicted in panel (*b*) of Figure 26-3 as an increase in aggregate demand.

a.   In panel (*a*) of Figure 26-4 (top of next page), the story told by Figure 26-3 is repeated; the higher investment causes real GDP to climb because output was initially (**well below / almost equal to / far above**) potential GDP.

b.   In panel (*b*), though, the higher investment causes only nominal GDP to climb, because (**real GDP / only prices**) **climb(s)**. The key here, of course, is that GDP was initially (**far below / almost equal to / well above**) potential.

17. a.   The difference between the nominal interest rate and the real interest rate is the ____.

b.   In the long run, a reduction in the money supply can

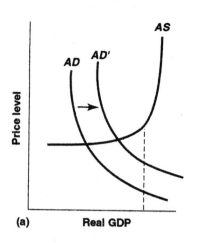
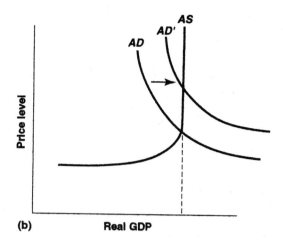

Figure 26-4

cause nominal interest rates to (**fall / climb**), even though they may (**fall / climb**) in the short run.

c. Initially, as the money supply contracts, (**the nominal / the real / both**) interest rate(s) climb(s), causing investment to fall, aggregate demand to fall, and, eventually, price inflation to slow down.

d. As a direct result of the slowdown in inflation, though, the (**nominal / real**) rate will fall. This change is supported by the slower growth in nominal GDP that causes the demand for money to shift (**to the right / nowhere / to the left**), where it can intersect an even smaller money supply at a lower nominal rate of interest.

e. One problem with this scenario is, though, that (**it may happen too fast for people to keep up / it may happen too slowly to avoid the costs of high unemployment**).

VIII. DISCUSSION QUESTIONS

Answer the following questions, making sure that you can explain the work you did to arrive at the answers.

1. Explain in words how the Fed uses open-market operations to control the money supply. Do not use any numbers or balance sheets—just words.
2. Explain why it is in the Fed's interest to set reserve requirements above what bankers would willingly hold by themselves.
3. Explain why changes in reserve requirements (especial-

ly increases) are so drastic. What is a better way to control the money supply?
4. What happened when the Fed began targeting M_1, M_2, and bank reserves in October 1979? How has the Fed modified this policy since 1982?
5. Is the Fed too independent? Argue pro and con.
6. Briefly discuss the reason why dollars might be held abroad.
7. Discuss the long-term effects of monetary policy on the economy and the neutrality of money.

IX. ANSWERS TO STUDY GUIDE QUESTIONS

III. Review of Key Concepts

5	Board of Governors
9	Federal Open Market Committee
14	Open-market operation
12	Discount-rate policy
10	Reserve requirements policy
3	Intermediate targets
11	Ultimate objectives
13	Transactions account
1	Non-transactions account
7	Sterilization
6	Monetary transmission mechanism
2	Money markets
8	Neutrality of money
4	Policy instruments of the Fed

VI. Multiple Choice Questions

1. E   2. D   3. C   4. A   5. A   6. D
7. E   8. C   9. B   10. A   11. B   12. C
13. A   14. E   15. E   16. D   17. E   18. B
19. C   20. E   21. D   22. E   23. E   24. E
25. C   26. A

VII. Problem Solving

1. a. a contraction, climb, contract
   b. more difficult, poorer, reduce
   c. fall, fall, fall, climb

2. All the statements are correct.

3.

TABLE 26-3 Federal Reserve

Assets		Liabilities	
Gold certs.	$10	FR notes	$15
		Deposits:	
Gov't. securities	45	U.S. Treasury	5
Loans	5	Bank reserves	40

Combined Commercial Banks

Assets		Liabilities	
FR deposits	$ 40	Demand deposits	$410
Vault cash	10		
Loans	360		

4. a. have excess reserves, will want to increase
   b. $50, $500

5.

TABLE 26-4 Federal Reserve

Assets		Liabilities	
Gold certs	$10	FR notes	$17.5
		Deposits:	
Gov't. securities	45	U.S. Treasury	5.0
Loans	5	Bank reserves	37.5

Combined Commercial Banks

Assets		Liabilities	
FR deposits	$37.5	Demand deposits	$500
Vault cash	12.5		
Loans	450.0		

6. a. increase, $100
   b. Increased lending by banks means that people are borrowing and spending more. GDP will increase.
   c. raise, easier
   d. fall
7. a. seller, lower, sales
   b. reducing
   c. decrease, down
8. a. may or may not
   b. do not have any, must
9. up, All the choices are possible.

10. a. purchase, sale
    b. selling
    c. lose, tight
    d. easyk
11. no single, Congress, everyone
12. a. totally, no, lower and minimal, savings
    b. partially, lapsing
13. use some of their "idle" money to buy securities, increase
14. buy, up, lower, encouraged
15. a. smaller, smaller
    b. more difficult
16. a. well below
    b. only prices, almost equal to
17. a. rate of inflation
    b. fall, climb
    c. both
    d. nominal, to the left
    e. it may happen too slowly to avoid the costs of high unemployment

VIII. Discussion Questions

1. Open-market operations refer to the Fed's purchase and sale of U.S. government securities or bonds. When the Fed sells a bond, the buyer of the bond (bank, business, individual) pays for it with money, usually a check. When the Fed presents the check to the bond purchaser's bank for payment, the bank loses demand deposits and reserves. This reduces the bank's ability to make loans and will ultimately affect other banks in the economy since they will no longer be receiving deposits from the first bank's loan recipients.

When the Fed buys bonds, it injects liquidity or reserves into the system. When the bond seller (whoever it is) deposits the payment from the Fed in the bank, the bank finds itself with excess reserves. This increases the bank's ability to make loans, and the money supply increases. As loan recipients spend their borrowings, other banks find themselves with excess reserves and the process continues.

2. If bankers willingly hold reserves beyond the Fed's requirements, this reduces the Fed's ability to use reserve requirements as a policy tool. If the Fed reduces reserve requirements to encourage lending, this may have a minimal effect since banks already had excess reserves that they chose not to lend. Alternatively, if the Fed increases reserves to slow down the money creation process, it may have little impact since banks may already have enough (excess) reserves to meet the new requirement.

3. When the Fed increases reserve requirements, many banks are likely to be short of reserves. (Even the most conservative banker knows that idle reserves earn no interest, so there is an incentive to keep reserves down to the legal minimum.) As the banking system as a whole tries to meet the new reserve requirement, there would be few available lenders. The "announcement effect" of this change in policy

could be dramatic. The Fed prefers to conduct its business in much more subtle ways. Open-market operations are more discreet and much less disruptive.

4. When the Fed focused its attention on the money supply, it had to give up its ability to control interest rates. Remember, interest rates are the price of money. When the Fed reduced the growth rate of the supply of money, it had to realize that interest rates would rise. (There is no way that the producer of a good can restrict its supply and also keep its price from rising.) While the Fed's strict attention to the money supply dramatically reduced inflation in the economy, many analysts believe it also pushed the economy into a recession. As the banking industry developed new types of money instruments, M_1—and to some extent M_2—became less reliable predictors of movements in aggregate demand. As a result, the Fed has recently paid closer attention *to real rates of interest in the economy.*

5. *Pro*: The Board of Governors is not elected. Fourteen-year term of office is too long. Bankers may be more concerned with the profits of fellow bankers and less with the health of the economy. *Con:* Bankers and economists are more likely to do a better job managing the money supply than politicians. Independence of the Fed insulates it from political pressure and enables monetary policy to counterbalance fiscal policy.

6. The dollar is recognized around the globe as a safe and stable currency. Foreign investors and those who trade with the United States hold dollars. Dollars are held for speculation, investing, and trade.

7. First of all, we should keep in mind that the long term here may be many decades. Research results suggest that in the long run the effects of changes in the money supply will be shown primarily as changes in the price level. Eventually prices, wages, and interest rates will all adjust to changes in the money supply, and there will be minimal impact on real output and employment in the economy.

CHAPTER

The Process of Economic Growth

I. CHAPTER OVERVIEW

Most of our attention thus far has focused on short- to medium-term changes in economic conditions associated with the business cycle. The focus here is on longer patterns of growth and the associated level of aggregate output in the economy. The approach used here is similar to the other models we have constructed in that it seeks to help explain another facet of the macroeconomy.

Economic growth, by definition, deals with changes in the level of *real* output, or GDP, in the economy. Without growth economies eventually stagnate and fade away. The chapter is divided into two parts: the first discusses several theories and trends in economic growth, the second part focuses on an analysis of economic growth in the United States.

II. LEARNING OBJECTIVES

After you have read Chapter 27 in your text and completed the exercises in this *Study Guide* chapter, you should be able to:

1. Discuss the four basic elements/factors in economic growth.
2. Trace the evolution of thought about economic growth from Smith and Malthus to the **neoclassical growth model** developed in large measure by Robert Solow.
3. Define **capital deepening** and explain why it tends to increase the real wage paid to labor and reduce the return earned by capital. Understand how and why reductions in the return to capital, in the absence of technological change, can bring capital deepening to a halt in a long-run **steady state.**
4. Explain how and why **technological change** can push a factor-price frontier out, thereby illustrating how a relatively high return to capital can be maintained even as continued capital deepening drives the capital-labor ratio upward.
5. Summarize briefly the (seven) basic trends in the economic development of advanced economies.

6. Understand the equations of **growth accounting,** and use that approach to identify the major sources of growth in per capita output in the United States.
7. Explain how technological change itself can be viewed as an output, produced by the economy.
8. Discuss the explanations of the productivity slowdown in the United States, and its subsequent increase in the late 1990s.

III. REVIEW OF KEY CONCEPTS

Match the following terms from column A with their definitions in column B.

A	B
___ Economic growth	1. Process by which the quantity of capital per worker (or the K/L ratio) increases over time.
___ Social overhead capital	2. An invention or innovation which has no major effect on relative demand for, or returns to, different factors.
___ Technological change	3. An invention or innovation that reduces the capital requirement more than the labor requirement. This raises wages relative to profits.
___ Neoclassical growth model	4. Level of real GDP the economy would produce if unemployment were at the "natural rate."
___ Capital-labor ratio	5. An invention or innovation that reduces the need for labor and increases the demand for capital. This increases profits relative to wages.
___ Capital deepening	6. Equals the growth of output minus the growth of the weighted-sum of all inputs. (This is another expression for *technological*

__ Aggregate
production
function

__ Long-run
steady state

__ Labor-saving
invention

__ Capital-saving
invention

__ Neutral invention

__ Growth
accounting

__ Total factor
productivity

__ Potential GDP

change, but do *not* put this
number with that term.)

7.   The expansion of a country's
real potential GDP or output.

8.   Total dollar value of capital
goods divided by the number of
workers, or the quantity of capital
per worker.

9.   A way of separating out the
contributions of the different
ingredients driving observed
trends in growth.

10.   Change in the processes of
production or the introduction of
new products such that more or
improved output can be obtained
from the same bundle of inputs.

11.   Assuming technology is held
constant, this describes a long run
equilibrium position in which
there is a cessation of capital
deepening and constant capital
returns, real wages, and interest
rates.

12.   Investments in a nation's
infrastructure undertaken by the
government, that precede and lay
the framework for a thriving private sector.

13.   Model in which a single
homogeneous output is produced
with two inputs: capital and labor.

14.   Relates total national output
to technology and all of a
country's inputs.

IV. SUMMARY AND CHAPTER OUTLINE

This section summarizes the key concepts from the chapter.

A. Theories of Economic Growth

1.   Economic growth ponders the processes by which the
American standard of living has improved so dramatically
and by which the stock of American capital has grown so
large. These are not merely topics of academic curiosity.
This topic is paramount when policymakers and economic
theorists question, for example, the sources of the recent
slowdown in American productivity and search for remedies
that can revitalize economic growth. It is also a topic that
needs to be understood if we are to be able to assist developing economies in their attempts to improve the lots of their
citizens. Economic growth is the single most important fac-

tor in the economic success of nations in the long run.

2.   The perspective of Chapter 27 is admittedly long-term,
and the analysis might appear at first blush to be a bit more
complex than that found in other chapters of the text. It may
help to point out that most models of economic growth are
explained almost exclusively in terms of the interplay
between the diminishing marginal productivity of the factors
of production and technological change. The three factors of
production—human resources (or labor), natural resources
(or land), and capital—along with technology are the four
main elements of economic growth.

The aggregate production function relates total national output to all of the economy's inputs and technology. It is written as:

$$Q = A F(K, L, R)$$

where Q is national output of GDP, A is the level of technological know-how in the economy and K, L, and R are the
capital, labor, and natural resource inputs in the economy.
The production function itself simply says that national output is some function of a combination of the inputs, weighted by the level of technology.

3.   Each new stage in the interplay between diminishing
marginal productivity and technology affects the distribution
of income between labor and capital. It is important to
understand that input proportions can change as economic
growth occurs. Furthermore, diminishing returns can apply
even when the supplies of all inputs are increasing—if they
are not increasing at the same rate.

4.   Consider a production function depending upon just two
inputs, *capital* and *labor*. The input with the slower rate of
growth (usually thought to be labor in a developed economy)
can, for purposes of studying growth, be considered to be the
(relatively) fixed input, while the other is viewed as the (relatively) variable input. Since the payment offered to the
variable input (capital, in this simple illustration) depends
upon its marginal product, and that marginal product should
decline as the supply of capital increases relative to labor,
diminishing returns work against the well-being of the owners of capital. In the extreme, in fact, diminishing returns
might drive the marginal product of capital to zero, so the
competitive return earned by capital would also move to
zero. It is, of course, unlikely that this circumstance would
come to pass; investment is likely to stop increasing the
capital stock well before the zero-payment level is reached.

Early (i.e., pre-industrial revolution) discussions of
economic growth were also based on two inputs, but in those
approaches *land* was viewed as the fixed factor and *labor*
was variable. With the emphasis on diminishing returns, it
was inevitable that economists like Malthus should conclude
that labor's future looked gloomy.

In more recent discussions, labor has been the fixed
input and capital the variable one (because the stock of capi-

tal is growing faster than population). Now the shoe is on the other foot. Capital, it would seem, is the input that is vulnerable to the ravages of diminishing returns; but capital has another card to play: *technological progress.*

The diminishing-returns effect, which continually works against the return to the owners of capital, is more or less continually being offset by technological advance.

5. **Capital deepening** occurs when the stock of capital grows more rapidly than the labor force. When we hold other factors constant, this accounts for the positive (though declining) slope of the aggregate production function (*APF*) in Figure 27-4 from your textbook (reproduced here as Figure 27-1). When **technology** changes, as in Figure 27-5 from your textbook (here, Figure 27-2), the entire *APF* schedule will shift. Capital and technology are the basic ingredients in the **neoclassical growth model.**

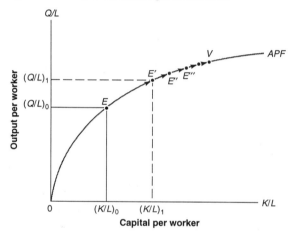

Figure 27-1 Economic Growth Through Capital Deepening

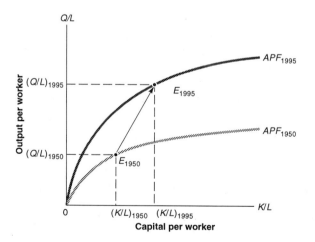

Figure 27-2 Technological Advance Shifts up the Production Possibilities

6. Recent theories of economic growth suggest that technological change may itself be an output of the economic system. Rather than assuming that technology is a "given" or determined exogenously (i.e., outside the economic system), newer economic models investigate how the private market and public policy contribute to technological progress.

Many aspects of technological change should also be viewed as public or "nonrival" goods. While new technologies may be expensive to develop, they tend to be rather inexpensive to reproduce. Further, once developed, many people and producers can use or share the same technology simultaneously without using it up. These public good attributes of technology suggest that the private market would tend to underproduce technology and that the government or public agency should be more involved in its development.

B. The Patterns of Growth in the United States

1. Aggregate U.S. statistics describe the following pattern of growth since 1900:

   a. The annual growth rate of labor and employment has been consistently smaller than the annual growth rate of capital. This is called capital deepening.

   b. For the most of this century, the real wage paid to labor has increased.

   c. The share of GDP paid to labor has increased only slightly, and been nearly constant for the last 20 years.

   d. There have been large fluctuations in both rates of profit and real interest rates and no discernible trends either up or down.

   e. The capital-output ratio has actually declined since 1990.

   f. The savings rate and the investment-output ratio has held stable, for the most part, except for a sharp decrease in the national savings rate since 1980.

   g. National output has grown at an average rate of about three percent per year. The weighted average annual growth rate of the three inputs (K, L, and R) has been less than three percent. This suggests that technology (or other factors) has played a key role in economic growth.

2. For those who read through the section on the **growth-accounting approach,** we offer the following explanation of equations (1) and (2) presented there. Samuelson and Nordhaus begin with:

$$(1) \ \% \ Q \ \text{growth} = 0.75 \times (\% \ L \ \text{growth}) + 0.25 \\ \times (\% \ K \ \text{growth}) + T.C.$$

The 0.75 and 0.25 represent the relative contributions of labor and capital, respectively, to economic growth.

There are a couple of intermediate steps between equations (1) and (2). First, subtract (% L growth) from both sides of the equation. Since the right-hand side of equation (1) already has $0.75 \times$ (% L growth) in it, we are left with negative one-quarter of (% L growth) on the right-hand side. This leaves:

(1a) % Q growth -% L growth =
$0.25 \times$ (% K growth) - $0.25 \times$ (% L growth) + *T.C.*

We can combine the capital and labor growth terms on the right-hand side of equation (la) since they are both premultiplied by 0.25.

(1b) % Q growth - % L growth =
$0.25 \times$ (% K growth - % L growth) + *T.C.*

Finally, when you calculate percentage changes, and two terms are subtracted, you can first form them into a ratio or fraction and then calculate the percentage change.
For example, let:

$Q_1 = 100$ and $Q_2 = 105$
$L_1 = 200$ and $L_2 = 202$.

The percentage change in Q is 5 percent, and the percentage change in L is 1 percent. So, we could write:

% Q growth - % L growth = 5% - 1% = 4%

Alternatively, we could first form the terms above into an output-labor ratio, and then calculate the percentage change in that ratio.

$(Q/L)_1 = 100/200$ and $(Q/L)_2 = 105/202$
$(Q/L)_1 = 0.5000$ and $(Q/L)_2 = 0.5198$

The percentage change in the ratio is 0.0396. (If the changes are very small, or if we calculate the change using the midpoint of the range, rather than the initial value as the base, then the two answers would be identical!)
This all leads to Samuelson's and Nordhaus's second equation:

(2) % Q/L growth = $0.25 \times$ (% K/L growth) + *T.C.*

About 60 percent of the growth in output in the United States can be attributed to increases in capital and labor. The rest is a residual factor and can, in large part, be attributed to technology and factors related to it: research and development, innovation, economies of scale, scientific advances, and education.
3. When compared with the period from 1948 to 1973, the rate of productivity growth in the United States from 1973 to the early 1990s slowed dramatically. While no clear-cut explanation for the **productivity slowdown** exists, studies point to several factors that have become more prevalent since the early 1970s. Stricter environmental regulations, the sharp increase in energy prices, a deterioration in labor quality, and a disproportionate share of research and development dollars (when compared to other industrialized economies) allocated to national defense and space exploration have all been proposed as contributing factors to the productivity slowdown.

However, during the late 1990s there was a dramatic increase in the labor productivity in the United States. Economists had been expecting to find increases in productivity due to the increased utilization of computers, and during the last few years of the century labor productivity returned to the levels it had been during the late 1960s and early 1970s. Economists attribute about half of the increase in labor productivity to the widespread investment in computer hardware and software as well as an overall increase in the productivity of the computer itself. It is estimated that the other half of the labor productivity increase is due to the strong growth in the U.S. economy and more accurate measurement of inflation indexes to reduce their upward bias. (For any given increase in GDP, the lower the measurement of inflation, the higher the real growth in output.)

V. HELPFUL HINTS

1. It has been mentioned previously that economic growth is always measured in *real* terms. Growth is also usually measured in *percent* per time period.
2. It may be helpful to keep in mind that when economists talk about the **steady state,** the level of technology is held constant. As long as technology keeps changing, an economy cannot be in a steady state position.
3. As we move along the aggregate production function *(APF)* in Figure 27-1, we add more capital per worker, holding all other factors constant. This is **capital deepening**.
4. The *APF* schedule will shift if there is a change in technology or natural resources.
5. If an invention or innovation is capital-saving, the firm will demand more labor relative to capital. Correspondingly, the amount of money paid in wages relative to profits will increase.
6. The classical approach to economics includes, for the most part, ideas that were developed in the eighteenth and nineteenth centuries. Economists of that time did not consider themselves as "classicals"—that is just what we call them now. Some of their ideas are very powerful and relevant today.

Neoclassical models are modern (twentieth-century) refinements of classical ideas.

VI. MULTIPLE CHOICE QUESTIONS

These questions are organized by topic from the chapter outline. Choose the best answer from the options available.

A. Theories of Economic Growth

1. Suppose agricultural output requires only two inputs, labor and land. The quantity of land available is fixed; the quantity of labor is variable. Then, as labor quantity is increased in order to increase output quantity, the law of diminishing returns will begin to operate, and:
   a. the ratio of labor to land will increase, but the ratio of land to output will fall.
   b. both the labor-land ratio and the land-output ratio will fall.
   c. both the labor-land ratio and the land-output ratio will increase.
   d. the labor-land ratio will fall, but the land-output ratio will not change.
   e. the labor-land ratio will increase, but the land-output ratio will not change.

2. In the simple labor theory of value, demand for goods plays the following role:
   a. It interacts with supply to determine price, as in any other case.
   b. It dominates over supply in the determination of price but does not influence quantities produced and consumed.
   c. It settles quantities produced and consumed but has no influence on price.
   d. It has no influence either on quantities produced and consumed or on price.
   e. It dominates over supply in determining not only the price but also the quantities produced and consumed.

3. The most important single factor accounting for increased productivity and growth in the American economy thus far appears to have been:
   a. a deepening of the capital stock.
   b. technological change.
   c. a widening of the capital stock.
   d. the use of growth-encouraging monetary and fiscal policy.
   e. the increase in skills of the labor force.

4. If the amount of capital employed increased while the amount of labor and other inputs stayed approximately fixed, and if the capital-output ratio remained constant, then:
   a. the capital-labor ratio must have fallen.
   b. the price of capital must have fallen.
   c. the law of diminishing returns must have been in operation.
   d. technological improvements must have been made.
   e. total output must have fallen.

5. A deepening of capital must, in the absence of technological change, eventually:
   a. increase the capital-output ratio.
   b. decrease the capital-output ratio.
   c. increase output by an amount that is more than proportionate to the increase in capital.
   d. increase output in proportion to the increase in capital.
   e. increase the share of capital-owners in the total of output.

6. "Deepening of capital" means:
   a. an increase in the stock of capital relative to the size of the labor force.
   b. the introduction of new capital goods which embody technological change.
   c. a change in either productivity or amount of capital which increases the share of capital-owners in total product.
   d. an increase in the productivity of capital which reduces, or at least does not increase, the total of the capital stock.
   e. none of the above.

7. If capital is considered to be the only variable input, then diminishing returns (without technological change) suggest that:
   a. the share of capital-owners in total output must increase as output is increased.
   b. the capital-output ratio must decrease as output is increased.
   c. the share of capital-owners in total output must decrease as output is increased.
   d. the capital-output ratio must increase as output is increased.
   e. the capital-output ratio must, by definition, remain constant as output is increased.

8. If a nation's capital-output ratio gradually increases over time despite capital deepening, then:
   a. the share of capital-owners in total output is increasing.
   b. the diminishing-returns stage has not yet been reached with respect to capital.
   c. the marginal physical product of capital must have reached zero.
   d. technological progress must be improving the productivity of capital.
   e. the law of diminishing returns is operating with respect to capital's productivity.

9. In economics, "capital formation" specifically refers to:
   a. the purchase of any new commodity.
   b. net investment.
   c. the borrowing of money.
   d. the sale of any new stock issue.
   e. none of these activities.

10. Which of the following have been presented as negative

side effects of too much economic growth?
a. Global warming.
b. Deforestation.
c. Species extinction.
d. All of the above.
e. Choices **a** and **b** only.

11. The neoclassical growth model developed by Robert Solow:
a. analyzes the growth of potential output.
b. assumes the economy is basically competitive.
c. expands earlier growth models by including capital growth and technological change.
d. includes all of the above.
e. includes none of the above.

12. What role does technological change have in Solow's neoclassical growth model?
a. Technological change is most important when capital deepening does not occur.
b. Technological change is not very important, only capital deepening matters.
c. Without technological change, incomes and wages end up stagnating.
d. Technological change is more important in Malthus's model.
e. Technological change has no role in the neoclassical growth model.

13. Recent models of economic growth have suggested that technological change:
a. is not as important as in previous time periods.
b. may be exogenous.
c. increases capital productivity more than labor productivity.
d. is an output of the economic system.
e. is all of the above.

B. The Patterns of Growth in the United States

14. Which of the following is *not* considered a trend in the recent economic growth of industrialized countries?
a. Average national product growth of about three percent per year.
b. Capital deepening.
c. Swings in real interest rates, especially during business cycles.
d. A decline in the share of wages and salaries in national income.
e. A decline in the capital-output ratio.

15. The **productivity slowdown** can be attributed to:
a. the depreciation of the capital stock.
b. an increase in energy prices.
c. stricter environmental regulations.
d. all of the above.
e. choices **b** and **c** only.

16. Since 1900, the stock of capital in the United States has increased:
a. eightfold, and operation of the diminishing-returns law has significantly reduced the capital-output ratio.
b. tenfold, and operation of the diminishing-returns law has significantly increased the capital-output ratio.
c. by an amount exactly proportionate to the increase in the labor force, so the diminishing-returns law has had no application.
d. threefold, and operation of the diminishing-returns law has significantly reduced the capital-output ratio.
e. eightfold, but the capital-output ratio has not increased significantly despite the diminishing-returns law.

17. Since 1900, the share of wages and salaries in national income:
a. has significantly increased.
b. has remained about constant, showing only a very slight upward trend.
c. has significantly fallen, except for a period during and immediately after World War II.
d. rose fairly steadily until about 1930 and remained constant until 1945 (excluding World War II), but has fallen perceptibly since then.
e. is not correctly described by any of the above.

18. According to the Council of Economic Advisors, how much of the increase in labor productivity in the late 1990s was due to the increased utilization of computers?
a. None.
b. About half of the increase in labor productivity was due to the computer.
c. About three quarters of the increase in labor productivity was due to the computer.
d. Nearly all of the increase in labor productivity was due to the computer.
e. None of the above. Labor productivity did not increase in the late 1990s.

19. Which of the following factors contributed to the increase in productivity in the late 1990s?
a. The productivity explosion in computer technology.
b. The widespread increase in investment in computer hardware and software.
c. Improvements in the measurement of price indexes which removed their upward bias.
d. Strong growth in the U.S. economy from 1995 through 1999.
e. All of the above.

VII. PROBLEM SOLVING

The following problems are designed to help you apply the concepts that you learned in the chapter.

A. Theories of Economic Growth

1. In very early attempts to construct economic theory (e.g., in Adam Smith's work), the discussion was often conducted as if production were exclusively a matter of labor cost. With only one input to consider, there could not be any conflict over the division of the output. Soon, however, it became evident (and this drew major emphasis in the work of Malthus) that land was likewise a productive input, one that was scarce or limited in supply. Moreover, there was no comparable limit to the size of population that might ultimately appear. "The law of diminishing returns" evolved, bringing along the need to ponder the distribution of output between the two input categories.

    a. In the Malthus approach to diminishing returns, (**land / labor / capital**) was the fixed input, and (**land / labor / capital**) was the variable one. Malthus felt that a final "equilibrium" would be reached when labor had (**increased / decreased**) sufficiently to make the wage per worker just equal to the minimum-subsistence level.

    b. This wage per worker would be labor's (**marginal / total**) product. The remainder of total product, after these wages were paid, would go to landowners.

2. The two ingredients in Malthus's diminishing-returns analysis were land and labor, with labor as the variable and increasing element. In modern growth theory, the participants have changed.

    a. The fixed input is considered to be (**land / labor / capital**), while the variable input is (**land / labor / capital**). When this variable input is increased relative to the fixed input, the condition is described by economists as capital (**widening / deepening / maintenance**).

If the stock of capital (i.e., machinery tools, and other such equipment) were to increase gradually over time, then we would expect to see at least some accompanied technological improvement, i.e., the appearance of different and more efficient capital goods. Suppose, for the sake of illustration, though, that we assume that this type of technological change is absent.

    b. An increase in capital with labor or population fixed—or more generally, an increase in the ratio of total capital to total labor—would lead to (**an increase / a decrease**) in the return to each unit of capital and (**an increase / a decrease**) in the wage paid to labor.

3. Consider the process indicated in question 2 in more detail. Designate the variable input capital as K, the fixed input labor as L, and quantity of total output as Q. Then, with no technological progress, the following results should be expected if K were increased relative to L:

    a. The capital-labor ratio K/L should (**increase / decrease**).

    b. The capital-output ratio K/Q should (**increase / decrease**). When the law of diminishing returns is operating, any increase in the variable input yields an

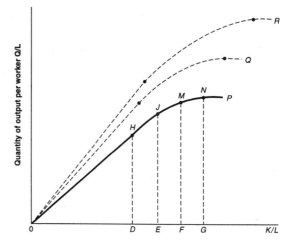

Figure 27-3

increase in output Q that is (**less than / exactly / more than**) proportionate to the increase in K.

    c. The interest or profit rate (price of K per unit) should (**increase / decrease**), and the wage rate (price of L) should (**increase / decrease**) as the K/L ratio increases.

    d. The fractional or percentage share of total output going to K owners (**must increase / might increase / must decrease**).

B. The Patterns of Growth in the United States

4. In the United States, over the past century the stock of capital has grown more or less steadily and has grown more rapidly than population or the labor force. But what about technological progress, which improves the performance of K (capital) and which was specifically ruled out in the last question? In terms of Figure 27-3 (where the variable input is now K *per worker*), technological progress lifts the output curve from $0P$ to $0Q$ and from $0Q$ to $0R$. (The first black dot on the $0Q$ and $0R$ lines marks the point at which curvature begins [the line begins to get flatter]—i.e., the point at which the influence of diminishing returns first begins to set in.)

    a. Thus even though K *is* increasing, the shift in position of the APF curve means that the marginal product of K will (**increase / decrease**). The rate of interest or profit (per unit of capital) will thus (**fall / rise**) relative to labor's wage rate.

    b. Combining the two effects (diminishing returns and technological progress), we see that the increase in the capital stock (**raises / lowers**) total output.

    c. Technological progress (**raises / lowers**) total output. The increase in the capital stock (disregarding technological progress) (**raises / lowers**) the demand for labor. Hence we would expect labor's wage or price to

(a) Output, Labor, Capital

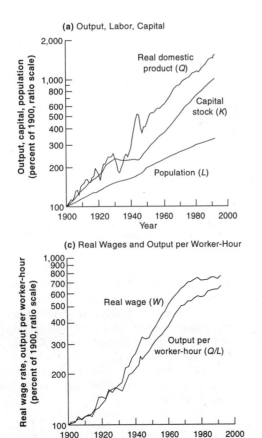

(b) Capital-Output Ratio

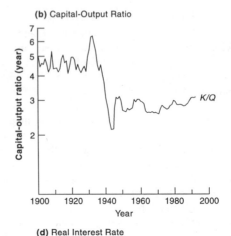

(c) Real Wages and Output per Worker-Hour

(d) Real Interest Rate

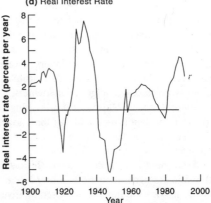

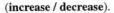

Figure 27-4

(**increase / decrease**).

d.   Moving against this trend is technological progress, which (**increases / decreases**) the interest or profit rate and tends to (**increase / decrease**) the demand for labor.

5.   The facts of economic growth in the United States are summarized below. Refer to Figure 27-6 from the text, which has been reproduced here as Figure 27-4 (on previous page), to deduce the answers.

a.   Since 1900, the labor force has (**remained roughly constant / nearly doubled / approximately tripled / increased more than sixfold**). The stock of capital has, meanwhile, (**remained roughly constant / nearly doubled / increased nearly fourfold / increased approximately eightfold / increased by more than elevenfold**). That is to say, the capital stock, in proportion to the labor force, has (**increased / decreased**) by a factor of approximately (**1 / 2 / 3 / 6**). There (**has / has not**) been a (**small / significant**) deepening of capital.

b.   Disregarding technological change, if both capital and labor had increased eightfold, then we would have expected to see output increase by a factor of 8. With

labor only tripled, though, we would expect to see output increase by (**more / less**) than 8 times its value in 1900.

c.   In fact, however, output has increased by a factor of approximately (**3 / 8 / 11**). This means that the ratio of the capital stock to annual output has (**increased / remained about constant / decreased slightly**). Things (**have / have not**) worked out as the simple law of diminishing returns would indicate, the reason evidently being (**that the law has been incorrectly set out / the effects of technological change / the higher real wage paid to labor**).

d.   Real wages (**have risen / have fallen / show no clear trend either up or down**). The interest or profit rate—the "price of capital"—(**has risen / has fallen / shows no clear trend either up or down**).

e.   Output per worker-hour, or Q/L, has (**risen / remained constant / fallen**). The increase in the wage rate (**has significantly exceeded / has been approximately equal to / has fallen behind**) the (**increase / decrease**) in output per worker-hour.

6. Seven basic trends in major economic variables have been typical of growth in the United States as well as in most developed countries. Indicate the direction of each in the spaces provided below:
    a. The capital-labor ratio has _____.
    b. The real wage has _____.
    c. The share paid to labor has _____.
    d. The real rate of interest has _____.
    e. After _____ from 1920 through 1945, the capital-output ratio has _____ since 1950.
    f. The savings-output ratio has _____.
    g. Output has _____.

7. a. Trend **f**, combined with a small level of net foreign investment, implies that the investment-output ratio has (**risen / remained steady / fallen**).
    b. Trends **a** and **b** are consistent with the neoclassical model of growth (**only when technological change is introduced / even without technological change**).
    c. Trends **d** and **e** (**do / do not**) depend on technological change because no progress would always combine with a deepening capital stock to predict (**higher / lower**) real interest rates and (**higher / lower**) capital-output ratios.

8. Complete Table 27-1 on the basis of the growth-accounting procedures presented in the text.

TABLE 27-1

	Case I	Case II	Case III
Rate of growth of labor (%)	1	0	1
Rate of growth of capital (%)	4	4	5
Rate of technological change (%)	2	2	2
Rate of growth of output (%)	__	__	__
Rate of growth of output per worker (%)	__	__	__

VIII. DISCUSSION QUESTIONS

Answer the following questions, making sure that you can explain the work you did to arrive at the answers.
1. Briefly describe Smith's and Malthus's approaches to economic growth.
2. How does Solow's neoclassical growth model differ from the classical approach to growth? How is it similar?
3. According to Table 27-1 in the text, Turkey and India both experienced greater annual growths of output per person than the United States during the period from 1973 to 1993. Nevertheless, citizens in the United States are much wealthier than people in either of these other two countries. How do you reconcile these two disparate facts?
4. Briefly explain the role of technology in the neoclassical growth model.

IX. ANSWERS TO STUDY GUIDE QUESTIONS

III. Review of Key Concepts
7   Economic growth
12   Social overhead capital
10   Technological change
13   Neoclassical growth model
8   Capital-labor ratio
1   Capital deepening
14   Aggregate production function
11   Long-run steady state
5   Labor-saving invention
3   Capital-saving invention
2   Neutral invention
9   Growth accounting
6   Total factor productivity
4   Potential GDP

VI. Multiple Choice Questions
1. A 2. C 3. B 4. D 5. A 6. A
7. D 8. E 9. B 10. D 11. D 12. C
13. D 14. D 15. E 16. E 17. B 18. B
19. E

VII. Problem Solving
1. a. land, labor, increased
   b. marginal
2. a. labor, capital, deepening
   b. a decrease, an increase
3. a. increase
   b. increase, less than
   c. decrease, increase
   d. must decrease
4. a. increase, rise
   b. raises
   c. raises, raises, increase
   d. increases, decrease
5. a. approximately tripled, increased approximately eightfold, increased, 3, has, significant
   b. less
   c. 11, decreased slightly, have not, the effects of technological change
   d. have risen, shows no clear trend either up or down
   e. risen, has been approximately equal to, increase
6. a. risen
   b. risen
   c. risen very slightly
   d. been trendless
   e. falling, remained constant
   f. been stable
   g. increased (at about 3 to 4 percent per year)

7. a. remained steady
    b. even without technological change
    c. do, lower, higher

8.

TABLE 27-1

	Case I	Case II	Case III
Rate of growth of output (%)	3.75	3.00	4.00
Rate of growth of output per worker (So)	2.75	3.00	3.00

VIII. Discussion Questions

1. Both Smith and Malthus stressed the importance of land in economic growth. Smith viewed land as an abundantly free resource; therefore, the value of all production belonged to, and would be returned to, labor. Malthus pointed out that land was fixed; therefore, the returns to labor would eventually have to decrease. As the population grew, and more and more labor was applied to the fixed supply of land, the marginal product of labor would fall and wages would be pushed to a subsistence level.

2. Solow's model is also based on two inputs: one variable and one fixed. In Solow's model, however, labor is the fixed input and capital is the variable. Indeed, capital has grown much more rapidly than labor in the twentieth century. Solow resolves Malthus's dilemma by recognizing the role of capital and technology in economic growth.

3. This question tempts the reader to confuse stocks and flows. The wealth of a nation and its citizens is a stock variable—it is measured at a particular point in time. Annual economic growth is a flow variable—it measures how a nation's output (or wealth) is changing. India and Turkey may have higher rates of growth, but their respective stocks of wealth are still far below that of the United States.

4. Technology is an important component of the neoclassical growth model. Technological change means that more output can be produced with a given amount of capital and labor. Technological change counterbalances the law of diminishing marginal returns (to capital) and helps keep the real wage of labor from falling.

CHAPTER 28

The Challenge of Economic Development

I. CHAPTER OVERVIEW

"Of the 5 billion people on this planet, perhaps 1 billion live in absolute poverty—barely able to survive from day to day." So begins Chapter 28 in your text. There exists, across the globe, a disparity in standards of living that boggles the mind; and it is this observation that raises a litany of questions which could turn out to be *the* critical questions for survival through the twenty-first century. What, first of all, could possibly be the source of this disparity? Second, what can be done by the developing countries to correct it? And finally, what does the future hold for further changes in economic development? Without some attempt to answer these questions, the growing gap between the wealthy and the poor nations of the world could foster economic, political, and military conflict that could wreak havoc across the planet.

In the first part of this chapter, Samuelson and Nordhaus document the characteristics of a developing nation. They discuss various issues in economic development and strategies for its eradication. In the second part of the chapter, alternative models of economic development are discussed. Particular attention is given to the economies of Asia and the former Soviet Union.

Only if we understand the sources of inequity between nations can we begin to work to correct it, and only if we sort out false strategies from productive strategies will progress be made. The major objective of the chapter is, therefore, an understanding of the dimension of the economic development problem.

II. LEARNING OBJECTIVES

After you have read Chapter 28 in your text and completed the exercises in this *Study Guide* chapter, you should be able to:
1. Discuss the aspects of life in developing countries.
2. Identify the four "wheels of development" and explain the problems faced by less developed countries in getting any one of them "rolling uphill."
3. Describe the vicious cycle of underdevelopment, and identify the means by which it might be broken.
4. Explain the backwardness hypothesis.
5. Discuss the pros and cons of each of the following issues in economic development: (a) industrialization vs. agriculture, (b) inward vs. outward orientation, and (c) state vs. market control.
6. Explain the approach used in the **newly industrialized** countries of Southeast Asia.
7. Discuss the various aspects of socialism.
8. Understand the historical underpinnings of Marx's radical theory and his contribution to economic thought.
9. Understand the economic history of the Soviet Union as it evolved from a czarist regime, to communism, to a newborn market economy.

III. REVIEW OF KEY CONCEPTS

Match the following terms from column A with their definitions in column B.

A	B
__ Developing country	1. Controlled prices which are artificially held below market clearing levels and which result in shortages.
__ Newly industrialized country (NIC)	2. Encompasses a wide variety of economic approaches ranging from democratic welfare states with nationalized industries to deregulation and privatization of the market.
__ Demographic transition	3. Strategy for development in which countries attempt to be self-sufficient and replace imports with domestic production.
__ Brain drain	4. Advocates a complete and quick transition from a command to a market-based system.
__ Infrastructure	5. An industry that is owned and operated by the state.
__ Vicious cycle of poverty	6. The less developed a country is, relative to other nations, the more advantages it has to develop.
__ Backwardness hypothesis	7. A country with low real per capita income relative to industrialized nations; also known as an LDC (less developed country).

355

___ Import
substitution

___ Outward
orientation

___ Free-market
absolutism

___ Communism

___ The Asian
managed-market
approach

___ Socialism

___ Command
economy

___ Nationalized
industry

___ Forced-draft
industrialization

___ Repressed
inflation

___ Soft budget
constraints

___ Step-by-step
reform

___ Shock-therapy
approach

___ Emerging
markets

8. Advocates a gradual and cautious transition to a market economy.

9. The questions of *how, what,* and *for whom* are determined by the government bureaucracy.

10. The transformation from high birth and death rates and a growing population to low birth and death rates and a stable population.

11. This establishes state-planned priorities for industrial development.

12. This country was a "developing country," but it has recently experienced significant and successful growth.

13. Social overhead capital.

14. Rapidly growing economies in low and middle income countries.

15. In a controlled economy, operating losses may be covered by state subsidies and therefore not lead to bankruptcy.

16. Specific type of totalitarian, collectivized economic system withgovernment ownership of land and capital.

17. Laissez-faire economy with minimal government involvement.

18. Economic system with both strong government oversight and powerful market forces.

19. Reinforcing obstacles of low income, low saving, low capital growth, and low productivity that keep a nation poor.

20. Strategy for development in which countries pay for imports by improving efficiency and competitiveness, by developing foreign markets, and by giving incentives for exports.

21. Intelligent citizens of LDCs are attracted to industrialized countries for education and training. When they do not return home after completing their education, this occurs.

IV. SUMMARY AND CHAPTER OUTLINE

This section summarizes the key concepts from the chapter.

A. Economic Growth in Poor Countries

1. Human resources, natural resources, capital formation, and technological advance are the four driving forces of development. Less developed countries typically have difficulty in exploiting all four.

2. Investments in the labor force (i.e., human capital) are critical to economic development. While the other factors of production can be imported if need be, labor is homegrown. Education, training, health, and nutrition are vital to the development of this resource and the economy.

The United Nations has developed a Human Development Index (HDI) which combines four different demographic, social, and economic statistics: life expectancy at birth, school enrollment, adult literacy, and real GDP per capita. The relationship between HDI and per capita output is strong and positive for most countries.

3. The vicious cycle of underdevelopment runs from low saving and investment to low capital accumulation, low productivity, and low incomes, and back again. It applies to many situations, but its general applicability varies from country to country depending upon the country's population, technology, resources, and capital base.

4. The **backwardness hypothesis** suggests that today's developing economies may have an advantage over countries in the 19th century simply because they can learn from and use technologies and supplies from more advanced economies. The key here is that some countries are backward, *relative* to others. As low-income countries learn and grow, economic *convergence* is expected to occur.

5. Strategies for promoting economic development abound. Some emphasize export goods; some emphasize import-competing goods; still others emphasize borrowing new technologies. Each has merit somewhere in the world, but none is universally applicable, especially in a world in which development must proceed with a cautious eye cast at its environmental consequences.

B. Alternative Models for Development

1. All societies are faced with the basic economic problem of scarce resources and unlimited wants. All societies need to determine *how* to produce goods and services, *what* to produce, and how to distribute them (i.e., *for whom*). The spectrum of alternative economic systems includes **market economies** at one end and **command economies** at the other. A market economy is based on voluntary decisions, and prices are determined by the interaction between buyers and sellers in the marketplace. In a command economy, the questions of *what*, *how*, and *for whom* are made by a government bureaucracy.

2. Some of the economies of eastern Asia (Japan, South Korea, Singapore, Hong Kong, Thailand) have experienced impressive rates of economic growth during the last few decades. There are several common threads to their success:

    a. All are market-oriented economies, albeit with differing levels of government involvement.

    b. All have above-average rates of investment.

    c. In each economy, macroeconomic policy has attempted to keep inflation rates low and investment rates high.

    d. Each economy is **outward-oriented**. These countries have encouraged exports and attempted to replicate the best technological advances of the high-income countries.

    e. Rather than relying entirely on the market, governments in some of these economies have organized non-market contests to allocate resources. After identifying strategic areas for development, the government, in these countries, sets up an internal contest among domestic firms to stimulate competition and promote efficiency.

3. China has enjoyed rapid economic growth during the past decade. The Chinese government has gradually decentralized some areas of economic decision making and established several special economic zones in which private and foreign-owned firms are permitted. There has, however, been limited political reform in China during this time period.

4. Karl Marx (1818-1883) said that the value of all commodities was determined by the amount of labor effort required to produce them. The value of commodities produced mainly by capital equipment was derived from the labor required to produce the capital. The profits received by the owners of the companies were viewed by Marx as "unearned income" since there was no productive labor embodied in their efforts. As the industrial revolution progressed and production became more capital intensive, Marx envisioned that the marginal product and rate of return on capital would fall and the unemployment rate would rise. As the masses of unemployed grew, discontent would spread and eventually the workers would rise up and overthrow the owners. One possible explanation as to why all of this did not occur can be found in the previous chapter. Technological change helped maintain the productivity of capital, increased the demand for labor, and contributed to economic growth!

5. Socialism, which was developed by Marx and others, lies between market and central-planned systems. Socialism encompasses a wide variety of alternative economic approaches ranging from democratic welfare states with nationalized industries to deregulation and privatization of the market. Nevertheless, there are some common threads running through most socialist economies:

    a. Government ownership of productive resources.

    b. Coordinated planning rather than "chaotic" market allocations.

    c. Redistribution of income.

    d. Control via peaceful, gradual, democratic evolution.

6. Central planning worked, more or less, in the Soviet Union for 70 years, but then the economy, and the union, fell apart. While researchers are still studying the collapse, it is clear that the Soviet planners paid much too little attention to their consumers. Emphasis was placed instead on the military, space exploration, and certain key industries. It also proved impossible to determine optimal production methods, product quality, and the distribution of goods and services by relying exclusively on centralized top-to-bottom decision making.

7. Most of the nations of the former Soviet Union are finding that the transition to market-based economies is both slow and painful. Economic hardships abound, and the obstacles are numerous. While each country is unique, they share some common economic problems.

    a. All resources and means of production must be released by the government and turned over to private ownership. Corporations must be developed, stock markets *created,* and banking and credit institutions modernized and greatly expanded.

    b. Prices must be determined by the forces of supply and demand in the marketplace. Government controls and subsidies must be removed.

    c. Individuals need to learn how to live in a market economy based on individual choice.

V. HELPFUL HINTS

1. The citizens of industrialized countries may be tempted to think of their economically poorer neighbors as slow or backward. This would be a grave mistake. Remember, GDP is not necessarily an accurate indicator of happiness or well-being. While not rich by industrialized standards, these nations have a wealth of culture, tradition, and history. Differences in lifestyle and/or values do not necessarily reflect impoverishment.

2. Duplication of Western technology in developing countries may or may not be successful. Production techniques need to be changed to fit the available supply of resources. Countries that are predominantly agricultural may be better served by trying to improve productivity in that area rather than industrializing the economy.

3. As we will see when we study international trade, even the richest of nations can benefit by trading with less developed partners.

VI. MULTIPLE CHOICE QUESTIONS

These questions are organized by topic from the chapter outline. Choose the best answer from the options available.

A. Economic Growth in Poor Countries

1. One area of economic development in which the country's government must take the initiative and also participate relates to:
   a. maintaining balanced growth.
   b. promoting heavy industry.
   c. transferring resources needed in the shift from agricultural predominance to industrial predominance.
   d. providing social overhead capital.
   e. none of the above, because there are no areas in which such government involvement is always needed.

2. The main reason population growth has spurted ahead so rapidly in many less developed countries in recent years is that:
   a. birth rates have increased sharply with improvements in nutrition.
   b. great strides have been made in keeping older people alive an extra 5 or 10 years.
   c. infant mortality and mortality due to epidemics have been drastically lowered.
   d. large-scale immigration has occurred into many countries since World War II.
   e. birth rates have risen markedly as the natural result of widespread reductions in the customary age of marriage.

3. Four of the following five statements identify a problem of economic development. Which one does *not*?
   a. Developing economies often have reasonable prospects of looking to "increasing returns to scale" as they expand their total output.
   b. Ordinarily, individual firms cannot undertake investment in social overhead capital, no matter how important such projects may be.
   c. Entrepreneurship and innovation are vital for the success of any developing economy.
   d. The principle of protecting import-competing industries is not necessarily a wise one for a developing nation to follow.
   e. In a probable majority of the less developed nations, excess saving is a significant problem.

4. As a country develops economically and builds its own industry, one of the following usually does *not* occur. Which one?
   a. It imports less and less from other developed and industrialized countries.
   b. Its total exports tend to rise.
   c. It imports more and more from other industrialized, highly developed countries.
   d. It imports more from less developed countries.
   e. Its total imports tend to rise.

5. "Social overhead capital" is:
   a. the money investment required before any return is obtainable from a particular natural resource.

   b. typically financed by foreign countries.
   c. investment in those projects considered to have the highest net productivity.
   d. projects which must be financed by the nation itself, as distinct from those financed by private corporations.
   e. any capital investment whose amount does not vary as the quantity of national output is increased.

6. An example of "social overhead capital" would be:
   a. a rural electrification project.
   b. state-financed hospitals and schools.
   c. the development of a domestic transportation system.
   d. all of the above.
   e. **a** and **c** above, but not **b**.

7. An absolute precondition for growth is the:
   a. development of some excess of income over consumption.
   b. creation of a surplus labor force for employment in manufacturing.
   c. discovery and exploitation of some internal economies.
   d. cultural acceptance of free enterprise principles of economic behavior.
   e. development of manufacturing to the point where it can begin to supplant agriculture.

8. Four of the following five statements identify a problem of economic development. Which one does *not*?
   a. In some less developed countries, considerable investment takes place but goes into items that are of low priority or even are undesirable from the standpoint of national economic development.
   b. The development of adequate social overhead capital is usually essential if there is to be much economic development.
   c. Historically, political revolutions have often taken place after some economic progress has been achieved.
   d. Most of the less developed countries are known to have substantial unexploited natural resources, if only the capital needed to bring them into effective use were available.
   e. In poor countries, especially rural ones, often a large part of the labor pool does almost nothing because there is nothing for it to do.

9. Less developed countries have lower per capita incomes than developed countries. Over the past several decades, that gap has been:
   a. diminishing between the "free enterprise" less developed countries but widening with respect to the socialist-oriented ones.
   b. almost impossible to measure because of differences in cultures, tastes, and climates.
   c. perceptibly diminishing, evidently as the result of foreign-aid programs.
   d. diminishing with respect to those countries which

have concentrated their investment upon social overhead capital.

e.   essentially stable, and in some areas may even be widening.

10. The human development index:

a.   combines economic and social indicators in an assessment of human conditions.

b.   has a strong negative correlation with per capita output.

c.   has been criticized by economists.

d.   is all of the above.

e.   is none of the above.

B. Alternative Models for Development

11. In "free-market absolutism:"

a.   the government has complete or absolute control.

b.   all goods and services are free.

c.   consumers have free choice in the marketplace, but jobs are assigned by the state.

d.   government has a very limited role in the economy.

e.   none of the above.

12. The "Asian managed-market approach:"

a.   has been used successfully in mainland China.

b.   coexists with communism in several nations.

c.   developed from socialism.

d.   all the above.

e.   none of the above.

13. In socialist economies:

a.   industries may be nationalized.

b.   tax rates tend to be higher and more progressive.

c.   the free market may be critically important to the nation's economic health.

d.   all the above.

e.   **a** and **b** only, not **c**.

14. The most impressive economic growth during the last 50 years has occurred in:

a.   Western Europe.

b.   North America.

c.   East Asia.

d.   Latin America.

e.   South America.

15. Investment is critical for economic growth because it:

a.   allows firms to focus less on current production and more on the development of new technology and the acquisition of capital.

b.   attracts foreign financial capital.

c.   encourages consumer spending on new products.

d.   raises tax revenues which are used to finance expenditures on social overhead capital.

e.   increases competition among firms.

16. The Chinese government has:

a.   successfully organized nonmarket contests between firms to encourage efficiency and growth.

b.   instituted political reforms since the Tiananmen Square incident in 1989.

c.   allowed foreign firms to operate alongside state-owned firms.

d.   a large trade deficit with the United States.

e.   restricted the operation of "special economic zones."

17. Marx's labor theory of value suggests that:

a.   the value of all goods and services is derived from the labor effort that went into making them.

b.   the profits of factory owners really belong to the workers.

c.   there is labor value even in capital equipment.

d.   all the above.

e.   **a** and **b** only, not **c**.

18. The "soft budget constraints" in the Soviet-style brand of communism can best be described as:

a.   an example of repressed inflation.

b.   subsidies from the government to cover operating losses of firms.

c.   cost restrictions on nontangible commodities such as services.

d.   budget restrictions on all sectors of the economy, except the military.

e.   none of the above.

19. Which statement below about the former Soviet Union is most accurate?

a.   While reform has been gradual, most of the citizens of Russia are economically better off now than they were under communism.

b.   Step-by-step reform has worked much better in the (former) satellite countries than has the shock-therapy approach.

c.   Economic reform in Russia has been more difficult than in the (former) satellite countries.

d.   All these statements are accurate.

e.   None of these statements is accurate.

20. Recent declines in socialist approaches to economic development have been attributed to:

a.   the overall decline in communism.

b.   stagnation in many European economies where socialism was popular.

c.   the successes of market-dominated economies.

d.   all of the above.

e.   choices **b** and **c** only.

21. The recessions that occurred in some of the countries in Southeast Asia during the 1990s were due to:

a.   a slowdown in economic growth.

b.   a series of banking crises.

c.   IMF requirements that countries pursue contractionary monetary and fiscal policies before providing them with loans.

d.   all of the above.

TABLE 28-1 Important Indicators for Different Groups of Countries

Country Group	Population, 1998 (million)	Gross Domestic Product at PPP			Adult Illiteracy, 1998(%)	Life Expectancy at Birth (years)
		Total, 1998 ($,billion)	Per Capita GNP			
			Level, 1998 ($)	Growth (GDP), 1990-1998 (% per year)		
Low-income economies:	3,515	7,475.1	2,130	7.3	32	63
Excl. China and India	1,296	1,821.3	1,400	3.6	39	56
Lower-middle-income economies	908	3,709.4	4,080	-1.3	15	68
(e.g., Peru, Philippines, Thailand)						
Upper-middle-income economies	588	4,606.3	7,830	3.9	11	68
(e.g., Brazil, Malaysia, Mexico)						
High-income economies	885	20,766.0	23,440	2.1	<5	78
(e.g., United States, Japan, France)						

Countries are grouped by the World Bank into four major categories depending upon their per capita incomes. In each, a number of important indicators of economic development are shown. Note that low-income countries tend to have highly illiteracy and low life expectancy.

[Source: World Bank, *World Development Report..*]

e.   choices **a** and **b** only.

22. The decline in Russia's GDP since 1990 can be attributed to:

a.   the slow pace of economic reform

b.   little prior experience with a market-based system.

c.   internal corruption.

d.   high rates of inflation.

e.   all of the above.

VII. PROBLEM SOLVING

The following problems are designed to help you apply the concepts that you learned in the chapter.

A. Economic Growth in Poor Countries

1.   The world's less developed countries are characterized by per capita income levels that are well below the worldwide average. Associated with low incomes are, moreover, human problems like poor health, widespread illiteracy, poor housing, poor diets, and demoralizing underemployment. This question asks you to record quantitative measures of these problems. Table 28-1 from your text, and reproduced here also as Table 28-1, analyzes country groups according to key indicators.

The data show that, compared with the high-income market economies, low-income countries display the following characteristics:

a.   Per capita levels of GDP that are (**about 50 percent lower / about 90 percent lower / over 90 percent lower**).

b.   Per capita GDP growth rates that are (**lower / higher / higher in China and India, but otherwise lower**).

c.   Adult illiteracy rates that are (**25 percent higher / nearly 50 percent higher / over 75 percent higher**).

d.   Life expectancies that are approximately (**20 per-cent lower / 33 percent lower / 50 percent lower**).

e.   Total population that is (**twice as great / between 3 and 4 times as great / 5 times as great**) as in high-income economies. (Note that more people live in low-income countries than in the other three groups *combined*.)

2.   Economists have identified four economic fundamentals which drive economic development: population, natural resources, capital formation, and technology.

a.   Focusing for a moment on *natural resources,* which of the following statements or questions accurately describe a resources-related issue? (Circle neither, one, or both.)

(1) Many less developed countries appear to be resource-poor. How then are they to develop?

(2) Land reform is necessary for development in many countries, since individual holdings are too small to be used to their best advantage.

b.   Turning now to *capital formation,* circle the numbers of all the statements that accurately record a development issue:

(1) Less developed nations find it very difficult to save (to refrain from consumption) in order to free resources for investment activity.

(2) The social customs in some less developed countries encourage rich people to hoard their saving or use them in nonproductive ways; they are not used to finance investment projects that would raise the national product.

3) The desire for development and the example of the developed nations have noticeably increased the amount of saving out of income in many less developed countries.

(4) In many poor countries, investment expenditure tends to go heavily into housing, an investment form which does not have the highest priority in devel-

opment.

(5) The amount of private lending for financing investment activity by citizens in developed areas is greater than it was in the nineteenth century, both absolutely and relatively; in less developed countries, it is not.

c. Finally, repeat the process one more time for the role of *technology*:

(1) Less developed countries have the advantage that imitation of techniques already worked out is easier than development of new and sometimes sophisticated techniques.

(2) Efforts by developed countries to export advanced "technological know-how" are frequently unsuccessful.

(3) Some advanced technologies are "capital-saving," and these are likely to be particularly well suited to adoption in less developed countries.

3. Figure 28-1 illustrates the vicious cycle of underdevelopment. Identify the boxes of the cycle in the spaces provided. Box C is already identified for the purpose of providing perspective.

A: _____

B: _____

C: Low productivity_____

D: _____

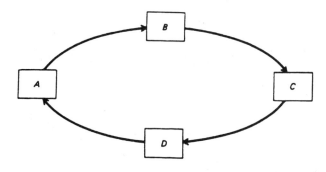

Figure 28-1

4. a. Higher saving will be useless and productive investment will not take place in any country unless it has a class of vigorous, creative ____.

b. Sometimes it is said that the recurring problem with which a developed country must cope during recession is that of (**too much / too little**) saving and hence (**too much / too little**) demand for consumption.

c. By contrast, the problem of the less developed country is that of (**too much / too little**) saving and hence (**too much / too little**) demand for consumption.

5. Strategies for development must confront and answer at least three general questions if they are to be successful.

First, is it more worthwhile to concentrate on industry or agriculture in initiating growth?

a. Investment in industry might provide a few high-paying jobs, but investment in agriculture might support industrialization by (**increasing the productivity of city workers / increasing the productivity of the farms and thereby releasing labor for industrial jobs / creating large agricultural surpluses that can replace imports**).

Second, it is important to decide whether to promote exports to generate growth supported by the worldwide marketplace or to protect import-competing industries to generate growth in domestic markets.

b. Care should be taken in considering the second alternative because protection can (**increase / decrease**) domestic prices, (**increase / decrease**) real incomes, and (**stimulate / retard**) investment at home and from abroad.

Third, many developing countries find themselves overspecialized and vulnerable to the whims of the world market for the few goods in which they have a comparative advantage.

c. The key to avoiding this difficulty is (**specialization / diversification**).

6. A less developed country is undertaking a large-scale development program and asks you to supply information on the points listed in parts **a** through **c**. What will you advise? (In each part, circle the number of the statement which you think furnishes the most likely scenario.)

a. Capital-formation policy:

(1) In view of the post-World War II experience, primary reliance can be placed on borrowing and aid from abroad.

(2) The primary problem will be achieving a better allocation of existing saving rather than increasing total saving.

(3) Historical experience suggests that the percentage of national product put into personal saving and into capital formation will have to be increased.

(4) Borrowing technology" will enable development at existing levels of saving.

b. Investment allocation:

(1) The government should make sure that it is undertaking adequate investment in social overhead capital.

(2) Private entrepreneurs can be relied upon to properly allocate available saving.

(3) Although inflation tends ultimately to discourage saving, it also tends to better allocate available saving.

(4) Modern technology makes heavy use of capital in production and hence should be avoided.

c.   Change in foreign trade:

(1) Imports are likely to fall as domestic manufactures replace foreign manufactures.

(2) Imports are likely to rise because of the need for foreign capital goods and possibly for food and fuel.

(3) Exports of primary products should be pushed, since this is where comparative advantage must lie.

(4) Exports should fall as the demand of developed countries for raw materials continues to decline.

B. Alternative Models for Development

7. Throughout Chapter 28 Samuelson and Nordhaus discuss the theories of many different writers and economic philosophers. Some of these theories of economic development are very broad and general, while others relate to specific aspects of growth. Match each of the individuals in column A with "their" theory, as briefly described in column B.

A	B
__ Francis Hackett	1. Advocated the shock-therapy approach with a more rapid move from a command to a market-based economy.
__ Thomas Malthus	2. Said that the relative backwardness of a country may actually aid in its development.
__ Max Weber	3. Led a group of economists who opted for more rapid economic changes rather than gradual reform in their country.
__ Mancur Olson	4. Instituted programs of collectivized agriculture and forced draft industrialization.
__ Alexander Gerschenkron	5. Argued that the value of all commodities is derived from the efforts of labor embodied in them. Also saw capitalism as inevitably leading to socialism.
__ Karl Marx	6. Argued that a nation's population growth would exceed its ability to produce more and more food.
__ Josef Stalin	7. Argued that a nation begins to decline when its decision making structure becomes inflexible and obstacles arise against further social and economic change.
__ Jerry Sachs	8. Believed in materialism and felt that the benefits of it should all be available for everyone.
__ Yegor Gaidar	9. Emphasized the "Protestant ethic" as a driving force behind capitalism.

8. It is clear that a wide range of economic development exists across the countries of the world. Furthermore, different approaches and strategies of economic development have been tried in various countries. Match each country in column A with the descriptions in column B.

A	B
__ South Korea	1. In 1990, Sachs persuaded this country's government to adopt a shock therapy approach to economic reform.
__ India	2. In the 1980s this country needed all of its export earnings just to pay the *interest* on its foreign debt.
__ Italy	3. Newly industrialized country with an outward orientation.
__ Bolivia	4. Has tried both step-by-step and shock-therapy approaches to economic reform. This country continues to face serious economic hardships.
__ China	5. Industrialized country.
__ Poland	6. Low-income country.
__ Russia	7. Has established "special economic zones" and allowed alternative forms of property ownership.

VIII. DISCUSSION QUESTIONS

Answer the following questions, making sure that you can explain the work you did to arrive at the answers.

1.   a.   Why is saving so important for economic growth?
     b.   Why is it so difficult, especially for developing countries, to save?

2.   Why is it both important and difficult for LDCs to acquire capital?

3.   a.   What is infrastructure?
     b.   Why is infrastructure necessary for economic development?
     c.   Why is it typically necessary for the government to finance infrastructure projects?

4.   Briefly describe some of the common factors contributing to the rapid economic development of the Asian dragons."

5.   List and briefly describe three factors that contributed to the economic collapse of the Soviet Union.

6.   List and briefly describe three problems that Russia must grapple with as it attempts to transform its economy from one that is command- to one that is market-based.

7.   Why did Marx view the profits received by capitalists as "unearned income?"

IX. ANSWERS TO STUDY GUIDE QUESTIONS

III. Review of Key Concepts

7	Developing country
12	Newly industrialized country (NIC)
10	Demographic transition
21	Brain drain
13	Infrastructure
19	Vicious cycle of poverty
6	Backwardness hypothesis
3	Import substitution
20	Outward orientation
17	Free-market absolutism
16	Communism
18	The Asian managed-market approach
2	Socialism
9	Command economy
5	Nationalized industry
11	Forced-draft industrialization
1	Repressed inflation
15	Soft budget constraints
8	Step-by-step reform
4	Shock-therapy approach
14	Emerging markets

VI. Multiple Choice Questions

1. D 2. C 3. E 4. A 5. D 6. D
7. A 8. E 9. E 10. A 11. D 12. E
13. D 14. C 15. A 16. C 17. D 18. B
19. C 20. D 21. D 22. E

VII. Problem Solving

1. a. over 90 percent lower
    b. higher in China and India, but otherwise lower
    c. over 75 percent higher
    d. 20 percent lower
    e. between 3 and 4 times as great
2. a. (1), (2)
    b. (1), (2), (4)
    c. (1), (2), (3)
3. a. Low saving and investment
    b. Low pace of capital accumulation
    c. Low productivity
    d. Low average incomes
4. a. entrepreneurs
    b. too much, too little
    c. too little, too much
5. a. increasing the productivity of the farms and thereby releasing labor for industrial jobs
    b. increase, decrease, retard
    c. diversification
6. a. (3)

b. (1)
c. (2)
7. 8 Francis Hackett
    6 Thomas Malthus
    9 Max Weber
    7 Mancur Olson
    2 Alexander Gerschenkron
    5 Karl Marx
    4 Josef Stalin
    1 Jeffrey Sachs
    3 Yegor Gaidar
8. 3 South Korea
    6 India
    5 Italy
    2 Bolivia
    7 China
    1 Poland
    4 Russia

VIII. Discussion Questions

1. a. Saving is important for economic growth for (at least) two reasons. First, it sends a signal to producers that consumers will want more goods and services in the future and less now. So producers need to postpone some current production and retool for the future. Second, saving provides the financial resources, via the credit market, that firms need to borrow to finance their investment projects. Other things held constant, the more households save, the greater the availability of funds in the credit market and the lower the interest rates will be.

    b. Developing countries have great difficulty saving because such a large proportion of their resources, time, and effort must be devoted to providing the basic necessities of food, clothing, and shelter for their citizens.

2. The acquisition of capital and investment are needed to improve the productive base in LDCs and raise productivity. LDCs, however, have not always proved to be good credit risks. Some LDCs have defaulted on loan payments, and lending institutions and nations have lost money on their loans.

3. a. Infrastructure, or social overhead capital, refers to the economic environment of a country and its ability to support and sustain economic growth. Infrastructure includes a nation's transportation system, communication industries, utilities, schools and hospitals.

    b. Once we see what infrastructure includes, its relationship to economic development is obvious.

    c. Many of the benefits of improved infrastructure accrue to the nation as a whole and not solely to private individuals. We all benefit from better highways, clean water, and telephone service, and it would be very difficult (not to mention impractical) to provide these commodities for just a few people and not everyone. The private market often has a difficult time providing these public types of goods, so the government taxes its citizens and provides these products for all.

4. First, the "Asian dragons" have had very high rates of investment. This has helped develop infrastructure and modernize production. Second, these nations have used their macroeconomic policies to keep inflation rates low and investment rates high. These governments have also spent a great deal on education and the development of human capital. Third, the "Asian dragons" have had an outward orientation to promote exports and adjust to external changes in technology. Finally, in some countries the government has sponsored competitions among firms, in certain industries, to encourage efficiency.

5. First, in the Soviet-style command economy it was decided to allocate resources to the military and investment. Consumers always received what was left over, and there was never enough. Second, it proved too difficult to centrally control such a huge and complex economy. Managers were not given proper incentives to produce quality output.

Finally, the political and economic repression that was necessary to have central control proved too unbearable for the citizens to take.

6. Russia faces many problems. First, prices need to be determined by the forces of supply and demand. Market-based economies change prices all the time and markets adjust, sometimes with hardly a notice. In Russia, prices have always been set by someone else. Grappling for *market-clearing* and *profit-maximizing* prices is a new challenge. Second, entrepreneurs must now realize that inefficiency can no longer be supported by the government. Profits are the reward for taking risk. Finally, the means of production have to be turned over to private hands. Stock markets need to be developed and credit markets created to finance business expansion. This is a huge adjustment that has to be made.

7. In Marx's model the only productive contributors to the production process are the workers. Even the machinery and capital equipment used to produce goods and services were first made by labor. Since labor contributes all the effort and value, they should receive all the rewards.

CHAPTER 29

Exchange Rates and the International Financial System

I. CHAPTER OVERVIEW

Chapter 29 begins a two-chapter discussion of the fundamentals of international economics—the issues surrounding the conduct of international trade and finance. The first chapter introduces the real factors involved in trade and describes how differences in resource endowments, tastes, and technology can generate the potential for all parties to receive substantial welfare benefits from trade. In this chapter, Samuelson and Nordhaus discuss trends in foreign trade and explain the role of the **foreign exchange market.** Samuelson and Nordhaus also discuss the details of the monetary mechanisms that have been developed to support international trade; the authors also point out some of the complexities of managing the global economy.

In Chapter 30 Samuelson and Nordhaus incorporate the international sector into our macroeconomic model of the economy. They also revisit the issue of fixed exchange rates and discuss the European Union in greater detail. The details of international economics *are* complex, and an introductory course can only scratch the surface of these issues. Nevertheless, with a little bit of work the fundamental welfare implications of international trade are easily understood.

II. LEARNING OBJECTIVES

After you have read Chapter 29 in your text and completed the exercises in this *Study Guide* chapter, you should be able to:

1. Discuss some of the recent trends in foreign trade and understand the economic factors that lie behind international trade patterns.
2. Define what is meant by a **foreign exchange rate,** and describe the supply-and-demand framework through which exchange rates are determined.
3. Differentiate between the terms **depreciation** and **devaluation** and between **appreciation** and **revaluation.**
4. Explain the **purchasing-power-parity theory of exchange rates.**
5. Outline the basic accounting procedure that is used

to keep track of the **international balance of payments.** Define the four components of balance-of-payments accounting.
6. Trace the evolution from young debtor nation to mature creditor nation.
7. Contrast the fixed-exchange-rate system of the gold standard with the pure floating of a flexible-exchange-rate system. Describe the intermediate managed float that characterizes the contemporary international system.
8. Explain David Hume's gold-flow equilibrating mechanism.
9. Sketch a brief chronology of the evolution of the international financial system from the Bretton Woods fixed-rate system that was created following World War II, through today's managed-float system.
10. Describe the crisis in the European monetary system and the creation of the monetary and economic union in Europe.

III. REVIEW OF KEY CONCEPTS

Match the following terms from column A with their definitions in column B.

A	B
— Open economy	1. Program and policies that make it difficult for a country to change its exchange rate.
— Foreign exchange rate	2. Contains data on a nation's exports and imports of goods and services.
— Depreciation	3. Item in a country's international balance-of-payments account that involves spending foreign currency.
— Appreciation	4. Item recorded in the balance-of-payments accounts when a country intervenes in the foreign exchange market.

__ Devaluation

__ Revaluation

__ Purchasing-power parity theory exchange rates

__ Balance of international payments

__ Credit

__ Debit

__ Current account

__ Financial account

__ Official settlements

__ Hard fix

__ Currency board

__ Floating exchange rates

__ Fixed exchange rates

__ Gold standard

5.   Systematic statement of all economic transactions between a country and the rest of the world.

6.   Contains data on financial flows (lendings and borrowings) into and out of a country.

7.   An economy that engages in of international trade.

8.   Item in a country's interntional balance-of-payments account that earns foreign currency.

9.   Deals with the *official* lowering of a country's foreign exchange rate in terms of other currencies or gold.

10.   The price of a unit of foreign currency in terms of the domestic currency.

11.   Monetary institution that only issues currency that is fully backed by foreign assets in a key foreign currency.

12.   A *market-determined* rise in the price of one currency in terms of others.

13.   A *market-determined* fall in the price of one currency in terms of others.

14.   Deals with the official raising of a country's foreign exchange rate in terms of other currencies or gold.

15.   In the long run, exchange rates tend to move with changes in *relative* prices of different countries. This doctrine also holds that countries with high inflation rates will tend to have depreciating currencies.

16.   Occurs when a government buys or sells its own or foreign currencies to affect exchange rates.

17.   Exchange rates are completely flexible and move purely under the influence of supply and demand.

18.   Exchange rates are basically determined by market forces, but governments intervene to affect exchange rates.

__ Four-pronged mechanism

__ Managed exchang rates

__ Intervention

__ Bretton Woods system

__ International Monetary Fund

__ World Bank

__ Monetary union

19.   The government specifies the rate at which its currency can be exchanged into other nation's currencies.

20.   Established a system of exchange rates that were fixed but adjustable; also laid foundations for the International Monetary Fund, the World Bank, and the General Agreement on Tariffs and Trade.

21.   Part of Hume's explanation of international payments equilibrium.

22.   Administers the international monetary system and operates as a central bank for the central banks of member countries.

23.   Fixed-exchange-rate system in which a country defines the value of its currency in terms of a fixed amount of gold.

24.   Industrialized nations lend money to this institution, which then makes low-interest loans to countries for projects which are economically sound but which cannot get private-sector financing.

25.   The decision of the countries in Europe to adopt a common currency.

IV. SUMMARY AND CHAPTER OUTLINE

This section summarizes the key concepts from the chapter.

A. The Balance of International Payments

1.   There are four components in the **balance-of-payments accounts:**
    a.   the *current account* (for goods and services)
    b.   the *financial account* (for capital goods and services)
    c   *official settlements*
    d.   *statistical discrepancy* (a catchall category)

Any transaction which requires foreign currency (e.g., the purchase of a commodity produced in another country) is recorded as a debit; any transaction which generates foreign currency (e.g., the sale of a domestic product in a foreign country) is recorded as a credit.

2.   Countries usually evolve through several stages in their balance-of-payments histories:
    a.   young debtor nation

    b.   mature debtor nation
    c.   new creditor nation
    d.   mature creditor nation

A less developed nation is typically one which borrows abroad to the full extent of its line of credit. A mature, developed nation is typically one which lends to other countries. As a nation develops over a long time period, it may change from borrower to lender, and this shift will affect its balance-of-payments position. The four-stage sequence, outlined above, is an attempt to describe the likely balance-of-payments changes involved.

3.   Some economists suggest that during the 1980s the United States may have entered a fifth stage of development, namely that of "senile debtor nation." Greatly diminished saving has caused heavy U.S. borrowing and turned the world's biggest creditor into the world's biggest debtor.

B. The Determination of Foreign Exchange Rates

1.   When producers in Country A sell their products to people in other countries, they prefer to be paid in their own currency. Therefore, before the people in Country B can purchase products from Country A, they must acquire some of Country A's currency. They purchase Country A's currency with their own currency in a **foreign exchange market.**

2.   An exchange rate is simply the price of some currency, A, in terms of some other currency, B. It is determined by the interaction of supply and demand in the foreign exchange market.

3.   In free markets, with relatively low transportation costs, a nation's exchange rate will move to equalize the cost of buying traded goods and services at home with the cost of buying those goods abroad. This known as *the law of one price* and it leads to **the purchasing-power-parity (PPP) theory of exchange rates.** In the long run, according to PPP theory, exchange rates will tend to move with changes in relative prices of different countries.

4.   When market exchange rates are used, many poor countries appear to have very small national output. Many of the goods and services in these countries which are *not* traded in international markets are relatively labor-intensive and therefore very *in*expensive. When PPP exchange rates are used to evaluate output, it raises the per capita GDP of low-income countries.

C. The International Monetary System

1.   In a system of pure floating exchange rates the forces of supply and demand determine the value of a nation's currency. The government neither announces a predetermined exchange rate nor takes steps to affect the exchange rate. If, for example, the price of Country X's currency is too high, it will find itself exporting fewer goods and services. Similarly, imports will be relatively cheaper for the citizens

of Country X and they will import more. The increase in imports will increase X's demand for foreign currencies, while the reduction in exports will, in turn, reduce the demand for its own currency. As a result, the market will "float" to a new equilibrium exchange rate.

2.   In 1752 David Hume discussed a **four-pronged mechanism,** based on the **gold standard** and **fixed exchange** rates, which automatically restored equilibrium if there was an imbalance in international payments between nations. Suppose that Country A has a trade deficit with Country B. According to Hume, the following sequence of events occurs to restore equilibrium in the international marketplace:

    a.   A must ship gold to B to pay for its trade deficit. Since A now has less gold, it must reduce its domestic money supply, and prices in A will fall. As a result, imports will become relatively more expensive and imports will decrease.

    b.   Since prices in A are now lower, A's exports will increase.

    c.   When B receives the gold from A its money supply will increase and prices there will go up. This increase in prices in B contributes to its decrease in exports—to A and elsewhere.

    d.   In response to higher domestic prices, citizens in B will import more goods and services from abroad.

So as a result of being on the gold standard, A's initial trade deficit will turn around, as will B's initial trade surplus. International trade equilibrium is restored, but Country A will suffer a decrease in its money supply and thereby will experience deflation, if not recession; Country B will have to deal with higher prices and inflation.

3.   In a system of **managed exchange rates,** market forces determine exchange rates, but governments or central banks may intervene when they want to influence the market exchange rate. **Intervention** occurs when the government buys or sells its own or foreign currencies, or changes its monetary policy with the goal of affecting exchange rates. For example, if a currency is appreciating in value, and the government has some holdings of this currency, it may sell this currency in the foreign exchange market. This action would increase the supply and, everything else held constant, tend to lower its price. Alternatively, the central bank could, via monetary policy, lower interest rates. This action would decrease the demand for the nation's currency by foreigners looking for high-interest investment opportunities.

4.   At the end of World War II the nations of the world recognized the need to coordinate economic policies and seek common solutions to their problems. The discussions held at Bretton Woods, New Hampshire, led to the creation of the **International Monetary Fund (IMF),** the **World Bank,** and the **General Agreement on Tariffs and Trade (GATT).** According to the Bretton Woods system, exchange rates would be fixed but adjustable.

    The intended goal behind the IMF's formation was to

maintain, to the extent possible, stable exchange rates. No nation would have to push itself deliberately into recession or depression just to maintain a steady international value for its currency, but each participating nation did deposit a supply of its own currency (and, in some cases, gold) with the IMF. These deposits established a "lending pool" from which any nation could borrow if it found itself temporarily losing reserves in its maintenance of a fixed rate. It was of course understood that persistent losses of reserves indicated some form of "fundamental disequilibrium" which could not be sustained by continual borrowing. A nation could then devalue its currency value by up to 10 percent if it wished. Further devaluation required "consultation with the fund"—in effect, international approval.

5.   Although the old international gold standard and Bretton Woods system are both gone, their influence persists, particularly in two important respects. First, nations still consider their gold stocks as reserves for settling international balances. (But now they tend to regard gold as an Emergency" reserve; they do not part with gold unless events force them to do so.) Second, the desire for relative stability in exchange rates persists. The gold standard is not the only possible mechanism to this end. You can hold the price of your currency steady by simply maintaining a sufficiently large inventory of foreign monies.

V. HELPFUL HINTS

1.   As with all diagrams, pay careful attention to how the axes are labeled when working with diagrams depicting foreign exchange markets. Like any supply-and-demand diagram, price is measured on the vertical axis and quantity on the horizontal axis. In this case, the *quantity* will always be the amount of some currency: French francs, German deutsche marks, Japanese yen, whatever. If we are considering the cost of these currencies from the U.S. perspective, the *price* (on the vertical axis) will measure how many dollars are needed to purchase each unit of the foreign currency. So in the foreign exchange market for Japanese yen, the price would be dollars per yen, or $/Y. (Note: Regardless of which currency market you are studying, the currency which is measured on the *horizontal* axis will always be in the denominator of the price on the *vertical* axis.)

     Consider Figure 29-1. Panel *(a)* illustrates the market for yen. Note how the axes are labeled. When people demand yen, they will pay for them with dollars. The suppliers of yen will sell them for dollars.

     Panel *(b)* illustrates the mirror image of panel *(a)*. The suppliers of yen (from panel [*a*]) are now the demanders of dollars, and the folks supplying dollars are demanding yen for dollars back in panel *(a)*.

2.   Samuelson and Nordhaus point out that "a rise in the price of a currency in terms of another currency is called an

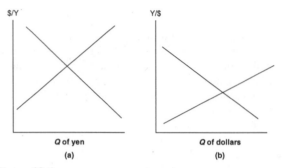

Figure 29-1

'appreciation.'" The key phrase here is "in terms of." Suppose that a dollar, *in terms of* deutsche marks (DM), costs 2 DM. For purposes of example, assume that a year later that same dollar now costs 3 DM. *In terms of* DM, the dollar is now more expensive—it costs more DM to get dollars. We would say that, at least relative to DM, the dollar has appreciated in value.

3.   A **devaluation** occurs when a country or government *intervenes* in the foreign exchange market to lower the value of its currency vis-à-vis other currencies. The result is similar to a **depreciation,** but that comes about via the forces of supply and demand in the market place.

4.   In the balance-of-payments account, the **current account** refers to the difference between exported and imported goods and services. This is the trade deficit that in recent years has been mentioned frequently on U.S. television news. Keep in mind that balance-of-payments accounts are only half the picture. Equally important are the flows of financial capital that are measured in the **financial account.**

5.   If a transaction earns foreign currency, it is called a **credit.** Exports earn foreign currency because foreigners who want to purchase goods and services from county A must sell their currency to buy some of Country A's currency. Borrowings, in the capital account, are also counted as credits, because when a country lends to Country A, it gives up some of its currency, again through the foreign exchange market, to Country A.

6.   Surpluses or deficits that exist in the current account must be financed or offset by lendings or borrowings in the financial account.

7.   The PPP exchange rate calculations, illustrated in Figure 29-6 in your text make China's GDP, and that of other low-income countries, much higher. Many of the products which are not traded internationally are labor-intensive services. These are very inexpensive, even in low-income countries. Therefore, when market exchange rates are used to evaluate output, GDP in low-income countries tends to be underestimated. Keep in mind, however, that the numbers in this table are "gross" and not "per capita." China remains the most populated nation on the earth.

VI. MULTIPLE CHOICE QUESTIONS

These questions are organized by topic from the chapter outline. Choose the best answer from the options available.

A. The Balance of International Payments

1. A "favorable balance of trade" means:
   a. an excess of merchandise exports and other capital account credits over merchandise imports and other capital account debits.
   b. an excess of foreign currency received by the home country over domestic currency received by foreigners.
   c. an excess of merchandise exports over merchandise imports.
   d. an excess of total credits over total debits in the entire balance of payments
   e. a situation in which the value of total imports exceeds the value of total exports.

2. The following five transactions are all entries to be made on the U.S. balance of payments. For balance-of-payments purposes, four of the five are fundamentally similar. Which one is different?
   a. The Federal Reserve Bank of New York sells dollars in the foreign exchange market.
   b. An American tourist on vacation spends francs in Paris.
   c. A South American country sells coffee in New York.
   d. A British shipping firm is paid to carry an American export commodity abroad.
   e. An American computer company receives an order for software programs from Germany.

3. A mature debtor nation is one whose balance of trade is:
   a. unfavorable, the import surplus being paid for by borrowing.
   b. unfavorable, thanks to the interest which is received from abroad.
   c. favorable, the interest on past borrowing being paid out of the surplus of exports.
   d. favorable, being made so by interest received from abroad.
   e. not correctly identified by any of these descriptions.

4. The **trade balance** consists of:
   a. the difference between the financial account and the current account.
   b. the difference between foreign investment and foreign saving.
   c. imports or exports of merchandise.
   d. a comparison of international exchange rates.
   e. none of the above.

B. The Determination of Foreign Exchange Rates

5. If we say that a country's currency has been devalued, we mean that:
   a. it has gone off the gold standard.
   b. the domestic purchasing power of its currency unit has increased.
   c. its government has increased the price it will pay for gold.
   d. it is experiencing an unfavorable balance of trade.
   e. the prices of at least some foreign currencies, as expressed in that country's domestic currency, have fallen.

6. In a stable exchange-rate situation, if the price of the French franc were 25 U.S. cents and the price of the U.S. dollar were 600 Italian lire, then the price of the French franc in Italian lire would be:
   a. 90 lire.
   b. 150 lire.
   c. 200 lire.
   d. 300 lire.
   e. 600 lire.

7. If the price of French francs in terms of U.S. dollars is 25 cents, then the price of dollars in terms of French francs is:
   a. 2 francs.
   b. 3 francs.
   c. 4 francs.
   d. 5 francs.
   e. cannot be determined from the information given.

8. If the British pound appreciates in value in terms of the Mexican peso, we can say that:
   a. there are now more pesos to the pound.
   b. there are now fewer pounds to the peso.
   c. other things held constant, British goods now cost more in Mexico.
   d. all the above.
   e. **a** and **c** only.

9. If the market exchange rate between Swiss francs and U.S. dollars were to change from Sfr. 4 to the dollar to Sfr. 3 to the dollar, then the franc's price must have:
   a. risen from 25 cents to 33 cents, and the dollar has appreciated relative to the franc.
   b. fallen from 33 cents to 25 cents, and the dollar has depreciated relative to the franc.
   c. risen from 25 cents to 33 cents, and the dollar has, been devalued relative to the franc.
   d. risen from 25 cents to 33 cents, and the dollar has depreciated relative to the franc.
   e. fallen from 33 cents to 25 cents, and the dollar has appreciated relative to the franc.

10. A substantial fall in the price of the dollar in foreign currencies could be expected to affect physical quantities of exports from the United States and imports into the United States in which of the following ways?
    a.   It would increase both exports and imports.
    b.   It would increase exports and decrease imports.
    c.   It would decrease both exports and imports.
    d.   It would decrease exports and increase imports.
    e.   It would have no perceptible effect on either imports or exports.

11. If a country depreciates the foreign exchange value of its currency, the results will typically be that:
    a.   its imports will seem cheaper (from the viewpoint of its own citizens), and its exports will seem more expensive (from the viewpoint of foreigners).
    b.   its imports will seem more expensive (from the viewpoint of its own citizens), and its exports will seem cheaper (from the viewpoint of foreigners).
    c.   both its imports and its exports will seem cheaper (from the viewpoint of both its own citizens and foreigners).
    d.   both its imports and its exports will seem more expensive (from the viewpoint of both its own citizens and foreigners).
    e.   none of the above will occur, since there is no reason why the prices of either imports or exports should be affected.

C. The International Monetary System

12. For a country to be fully on the gold standard, the government of that country must:
    a.   set a fixed price at which it is prepared to buy or sell gold in any quantity without restriction.
    b.   be prepared to buy or sell gold at any time without restriction, but at a price which it is free to vary from day to day as it chooses, provided the same price (or almost the same price) applies to both purchases and sales.
    c.   be prepared to buy gold in any quantity without restriction at a fixed price, but not necessarily to sell it.
    d.   be prepared to sell gold in any quantity without restriction, but not necessarily to buy it.
    e.   maintain a fixed gold content in its money unit, but not necessarily be prepared to buy or sell gold at any fixed price or without restriction.

13. Suppose that the exports of Country A to Country B have increased substantially and that both A and B operate on the gold standard. According to David Hume's gold-flow mechanism:
    a.   A's domestic price level will fall, but B's domestic price level may or may not change.
    b.   A's price level may or may not change, but B's will fall.
    c.   A's price level will rise; B's will fall. d.   A's price

level will fall; B's will rise.
    e.   none of the above will happen.

14. If the exchange rate between Canadian and U.S. dollars is a floating one, and if the demand for Canadian dollars increases, then:
    a.   the supply of Canadian dollars has decreased or will decrease.
    b.   the price of the Canadian dollar in U.S. currency will fall.
    c.   the supply of U.S. dollars has decreased.
    d.   the price of the U.S. dollar in Canadian currency will fall.
    e.   the U.S. dollar has been devalued.

15. The primary advantage of the gold standard, or any other fixed-exchange-rate system, is its:
    a.   flexibility.
    b.   predictability.
    c.   link to a precious metal.
    d.   universal acceptance.
    e.   relationship to the International Monetary Fund.

16. The main difficulty in all fixed-exchange-rate systems is that:
    a.   one currency may dominate the others.
    b.   gold is expensive to mine.
    c.   economic adjustment may be impeded if prices fluctuate widely.
    d.   there is no mechanism to counteract trade surpluses.
    e.   none of the above.

17. Under a system of managed exchange rates:
    a.   exchange rates are basically determined by market forces.
    b.   a government may purchase its own currency in the foreign exchange market.
    c.   monetary policy may be used to influence exchange rates.
    d.   all the above.
    e.   none of the above.

18. If GDP falls in the United States and exchange rates are floating, then:
    a.   imports will tend to decrease and the price of the U.S. dollar will tend to increase.
    b.   imports will tend to decrease and the price of the U.S. dollar will tend to decrease.
    c.   imports will tend to increase and the price of the U.S. dollar will tend to increase.
    d.   imports will tend to increase and the price of the U.S. dollar will tend to decrease.
    e.   none of the preceding statements will be true.

19. One of the principal tasks of the International Monetary Fund is to:
    a.   serve as a partial substitute for the gold standard in maintaining stable exchange rates.
    b.   help countries with short-term balance-of-payment difficulties.

c. make loans to private companies in any country where the funds could not otherwise be borrowed at any reasonable interest rate.

d. facilitate the development of free-trade "regions" similar to the European Common Market.

e. coordinate the views of the larger and more developed nations concerning exchange-rate and trade problems.

20. It could also be said that a principal task assigned to the International Monetary Fund is to:

a. act as the world's banker in matters of both short-term and long-term credit.

b. make direct long-term loans to less developed nations when necessary, so as to assist in their economic development.

c. control international credit sufficiently to enable member nations to maintain their price levels at reasonably noninflationary levels.

d. work toward the gradual reduction of tariffs and the elimination of protectionist policies among nations.

e. none of the above.

21. Which alternative in question 9 would be correct had that question referred to the World Bank rather than the International Monetary Fund?

a.

b.

c.

d.

e.

22. A disturbance in its balance of payments may cause any nation to lose gold or foreign exchange reserves.

This danger of loss is most acute whenever that nation:

a. increases its exports.

b. seeks to maintain a flexible exchange rate.

c. seeks to maintain a fixed exchange rate.

d. increases its borrowing from other nations.

e. experiences a drop in GDP—i.e., whenever a recession occurs.

23. A "managed float" means:

a. an increase in the protectionist policies by some device other than a tariff increase.

b. refusal by a nation to allow its currency to appreciate even though its reserves are large and increasing.

c. a beggar-thy-neighbor policy.

d. introduction of a split exchange rate—a fixed rate for some transactions, a floating rate for others.

e. periodic intervention by a central bank to check excessive fluctuation in an otherwise floating exchange rate.

24. As part of the Bretton Woods system:

a. the industrialized economies adopted a system of floating exchange rates.

b. the ideas of John Maynard Keynes were widely discredited.

c. the U.S. dollar was recognized as the preeminent currency of the world.

d. all the above.

e. none of the above.

25. Which of the following is typically expected to have the largest influence on the rate of investment in a country?

a. The policies of the World Bank.

b. The rate of saving in that country.

c. The productivity of capital in that country.

d. The foreign exchange rate.

e. None of the above.

26 If a country wants to increase its own real income it should probably attempt to:

a. overvalue its currency.

b. depreciate its currency.

c. export its inflation problems.

d. coordinate its economic policies with other nations.

e. employ a beggar-thy-neighbor policy.

VII. PROBLEM SOLVING

The following problems are designed to help you apply the concepts that you learned in the chapter.

A. The Balance of International Payments

1. A country's balance of payments is the official record of all its transactions with foreign countries for some specified period of time, usually 1 year. There are four main categories; list them in the spaces provided:

a. _____

b. _____

c. _____

d. _____

The key to entries in any of these categories is the effect that the transaction has on domestic holdings of foreign currencies.

e. If a transaction generates foreign currency, then it is recorded as a (**debit / credit**); if it costs currency because a foreign citizen (or institution) requires payment in his or her (or its) own currency, then it is a (**debit / credit**).

2. A less developed nation is likely to try to build up its stock of capital goods through sales of its IOUs to more developed countries.

a. On its balance of payments, these security sales will be recorded as a (**credit / debit**).

b. The import of capital equipment or other goods purchased with security-sale proceeds will appear on the merchandise line as a (**credit / debit**).

c. This country has (**a favorable / an unfavorable**) balance of trade.

These facts make it a "young debtor" nation.

As time passes, the country ceases to borrow, or borrows

in smaller quantities. It still pays interest and dividends on earlier years of bond and stock financing, but its exporting capacity has increased.

    d.   It now shows a surplus of merchandise exports over imports, or an excess of (**credits over debits / debits over credits**).

    e.   This (**favorable / unfavorable**) balance of trade is matched, or approximately so, by a surplus of debits on the investment income line of the balance of payments.

The "mature debtor" stage has been reached.

    Further down the road, the country may begin not only to repay its own earlier borrowings but also to lend to other countries.

    f.   This means a surplus of (**credits over debits / debits over credits**) in the balance-of-payments capital account.

If this is matched, or approximately so, by a surplus of merchandise exports over imports, the "knew creditor" stage has been reached.

    Ultimately, the "mature creditor" stage may be attained. At this point, the country may still be lending capital abroad, but its inflow of interest and dividend payments is more than sufficient to offset this lending.

    g.   In the balance-of-payments merchandise account, therefore, there is a surplus of (**credits over debits / debits over credits**), and the balance of trade is (**favorable / unfavorable**).

    h.   This balance is supported by the (**debit / credit**) balance in the investment income account.

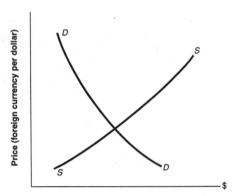

Figure 29.2

B. The Determination of Foreign Exchange Rates

3.   For each of the following statements, indicate whether its effect would be to increase (**I**) or to decrease (**D**) the dollar's price in foreign-currency terms. Use the supply-demand framework reflected in Figure 29-2 to inform and illustrate your answers.

    ___ a.   American demand for imports increases.

    ___ b.   Foreign demand for U.S. goods decreases.

    ___ c.   A recession in the United States results in falling GDP, employment, and imports.

    ___ d.   The rate of inflation in foreign countries is more rapid than that in the United States.

    ___ e.   Americans decide to invest less abroad— i.e., their demand for foreign assets decreases.

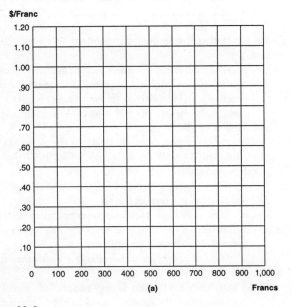

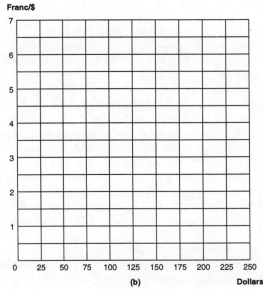

Figure 29-3

____ f.   Foreign firms increase their dividend payments, and some of the shareholders are Americans.

____ g.   Foreigners decide to hold fewer U.S. dollars.

4.   A demand schedule for francs, at various dollars-and-cents prices, is outlined in Table 29-1.

TABLE 29-1

P of Franc (in $)	Q of Francs Demanded	P of Dollar (in francs)	Q of Dollars Supplied
1.00	0	___	___
0.90	100	___	___
0.80	200	___	___
0.70	300	___	___
0.60	400	___	___
0.50	500	___	___
0.40	600	___	___
0.30	700	___	___
0.20	800	___	___
0.10	900	___	___

a.   Convert the table into a supply schedule for dollars, at various franc prices.

Hint: A "straight-line" demand schedule results in a supply schedule of quite unexpected shape. Convert in this way: If the price of 1 franc is 90 cents, then 1 franc = 90 cents, and so $1 = 100/0.90 franc (i.e., the price of $1 is about 1.1 francs). The schedule in Table 29-1 says that 100 francs will be demanded when the price of the franc is 90 cents; i.e., $90 will be supplied to buy them. In sum, then, $90 will be supplied when the dollar's price is 1.1 francs. Work out other points on the supply schedule similarly.

b.   Plot both curves in the appropriate panels of Figure 29-3. The demand schedule goes in panel (*a*) and the mirror-image supply schedule goes in panel (*b*).

5.   What effect, if any, is each of the following events likely to have on the price of the franc in dollars? For each statement below, put (**U**) in the blank if the effect should be to push the price of the franc (in terms of dollars) up, (**D**) if it should push the price down, and (**N**) if there is no reason why the price of the franc should be affected at all.

____ a.   French corporations have a large interest payment to make, in dollars, to American bondholders.

____ b.   French corporations have a large interest payment to make, in francs, to American bondholders.

____ c.   France emerges from a recession, and with this increase in incomes, the French people want to buy more American merchandise.

____ d.   American residents decide to buy French bonds.

____ e.   French corporations sell bonds to Americans, borrowing in dollars in New York because the interest rate is lower there. The proceeds of the bond issue are to be spent on French labor and materials.

____ f.   Foreign exchange speculators decide that the price of the dollar in francs is going to fall.

____ g.   The taste of American gourmets for French wine is replaced by a taste for California wine.

____ h.   The French government decides that American movies are immoral and refuses to admit them into France.

____ i.   An American citizen sends a package of merchandise to her French relatives as a gift.

____ j.   An American citizen sends a remittance of dollars to his French relatives as a gift.

____ k.   A French bank, in possession of a dollar bank account, decides to convert the dollars into francs.

6.   Canada relies heavily on exports to, and imports from, the United States. Suppose that the Canadian authorities (to whom the exchange rate is consequently important) decide that it would be desirable for trading purposes to keep the price of the U.S. dollar at $(Can.) 1.15.

a.   If the price of the U.S. dollar begins to drift below this figure, then Canada could enter the foreign exchange market and support the price by (**selling / buying**) U.S. dollars.

b.   It would, for this purpose, supply (sell) (**Canadian / American**) dollars.

c.   If the U.S. dollar's price started to move above $(Can.) 1.15, on the other hand, Canada could (**buy / sell**) U.S. dollars.

Alternatively, Canada might choose a modified version of the same plan, keeping the price of the U.S. dollar within a "band" of, say, $(Can.) 1.12 and $(Can.) 1.18. Canada could not, of course, keep the exchange rate indefinitely at a level not justified by supply and demand.

d.   If the price of the U.S. dollar kept trying to push above $(Can.) 1.18, then Canada would (**accumulate too many / run out of**) U.S. dollars.

7.   The word "devaluation" goes back to the days of the gold standard, in which the currency unit allegedly had a "gold content" and gold consequently had an "official price" per ounce.

a.   Devaluation meant a government-decreed (**reduction / increase**) in that gold content—i.e., (**a reduction / an increase**) in the official price of gold.

b.   President Roosevelt's 1933 declaration that the dollar's gold content would be reduced from 1/21 to 1/35 of an ounce (**was / was not**) an instance of devaluation.

Depreciation, in the context of foreign exchange, refers to a reduction in the price of a currency relative to other monies.

c.   Suppose that the price of the Canadian dollar is 90 U.S. cents. If this price were to drop to 85 U.S. cents, then the Canadian dollar would be worth, in U.S. funds, (**more / less**); this would be an instance of depreciation.

d.   If the price were to rise from 90 U.S. cents to 95 U.S. cents, on the other hand, this would indicate (**a depreciation / an appreciation**) of the Canadian dollar.

e.   Any depreciation of a foreign currency (relative to

the U.S. dollar) makes that foreign country's goods appear (**cheaper / more expensive**) to Americans. To residents in that other country, in terms of their own currency, American goods appear (**cheaper / more expensive**).

f.   When a country's currency is depreciated, therefore, this move tends to (**increase / decrease**) the volume of its exports and to (**increase / decrease**) the volume of its imports.

C. The International Monetary System

8. Suppose that a widespread taste for Scotch whiskey develops in the United States.

a.   This would create an increase in the demand for (**dollars / pounds sterling**).

b.   If the United States were on the gold standard and if this demand increase were sufficiently large, then there would be a flow of gold (**away from / toward**) the United States.

c.   If this demand increase persisted without a countering effect for a long time, then the United States might be drained of its entire stock of (**gold / Scotch whiskey**).

The gold standard kept exchange rates steady by definition, but demand-and-supply forces were still at work. Why didn't some nations run out of gold while trying to maintain that standard? A nation did, indeed, have to "go off" the gold standard if it lost all or most of its gold because of a major rise in imports or a sufficient drop in exports. There were, however, some "equilibrating" forces that operated to brake any such overwhelming gold outflow. The first major attempt to describe an equilibrating mechanism was laid out by David Hume in the eighteenth century.

9. Suppose, as in question 1, that the U.S. demand for imports increases to a point where imports exceed exports.

a.   According to Hume's analysis, the resulting gold flow (**out of / into**) the United States (**increases / decreases**) the U.S. money supply, causing the price level to (**rise / fall**).

b.   The (**same / reverse**) situation occurs in one or more foreign exporting countries. The gold which has left the United States flows into these countries, increasing their money stock and causing their prices to (**climb / fall**).

c.   Since American prices have gone down while foreign prices have gone up, (**more / fewer**) American goods will be bought by foreigners, while Americans will tend to buy (**more / fewer**) foreign goods.

d.   That is, in America, exports will (**rise / fall**), imports will (**rise / fall**), and the rise in the U.S. imports which began the process would be offset.

In rough outline, for sufficiently large movements, Hume's analysis may have some validity. There is today, however, almost no link between a nation's total gold stock and its total money supply. Moreover, Hume's analysis

relies heavily on the quantity theory of money and its assumption of full employment. Both of these caveats leave the Hume analysis wanting as a description of modern-day responses to an imbalance in its current account.

10. Assume that the nations of Germany and France have agreed to maintain fixed exchange rates between themselves. In Figure 29-4 the initial exchange rate is 3 French francs per German mark. Suppose something happens so that the demand for marks increases (dotted demand curve).

a.   What is one possible reason for the rightward shift in the demand curve?

Suppose that the German government wants to reestablish the original exchange rate.

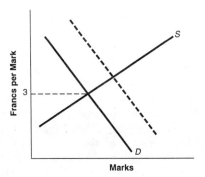

Figure 29-4

b.   What is one reason why the German government might want to do this?

c.   What action might the German government take to bring about this change?

11. Assume that Japan and England have agreed to a system of floating exchange rates. Figure 29-5 illustrates the foreign exchange market between these two countries. Assume that the initial exchange rate is 320 Japanese yen per English pound.

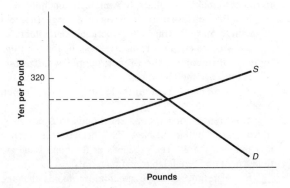

Figure 29-5

a. At the initial exchange rate, there is an excess supply of (**pounds / yen**).

b. One possible explanation for the excess supply is that relative prices of goods and services in England may be too (**high / low**).

c. As the exchange rate falls, Japanese citizens will want more (**Japanese / British**) goods and services.

d. As this happens, there will be a (**movement along / shift in**) the demand and supply curves to a new equilibrium point.

12. The World Bank's task, in brief, is to channel money from richer nations to less developed ones.

a. In slightly more detail, the bank's function is to (**make short-term loans / make long-term loans / provide foreign exchange for balance-of-payments shortages**) to the world's poorer countries.

b. It provides funds for a less developed nation (**even if that nation can / only if that nation cannot**) borrow privately at a reasonable interest rate.

13. One of the most significant problems of international finance in the early 1980s was the overvalued U.S. dollar.

a. The dollar was estimated by some to have been (**10 / 25 / 50**) percent overvalued from 1981 into 1984.

b. The scenario that produced this overvaluation began with the (**tight / loose**) monetary policy and (**stimulative / contractionary**) fiscal policy of the Reagan administration that drove real interest rates in the United States (**up / down**).

c. Foreign investment therefore flowed (**into / out of**) the United States, (**increasing / decreasing**) the demand for dollars and thus causing the dollar to (**appreciate / depreciate**) in money markets all around the world.

d. Exports from the United States therefore became (**more / less**) expensive, while imports from abroad became (**more / less**) costly.

e. Net exports (**expanded / contracted**) by nearly (**$50 / $140 / $250**) billion, as a result, and created an enormous (**deficit / surplus**) in the current account.

f. This discrepancy was, though, almost canceled by a (**deficit / surplus**) in the capital account, so the overvaluation persisted and drove interest rates abroad (**up / down**).

g. The result was a tendency for foreign economies to move into (**recession / boom**), and (**depressed / overextended**) export- and import-competing industries called for (**free trade / protection and subsidy**) in the United States.

VIII. DISCUSSION QUESTIONS

Answer the following questions, making sure that you can explain the work you did to arrive at the answers.

1. Why does the use of PPP exchange rates, as opposed to market exchange rates, increase the value of GDP in low-income countries?

2. According to the PPP doctrine, why do countries with high inflation rates tend to have depreciating currencies?

3. Briefly explain the four steps in Hume's gold-flow equilibrating mechanism.

4. Briefly discuss the two main ways in which a country can intervene in the foreign exchange market to influence the exchange rate of its currency.

5. What factors contributed to the collapse of the Bretton Woods exchange-rate system?

6. Discuss some of the economic considerations that must be addressed before Europe can act as a truly unified single economy.

IX. ANSWERS TO STUDY GUIDE QUESTIONS

III. Review of Key Concepts

7	Open economy
10	Foreign exchange rate
13	Depreciation
12	Appreciation
9	Devaluation
14	Revaluation
15	Purchasing-power-parity theory of exchange rates
5	Balance of international payments
8	Credit
3	Debit
2	Current account
6	Financial account
4	Official settlements
1	Hard fix
11	Currency board
17	Floating exchange rates
19	Fixed exchange rates
23	Gold Standard
21	Four-pronged mechanism
18	Managed exchange rates
16	Intervention
20	Bretton Woods system
22	International Monetary Fund
24	World Bank
25	Monetary union

VI. Multiple Choice Questions

1. D 2. E 3. C 4. C 5. C 6. B
7. C 8. D 9. D 10. B 11 B. 12. A
13. C 14. D 15. B 16. C 17. D 18. B
19. B 20. E 21. B 22. C 23. E 24. C
25. C 26. D

VII. Problem Solving

1. a. current account
    b. financial account
    c. official settlements
    d. statistical discrepancy
    e. credit, debit
2. a. credit
    b. debit
    c. an unfavorable
    d. credits over debits
    e. favorable
    f. debits over creditgs
    g. debits over credits, unfavorable
    h. credit
3. a. D
    b. D
    c. I
    d. I
    e. I
    f. I
    g. D
    See Figure 29-2 for the appropriate shifts.
4. a.

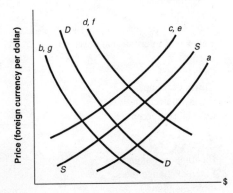

Figure 29-2

TABLE 29-1

P of Franc (in $)	Q of Francs Demanded	P of Dollar (In francs)	Q of Dollars Supplied
1.00	0	1.00	0
0.90	100	1.11	90
0.80	200	1 25	160
0.70	300	1 43	210
0.60	400	1 67	240
0.50	500	2.00	250
0.40	600	2 50	240
0.30	700	3.33	210
0.20	800	5.00	160
0.10	900	10.00	90

    b. See Figure 29-3.

5. a. D
    b. D
    c. D
    d. U
    e. U
    f. U
    g. D
    h. U
    i. N
    j. U
    k. U
6. a. buying
    b. Canadian
    c. sell
    d. run out of
7. a. reduction, an increase
    b. was
    c. less
    d. an appreciation
    e. cheaper, more expensive
    f. increase, decrease
8. a. pounds sterling
    b. away from
    c. gold
9. a. out of, decreases, fall
    b. reverse, climb
    c. more, fewer
    d. rise, fall
10. a. There could be an increase in demand by the French for German goods and services. There could also be an increase in the flow of financial capital from France into Germany.
    b. As the mark appreciates, German exports become more expensive for the French. Also, the relative price of French goods and services will fall in Germany, so German citizens will import more products from France and purchase fewer domestic goods and services.
    c. The German government could sell marks, or it could purchase francs. Germany could also use an expansive monetary policy to lower domestic interest rates. This would encourage investors to move funds out of Germany and toward France. As a result, the demand for marks would decrease.
11. a. pounds
    b. high
    c. British
    d. movement along
12. a. make long-term loans
    b. only if that nation cannot
13. a. 50 percent
    b. tight, stimulative, up
    c. into, increasing, appreciate
    d. more, less
    e. contracted, $140, deficit

f. surplus, up

g. recession, depressed, protection and subsidy

VIII. DISCUSSION QUESTIONS

1. Low-income countries tend to have large, low-income, labor-intensive service sectors. The output from these sectors tends, by its nature, not to be traded in international markets. The use of market-established exchange rates is an accurate way to establish a common value for traded goods, but it is less accurate in assessing the value of nontraded products. PPP exchange rates may more accurately reflect the true value of a nation's output when there are different products and means of production across countries.

2. Countries with relatively high rates of inflation will experience higher prices. Higher prices hurt exports, and the demand for the nation's currency on the foreign exchange markets will fall. In other words, the country's currency will depreciate in value.

3. a. When a country runs a trade deficit, it must pay for it with gold. The reduction in gold decreases its money supply and price level. The fall in prices makes imports relatively more expensive, so imports decrease.

b. Exports will increase due to the fall in prices.

c. The country receiving the gold will experience an increase in its money supply and an increase in prices. Since prices are higher, exports will decrease.

d. The increase in prices will also encourage citizens to import more goods and services.

4. A country can purchase or sell its own currency or the currency of other nations. A country can also use monetary policy to change domestic interest rates. This will influence the flow of foreign financial capital and thereby affect the demand and exchange rate for its currency.

5. As the economies of the world recovered from the Second World War, nations (especially Germany and Japan) developed trade surpluses with the United States. Trade barriers were lowered, and technological advances quickened the pace of financial capital flows between countries. Large federal budget deficits in the United States, which kept upward pressure on interest rates, attracted financial resources from abroad. All these factors made it more and more difficult for the United States to maintain the exchange-rate parities that were established at Bretton Woods.

6. Once a common currency is agreed upon, a single central bank needs to be established to create a uniform monetary policy (no small matter). Price and wage rigidities need to be reduced so that markets can adjust to shocks and disturbances. For the same reason, labor needs to be mobile between regions and countries! Both interest rates and the inflation rate need to be similar among the nations—hopefully at a low level. In addition, participating countries need to control their federal government budget deficits and national debt. A great deal needs to be accomplished, but the payoff could be enormous!

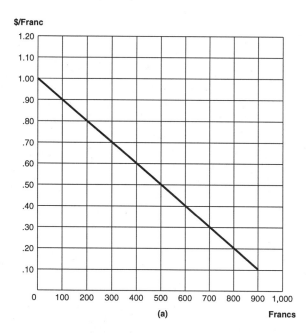

(a)

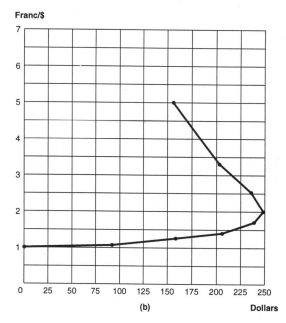

(b)

Figure 29-3

CHAPTER 30

Open-Economy Macroeconomics

I. CHAPTER OVERVIEW

Chapter 30 returns to our earlier multiplier model and incorporates foreign trade into the analysis. Not only does the inclusion of a foreign sector change the composition of aggregate demand, but the overall effects of changes in fiscal policy and investment are altered when imports are sensitive to changes in GDP. Adding a foreign sector also brings questions of exchange-rate effects and international policy coordination to the fore, and these are discussed as well.

The second section of the chapter focuses on the increased interdependence among nations in the global economy and returns to the concept of economic growth in an open environment. Of critical importance here will be the relationships between saving and investment, and national and global interest rates. The international coordination of macroeconomic policies and the economic linkages that exist between economies are also central to this discussion. The impact of recent wide swings in the value of the dollar on both the United States and the rest of the world is also discussed.

In the final section there is as an assessment of the main international economic issues that we face at the dawn of the new millennium. At the forefront here is a discussion of the new monetary union in Europe. If nothing else, it should be clear that no nation is an island—at least as far as the global economy is concerned.

II. LEARNING OBJECTIVES

After you have read Chapter 30 in your text and completed the exercises in this *Study Guide* chapter, you should be able to:

1. Appreciate the importance of foreign trade and finance in the contemporary world economy.
2. Understand the bearing that flexible and fixed exchange rates have on international trade and trade policy.
3. Understand how trade is incorporated into an **open model** of the economy.
4. Calculate the **marginal propensity to import** and

the **open-economy multiplier**.
5. Discuss recent trends in net exports in the United States.
6. Understand how domestic economic growth can be affected by international trade and economic circumstances abroad.
7. Understand the relationship between saving and investment in an open economy.
8. Discuss the strategies for promoting growth in an open economy.
9. Discuss the economic linkages that exist between nations and provide a rationale for the need for international coordination of macroeconomic policies.
10. Describe how the wide swings in the value of the U.S. dollar have been caused by, and have been the causes of, major worldwide economic events.
11. Understand the difference between *competitiveness* and *productivity* especially as these terms apply to the United States' position in the global economy.
12. Describe the crisis in the European monetary system and the resulting plans for monetary union in Europe.

III. REVIEW OF KEY CONCEPTS

Match the following terms from column A with their definitions in column B.

A	B
__ Open economy	1. Occurs when the value of a nation's currency increases, relative to the currency of other nations.
__ Closed economy	2. Refers to a situation in which the value of a nation's money is high relative to its long-run sustainable level.
__ Net exports	3. Exposure to competition with the world leader in a particular industry.
__ Domestic demand	4. Economy without foreign trade or finance.

__ Marginal propensity to import

__ Net foreign investment

__ Depreciation

__ Appreciation

__ High capital mobility

__ Intangible capital

__ Overvalued currency

__ Competitiveness

__ Productivity

__ Globalization

__ Optimal currency area

5.   Occurs when financial capital can flow easily among countries.

6.   Occurs when the value of a nation's currency falls, relative to the currency of other nations.

7.   Country which participates in the world economy and is linked with other countries through trade and finance.

8.   Includes human capital and other types of nonphysical capital.

9.   Area in which wage adjustments can be made and labor mobility is high enough to adjust to economic changes.

10. Total spending on goods and services in a closed economy, i.e., C+I+G, or GDP-X.

11. The change in spending on imports for each dollar change in GDP.

12. Value of imported goods and services subtracted from the value of exports.

13. Denotes net saving or investment abroad and is approximately equal to the value of net exports.

14   Measured by the output per unit of input; e.g. output per person-hour of labor.

15. Refers to the extent to which a nation's goods can compete in the marketplace.

IV. SUMMARY AND CHAPTER OUTLINE

This section summarizes the key concepts from the chapter.

A. Foreign Trade and Economic Activity

1.   Our model of total spending or aggregate demand in the economy becomes complete when we include trade in the analysis.

$$\text{Total aggregate demand } = C+I+G+X$$

2.   Net exports (X), are the difference between a nation's exports (*Ex*) and imports (*Im*):

$$X = Ex - Im$$

Imports and exports are determined primarily by incomes, relative price differences, and foreign exchange rates. When a nation's exchange rate rises, the prices of imported goods fall while its exports become more expensive to foreigners.

3.   There are two basic exchange rate systems: **flexible** and **fixed exchange rates**. With flexible exchange rates, the market forces of supply and demand determine the rate at which currencies are traded. Under a fixed exchange rate system, the government specifies the rate at which its nation's currency will be traded for other currencies.

4.   When trade is included in our macroeconomic model, we need to adjust the *I* and *G* expenditure multiplier because some of that spending typically leaks out to the rest of the world.

Exports are treated as an exogenous variable since they are determined largely by factors outside the domestic economy, such as foreign incomes, prices abroad, and exchange rates. Imports also depend on exogenous foreign variables, but they vary directly with (domestic) GDP as well. As income and GDP increase, other things held constant, so does spending on foreign goods and services, such as coffee, bananas, and kiwi fruit.

When net exports are included in the model, the equilibrium level of GDP may be higher, lower, or unchanged.

5.   Recall our earlier discussion of the relationship between the terms *margin* and *change*. The *marginal propensity to import*, *Mpm*, measures the *changes* in spending on imports for each dollar *change* in GDP. We can write this as:

$$Mpm = \frac{\text{change in } m}{\text{change in GDP}}$$

We now have an additional factor influencing the slope of the C + I + G + X or total spending line. The slope is determined by both the *MPC* and the *Mpm*. Other things held constant, as GDP increases, so too will spending on *foreign* goods and services. Therefore, the *Mpm* represents a drain or leakage on the economy and, as such, will reduce the slope of the total spending line.

In the example in the text, the *MPC* is 0.67 and the *Mpm* is given as 0.10. If GDP increases by $300, *C* will increase by $200 ($300 × 0.67) and imports will increase by $30 ($300 × 0.10). Remember, this increase in imports means that there is a $30 increase in spending on foreign goods and services—this is $30 that is no longer spent at home. The total change in spending (*C* and *m* combined) is $170 ($200-$30). Since slope is a measure of margin or change, we can write:

$$\frac{\text{Slope of total}}{\text{spending line}} = \frac{\text{total change in spending}}{\text{change in GDP}} = \frac{170}{300}$$
$$= 0.567$$

Given the assumptions made in this model, in a *closed* economy, the slope of total spending is the *MPC*. In an open economy, the slope of total spending is flatter due to the leakage of spending on imports. Changes in **exports** will shift the entire spending line up or down, just like changes in *I* and *G*.

6. The *open-economy multiplier* is less than the closed economy expenditure multiplier.

$$\text{Open – economy multiplier} = \frac{1}{MPS + Mpm}$$

(As the denominator of a fraction increases, the value of the expression decreases.)

7. When two countries pursue a policy of fixed exchange rates, they must make sure that their interest rates move in tandem. If there is a divergence in interest rates speculators will have an incentive to move financial capital into the country with higher rates. In essence, the smaller of the two countries can no longer follow an independent monetary policy—its monetary policy must be devoted to aligning its interest rates with its fixed-exchange-rate partner.

8. Under a system of flexible exchange rates, monetary policy may become more effective. In the early 1980s the Fed raised interest rates in the United States to fight inflation and slow down the economy. On the international market, the higher interest rates attracted foreign financial capital, increased the demand for the dollar, which then appreciated in value and subsequently reduced exports and increased imports. This helped to slow the economy further!

B. Interdependence in the Global Economy

1. In a closed economy, deficit spending by the government tends to lower savings and investment. As government saving, T - G, decreases, this tends to reduce the overall level of saving in the economy. At any given interest rate, there is less saving available for lending, so this tends to push the equilibrium real interest rate up.

2. In an open economy, real interest rates are determined in world capital markets. If domestic saving and investment are not in balance exchange rates will move to ensure that the appropriate level of net exports is reached. It is important to realize that net exports will be the same as net foreign investment. If a country has a trade surplus, i.e., Ex > Im, then foreigners are purchasing more of the country's goods and services than its citizens are purchasing abroad. Therefore, the country will be left with a surplus of foreign currency. Whether this is invested abroad or not, this can be considered as *net foreign investment*.

3. There are several policies that a nation can pursue to promote economic growth in an open system. In order to encourage foreign investment countries need to strive to select the best technological processes. Care needs to be exercised here. What works well in Country A may not suc-

ceed in Country B. Differences in resources as well educational and cultural dissimilarities may make it difficult to adapt to new technology. Nevertheless, foreign investors need to be assured that their investments are secure. Trade policies need to be open and competition needs to be encouraged. Countries also need to invest in their *human* as well as their physical capital.

C. International Economic Issues at Century's End

1. While U.S. competitiveness declined during the 1980s, U.S. productivity did not. Samuelson and Nordhaus contribute the declining position of the United States in the global marketplace to the appreciation of the dollar, which increased U.S. prices relative to prices in other nations.

Domestic productivity is enhanced when foreign leaders in productivity invest abroad. For example, the U.S. automobile industry has benefited from Japanese production facilities in the United States. Open markets increase the exposure of new technology and stimulate competition.

2. In 1978 many of the large economies of Europe agreed to keep exchange rates, amongst themselves, within a rather narrow range of prices. This attempt to insulate themselves from exchange-market fluctuations could only be successful if each country was willing to sacrifice some autonomy over its domestic interest rates.

When Germany was reunited in 1990 it experienced a large increase in inflation as it converted East German marks into West German marks. The German central bank raised interest rates to reduce inflationary pressure. The higher interest rates attracted financial resources from foreign countries and increased the demand for the German mark. As a result, other members of the European Monetary System (EMS) had to raise their interest rates to keep their currencies from depreciating vis-à-vis the mark. Before long, this became too costly for the other countries to sustain, and the market reacted as speculators realized that the currencies were artificially overvalued. The EMS collapsed.

3. As a result of the EMS crisis, a plan was developed to create a common currency (the "Euro") for Europe. A common currency would eliminate all exchange rate problems between the countries, eliminate speculation and lower transaction costs. A newly-created European central bank would conduct monetary policy for the nations in this new European Union. Some economists worry that due to wage and price rigidity, and lack of labor mobility, that some areas will be left behind with chronic unemployment and low growth.

4. While no one can say precisely what lies ahead, most countries now agree that international cooperation and coordination is the best way to avoid global economic problems and increase the welfare of all. Finally, it remains for society, not the economist, to decide how to allocate scarce resources: for guns or butter, for the present or the future.

V. HELPFUL HINTS

1. Remember, the *open*-economy expenditure multiplier is less than the *closed*-economy expenditure multiplier. This is because imports (a leakage) increase as income or GDP rises. Exports are primarily determined by the economic health of other countries and are treated as exogenous.

2. We have talked at length in previous chapters about the importance of saving and investment for economic growth. The discussion in this chapter should reinforce this point.

3. Keep in mind that when Samuelson and Nordhaus refer to "capital mobility" in this chapter, they are referring to financial capital, not the physical capital which we consider a factor of production.

VI. MULTIPLE CHOICE QUESTIONS

These questions are organized by topic from the chapter outline. Choose the best answer from the options available.

A. Foreign Trade and Economic Activity

1. Assume that the following conditions hold:
   A. GDP is initially in equilibrium.

   B. The government then increases its total expenditure on goods and services by $2 billion.
   E. There is no increase at all in tax collection.
   D. The marginal propensity to consume is 0.75.
   E. The marginal propensity to import is 0.25.
   Assuming that there is no price-inflationary consequences in the new equilibrium thus produced, GDP will:
   a. fall by $4 billion.
   b. rise by $2 billion.
   c. rise by $6 billion.
   d. rise by $8 billion.
   e. rise by $4 billion.

2. Which answer to question 1 would be correct if instead of the increase in government spending, exports respond to a depreciation in the value of domestic currency and increase by $2 billion?
   a.
   b.
   c.
   d.
   e.

3. Which answer to question 1 would be correct if instead of the increase in government spending, exports respond to an appreciation in the value of domestic currency and decrease by $2 billion?
   a.
   b.
   c.
   d.

e.
4. Over most of the twentieth century:
   a. the United States pursued isolationist policies.
   b. the United States ran a trade surplus.
   c. the volume of trade between the United States and Canada declined.
   d. all the above.
   e. none of the above.

5. The difference between national output and domestic expenditure is:
   a. net imports.
   b. exports minus imports.
   c. imports minus exports.
   d. saving.
   e. none of the above.

6. Assume that the exchange rate of Japanese yen to U.S. dollars falls. Which of the following statements is true?
   a. It will now take more dollars to purchase the same amount of yen.
   b. Other things held constant, Americans will probably purchase fewer Japanese goods and services.
   c. Other things held constant, the Japanese will probably purchase more American goods and services.

   d. We would say that, relative to the yen, the dollar has depreciated in value.
   e. All of the statements above are true.

7. When we move from a closed to an open model of the economy:
   a. private saving decreases.
   b. the expenditure multiplier increases.
   c. lump-sum taxes will not change.
   d. the slope of the total spending line does not change.
   e. exports and imports will have the same *absolute* impact on the economy, just the *direction* of the change will be different.

8. The open-economy multiplier:
   a. is linked to the slope of the total spending line.
   b. equals the expenditure multiplier multiplied by the *MPC*.
   c. is equal to 1/*Mpm*.
   d. will decrease when imports exceed exports.
   e. is none of the above.

9. The key feature of countries with fixed exchange rates and high capital mobility is that:
   a. except for capital, their economies must be closed.
   b. they should trade primarily with each other.
   c. their interest rates must basically be the same.
   d. they must be on the gold standard.
   e. all of the above.

10. The United States adopted a policy of flexible exchange rates in:
    a. 1962.
    b. 1973.

c. 1979.

d. 1987.

e. None of the above, the United States follows a system of fixed exchange rates.

11. When the dollar appreciates in value:

    a. imports tend to increase.

    b. exports tend to increase.

    c. monetary policy is used to counteract the appreciation.

    d. the government budget deficit tends to decrease.

    e. the marginal propensity to import tends to decline.

B. Interdependence in the Global Economy

12. Developing a program of economic growth entails:

    a. encouraging saving.

    b. expanding capital.

    c. developing appropriate trade policies.

    d. adopting the best technological advances.

    e. all of the above.

13. High domestic interest rates tend to:

    a. attract funds from abroad.

    b. contribute to an appreciation of the domestic currency.

    c. lead to a reduction in exports.

    d. lead to an increase in imports.

    e. contribute to all of the above.

14. A country's foreign trade balance is primarily determined by:

    a. domestic saving.

    b. domestic investment.

    c. its level of productivity.

    d. all of the above.

    e. choices **a**. and **b**. only.

15. Over the long run, the single most important way of increasing per capita output and living standards in a country is to:

    a. increase the savings rate.

    b. increase foreign investment.

    c. increase domestic investment.

    d. adopt the best possible technological advances in production.

    e. lower per capita tax rates.

16. When there is a gap between savings and investment, the gap tends to be offset:

    a. by changes in net exports.

    b. by changes in the world interest rate.

    c. when the country adopts a policy of fixed exchange rates.

    d. when monetary policy intervenes.

    e. in the long run.

17. When world interest rates exceed domestic rates:

    a. the domestic currency appreciates in value.

    b. saving tends to flow abroad.

    c. imports will exceed exports.

    d. all of the above.

    e. none of the above.

18. *Intangible capital*:

    a. is hidden in the underground economy.

    b. includes investment in the service sector of the economy.

    c. includes capital investment in off-shore corporations.

    d. includes investment in human capital.

    e. is composed primarily of investments in less developed countries.

C. International Economic Issues at Century's End

19. When interest rates in France increase, we should expect:

    a. domestic investment in France to decrease.

    b. foreign financial capital to flow into France.

    d. interest rates in Belgium to increase.

    d. the French franc to appreciate.

    e. all the above.

20. The U.S. dollar's sharp decline in the mid-1980s can be attributed to:

    a. the sale of dollars by some governments.

    b. the actions of speculators who sold dollars.

    c. higher relative interest rates outside the United States.

    d. all the above.

    e. none of the above.

21. A speculative attack occurs when speculators:

    a. believe a currency is about to be devalued and start purchasing it.

    b. believe a currency is about to be devalued and start selling it off.

    c. coordinate their activities in a financial cartel.

    d. move assets from stocks to bonds to currency.

    e. do any of the above.

22. One reason for the decline in U.S. competitiveness during the 1980s was:

    a. the decrease in U.S. productivity.

    b. the U.S. recession.

    c. the appreciation of the U.S. dollar.

    d. all the above.

    e. none of the above.

23. The trade deficit that the United States had in the late 1990s was related to:

    a. a strong increase in the value of the dollar.

    b. weak economic growth abroad.

    c. the low inflation rates that the U.S. enjoyed during the time period.

    d. all of the above.

    e. choices A and B only.

24. When world interest rates increase, a small open economy would tend to experience:
    a. an *increase* in exchange rates, an *increase* in investment, and an *increase* in net exports.
    b. an *increase* in exchange rates, a *decrease* in investment, and an *increase* in net exports.
    c. a *decrease* in exchange rates, an *increase* in investment, and an *increase* in net exports.
    d. a *decrease* in exchange rates, a *decrease* in investment, and an *increase* in net exports.
    e. a *decrease* in exchange rates, a *decrease* in investment, and a *decrease* in net exports.

25. When the countries of Europe created the European Monetary System in 1978 they committed to keeping their exchange rates within narrow prescribed bands. One result of this agreement was:
    a. a decrese in net exports.
    b. a loss of control over domestic interest rates.
    c. a decline in the risk of speculative attacks against their currencies.
    d. all of the above.
    e. A and C only.

26. If a country wants to have free flows of financial capital across its borders, as well as an independent monetary policy, then it must also have:
    a. a trade surplus.
    b. fixed exchange rates.
    c. floating exchange rates.
    d. a government budget surplus.
    e. a government budget deficit.

27. Before joining the European Union, prospective members had to adhere to guidelines on their domestic:
    a. inflation rates.
    b. interest rates.
    c. government budget deficit.
    d. national debt.
    e. all of the above.

28. In order for the "Euro" to succeed as a common European currency:
    a. a European central bank needs to be created.
    b. wage and price rigidities in some European economies need to be reduced.
    c. labor should be freely mobile between markets.
    d. participating countries need to have inflation and interest rates that are close to those in the lowest countries.
    e. all of the above.

VII. PROBLEM SOLVING

The following problems are designed to help you apply the concepts that you learned in the chapter.

A. Foreign Trade and Economic Activity

1. Consider the open economy defined in Table 30-1.

TABLE 30-1

GDP	C	I	G	T	Ex	Im
900	340	200	500	500	250	90
950	370	200	500	500	250	95
1,000	400	200	500	500	250	100
1,050	430	200	500	500	250	105
1,100	460	200	500	500	250	110
1,150	490	200	500	500	250	115
1,200	520	200	500	500	250	120
1,250	550	200	500	500	250	125
1,300	580	200	500	500	250	130
1,350	610	200	500	500	250	135
1,400	640	200	500	500	250	140
1,450	670	200	500	500	250	145
1,500	700	200	500	500	250	150
1,550	730	200	500	500	250	155
1,600	760	200	500	500	250	160
1,650	790	200	500	500	250	165
1,700	820	200	500	500	250	170
1,750	850	200	500	500	250	175
1,800	880	200	500	500	250	180
1,850	910	200	500	500	250	185
1,900	940	200	500	500	250	190
1,950	970	200	500	500	250	195
2,000	1,000	200	500	500	250	200
2,050	1,030	200	500	500	250	205

a. Solve GDP = $G + I + G + X$ to compute the equilibrium level of GDP for the open economy. The equilibrium level of GDP or GDP* = \$___.

b. Record the values assumed by the following variables at GDP*:
    (1) I = \$__
    (2) S = \$__
    (3) $T - G$ = \$__
    (4) $Im - Ex$ = \$__

When the economy is at equilibrium, investment should again be equal to all saving. Just as we added government saving in the last problem, we must, in addition, include foreign saving here. A positive figure for foreign saving will occur when imports are greater that exports. ("Foreign saving" means that U.S. buyers are spending more on foreign goods and services than foreigners are spending on U.S. products.) So, we need to include the *Im—Ex* term above as part of saving.

c. At GDP* the sum of private saving, government saving, and foreign saving is \$___; this (**matches / falls short of / exceeds**) investment at GDP*.

d. If this economy were closed, and thus exports and imports were both zero, then equilibrium GDP would be \$___.

e. Opening the economy according to the data provided in Table 30-1 therefore (**increases / has no effect on / decreases**) GDP by ___ percent.

Opening an economy can distort the Keynesian multipliers because the level of imports can change with the level of domestic economic activity; and if imports change while exports hold constant, then net exports must change.

One measure of the sensitivity of imports to GDP is the *marginal propensity to impost (Mpm)*. Given any change in GDP, the *Mpm* is defined as the ratio of the resulting change in imports to the change in GDP.

   f.   The import schedule displayed in Table 30-1 exhibits a marginal propensity to import of ___.

Given any marginal propensity to import, the expenditure multiplier for a change in government spending and/or a change in domestic investment is no longer 1/*MPS*. It is, instead:

$$\frac{1}{(MPS + Mpm)}$$

   g.   As long as the *Mpm* is greater than zero, the open-economy multiplier is (**larger than / equal to / smaller than**) the closed-economy multiplier.

Changes in either investment or government spending therefore have a smaller effect on GDP in an open economy than in a closed economy. Why? Because any stimulus that might be created by an increase in investment or government spending in an open economy is partially vented abroad.

   h.   Compute the marginal propensity to consume exhibited by the consumption function in Table 30-1; *MPC* equals ___.

   i.   The closed-economy multiplier would then be ___, but the open-economy multiplier is ___.

2.   Use Table 30-1 to answer the following questions.

   a.   Suppose that investment increases by $250 billion. If the economy were *closed*, you would expect GDP to (**increase by / hold steady at / decrease by**) $___.

   b.   In the *open* economy illustrated in Table 30-1, though, GDP should (**increase by / stay the same at / fall by**) $___.

   c.   Verify your second calculation using the investment equals saving approach:

      (1) GDP** = $___.
      (2) *I* = $___.
      (3) *S* = $___.
      (4) *T - G* = $___.
      (5) *Im - Ex* = $___.

   d.   Suppose that the trading partner of the economy depicted in Table 30-1 follows a "beggar thy neighbor" trade policy by prohibiting our economy's exporting of any product; i.e., let *x* fall to $0. Equilibrium CDP would (**rise / fall**) to $___.

   e.   Now suppose that a change in the exchange rate makes imports more expensive, causing exports to rise by $100 and the import schedule to fall by $30 at every

level of GDP. The economy's currency must, therefore, have (**appreciated / depreciated**). Equilibrium GDP would (**rise / fall**).

3.   This problem is based on Table 30-1 in the text. Table 30-2 here is identical to the one in the text, *except* exports have been changed from 250 to 350.

Table 30-2: Output Determination with Trade

(1) Initial GDP	(2) Domestic Demand C+I+G	(3) Exports Ex	(4) Imports Im	(5) Net Exports X=Ex-Im	(6) Total Spending C+I+G+X
4100	4000	350	410	___	___
3800	3800	350	380	___	___
3500	3600	350	350	___	___
3200	3400	350	320	___	___
2900	3200	350	290	___	___

   a.   Complete columns (5) and (6) in the table and estimate the new equilibrium of GDP in the economy. (Your answer at this point may not be exact because the GDP numbers in the table always change by 300. The exact answer lies in between two of the numbers.) GDP is (approximately) equal to $___.

   b.   The *MPC* = ___.

   c.   The *Mpm* = ___.

   d.   The open-economy expenditure multiplier = ___.

   e.   The change in exports was 100. If you multiply that change by the open-economy multiplier, you get $___, which is precisely the change in GDP! The new equilibrium level of GDP is $___.

   f.   Figure 30-2 from the text is reproduced here as Figure 30-1. Add the new spending line to this diagram.

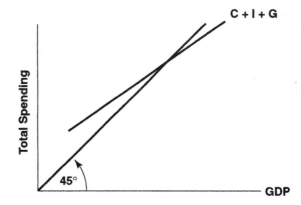

Figure 30-1

B. Interdependence in the Global Economy

4.   Figure 30-2 illustrates the relationship between saving and investment in a closed economy. Recall that *S* includes total private saving by households and businesses, and public

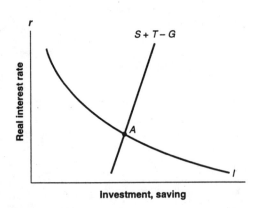

Figure 30-2: Saving and Investment in the Closed Economy

saving is the difference between government tax receipts (T) and expenditures (G). The economy begins at equilibrium at point *A*. Suppose now, other things held constant, that the government increases taxes.

  a.   As a result, the government budget deficit should **(increase / decrease / remain the same)**.

  b.   Draw a new line in Figure 30-2 which includes the change in taxes.

  c.   At the new equilibrium point in the economy, the real interest rate is **(lower / higher / unchanged)** and the level of investment spending in the economy has **(decreased / increased / remained the same)**.

  d.   Why do you think the government decided to raise taxes in the first place?

5.   Figure 30-3 shows the relationship between saving and investment in an open economy, which is too little to influence the world interest rate, r^W. Recall that an open economy has alternative sources of investment and alternative outlets for saving. Initially, total national savings equals

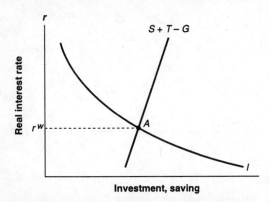

Figure 30-3: Saving and Investment in an Open Economy

total national investment and the   economy is at equilibrium at point A.

  a.   Suppose there is an increase in national frugality and the savings rate increases. Illustrate this change on the diagram. Label the new line S-S.

  b.   As a result domestic interest rates will (**increase / decrease/ remain unchanged**) relative to the world rate, and foreign investment will (**increase / decrease/ remain unchanged**).

  c.   In turn, the domestic currency will (**appreciate / depreciate / remain the same**) in value, and exports will (**increase / decrease / remain unchanged**).

  d.   Suppose instead, that world interest rates increase relative to rates in the domestic economy. As a result, domestic investment will (**increase / decrease / remain unchanged**) and domestic interest rates will (**increase / decrease / remain unchanged**).

  e.   This will lead to a/an (**increase / decrease / no change**) in domestic saving. Since people are saving (**more / less / the same**), spending will (**decrease / increase / remain the same**) and the domestic currency will (**appreciate / depreciate / remain the same**) in value.

  f.   Finally, net exports and foreign investment will (**increase / decrease / remain unchanged**) and equilibrium will be restored.

  g.   Illustrate the changes that occur in Figure 30-3.

C. International Economic Issues at Century's End

6.   One of the most significant problems of international finance in the early 1980s was the overvalued U.S. dollar.

  a.   The dollar was estimated by some to have been (**10 / 25 / 50**) percent overvalued from 1981 into 1984.

  b.   The scenario that produced this overvaluation began with the (**tight / loose**) monetary policy and (**stimulative / contractionary**) fiscal policy of the Reagan administration that drove real interest rates in the United States (**up / down**).

  c.   Foreign investment therefore flowed (**into / out of**) the United States, (increasing / decreasing) the demand for dollars and thus causing the dollar to (**appreciate / depreciate**) in money markets all around the world.

  d.   Exports from the United States therefore became (**more / less**) expensive, while imports from abroad became (**more / less**) costly.

  e.   Net exports (**expanded / contracted**) by nearly (**$50 / $140 / $250**) billion, as a result, and created an enormous (**deficit / surplus**) in the current account.

  f.   This discrepancy was, though, almost canceled by a (**deficit / surplus**) in the capital account, so the overvaluation persisted and drove interest rates abroad (**up / down**).

  g.   The result was a tendency for foreign economies to move into (**recession / boom**), and (**depressed / overex-**

tended) export- and import-competing industries called for (**free trade / protection and subsidy**) in the United States.

7. In a global economy, higher interest rates in one country may have a series of effects on its neighbors.

   a. As interest rates in Germany increase, Germany will attract (**more / less**) foreign financial resources from the United States.

   b. This will lead to (**an appreciation / a depreciation**) of the dollar.

   c. As a result, both exports and GDP in the United States should (**increase / decrease**).

   d. At the same time, the higher interest rates in Germany should cause interest rates in the United States to go (**up / down**), since financial resources may be leaving (**the United States / Germany**).

   e. Consequently, investment spending and GDP in the United States would go (**down / up**).

   f. In conclusion, the effect of higher interest rates in Germany on the U.S. economy is (**ambiguous / clear cut**).

8. Figure 30-4 illustrates the relationship between industry, productivity and globalization.

   a. List two ways in which domestic industries are exposed to the world leaders in their industry.

      (1) _____

      (2) _____

   b. According to Figure 30-4 there is (**a positive / a negative / no**) relationship between the degree of globalization and productivity in an industry.

VIII. DISCUSSION QUESTIONS

Answer the following questions, making sure that you can explain the work you did to arrive at the answers.

1. Explain why the slope of the total spending line is flatter in an open economy than a closed economy.
2. Take another look at Figure 30-3 in your textbook. What caused the large drop in real net exports in the early 1980s, their recovery in the late 1980s and early 1990s, and their decline since then?
3. Explain the relationship between the savings rate in a country and the investment rate. Differentiate between the short and long run in your answer.
4. What has happened to competitiveness and productivity in the U.S. economy in the last 10 years?
5. Discuss some of the economic considerations that must be addressed before Europe can act as a truly unified single economy.

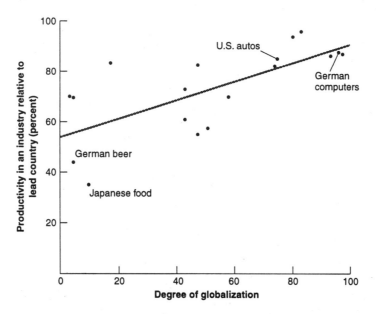

Figure 30-4 Exposure to Leading Technologies Improves Relative Productivity

The globalization index measures the extent to which an industry is exposed to the world leader in that industry either through free and unprotected trade or through transplants from the leader country. When industries are exposed, as were U.S. automakers and German computer manufacturers, they must compete vigorously to survive and they therefore close the gap with the leading country. When domestic industry is protected, as were German beer and Japanese food producers, competition is weak and relative productivity is low. [Source: McKinsey Global Institute, *Manufacturing Productivity* (Washington, D.C., 1993).]

IX. ANSWERS TO STUDY GUIDE QUESTIONS

III. Review of Key Concepts

7   Open economy
4   Closed economy
12 Net exports
10 Domestic demand
11 Marginal propensity to import
13 Net foreign investment
6   Depreciation
1   Appreciation
5   High capital mobility
8   Intangible capital
2   Overvalued currency
15 Competitiveness
14 Productivity
3   Globalization
9   Optimal currency area

VI. Multiple Choice Questions

1. E   2. E   3. A   4. B   5. B   6. E
7. C   8. A   9. C   10. D   11. A   12. E
13. E   14. C   15. D   16. A   17. A   18. D
19. E   20. D   21. B   22. C   23. D   24. D
25. B   26. C   27. E   28. E

VII. Problem Solving

1. a. GDP* = $1500
    b. (1) $I = \$200$
        (2) $S = \$300$
        (3) $T - G = \$0$
        (4) $m - e = -\$100$
    c. $200, matches
    d. $1250
    e. increases, 20
    f. 5/50 = 0.10
    g. smaller than
    h. 30/50 = 0.60, $C = 100 + (0.6 \yen DI)$
    i. 2.5, 2.0
2. a. increase by, $250 \times 2.5 = \$625$
    b. increase by, $250 \times 2.0 = \$500$
    c. (1) GDP** = $1500 + 500 = \$2000$
        (2) $I = \$200 + 250 = \$450$
        (3) $S = \$500$
        (4) $T - G = \$0$
        (5) $m - e = -\$50$
    d. fall, $250 \times 2 = \$500$, GDP*** = $2000 - 500 = \$1500$. To check your answer, compare investment with all savings: $I = \$450$, $S = \$300$, $T - G = \$0$, $m - e = \$150$
    e. depreciated, rise
3. a.

Table 30-2: Output Determination with Trade

(1) Initial GDP	(2) Domestic Demand C+I+G	(3) Exports Ex	(4) Imports Im	(5) Net Exports X=Ex-Im	(6) Total Spending C+I+G+X
4100	4000	350	410	-60	3940
3800	3800	350	380	-30	3770
3500	3600	350	350	0	3600
3200	3400	350	320	30	3430
2900	3200	350	290	60	3260

GDP is approximately equal to $3700.
    b. 0.67
    c. 0.10
    d. 1/0.43 = 2.33
    e. $233, $3733
    f.
4. a. decrease
    b.
    c. lower, increased
    d. Taxes were probably increased to fight inflation and slow the economy down. Alternatively, taxes may have been increased to finance a new spending project.
5. a.
    b. decrease, decrease
    c. depreciate, increase
    d. decrease, increase
    e. increase, more, decrease, depreciate
    f. increase
    g. The world interest rate is $r^{w'}$. BC indicates exports or foreign investment.
6. a. 50 percent
    b. tight, stimulative, up
    c. into, increasing, appreciate
    d. more, less
    e. contracted, $140, deficit
    f. surplus, up
    g. recession, depressed, protection and subsidy

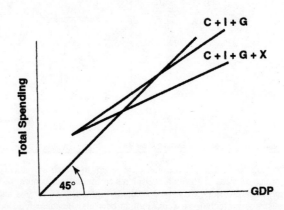

Figure 30-1

7. a. more
    b. a depreciation
    c. increase
    d. up, the United States
    e. down
    f. ambiguous
8. a (1) Through free trade
       (2) Through transplants from the leader country
    b. a positive

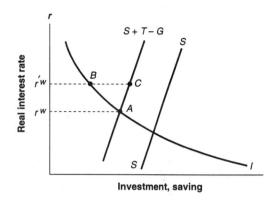

Figure 30-3: Saving and Investment in an Open Economy

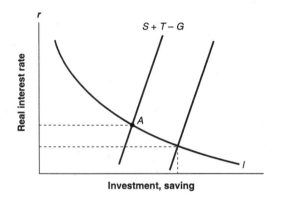

Figure 30-2 Saving and Investment in the Closed Economy

VIII. Discussion Questions

1. In an open economy, imports are related to the level of GDP in the domestic economy. When income increases, some of that income will be spent on foreign goods and services. Likewise, when income falls, domestic spending will not bear the full brunt of the decline since citizens will cut back on their imports as well. As a result, the slope of the spending line and the multiplier are reduced.

2. After the 1982 recession the U.S. economy experienced strong growth relative to most of its major trading partners. This led to an increase in U.S. imports and a decline in U.S. exports. Analysts also point out that an over-valuation of the dollar also contributed to the decline in net exports. The declining value of the dollar and the recovery of foreign economies helped decrease the trade deficit in the late 1980s and early 1990s. Since then, strong domestic growth and recessions abroad have contributed to the decline in net exports.

3. A major determinant of investment in a country is the productivity of capital in that country. As long as financial resources are globally mobile, they should flow into countries where the productivity of capital is the highest. If domestic savings are too low, relative to the rate of investment, the shortfall in savings can be compensated by an inflow of foreign financial capital. This appears to have happened, at least in the short run, in the United States.

4. Competitiveness depends upon the relative prices of goods and services in the marketplace. The competitiveness of U.S. products was diminished during the 1980s by the appreciation of the dollar. Productivity, which measures output per unit of inputs, increased during the 1980s. A study by the McKinsey Global Institute indicates that productivity in an industry is enhanced by free market competition and direct exposure to industry leaders. The productivity in domestic industries appears to be improved when foreign industry leaders produce in the domestic economy.

5. Once a common currency is agreed upon, a single central bank needs to be established to create a uniform monetary policy (no small matter). Price and wage rigidities need to be reduced so that markets can adjust to shocks and disturbances. For the same reason, labor needs to be mobile between regions and countries! Both interest rates and the inflation rate need to be similar among the nations—hopefully at a low level. In addition, participating countries need to control their federal government budget deficits and national debt. A great deal needs to be accomplished, but the payoff could be enormous!

CHAPTER

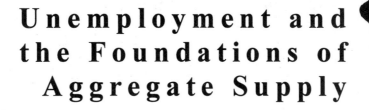

Unemployment and the Foundations of Aggregate Supply

I. CHAPTER OVERVIEW

Chapters 27 and 28 focused on economic growth and development. In the first part of this chapter we study the foundations of aggregate supply. While the concept of aggregate supply (AS) was first introduced in Chapter 20, after working through Chapter 31 you should have a deeper understanding of both national output and the underpinnings of economic growth. Obviously, without output there can be neither growth nor development.

Unemployment is, to some, a major macroeconomic issue, especially when growth and development stagnate. To others, it is simply a measure of how many people do not want to work at the going wage. Chapter 31 explores both of these points. A precise definition of unemployment is presented, in terms of both economic content and statistical expedience. The social costs of unemployment are also discussed at some length. Interpretation of the scope of involuntary *unemployment* will command some of our attention, as will the effect of unemployment on various subgroups of the population.

The focus here is not on macroeconomic policies that might help reduce unemployment by pushing output higher; those are the topics of past and future chapters. Instead, some of the micro-based sources of unemployment are discussed along with some of the policies that might be designed specifically to alleviate this problem.

II. LEARNING OBJECTIVES

After you have read Chapter 31 in your text and completed the exercises in this *Study Guide* chapter, you should be able to:

1. Describe the two fundamental sets of forces behind the **aggregate supply** schedule.
2. Explain the difference between the *classical* view and the *Keynesian* view of the aggregate supply curve.
3. Explain the difference between the short-run shape and the long-run shape of aggregate supply.
4. Understand the meaning, significance, and empirical validation of **Okun's Law**.
5. Understand the dimension of the economic and social consequences of unemployment: forgone GDP, forgone investment, increased stress, heightened illness, and lost skills.
6. Explain how the **unemployment rate** is calculated and discuss the problems associated with the measurement procedure.
7. Differentiate between **frictional, structural,** and **cyclical** unemployment.
8. Differentiate between **voluntary** and **involuntary** unemployment. Understand the role of wage stickiness in explaining the existence of involuntary unemployment.
9. Recognize that unemployment is distributed unevenly over different classifications of workers.
10. Understand the reasons for the recent increase in unemployment rates in Europe.

111. REVIEW OF KEY CONCEPTS

Match the following terms from column A with their definitions in column B.

A	B
__ Aggregate supply curve	1. Unemployment that exists because people seek employment at wage rates above the prevailing market wage rate.
__ Potential output	2. The number of people unemployed divided by the total labor force.
__ Employed	3. Highly organized and competitive market where price floats up or down to balance supply and demand.
__ Unemployed	4. Unemployment that exists because more people seek work at the prevailing market wage than there are jobs available.
__ Not in labor force	5. Unemployment due to a mismatch between the type of job openings and the skills or type of job seekers.

___ Labor force

___ Unemployment
rate

___ Frictional
unemployment

___ Structural
unemployment

___ Cyclical
unemployment

___ Voluntary
unemployment

___ Involuntary
unemployment

___ Non-clearing
labor market

___ Auction market

___ Administered
market

___ Okun's Law

6.   For every 2 percent shortfall between actual GDP and potential GDP, the unemployment rate increases by 1 percent.

7.   Maximum output that the economy can produce without triggering rising inflationary pressures.

8.   Unemployment due to a decline in the *overall* demand for labor. This corresponds to a downturn in the business cycle.

9.   Schedule showing the level of total national output that will be produced at each possible price level other things equal.

10. Labor market in which the *prevailing* market wage is different from the market-clearing equilibrium wage.

11. People who perform any paid work and those who have jobs but are absent due to illness, strikes, or vacation.

12. Market in which prices are set according to some scale or predetermined criteria.

13. Unemployment due to the movement of people between jobs or geographical locations (considered as *voluntary* unemployment, but do not put this number in that space).

14. Not working in the market place and not looking for work.

15. People who are not employed but who are actively seeking work or waiting to return to work.

16. Includes the employed and the unemployed.

IV. SUMMARY AND CHAPTER OUTLINE

This section summarizes the key concepts from the chapter.

A. The Foundations of Aggregate Supply

1.   The level of **aggregate supply** in the economy is determined by the economy's *potential* to produce goods and services and the behavior of wages and prices in the economy.

2.   The classical view of the world envisions wages and prices responding so quickly that an economy's performance is determined almost exclusively by its potential GDP. In the arena of aggregate supply and demand, this view is represented by a vertical aggregate supply curve at potential GDP.

3.   The Keynesian view of the world envisions wages and prices responding slowly such that an economy can be in equilibrium well below its potential. In terms of aggregate supply and demand, this view is represented by an aggregate supply curve which is horizontal or very flat, at least to the left of potential GDP.

B. Unemployment

1.   **Okun's Law** is one of the miracles of statistics—a simple rule that fits reality. It tells us that every 2 percent reduction in actual GDP relative to potential GDP causes unemployment to *increase* by 1 percentage point. If real GDP simply grows at the same rate as potential GDP (which does tend to increase marginally every year), the unemployment rate would remain unchanged.

2.   The unemployed (U) are people without jobs who are actively looking for work. The employed (E) are people who work for pay in the marketplace. The labor force (LF) includes both the employed and the unemployed (U + E). The unemployment rate (measured as a percent) is the proportion of people in the labor force who are unemployed.

$$\frac{\text{Unemployment}}{\text{rate}} = \frac{U}{U+E} \times 100\% = \frac{U}{\text{labor force}} \times 100\%$$

People who work outside the labor force (e.g., at home taking care of a family) are not in the labor force. As far as the government unemployment statistics are concerned, they are neither employed nor unemployed!

3.   Economists have, after decades of study, identified three different sources of unemployment. **Frictional unemployment**, caused by the usual turnover of some workers, reentry of others, and migration by still others, is the first major category. It is generally viewed as a lubricant for the overall labor market because it improves that market's economic efficiency. It can, however, be taken to an extreme. Teenagers typically change jobs frequently, and their unemployment rate is among the highest in the country.

Structural unemployment, meanwhile, arises from the contraction of some industries whose time has come and is now going. Even in a growing economy, some industries contract as the demand for their products contracts, and they must therefore lay workers off.

Finally, **cyclical unemployment** is the natural manifestation of the business cycle in the labor market; an overall contraction in business activity means that fewer people are required to produce the desired level of output, and employment must therefore fall.

4.   In another attempt to understand unemployment and the reasons behind it, economists have made a distinction between **voluntary unemployment** (people who choose not

to work at the offered wage) and **involuntary unemployment** (people who would gladly work at the offered wage but who cannot find work). Involuntary unemployment is the result of *sticky* wages which do not fall in response to excess supply in the labor market.

5.   Different types of unemployment suggest different policy responses. Frictional and/or voluntary unemployment is perhaps not very troublesome. Cyclical unemployment can be reduced by policies which smooth out the troughs of the business cycle. Structural unemployment requires more than that; the structurally unemployed frequently need retraining to acquire new skills.

6.   Recessions, and the unemployment they create, affect different types of people differently; but nearly every demographic category suffers. The unemployment rate in every category generally rises (the rise is often proportionate across categories), and the duration of unemployment for each rises as well.

7.   Recently, unemployment rates in Europe have surpassed those in the United States. The German economy is the strongest on the European continent and the other European countries have tied their monetary policies to those of Germany. The Bundesbank, Germany's central bank, has (logically) been more concerned with economic conditions in Germany than in Europe as a whole. The Bundesbank's efforts to control inflation in Germany after the 1990 reunification, thereby contributed to higher unemployment rates in the rest of Europe. Another factor contributing to European unemployment rates is an increase in the rate of structural unemployment as compared with the United States. This is related to both philosophical and actual differences in unemployment benefits between the U.S. and European nations.

V. HELPFUL HINTS

1.   To be counted as unemployed, you must be looking for work. Full-time students, household caregivers, and retirees are generally not looking for work—they are not unemployed, and they are not in the labor force. Once you look, though, you should be counted, and you become part of the labor force, whether you have a job or not.

2.   All part-time workers are counted as employed. These individuals may want to work longer hours *and* they may actually be seeking more work, but they are nonetheless counted as employed. To the extent that this problem exists, the unemployment rate is an *under*estimate of the true unemployment problem.

3.   The individuals without work may not know, nor particularly care, what category of unemployment they fall into. However, from a policy perspective it is very important to know whether people are frictionally, structurally, or cyclically unemployed. For example:

  a.   Frictionally unemployed workers do not need a

government-financed retraining program, but the structurally unemployed may.

  b.   Structurally unemployed workers will not be helped very much by a general tax cut, but the cyclically unemployed may be.

4.   The unemployment rate is an average measure of unemployment for the entire labor force. Pay careful attention to the different rates of unemployment for various subgroups of the population. The national unemployment rate may be 6 percent, but the individual seeking a job may consider his or her *personal* rate of unemployment to be 100 percent!

VI. MULTIPLE CHOICE QUESTIONS

These questions are organized by topic from the chapter outline. Choose the best answer from the options available.

A. The Foundations of Aggregate Supply

1.   Which of the following should be expected to shift the aggregate supply curve out to the right?
  a.   an increase in government spending.
  b.   a reduction in net exports.
  c.   a reduction in labor force participation.
  d.   the adoption of an improved production technology.
  e.   a reduction in the value of the dollar.

2.   Suppose that government spending rises. Assuming that the economy is operating at potential GDP, the long-run effect of this policy change should be:
  a.   higher prices with no change in output.
  b.   higher prices with higher output.
  c.   higher prices with lower output.
  d.   lower prices with higher output.
  e.   lower prices with no change in output.

3.   Which answer to question 2 would have been correct had that question referred to the short-run effect with output close to but beneath potential GDP?
  a.
  b.
  c.
  d.
  e.

4.   Which answer would have been correct if question 2 had referred to the long-run effect expected from the Keynesian perspective?
  a.
  b.
  c.
  d.
  e.

5.   Which answer to question 2 would have been correct had that question referred to the long-run effect expected from the classical perspective of improved technological productivity?

a.
b.
c.
d.
e.

6. Which answer to question 2 would have been correct if that question had referred to the long-run effect expected from the Keynesian perspective and there was a simultaneous contraction in available inputs?
   a.
   b.
   c.
   d.
   e.

7. In the short run, "sticky elements of cost" contribute to:
   a. firms' ability to make profits.
   b. a willingness to produce more as prices rise.
   c. the positive slope of the short-run aggregate supply curve.
   d. all of the above.
   e. none of the above.

B. Unemployment

8. According to Okun's Law, if potential GDP rose by 9 percent between 1979 and 1982 but actual GDP did *not* change, then unemployment should have climbed from 5.8 percent in 1979 to:
   a. 6.1 percent.
   b. 10.3 percent.
   c. 11.2 percent.
   d. 8.8 percent.
   e. 9.7 percent.

9. A computation of forgone output of the 1975-1984 period of high unemployment estimated the loss at:
   a. $2100 billion.
   b. $40 billion.
   c. $1333 billion.
   d. $3000 billion.
   e. an amount roughly comparable to the deadweight loss created by the abuse of market power.

10. Psychological studies indicate that being fired from a job is:
    a. a positive factor in an individual's labor-market experience.
    b. something everyone should experience, at least once.
    c. generally as upsetting as the death of a close friend.
    d. on average, neither harmful nor beneficial to most individuals.
    e. both **a** and **b**.

11. A person who is waiting to be recalled to a job would be classified as:
    a. employed.
    b. unemployed.
    c. not in the labor force.
    d. underemployed.
    e. a discouraged worker.

12. Which answer to question 11 would have been correct had that question asked for the classification of a person who was too sick to work?
    a.
    b.
    c.
    d.
    e.

13. Suppose a college graduate starts work in a family business the day after graduation. As a result, we should expect the unemployment rate:
    a. not to change at all.
    b. to go up slightly.
    c. to go down slightly.
    d. to fluctuate slightly, first up and then down.
    e. none of the above—more information is needed.

14. The existence of involuntary unemployment:
    a. depends critically on the Keynesian assumption that wages do not rise in response to excess demand in the labor market.
    b. depends critically upon the Keynesian assumption that wages do not fall in response to excess supply in the labor market.
    c. is accepted even by classical economists.
    d. plays a small role in the overall unemployment statistics.
    e. is described by none of the above.

15. Which of the following statements is accurate?
    a. Unemployment rates are generally different for different demographic categories of people.
    b. Unemployment rates tend to move in parallel as the economy proceeds through the business cycle.
    c. The duration of unemployment tends to increase during recession.
    d. An increase in frictional unemployment is not necessarily bad.
    e. All the above are accurate.

16. Someone who loses his or her job because of a recession would fall into the category of:
    a. frictionally unemployed.
    b. structurally unemployed.
    c. cyclically unemployed.
    d. permanently unemployed.
    e. none of the above.

17. Which of the answers to question 16 would have been correct if the person in question became unemployed because of the decline of the U.S. steel industry?
    a.
    b.
    c.
    d.
    e.

18. Which of the answers to question 16 would have been correct if the person in question had just entered the labor force but had not yet found a job?
    a.
    b.
    c.
    d.
    e.
19. The recent increase in unemployment rates in Europe can be attributed in part to:
    a. a world-wide recession.
    b. the elections in France and the political business cycle.
    c. the slow down in growth in the United States.
    d. the monetary policies of the Federal Reserve System.
    e. the monetary policies of the Bundesbank.

VII. PROBLEM SOLVING

The following problems are designed to help you apply the concepts that you learned in the chapter.

A. The Foundations of Aggregate Supply

1. a.   The two major determinants of aggregate supply are categorized as _____ and _____.
    b.   Table 31-1 lists a series of changes in economic circumstances. For each change, indicate in column (2)

which of the aggregate supply determinants from part **a** is involved.
    c.   Use column (3) to designate whether panel (*a*), (*b*), or (*c*) of Figure 31-1 best illustrates the effect graphically as a shift from *AS* to *AS'*, and explain your reasoning in column (4). The first row has been completed for your reference.
2.   A number of events are listed below. For each one, determine what a Keynesian and a classicist would expect in terms of the event's effect on GDP and prices. In the spaces provided in Table 31-2 indicate only the direction of the expected effect by recording **U** for "up," and **D** "down," **0** for "no change," and **?** for an ambiguous effect. It may be useful (as it always seems to be) to represent the event on a graph with the appropriate aggregate supply curve drawn beforehand. Use Figures 31-2 and 31-3 (top of next page) to help you with your answers.
    a.   An increase in potential output
    b.   A large increase in aggregate demand
    c.   An increase in interest rates that depresses aggregate demand
    d.   A dramatic reduction in foreign oil suppliers which increases oil prices, depresses the demand for domestic goods and services, and increases overall input prices
    e   A major catastrophe that reduces potential output by 25 percent

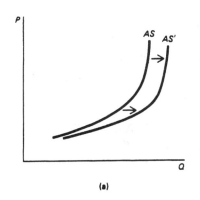

(a)

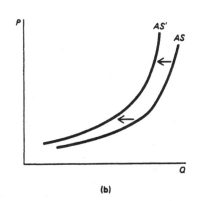

(b)

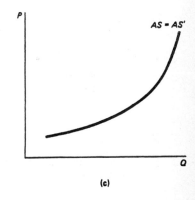

(c)

Figure 31-1

TABLE 31-1

	(1) Change	(2) AS Category	(3) Panel	(4) Explanation
a.	Population increase	Potential output	(*a*)	More inputs available
b.	Higher wage rates	____	____	_____
c.	Higher input prices	____	____	_____
d.	Improved production technology	____	____	_____
e.	Destructive earthquake	____	____	_____
f.	Increase in consumption	____	____	_____

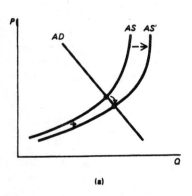 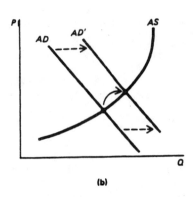 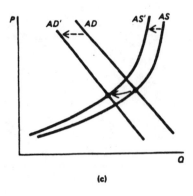

(a)　　　　　　　　(b)　　　　　　　　(c)

Figure 31-2

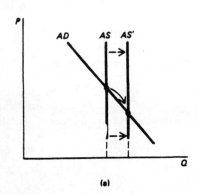 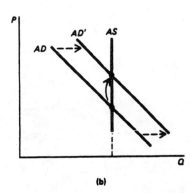 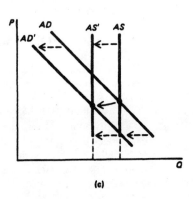

(a)　　　　　　　　(b)　　　　　　　　(c)

Figure 31-3

TABLE 31-2

Case	Keynesian		Classicist	
	Price	Output	Price	Output
a.	___	___	___	___
b.	___	___	___	___
c.	___	___	___	___
d.	___	___	___	___
e.	___	___	___	___

3. A "pure" Keynesian model might envision a perfectly horizontal aggregate supply curve, at least for GDP less than potential.

　　a. As a result, any stimulus to aggregate demand created in that region by an adjustment in either taxes or government spending produces (**no / a positive / a negative**) effect on GDP and (**no / a positive / a negative**) effect on prices.

　　b. At the other extreme, the classical view holds that stimulative fiscal policy will produce (**no / a positive / a negative**) effect on GDP and (**no / a positive / a negative**) effect on prices.

　　c. In between these two extremes, changes in fiscal policy can be expected to affect (**both prices and GDP / only GDP / only prices**).

4. Fill in the spaces provided in Table 31-3 with the expected effects of the policy changes indicated. As before, use **U** for "up," **D** for "down," and **0** for "no change." Take care to note that you must answer according to the specified philosophy.

TABLE 31-3

Case	Keynesian View		Classical View	
	Price	Output	Price	Output
a. Increase in taxes	___	___	___	___
b. Increase in government spending	___	___	___	___
c. Reduction in taxes	___	___	___	___
d. Reduction in government spending	___	___	___	___

B. Unemployment

5. Consider Table 31-4. Record your prediction for the actual unemployment rate for the years indicated by applying Okun's Law to the data provided. For purposes of comparison, the actual unemployment rates are listed in Table 31-5.

TABLE 31-4

Calendar Year	Annual Growth Rates		Unemployment Rates	
	Potential GDP (%)	Actual GDP (%)	Initial (%)	Predicted (%)
1960	3.3	2.2	5.5	___
1965	3.3	6.0	4.8	___
1970	3.3	- 0.2	3.5	___
1975	3.3	- 1.1	5.6	___
1980	2.7	- 1.3	7.5	___

TABLE 31-5

Year	Actual Unemployment Rate (%)
1960	6.7
1965	3.8
1970	4.9
1975	8.5
1980	9.8

6. To bring the unemployment rate down, actual GDP must grow faster than potential GDP. Assume that potential GDP is growing at 2 percent per year and the current rate of unemployment is 9 percent. Suppose Congress wants the unemployment rate to fall to 6 percent in three years. According to Okun's Law, what must be the annual growth rate in real actual GDP to achieve this objective? __

7. a. The unemployment rate is measured every month by sampling across (**10,000 / 30,000 / 60,000**) households to determine their employment status.

b. There are three categories: employed, unemployed, and not in the labor force. In the spaces provided, indicate the category into which the people in the following circumstances would be classified; designate employed by (**E**), unemployed by (**U**), and not in the labor force by (**N**):

___ (1) A laid-off autoworker looking for work

___ (2) A laid-off autoworker employed part-time at Wendy's

___ (3) A lawyer too sick to work

___ (4) An unemployed steelworker too discouraged to look for a job

___ (5) A full-time college student

___ (6) A car mechanic going to college at night

___ (7) An executive on leave to go to law school

___ (8) A housewife who works full-time at home

___ (9) A housewife who works part-time at the library

___ (10) A housewife who volunteers part-time at the library

8. For each person listed below, identify the type of unemployment that his or her situation most closely exemplifies; denote structural unemployment by (**S**), frictional unemployment by (**F**), and cyclical unemployment by (**C**):

___ a. A graduating senior who cannot find a job

___ b. A steelworker who loses his job because of permanent foreign competition

___ c. An autoworker who loses her job in a recession

___ d. An executive who loses her job because higher oil prices cause aggregate demand to fall

___ e. An executive who loses his job because higher oil prices cause the demand for oil burners to fall

___ f. A spouse who quits a job because the family has to move

___ g. A member of the garment union who loses his job because union wages refuse to fall when faced with inexpensive foreign labor

9. To explore the distinction between voluntary and involuntary unemployment, consider Figure 31-4. Curve SS represents a typical supply schedule for labor. Let the size of the available labor force be 1000 workers. Curve DD reflects the demand for labor.

a. The equilibrium wage is $___, with ___ people desiring and finding employment and ___ people choosing not to work.

b. Therefore, the number of people voluntarily unemployed is ___, and the number of people involuntarily unemployed is ___.

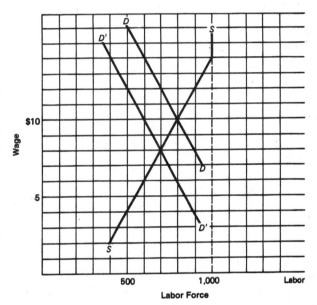

Figure 31-4

Suppose, however, that demand conditions deteriorate so that D'D' now represents the demand for labor.

c. If the wage could fall, then the new equilibrium wage would be $___, and total employment would be ___.

d. Total involuntary unemployment would be ___ and total voluntary unemployment would be ___.

e. If the wage could not fall, though, then total employment would be ___, total involuntary unemployment would be ___, and total voluntary unemployment would be ___.

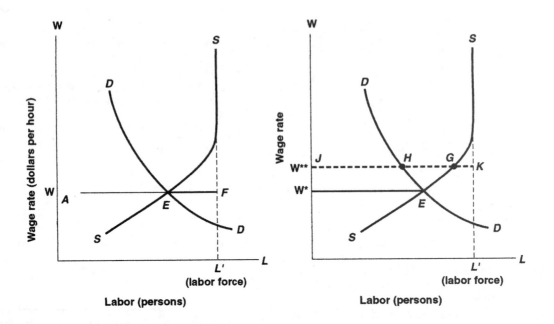

Figure 31-5

The important point to note from this exercise is that the existence of involuntary unemployment depends critically upon the inability of the wage to fall in response to excess supply in the labor market. Quite simply, no one who wanted to work at the going wage would be unable to do so if wages were sufficiently flexible.

f.   This (**is / is not**) to say that total employment would

not fall if the demand for labor were to fall; it is simply a statement about the ability of people to find a job if they want to work even at the lower wage.

10.   Figure 31-6 from the text is reproduced here as Figure 31-5.

a.   In the Flexible Wage diagram, the market clears at wage rate, w*. Using the letters on the diagram, the level of employment is _____. the level of unemployment is _____ and this is considered (**voluntary / involuntary**) unemployment.

b.   In diagram (b), the wage rate is stuck at w**. The level of employment is _____. The level of voluntary unemployment is _____. The level of involuntary unemployment is _____.

11.   a.   Figure 31-8 from the text is reproduced here as Figure 31-6. This diagram shows us that recession tends to increase the unemployment rate by increasing the percentage of those in the labor force who are unemployed because they have (**reentered the labor market / lost their jobs / left their jobs voluntarily / entered the labor market for the first time**).

b.   The unemployment rate in 1982 was ____ percent, and in 1999 it was ____ percent.

c.   According to Figure 31-6, there are four main reasons why people are unemployed. Complete Table 31-6 by calculating the percent of unemployment in each year that is attributable to each of the reasons. (The first entry is already filled in for 1982.)

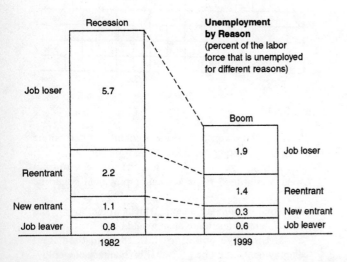

Figure 31-6

TABLE 31-6

Reason	Percent of Unemployment In 1982	Percent of Unemployment An 1999
Job loser	58.2	___
Reentrant	___	___
New entrant	___	___
Job leaver	___	___

d.   In which year are entrants (both "New" and "Re") a larger percent of the total? ___

e.   In which year are job losers a larger percent of the total? ___

f.   Reconcile your answers to parts **d** and **e** with what you have learned about patterns of unemployment during the business cycle.

g.   During which year are workers more likely to leave their jobs and search for something better? Please explain briefly.

VIII. DISCUSSION QUESTIONS

Answer the following questions, making sure that you can explain the work you did to arrive at the answers.

1.   Explain the differences between the short-run and long-run aggregate supply curves.

2.   Explain the differences between the Keynesian and classical views of aggregate supply.

IX. ANSWERS TO STUDY GUIDE QUESTIONS

III. Review of Key Concepts

9	Aggregate Supply Curve
7	Potential output
11	Employed
15	Unemployed
14	Not in labor force
16	Labor force
2	Unemployment rate
13	Frictional unemployment
5	Structural unemployment
8	Cyclical unemployment
1	Voluntary unemployment
4	Involuntary unemployment
10	Non-clearing labor market
3	Auction market
12	Administered market
6	Okun's Law

VI. Multiple Choice Questions

1. D   2. A   3. B   4. A   5. D   6. C
7. D   8. B   9. A   10. C   11. B   12. C
13. C   14. B   15. E   16. C   17. B   18. A
19. E

VII. Problem Solving

1.   a.   wages and costs, potential output
      b. and c.

TABLE 31-1

(1)	(2)	(3)	(4)
b.	wages and costs	(b)	increased costs shift AS left
c.	wages and costs	(b)	increased costs shift AS left
d.	potential output	(a)	greater Q at every price level
e.	potential output	(b)	inputs and resources are destroyed
f.	neither	(c)	consumption affects AD

2.

TABLE 31-2

Case	Keynesian Price	Keynesian Output	Classicist Price	Classicist Output
a.	D	U	D	U
b.	U	U	U	0
c.	D	D	D	0
d.	?	D	?	D
e.	U	D	U	D

3.   a.   a positive, no
      b.   no, a negative
      c.   both prices and GDP

4.

TABLE 31-3

Case		Keynesian View Price	Keynesian View Output	Classical View Price	Classical View Output
a.	Increase in taxes	0	D	D	0
b.	Increase in government spending	0	U	U	0
c.	Reduction in taxes	0	U	U	0
d.	Reduction in government spending	0	D	D	0

5.   6.05 percent, 3.45 percent, 5.25 percent, 7.80 percent, 9.50 percent

6.   4 percent (If actual GDP grows 2 percent faster than potential GDP for a year, the unemployment rate will fall 1 percent. If this continues for three years, the unemployment rate will fall 3 percent.)

7.   a.   60,000
      b.   (1) U
            (2) E
            (3) N

(4) N
(5) N
(6) E
(7) N
(8) N
(9) E
(10) N

8. a. F
   b. S
   c. C
   d. C
   e. S
   f. F
   g. S
9. a. $10, 800, 200
   b. 200, 0
   c. $8, 700
   d. 0, 300
   e. 600, 200, 200
   f. is not
10. a. AE, EF, voluntary
   b. JH, GK, HG
11. a. lost their jobs
   b. 9.8 percent, 4.2 percent
   c.

TABLE 31-6

Reason	Percent of Unemployment In 1982	Percent of Unemployment In 1999
Job loser	58.1	45.2
Reentrant	22.5	33.3
New entrant	11.2	7.1
Job leaver	8.2	14.3

d. 1999
e. 1982
f. In boom years more entrants are attracted into the labor force. In recession years the unemployment rate swells with job losers. The data in the table support this.
g. 1999. When the economy is growing, new job opportunities abound. Workers are more apt to leave their job and search for something better.

VIII. Discussion Questions

1. The short-run aggregate supply curve is positively sloped. Higher prices are associated with increases in output. In the long run, however, aggregate supply is determined by the level of potential output in the economy. Potential output is in turn determined by population growth, technological advances, and other factors, but not the price level. So the long run aggregate supply curve is drawn as a vertical line.

2. Keynes, focusing on the Great Depression, viewed the aggregate supply curve as a horizontal line. Keynes looked at the economy and saw massive unemployment and idle resources. Hence, in his eyes, it was possible for real GDP to increase substantially without exerting any upward pressure on prices. Classical economists, on the other hand, thought the economy would always adjust to any disturbances (like unemployment) and return to a position of long-run equilibrium. For them, the aggregate supply curve was a vertical line right at potential GDP.

CHAPTER 32

Ensuring Price Stability

I. CHAPTER OVERVIEW

We have seen the terms **inflation** and **price** mentioned in nearly every previous chapter in the text. It is time that we devoted an entire chapter to these critically important topics. Earlier chapters have concentrated your attention on how changes in economic conditions can move real GDP up or down. Previous chapters have conducted analyses of these changes in the context of both the aggregate supply-and-demand model of macroeconomics and the total-spending construction of the basic Keynesian model. Most recently, Okun's Law has been used to translate changes in actual real GDP into changes in employment. It is now time to extend our field of vision to include changes in the price level. It is time, more specifically, to ponder the sources and costs of inflation.

As you work through this material, you will confront some of the fundamental economic issues of today (and yesterday and tomorrow). Why has history recorded an occasional episode of hyperinflation, and what can be done to guard against its recurrence? What are the costs of inflation, and how are those costs dependent upon economic circumstance? Are there different strains of inflation that are more or less costly than others?

We also need to explore the purported tradeoff between unemployment and inflation. Is an economy forever doomed to endure high levels of one or the other, or can fiscal and monetary policies be employed to reduce the severity of the tradeoff? Can some type of incomes policies be employed to lower inflation without creating intolerable levels of unemployment? And, finally, can the cost of reducing inflation by enduring high levels of unemployment be assessed in either the short or the long run?

As you can see, we have a great deal of new ground to cover.

II. LEARNING OBJECTIVES

After you have read Chapter 32 in your text and completed the exercises in this *Study Guide* chapter, you should be able to:

1. Describe the means by which inflation is measured, and understand the distinction between **inflation, deflation**, and **disinflation.**
2. Outline the history of inflation for the United States (and, to some degree, for other countries).
3. Delineate the differences between *moderate* inflation, *galloping* inflation, and *hyper* inflation.
4. Relate how inflation has an economic impact on the distribution of wealth, the allocation of resources, and relative prices.
5. Decipher the distinction between **anticipated** and **unanticipated** inflation, on the one hand, and **balanced** and **unbalanced** inflation, on the other.
6. Differentiate between **inertial** inflation, **demand-pull** inflation, and **cost-push** inflation. Relate how shocks to an economy can contribute to increases in the inertial rate of inflation.
7. Illustrate each type of inflation in the context of graphs of aggregate supply and demand.
8. Outline the role of inertial inflation in short- and long-run **Phillips curves.**
9. Define the **nonaccelerating inflationary role of unemployment** (NAIRU) and explain some of the challenges of lowering it.
10. Use both the short-run and the long-run Phillips curve constructions to derive the spiral patterns of unemployment and inflation combinations that describe the U.S. experience of the 1970s, 1980s, and 1990s.

III. REVIEW OF KEY CONCEPTS

Match the following terms from column A with their definitions in column B.

A	B
__ Inflation	1. Nominal or money wage divided by consumer prices.
__ Price index	2. A way of adapting to inflation, in which wages, prices, and contracts are partially or wholly compensated for changes in the general price level.

___ Real wages

___ Inertial rate of inflation

___ Demand-pull inflation

___ Cost-push Inflation

___ Stagflation

___ Philips curve

___ Nonaccelerating inflationary rate of employment

___ Indexing

___ Disinflation

___ Income policies

3.   High inflation in periods of high unemployment.

4.   A reduction in the *rate of increase* in the price index.

5.   Occurs when *AD* rises more rapidly than the economy's productive potential.

6.   Represents the highest sustainable level of employment at which the inflation rate is stable—also corresponds to potential GDP.

7.   An increase in the general level of prices.

8.   Rate of inflation that is expected and built into contracts and informal arrangements—also called the core, underlying, or expected inflation rate.

9.   Government actions that attempt to moderate inflation by direct steps, whether by verbal persuasion, legal controls, or other incentives.

10   Inflation resulting from rising costs during periods of high unemployment and slack resource utilization—also known as supply-shock inflation.

11.   A weighted average of the prices of a group of goods and services.

12.   Illustrates the "tradeoff" theory of inflation—inflation is the tradeoff for low levels of unemployment.

IV. SUMMARY AND CHAPTER OUTLINE

This section summarizes the key concepts from the chapter.

A. Definition and Impact of Inflation

1.   Inflation is measured as a rate of change in a price index from one period (e.g., 1 year) to the next. If P_1 represents the price index recorded in year 1 and P_2 represents the index recorded in year 2, then inflation between years 1 and 2 would be:

$$\frac{P_2 - P_1}{P_1} \times 100\%$$

A major issue, therefore, is how the price indexes are constructed. *Inflation* is not an increase in all prices. It is, instead, an increase in the *general* level of prices and costs.

2.   Despite the occasional occurrence of hyperinflation throughout history, it is happy news that even galloping inflation does not necessarily accelerate to unmanageable levels in the absence of heroic anti-inflationary policy measures. Moderate inflation, meanwhile, does not seem to be terribly troublesome because relative prices are not terribly distorted, people do not spend too much time and energy in managing their money balances to avoid losses in real purchasing power, and inflationary expectations are fairly stable and predictable. Expectations of moderate inflation can, in fact, be self-fulfilling prophesies if they generate moderate wage settlements.

3.   Balanced inflation affects the prices of all goods or most goods (roughly) proportionately. Unbalanced inflation focuses its effects on specific goods or categories of goods. Unbalanced inflation can breed inefficiency by causing people to spend more time managing their money (recall the example of "shoe leather" costs from the chapter) and by eroding the informational content of prices.

4.   Anticipated inflation can be handled by advance planning. Unanticipated inflation can cause distributional effects (from lenders to borrowers, for example) which breed potentially costly hedging strategies. The most damaging inflation is unbalanced and unanticipated.

5.   Most economists agree that stable prices, with only a small annual increase, are the best prescription for an economy. While it may be politically unpopular to fight inflation (because of resulting unemployment), the central banks of most of the industrialized economies are ardent inflation fighters.

B. Modern Inflation Theory

1.   **Demand-pull** inflation is the result of excessive aggregate demand and can be associated with higher levels of real as well as nominal GDP. (If an economy is operating at its potential, then the increase in GDP will be entirely nominal.) **Cost-push** inflation is caused by increased costs which push aggregate supply up; it is therefore associated with lower levels of real GDP, so nominal GDP can be higher or lower.

2.   The "rate of inertial inflation" is a bit of a misnomer. The inflation rate itself has some inertia—that is, a tendency not to move unless pushed—only because prices have a consistent momentum that translates into a stable rate of increase. **Inertial inflation** therefore reflects an internal rate of inflation with which an economy seems to be comfortable. Individuals expect it, and the expectations tend to become self-fulfilling prophesies. Policies are written in acceptance of those expectations; interest rates include premiums to accommodate those expectations; transfer payments are amended to keep up with those expectations; and so on.

Either demand-pull or cost-push inflation can contribute to inertial inflation, the best reflection of which is a simultaneous shifting up of both the aggregate supply curve and the aggregate demand curve.

3. Due to the dynamic nature of the economy, we should never expect unemployment to be completely eradicated. People are constantly searching for new jobs (frictional) and new industries are continually emerging from the ashes of old ones (structural). In order to provide employment, at acceptable pay levels to *all* workers, the wage rate would have to higher than what many firms are otherwise willing to pay. The upward pressure on inflation in the economy would be very great. The NAIRU is the lowest sustainable unemployment rate. This is as low as we can realistically expect the unemployment rate to get without putting a great deal of upward pressure on the inflation rate in the economy. The evidence suggests that the declining influence of American labor unions and the strengthening of competition in the economy have contributed to a decline in the NAIRU during the last ten years.

4. The **Phillips curve** displays an inverse relationship between inflation and unemployment. It is anchored by the NAIRU and the inertial rate of inflation. Moving unemployment below (above) the NAIRU can, in particular, be expected to move inflation above (below) the inertial rate in the short run and contribute to an increase in the inertial rate in the long run. The short-run Phillips curve can, therefore, shift around.

5. Modern theory suggests that there is no tradeoff between inflation and unemployment in the long run; the long-run Phillips curve is therefore vertical at the NAIRU..

C. Dilemmas of Anti-inflation Policy

1. An economy can, to some extent, insulate itself from the effects of inflation. This insulation would, in particular, include such things as the indexing of transfer payments like social security and the adjustment of nominal interest rates to preserve the desired real rate. If 10 percent inflation were expected, for example, then banks that wanted a 3 percent real return would charge 13 percent.

2. To reduce the rate of inertial inflation, an economy must be willing to accept an economic slowdown and higher unemployment. It is estimated that it would cost the United States about $304 billion (in 1996 prices) in lost jobs and output to reduce the inflation rate by 1 percentage point. Other tools have been suggested: wage and price controls, voluntary guidelines, and tax-based incomes policies. No economy has yet managed to maintain full employment over long periods of time with completely stable prices and free markets.

V. HELPFUL HINTS

1. Sometimes it is not easy to identify the cause of inflation as being strictly demand-pull or cost-push. Suppose, for example, workers demand higher wages in response to an increase in prices that were caused by an increase in government spending. If we focus our attention solely on the workers, this *looks like* cost-push inflation. However, all labor is doing is reacting to higher prices—which were caused by an increase in aggregate demand. If we are going to point a finger here, we need to back up and collect all the relevant information. The root problem, in this example, would be demand-pull inflation, not cost-push inflation.

2. If you try to push the unemployment rate beneath the NAIRU without changing the underlying structure of the economy, you are asking for inflationary trouble.

3. The analysis of shifts in the AS and AD curves in Figure 32-7 (and others) assumes "...that potential output is constant...". You should realize that in a growing economy more real goods and services can be produced and that inflation does not *necessarily* have to increase.

4. Historically, wage and price controls have not done a very good job in reducing inflation. Wage and price controls are similar to placing a lid on a boiling kettle of soup to keep it from boiling over. However, nothing is done to lower the heat, or in this case, the inflationary pressure in the economy. Occasionally, when wage and price controls have been left on for a long period of time, they have been successful in lowering inflationary expectations and thereby inflationary pressure in an economy.

5. The United States was very fortunate in the last few years of the 1990s in that the economy enjoyed strong growth, low inflation and declining rates of unemployment. It would be foolish to assume that this type of experience has become the status quo.

VI. MULTIPLE CHOICE QUESTIONS

These questions are organized by topic from the chapter outline. Choose the best answer from the options available.

A Definition and Impact of Inflation

1. Prices in the United States:
   a. became less volatile after World War II.
   b. have stabilized since the Depression.
   c. have increased faster than wages since World War II.
   d. have increased since World War II only because of the Vietnam war and the OPEC oil shock.
   e. have done none of the above.

2. Moderate inflation:
   a. is characterized by less than double-digit rates.
   b. is characterized by relatively stable relative prices.
   c. does not seem to cause people to spend excessive amounts of time and energy managing their account balances.
   d. creates fairly stable inflationary expectations.
   e. is described by all the above.

3. Inflation can be associated with:
   a. only increasing nominal GDP.
   b. increasing or decreasing real GDP, depending upon its source.
   c. only decreasing real GDP.
   d. only increasing nominal GDP when the economy is operating past its full potential.
   e. none of the above.

4. One of the potential costs of unanticipated inflation is:
   a. the redistribution of wealth from lenders to debtors.
   b. the redistribution of wealth from debtors to lenders.
   c. the redistribution of wealth from the government to those who have helped finance its debt.
   d. the indexing of transfer payments to inflation.
   e. the elimination of variable-rate mortgages.

5. In response to increased risk of unanticipated inflation, you should expect:
   a. that banks will charge a risk premium on loans that they write.
   b. that socially motivated governments will try to index transfer payments to people on fixed incomes.
   c. that banks will try to sell variable-rate mortgages to home buyers.
   d. that people will look for assets whose value is insulated from inflation.
   e. all the above.

6. Unbalanced and unanticipated inflation usually causes:
   a. no harm.
   b. efficiency losses.
   c. the redistribution of income and wealth.
   d. efficiency losses accompanied by a redistribution of income and wealth.
   e. none of the above.

7. One potential cost of anticipated and balanced inflation is:
   a. the lost resources devoted to the management of money.
   b. the loss of employment required to raise the inflation rate for political reasons.
   c. the excessive inflation of real estate prices.
   d. a reduction in the flow of imports into the country.
   e. none of the above.

8. Which of the following is a hedge that you might expect to see an individual pursue in an effort to protect *only* himself or herself from the risk of unanticipated inflation?
   a. Negotiate a cost-of-living clause in a long-term wage contract.
   b. Accept an adjustable-rate mortgage whose rate of interest would be expected to climb with inflation.
   c. Offer a friend a loan at a rate of interest lower than that charged by a hedging bank.
   d. Start a new business with cash withdrawn from a variable-rate savings account.

   e. All the above.

9. Two common features associated with most hyperinflations are:
   a. a decline in the real demand for money and a decrease in the stability of relative prices.
   b. an increase in the real demand for money and a decrease in the stability of relative prices.
   c. a decline in the real demand for money and an increase in the stability of relative prices.
   d. an increase in the real demand for money and an increase in the stability of relative prices.
   e. an increase in the overall savings rate.

10. Recently, in the United States, the most vigorous and successful fighter of inflation has been:
    a. the President.
    b. Congress.
    c. the Federal Reserve.
    d. the Fortune 500 companies.
    e. organized labor.

11. The nonaccelerating inflationary rate of unemployment (NAIRU) is the rate at which:
    a. upward and downward forces on price and wage inflation are in balance.
    b. inflation is stable.
    c. the economy has the lowest level of unemployment that can be maintained without upward pressure on inflation.
    d. all of the above.
    e. choices **b.** and **c.** only.

B. Modern Inflation Theory

12. Inertial inflation:
    a. can usually be traced to some sort of supply-side price shock.
    b. can usually be traced to some sort of increase in aggregate demand.
    c. reflects an expected rate of inflation to which the major institutions of an economy have adjusted.
    d. is highly volatile and unpredictable at best.
    e. is described by none of the above.

13. Which answer to question 12 would have been correct had that question referred to cost-push inflation?
    a.
    b.
    c.
    d.
    e.

14. Which answer to question 12 would have been correct had that question referred to demand-pull inflation?
    a.
    b.
    c.
    d.
    e.

15. The inertial rate of inflation is reflected in:
    a. interest rates.
    b. wage settlements.
    c. long-term price specifications.
    d. federal macroeconomic-policy specifications.
    e. all the above.

16. In Figure 32-1 AS_1 and AS_2 represent aggregate supply curves for two successive years; AD_1 and AD_2 depict the corresponding aggregate demand curves. In moving from year 1 to year 2, then:
    a. prices climb in classic illustration of cost-push inflation.
    b. prices climb, illustrating inertial inflation.
    c. prices are stable, but real GDP falls.
    d. prices climb in illustration of demand-pull inflation.
    e. prices are stable, but real GDP falls in response to lower aggregate demand.

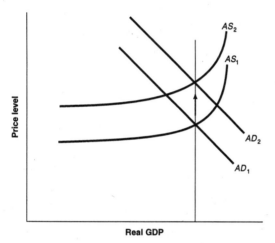

Figure 32-1

17. The occurrence of stagflation can be explained as a consequence of:
    a. a cost-push inflationary episode caused by a supply shock.
    b. an increase in the rate of inertial inflation.
    c. a demand-pull inflationary episode caused by an increase in aggregate demand.
    d. all the above.
    e. none of the above.

18. Which of the following correctly states the correlation between the NAIRU and the rate of inertial inflation?
    a. Any inertial rate of inflation can be maintained at the NAIRU as long as nonlabor costs increase at the same rate as labor costs.
    b. If the rate of unemployment falls below the NAIRU, then the inertial rate of inflation can be expected to climb, and vice versa.

c. If the rate of unemployment is driven above the NAIRU, then the inertial rate of inflation can be expected to climb, and vice versa.
    d. Answers **a** and **b**.
    e. Answers **a** and **c**.

Use Figure 32-2 to answer questions 19 through 22. Assume that the NAIRU is 5 percent and the dots correspond to successive years (i.e., dot 1 to year 1, dot 2 to year 2, etc.).

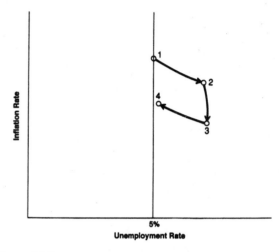

Figure 32-2

19. This figure illustrates:
    a. an austerity cycle.
    b. a boom cycle.
    c. a complete business cycle.
    d. a supply-side price shock.
    e. none of the above.

20. Movement from dot 1 to dot 2 represents:
    a. movement along a short-run Phillips curve toward higher levels of unemployment.
    b. a shift in Phillips curves caused by increased supplies.
    c. a shift in Phillips curves caused by a reduction in the rate of inertial inflation.
    d. movement along a short-term Phillips curve toward lower levels of unemployment.
    e. movement along a long-run Phillips curve.

21. Which answer to question 20 would have been correct had that question referred to movement from dot 2 to dot 3?
    a.
    b.
    c.
    d.
    e.

22. Which answer to question 20 would have been correct if the question had referred to movement from dot 3 to dot 4?

a.

b.

c.

d.

e.

C. Dilemmas of Anti-Inflation Policy

23. The short-run Phillips-curve tradeoff might be made more favorable by:

    a.   a policy that lowers export competition.

    b.   an incomes policy that reduces inertial inflation.

    c.   a trade policy that deflects inflationary price shocks from abroad.

    d.   a constitutional amendment mandating that the fraction of GDP supported by government spending cannot climb.

    e.   none of the above.

24. The point of an incomes policy would be to:

    a.   lower inertial inflation without the country's suffering a period of high unemployment.

    b.   simultaneously moderate the wage demands of as many workers as possible.

    c.   lower the inflationary expectations of bankers so that the inflationary premiums built into interest rates might fall.

    d.   facilitate a monetary policy designed to support a lower rate of inflation without creating unemployment.

    e.   do all the above.

25. Among the paradoxes of the study of inflation is (are):

    a.   that lower unemployment is sometimes associated with higher inflation and sometimes not.

    b.   that indexing an economy to protect it from inflation may tend to make inflation worse.

    c.   that inflationary expectations are sometimes as important as actual events in the economy.

    d.   that foreign trade is affected by rates of domestic inflation.

    e.   all the above.

26. Which of the following reasons have been suggested to explain the declining rates of both inflation and unemployment in the United States during the last years of the 20th century?

a.   An increase in low-cost labor-displacing equipment.

b.   Increased deregulation of the U.S. economy.

c.   A decrease in Cold War spending.

d.   All of the above.

e.   Only choices A and B.

VII. PROBLEM SOLVING

The following problems are designed to help you apply the concepts that you learned in the chapter.

A. Definition and Impact of Inflation

1. a.   Three "strains" of inflation, distinguished by their virulence, have been identified; they are:

         (1) _____

         (2) _____

         (3) _____

    b.   Use Figure 32-3 to diagnose the strain infecting the countries listed in Table 32-1 during the years indicated. For each country, record the approximate rate of inflation in the first blank and identify the strain in the second blank.

TABLE 32-1

Country/Period	Inflation Rate(%)	Strain
1. United States (1970s)	___	___
2. Germany (1922)	___	___
3. Germany (1923)	___	___
4. Israel (1980s)	___	___
5. Germany (1960s)	___	___
6. Brazil (1970s)	___	___
7. Poland (1923)	___	___

2. a.   Consider the impact of inflation on GDP. In the top three panels of Figure 32-4 (top of next page), draw a new aggregate demand curve that illustrates the potential that higher demand (caused by, e.g., higher government spending or a tax cut) might cause inflation; label the new curve *AD'*. In each case, *AS* indicates the aggregate supply curve and *AD* represents aggregate demand before the increase.

THREE KINDS OF INFLATION

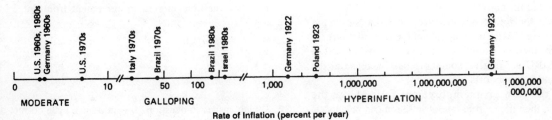

Figure 32-3

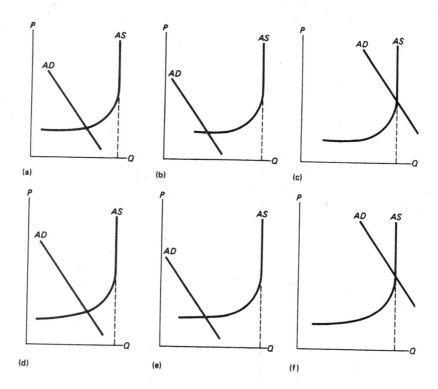

Figure 32-4

b.   It is clear from this analysis that higher aggregate demand is most likely to produce higher prices when equilibrium GDP is (**nearly equal to / far above / far below**) potential GDP.

c.   Moreover, real GDP can be expected to (**rise / fall / hold roughly constant**) when the economy is close to its potential.

d.   When a moderate increase in prices is expected, though, real GDP might actually (**fall / rise**).

e.   In the bottom three panels of Figure 32-4, draw the change in aggregate supply that might produce inflation as the result of an outside price shock that leaves potential GDP fixed. Label the new curve AS.

f.   In each of these three cases, real GDP can be expected to (**fall / rise**).

3.   Inflation can cause two general types of effects. The first surrounds the distribution of wealth and income; the second concerns the efficiency of relative prices and the information that they contain. The incidence of these effects can be expected to depend critically upon whether or not the inflation is (a) anticipated or unanticipated and (b) balanced or unbalanced.

   a.   If all prices were to increase at the same rate, for example, then the resulting inflation would be _____ .

   b.   If it were anticipated, then it (**would also / would not**) be expected to produce "winners and losers"

depending upon what types of goods and services individuals and institutions purchased or produced. There (**would / would not**), in other words, be troublesome efficiency losses created by the inflation.

c.   If the prices of some goods rose disproportionately, though, then some people could win at the expense of others. People might therefore spend (**more / less**) time managing their money to avoid becoming locked into a disadvantageous financial position.

d.   In extreme cases, the information contained in relative prices could be (**increased / distorted**), because they would change so quickly that nobody could keep up.

e.   If balanced inflation were fully anticipated, then there would be (**almost no / surely a significant**) cost. The inflation would look like a situation of stable prices to all those people who could insulate themselves from the rising prices.

f.   If the inflation were unanticipated, then (**distributional / governmental**) effects would be expected even if it were balanced. Borrowers would, for instance, be (**worse off / better off / unaffected**) because they could pay off their debts with currency that was (**worth more / worth less**). Lenders would experience the opposite effect. Under conditions of high inflationary risk, therefore, lenders can be expected to hedge against unanticipated inflation by charging (**higher / lower / exactly the same**) interest rates on new loans.

   g.   Alternatively, they might try to shift the risk to the borrower through (**policy lobbying / offering no loans / offering adjustable-rate loans**).

4.   Summarize the potential costs of inflation in Table 32-2 by noting the appropriate cost that is associated with each type of inflation. Put the letters of the costs below in the boxes of the table. (There is one letter for each box.)

Costs

a.   Essentially costless
b.   Efficiency losses
c.   Distribution losses
d.   Both efficiency and distribution losses

TABLE 32-2

	Balanced Inflation	*Unbalanced Inflation*
Anticipated inflation		
Unanticipated inflation		

5.   a.   Fill in the inflation rates for the years noted in the spaces provided in Table 32-3.
      b.   Notice that high rates of inflation seem to be associated with high nominal rates of interest. Do you see any evidence that interest rates in the 1980s included a hedge against the possibility that inflation might be unexpectedly rekindled? Explain.

TABLE 32-3

Year	CPI (1967 = 100)	Inflation Rate (%)	Nominal Rate of Interest (%)
1977	181.5		5.5
1978	195.4	——	7.6
1979	217.4	——	10.0
1980	246.8	——	11.4
1981	272.4	——	13.8
1982	289.1	——	11.1
1983	298.4	——	8.8
1984	312.7	——	9.8

B. Modern Inflation Theory

6.   Suppose that labor is the only productive factor available to an economy, so it has only one type of production cost—the wage paid to the labor that it employs. Let the rate of *growth of labor productivity* be zero, and assume that labor expects prices to climb over the next year at a rate of 5 percent. When the workers negotiate their contracts for that year, therefore, they should demand and receive a 5 percent raise.

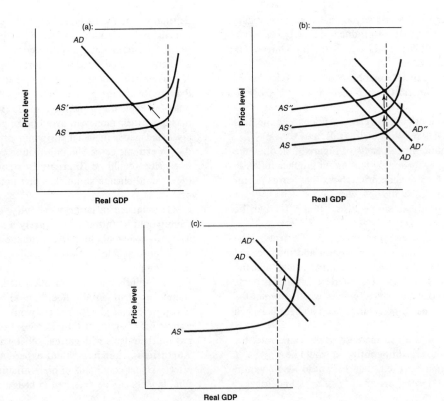

Figure 32-5

a. The result must be a ___ percent increase in the average cost of production, a ___ percent increase in the price of output, and thus a ___ percent rate of inflation. Labor's inflationary expectations are thereby (**exceeded / met exactly / found to be excessive**).

b. Reinforced by this experience, labor should be expected to demand a second-year raise that would be (**higher than / identical to / lower than**) the first-year raise that initiated the process. (**Declining / Stable / Increasing**) price and wage inflation could therefore be perpetuated in the absence of any outside shocks.

Now suppose that the economy suffers an outside shock that produces an additional 5 percent increase in prices, so the overall rate of inflation in year 2 is 10 percent.

c. If labor expects year 2 inflation to continue into year 3, then labor would demand a (**5 / 10 / 15**) percent raise for year 3, which would support a (**5 / 10 / 15**) percent wage-based inflation rate in year 3 even without another outside shock. Once again, labor's expectations would be (**exceeded / met exactly / found to be excessive**), and the inertial rate of inflation would have (**increased / remained the same / decreased**).

7. a. Use the spaces provided in the three panels of Figure 32-5 to label each one according to the type of inflation that it illustrates.

b. On the basis of that labeling, it appears that cost-push inflation can occur when the economy is operating (**above / at / below**) its potential and causes (**an increase / no change / a reduction**) in real GDP. (**Cost-push / Demand-pull**) inflation can, therefore, be identified as one source of stagflation.

Turn now to the specific sources of inflation, and indicate in the spaces provided which type of inflation each of the following is more likely to create; denote cost-push with a (**C**), demand-pull with a (**D**), and inertial inflation with an (**I**).

___ c. A dramatic increase in oil prices

___ d. A dramatic increase in government expenditure to finance a war

___ e. An automatic wage increase produced by a cost-of-living clause that follows inflation closely

___ f. A sudden reduction in the saving of an entire population

___ g. A wage settlement that increases the cost of steel

___ h. A sudden and large reduction in personal income taxes

8. Refer now to Figure 32-6. Three aggregate supply curves are drawn there. AS_1 represents aggregate supply at the beginning of year 1; AS_2 represents aggregate supply at the beginning of year 2; and AS_3 represents aggregate supply at the beginning of year 3. The corresponding aggregate demand curves are indicated by AD_1, AD_2, and AD_3.

a. The rate of inflation during year 1 was ___ percent, while the rate of inflation during year 2 was ___ percent.

b. If potential GDP were growing at 4 percent per year throughout this two-year period, then an initial unemployment rate of 6 percent would, by application of Okun's Law, (**grow / fall**) to ___ percent by the end of year 1 and ___ percent by the end of year 2.

9. The geometry of the Phillips curve can be displayed with either price inflation or wage inflation on the vertical axis.

a. This arithmetic equivalence can be supported by a markup theory of pricing that equates the difference between the rate of wage inflation and the rate of price inflation with (**a constant 2.45 percent / the rate of growth of labor productivity / the rate of conservation of scarce energy resources**).

b. On the basis of this equality, complete Table 32-4.

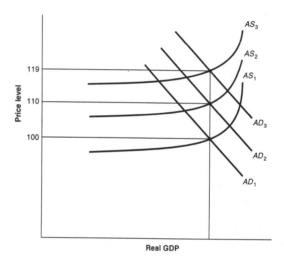

Figure 32-6

TABLE 32-4

Rate of Wage Inflation (%)	Rate of Price Inflation (%)	Rate of Productivity Growth (%)
10	___	3
10	___	0
3	5	___
___	7	2
___	150	0

10. Assume that labor has a long-term contract guaranteeing that wages will climb by 80 percent of the rate of increase of prices during the previous year. Using the equation that you employed in question 9 (namely, that the rate of inflation equals the rate of wage increase minus the rate of productivity growth), complete Table 32-5 given a constant rate of growth of labor productivity of 2 percent per year and an initial rate of price inflation of 20 percent.

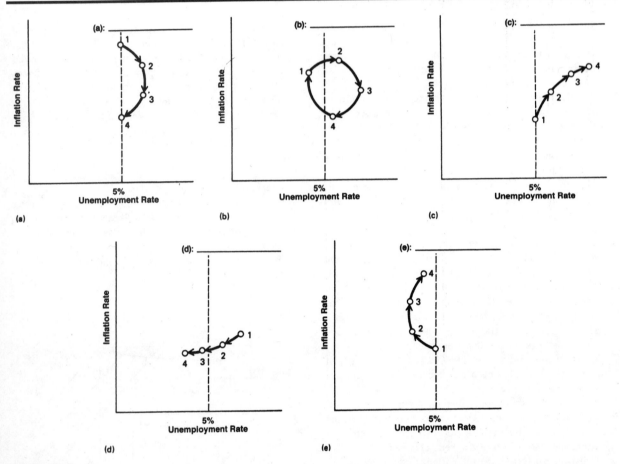

Figure 32-7

TABLE 32-5

Year	Rate of Wage Inflation (%)	Rate of Price Inflation (%)
1	—	—
2	—	—
3	—	—
4	—	—

The rate of growth of labor productivity acts as a buffer between wage and price inflation that can serve to reduce inertial inflation over periods of time in an economy. Note too that no indexation scheme in the world will allow the standard of living to increase faster than real output—the rate of growth of labor productivity in this question.

C. Dilemmas of Anti-inflation Policy

11. Figure 32-7 shows five panels. Among the set are portraits of *a boom cycle, an austerity cycle, an inflationary supply shock,* and *a complete political business cycle.* The 5 percent level indicates the NAIRU, and the dots along the schedules indicate years (dot 1 for year 1, dot 2 for year 2, etc.).

Match each cycle with its most appropriate portrait;

write your answers in the spaces provided in the graphs. (*Note*: One of your responses should be "none of the above.")

12. Suppose that a tiny economy has only 1000 workers. In the absence of any growth in their productivity and any outside shocks, suppose further that any wage increase that they all receive is passed on, percentage point for percentage point, to the price of the economy's output. Thus, an *X* percent rate of wage inflation would always be translated into an *X* percent rate of price inflation.

If these workers expected inflation to be 10 percent in the following year, then they would demand a 10 percent wage increase to preserve their real standard of living.

a.   That would, of course, produce a ___ percent rate of inflation.

If one worker were to realize that his or her wage increase would contribute to inflation, then he or she could, of course, refuse the offer of a 10 percent wage increase in the interest of being a "good citizen."

b.   In that case, his or her real wage would (**rise / fall / remain the same**) by ___ percent, but the rate of inflation would (**rise / fall dramatically / remain almost exactly the same**) because the increase in the average cost of production would (**rise / fall dramatically / fall ever so slightly**).

c. If, by way of contrast, everyone were to realize that his or her wage settlement contributed to inflation and were to demand only a 5 percent wage increase, then inflation would be __ percent. If all the workers agreed to no wage increase, in fact, then inflation in this simple economy would be __ percent.

The key, therefore, is to get everyone to adjust his or her wage demand at the same time. Nobody would want to be alone in taking a lower wage settlement, but something that would encourage everyone to react in the same moderating way could have a moderating effect on price inflation. It would be the purpose of an incomes policy to provide the incentive for everyone to behave in that way.

VIII. DISCUSSION QUESTIONS

Answer the following questions, making sure that you can explain the work you did to arrive at the answers.

1. Briefly discuss three features common to different hyperinflations.

2. Explain why workers should be more concerned about their real wage than their nominal wage. Are most labor contracts written in real or nominal terms?

3. Explain how wealth gets redistributed by inflation.

4. What reasons can be given for the recent decline in the NAIRU? What sorts of policies could be pursued to lower the NAIRU?

IX. ANSWERS TO STUDY GUIDE QUESTIONS

III. Review of Key Concepts

7	Inflation
11	Price index
1	Real wages
8	Inertial rate of inflation
5	Demand-pull inflation
10	Cost-push inflation
3	Stagflation
12	Phillips curve
6	Lowest sustainable unemployment rate
2	Indexing
4	Disinflation
9	Incomes policies

VI. Multiple Choice Questions

1. A   2. E   3. B   4. A   5. E   6. D
7. A   8. A   9. A   10. C   11. D   12. C
13. A   14. B   15. E   16. B   17. A   18. D
19. A   20. A   21. C   22. D   23. B   24. E
25. B   26. D

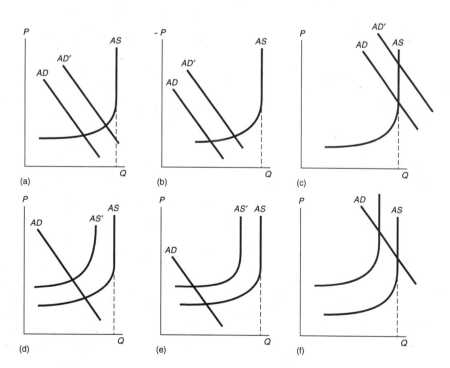

Figure 32-4

VII. Problem Soaring

1. a. (1) moderate inflation
        (2) galloping inflation
        (3) hyperinflation
    b.

TABLE 32-1

Country/Period	Inflation Rate (%)	Strain
1. United States (1970s)	7	moderate
2. Germany (1922)	≥ 1000	hyperinflation
3. Germany (1923)	≥ 1 bil	hyperinflation
4. Israel (1980s)	≥ 100	galloping
5. Germany (1960s)	4	moderate
6. Brazil (1970s)	45	galloping
7. Poland (1923)	≥ 1000	hyperinflation

2. a. See Figure 32-4 (top panels).
    b. nearly equal to
    c. hold roughly constant
    d. rise
    e. See Figure 32-4 (bottom panels).
    f. fall
3. a. balanced
    b. would not, would not
    c. more
    d. distorted
    e. almost no
    f. distributional, better off, worth less, higher
    g. offering adjustable-rate loans
4.

TABLE 32-2

	Balanced	Unbalanced
Anticipated	a	b
Unanticipated	c	d

5. a. The inflation rates in Table 32-3 are 7.7, 11.3, 13.5, 10.4, 6.1, 3.2, 4.8.
    b. Inflation decreased dramatically after 1981. Nevertheless, nominal (and real) rates of interest remained high in 1982, 1983, and 1984.
6. a. 5 percent, 5 percent, 5 percent, met exactly
    b. identical to, Stable
    c. 10 percent, 10 percent, met exactly, increased
7. a. (a) cost-push, (b) inertial, (c) demand-pull
    b. below, a reduction, cost-push
    c. C
    d. D
    e. I
    f. D
    g. C
    h. D
8. a. 10 percent, 8 percent (The price index in year 2 increased from 110 to 119.)
    b. grow, 8 percent, 10 percent

9. a. the rate of growth of labor productivity
    b. Reading across each row in Table 32-4, the entries are: 7, 10, -2, 9, 150

TABLE 32-4

Wage (%)	Price (%)	Growth (%)
10	7	3
10	10	0
3	5	-2
9	7	2
150	150	0

10.

TABLE 32-5

Year	Rate of Way Inflation (%)	Rate of Price Inflation (%)
1	16.0 (20 × .8)	14.0 (16 - 2)
2	11.2	9.2
3	7.4	5.4
4	4.3	2.3

11. (a) austerity cycle, (b) complete political business cycle, (c) inflationary supply shock, (d) none of the above, (e) boom cycle
12. a 10 percent
    b. fall, 10 percent, remain almost exactly the same, fall ever so slightly
    c. 5 percent, 0 percent

VIII. Discussion Questions

1. Three features common to all hyperinflations are: (1) a dramatic decrease in the demand for real money, (2) the distortion and destabilizing of relative prices, and (3) a very significant alteration of the distribution of wealth.
2. Workers should be concerned with the cost of purchasing goods and services. A nominal wage increase of 10 percent that just equals an inflation increase of 10 percent amounts to a real wage increase of 0 percent! Many workers have automatic cost-of-living adjustments (COLAs) written into their contracts. This was a much greater concern during the early 1980s when inflation was much higher.
3. Unanticipated inflation redistributes wealth from lenders to borrowers. People and institutions (like the government) that borrow get to pay back their loans with cheaper dollars. Furthermore, everyone with saving is made poorer by inflation. The purchasing power of saving is reduced as prices increase. The German hyperinflation wiped out decades of saving by German citizens.
4. Part of the decline in the NAIRU could be attributable to the decreased power of American labor unions. The percent of the labor force that is unionized has been declining and with it, the ability of organized labor to dictate conditions of employment or pay. Hence the wage rate has become more responsive to changes in the market place. As the economy has become more competitive, both internally and through

trade and immigration, there has been a further downward pressure on the NAIRU. Other factors that have contributed to the decrease in the NAIRU include the increased productivity of American workers and the expanding markets (for U.S. goods and services) in the former Soviet block countries. The end of the Cold War and increased deregulation of markets have also improved the efficiency of resource allocation in the U.S. economy.

To lower the NAIRU, efforts could be made to increase labor market information. Better information could bridge the gap between job seekers and job openings. Improved training programs could decrease structural unemployment and a general revamping of government programs could help send the appropriate signals to (potential) labor market participants.

CHAPTER 33

The Warring Schools of Macroeconomics

I. CHAPTER OVERVIEW

You have spent a great deal of time and effort learning the basics of the macroeconomy. You have learned about fiscal policy and the Keynesian multiplier. You have learned about monetary policy and the Federal Reserve System. You have learned about the problems of unemployment and inflation and the various approaches used to deal with each malady. While there is general agreement among economists about what the fundamental economic problems are, there is much less agreement about the methods used to solve these problems.

Economists, like other scientists, have different backgrounds and different philosophical points of view. Moreover, the solutions proposed by alternative schools of thought often seem to be more contradictory than supportive of each other. We must keep in mind that economics does not exist in a vacuum or in a controlled laboratory. Policymakers do not have the luxury of first trying new ideas out in a controlled environment to see how they will work.

In Chapter 33, Samuelson and Nordhaus discuss four different schools of economic thought. The first two, **classical economics** and **Keynesianism**, are already somewhat familiar to you. The other two—**monetarism,** and **the new classical economics**—are new, but they rely to a considerable extent on concepts you already know. For example, throughout the analysis, Samuelson and Nordhaus employ the aggregate demand-aggregate supply diagram and the Phillips curve to explain the differing philosophical viewpoints. Your general objective is to develop sufficient "feel" for the various schools of thought to enable you to sort through their similarities and differences.

II. LEARNING OBJECTIVES

After you have read Chapter 33 in your text and completed the exercises in this *Study Guide* chapter, you should be able to:

1. Understand that the **classical** view of the world envisions wages and prices responding so quickly that an economy's performance is determined almost exclusively by its potential GDP.

2. Understand that the **Keynesian** view of the world envisions wages and prices responding so slowly that an economy can be in equilibrium well below its potential.

3. Define the **income velocity of money** and explain its role in (a) the classical **quantity theory** and (b) the modern **monetarist** view of macroeconomic policy.

4. Relate the lessons of the **monetarist experiment** in the United States during the early 1980s.

5. Understand the **new classical economics** and the two fundamental assumptions of **rational expectations**.

6. Discuss the criticisms leveled against rational expectations, and explain the responses of its proponents to the criticisms.

7. Recall the "**Lucas critique**" of monetarist rules and the new classical economics.

8. Explain and appraise the **supply-side** approach to economic policy.

III. REVIEW OF KEY CONCEPTS

Match the following terms from column A with their definitions in column B.

A	B
__ Classical theory	1. People incorporate all available information into their economic decision making. Since they anticipate predictable changes in policy and react accordingly, the policy action itself becomes less effective.
__ Say's Law	2. Monetary policy that sets the growth of the money supply at a fixed rate and holds to that rate through *all* economic conditions.
__ Crowding out	3. Emphasizes *incentives* for people to work and save more, thereby stimulating output and lowering prices.
__ Keynesian revolution	4. Dramatic change in Fed operating procedure in the late 1970s in which the Fed decided to stop focusing on interest rates and

__ Monetarism

__ Income velocity of money

__ Quantity theory of money and prices

__ Monetary rule

__ Monetarist experiment

__ New classical macroeconomics

__ Rational-expectations hypothesis

__ Real business-cycle theory

__ Policy ineffectiveness theorem

__ Lucas critique

__ Adaptive expectations

__ Supply-side economics

instead endeavored to keep bank reserves and the money supply on predetermined growth paths.

5.   With rational expectations and flexible prices and wages, anticipated government policy can not affect real output or unemployment.

6.   Approach to macroeconomics that emphasizes the powerful self-correcting forces in an economy due primarily to flexible wages and prices.

7.   People form their expectations simply and mechanically on the basis of *past* information.

8.   When the government increases its spending, production of private goods and services will be displaced.

9.   Explains business cycles purely as shifts in *AS*, without any reference to monetary or other demand-side forces.

10. Supply creates its own demand—overproduction is impossible by its very nature.

11. Dramatic change in economic thought that overthrew the classical model of macroeconomics

12. Maintains that prices move in proportion with the supply of money.

13. Maintains that the money supply is the major determinant of short-run movements in nominal GDP and of long-run movements in prices.

14. Emphasizes the role of flexible wages and prices but adds rational expectations as well.

15. Measures the rate at which the stock of money turns over or gets spent relative to the total output of the nation—the ratio of nominal GDP to the stock of money.

16. Criticizes the fixed rules of monetarism and the new classical economics because people may change their behavior when policy changes.

IV. SUMMARY AND CHAPTER OUTLINE

This section summarizes the key concepts from the chapter.

A. Classical Stirrings and Keynesian Revolution

1.   The most straightforward summary of the classical model is contained in Say's Law of Markets, which states that "Supply creates its own demand," or, in today's jargon, "Supply rules!" Say lived in the very early 1800s, at the dawn of the industrial revolution, long before the birth of huge conglomerates and multinational corporations. In such a competitive economy with flexible wages and prices, resources were more likely to be allocated efficiently, and the income that labor earned could be used to purchase the commodities produced. Think back to the circular-flow model of the economy in which households provide the factors of production and get paid wages, rent, interest, and profits. Any unemployment that exists, in this view, is temporary and more *micro* in nature. Workers could be moving between jobs or may temporarily demand above-market wages.

There is no need or role for *macro*economic policy (either fiscal or monetary) here. The price flexibility that is assumed to exist in all markets assures us that full employment equilibrium will be achieved. Government interference in markets is unnecessary and impacts only the price level. Since the economy always adjusts and moves to full employment, the aggregate supply curve is a vertical line at potential GDP.

2.   The Keynesian view of the world envisions slower wage and price adjustments, so the aggregate supply curve is thought to be positively sloped, not vertical, in the short run. Demand-side manipulation is therefore expected to have some ability to alter the level of GDP in the short run. Potential GDP nonetheless defines a vertical long-run aggregate supply curve.

One critical difference in the classical-vs.-Keynesian debate concerns prolonged periods of unemployment. Keynesians think that *equilibrium* can be sustained, at least for a period of time, *below* potential GDP and thus can be accompanied by prolonged unemployment. (Remember, Keynes was writing during the Depression.) This is because wages and prices respond slowly to changes in the economy especially during contractions, when firms are initially reluctant to lower prices and workers are adamant about refusing cuts in pay. Of course, during recessions, when prices are falling, labor's *nominal* wage could be constant, but the *real wage* could be rising. The problem is that most workers are not immediately aware of this.

Note, too, Keynes's emphasis on demand. In the Keynesian view, fiscal and monetary policies can be both helpful *and* necessary to move an economy to its potential.

B. The Monetarist Approach

1. Keynes recognized the importance of money in an economy, but **monetarism** holds that the money supply is *the major* policy variable. Modern monetarism rests on three major propositions: (a) growth in the money supply is the primary determinant of growth in nominal GDP; (b) prices and wages are quite flexible in response to excess supply and/or demand; and (c) the private economy is very stable. Derived from these propositions are beliefs that (a) macroeconomic fluctuation is caused by erratic money-supply growth; (b) active government intervention into economies should be avoided; and (c) stable money growth at 3 to 5 percent per year should painlessly produce stable prices and steady growth.

2. The **income velocity of money** is one of two factors in the **quantity theory of money** which strict monetarists hold as constant. The other constant term is real GDP (equal to potential GDP, since the economy has flexible wages and prices and will thereby self-adjust to full employment). Velocity measures the rate at which the stock of money turns over or gets spent. It can be defined as:

$$V = \frac{GDP}{M} = \frac{PQ}{M}$$

This can be rewritten as follows:

$$VM = PQ$$
$$P = \frac{VM}{Q}$$
$$P = kM$$

where k, the ratio of V to Q, is constant, or close to it in the short run. In this view, money has no *real* effect on the economy, just on prices.

3. In what has come to be known as the *monetarist experiment* of the early 1980s, the Fed stopped focusing on interest rates and instead endeavored to keep the money supply on a predetermined and rigid growth path. The Fed's determined adherence to this tight policy taught us that (a) money *is* a powerful determinant of aggregate demand; (b) the money supply can be an effective inflation fighter; and (c) anti-inflationary tight monetary policy is not appreciably less expensive (in terms of lost employment and output) than alternative macroeconomic tools.

C. The New Classical Economics

1. The **new classical economics**, like the classicals and monetarists, emphasizes the role of flexible wages and prices; however, the new classical economics adds a new feature called **rational expectations**. Believers in rational expectations hold that individuals efficiently and rationally use the available information in the economy to form their expectations of what will happen in the future. It follows that any predictable policy designed to move aggregate demand will be ineffective because the people will see through its mechanism and undermine its power, thereby keeping GDP at its potential. For example, a tax cut would be undermined by people who, realizing that the resulting deficit would have to be repaid with interest in the future, would save the proceeds in anticipation of the "bill's coming due." It follows that policy rules are better than discretionary changes in policy.

2. Critics of the theory of rational expectations are particularly quick to point out that it falls short of explaining prolonged periods of unemployment.

3. The **real business cycle (RBC) theory** explains business cycles purely as shifts in aggregate supply. Shifts in the long run (vertical) aggregate supply curve are independent of aggregate demand and cause changes in real output. Proponents of the RBC theory argue that these shifts in AS may give the appearance of a short-run Phillips curve.

4. The efficiency-wage theory brings together parts of both classical and Keynesian economics. It suggests that firms may increase wages above market-clearing levels to increase labor productivity. As workers compete for these high paying jobs, the labor market may not clear and involuntary unemployment may persist over the long term. Proponents of the efficiency wage theory argue that long-term increases in the LSUR may be due to a worsening in efficiency-wage attributes in the labor market.

5. The **supply-side** policies of the Reagan and Thatcher administrations emphasized the role of fiscal policy in the determination of economic growth and aggregate supply. They provided *incentives,* in the form of large tax cuts to consumers and businesses, to encourage work effort, saving, and investment. They believed that even though tax rates were lower, the increased growth and output in the economy could generate more tax revenue.

The U.S. economy did grow strongly throughout most of the 1980s, but many economists believe the rightward shift in aggregate demand was much more influential than any changes in aggregate supply. Furthermore, national saving did not increase as the supply siders expected, and the tax cuts produced enormous federal budget deficits that still hinder the economy today.

V. HELPFUL HINTS

1. To keep track of these models, it might be helpful to view them in historical context.

   a. The classical model was developed at the beginning of the industrial revolution. England and other

European countries experienced unprecedented economic growth. It is no wonder that this model called for limited government involvement.

b.   Keynes was reacting to the Great Depression and the inability of the classical model to deal with it.

c.   Monetarism, the new classical economics, and supply-side economics are all related to the classical model. The inability of the Keynesian model to deal with some of the macroeconomic problems of the 1970s encouraged their development.

2.   The term *new classical* should not be confused with the "neoclassical growth model" of Chapter 27. They are different models and address different issues.

3.   Monetarists adhere to a fixed growth rate of the money supply. This is not because they view money as unimportant, but rather that they view discretionary swings in the money supply as potentially upsetting to the economy and doing more harm than good.

4.   In footnote number 5 in this chapter of your text, Samuelson and Nordhaus describe the aggregate demand curve, in the monetarist view, as a rectangular hyperbola. This is illustrated in panel *(a)* of Figure 33-5, which is reproduced here as Figure 33-1. Recall that the quantity theory of money states that $MV = PQ$. So if V is constant (as monetarists contend) and the money supply does not change, then the multiplication of P and Q must remain constant as well. This is precisely the characteristic of a rectangular hyperbola—the area underneath the curve is the same at every point along the curve. We have drawn two rectangles underneath the *AD* curve, one touching at point *A* and another touching at point *B*. The area of each rectangle (P times Q) is identical.

5.   During a year's time every dollar in the economy is spent several times. This is what velocity measures. Get a dollar bill out of your wallet (any denomination will do). On the front of the bill, to the left of the picture, is a capital letter (A through L). The letter, and the seal around it, represent one of the twelve Federal Reserve district banks. A is Boston, D is Cleveland, L is San Francisco, and so on. (You can find the name of the Federal Reserve Bank, written in small letters, in the seal around the big letter.) Chances are, most of the money in your wallet is from the Federal Reserve Bank(s) in your area. But some bills may be from far away. This money has changed hands many times before it found its way into your wallet. Money that is spent does not go out of circulation. It continues to be turned over and spent again.

VI. MULTIPLE CHOICE QUESTIONS

These questions are organized by topic from the chapter outline. Choose the best answer from the options available.

A. Classical Stirrings and Keynesian Revolution

1.   Which of the following economists would *not* be considered a classical economist?
a.   John Stuart Mill
b.   Adam Smith
c.   David Ricardo
d.   A. C. Pigou
e.   They are all considered classicals.

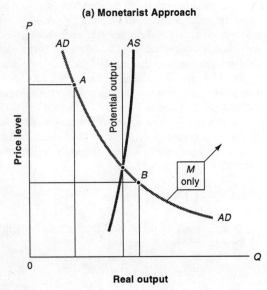

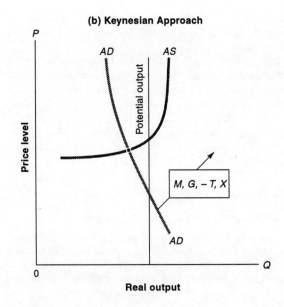

Figure 33-1

2. Why do classical economists contend that the economy moves to its long-run equilibrium position very quickly?
   a. People process information efficiently and respond accordingly.
   b. Fiscal policy is effective in shifting *AD*.
   c. The money supply grows at a fixed rate.
   d. Prices and wages are flexible.
   e. The short run is too short to be meaningful.

3. Stimulative aggregate demand policies are ineffective in the classical model because:
   a. the economy is already at, or moving toward, potential GDP.
   b. they will only drive up prices.
   c. unemployment is more of a short-run micro problem.
   d. all the above.
   e. none of the above.

4. Keynes argued that:
   a. the economy would tend to move toward potential GDP in the long run.
   b. the AS curve had shifted to the left during the Depression.
   c. demand creates its own supply.
   d. workers respond quickly to changes in *real* wages but not to changes in *nominal wages*.
   e. none of the above.

5. Keynesian economics contends that the aggregate supply curve:
   a. is flat or upward-sloping when output is beneath potential GDP.
   b. is flat or upward-sloping throughout.
   c. is no longer relevant—only aggregate demand matters.
   d. shifts when the unemployment rate changes.
   e. shifts when the government cuts taxes.

6. The retreat from Keynesianism came in part from:
   a. the failed fiscal policies of the 1960s.
   b. its overemphasis on incentives for long-run growth.
   c. Richard Nixon's declaring, "We are all Keynesians now."
   d. its overemphasis on wage and price rigidity.
   e. none of the above.

7. In terms of the saving-investment diagram used extensively in earlier chapters, the introduction of a tight-money policy by the Federal Reserve would be intended to:
   a. lower both the investment (*I*) and savings (*S*) schedules and hence lower GDP.
   b. raise the *I* schedule and hence lower GDP.
   c. raise the *I* schedule and hence raise GDP.
   d. lower the *S* schedule and hence raise GDP.
   e. lower the *I* schedule and hence lower GDP.

B. The Monetarist Approach

8. The quantity theory of money assumes:
   a. that both *V* and nominal GDP are fixed.
   b. that both *V* and real GDP are fixed.
   c. that only *V* is fixed.
   d. that *V* and the price level are fixed.
   e. none of the above.

9. Monetarists believe:
   a. that the money supply determines nominal GDP in the short run.
   b. that the money supply determines prices in the long run.
   c. that fiscal policy is essentially ineffective.
   d. that market forces will maintain potential GDP in the long run.
   e. all the above.

10. The lessons of the past decade or so include which of the following?
    a. Strict adherence to money-supply growth targets can cause substantial unemployment.
    b. The Keynesian view is entirely wrong.
    c. There is nothing to the monetarist view of the world that should be accepted in constructing policy.
    d. Money matters, but so does fiscal policy.
    e. Answers **a** and **d**.

11. The **monetary rule** states that:
    a. the economy should grow at a fixed rate and that money supply growth should vary.
    b. the money supply should grow at a fixed rate, regardless of economic conditions.
    c. monetary policy should maintain a steady trend in real interest rates.
    d. the Federal Reserve should fight inflation.
    e. the money supply should grow more during recessions.

12. The instability of velocity since the early 1980s can be attributed to:
    a. more active monetary policy.
    b. the increased volatility of interest rates.
    c. innovations in the financial sector.
    d. all of the above.
    e. choices A and C only.

C. The New Classical Economics

13. The basic assumptions of rational-expectations macroeconomics include:
    a. a presumption that people form their expectations about the future efficiently and rationally.
    b. a presumption that prices are extremely flexible in both directions.
    c. a presumption that wages are extremely flexible in both directions.
    d. all the above.
    e. answers **a** and **c** only.

14. It follows from the assumptions of rational expectations that:
    a. most unemployment is voluntary.
    b. monetary policy can work in the short run but not in the long run.

    c. fiscal policy can affect the long term but not the short term because of delays in Congress.
    d. any policy might work, independent of the circumstance.
    e. none of the above.

15. It follows from the assumptions of rational expectations that a reduction in taxes to stimulate consumption:
    a. would work as advertised.
    b. would not work unless accompanied by accommodating monetary policy.
    c. would not work because people would save their tax break in anticipation of future higher taxes.
    d. might work unless there were substantial leakages into foreign markets.
    e. would involve none of the above.

16. According to rational-expectations macroeconomics, the short-run Phillips curve is effectively:
    a. horizontal.
    b. positively sloped.
    c. vertical.
    d. negatively sloped.
    e. sloped in either direction depending upon conditions.

17. Should an economy attempt to move up its short-run Phillips curve to reduce unemployment below the natural rate, the rational-expectations macroeconomist would expect that:
    a. people would not be fooled, and only inflation would result.
    b. people would gradually find out that real wages had climbed, turning the curve vertical in the long run.
    c. the economy would be successful in the short term, but successful in the long term only if there were substantial economic growth.
    d. the natural rate would indeed fall as potential output grew.
    e. none of the above would occur.

18. The policy prescription of rational-expectations macroeconomics includes:
    a. the notion that stable monetary-policy rules should be constructed and followed so that changes in velocity can maintain equilibrium at potential GDP.
    b. the notion that discretionary policy should be avoided.
    c. the notion that no policy adjustment would be required to help an economy overcome an oil crisis like the one that occurred in 1973.
    d. the notion that fiscal policy should determine the mix of public and private spending once and for all and

then leave it alone.
    e. all the above.

19. The existence of periods of prolonged unemployment in our history does damage to:
    a. the expectations assumption of rational expectations only.
    b. the flexibility assumption of rational expectations only.
    c. both assumptions of the rational-expectations theory.
    d. either assumption of rational expectations, depending upon conditions.
    e. neither assumption of rational expectations in any circumstance.

20. Without the flexibility (of prices) assumption of rational expectations:
    a. periods of unemployment could exist.
    b. the short-run Phillips curve would have some negative slope.
    e. policy could be used to exploit the short-run trade-off.
    d. the expectations hypothesis would be damaged but not necessarily destroyed.
    e. all the above would be true.

21. A policy mix that targets monetary policy at inflation and fiscal policy at unemployment seems to produce high-consumption, low-investment, high-deficit economies because:
    a. monetary policy is ineffectual against inflation.
    b. fiscal stimulus during recession is never turned off, so monetary policy must become increasingly contractionary over time.
    c. Congress never writes fiscal policy fast enough to avoid a recession.
    d. fiscal policy is ineffective in stimulating an economy past its potential GDP.
    e. none of the above.

22. The real business cycle theory (RBC) theory:
    a. also relies on rational expectations and competitive markets.
    b. explains business cycles purely as shifts in AS.
    c. contends that changes in the unemployment rate are the result of movements in the LSUR.
    d. is all of the above.
    e. is none of the above.

23. The efficiency wage theory:
    a. argues that the LSUR should fall over time.
    b. offers an explanation for the rigidity of real wages and the existence of involuntary unemployment.
    c. says there is little or no relationship between wage rates and worker productivity.
    d. was first developed by Keynes.
    e. says more about production and output than it does about wages.

24. The Ricardian view of fiscal policy is that tax changes have no impact on consumption because:
   a. households save more when taxes are cut because they realize that the government will have to raise taxes at some point in the future to pay interest on the new loans.
   b. the government has a budget surplus.
   c. households save less when taxes are cut to take advantage of the multiplier and the growing economy.
   d. the benefits from trade and comparative advantage will pay for the tax cut.
   e. investment spending changes to counteract the effect of the tax cut.

25. Which of the following statements is (are) true about the supply-side program for economic recovery offered by the Reagan administration in 1981?
   a. It represented a retreat from belief in the Keynesian model of macroeconomic behavior.
   b. It represented a belief that price and wage adjustments would keep any recession short.
   c. It included a prescription to increase potential output that depended upon a nearly vertical aggregate supply curve to be most effective.
   d. It attempted to increase aggregate demand by cutting personal taxes.
   e. All the above.

26. The supply-side approach placed a key role on incentives to:
   a. save.
   b. invest.
   c. increase production.
   d. work harder.
   e. all the above.

27. The Reagan tax cuts of the 1980s:
   a. pushed the economy into recession.
   b. actually generated more revenue for the government via the Laffer curve.
   c. probably stimulated *AD* more than *AS*.
   d. all the above.
   e. none of the above.

VII. PROBLEM SOLVING

The following problems are designed to help you apply the concepts that you learned in the chapter.

A. Classical Stirrings and Keynesian Revolution

1. a. The (**Keynesian / classical**) view holds that a reduction in aggregate demand will cause no significant change in GDP because there will be (**an immediate / some / no significant**) change in prices. The appropriate representation of the aggregate supply curve is there-

fore (**a horizontal line up to / a positively sloped line through / a vertical line directly above**) potential output.
   b. The (**Keynesian / classical**) view, meanwhile, holds that a reduction in aggregate demand will cause GDP to fall by more than the initial reduction in demand because there will be (**an immediate / some / no significant**) change in prices. The appropriate representation of the aggregate supply curve is therefore (**a horizontal line up to / a positively sloped line up to / a vertical line directly above**) potential output.

2. The classical view of the economic world is based upon the immediate responsiveness of wages and prices to disequilibrium.
   a. Belief in this responsiveness was dealt a severe blow by (**World War II / the stock market crash of 1989 / the Great Depression**). A persistent unemployment rate of about (**8 / 25 / 34**) percent during the early 1930s cast serious doubt on the ability of wages to fall in response to excess supply of labor.
   b. Even today, there are many reasons why wages appear to be sticky. Use the spaces below to list four:
      (1) _____
      (2) _____
      (3) _____
      (4) _____
   c. If you accept the stickiness of wages, as the Keynesians do, then it (**is / is not**) possible for an equilibrium to persist with a high rate of unemployment of not only labor but also other productive resources. In response to this situation, a Keynesian would prescribe (**nothing, because nothing would work / some kind of increase in aggregate demand / some kind of reduction in aggregate demand**) that would increase equilibrium GDP and thus employment.
   d. A classicist, on the other hand, would prescribe (**nothing, because nothing is required / some sort of increase in aggregate demand / some sort of reduction in aggregate supply**); he or she would remark either that the existing unemployment was voluntary or that artificial barriers had prevented the necessary movement of wages down to equilibrium.
   e. List three possible policies that a Keynesian might suggest to reduce unemployment:
      (1) _____
      (2) _____
      (3) _____

B. The Monetarist Approach

3. a. In the space provided, record the quantity exchange equation: _____
   b. According to the quantity theory, velocity and real GDP are assumed to (**vary proportionately / be fixed /**

be wildly variable) . The result is, according to the theory, that any change in the money supply will be immediately reflected in (**prices / output / investment**) .

c.   While this is a reasonable explanation of (**recession / hyperinflation / hyperventilation**), it is not very satisfactory in a world where the velocity of money has been (**climbing / falling**) for the past three decades and was quite variable during the monetarist experiment of 1980, 1981, and much of 1982.

4.   The problems with the crude theory aside, modern monetarists use a fairly stable velocity and the quantity theory of money to make their points.   Rough stability in V is all that they need.   Their first proposition is that the money supply determines nominal GDP in the short run.

a.   If V is fixed in the short run, then any change in the money supply will, by application of the quantity equation, be (**proportionately / progressively**) reflected in (**nominal / real**) GDP.

Their second proposition is that the money supply determines prices in the long run.

b   This follows from the quantity theory and their (**conservative political views / belief in the market responsiveness of wages and prices / belief in the proportional variation of velocity**).   In particular, market clearing sets real GDP at its (**potential / nominal level / second-best optimum**), so the quantity equation has, in effect, (**one / two / three**) constants, namely _____.

Any change in the money supply is therefore translated directly and proportionately into changes in prices.

As an aside, the quantity theory of modern monetarism still precludes the effectiveness of fiscal policy to move GDP around.   There is, quite simply, no place in the quantity equation for either government spending or taxes to appear.   The only role for fiscal policy is to determine the mix of spending between the public and private sectors.

5.   a.   The Fed conducted a monetarist experiment in the United States from (give month and year) _____ through _____ under the leadership of Chairman Paul Volcker.

b.   During this time, it stopped trying to (**maintain stable interest rates / maintain stable exchange rates / keep bank reserves and the money supply moving along predetermined growth paths**) and focused instead on (**smoothing interest rates / maintaining stable exchange rates / keeping bank reserves and the money supply moving along predetermined grown paths**).

c.   Which of the following statements accurately describe the lessons that were learned from the experiment?   (Circle the number of each accurate statement.)

(1)   The velocity of money proved to be quite stable in the context of firm monetary policy.

(2)   The short-run effects of tight money were felt more in prices than they were in output.

(3)   Money proved to be relatively impotent in determining aggregate demand.

(4)   Firm monetary policy proved to be a relatively inexpensive way to curb high rates of inflation.

6.   The effectiveness of monetary policy is still an issue of current debate.   Consult Figure 33-2.   There, initial equilibrium is given by E and is supported by long-run aggregate supply AS and aggregate demand AD.   Short-run aggregate supply below equilibrium is shown by AS'.

a   A contraction in the money supply should move aggregate demand to (**AD'/ AD''**).   In the short run, output should fall to (**$0B$ / $C0$ / $F0$ / $0G$**) .   In the long run, prices should fall to (**$0B$ / $C0$ / $F0$ / $0G$**).

b.   Figure 33-2 can therefore be used to explain why the effect of monetary policy seems to be felt more in (**output / prices**) in the short run and more in (**output / prices**) in the long run.

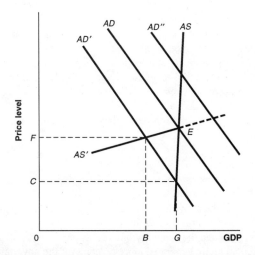

Figure 33-2

Because potential GDP determines output in the long run, contractionary monetary policy eventually produces lower prices (deflation); it does not, however, avoid the cost of recession required to initiate the process.

C. The New Classical Economics

7.   a.   Proponents of rational expectations contend that most unemployment that is observed during a recession is (**voluntary / involuntary**).

Consider the supply and demand curves representing a labor market in Figure 33-3; SS represents the supply curve, and DD represents an initial demand curve.

b.   The initial equilibrium wage is $___, with ___ people voluntarily unemployed; i.e., they (**are / are not**) willing to work for the going wage because (**it is too low / they cannot find a job**).

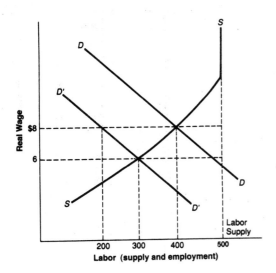

Figure 33-3

c. If the demand curve were to fall to *D'D'*, the rational expectations theory would predict (**an immediate / a slow and tortured**) decline in wage to $___ with ___ people in voluntary unemployment and ___ people in involuntary unemployment.

d. If the wage did not fall, though, ___ people would be employed and ___ people would be out of work— ___ voluntarily and ___ involuntarily.

8. The proponents of rational-expectations macroeconomics hold that the observed slope in the short-run Phillips curve is a source of confusion and misperception. Consult Figure 33-4.

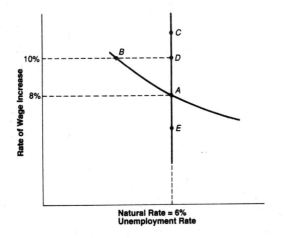

Figure 33-4

a. Beginning at point *A*, wage inflation would be running at ___ percent, with unemployment holding at the natural rate of 6 percent.

Suppose, now, that government policy is initiated to try to stimulate employment and to move the economy along the short-run Phillips curve to a point like *B*.

b. Rational-expectations theory states that unemployed workers would (**have to be offered higher real wage increases / have to be tricked into thinking that higher nominal wage increases were higher real wage increases**) to accomplish that move. Only if labor thought that the (**nominal / real**) wage were rising would the workers be attracted to work (remember, the 6 percent natural rate includes a significant number of voluntarily unemployed workers), and the unemployment rate would fall.

c. The ___ percent wage increase noted at point *B* would, according to the theory, be exhausted by price inflation, so the increase in the real wage would be (**the expected positive increment / zero / actually negative**) and those who were voluntarily unemployed at point *A* would again leave the labor force.

d. As a result, the economy would have moved to point (**C / D / E**) instead of *B*.

Even in the short run, because labor would not have been so fooled in the first place, the policy stimulus would have been vented entirely in price and wage inflation and not in the intended reduction in the rate of unemployment.

e. Notice that it (**does / does not**) matter whether the stimulus was the result of a change in monetary policy or of a change in fiscal policy; the result (**would / would not**) be the same in either case—a short-run Phillips curve that is unstable and, for policy purposes, effectively (**vertical / horizontal**) in the region directly above the (**current rate / natural rate**) of unemployment.

9. a. If employment policy can (a) always be immediately undone and (b) create bad things like inflation, then it follows that discretionary changes in policy (**should nonetheless be allowed because they are currently expected / should be discontinued because they are only harmful**).

b. The money supply should increase at a (**targeted / variable**) rate with the clear understanding that the velocity of money will (**be fixed / vary to preserve potential GDP**).

10. There were three components of the supply-side recovery packages enacted in the early 1980s by the Reagan administration in the United States and the Thatcher administration in the United Kingdom. The *first* was a retreat from the short-run stabilization prescriptions of the Keynesian model, turning attention instead to the medium run.

a. This retreat was supported by a view that the aggregate supply curve was (**nearly vertical / nearly horizontal**), so any recession that might be forthcoming would be short and mild.

b.   Prices and wages would, in particular, (**quickly / slowly**) adjust to any excess supply in the labor market, and changes in aggregate demand would have a (**large / little**) effect on GDP.

The *second* was a set of tax incentives designed to move the aggregate supply curve up and (mostly) out by boosting potential GDP, as shown in Figure 33-5 by the shift from *AS* to *AS'*. The effectiveness of this policy also depends upon the shape of the aggregate supply curve.

c.   If the curve were vertical (or if the economy were represented by AD_1 on the vertical portion of the *AS* curve), then the shift would be effective in (**increasing / reducing**) actual GDP and (**lowering / increasing**) prices.

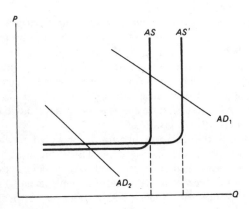

Figure 33-5

d.   If the curve were closer to horizontal in slope (or the economy represented by AD_2 on the flat portion of *AS)*, though, then the supply shift would (**increase actual GDP slightly / reduce actual GDP slightly / still be effective in increasing GDP substantially**) and actually (**increase / reduce**) prices.

Again, support for the program was based upon a rejection of either the sloped or the horizontal *AS* curve of the Keynesian model. The *third* arm of the program was a substantial reduction in personal income taxes.

e.   The effect of this reduction would, of course, influence (**aggregate demand / aggregate supply**). As such, one should have expected that it would increase actual GDP with stable prices only if the aggregate supply schedule were (**nearly vertical / nearly horizontal**).

f.   Otherwise, the increase in aggregate demand would be vented almost exclusively in (**prices / potential GDP / output**).

In supporting this final component of the program, it would appear that the architects of the program were not ready to discard Keynes entirely. Indeed, the Reagan people

campaigned for the program by comparing it favorably with the Kennedy round of tax cuts of the early 1960s—the beginning of the high point for Keynesians in making federal policy.

11. The record of the supply-side experiment in the United States ran its course over two presidential terms.

a.   The 1981 Economic Recovery Program forecast annual growth rates for real GDP averaging 4.8 percent into the middle of the 1980s; actual experience showed growth (**significantly greater than / roughly equal to / significantly lower than**) the forecast.

The program aimed to support this growth by significant increases in saving, investment, and productivity.

b.   Over the course of the 1980s, in fact, the national savings rate (**rose significantly / held roughly constant / fell significantly**) . Investment was (**down / stable / up**), and productivity growth (**increased / held steady / declined**).

The record was not what was hoped.

VIII. DISCUSSION QUESTIONS

Answer the following questions, making sure that you can explain the work you did to arrive at the answers.

1.   Why did velocity in the United States become unstable in the early 1980s? What did this do to monetarism?

2.   Both monetarists and new classical economists call for fixed rules. Explain the role of fixed rules in each of these approaches.

3.   Given your expanding knowledge of economics and the macroeconomy, which of the schools of thought presented in this chapter do you think is most accurate right now? Which is least accurate?

4.   Explain the major components of supply-side economic policy.

5.   Discuss the results of the Reagan supply-side package in the early 1980s.

IX. ANSWERS TO STUDY GUIDE QUESTIONS

III. Review of Key Concepts

6	Classical theory
10	Say's Law
8	Crowding out
11	Keynesian revolution
13	Monetarism
15	Income velocity of money
12	Quantity theory of money and prices
2	Monetary rule
4	Monetarist experiment
14	New classical macroeconomics
1	Rational expectations hypothesis
9	Real business-cycle theory

5   Policy ineffectiveness theorem
16 Lucas critique
7   Adaptive expectations
3   Supply-side economics

VI. Multiple Choice Questions

1. E   2. D   3. D   4. C   5. A   6. E
7. E   8. B   9. E   10. E 11. B 12. D
13. D 14. A 15. C 16. C 17. A 18. E
19. C 20. E 21. B 22. D 23. B 24. A
25. E 26. E 27. C

VII. Problem Solving

1. a. classical, an immediate, a vertical line directly above
   b. Keynesian, some, a positively sloped line up to
2. a the Great Depression, 25 percent
   b. (1) multiyear-labor contracts
      (2) cost-of-living clauses
      (3) regulated prices
      (4) inertia of prices charged by large corporations
   c. is, some kind of increase in aggregate demand
   d. nothing, because nothing is required
   e. (1) increase in government spending
      (2) a reduction in taxes
      (3) an increase in the money supply
3. a. $MV = PQ$
   b. be fixed, prices
   c. hyperinflation, climbing
4. a. proportionately, nominal
   b. belief in the market responsiveness of wages and prices, potential, two, potential real GDP and velocity
5. a. October 1979, August 1982
   b. maintain stable interest rates, keeping bank reserves and the money supply moving along predetermined growth paths
   c. All the statements are inaccurate.
6. a. AD', 0B, C0
   b. output, prices
7. a. voluntary
   b. $8, 100, are not, it is too low
   c. an immediate, $6, 200, 0
   d. 200, 300,100, 200
8. a. 8 percent
   b. have to be tricked into thinking that higher nominal wage increases were higher real wage increases, real

c. 10 percent, zero
d. D
e. does not, would, vertical, natural rate
9. a. should be discontinued because they are only harmful
   b. targeted, vary to preserve potential GDP
10. a. nearly vertical
    b. quickly, little
    c. increasing, lowering
    d. reduce actual GDP slightly, increase
    e. aggregate demand, nearly horizontal
    f. prices
11. a significantly lower than
    b. fell significantly, down, declined

VIII. Discussion Questions

1. The high interest rates of the early 1980s encouraged financial innovation and the development of interest-bearing checking accounts. These new types of money contributed to the instability of velocity. It has also been suggested that the heavy reliance on monetary policy itself contributed to the increase in velocity. The instability of velocity diminished the linkage between the money supply and both prices and nominal GDP.
2. The private economy is viewed as being stable, and government policies tend to destabilize the economy. Classical economists contend that changes in the money supply affect only prices, while monetarists believe that money affects output only after long and variable lags. Consequently, both approaches call for a fixed rate of growth of the money supply.
3. Your choice. Do a great job!
4. There were three components of the Reagan supply-side approach. First, more attention was paid to the medium run rather than the short run. Second, individuals were given incentives to work harder, produce more, and invest more. Third, it was expected that tax cuts would influence aggregate supply more than aggregate demand. The increased productivity and output generated by the tax cut was expected to increase tax revenues.
5. During the 1980s the savings rate fell and economic growth slowed. Investment and productivity growth both declined. While other factors may have contributed to these changes, supply siders certainly did not observe the results they had hoped for.

CHAPTER

Policies for Growth and Stability

34

I.   CHAPTER OVERVIEW

Several chapters ago, you were introduced to the concept of economic growth (see Chapters 27 and 28). Samuelson and Nordhaus discussed trends in economic growth and examined several economic growth models. You have also learned about the business cycle (Chapter 23) and the problems of unemployment (Chapter 31) and inflation (Chapter 32). By now, you can also appreciate that there are different points of view, especially among economists, about how to deal with these problems (Chapter 33).

With all of this new information in hand, the focus in this chapter becomes more applied and policy-oriented. In the first section we confront one of the most controversial political and economic issues of our time: what to do about the federal deficit and the resulting federal debt. Are deficits recession-induced or policy-induced? Are there burdens associated with deficits that should cause us to avoid them at all cost? In the second section, Samuelson and Nordhaus consider the possibility of fiscal and monetary policy working together to provide stability and growth for the economy. In the final section, the discussion moves to long-term growth alternatives for increasing saving, investment, and productivity.

II.   LEARNING OBJECTIVES

After you have read Chapter 34 in your text and completed the exercises in this *Study Guide* chapter, you should be able to:

1.   Differentiate between the **structural budget** and the **cyclical budget**.

2.   Explain why there is a **crowding out** (of investment) controversy and discuss its relationship to monetary policy.

3.   Differentiate between **internal** and **external** debt and discuss the relationship between the national debt and the foreign trade deficit.

4.   Explain how the burden of the debt is affected by efficiency losses from taxation and the potential displacement of capital.

5.   Evaluate the relative effectiveness of fiscal and monetary policy in managing aggregate demand.

6.   Form an educated opinion on the appropriate **fiscal-monetary mix** for the economy.

7.   Understand the two sides of the *fixed-rules-vs.-discretion* debate.

8.   Discuss the components of the **national savings rate** and explain the long-term decline in saving in the United States.

9.   Understand the 1993 Budget Act and discuss its main features.

10.   Point out the components of **total national wealth** and discuss the relative importance of each.

11.   Appreciate the spirit of enterprise in the U.S. market-based economy.

III.   REVIEW OF KEY CONCEPTS

Match the following terms from column A with their definitions in column B.

A	B
__ Budget	1. As the government debt grows, people will accumulate government debt instead of private capital, and the nation's private capital stock will be displaced by the public debt.
__ Budget surplus	2. Calculates what government revenue, expenditures, and deficit would be if the economy were operating at potential output.
__ Budget deficit	3. To pay interest on the debt, the government has to raise taxes; these tax increases may cause people to work less or save less.
__ Balanced budget	4. Shows, for a given year, the planned expenditures and expected revenues of the government.
__ Government debt	5. Debt owed by a nation to its own citizens—occurs when U.S.

__ Fiscal policy

__ Discretionary
fiscal policy

__ Structural
budget

__ Cyclical budget

__ Crowding out

__ Internal debt

__ External debt

__ Displacement
of capital

__ Distortion from
taxation

__ Demand
management

__ Fiscal-monetary
mix

__ Gramm-Rudman
Act

__ Pay-as-you-go
provision

__ Purchasing-
power parity

__ National savings
rate

citizens purchase U.S. government bonds.

6.   Increases in the structural
deficit through tax cuts or higher
government spending; tends to
raise interest rates and thereby
reduce investment.

7.   Occurs when expenditures
exceed taxes and other revenues.

8.   Government taxation and
spending programs.

9.   Consists of the total or accumulated borrowings by the government; also called the public
debt or national debt.

10.   Debt owed by a nation to foreigners; occurs when foreigners
buy U.S. government bonds.

11.   Occurs when expenditures
and all revenues are equal.

12.   Exists when the government
changes tax rates or spending
programs, usually by new
legislation.

13.   Difference between the actual
budget and the structural budget;
it measures the impact of the
business cycle on the budget.

14.   Occurs when all taxes and
other revenues exceed government expenditures for a year; this
does not happen very often in the
United States.

15.   Measure of technological
change which measures total output per unit of all inputs.

16.   Total saving, both private and
public, divided by net domestic
product (NDP).

17.   Includes reproducible capital,
capital, human capital, technological and land resources.

18.   Attempt to increase national
saving by raising rates of return
on saving or investment by lowering taxes on capital gains and
rewarding investment with investment tax credits.

19.   The use of monetary and l
fisca policy to set AD at a desired
level.

20.   Attempt to increase national
saving by lowering government
dissaving and private consump-

__ Income-oriented
approaches

__ Price-oriented
approaches

__ Total factor
productivity

__ Total national
wealth

tion while stimulating investment
through lower interest rates.

21.   Refers to the relative strength
of fiscal and monetary policies
and their effect on different
components of output.

22.   Requires that Congress find
the necessary revenue before
enacting any new spending
program.

23.   Method of comparing living
standards across countries by
measuring the quantity of goods
and services that can be purchased.

24.   Congressional bill passed in
1985 which required the deficit to
be reduced by a specified dollar
amount each year and balanced in
1991.

IV. SUMMARY AND CHAPTER OUTLINE

This section summarizes the key concepts from the chapter.

A. The Economic Consequences of the Debt

1.   The **structural** component of the budget reflects what
the government would collect and spend if it were operating
at its full potential; it is the measure which best indicates the
impact of fiscal policy. The **cyclical** component reflects the
effect of the business cycle on what the government collects
and spends. When the economy is contracting or in a recession, the government brings in less revenue in the form of
tax receipts and pays out more money in the form of transfer
programs (unemployment compensation, food stamps, etc.).
In such years, the *structural* budget may actually be balanced, but the *actual* budget may show a large deficit due to
the large cyclical component.

Cyclical budget + structural budget = actual budget

Actual budget deficits during these "lean" years are not
as problematic as deficits during years of prosperity and
strong economic growth. In "good" years, the positive cyclical component should help push the actual budget into a surplus. This did not happen during the mid- and late 1980s, a
period of prolonged economic growth in the United States.

2.   Concern is often voiced that government deficits **crowd
out** private investment by driving up interest rates. The strict
monetarist view of the world holds, in fact, that crowding out
would be immediate and complete as government dissaving
shrinks the pool of available financing. Others look for considerably less than 100 percent crowding out in the short run,
particularly during periods of recession.

3. The nominal level of the federal debt has been growing steadily since World War II, but it exploded in the early 1980s. The Reagan structural deficit, combined with enormous cyclical components, brought in government revenues more than $200 billion short of government expenditures.

4. There are some serious sources of concern about the burden of the debt which cannot be overlooked in using deficit spending as an arm of fiscal policy:

    a. the cost of servicing external debt

    b. the distortions created by the taxes required to service even internal debt

    c. the potential crowding out of capital

    d. the possibility that the cost of servicing the debt may grow more quickly than GDP

B. Stabilizing the Economy

1. In addition to determining the appropriate level of output and growth for an economy, policymakers must also decide on the mix or combination of fiscal and monetary tools to use to achieve their objectives. For example, to achieve high investment (which is crucial for economic growth), the budget should be balanced or have a surplus (to reduce the possibility of crowding out) and monetary policy should be expansionary or loose to help keep interest rates low. Until recently the federal government budget has been running very high deficits because the government either spends "too" much or taxes "too" little; and monetary policy has been relatively tight to keep the lid on inflation and inflationary expectations.

2. Fiscal policy, at least in the United States, has become the "weak sister" when it comes to providing stabilization for the economy. Timing lags delay the responsiveness of fiscal policy to swings in the business cycle. It takes time to recognize problems; debate appropriate policy responses and pass new legislation; and then (via the multiplier) affect output, employment, and income. By the time an impact is felt on the real side of the economy, it is possible for the economic winds to have changed and be blowing in the opposite direction. What was to have been a beneficial policy response may thus become the wrong medicine for the economy.

3. Monetary policy operates more indirectly than fiscal policy. It affects spending through changes in interest rates, credit conditions, and exchange rates. Nevertheless, the Fed has become a more effective stabilizer in the U.S. economy. Empirical results indicate that money-supply changes have their primary impact on output in the short run. Over longer time spans, more of the changes in nominal GDP are manifested instead in prices and wages.

C. Economic Prospects in the New Century

1. There are several reasons for the slowdown in labor productivity in the United States since the 1970s:

    a. Environmental and health-and-safety regulations may have improved the quality of life, but they have had no positive impact on output.

    b. Large increases in the cost of energy encouraged firms to substitute labor and capital for it. As these other factors of production were used more intensively, their productivities declined.

    c. There has been a large infusion of inexperienced, low-wage workers into the labor force.

2. The decline in the national savings rate in the United States has been dramatic. All the components of national saving—government saving, business saving, and personal saving—have declined.

3. The nation's total wealth includes more than just its tangible assets and physical capital. In today's global economy with highly mobile resources, a nation's labor force and the human capital embodied in it are key to long-term prosperity. Consider the economic recovery of Japan with few natural resources, small size, and a capital base that was in large part destroyed by the Second World War.

V. HELPFUL HINTS

1. The government *debt is* the *accumulation of* all the yearly budget *deficits*. Every year that the government does not balance its budget, it borrows more money to pay its bills. This adds to the debt. If the government runs $200-billion-dollar deficits five years in a row, this would add $1 trillion to the national debt! In fiscal year 1995, approximately 14 percent of the federal government's expenditures were being used just to pay the interest on the debt. These payments do nothing to reduce the principal of this huge loan, which grows larger every year.

2. When the government borrows money it sells bonds. The government sells bonds because it does not bring in enough revenue, in the form of taxes, to pay for all of the programs that it wants to fund. Selling bonds is viewed as politically less costly than raising taxes or cutting spending, which are the only alternatives to selling bonds.

3. As an economy grows, a nation can handle more debt. This is analogous to individuals' being able to borrow more money as their income increases. Unlike individuals, the federal government does not, at least at the present time, seem to worry about paying the debt off. Creditors do not seem to be overly concerned about this either. This is partly because the federal government, unlike an individual, does not age or become less inclined to saddle itself with long-term debt as the years go by. U.S. government bonds continue to be one of the safest, most secure instruments in the world for financial investment.

4. Whether or not crowding out occurs depends upon several different factors: slack in the economy, monetary policy, business expectations. Keep an open mind and try to collect

as much information as possible before forming an opinion about this important issue.

5. There exists a relationship between the national debt and the balance of trade.

    a. As the government borrows more, this puts upward pressure on interest rates.

    b. Higher interest rates in the United States attract more foreign financial capital.

    c. The demand for dollars increases in the foreign exchange markets. (The United States sells bonds to get money, i.e., *dollars*. If foreigners want to buy U.S. bonds, they must first convert their currency into dollars.)

    d. The dollar appreciates in value.

    e. U.S. goods and services become more expensive to foreigners, and foreign goods and services become cheaper to U.S. citizens.

    f. Result: The United States exports less and imports more.

6. Before screaming that the government is running up yet another budget deficit, look at the state of the economy. Is the business cycle in contraction or expansion? Look for the *structural* budget.

7. One of the key points of this chapter is that getting the economy to a particular place with regard to output, employment, and growth is only part of the problem. How the economy gets there and the mix of monetary and fiscal policy tools used are also very important.

8. The Federal Open Market Committee (the key policy-making arm of the Fed) meets often: 10 times a year. These frequent meetings in addition to the Fed's political independence—help it to maintain its focus.

9. While there is controversy over the appropriateness of establishing fixed budgets and policy rules for legislatures and the Fed, *credibility is* the most important attribute of an effective policy.

VI. MULTIPLE CHOICE QUESTIONS

These questions are organized by topic from the chapter outline. Choose the best answer from the options available.

A. The Economic Consequences of the Debt

1. Structural deficits:

    a. vary in size with changes in discretionary fiscal policy.

    b. vary in size with the sensitivity of the tax revenues to upswings in the economy.

    c. vary in size depending upon the latitude of welfare entitlement programs during economic downturns.

    d. are reflections of the degree of stimulus embodied in monetary policy.

    e. are described by none of the above.

2. Cyclical deficits are:

    a. the products of discretionary fiscal policy.

    b. the appropriate reflection of the stimulative character of fiscal policy.

    c. dependent in part on the unemployment rate in the economy.

    d. never considered until strict monetary control raises the specter of crowding out.

    e. none of the above.

3. A $50 billion increase in defense spending is an example of:

    a. monetary policy directed at reducing inflation.

    b. fiscal policy directed at reducing inflation.

    c. fiscal policy that would contribute directly to increasing the structural deficit.

    d. fiscal policy that would contribute directly to increasing the cyclical deficit.

    e. none of the above.

4. Which answer to question 3 would have been correct had that question asked about an increase in tax revenues caused by a growing economy and a progressive income tax?

    a.

    b.

    c.

    d.

    e.

5. Which answer to question 3 would have been correct if the question had asked about an open-market operation that purchased bonds?

    a.

    b.

    c.

    d.

    e.

6. Discretionary fiscal policy:

    a. is more effective in fighting recessions.

    b. is more effective in fighting inflation.

    c. would include a new public-works project.

    d. must be approved by Congress.

    e. none of the above.

7. Monetary policy:

    a. can typically be changed more quickly than fiscal policy.

    b. has a limited discretionary component.

    c. has been relatively ineffective in fighting inflation.

    d. is conducted by an independent agency and therefore cannot be coordinated with fiscal policy.

    e. is changed only when the Board of Governors meets.

8. Deficits in the early 1980s were enormous, in part because the Reagan administration:

    a. pursued expansionary fiscal policy with high structural deficits.

b. received the tight monetary policy that it wanted.

c. suffered a recession that enlarged the cyclical deficit.

d. did all the above.

e. did none of the above.

9. In the face of a stagnant economy, a government should:

a. spend more, tax less, and/or pursue a contractionary monetary policy.

b. spend less, tax less, and/or pursue an expansionary monetary policy.

c. spend more, tax less, and/or pursue an expansionary monetary policy.

d. spend less, tax more, and/or pursue an expansionary monetary policy.

e. do nothing and rely on the ability of the economy to rapidly return to potential GDP just as it did in the 1983 recovery.

10. The linkage between government spending that could lead to the crowding out of private investment is best outlined by a causal connection from spending growth to:

a. output growth, to an increase in the assets demand for money, and eventually to higher interest rates, which cause reduced investment.

b. output contraction, to an increase in the transactions demand for money, to a lower assets demand for money, and finally to lower interest rates, which encourage more investment.

c. output growth, to an increase in the transactions demand for money, to a lower assets demand for money, and finally to higher interest rates, which cause reduced investment.

d. output growth and to higher investment with higher transactions and assets demands for money.

e. none of the above.

11. Strict monetarists believe in a vertical aggregate supply schedule. They believe, as a result, that every increase in government spending of one dollar should cause private investment to fall by:

a. 50 cents.

b. 75 cents.

c. 90 cents.

d. $1.

e. none of the above.

12. Which of the following is a valid reason for being concerned about the size of the federal debt?

a. It has grown, in the recent past, as a proportion of GDP.

b. It has grown, in the recent past, so much that interest payments are growing faster than GDP.

c. High deficits may displace capital by distorting the financial markets.

d. The taxes required to pay the interest result in losses in efficiency.

e. All the above.

13. Which of the following statements about the relationship between the federal budget deficit and the government debt is true?

a. If the debt is getting smaller, the budget must have a surplus.

b. Large *cyclical budget* surpluses could reduce the debt.

c. Every single-year deficit adds more to the debt.

d. All these statements are true.

e. These statements are all false.

14. Internal debt:

a. is owed by a nation to its own citizens.

b. can result in efficiency losses due to the taxes required to pay the interest.

c. can redistribute wealth from taxpayers to bondholders.

d. is all of the above.

e. is just **a** and **b**.

15. A displacement of capital can occur when:

a. foreigners own more of the debt.

b. interest rates are rising.

c. people start to save less.

d. people accumulate more government bonds and less private capital.

e. all the above.

B. Stabilizing the Economy

16. To revive a lagging economy, the government can:

a. manage aggregate demand by raising monetary growth.

b. manage aggregate demand by cutting taxes.

c. manage aggregate demand by increasing the structural deficit.

d. both **a** and **b**.

e. all the above.

17. The *biggest* current impediment to effective fiscal policy is:

a. the size of the federal deficit.

b. tight monetary policy.

c. the foreign trade deficit.

d. disagreements between the White House and Congress.

e. the decline in labor productivity.

18. Other things held constant, when interest rates increase, this tends to:

a. decrease investment and decrease imports.

b. increase investment and increase imports.

c. decrease investment and decrease exports.

d. decrease investment and increase *net* exports.

e. decrease investment but have no predictable impact on trade.

19. How was the Reagan administration able to have a large defense buildup without inflation?

a.   The administration raised taxes to finance the increased expenditures on defense.

b.   An increase in personal saving financed the buildup.

c.   The administration's goal was helped by the Fed's tight-money policy.

d.   Wage and price controls were used to keep inflation down.

e.   Private investment was increasing and the subsequent economic growth helped finance the increased defense expenditures.

20. If policymakers are concerned about the low national savings rate they can:

a.   cut taxes and the growth rate of the money supply.

b.   raise taxes and interest rates.

c.   "tax and spend" more.

d.   remove interest rate ceilings.

e.   balance the budget.

21. Partly as a result of the Gramm-Rudman bill:

a.   the government debt decreased.

b.   the federal government deficit decreased.

c.   the national savings rate increased.

d.   all the above.

e.   none of the above.

22. Data from the Federal Reserve Board and the U.S. Department of Commerce indicate that:

a.   the variability of M_2 exceeds the variability of M_1.

b.   the variability of M_1 is less than the variability of nominal GDP.

c.   nominal GDP is more variable than either measure of the money supply.

d.   a fixed monetary growth rule may not work.

e.   none of the above.

C. Economic Prospects in the New Century

23. During the past 15 years, which component of national saving has decreased the most?

a.   government saving.

b.   business saving.

c.   personal saving.

d.   They have all fallen by about the same amount.

e.   The data are not precise enough to measure this.

24. The decline in business saving is due primarily to:

a.   increased corporate mergers.

b.   the increase in multinational firms operating in the United States.

c.   the trade deficit.

d.   high real interest rates.

e.   the declining share of corporate profits in the total economy.

25. Which of the following has contributed to the decline in personal saving?

a.   the slowdown in the growth of incomes.

b.   declining imperfections in capital markets.

c.   the increase in government transfer programs.

d.   all the above.

e.   none of the above.

26. The 1993 Budget Act:

a.   hoped to eliminate the deficit by 1998.

b.   hoped to reduce the deficit by approximately $144 billion by 1998.

c.   continued the cycle of "tax and spend."

d.   was not passed by Congress

e.   none of the above.

27. In addition to reproducible capital, the country's total wealth includes:

a.   human capital.

b.   technological capital.

c.   renewable land resources.

d.   all the above.

e.   **a** and **b** only.

VII. PROBLEM SOLVING

The following problems are designed to help you apply the concepts that you learned in the chapter.

A. The Economic Consequences of the Debt

1.   In the spaces provided, record whether the following policies would affect the structural budget (**S**), the cyclical budget (**C**), or neither (**N**).

___ a.   A reduction of 25 percent in tax rates

___ b.   An increase in unemployment compensation during recession

___ c.   An increase of $50 billion in defense spending

___ d.   A reduction in social security tax rates

___ e.   An expansion of the money supply

___ f.   An expansion in tax receipts during an economic upswing

___ g.   A reduction in funding for Head Start and other welfare programs

2.   A number of changes in economic condition are listed in Table 34-1. In the spaces provided in the table, indicate the likely short-term effects of each change on the structural and cyclical deficits. Denote a reduction with (-), an increase with (+), and no change with (**0**).

TABLE 34-1

	Change In Condition or Policy	Structural Deficit	Cyclical Deficit
a.	A permanent tax cut	___	___
b.	A sharp increase in private investment	___	___
c.	Tighter monetary policy	___	___
d.	A corn blight	___	___
e.	An increase in welfare payments	___	___
f.	An increase in tax evasion	___	___

3. a. From 1979 through 1982, the actual budget deficit (**fell / rose**) in response to (**active fiscal policy / passive fiscal policy**). The result was actually (**an increase / a reduction**) in the (**structural / cyclical**) deficit that signaled (**more stimulative / no change in the degree of stimulus applied by / less stimulative**) fiscal policy.

b. In 1982, though, the supply-side tax cuts and the massive defense buildup of the Reagan administration came on line. The result was fiscal (**stimulus / contraction**), reflected by a dramatic increase in the (**structural / cyclical**) deficit. In fact, from 1982 through 1986 the cyclical deficit (**fell / rose**) while the structural deficit (**fell / rose**).

Numbers supporting your answers to these questions can be found in Table 34-2 (use this table to answer the questions that follow).

c. The federal government ran an actual deficit of $___ in 1986. This was up $___ from 1979 and $___ from 1982.

d. A deep recession in 1982 increased the cyclical deficit by $___ from 1979, but that increase fell to $___ by 1986.

e. The structural deficit, meanwhile, climbed by only $___ through 1982, but by $___ through 1986.

TABLE 34-2 The Source of Rising Federal Deficits

Deficit or Contributing Factor	Year		
	1979	1982	1986
A. Budget deficit:			
Actual	$16	$146	$204
Cyclical	0	91	26
Structural	16	55	178
B. Increase in budget deficit from 1979:			
Actual	0	130	188
Cyclical	0	91	26
Structural	0	39	162
C. Contributing factor:			
Decreased share of taxes	0	5	26
Increased share of defense	0	40	72
Increased transfer payments	0	58	44
Increased interest payments	0	31	64
Total, Contributing Factors	0	134	206

Source: U.S. Department of Commerce.

f. It is clear, therefore, that fiscal policy was (**stimulative / contractionary**) over the second period.

g. Under "Contributing Factors," it is important to note that higher interest payments added $___ to the actual deficit from 1979 through 1986.

Why? Certainly because the government borrowed a lot more money, but that is not the only reason. The federal government turns over the equivalent of its entire debt every three or four years; large increases in current interest rates can therefore have large effects on the cyclical deficit. Also notice that the combined effect of the listed contributing factors sums to more than the increase in the actual deficit (i.e., $206 billion, which is greater than $188 billion). How is that possible? Other items in the spending budget were slashed by the difference ($18 billion) .

4. Suppose, in the face of stagnation, the President wants to stimulate recovery without adjusting monetary policy.

a. You, as adviser to the President, should recommend a policy that would (**increase / decrease**) government spending and/or (**increase / decrease**) federal taxes.

b. The immediate result of your recommendation would be (**a reduction / an increase**) in the size of the (**structural / cyclical**) deficit.

c. If your policies were implemented and worked to stimulate recovery, the ultimate result would be (**a reduction / an increase**) in the (**structural / cyclical**) deficit.

d. To bring the actual deficit down, though, you would have to also recommend (**the eventual cancellation of the active policy / no further change**).

Facing the opposite problem, of course, you would recommend the opposite policies.

e. If you were free to suggest changes in monetary policy to support the stimulus package that you proposed above, though, you should recommend (**a reduction / an increase**) in the money supply, probably instituted by (**an open-market operation / a reduction in the reserve requirement / an increase in the discount rate**).

f. The desired result would be (**an increase / a decrease**) in investment because of (**higher / lower**) interest rates and perhaps induced investment (crowding in).

5. The Reagan Economic Recovery Program instituted in January 1981 called for (a) substantial cuts in personal taxes, (b) substantial cuts in business taxes, (c) substantial increases in defense spending, and (d) moderate cuts in social spending. President Reagan also asked the Fed to pursue fairly tight monetary policy.

a The ultimate result was (**stimulative / contractionary**) fiscal policy, reflected halfway through his first term by an increase in the (**cyclical / structural**) deficit but also by lower investment caused by high interest rates.

Some contend that the recession of 1982 was caused in large part by the high interest rates.

The Carter administration had tried to stimulate investment in the late 1970s by (a) increasing taxes, (b) maintaining government spending, and (c) encouraging expansionary monetary policy.

b. The idea was to (**increase / reduce**) the structural deficit and thereby (**increase / decrease**) public saving, lower interest rates, and promote investment.

Monetary policy turned out to be too tight, though, and investment did not climb.

c. Combined with the oil shock of the Iran-Iraq war, a recession developed because the change in the (**structural / cyclical**) deficit actually signaled a move toward more (**contractionary / expansionary**) fiscal policy.

6. The basic mechanism behind the concern that increased government spending "crowds out" private investment can be traced through expected changes in interest rates.

a. An increase in government spending initially causes GDP to (**rise / fall**). As a result, the transactions demand for money (**rises / falls**), so interest rates must (**rise / fall**) to engineer the change in the assets demand for money that is required to cancel the change in transactions demand.

And because interest rates respond, investment must decline. The problem is particularly acute in the monetarist view of the world, in which GDP does not increase with G because government spending replaces investment spending, dollar for dollar. The economy is, by assumption, at its potential, and further increases in GDP are impossible. An increase in aggregate demand caused by an increase in government spending must, therefore, be matched by an equal reduction in investment.

The evidence on crowding out is mixed. The expansionary fiscal policy of the early 1960s did not cause any substantial crowding out.

b. However, that was not really a fair test because during the 1960s, (**the natural rate of unemployment was lower / the Fed accommodated fiscal policy to keep interest rates constant / the Keynesian model was widely accepted**).

c. The empirical evidence suggests that (**25 / 50 / 75**) percent of the stimulative effects of increases in government spending are canceled in the short term and that (**75 / 90 / 100**) percent of the effects may disappear in the long term. This is because the long run aggregate supply curve is (**horizontal / vertical**) over potential GDP.

d. Even in the long term, though, crowding out appears to be a problem associated only with the (**cyclical / structural**) deficit.

There is reason to believe that an increase in government spending caused by automatic stabilizers during a recession might actually increase investment.

e. If the spending does in fact promote recovery, then GDP will begin to rise, and (**higher / lower**) investment might be induced by the prospect of a more vigorous economy. By the time the potential for crowding out appears (i.e., by the time the economy approaches its level of potential GDP), the cyclical spending will have (**disappeared / accelerated**) and there will be (**nothing left / even more spending**) to do the crowding.

7. Indicate which of the following arguments for or against large budget deficits are valid (**V**) and which are invalid (**I**).

___ a. I can't run a deficit forever, so neither can the government.

___ b. The debt is internally held, so there is no problem.

___ c. There are efficiency losses associated with the taxes required to pay the interest.

___ d. Private debt is high, too, and that is not a source of concern.

___ e. There is a significant likelihood that large deficits displace capital from private borrowers to public ones.

___ f. If interest payments grow faster than GDP, then increasingly large proportions of GDP will have to be taxed away to pay for the debt service.

___ g. Other things held constant, the more debt that is owned by foreigners, the larger will be the trade surplus.

D. Stabilizing the Economy

8. Table 34-4 from the text is reproduced here as Table 34-3.

TABLE 34-3 Money, Output, and Prices

Affected Variable	Response of Affected Variable to 4 Percent Change in Money Supply (% change in affected variable from baseline path)				
	Year 1	*Year 2*	*Year 3*	*Year 4*	*Year 5*
Real GDP	0.9	1.1	1.2	1.1	0.8
Consumer prices	0.2	0.7	1.1	1.5	1.8
Nominal GDP	1.1	1.8	2.3	2.5	2.7

A survey studied the impact of a change in monetary policy in eight different econometric models. in each case, a baseline run of the model was "shocked" by adding 4 percent to the money supply in year 1 and holding the money supply 4 percent above the baseline in all years thereafter. Estimates in the table show the average calculated response of the models.

Note an initial response of real output to a monetary-policy shift, with the peak response coming in year 3. The impact upon the price level builds up gradually because of the inertial response of price and wage behavior. Note that the impact on nominal GDP is less than proportional to the money growth even after 5 years. [Source: Ralph C. Bryant, Peter Hooper, and Gerald Holtham, "Consensus and Diversity in the Model Simulations," in Ralph Bryant et al. (ads.), *Empirical Macroeconomics for Interdependent Economies* (Brookings, Washington, D.C., 1988).]

a. Why does the percentage change in real GDP increase and then decrease?

_____

_____

b. Why does the percentage change in nominal GDP get larger and larger?

_____

_____

c. What does it mean if the percentage change in nominal GDP is increasing while the percentage change in real GDP is falling? When does this occur?

_____

_____

d. Given the material you have read in this chapter, what do you think the results of this study would have been if fiscal policy had been changed instead?

_____

_____

_____

C. Economic Prospects in the New Century

9. Two alternatives which have been suggested to increase national saving are the *income-oriented* and *price-oriented* approaches. For each of the following policy options, write **I** if the proposal is income-oriented and **P** if it is price-oriented.

___ a. Lowering government dissaving

___ b. Raising the real rate of return to saving

___ c. Lowering taxes on capital income

___ d. Increasing taxes to reduce the deficit

___ e. Increasing capital depreciation allowances

10. Consider Figure 34-1.

a. What reasons lie behind the fall in the personal savings rate? _____

b. To what do you attribute the decrease in the overall national savings rate? _____

VIII. DISCUSSION QUESTIONS

Answer the following questions, making sure that you can explain the work you did to arrive at the answers.

1. Explain why it may be difficult to get a clear picture of what the structural budget actually is.

2. When is crowding out most likely to occur?

3. Briefly discuss some of the problems associated with a government debt that is entirely *internal*.

4. How may the foreign inflow of financial capital in the 1980s have helped reduce the crowding out that was caused by the increasing federal budget deficits?

5. Briefly discuss the long-run impact of the government debt on economic growth.

6. Briefly explain the essence of the "rules vs. discretion" debate.

7. Explain the fall in the national savings rate from 8 percent of net domestic product to less than 2 percent in the early 1990s.

8. What did Congress do when it could not meet the deficit-reduction targets established by the Gramm-Rudman bill?

9. Give several examples of public investments and explain how they would increase total national wealth.

10. What can an economy do to encourage new technology?

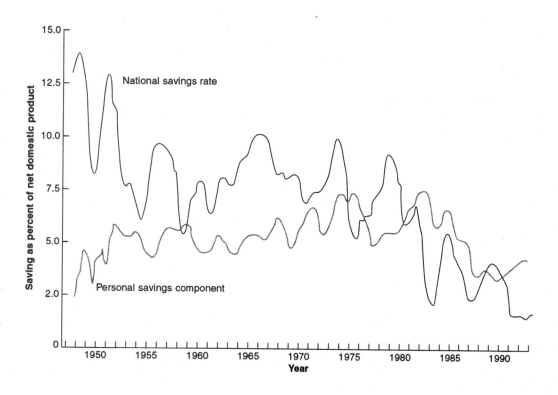

Figure 34-1

IX. ANSWERS TO STUDY GUIDE QUESTIONS

III. Review of Key Concepts

4	Budget
14	Budget surplus
7	Budget deficit
11	Balanced budget
9	Government debt
8	Fiscal policy
12	Discretionary fiscal policy
2	Structural budget
13	Cyclical budget
6	Crowding out
5	Internal debt
10	External debt
1	Displacement of capital
3	Distortion from taxation
19	Demand management
21	Fiscal-monetary mix
24	Gramm-Rudman Act
22	Pay-as-you-go provision
23	Purchasing-power parity
16	National savings rate
20	Income-oriented approaches
18	Price-oriented approaches
15	Total factor productivity
17	Total national wealth

VI. Multiple Choice Questions

1. A 2. C 3. C 4. E 5. E 6. C
7. A 8. D 9. C 10. C 11. D 12. E
13. D 14. D 15. D 16. E 17. A 18. C
19. C 20. E 21. E 22. D 23. A 24. E
25. D 26. B 27. D

VII. Problem Solving

1. a. S
    b. C
    c. S
    d. S
    e. N
    f. C
    g. S
2. a. +, – (perhaps 0, depending on the stimulus of the cut)
    b. 0, –
    c. 0, +
    d. 0, +
    e. +, – (perhaps 0, depending on the stimulus of the payments)
    f. +, 0 (assuming that evasion is not related to the business cycle)

3. a. rose, passive fiscal policy, an increase, cyclical, no change in the degree of stimulus applied by
    b. stimulus, structural, fell, rose
    c. $204, $188, $58
    d. $91, $26
    e. $39, $162
    f. stimulative
    g. $64
4. a. increase, decrease
    b. an increase, structural
    c. a reduction, cyclical
    d. the eventual cancellation of the active policy
    e. an increase, an open-market operation
    f. an increase, lower
5. a. stimulative, structural
    b. reduce, increase
    c. structural, contractionary
6. a. rise, rises, rise
    b. the Fed accommodated fiscal policy to keep interest rates constant
    c. 50 percent, 100 percent, vertical
    d. structural
    e. higher, disappeared, nothing left
7. a. I
    b. I
    c. V
    d. I
    e. V
    f. V
    g. V
8. a. The response of prices and wages to the increase in the money supply is sluggish. It takes time for them to adjust to the increased money supply. So, initially there is a larger impact on real GDP. However, as prices and wages adjust, the changes in real GDP peak and then taper off.
    b. As prices and wages react and adjust, nominal GDP changes accordingly. There is some rigidity to prices and wages, and they cannot respond immediately to the increase in the money supply.
    c. This means that the effect on the economy is becoming less and less real (in terms of output) and more and more inflationary. This occurs during years 4 and 5 in Table 33-3.
    d. The effectiveness of fiscal policy depends on how close the economy is to potential GDP. The closer to potential the economy is, the more crowding out there will be and the more inflationary the fiscal policy stimulus. Given the size of the national debt, many economists believe that fiscal policy can no longer be used as a major stabilization tool in the United States.
9. a. I
    b. P
    c. P

d. I

e. P

10. a. The personal savings rate has fallen due to a decrease in the rate of income growth, the increased growth of government transfer programs (like social security), and the deregulation of the banking industry, which has made it easier for consumers to borrow.

b. The national savings rate is made up of three components: government, business, and personal saving. The huge federal budget deficits during the past decade are the single biggest reason for the decline in the national savings rate. Due to a declining share of corporate profits in the economy, business saving has fallen as well.

VIII. DISCUSSION QUESTIONS

1. The economy is always in some phase of the business cycle, and it is only with hindsight that we can determine the economic climate with precision. While we observe the actual budget, it is difficult to separate that into structural and cyclical components.

2. Crowding out is most likely to occur when the economy is not in a recession. During recessions, the demand for money and interest rates fall, so there is apt to be less of an influence of government borrowing on interest rates. If interest rates do not respond to the government's increase in borrowing, there will be less crowding out. If the economy is at potential GDP, crowding out should be greatest.

3. If the debt is held internally, there would be a redistribution of wealth from taxpayers to bondholders (who are owed interest for lending money to the government) . If the government needs to raise taxes to make interest payments, this will have an effect on patterns of work and saving. The greater the debt, the more the government has to use its (finite) budget to service the debt rather than provide programs for its citizens.

4. To the extent that foreigners willingly purchased U.S. government bonds, the funds from domestic saving were still available to private industry without pushing interest rates higher.

5. As the government borrows more and more, people will acquire more public debt (government bonds) and less private debt. As the funds for private investment dry up, there will be less investment spending and less expansion of capital and thereby less growth in the nation's ability to produce goods and services. Private investment spending is a vital component of economic growth.

6. Proponents of discretion argue that the Fed needs to have flexibility in setting monetary policy so that it can react to economic shocks and disturbances. A good example is the Fed's immediate response to the stock market crash of October 1987. Proponents of fixed rules state that a predetermined monetary growth path is needed to remove uncertainty from the financial markets and enhance the Fed's credibility as an inflation fighter.

7. The primary reason for the fall in the national savings rate has been the ballooning of the national debt. The structural deficits of the Reagan administration added over a trillion dollars to the national debt. Lower economic growth rates and the recession of 1990-1991 contributed to the decline in saving as well.

8. Congress has amended the Gramm-Rudman bill several times when it became clear that its guidelines for deficit reduction could not be met. In 1993, Congress did pass a pay-as-you-go provision that required that any new spending programs be fully funded before being put into place. This by itself will do nothing to reduce the deficit, but it will at least help prevent the deficit from getting bigger.

9. Government programs to repair and improve the nation's infrastructure can facilitate economic growth and increase national wealth. Examples include highways, airports, utilities, and even the information superhighway. Additionally, the government can invest in the nation's human capital by providing funds for higher education and training programs to help labor adapt to the structural changes occurring in the economy.

10. A free marketplace seems to be the best setting for the development of new ideas and technology. Competition brings out the best in both individuals and industry. In this market setting, the government needs to encourage and support research and development by private industry. The government can also encourage foreign investment and technology to do business with, and in, the U.S. economy.

Notes

Notes